The Making of a New Rural Order in South China

This volume is written for anyone who has wondered about the growth of Chinese businesses and their relation to Chinese family and government institutions. Making full use of its partner volume's findings on village institutions in the southern prefecture of Huizhou, this volume explains how late imperial China's key regional group of merchants emerged from this prefecture's village lineages. It identifies the strategies they deployed to overcome the serious obstacles to their domination of major financial transactions and commodity markets throughout much of China from 1500 to 1700. At the same time it describes how the commercial success enjoyed by these "house firms" undermined their lineages' social stability, making them vulnerable to competition from popular religious cults back home. In recounting how rural and urban institutions interacted through state and economic development, McDermott provides a powerful new framework for understanding late imperial China's distinctive trajectory to social and economic transformation.

A Fellow of St John's College, Cambridge, Joseph P. McDermott has published and lectured widely on the social and economic history of premodern China. His recent books include *The Making of a New Rural Order in South China, v. 1*, and *A Social History of the Chinese Book*.

The Making of a New Rural Order in South China

II. Merchants, Markets, and Lineages, 1500–1700

JOSEPH P. MCDERMOTT
University of Cambridge

CAMBRIDGE
UNIVERSITY PRESS

University Printing House, Cambridge CB2 8BS, United Kingdom

One Liberty Plaza, 20th Floor, New York, NY 10006, USA

477 Williamstown Road, Port Melbourne, VIC 3207, Australia

314–321, 3rd Floor, Plot 3, Splendor Forum, Jasola District Centre, New Delhi – 110025, India

79 Anson Road, #06–04/06, Singapore 079906

Cambridge University Press is part of the University of Cambridge.

It furthers the University's mission by disseminating knowledge in the pursuit of education, learning, and research at the highest international levels of excellence.

www.cambridge.org
Information on this title: www.cambridge.org/9781107048515
DOI: 10.1017/9781107261471

© Joseph P. McDermott 2020

This publication is in copyright. Subject to statutory exception and to the provisions of relevant collective licensing agreements, no reproduction of any part may take place without the written permission of Cambridge University Press.

First published 2020

A catalogue record for this publication is available from the British Library.

ISBN 978-1-107-04851-5 Hardback

Cambridge University Press has no responsibility for the persistence or accuracy of URLs for external or third-party internet websites referred to in this publication and does not guarantee that any content on such websites is, or will remain, accurate or appropriate.

To three great scholars and teachers of Chinese history

Shiba Yoshinobu
Tanaka Masatoshi
Yanagida Setsuko

Contents

List of Tables		*page* viii
List of Maps		ix
Acknowledgments		x
	Introduction	1
1	Ming Markets and Huizhou Merchants	7
2	Ancestral Halls and Credit: Building, Investing, and Lending	60
3	The Working World of Huizhou Merchants: Travel and Trade, Problems and Resolutions	125
4	Huizhou Merchants and Their Financial Institutions	202
5	Huizhou Merchants and Commercial Partnerships	252
6	Huizhou House Firms: The Binds of Kinship and Commerce	308
7	Conclusion	384
Bibliography		421
Index		462

Tables

1.1	Commercial tax quota and revenues at eight big customs stations in the late Ming	page 14
2.1	Number of ancestral halls built in a single Huizhou village	63
2.2	Individual ancestral halls' construction costs	79
2.3	Funding sources for the construction of the ancestral hall dedicated to Luo Dongshu in Chengkan, She county	96
2.4	Revenues and disbursement schedule in the construction of the ancestral hall dedicated to Luo Dongshu in Chengkan, She county	97
3.1	Non-Huizhou native-place associations and public places in Suzhou prefecture during the Yuan and Ming dynasties	188
3.2	Huizhou native-place associations and public places in Suzhou prefecture during the Ming and Qing dynasties	189
4.1	Special pawnbrokerage tax levy quotas for specific provinces and metropolitan areas, 1623	227
4.2	Pawnbrokerage tax levy quotas for specific prefectures in the Northern Metropolitan Area, 1623	228
4.3	Pawnbrokerage tax levy quotas for specific prefectures in the Southern Metropolitan Area, 1623	229
4.4	Huizhou loan contracts' interest rates: lowest, highest, average, and median	236
4.5	Capital assets of Cheng Yujing and annual net rate of increase	244
6.1	External market bases of the Taitang Chengs during the early Ming	347

Maps

1.1 Huizhou in the Ming *page* 9
1.2 Distribution of major marketplaces in *c.*1077, 1429, and *c.*1580   17

Acknowledgments

This volume's study of the wealthiest regional group of merchants in Ming China builds on my earlier volume's findings on lineage growth in Huizhou villages roughly from 900 to 1600. Like that earlier volume it has benefited from the aid of a large number of institutions and people in Britain, the United States, China, Hong Kong, Taiwan, and Japan. To those institutions and staff who have opened their collections to me, especially those in Shanghai, Beijing, Cambridge, and Tokyo, I wish to express my gratitude, with the hope that other scholars will find much of interest in these pages. To the many scholars whom I acknowledged in the previous volume for helping me carry out my Huizhou studies, I would now like to add others who read and commented on a portion of this book: David McMullen, Ghassan Moazzin, and Adam Chau of Cambridge; my brother Edward McDermott of New York; John Lagerwey of Hong Kong; and Michael Robbins, William Steele, and Iiyama Tomoyasu of Tokyo. And to Lucy Rhymer, James Baker, and the rest of the editorial staff at Cambridge University Press, my warm thanks once again.

Also, I wish to express my gratitude to a group of scholars who in the past few years have helped me greatly by inviting me to seminars and conferences to discuss issues addressed in this volume. Over the past decade François Gipouloux generously asked me to present papers at the stimulating Eurasia Trajeco conferences and seminars he has run on Chinese economic history; his friendship, honest discussions, and warm encouragement, along with those of the other conference participants, have made learning from my errors very enjoyable and rewarding and made this volume a much better book. More recently, Manuel Garcia Perez has successfully run similarly fruitful seminars in Seville, Shanghai, and Boston, where the question-and-answer sessions happily rolled into memorable dinners. Also, Wang Jinping of the National University of Singapore; Cheung Sui-wai, Choi Chi-cheung, David Faure, and Puk Wing-kin of the Chinese University of Hong

Acknowledgments

Kong; Billy So of the Hong Kong University of Science and Technology; Miura Toru and Kishimoto Mio of Ochanomizu Women's University; Wu Cuncun and Joseph Poon of the University of Hong Kong; Wang Zhenzhong of Fudan; Michael Szonyi of Harvard; Cynthia Brokaw of Brown; Alain Arrault and Michela Bussotti of the EFEO and Christian Lamouroux of the CNRS in Paris; Beverly Bossler and Mark Halperin of the University of California, Davis; and my former student Zhang Ling of Boston College have all hosted discussions of this book's findings. The insights gained from these meetings have, I hope, found their way into this volume, which is undoubtedly much better for their questions and criticisms. I am sincerely grateful to them for their generous help. As an Isaac Manasseh Meyer Fellow at the University of Singapore, I was asked to introduce many of my findings in Chapter 5 to a public audience that proved lively and generous. I was once again fortunate, when Billy K.L. So asked me to submit an essay to a conference in Taipei that resulted in his fine volume *The Economy of Lower Yangzi Delta in Late Imperial China* (Routledge, 2013); I am grateful for permission to reprint much of that essay in Chapter 6 here.

Special thanks is due to the CUP map section for help with Map 1, and to Professor Song Chen for his skillful drafting and editing of Map 2 from the digital map of China jointly developed for the China Historical GIS Project by Harvard's Center for Geographic Analysis and the Historical Geography Research Center of Fudan University. Professor Chen's expertise in the mapping of historical information has become a byword among social and economic historians of China, and I am deeply grateful to him for his work on this particular map. Any problem with it, needless to say, remains my full responsibility.

Finally, this volume is dedicated to three great scholars, vastly different in their historical interests but strikingly similar in their intelligence, integrity, and openheartedness. During the many happy years I spent in Japan, it was my great good fortune to study with these students of Chinese history. Sadly, Professors Tanaka Masatoshi and Yanagida Setsuko are not able to see this fruit of their kindnesses. But fortunately Professor Shiba is still here, and I hope this volume captures some of his wisdom and erudition. I wish to express my unending gratitude to them for sharing with me their profound learning about China and for teaching me through their actions how to teach and how to be a better human being. I am sure that their instruction and writings have made this a much better book. What I hope is that this work has captured even a portion of the humanity I have tried to learn from them and – as they all would have wanted – from the people of Huizhou.

Introduction

The sixteenth and seventeenth centuries in Ming China (1368–1644) were years of turmoil. In Beijing official factionalism and eunuch intrusion led to decades of political infighting and policy indecision. Not just the inner and outer courts but also groups within each of these palace bases vied for dominance over the throne and officialdom. Inept emperors failed to bridge the divisions, allowing generals, eunuchs, family members, and officials to carve out separate spheres of influence. Denied appointments by this deadlock, officials resigned or protested in vain.

Meanwhile, in the provinces the dynasty's defenses fell under constant strain. Along the coast Chinese and Japanese piracy was rampant. With the coming of European boats into East Asian waters, maritime tensions worsened. Upon casting anchor in Guangzhou harbor in 1520 Portuguese boats issued a balustrade of cannon fire to declare their wish to initiate trade and negotiate for an overseas fort in China. Over the next century or so well-armed Spanish, Dutch, French, and English ships pressed the Chinese for similar privileges. Even more relentless pressures piled up along the northeast frontier, where from the 1610s onward bands of semi-nomadic warriors known as Manchus routinely raided undermanned Ming garrisons and plundered cities guarded by underpaid troops. In sum, by the early seventeenth century the empire faced serious challenges along its eastern, southern, and northern borders.

For sure, these political and military threats could have been thwarted – how could a semi-civilized people like the Manchus even contemplate subjugating the world's largest, richest, and most civilized empire holding a quarter of the world's population? But the distant border rumble of these centuries was not divorced from the empire's heartland and its combustible problems. Just as Chinese discontents far outnumbered Japanese renegades in the ranks of raiding pirates, so did disaffected Ming generals and troops often provide crucial support for raiding Manchus. The institutions established by the founding Ming emperors, as countless commentators have remarked, soon failed to fit the country's new needs. The basic units of local government had been set up on the assumption that local rule consisted of little more than the registration of households, the collection of taxes, the transmission of government orders, the arrest of criminals, and the maintenance of a well-recognized moral code. By the late fifteenth century, however, these institutions had already begun to flounder, at least in the southeast.[1] Moralistic denunciations of expensive funerals and other "luxuries" failed to solve growing problems like poverty, corruption, and uneven commercial development. Semiprivate institutions like community pacts and private academies attracted limited local support, and so they stopped meeting or were closed by a frightened court. Other state institutions lumbered on for decades, ill-suited to a new world of rapid change.

In the early 1570s a Nanjing scholar-official alarmed about this flux assembled twenty-four local men, all in their eighties, to air their reflections on the last half-century. In silence he listened to their longings for a lost world of simple duties and few pleasures. Back in that never-never land of their youth men had worked hard in the fields, wives had woven cloth at home, sons had practiced filial piety, and indeed people had repaid loans.[2] Now, by contrast, all was inconstant. The changes men noted were no longer of a distant past, but of their own lifetime and experiences. Their villages were shells of once active communities, left by youths who no longer showed their elders proper respect and who thought solely of landing better-paid work elsewhere. Money and status were all that men and women talked of, and the only things they now wove were schemes of deception. Living off the labor of others, the remaining youths were given to donning silk gowns for their strolls. Even more than the social order, these Nanjing elders warned, the social code lay in tatters.

Over the remaining seven decades of Ming rule these fears about the fallen state of public and private morality gained force. Large numbers of men in search of land to till and work lists to fill abandoned homes with scant regard for ancestral ties. Some, like the shepherds of Shanxi province, traveled virtually all year long in search of edible pasture.

---

[1] *Changshu xianzhi* (1539), 4.20b.
[2] He Qiaoyuan, *Mingshan cang*, huozhi ji, 6a–12b.

Introduction

Tending large herds of sheep, every winter they trekked south across bare mountain ranges into the Lake Dongting area of the central Yangzi Valley. Come spring, they led them back another 400 miles to the green grass of southern Shanxi.[3]

Whereas some men went on the road in search of forage for their sheep, others, women as well as men of all ages, left hungry villages in search of food for themselves. While performing the legendary "flower drum songs," thousands of northern Anhui peasants spent their winters walking to and around the delta counties where their ancestors had lived until being uprooted by the first Ming emperor. "Our family lives in Luzhou and Fengyang," they would sing out to the delta houses they approached. "Fengyang was once upon a time a fine place, but then it produced Emperor Zhu [Yuanjiang], and ever since it has had famines nine years out of ten."[4] As their pleas for food rarely reached the ears of long-lost relatives, these beggars each spring returned home to seed another crop of grain.

Other ex-villagers from throughout central China landed jobs and housing on trading and fishing boats. Sailing along the empire's canals, rivers, and lakes, they saw months pass without need to set foot on land. Other migrants moved to cities, where they scrambled for unskilled jobs as stevedores and servants. The more skilled found work in resurgent industries like ceramic kilns and iron forges or in new sectors like cotton textiles and lens manufacture. Many of these migrants retained their dream of striking it rich. But the longer they stayed away from home, the more prone they were to fall for the latest cult's promises of protection and fortune. Although movement had become the order of the day, many ordinary Chinese remained worried about the wisdom of their own moves.

Their anxieties flourished on fertile ground. From 1580 to 1644 the towns and cities of the Yangzi delta, when not wracked by epidemics, were continually disrupted by urban protests and riots, by fiery attacks on granaries and pawnshops, and by famines brought on by interrupted grain-supply lines. In northwest China, the countryside was overrun by peasant rebel armies, which from the 1620s fanned out over the Central Plain and into the capital area. Between 1626 and 1640 freezing temperatures, extreme drought, and great floods repeatedly struck much of east China, driving millions of hungry villagers

[3] Wang Shixing, *Guangzhi yi*, 3, 66.   [4] Wang Zhenzhong, *Shehui lishi*, 16–28.

onto hard-hearted roads.[5] And, from 1638 onward, when the Beijing court was overwhelmed by these northern problems, the Yangzi delta was thrown into turmoil by a succession of famines, urban uprisings, and further breakdowns in transport and grain deliveries.[6] The worsening military news from the northern border echoed ominously hundreds of miles away in the cultural and economic center of this tottering empire.

This tale of dynastic decline and social disorder, however, did not constitute the entire history of the late Ming. Usually ignored by court chronicles, a string of local initiatives and institutions slowly replaced some of those in decay. Linked more to the long-term development of the market-oriented economy of the Song dynasty (960–1279) than to the command-like economy of the early Ming, this new social order took shape in the sixteenth and seventeenth centuries, first in the countryside and later in the cities. In the villages of south China, where Buddhist temples and village worship associations had lost considerable social and economic clout, powerful lineages increasingly held sway. While individual villagers were taking up rootless careers on the road or lowly jobs in riverside towns, the families and graves they left behind often fell under tighter control by lineages and other large kinship groups. Even in the world of imperial politics, frustrated scholars and officials took steps to assert independence. They established over a thousand literary and scholarly associations, hundreds of whose members, emboldened to assemble, came from eight or more provinces to propose reforms of *their* dynasty. Having woken from the nightmare at the court to find others raging in their home locales, they demanded reforms on both imperial and local fronts.[7]

And, to complete this account of countercurrents, the itinerant merchant merits attention. Long disparaged in official records as bit players with the basest motives, these sojourners traveled the roads and rivers of the empire. Virtually wherever they settled, they were considered outsiders with few commitments to the well-being of communities they milked for profits. For sure, their crisscrossing of administrative boundaries to do what Chinese merchants had always done – buying up goods local producers wanted to sell and then

---

[5] Wakeman, *The Great Enterprise*, v. 1, 7.
[6] Horichi, *Min Shin shokuryō*, 56–63, 65.
[7] Li Yushuan, *Mingdai wenren*, 2 and 3 of preface by Li Shiren.

Introduction 5

profitably trading them on to other places demanding them – often set them at odds with a Ming bureaucratic order that strove to silo their transactions and communications to within a strict administrative hierarchy of government offices and registered settlements. Yet, in moving goods between private markets these merchants were responding to the different needs and demands of different places in the Yangzi Valley.

More significantly, their travel linked up not just separate places and markets but also separate product parts and workers in discrete stages of the production process for one type of commodity. It introduced silver and credit into an ever widening variety of transactions, led to the establishment of commercial partnerships with people sometimes far from home, and spurred on the formation of native-place associations for fellow travelers. Although many pre-1500 institutions and economic practices remained unchanged, others significantly did change, largely due to the greater circulation of things and people pursuing opportunities elsewhere. The sixteenth- and seventeenth-century world of commercial partnerships and pawnshops, of numerous ancestral halls and a few native-place associations, functioned as a relatively stable set of newly accepted institutions within a larger world of military turmoil and political conflict. In effect, a transformation, however incomplete, of the early Ming economy gathered pace over the last half of the dynasty.

It is all too facile to regard these changes as essentially the responses of an organic economy casting off a rigid social and economic order decreed by early Ming autocrats. Not only were some early Ming institutions like the *lijia* 里甲 easily and profitably adapted to local circumstances in ways unimagined by their court creators.[8] But also the emergence of a new social order in the mid and late Ming was arguably prompted and shaped by the *dirigiste* policies of the early Ming. Just as punitive land taxes in the early Ming drove many Yangzi delta landholders to shift their investments from agriculture and land into commerce and crafts,[9] so did the relatively low level of commercial tax on long-distance trade persuade many peasants to risk leaving their rocky fields to peddle others' products elsewhere.[10] In other words,

---

[8] Liu Zhiwei, *Zai guojia*; Cheng Yizhi, *Cheng dian*, 6.1a ff.
[9] Nishijima, "The Formation of the Early Chinese Cotton Industry."
[10] As discussed below in Chapter 3.

a merchant-based account of these changes promises to disclose much about the complex intertwining of economics and politics in late imperial times.

For detailed insight into these widely reported commercial changes, few places in Ming China provide as revealing a documentary record as Huizhou prefecture. Perched high in the mountains of southern Anhui province, this prefecture was by 1200 famed for its paper, tea, and timber, as well as for its ink cakes and inkstones. From 1500 it also became celebrated for its merchants, probably Ming China's most successful group of sojourning merchants. How they took not just their goods but also their rural practices and institutions (not least their lineages) out of their villages and thereby changed China's commercial and financial world is a central concern of this volume. Beneath the turmoil of the late Ming another order, fragile but dynamic, was emerging, as Huizhou merchants established a set of rural and urban institutions that linked their lineages and villages to urban markets throughout much of the country and thereby profoundly shaped life in south China and especially the Yangzi Valley up until our time.

1 | *Ming Markets and Huizhou Merchants*

During the last two centuries of the Ming dynasty hundreds of thousands of young men left the rocky fields and narrow prospects of their overcrowded Huizhou villages in search of fortune elsewhere. Often abandoning their recent brides, these youths joined their fathers in repeated cycles of travel and trade, in order to learn firsthand the skill of peddling and trading far from home. In the first generation or two of this large-scale Ming emigration, some made the move tentatively. They tended to trade first in another hilly prefecture nearby, and then, if successful, moved down to the more competitive markets of the Yangzi Valley's cities. Later in the Ming, however, most of Huizhou's merchants, the aspiring as well as the experienced, showed less hesitation. They headed directly to the lowland markets and trading routes that their Huizhou predecessors had helped to develop.

Journeying long distances from one town or periodic market to another, many passed a rootless adolescence on foot or, if lucky, on carts and boats. Some returned home with profits at the year's end. Some, either because they had not yet succeeded or because they were too busy succeeding, returned to Huizhou to celebrate the New Year's festivities at home just once every few years. Others never returned. Their leaky vessels, operated by inexperienced crews, crashed into rocks, ran aground on river shoals, were raided by pirates, or simply sank in the muddy Yangzi with their cargo. Or on land they fell victim to daytime highwaymen eager to snatch their goods and purses and leave them knocked unconscious by the roadside. Others suffered an even worse fate: stricken by illness along deserted roads, they died at night in lonely inns, forgotten and never buried by kinsmen.

Over time, the more fortunate in the ranks of these traveling merchants survived these trials and settled down with their concubines, sons, and silver holdings to live the "Chinese dream" in the thriving towns and cities of the Yangzi Valley, on the Grand Canal, and along the southeast coast. At the very least, they retained ties to their home village in Huizhou by having their corpses returned there for burial amongst their ancestors on the surrounding hillsides.[1] Meanwhile, even as ambitious youths continued to stream out of Huizhou to find their fortune in distant places, Huizhou's population kept on expanding, from 131,622 registered households in 1391 to more than double that figure by 1578.[2]

This book is about these Huizhou men and their families, their wealth and institutions, their plans and loans, the problems they faced as merchants and especially the solutions they found to these problems – in short, the commercial and financial world they sought to shape and often came to dominate. Previous migrants to south China's lowlands had commonly been northern Chinese, who craved farmland, jobs, and security in their new settlements. These Huizhou emigrants in the Ming were different. Not only were they southern Chinese moving to somewhere else in south China.[3] But also, in fleeing the stony soil of Huizhou and its endemic poverty, they had their eyes fixed on urban marketplaces and their commercial potential. With remarkable alacrity they adapted to their new lowland urban environment, set up partnerships and branch offices, and thereby often formed networks of exchange with distant places. In the face of challenges as daunting as those that centuries earlier had confronted their ancestors when struggling to open wild forests in Huizhou and to carve terraced paddies out of its mountain slopes, they became a dominant force in the wharves, marketplaces, and moneylending shops in the Yangzi Valley; that is, in the heart of the late imperial economy.

Whereas the preceding volume in this pair of studies on Huizhou focused on changes both in agricultural life and among four kinds of institutions common to Huizhou villages (a tutelary village worship association, popular shrines, Buddhist and/or Daoist establishments, and large kinship organizations such as lineages), this volume is largely concerned with the expanding role of Huizhou merchants and lineages outside Huizhou, in the commercial and financial sectors of the Ming economy at large. This study of Huizhou from the mid Ming to the early

---

[1] *MQHS*, 25; Usui, *Kishū shōnin*, 19–51; *Xiuning xianzhi* (1693), 1.63a, quoting the "former" 1603 gazetteer (Ibid., pref. 9b); *Huizhou fuzhi* (1699), 2.67b–68b.
[2] Ye Xian'en, *Ming Qing Huizhou*, 32.
[3] Already in the late twelfth century a severe land shortage had driven some Huizhou residents to migrate to war-torn but underpopulated prefectures north of the Yangzi (*Xin'an zhi*, 1, 16).

Ming Markets and Huizhou Merchants

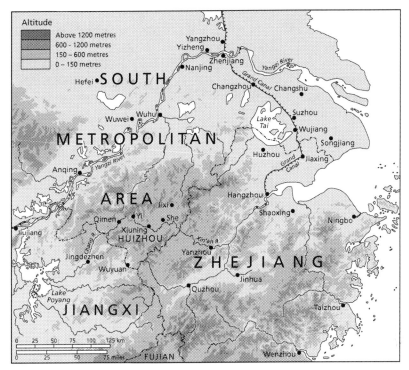

Map 1.1 Huizhou in the Ming

Qing, roughly 1500 to 1700, would seem, then, to contrast with the previous volume by dealing with a strikingly different list of subjects: urban as opposed to rural, commercial as opposed to agricultural, merchants as opposed to farmers, interest rates as opposed to harvests, and then the frequent primacy of secular as opposed to religious commitments (Map 1.1). Put in terms of the institutions discussed, this volume's early and later chapters will deal with the "village quartet" of institutions introduced in the previous volume. But elsewhere it will mainly concentrate, in turn, on ancestral halls (*citang* 祠堂) and then on a handful of usually urban, commercial, and financial institutions, such as native-place associations (*huiguan* 會館), the salt monopoly (*yanyun si* 鹽運司), pawnshops (*dianpu* 典鋪), commercial partnerships (*hehuo* 合夥), and house firms (*hao* 號, *tang* 堂).

Underlying these differences in place and topic, nonetheless, is a set of concerns common to these two volumes. In general, both volumes discuss the same relatively large Huizhou lineages, concentrate on the institutional framework in which problems of resource shortage and conflict resolution arose within and among lineages, and seek to identify the institutions and practices that these Huizhou lineages and their merchant members used to overcome these difficulties. More specifically, this volume will explore such challenges as the competition among ancestral halls for members, tensions over the interest rates for loans, Huizhou merchants' struggles to penetrate local markets and secure their place in an often hostile commercial environment, and the engagement of village-born lineage members in running and working for large branch and lineage-shaped "house firms," that functioned often as ensembles of commercial partnerships. All these subjects bespeak a complex social order riven by intense competition for capital (in place of the previous volume's land) and averse to the easy inclusion of merchant outsiders (in place of the previous volume's rival branches and surname groups). We thus can discover how recurring problems of resource shortages and governance shaped the development of Huizhou's lineages both inside and outside Huizhou.

Over the past century scholars have repeatedly linked these changes in the late Ming economy and society to the expansion of its cotton and silk textile production, to the government's continuing efforts in the sixteenth century to commute all land tax and labor service levies to a single payment in silver (commonly called the "Single Whip tax"), and especially to the infusion of a great amount of foreign supplies of silver into China's bimetallic currency system of copper coins and silver ingots. To be sure, during at least the last century of the Ming the regular arrival of large supplies of Japanese, New World, and European silver helped to satiate the Chinese market's persistent thirst for this metal currency. According to a relatively modest estimate, the Chinese economy between 1550 and 1644 is thought to have imported 7,300 (or, in the same author's most recent estimate, 7,000 to 10,000) metric tons of silver ingots: "In the first half of the seventeenth century the amount of silver imported into China each year averaged 116,000 kgs., or 250 percent more than in the second half of the sixteenth century," with more than half coming from Japan and almost all the rest from the New World.[4] Or, put more concretely and comprehensively, the silver

---

[4] Von Glahn, *Fountain of Fortune*, 138–39, 141; or, more recently, his "Cycles of Silver," 31–44; and *The Economic History of China*, 308, which estimate the

Ming Markets and Huizhou Merchants 11

imports into China for the years 1573, 1590, 1581, 1620, 1621, 1622, 1623, 1625, and 1626 average out at 3.56 million taels (*liang* 兩) a year.[5] Some scholars would put this average higher. But even this conservative estimate has the Chinese economy profit greatly from the sale of its manufactured products for foreign silver. From 1550 to 1600 silver imports added eight times more silver to China's supply of this precious metal than did domestic silver mining; and from 1600 to 1650 the total gap between new foreign imports and domestic production of silver was even greater – twentyfold.[6]

This volume will focus instead on social and economic developments within Ming China both before and during this period of great silver imports. In exploring the rise and reign of south China's premier regional group of merchants in the Ming, it will be concerned with five interrelated questions: how did Huizhou merchants acquire the capital to become the wealthiest regional merchant group in all of Ming China? How did they handle the risks to their person and their wealth both on their travels and during their stays at their points of destination? What links can we discern between Huizhou merchants' kinship ties and organizations and their distinctive ways of doing business and use of capital? How did merchant relations with the government change over the Ming? And how did Huizhou lineages' commercial success outside Huizhou affect their position among the "village quartet" of institutions back in their Huizhou villages? In building on the findings of the previous volume about the mid-Ming ascendance of the lineage in Huizhou village life, this volume will highlight the institutional innovations and obstacles undertaken by Huizhou lineages to become the principal institution in the collective life of their villages and their residents.

To provide a historical context for this analysis, this particular chapter will map and discuss the long-term expansion and spread of domestic markets and market networks from the late eleventh to the

---

annual silver import figure as at least fifty tons from 1550 to 1599 and 115 tons from 1600 to 1639.

[5] This volume has followed a convention of translating the Chinese unit *liang* 兩 as tael. The official weight of a tael equals about 1.3 (European) ounces of silver, hence my reluctance to translate it, as some do, as ounce. Regardless of the translation, persistent debasements of silver greatly complicate the conversion of these taels into any standard silver equivalent.

[6] Quan Hansheng, "Zi Song zhi Ming," 359–62.

late sixteenth century, the accompanying changes in the social position of Chinese merchants, and what distinguished Huizhou merchants in the Ming from their pre-Ming forebears and then from their regional merchant rivals in the Ming. The aim of this chapter, then, is to provide a broader historical framework for the subsequent chapters' separate analyses of the innovative uses of those institutions – ancestral halls, local-place associations, pawnshops, the salt monopoly trade, commercial partnerships, and merchant firms – that were key to Ming Huizhou merchants' commercial and financial ascendance in what historians increasingly regard as premodern China's "second economic revolution" (the first having occurred in the Song dynasty).[7]

Market Changes: From c.1077 to c.1580

A key underlying feature of this "second economic revolution" was an unprecedented expansion of the market and related institutions of Chinese economic life. Quantitatively, any claim of "unprecedented market expansion" is hard to prove definitively, as we lack empire-wide figures of functioning marketplaces from both the Song and Ming dynasties. Our official figures, instead, are for these periods' commercial tax stations, and these numbers, if taken to indicate markets, suggest great decline rather than expansion. Whereas in c.1077 the Song dynasty had 2,060 commercial tax stations, plus 20,606 additional sites for collecting salt and wine levies, spread throughout the Northern Song empire, corresponding figures for the Ming are close to 1,000 for the early Ming, 380 in c.1488, and 111 in 1583.[8] Upon

---

[7] Rowe, "Approaches to Modern Chinese Social History," 236–96.
[8] Aramiya, *Min Shin toshi*, 307. An incomplete list of markets and market towns found in twelve provinces (unfortunately omitting all provinces of western China but for Shaanxi and Sichuan) shows that of the 7,682 markets in the late Ming and early Qing south China clearly had a preponderant share. Three areas of relatively high market concentration were the Yangzi and Grand Canal corridors and the far southeast coastal area. Provincial shares of registered markets were Guangdong (16.6%), Shandong (14.7%), Jiangsu (14.5%), Anhui (9.2%), Hubei (9.1%), Jiangxi (8.8%), Zhejiang (7.9%), Zhili (6.7%), Hunan (5.0%), Shaanxi (3.1%), Fujian (2.7%), and Sichuan (1.8%). The top share for Guangdong probably reflects the disproportionate amount of information collected on this province and the small number of markets in Jiangsu north of the Yangzi (Ren Fang, "Ming Qing shizhen," 201). In the Qing the number of markets in imperial China would peak at c.22,000 (Fang Xing, Jing Junxian, and Wei Jinyu, *Zhongguo jingji tongshi, Qing*, v. 2, 778).

Market Changes: From c.1077 to c.1580

inspection, however, this long-term dramatic drop in official tax station numbers turns out to reflect mainly administrative changes; that is, a decline in the relative importance of commercial taxes in the Ming dynasty's tax revenues and its concentration of commercial tax collection activities in fewer sites, each of which was increasingly expected to collect more commercial taxes. In fact, as the number of tax stations declined during the Ming, the dynasty's overall commercial tax quota rose.

For indications of the spread of the market between c.1077 and c.1580 we instead have a very large body of other quantitative and nonquantitative regional evidence.[9] According to recent Chinese studies, the number of markets operating in the middle Yangzi Valley during these five centuries increased fivefold and, depending on the modern historian, between twofold and fivefold in the lower Yangzi delta.[10] Focusing on just the century and a half between 1500 and 1650, the Taiwan scholar Liu Shiji has estimated the surge in the number of markets as two-and-a-half-fold in the delta alone.[11] Within the single delta county of Wujiang 吳江, a relatively agricultural area of Suzhou prefecture, the three markets and four market towns of c.1510 became ten markets and four market towns by 1561 and then ten markets and seven market towns by the close of the sixteenth century.[12] By then, the delta's five core prefectures had four market towns with a population of over 50,000 apiece, another of 35,000 people, and seven more with 10,000 to 20,000 apiece.

The increased volume of trade in these years can be glimpsed, if only tangentially, through tax data (Table 1.1). Even though Table 1.1's statistics are incomplete and their "old quota" can be dated no more precisely than to the preceding Wanli reign (1573–1620), these figures for commercial tax revenues collected at eight major internal customs stations – seven along the Grand Canal and just one along the Yangzi

---

[9] McDermott and Shiba, "Economic Change in China," 379, 384.
[10] Mei Xinlin and Chen Guocan, eds., *Jiangnan chengshihua,* 170–71; Ren Fang, "Ming Qing shizhen," 187–227.
[11] Shiba, "Pattern of Rural–Urban Continuum," 176, quantifies the increase graphically: "If we take the early Ming figure of towns and markets as the index number 100, at the end of the Ming there were 222 for Suzhou, 179 for Songjiangfu, and 209 for Hangzhou."
[12] Liu Shiji, *Ming Qing shidai*; and his "Ming Qing shidai Jiangnan shizhen zhi shuliang fenxi," 128–49; Heijdra," Socio-economic Development," 509; Chen Xuewen, *Ming Qing shehui jingji,* 88–91.

Table 1.1 Commercial tax quota and revenues at eight big customs stations in the late Ming (all figures in terms of 10,000 taels)*

Date	Chongwen Gate (Beijing)	Beixi Station	Hushu Station	Jiujiang Station	Huai'an Station	Yangzhou Station	Linqing Station	Hexi Station	Total
Old Quota	6.8929	4.0	4.5	2.5	2.2	1.3	8.38	4.6	34.3729
1621 income	-------	6.0	6.75	3.75	2.96	5.6	---	---	------
1626 income	8.8929	8.0	8.75	5.75	4.46	2.56	6.38	3.2	47.9929

* Source:: Wang Qi, *Xu Wenxian tongkao*, 18, 2,937.

river – suggest a significant upturn in commercial activity during the Wanli reign and the first half of the 1620s. The increase was particularly evident in the lower stretches of the Yangzi river from Jiujiang 九江 to Yangzhou and in the Yangzi delta thanks to the inclusion of the Hushu 滸墅 Customs Station just northwest of Suzhou city.

Clearly, at the very time when hundreds of thousands of Huizhou men were winning ill repute for their cunning at trade, the value of Ming trade and by extension its volume (since the tax rate remained the same) were expanding in the very areas, the Yangzi Valley and the Grand Canal, where these Huizhou merchants were most active. In fact, the Ming located these stations preponderantly on the Grand Canal, letting passage in most of the Yangzi Valley remain relatively undertaxed throughout the dynasty and thus in this list account for roughly just a third of the total commercial tax quota in 1626. A slightly earlier list of fifteen important commercial tax stations (but without tax quotas) roughly confirms most of these conclusions: two-thirds of these major commercial tax stations were located on the Grand Canal, all but one station was either in the Yangzi Valley or on the Grand Canal, six were in the delta, and just two were on the Yangzi river west of Nanjing.[13]

Much development of new markets, however, took place far beyond the Grand Canal and the lower Yangzi delta. By the end of the Ming, markets were operating over the full breadth of the Chinese empire at an unprecedented span and number. This broader historical and geographical assessment of market expansion is confirmed through a comparison of three empire-wide lists of important Chinese commercial centers compiled between the eleventh and the late sixteenth centuries. The earliest, a comprehensive commercial tax survey, dates from *c.*1077 in the heyday of Northern Song rule.[14] It is followed by a 1429 government list of those locations "where merchants assemble from throughout the empire." In accompanying a reorganization of the Grand Canal grain traffic this 1429 list signaled the early stages of the Ming economy's delayed recovery from the century and a half of Mongol misrule and ruin of north China. The last of our three lists is

---

[13] Wu Shiqi, *Lüzi guan zhengxin bian*, 5.28a–b.
[14] Ma, *Commercial Development*, Appendix, 165–71, lists all sixty-three cities bearing in *c.*1077 a commercial tax quota of 20,000 or more strings of cash.

found in a survey of important commercial places in c.1580 during the boom years of the late Ming (see Map 1.2).

These lists need to be compared with care. Not all their aims are identical; nor are the number of locations each includes, nor the identity of the object each claims to measure. Whereas the first two lists were drafted by serving officials to determine commercial tax quotas, the third was drawn up as a retired official's personal overview of important late Ming centers of commercial activity. Nonetheless, all three lists had a common purpose of identifying major commercial centers in the China of their time. Useful, then, for our purposes, a simple comparison of the locations in these lists suggests changes in the nature, location, and organization of China's major markets over five centuries, when its population rose from roughly 100 million to more than 150 million.

First, even though this comparison shows a noticeable expansion of the market as an institution from the eastern coastal provinces into the southwest quarter of the Ming empire, it is the north–south differences in market numbers and location that Map. 1.2 most clearly highlights. In fact, the preponderance of south China's commercial economy over north China's, as seen in their relative number of market sites, persists throughout these five centuries. In the early and late Ming the growth of this southern preponderance is largely due to the increased market presence in the middle and lower Yangzi areas and, by the late Ming, the southwest. The fact that no less than 20 percent of this map's place names appear solely in the c.1580 list and that virtually all of these additional sites are situated in south China is strong evidence that south China's marketing area had increased its dominance and expanded its geographical range by the late Ming.[15]

Second, north China's markets have a distinctive history. The inclusion of virtually all thirty-three places in the 1429 list in also the c.1077 and c.1580 lists appears to indicate that north China's most important centers of market activity enjoyed considerable continuity as market centers from the Northern Song to the end of the Ming. In fact, it is discontinuity rather than continuity that distinguishes north China's significant market locations and, by implication, its commercial development during these centuries. Consider the dire fate, come the Ming, of two of the Northern Song's (960–1126) most thriving commercial

[15] Ren Fang, "Ming Qing shizhen," 187–228, confirms these trends.

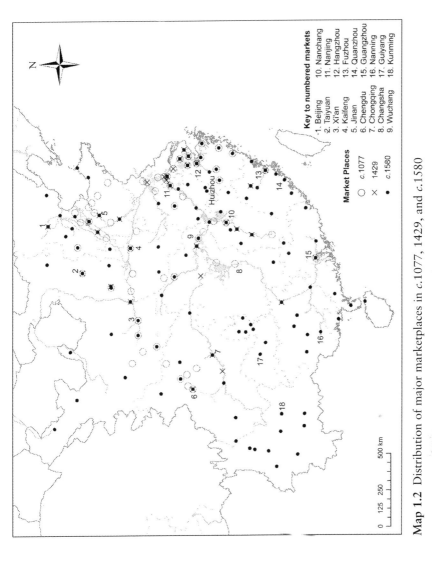

Map 1.2 Distribution of major marketplaces in c.1077, 1429, and c.1580

regions, Sichuan and the Huai area. In the 1429 list a major market is recorded for just three, very disparate, prefectural seats of the vast province of Sichuan and for just one prefecture in the Huai area (where three prefectural seats had ranked among the empire's top seven commercial taxpaying tax stations in the c.1077 list). Similarly, the northern province of Shaanxi, the site of the imperial capital for virtually the entire first millennium of Chinese imperial history, had no site in the 1429 list, and the two Central Plain areas of Hebei and Henan (in the Ming they roughly corresponded to the Northern Metropolitan Circuit and Henan province) had just one site apiece.[16] Even more telling is the absence from the 1429 list of eight of the top ten north China commercial sites with the highest commercial tax quotas in c.1077.

Third, and most interestingly, by the sixteenth century at the latest some southern and northern markets differed qualitatively in the spatial relationship of some of their market towns to the government's administrative hierarchy and thus the degree of government control over low-level market activities. The thirty-three sites included in the 1429 list formed an urban commercial network whose sites tightly overlapped with those of the early Ming government's administrative hierarchy (all but two of the 1429 list's thirty-three sites were county or prefectural seats, and the other two were market towns, Linqing 臨清鎮 in Shandong in the north and Qingjiang 清江鎮 in Jiangxi in the south). Furthermore, commercial travel and transport routes between these 1429 sites also continued to follow the imperial-run waterway network that ever since the Sui dynasty (581–618) had consisted of the Grand Canal, Yellow River, and Yangzi river waterways (all central and northern locations in the 1429 and c.1580 lists are situated along one or more of these waterways or on one of their major tributaries).[17] Maintained by the government, the Grand Canal was restored in the early Ming as part of the government's efforts to repair the transport infrastructure and battered countryside of north China after two centuries of severe military destruction and environmental damage. The court's decision to shift the capital from Nanjing to Beijing in 1419 also led to a great expansion of its use by government and private vessels alike.

---

[16] Also sorely underrepresented in the 1429 list are the two southwest provinces of Yunnan and Guizhou, each given no market, and the two southeast provinces of Guangdong and Guangxi, each given just one.
[17] Guo Hou'an, *Ming shilu jingji*, 548.

Although the role of the state in the running and supervision of these important markets in north China seems to have been strong, it does not signify a straight continuation of state predominance from the Northern Song. The 1429 list contains just one market town in north China (and another in south China), while in most Northern Song circuits, or provinces, market towns collectively paid more commercial tax than did the county seats collectively.[18] The marketing order of north China in the early fifteenth century – and all it implies about the vitality or otherwise of local commercial life and the volume of private trade – was a far more top-down order than in c.1077, when the north's many market towns had supplied numerous privately made specialized agricultural and handicraft goods. The Song breakthroughs for an expansion of private organization of commercial life had, after centuries of foreign invasion and political disturbance, been tamed, if not reversed, in north China.[19]

Fourth, note the great shift between the early and late Ming governments' handling of foreign trade. All but one (that is, Guangzhou in the far southeast province of Guangdong) of the thirty-three sites mentioned in the 1429 list were located on interior waterways, indicating the early Ming government's overwhelming concentration on domestic production and transportation. The early Ming ban on private overseas trade lasted up to at least 1567, and the government's overriding concern with northern border control lay behind not just its 1419 shift of the capital to a fortress-like Beijing but also its enforced withdrawal of the major northern frontier market sites of earlier dynasties back to Beijing and Taiyuan 太原, each located more than a hundred miles south of the nearest border. These inward shifts of significant market sites, however, did not reduce the self-absorbed court's tendency to view both foreign and domestic trade as anything other than its cash cow. Anxious to replenish the dynasty's coffers, court officials recommended that all thirty-three sites in the 1429 list be ordered to pay a flat 4,000 percent rise in their commercial tax quota. The Xuande emperor (r. 1426–35) demurred. Judging this level of increase "too onerous," he demonstrated his enlightenment by declaring a rise in the tax quota of just 500 percent.[20]

[18] McDermott and Shiba, "Economic Change in China," 381–85.
[19] Von Glahn, "Towns and Temples," 176–211.
[20] Guo Hou'an, *Ming shilu jingji*, 548; Brook, "Communications and Commerce," 673–77; Huang, *Taxation*, 226–36.

A century and a half later, the commercial landscape in all parts of China had changed profoundly. In his empire-wide survey of major commercial centers in the late sixteenth century the ex-official Zhang Han 張瀚 (1511–93) drew upon his travels to portray a world of commerce flourishing far more widely than in any previous post-Song account of the Chinese economy.[21] As already indicated, four times as many sites (that is, 120) are mentioned in his *c*.1580 text than in the 1429 report, and so widely are they now scattered that all Ming provinces and metropolitan circuits are represented, each by no fewer than four major commercial centers.[22] Extending earlier mid-sixteenth-century reports of merchant boats traveling both northward and southward "bumping one another night and day for months at a time" on their Grand Canal voyages,[23] Zhang Han identifies the embarkation and destination points of these busy merchants' journeys: "Merchants from the north and south of the empire clamor to come to the Yangzi delta ... Even the big merchants from Shaanxi, Shanxi, Shandong, and Henan provinces do not consider traveling several thousand *li* [to Zhejiang province] too long a journey to make."

Border sites and their foreign trade also receive far greater attention from Zhang. Along the southeast coasts of Zhejiang, Fujian, and Guangdong provinces the Ming dynasty's 1567 relaxation of its two-century-old ban on private parties' engagement in foreign trade had allowed far more people to trade abroad or in Chinese ports with foreigners. In the far southwestern provinces of Sichuan, Guangxi, and Yunnan an unprecedented number of thriving market sites suggests a stretching of central and south China's market network to these distant reaches as well as these same provinces' expanded overland and riverine contact with foreign traders to their west and south. At the same time, the more central marketing sites mentioned in the 1429 list

---

[21] Brook, "Merchant Network," 165–214. The *c*.1580 date given to this survey follows the judgment of Brook, *Confusions of Pleasure*, but the conditions Zhang describes doubtless largely existed in the two or three preceding decades as well (Brook, "Merchant Network," 175). All references here to Zhang Han and his text can be found in this study by Brook.
[22] A far shorter list in Ye Quan (1522–78), *Xianbo bian*, 179, includes Xingzhou 荊州, Zhangshu 樟樹, Wuhu 蕪湖, Shangxin he 上新河, Fengqiao 楓橋, Nanhao 南濠, Huzhou 湖州市, Kuazhou 瓜州, Zhengyang 正陽, and Linqing 臨清 as "places where commercial goods most assemble." All these places (or their larger administrative unit) are found in Zhang's list.
[23] *MQHS*, 5.

(the only one of its thirty-three sites not relisted by Zhang Han is Qingjiang 清江 in Jiangxi, despite its continuing prosperity[24]) have retained their critical importance in Zhang's depiction of commodity distribution, north–south as well as east–west, in the late sixteenth century.[25]

The successful spread of the market into the far reaches of the Yangzi and other major river valleys prompts us to wonder if and how these thousands of markets were integrated in any coherent and efficient way. In a series of seminal publications G. William Skinner presented a comprehensive answer to these questions. Inspired by central-place research on market distribution patterns in the north German plain, he sketched an eight-tiered marketing hierarchy that with periodic markets constituted an integrated infrastructure for each of "the nine macro-regions" of late imperial China. In a classic statement of his views on the circulation of goods within this marketing network, he described the basic operating principles for the interlinkage of multiple marketing tiers for commodity circulation within each macro-region:

Economic central places are shown to have formed regional systems of cities, each system a multilevel hierarchy internally differentiated by the degree of economic centrality of its components and their position in the core-periphery structure of the region. The commercial hinterlands of economic central places were hierarchically stacked in a manner that involved systematic overlap from one level to the next – a structural arrangement that conditioned politics and social structure as well as economic activity.[26]

Skinner's conceptual framework rightly won admiration for its bold comprehensive vision of an extensive circulation of goods within

---

[24] *Qingjiang xianzhi* (1642) reports, "By custom [Qingjiang] has many merchants, who happen to abandon wife and children and tread off on foot for several thousand *li*, so much that they have families outside in Guangdong, Guangxi, Guizhou, and Yunnan [provinces] – there is nowhere they don't get to." By the Ming's close, trade in Qingjiang had been hard hit by commercial tax increases that drove merchants from this once thriving commercial center. Ibid., 1.25a–b, 34a–b, Long Denggao, *Jiangnan shichang*, 79–80, identifies six delta market towns which declined despite general delta prosperity.
[25] Li Xianting (1648–95), *Guangling zaji*, 193, confirms these trends by identifying the empire's four "gathering points": Beijing in the north, Suzhou in the east, Foshan in the south, and Hankou in the west (the last two are market towns).
[26] Skinner, *The City in Late Imperial China*, "Introduction," 253, and "Regional Urbanization," 211–49.

China's macro-regions and of limited long-distance trade between these macro-regions. Presented at a time when other scholars were detailing the significance and scale of late imperial commerce, his research suggestively described how some traders moved between upper and middle-upper levels of this market scaffolding while peddlers and others tended to operate at its lower levels.

Yet Skinner's model of market development has never been empirically confirmed for premodern China.[27] It is built on a string of hypotheses and evidence from post-1800 China, that ill fits the crisscrossing of merchant travel routes detailed in Huizhou merchants' guide books from the Ming and early Qing.[28] These ambitious merchants, aware of the great complexity of the Yangzi Valley's marketing structure and of great variations in the profitability of its different market levels, tended to have their eyes fixed on the far more profitable higher levels of interregional trade rather than on the more local, or intra-regional, deals of a resident merchant. In the cry of one mid-Ming Huizhou merchant desperate to escape the boredom and poverty of his lower-level trading place in the Zhejiang interior – "I want to be a sojourning merchant and get double the cash"[29] – one hears the despairing longings of those Huizhou merchants unable to achieve the glamorous career of a big-city sojourning trader they had once imagined for themselves and then seen others realize. Such disenchanted local merchants, the peddlers as well as the shopkeepers, certainly existed in large numbers. Even if they became rich, they would have regarded themselves as failures relative to those who circulated among the bigger cities and their markets.

Admittedly, Skinner was aware of the inadequacy of his model for long-distance shipping between the middle and lower reaches of the

---

[27] Even Shiba Yoshinobu's exemplary regional study "Ningbo" (Skinner, ed., *The City in Late Imperial China*, 275–346) makes limited use of a macro-regional analysis.

[28] Huang Bian, *Tianxia shuilu lucheng*, has 143 long-distance routes, most of which sensibly make use of rivers whenever possible to crisscross the country with blissful disregard for any micro- or macro-regional marketing hierarchy. By and large, these routes connect large marketing centers with stops or pass-through points along the way. These smaller locations might well have been additional sites of commercial transaction, but many listed here served merely as merchant signposts to the correct route.

[29] FKSFC, 171–72.

Yangzi Valley.[30] But the problem with Skinner's theory, as Martin Heijdra, among others, has noted, extends as well to trade along other major Chinese waterways, which "were the mainstay of the economic structure of the empire as a whole." Regardless of whether or not Heidjra is also right to argue that "most trade took place and most profits were made and *could only* be made inter-regionally" (my italics), he surely is correct to question Skinner's additional claim "that every city within a macro-region had more trade with every other city within the macro-region than with any city outside the region."[31] Compared to the feudal and early modern kingdoms of Central Europe (from whose pattern of economic development Skinner's theory ultimately derived), traders in Ming China faced relatively few formal government restrictions on the geographical extension and scope of their transactions.

Two additional deviations from Skinner's model concern the formation of horizontally interlinked market-town clusters in the Yangzi delta economy and the expansion of direct transhipment trading between large commercial nodes along major waterways. Though located at opposite levels in Skinner's regional market schema, the clusters at the lower levels in the delta's economy and the nodes along the Grand Canal and Yangzi river at higher levels in the market structure tended to be dominated by Huizhou merchants. More to the point, both of these types of market growth in the Ming developed along distinctive lines ill-suited to notions of markets functioning mainly to meet local demand.

Since at least the Tang dynasty (618–907), market towns in the Yangzi delta had grown out of various kinds of preexisting settlement, ranging from a temple complex, military garrison, and river fording point to a travelers' inn and a periodic market. In general, these market towns enjoyed links by stream or road to the surrounding countryside, allowing for their channeling of other places' products down to nearby periodic markets or of these villages' raw materials and products for use higher up in the local marketing hierarchy. As Shiba Yoshinobu noted for the Ningbo plain, three types of businesses would play a crucial role in interconnecting the delta's markets: shops involved in

---

[30] Skinner, *The City in Late Imperial China*, 217–18, 235, Table 5, 242, 248, attributes this divergence to the cheapness of river, as opposed to land, transport, and the extensive stretch of the Yangzi's four major tributaries.
[31] Heijdra, "Socio-economic Development," 499; von Glahn, *Economic History of China*, 334; Brokaw, "Empire of Texts," 187–235.

textile production, shops with goods from elsewhere in China, and money shops or pawnshops involved in giving loans to finance these concentrated commercial activities.[32] And, in almost every case, these traders would have experienced minimal government supervision, particularly in comparison to the controls imposed on them in county and prefectural seats.

From the mid fifteenth century, some neighboring market towns in the northeast corner of the delta underwent a far more complicated form of economic integration. An archipelago of market towns – and not just periodic markets – functioned increasingly as a single, if dispersed, unit in the production of a single type of product like cotton textiles. Horizontal clusters of markets and market towns performed different specialized steps in a cotton textile production process (cultivating and harvesting the cotton plant, ginning, spinning cotton yarn, weaving the cloth, dyeing and finishing the cloth for particular markets) that by the Ming's end engaged most of the land and population of the eastern counties of Suzhou prefecture and all of Songjiang prefecture (in 1621 the Portuguese Jesuit Alvaro Semedo reported the operation of over 200,000 looms in the town and county of Shanghai in Songjiang prefecture).[33] In other words, some of the distribution sites where merchants "assembled to trade" had become production centers as well and were beginning to attract merchant money for finished products, advanced orders, and eventually also infrastructure and simple technical investment. Cotton spinning and weaving were concentrated in the various market towns of Jiading 嘉定 and Changshu 常熟 in Suzhou and elsewhere in Songjiang, areas conveniently located to acquire abundant supplies of raw cotton, ginned cotton, and cotton thread, as well as spinners and weavers from neighboring Jiaxing 嘉興 and Jiashan 嘉山 counties. Dyeing and finishing were done in Zhujing 洙涇 and Fengjing 楓涇 market towns, where there were several hundred cloth shops as well as dyeing and calendaring houses. Their interlinkage, both vertical and horizontal, of raw materials, labor, marketing, and simple technology factors transformed the northeast quarter of the delta into China's cotton textile production center from the sixteenth century onward, thereby laying the basis for

---

[32] Shiba, "Pattern of Rural–Urban Continuum," 180. As Shiba found in the late Qing Ningbo plain, few Jiangnan shops in the Ming specialized in overseas products.
[33] Nishijima, "Chinese Cotton," 63.

the establishment of China's modern textile industry in nearby Shanghai at the end of the nineteenth century.

Furthermore, to help the market towns of Songjiang meet the growing demand for their textiles elsewhere in China, merchants from Huizhou and other regions shipped in large amounts of raw cotton from locations in north and south China hundreds of miles away from the delta. Along with local merchants they further expanded these market towns' connections by selling directly and indirectly to Fujianese and Cantonese merchants an increasing amount of delta textiles, including high-end luxury items like velvet and cotton cloth interwoven with silk. To intensify its concentration on the production of cotton textiles for the rest of the country (by the end of the fifteenth century most of the early Ming rice paddies in western Songjiang had been converted to cotton plant cultivation), Songjiang's growing population likewise required great amounts of grain shipped often from nearly a thousand miles away and often by Huizhou merchants.[34]

In other words, market towns in much of the northeast portion of the delta were now woven into a larger, more organic long-distance marketing hierarchy that extended far beyond the delta. By the mid Ming, rice-surplus areas far up the Yangzi Valley, thanks to their expansion of production, population, and markets, formed at their greatest extent a nearly thousand-mile-long chain of distribution and consumption for the delta's residents, urban as well as rural.[35] In addition, the delta's market towns received cotton harvested or spun into thread in north China and then shipped it back as woven cloth to north China or onward to provinces in the southeast.

Another feature of Ming market development that Skinner's model downplays is the direct trans-regional river trade conducted among a long string of commercial nodes that stretched from the start of the Grand Canal in Beijing to Yangzhou and then westward from the mouth of the Yangzi river to virtually the start of its gorges.[36] It was

---

[34] Ibid., 17–77; Zurndorfer, "Cotton Textile Production," 72–98; Gong Shengsheng, "Lun 'HuGuang shu'," 130–40. Long Denggao, *Jiangnan shichang*, 63–66, discusses clusters of silk textile production in the southern half of the delta, as does Tang Lixing, *Suzhou*, 230, for Suzhou market town clusters of iron production and cotton and silk weaving.

[35] Gong Shengsheng, "Lun 'HuGuang shu'," 130–40.

[36] Finnane, *Yangzhou*, 36–38, notes the greater utility of network over central-place theory for analyzing China's urban development.

at these riverside ports that Huizhou's long-distance merchants tended to congregate and carry out their transactions. Without first establishing close links with nearby local markets and then working themselves up any regional marketing hierarchy in the way Skinner described, they preferred to set up operational bases far from home in very disparate nodes for traffic along the Yangzi Valley and the Grand Canal (see the destination places listed in Ming merchant travel guides like Huang Bian's 黃汴 *Tianxia shuilu lucheng* 天下水陸路程, as well as the travel routes mentioned in Chapter 6's case histories of specific merchant families).

This kind of commercial node was far from new in the Chinese economy. Every dynasty since at least the construction of the Grand Canal in the Sui dynasty, had made use of riverine nodes, the classic example being Yangzhou city, adjacent to the empire's biggest salt-producing area at the juncture of the Yangzi river and the Grand Canal. During the Ming, what was new was the number of these nodes on the country's major waterways and the volume of trade passing through them in east–west as well as north–south directions. Along the Yangzi's final thousand miles to the sea, we have by the Ming's end no fewer than seven such major nodes (the famous ports of Yuezhou 岳州, Hankou, Huangzhou 黃州, Jiujiang, Wuhu 蕪湖, Nanjing (Longjiang 龍江), and Zhenjiang 鎮江, plus three major nodes along the Grand Canal in the delta: Hangzhou, Suzhou, and Changzhou). And, along the Grand Canal in central and north China, long-distance merchants, according to Fu Chonglan's research, frequented another eight Ming nodes: Yangzhou, Huai'an 淮安, Xuzhou 徐州, Jining 濟甯, Linqing, Dezhou 德州, Tianjin 天津, and Beijing.[37]

Foremost of these northern Grand Canal nodes in its fame, commercial growth, and impact, and in the number of its Huizhou settlers, was Linqing, a Ming and Qing emporium far too little studied outside China. Just as the market town of Hankou fused the markets of east and west China along the Yangzi during the Qing dynasty, so did Linqing in Ming and Qing times help to integrate many of the markets of north and south China, and not just those along the Grand Canal. Once the goods of all four quarters of the Ming empire started arriving in great volume at its wharves, its warehouses filled up with goods, more so than anywhere else in north China but for Beijing. Situated

[37] Fu Chonglan, *Zhongguo yunhe*.

conveniently at the intersection of the Grand Canal, the Wen 汶 river, and the Wei 衛 river in the northwest corner of Shandong province, it was a transhipment point less for immediately adjacent counties and prefectures in Henan and Shandong than for the more distant county and prefectural seats of these two provinces, to the southwest of Henan and the east of Shandong.[38] Attracting merchants from throughout much of the northeast quarter of the empire (Beijing; the provinces of Henan, Shanxi, and Shaanxi; the towns and cities of Shandong; and Liaodong – and from several regions of the southeast: Xuzhou, Huai'an, Yangzhou, southern Jiangsu, Zhejiang province, and, not least, Huizhou), it supplied markets in these areas with both its shipped-in goods and its own products of bricks, iron goods, silk and cotton textiles, boats, tiles, and other construction materials. So broad was its reach that its annual volume of private grain trade (excluding taxes) by the late sixteenth century fluctuated between five million and ten million bushels, making it second only to Beijing as the preferred site for private and government grain warehouses in all of north China.[39] The annual volume of its cotton cloth trade, then, is estimated to have ranged from half a million to a full million bolts as well.

The city wall of Linqing, a mere market town at the start of the Ming, was built in 1449 and its administrative status was elevated to that of prefecture (*zhou* 州) in 1484. A town with a five-thousand-household population at the start of the Ming mushroomed over the next two centuries into one of north China's largest cities with a population of over 150,000 in *c*.1580 and close to 200,000 by the Ming's end. By the mid fifteenth century this population boom had expanded the town's perimeter to a length of about ten miles, and later on (the Ming date is unclear) its shops, warehouses, and markets stretched ten or more miles along the Grand Canal. With a constant stream of boats and travelers passing through its port in the canal's ice-free months, Linqing's registered shops by the end of the sixteenth

---

[38] Exceptionally detailed Japanese field research reports from wartime Suzhou (March 1941) indicate that long-distance merchants would have unloaded their goods onto other long-distance merchants' vessels heading north and south of the Yangzi, or, more commonly, onto local merchants' junks or carts that wended along branch waterways and roads to smaller markets in the same node's marketing area. Mantetsu chōsabu, ed., *Chū Shi no minsengyō*, 274–91. Ibid., 293–364, describes the methods of operating these local boat businesses; long-distance merchants did not do this local marketing.

[39] Hoshi, *Mindai sōun*, 275–304.

century had so proliferated that their product range was rivaled only by Beijing and the larger cities of the Yangzi Valley: seventy-three cloth shops, thirty-two silk shops, sixty-five shops for miscellaneous goods, twenty-odd shops for lacquerware, twenty-four paper shops, thirteen big shops for goods from Liaodong, a hundred-odd pawnshops, and countless shops for grain and tea (one large street had over twenty grain shops).[40]

With these shops' owners, other northern merchants, and Huizhou sojourners all buying one another's goods, Linqing in the Ming served as a major junction of the commercial worlds of north and south China. Even so, it is startling that its boat traffic and commercial transactions, largely along the Grand Canal, earned its customs station the top commercial tax quota in the entire empire for most of the Ming; its quota was twice that of Hushu Station just northwest of Suzhou and 20 percent more than that of even Chongwen Gate Station, the Grand Canal's terminus in Beijing. Even though large increases in its commercial tax quota in the Wanli era (1573–1620) forced many Linqing stores to close down and thus by 1625 reduced its actual commercial tax revenues to just three-quarters of its new (and higher) quota, Linqing's customs tax payment in 1625 still ranked as the second-highest from all tax stations in the empire (the top position that year fell to Hushu Station in Suzhou). In other words, Linqing's commerce, most of it dominated by Huizhou merchants, flourished so greatly that this former market town of the 1429 list had by the end of the Ming become a Grand Canal emporium representing the economic power of Huizhou merchants in north China far from their bases in the Yangzi Valley.

Imagine, then, along just the Grand Canal as many as ten smaller versions of this flourishing site, and one can grasp the degree of commercial expansion and urban transformation that the Ming's economic growth had attained. The great majority of Linqing city's residents, however, were, like those down in Hankou, merchants from elsewhere, especially Huizhou.[41] "Sojourning" far from home, they made their wealth by shipping north the grain, timber, silk cloth, and

---

[40] Xu Tan, "Ming Qing shiqi," 135–57; Xin Shufang, "Gudai yunhe," 68–75, 83–85, 287–304; Okano, "Minmatsu Rinshin," 103–33.

[41] Xie Zhaozhe, *Wu zazu*, 14, 413, claims that 90 percent of Linqing's candidates in the civil service examinations "are Huizhou merchants with registration [in Huizhou]."

cotton textiles they had purchased in the Yangzi Valley and on return sending on to the Yangzi the furs, metals, raw cotton, dried fish, and other products acquired in north China.

In sum, despite advances into western China the major trading network used by Huizhou's long-distance merchants in the Ming was built out of the larger ports along the major trunk routes of the empire in eastern China: the Yangzi river, the Grand Canal, and some stretches of the Huai and Yellow rivers. Their ships and shipments regularly stopped at smaller harbors in between their major stops,[42] but it was these larger meeting points, or nodes, where Huizhou merchants in the sixteenth and seventeenth centuries tended to congregate and make the fortunes that won them empire-wide fame and envy. Unlike the early Ming rulers they had seen the possibility of forming this network of largely private trade and taken the steps and risks necessary to achieve it. Skinner's work, so intent on describing the structure of this network, seems singularly devoid of human agents, and so I suggest that we consider Huizhou merchants its main creators, if not its heroes, during the last two dynasties. Some lost their lives in moving about to find better deals and higher profits, while others eventually settled down and dealt in goods and credit in the thriving towns and cities of the Yangzi Valley, the Grand Canal, and the southeast coast.[43] It is their fate and fortune that this volume will explore both inside and outside Huizhou.

Changes for Ming Merchants

In the latter half of the Ming these travel routes and nodes became crowded with fortune seekers, men who abandoned the "essential work" of agriculture for the "nonessential" work of being an artisan, a merchant, or, worse, a vagabond,[44] and thereby fell subject to their betters' moral contempt. The empire-wide figure for all these escapees

---

[42] As is evident from the list of places passed by on long-distance merchants' trading routes, as detailed in, for example, Huang Bian, *Tianxia*, 23, 35, 248–49.

[43] Of course, not all such efforts succeeded consistently; witness the vagaries of the periodic market from the late Tang to the Qing, as in Tuncun (*Tuncun zhi*, 313–38, in *Tongli zhi (liang chong)*, and Puyuan 濮院 market town (von Glahn, "Towns and Temples").

[44] Brook, *Confusions of Pleasure*, 139–52.

from the real work of agriculture was put by a native Fujianese at over 50 percent.[45] It was even higher for some parts of the Yangzi delta: 60 to 70 percent in Songjiang prefecture[46] and 70 to 80 percent on islands in nearby Lake Tai.[47] By the close of the sixteenth century natives of Yangzhou city accounted for just a thirtieth of their city's population. Its markets, along with those in nearby Yizhen 儀鎮 and Guazhou 瓜洲, were home to no fewer than 10,000 brokers, all engaged in handling traveling merchants.[48] Already in 1435, long before the late Ming economic surge began in the hinterlands of south China, the official head of Yaoan 姚安 commandery in far-off Yunnan province reported that a total of 30,000 to 50,000 merchants – these figures are surely excessive – were active there from Anfu 安福 county in Jiangxi province and from Longyu 龍游 county in Zhejiang province.[49] Even in relatively underdeveloped Guangdong province, mid Ming officials reported that "many [people] practice trade."[50] And, in Huizhou, one of the epicenters of this explosive rush into commerce, the share of late Ming locals who left its paddy fields for marketplaces elsewhere in the empire was often estimated at 70 or 80 percent.[51]

The authors of these reports were by and large convinced that the expanded role of money and the market in everyday life had proven corrosive of the social order and particularly of the centuries-old hegemony of scholar-official rule in both government and local society. Their figures surely need serious qualification, as they refer almost entirely to those parts of south China where market expansion was most widely experienced and where many "merchants" actually were temporary or part-time traders supplementing their family's farm income. These figures also consistently omit the half of the populace in Huizhou and elsewhere that was bound-footed to stay at home. But, even if we conclude that these numbers and their accompanying critiques are best understood as expressions of Ming scholars' and

---

[45] Lin Xiyuan, *Lin Ciya xiansheng wenji*, 2.8a.
[46] He Liangjun, *Siyou zhai congshuo*, 13, 112.
[47] Fu Yiling, *Ming Qing shidai shangren*, 96.
[48] Han Dacheng, "Mingdai Huishang," 41–42.
[49] Zhang Haipeng and Zhang Haiying, *Zhongguo shida shangbang*, 369; they mostly engaged in lending at usurious rates to local tribesmen.
[50] Chen Dakang, *Mingdai shanggu*, 73.
[51] To cite just three such claims: *THJ*, 52, 1,101; Fu Yiling, *Ming Qing shidai shangren*, 53; *MQHS*, 44; Zhang Zhengming, *Ming Qing Jinshang*, 94, for similar reports elsewhere.

officials' discontent with meagre agricultural incomes and with recent social changes, they rightly point to real changes in the place of merchants in Ming society – an expansion in merchant numbers and activities, a division of labor in their ranks and a resultant stratification of their jobs, a greater complexity of their social position, and new means of organization, as well as a greater variety in their commodities, destinations, level of wealth, and actual types of work.

In a common historical interpretation, the final legal status differences and disabilities for merchants in China were dismantled during the Ming. Not only were merchants and their sons eligible for civil service examinations, but also they as individuals and groups won greater appreciation in society at large, particularly in comparison to their past position and the continued privileges of the social and legal position of "official households" (*guanhu* 官戶, *guanren* 官人).[52] This perception is generally accurate, but it has unfortunately given birth to the far less accurate assumption that one can capture and describe elite male social change in late imperial China in terms of their movement from one of these categories to the other.

Strictly speaking, the categories "merchant" and "official" (or "official household") are different *kinds* of category. They may generally refer to two distinct occupations (*ye* 業), but the fundamental difference between these two categories is that "official household" indicates a legal status and "merchant" an economic class. The legal status of "official household" was conferred by the government normally upon a male's acquisition of an examination degree, even if he never proceeded to hold a government office and own property.[53] Linked to the dynasty's system of household register categories and to its sumptuary laws, this legal status accorded its holders a high social status; certain legal privileges and powers, such as eligibility for official appointment; tax breaks; penal exemptions; and a wide swathe of consumption distinctions manifested in superior means of transport, type of clothing, and housing materials. Yet, in contrast to the ruling elites of other contemporary East Asian polities, the Ming "official household" status did not confer land, income, or an official position. A Ming official household's land and landed income came to him through

---

[52] For a more detailed treatment of this subject, see my essays, "Merchants and Trade Networks in Late Imperial China" and "Merchants in Late Imperial China."

[53] Beattie, *Land and Lineage*, 17–19.

purchase, gift, and inheritance, not directly from holding a government position. He was expected to look after whatever economic assets his family held (his official salary was relatively low), and so he faced strikingly few legal restraints on his actual work and income when out of office. Even fewer work regulations were imposed on his sons, many of whom in Huizhou would have invariably entered trade while their family's household status remained that of an "official household" during their father's lifetime.

By contrast, merchants shared, but perhaps for a brief period at the start of the Ming, an identical legal status with the vast majority of Ming households, that of "commoner" (*minhu* 民戶), and thus were distinct from the other main Ming legal status groups, such as military households (*junhu* 軍戶), base people (*jianmin* 賤民), and "official household."[54] By itself, a merchant's commoner legal status blocked neither his exit from the occupation of merchant nor his entrance into any other household category. In theory and in fact, male members of a merchant household could and did hold virtually any legal status or social position, just as virtually no one – except, as prescribed in a 1394 law, certain high-ranked members of the imperial family, some very high officials and their sons, and serving officials – was barred from trading or becoming a merchant (*shangren*).[55] To cite two extreme cases, not only did some Buddhist monks at Suzhou's celebrated Chengtian temple 承天寺 routinely make and sell wine,[56] but also some members of the Ming imperial clan ran their own shops in Beijing from no later than the mid sixteenth century.[57] The door was thus legally open for holders of "official household" status and their sons to spend, if they chose, some, if not a great deal, of their life as a merchant; it was open more widely for merchants to purchase degrees (and the attendant legal status of "official household") and even more widely for their descendants to seek and sometimes gain an official appointment through the examinations. Already in the reign of the

---

[54] *Huizhou fuzhi* (1699), 2.72b–73a; Usui, *Kishū shōnin*, 55–57.
[55] Ibid., 81; this 1394 law proved unenforceable even in the early Ming.
[56] Huang Zongxi, *Ming wenhai*, 420, 4,392; Chen Baoliang, *Piaoyao de chuantong*, 288–92, and Ye Shaoyuan, *Qi Zhen*, 2.8a.
[57] *Ming shilu*, 138.5a (on imperial family members trading in Beijing); Liu Ruoyu, *Zhuozhong zhi*, 16, 132–33 (on six imperial shops in Beijing, whose luxury goods sales from the Jiajing reign era to the Tianqi reign era (1621–27) were annually worth several tens of thousands of taels; the buyers aimed to sell them on).

Jiajing emperor (r. 1522–66) some merchants reportedly bought official titles and official appointments.[58] Even if these latter instances were rare (a large sum of silver won only lower-rank provincial postings such as the magistracy of a large county), the fluidity of merchants' and their family members' legal and social status in the Ming was virtually unprecedented among the premodern sedentary societies of East Asia.

In the second half of the Ming, then, elite social change conceivably consisted not just of a man's passage from one legal status to another but also of a far more complicated passage from commoner (including merchant) to official, vice versa for sons, and one person's combination or mixture of official and merchant work in his own lifetime in an endless variety of patterns. And, if that overlapping of merchant and official interests held true for individuals and families, it would have been doubly so for the state within which they worked. As Marianne Bastid has argued, premodern Chinese had difficulty conceiving of the economy as a separate domain from the political world.[59] Not surprisingly, the mixture and at times merger of the political and economic domains led, on an individual as well as on a state level, to not just a collision of values but also collusion. For many individual Chinese, the dream career combined the legal status of an official and the wealth of a successful merchant, such as a salt merchant successful in the government's salt monopoly.

In fact, a push towards the realization of this dream can be discerned over the course of the Song and Ming dynasties. During the Northern Song some Song merchants were themselves taking these examinations and, when successful, changing their careers to become officials, while by c.1040 their sons were eligible for the examinations and official life.[60] Furthermore, government restrictions and social emphases did not prevent successful examinees, once they became high court officials, from accumulating and profiting from urban real estate, including the ownership of many shops and businesses.[61] As Charles Hartman reminds us, no social or legal restrictions on holding extra-

---

[58] Han Dacheng, *Mingdai shehui jingji*, 199–200.
[59] Bastid, "The Structure of the Financial Institutions," 51–79.
[60] Yu Ying-shih, *Chinese History and Culture, v. 2*, 242–44; John Chaffee, *Thorny Gates*, 33, 39–40, 55.
[61] Miyazaki, *Ajiashi kenkyū, v. 3*, 179–80; Quan Hansheng, "Songdai guanli," 199–253.

official interests applied to officials or their family members in periods between their official appointments. "Many [Song] officials led double lives as businessmen."[62] Come the Ming dynasty, government efforts to distinguish sharply between merchant work and official work were frustrated by commerce's penetration of occupations held by all strata of Ming society. In the words of the scholar-official Qiu Jun 邱濬 (1420–95), "Nowadays, few do not engage in commercial activities. Scholars who study rely on commerce in place of their official salaries. Peasants who work hard on their farms, rely on commerce for their food; artisans, officials, Buddhists, and Daoists, all go beyond their nominal work to practice commerce."[63]

Even in as arch a center of high-gentry culture as mid-Ming Suzhou, members of the gentry and scholar-official elite engaged in business. Whereas individual Suzhou merchants were praised in the early Ming for doing good (*shan* 善), being a good man, "being good at money making" (*huozhi* 貨殖), and not living beyond their station (*fen* 分),[64] by the 1530s the world of business had been transformed by the intrusion of local elite families into the worlds of trade, manufacture, and moneylending, foretelling the end of a social order that had strictly distinguished official from merchant. In fact, according to the Suzhou literatus Huang Xingceng 黃行曾 (1490–1540), "Everyone in Suzhou regards a scholar (*shi* 士) as a merchant (*gu* 賈)," if only because they had seen fellow locals, having passed the examinations, "end up very rich by finding a powerful patron at the court and giving just two or three years of official service … The few who remain modest and do not manage their properties were viewed by others as 'idiots' (*chi* 痴)." Huang tells of scholar-official families who profited from metalworks and warehouses, but his interest seems greatest in those who had made their fortunes out of money:

So far, many gentry and scholar officials (*jinshen shifu* 縉紳士夫) [in Suzhou] have regarded moneymaking (*huozhi*) as urgent. When it comes to [running] official shops (*guandian* 官店) in the capital [presumably Beijing], operating lending and pawn brokering in its six suburbs, and dealing in salt and liquor, their [commercial] skill is twice that of ordinary people (*qimin* 齊民).[65]

---

[62] Hartman, "Sung Government," 79.
[63] Qiu Jun, *Chongbian Qiongtai gao*, 10.25b.
[64] Wang Guoping and Tang Lixing, *Ming Qing yilai Suzhou*, 86, 89, 98, 101.
[65] Huang Xingceng, *Wufeng lu*, 3, 4. Kang-i Sun Chang, "Literature of the Early Ming to Mid Ming (1375–1572)," 37–38, has noticed "an unprecedented

Two generations later, shortly after Huang Xingzeng's spendthrift son Huang Jishui 黃姬水 had depicted the dire living conditions of many earlier scholars in his *Lives of Poor Scholars* (*Pinshi zhuan* 貧士傳), the social commentator Guan Zhidao 管志道 (1536–1608) revealed in 1602 the path to wealth traveled by many retired officials in the Yangzi delta. When they found their landholdings of a thousand *mu* barely sufficient to support a poor official (*pinhuan* 貧宦) like themselves and feed a hundred men, they turned to brokering behind-the-scenes transactions among very wealthy individuals or between them and local government offices: "*If one does not acquire income from mediating (zhujian* 居間*), then where does one?*" (italics added).[66]

For many late imperial Chinese, nowhere in the empire was more closely associated with this heightened regard for commerce and merchants than the prefecture of Huizhou. From no later than the early sixteenth century its county and prefectural gazetteers routinely mention this appreciation, asserting baldly that Huizhou people evaluated commerce more highly than scholarship and preferred the career of a merchant to that of an official.[67] Slightly later, the Huizhou scholar Wang Xun 汪循 observed that some better-off merchants from Huizhou regarded themselves as superior to their overeducated but struggling scholarly neighbors, preferring neither to lend them money nor to marry their children.[68] By the mid sixteenth century the Suzhou writer Tang Shunzhi 唐順之 (1507–60) stressed Huizhou men's universal practice and appreciation of trade as a socially respectable occupation: "As virtually all men [there] make a living by relying on trade, even families of considerable accomplishment (*fachang zhi jia* 閥閱之家) are not ashamed of being traders."[69]

---

number of poems on money" in Suzhou poetry in the mid Ming. This period, she adds, "was the first time in Chinese history that money was openly discussed in literature." The belief that Suzhou did not have its own regional group of merchants (other than those from Dongting shan) is perhaps shaped by the fact that it had this kind of very commercialized "gentry elite," a social world where money, official title, and classical learning were closely interlinked in fact, if not simply in their own publications, paintings, and calligraphy pieces.

[66] Guan Zhidao, *Congxian*, 5.36a–b; for a case study, Jie Zhao, "Ties That Bind," 136–64.
[67] *Huizhou fuzhi* (1502), 1.10b; (1566), 2.39b–40a; (1699), 2.67b; (1827), 2.5.4a.
[68] Wang Yuming, "'*Renfeng ji*'," 110.   [69] *MQHS*, 5.

These changes eventually had great repercussions on official life, not least because a merchant's income was estimated in the early Qing to be in most years two to three times greater than an official family's (which usually was drawn from salary and land rents).[70] Furthermore, examination success increasingly required the resources of a rich merchant family.[71] No wonder that in 1826 Shen Qiqian 沈起潛 (1799–1845) wrote of his fellow students in a private Hangzhou academy that "they regarded a career in money (*qianye* 錢業) as fine (*jia* 佳)" and showed little interest in the examination circus.[72] For them and many others, long before Western gunboats hit China's shores, the examination dream had become an unending nightmare, leading only to poverty and an abiding sense of failure. As merchants and their sons could and did become officials, the more pertinent questions for many officials might have become, how and when can we officials become merchants?

At this point it is wise to pause and reiterate what is obvious to anyone remotely conversant with Ming and Qing dynasty records. Official status, as opposed to official income and the scholar's life, retained great attraction and social clout for the vast majority of educated Chinese men throughout the imperial period and beyond. If reports of overcrowded examination halls in Huizhou and elsewhere in the Ming and Qing fail to persuade, then observe the determination of the scholar-official founders of the She county native-place association (*huiguan* 會館) in Beijing to exclude mere merchants from their association well into the eighteenth century.[73] For Ming Huizhou, notice also the obsession with examination successes, official appointments, and literary writings and omission of information on merchants in the well-known book *A Record of Famous Lineages of Huizhou* (*Xin'an mingzu zhi* 新安名族志, 1551). Some modern scholars have treated this book's compilation of 700-odd "famous lineages" in eighty-four surname groupings as a comprehensive list of Huizhou's merchant elite,[74]

---

[70] As claimed by a Suzhou native in the late Ming and by the knowledgeable court official Zhang Ying two generations later (Beattie, *Land and Lineage*, 143–44, 180 n.12).
[71] Shen Yao, *Luofan lou wenji*, 24.12a.
[72] Shen Qiqian, *Xianyuan zashuo*, shang, 43a.
[73] Xu Shining and Xu Zeng, *Chongxu Shexian huiguan*, 31.
[74] Dai Tingming and Cheng Shangkuan, *Xin'an mingzu zhi* (henceforth *Xin'an mingzu zhi*); Zurndorfer, *Change and Continuity*, 15; Yamane Naoki, "Tō Sō kan no Kishū," 37–56.

but this assessment ignores how consistently this book and its seven prefaces celebrate Huizhou lineage members' official careers and downplay their commercial success. Even when the follow-up survey for one Huizhou county, *A Record of Famous Lineages of Xiuning* (*Xiuning mingzu zhi* 休寧名族志, 1621–27) includes information on some twenty successful merchants, it still omits all mention of Xiuning's pawnbrokers, the wealthiest not just in Huizhou but also in the entire empire.[75] For instance, the section devoted to the Wu lineage of Shangshan 上 (aka 商) 山吳 – a lineage which over ten generations built up the largest and most profitable pawnbrokering business in the empire – includes only their pre-Ming officials and scholars or their wives.[76] In short, the traditional Confucian-statist values that had for so long dominated elite official life in China retained a strong pull even among those Huizhou groups supposedly trying to break down its narrow gates with satchels of silver.

An even greater obstacle to an understanding of "merchants" in late imperial times is the overuse of this single term "merchant" for all traders regardless of their work, wealth, and status. If variety, then, is recognized for the types of merchants, so should it serve as a guide to the types of category Chinese devised for merchants. Some categories refer to a merchant's place of origin (for example, Huizhou) or site of trading (Yangzhou), and yet others to their proximity to the government (such as imperial merchants or official merchants). Also, Chinese traditionally distinguished between traveling merchants (*xingshang* 行商) and settled shopkeepers (*zuogu* 座賈), who traded usually at just one urban site.[77]

To these largely descriptive distinctions, late Ming writers in Huizhou and elsewhere added four sets of economic categories, two of them primarily functional and the other two essentially quantitative. Two types of merchant work appeared, then, very frequently for the first time in Chinese discourse: the broker (*yaren* 牙人) and the long-distance outsider, itinerant merchant, or "sojourning merchant" (*keshang* 客商),[78] be they sun-bronzed peddlers or pale-faced salt

---

[75] Cao Sixuan, *Xiuning mingzu zhi* (henceforth *Xiuning mingzu zhi*), editor's preface, *Xiuning mingzu zhi*, editor's pref., 4, for the 1626 or later date.
[76] *Xin'an mingzu zhi*, 2, 396.
[77] Tang Lixing, *Shangren*, 14–18, lists several uncommon means of distinguishing merchants.
[78] Adachi, *Min Shin Chūgoku*, 521–51.

merchants sailing on their own boat over the empire's waves. Among these long-distance merchants other writers discerned important differences by work: the peddling of commodities in far-away places, the storage of these goods to play the market, the opening and running of retail shops, pawnbrokering, and trading (*huiyi* 回易).[79] A 1609 breakdown of Huizhou merchant jobs, like the similar list of merchant jobs in mid-sixteenth-century Suzhou, shows that just as a pawnbroker might have his own retail shops and warehouses for commodity trading, so might the practice of "commodity accumulation" (a euphemism for "cornering the market") not be restricted to warehouse owners. In other words, members of the same merchant family performed different merchant jobs in different types of businesses.

Two further Ming sets of categories, when linked to these job types, help us assess a Ming merchant's assets in terms of his capital worth or, more roughly, their rank in merchant circles – top, middling, or lower (*shang, zhong, xia* 上, 中, 下).[80] The largest capital assets, held reportedly by salt merchant families in She county during the early seventeenth century, ranged from several hundred thousand taels to over one million taels. Below this top rank one finds a variety of middling positions, beginning with thousands of successful pawnbrokers with assets varying from several tens of thousands of taels up to hundreds of thousands. Next down were the itinerant traders in costly and season-sensitive bulk commodities like timber, grain, and quality tea, which they stored in large warehouses until a price change made their sale highly profitable; these traders' assets often totaled tens of thousands of taels. Beneath them were the lower-rank businesses, the start-up pawnshops, the struggling shops and businesses, and the mass of itinerant traders moving from city to city with a wide variety of goods to sell and buy, all forced to eke out a living with well below 10,000 taels and often in the mere hundreds for most of their lives.

Such a rough sketch of the merchant ladder of success should warn us off continually treating merchants, and especially the Huizhou merchants, as a single uniform group. It gains further complexity and

---

[79] *She Zhi* (1609), 20.shihuo, 1a–3b. Wang Tingyuan, "Lun Ming Qing shiqi," 54, broadly translates *huiyi* as "exchanging one thing for another," thereby encompassing both money purchase and barter methods (for example, raw cotton for cotton cloth).

[80] See Chapter 6 on the Fang lineage; Fujii, "Shin'an shōnin no kenkyū," 36.3, 75; *She zhi* (1609), 20.shihuo, 1a–3b.

credibility once these distinctions in wealth are recognized as fluid and that some of these jobs were performed concurrently or successively by the same merchant and his family members for different markets. Not only did most merchants, even salt merchants, deal in a variety of goods, if necessary in different ports of the Yangzi. But also a merchant's type of work might change over time, as his circumstances changed. He might rise from being a common peddler to become a dealer in expensive commodities, then an owner of warehouses and storeholds in market towns and cities in the delta; to trading in profitable commodities like textiles, timber, and tea; to dealing in credit as a moneylender and pawnbroker; to dealing as a salt merchant in Hangzhou and then, if he were fortunate, in Yangzhou; and if most fortunate, to be appointed head of the salt merchant community in either of these cities.

This description of the Ming merchants' ladder of success encompasses huge differences in capital holdings, social status, and political power. Whereas salt merchants were required by their job to maintain close ties with officials and whereas large commodity shippers sought government protection for their cargo and warehouses, pawnbrokers strove strenuously to restrict government involvement in their work to personal arrangements on their own terms. Moreover, the more capital a merchant had in his hands, the more likely it was that, pawnbrokers aside, he desired good and close ties with officialdom. Such success, as he knew, courted danger. A rich and powerful merchant, regardless of his purchased degree and family connections with officials, simply did not have an active place within government offices, and so his and his family's rise in the world remained constantly vulnerable to sharp reversals in fortune, if subjected to official criticisms of practicing collusion, as was arguably intrinsic to the Ming's political economy. He was a tightrope walker, liable to fall at just one official's flick of the rope.

Thus, accounts of an improvement in the social status of the merchant in the late imperial hierarchy from the sixteenth century onwards need to distinguish between different kinds of merchants, the different kinds of place they traded in, and the diversity of these individuals' relations to the Ming government and its officials. This overall diversity will also be evident in the different markets and commodities Huizhou merchants dealt with and in their use of designations such as top-, middling-, and lower-rank to acknowledge rough differences in their wealth and status.[81] But in a society whose uppermost ranks were overwhelmingly shaped by the examination system, the rich merchant had to tread carefully. His wealth attracted both the resentment of ordinary locals and kinsmen and predatory claims by officials and even scholars.[82] Witness the reported repartee between the king-maker of late Ming gentry culture in the delta, the Taicang 太倉 scholar-official Wang Shizhen 王世貞 (1526–90), and Zhen Jingfeng, a Huizhou commoner long resident in the delta. To Wang's insult, "When Huizhou merchants see Suzhou literati, they are like flies converging on a carcass," Zhen retorted, "And, when Suzhou literati see Huizhou merchants, they too are like flies converging on a carcass."[83] Note that Zhen's comeback line did not go beyond the framework and terms of Wang's wit, as if a merchant had to avoid toppling an official, especially when replying in public.

Changes for Huizhou Merchants

From the late Tang, long-distance traveling merchants gradually grew in numbers,[84] so that by the eleventh century some were considered to form distinct regional groups. In the Song such regional merchant groups numbered just three or four, emanating from Fujian, Sichuan, and the capitals, Kaifeng and Hangzhou.[85] During the Ming the spread of the market expanded the number of these groups to no fewer than eight – two in north China (Shanxi, Shaanxi) and six in south China (Jiangxi, Longyou 龍游 (Zhejiang), eastern Fujian, southern Fujian, Guangdong (divided into Guangzhou and Chaozhou groups), Dongting 洞庭 islands (Suzhou), and Huizhou), and all but one (Shaanxi) from the eastern half of the country.[86] The grounds for a

[81] Ibid.
[82] Writing in the early Qing, Sun Zhilu, *Ershen yelu* (1721 ed.), 4.20a–b, describes this resentment in terms of a more general antipathy of locals towards outsiders: "In the Hongzhi reign (1488–1505) the hereditary ministers got rich. In the Zhengde (1506–21) reign the eunuchs got rich. In the Jiajing reign (1522–66) the southern merchants got rich. In the Longxing (1567–72) and Wanli (1573–1620) reigns the wandering knights-errant got rich. And so, the migrating sojourners got rich, and the locals got poor."
[83] Sawada Masahiro, "Bun Chōmei," 534.
[84] Hino Kaisaburō, "Kyakushō no torihiki sosei," 154–98.
[85] Smith, *Taxing Heaven's Storehouse*; Shiba, "Sōdai no toshika," 4.
[86] Zhang Haipeng and Zhang Haiying, *Zhongguo shida shangbang*, is the standard account, though Usui, *Kishū shōnin*, 75–92, lists fifteen regional

merchant's affiliation or admission to one of these regional groups seem to have been self-evident: the location of his family's homestead and ancestral graves, a claim presumably backed up by an informal introduction from an older group member and confirmed, of course, by the new member's preferred dialect, diet, and living habits.[87]

Significantly, ascription of membership is usually made in our sources by nonmembers, not by a merchant himself, and so a term like "Huizhou merchants" more often than not expresses a non-Huizhou designation of a diverse body of traders, pawnbrokers, dealers, and their families with a Huizhou homestead and ancestral graves. Ming Huizhou merchants had no formal regional organization representing their collective or occupational interests inside Huizhou and rarely any elsewhere.[88] Nor did they, at least to the extent we know, commonly engage in collective economic, social or political action as "Huizhou merchants."[89] Admittedly, clusters of Huizhou merchants regularly cooperated commercially and financially with one another away from home more than they did with merchants of other Ming regional groups. Such informal ties could form very strong alliances; but even when added up, these relationships did not coalesce into a single unified group of merchants representing merchant interests either at home or away from it. As we have already seen, they were as likely to compete as to co-operate with one another. Admittedly, some Huizhou families had formal and informal alliances with one another inside Huizhou, but these alliances, so far as we now can tell, tended to remain focused on village, kinship, religious affairs, marriage, and land matters – not with trade, commodities, or even the places they traded in. Rarely, if ever, during the Ming did Huizhou merchants act as a

merchant groups. Ningbo and Shandong merchant groups emerged, it seems, only in the Qing, though one wonders which coastal merchant group dominated Chinese trade with Japan during the Ming.
[87] The demand for evidence of authentic Huizhou ties becomes more prominent in the eighteenth than in the sixteenth century (Xu Shining and Xu Zeng, *Chongxiu Shexian huiguan lu*, 31). As Steven Miles, *Upriver Journeys*, 114, has shown, in as late as 1756 "many of the largest merchants in the Lingnan [aka Guangdong salt] monopoly were from northern Zhejiang."
[88] See the related discussion in Chapter 3 below.
[89] Tellingly, their most reported collective action concerned their place not in the marketplace but in the operation of the civil service examinations: they won a distinct degree quota for the sons of Huizhou salt merchants residing in two delta prefectures, Hangzhou and Yangzhou (Puk, *Rise*, 121–26; Usui, *Kishū shōnin*, 57).

single body, hence my preference for the term "Huizhou merchants" over the more precise terms "the Huizhou merchant" and "the Huizhou merchants." Thus, by definition, the geographical scope of these Huizhou lineages' alliances would have been far narrower than that of an association based on common county and especially prefectural ties.[90]

During the Ming, "Huizhou merchants" (*Huishang* 徽商) were the foremost of these eight identifiable regional groupings. Foremost in the size of their membership, fame, wealth, and power, and the geographical span of their commercial activities, they were said to travel to distant markets, open shops, and make loans in places that most comfortable merchants shunned. Although they encompassed the widest variety of Ming merchant types with a high percentage of peddlers, Ming fiction writers preferred to portray them as highly successful and self-indulgent salt merchants, whose lifestyle and values were worlds away from those of the peddler haggling with stubborn customers at a Wuhu wharf. Indeed, the more elevated Huizhou salt merchants hired others to do all this work in the "dust and dirt" of the marketplace.

The term "Huizhou merchants" and by strong implication the notion of the "Huizhou merchants" date from the last third of the fifteenth century.[91] The ninth-century or earlier Huizhou practice of regularly growing timber and tea for long-distance commerce would seem to counter this view, but Huizhou merchants' involvement in marketing and transporting these local products at this time seems

---

[90] What Zelin writes of the Shanxi merchants in the Qing dynasty ("Chinese Business Practice," 781) – "there is no evidence of institutional links among Shanxi merchants extending across China" – holds true for Huizhou merchants in the Ming.

[91] Wang Tingyuan, "Lun Huizhou shangbang," 39–41; Fan Jinmin, "Cantian Dongting," 97–101. Initially, the term *Huishang* referred to merchants from one of the three Huizhou counties of She, Xiuning, and, to a lesser extent, Qimen. Then, from the latter half of the sixteenth century its scope widened to encompass merchants from Huizhou's three other counties of Jixi, Wuyuan, and Yi as well. According to the *Yi xianzhi* (1812), 3.3a, "Merchants did not go forth from Huizhou before the Zhengde era (1505–21)." This view, clearly an exaggeration, needs to be understood in the context that in 1683 Yi county merchants were still few and as of 1756 Jixi merchants were fewer than their counterparts in She and Xiuning and their movements more restricted (*MQHS*, 28).

negligible.⁹² According to Fan Jinmin, the Huizhou merchants acquired a collective consciousness as "Huizhou merchants" only six centuries later, when large numbers of Huizhou men began to constitute a self-conscious commercial group far richer, larger, and more diverse and powerful than ever before. Certainly, support for Fan's claim can be found in Huizhou's cultural history. Although Huizhou's local identity was strong long before the mid Ming thanks to its distinctive dialect, deities, cuisine, teacher–student ties, and literary and philosophical commitment, the late fifteenth century saw its wealthy residents promulgate its significant literary accomplishments for the first time through printings of the first and second compilations of Huizhou's literary writings in 1460 and 1491.⁹³ The publication of Cheng Tong's history of neo-Confucian thought in Huizhou, the first ever on Huizhou's intellectual tradition, followed shortly afterwards in 1506.⁹⁴ When placed within this wider cultural context, Fan's claim of Huizhou merchants' enhanced local consciousness at this time gains credibility.

Information about the Huizhou merchants' heightened economic activity, then, in the Yangzi Valley provides even stronger support.⁹⁵ Suzhou's revived urban economy created a strong demand for Huizhou timber, and in Yangzhou the salt monopoly reforms of 1492 by all accounts greatly enriched Huizhou merchants based there.⁹⁶ When many Huizhou natives were suddenly priced out of their village's landownership market in the late fifteenth century, a fair number of them understandably preferred a life on the road with its enhanced

---

⁹² The origin of the Huizhou merchants and their practice of trading widely outside it remains unclear. *SSXT*, 28, 930, traces the Huizhou practice of moving elsewhere to Sima Xi 司馬晞, a Huizhou native who lived away from Huizhou for much of the Western Jin dynasty (265–316). Yet no text mentions his dealing in Huizhou products, let alone trading. Likewise, the oft-quoted 808 report about the sale of Qimen county tea mentions "merchant boats" coming from outside Qimen to sell its tea elsewhere, suggesting that local Qimen (if not all of Huizhou's) merchants did not market this tea outside Huizhou (Shiba, *Sōdai Kōnan keizaishi*, 400). These issues clearly require further research.

⁹³ That is, the *Xin'an wencui* 新安文粹 (1460) compiled by Jin Dexuan 金德 and *Xin'an wenxian zhi* 新安文獻志 (1491) compiled by Cheng Minzheng 程敏政.

⁹⁴ That is, *Xin'an xuexi lu* 新安學系錄.

⁹⁵ The use of the term "Huizhou merchants" came far more frequently and smoothly off the brush of outsiders, of non-Huizhou people, than of Huizhou people, who preferred to publicize their literati and official achievements, not their commercial.

⁹⁶ McDermott, *Making*, v. 1, 179, 268–69, 283.

commercial attractions. This combination of "push" and "pull" factors transformed the fortune of Huizhou's merchant families and made them, the rich as well as the poor, a larger, more mobile and visible group outside Huizhou.

Their economic activities there also started to change significantly at this time. Whereas in the Song merchants from Huizhou had dealt predominantly in Huizhou products, such as tea, timber, alum, and ink,[97] from no later than the mid Ming they were trading a much wider range of goods, many produced outside Huizhou. These new products and materials from elsewhere included not just luxury items (such as porcelain, jade, finely illustrated books, and antiquities) that in the past had garnered for others high profits, or goods like Guizhou timber that required traders to have deep reserves of capital.[98] But also, to an unprecedented degree, Huizhou merchants' ship holds, horse packs, and road carts held large amounts of daily commodities (such as rice, tea, dried fish, pickles, and, of course, salt) that, when sold in bulk, acquired considerable profits. If only to spread risks, Huizhou merchants tended not to specialize in a single product for a single sector in all places. Like most Ming dynasty merchants, they diversified their investments in a variety of businesses, so that the career of the She county merchant Wu Yigong 吳逸公 was representative of career patterns in highly successful merchant circles: he traded in salt in Yangzhou; pawnbrokered in another large delta city like Nanjing; and bought, sold, and shipped rice and textiles along the Grand Canal and the Yangzi Valley.[99] As a result, the same merchant could be termed both a resident and an itinerant merchant, and he could engage in trade, finance, and running a shop in one delta city that served as his headquarters for deliveries and travels to branch shops elsewhere.[100]

Nonetheless, as these merchant families' capital accumulated over the course of the Ming, the relative level of their financial involvement in different sectors changed. Whereas Huizhou individuals and families in the mid Ming competed to climb a capital-hungry ladder with rungs rising from local products like tea and timber, to relatively cheap commodities like cotton textiles and fish, and then up to more capital-intensive products like silk and salt, and finally onto financial

---

[97] Shiba, *Sōdai Kōnan keizaishi*, 390–402. [98] *MQHS*, 179.
[99] Long Denggao, *Jiangnan shichang*, 162; Fan Jinmin, *Fushui jia tianxia*, 328.
[100] Ibid., 329.

activities like moneylending and pawnbrokering, by the late Ming certain family and lineage groups had at the same time come to dominate specific lines, even while continuing to trade in other goods.[101]

In implementing a comprehensive strategy of investment diversification Huizhou merchants or their agents appear to have invested to secure the most promising opportunities for profit making in various local markets. An arch-proponent of this high-flying strategy was the notorious millionaire Ximen in the celebrated late Ming novel *The Plum in the Golden Vase* (*Jinping mei* 金瓶梅):

> His Honor, Ximen Qing, whose residence is located in front of the county yamen, currently occupies the post of assistant judicial commissioner of the local office of the Provincial Surveillance Commission. His household not only engages in money lending to both officials and functionaries, but also operates four or five businesses, including a satin piece goods store, a pharmaceutical shop, a silk goods store, and a knitting and sewing supplies story. In addition, he operates fleets of merchant vessels with armed escorts on the rivers and lakes, trades salt certificates in Yangzhou, and purveys incense and wax in Dongping prefecture for use by the imperial household.[102]

To handle this far-flung network of commercial and political connections, the successful Huizhou merchants commonly settled their sons and kinsmen in one or more areas outside Huizhou, where the levels of their trade surpassed the previous capacity of Chinese businesses' capital and human resources.

In fact, salt produced in the Huainan and Zhejiang areas proved the Huizhou merchants' most profitable commodity thanks to a sale price fixed by the government at levels far above production costs and any putative market value. These merchants' shipments of salt coursed throughout the lower and middle Yangzi Valley, wending their way among the delta's labyrinthine streams and canals, and even sailing along the Zhejiang coast from the late fifteenth century onwards.[103] Once released in 1492 from the legal obligation to transport grain provisions to northern frontier garrisons in order to qualify for trading

---

[101] Wang Tingyuan, "Ming Qing Huishang," 61–69; Chapter 6 below.
[102] Roy, *The Plum in the Golden Vase*, v. 4, 248.
[103] *THJ*, 54, 1,143; Gui Youguang, *Zhenchuan xiansheng ji*, 13, 319, also lists soy sauce, animal fat, and precious stones.

in the salt monopoly, Huizhou's salt merchants focused on the far more profitable Yangzi river run with its artificially conflated prices for salt, on its booming demand for many other kinds of commodities, and on improving security on the rivers of south China.

Trading in this range of goods and profiting greatly from the salt business, many Huizhou merchants were induced to travel to and trade with a much more widely dispersed selection of places in the Ming than in the Song. Whereas they had sought their fortunes during the Northern Song mainly in the emporium of Yangzhou, the capital Kaifeng, and Grand Canal ports in Shandong province, and during the Southern Song in the Yangzi delta (especially the capital Hangzhou) and Fujian and Guangdong circuits (or provinces), they acquired during the Ming a reputation for trading everywhere. They – the peddlers and the long-distance merchants – eyed markets not just in the relatively prosperous stretches of the lower and middle Yangzi Valley but also throughout virtually the rest of the country. In Zhang Han's view merchants from She and Xiuning counties "cover almost the entire empire," a claim that the 1609 gazetteer for She county vigorously supported: "She [county] merchants go to not only ... the great metropolises (*duhui* 都會). All places [in the empire] have them: the mountain slopes, the ocean wharves, the lonely villages, and the isolated hamlets all have our [She county] men."[104] In other words, Huizhou merchants, even if they still concentrated on the Yangzi Valley and delta and Grand Canal markets, played a vital role in the expansion of the market to the far south and southwest corners of the Ming empire.

Three related changes occurred in their role in this Ming commercial expansion. First, even more deeply than Zhang Han indicated, they penetrated south China's markets, some of them even settling down permanently or for long periods in distant places outside Huizhou, turning some places into "little Huizhous."[105] In Linqing of Shandong province, for example, Huizhou natives constituted a very sizeable share (unreliably estimated at 90 percent) of the registered population of this thriving emporium.[106] Second, merchants from Ming Huizhou's separate counties tended to acquire for their operations specific urban

---

[104] *She zhi* (1609), 20.shihuo 3b. The other major urban sites they frequented were Beijing, Nanjing, Hangzhou, Fuzhou (in Fujian), Suzhou, Yangzhou, Songjiang, Jining and Linqing in Shandong, Wuhu, Guazhou, and Jingdezhen.
[105] Du Yongtao, *Order of Places*, 62–65.
[106] Okano, "Minmatsu Rinshin," 103–33; Xie Zhaozhe, *Wu zazu*, 14, 413.

bases outside Huizhou. Xiuning merchants were recognized as a powerful group in the markets of Nanchang 南昌, Nanjing, and other delta towns and cities, often as pawnbrokers. Likewise, She merchants were strong in the Yangzhou timber and salt markets,[107] Yi county merchants in the delta and Zhejiang province, and Wuyuan and Qimen merchants in Jingdezhen.[108] Some Yi county merchants operating in Jiangxi stayed there for several successive generations,[109] even though, as late as 1883, the gazetteer for Yi county grandly declared that its residents were more likely to be scholars than merchants.[110]

Third, the work and social position of some long-distance Huizhou merchant families underwent a fundamental transformation. Despite uniform claims in their genealogies of a perfectly honorable ancestry, not all Song and earlier ancestors of Huizhou merchants had operated consistently on the right side of the law, especially during their early involvement in the salt trade. Following a pattern readily seen in other countries' early merchant families,[111] Huizhou's merchant families in the salt monopoly transport business were reported in 1089 by the famous scholar-official Su Shi 蘇軾 to be working not just as peddlers of salt but also as bodyguards for salt smugglers:

Many of the strong and brave [along with some residents of the neighboring prefecture, Xuanzhou 宣州] make groups of tens and hundreds [of people]. Coming and going in the Liangzhe 兩浙 region (*Zhezhong* 浙中 [present southern Jiangsu and Zhejiang provinces]), they use weapons and wooden staves to guard and escort private dealers of salt. The officials, on the understanding that they commit no other robberies, by and large make no enquiries about them.[112]

In light of Chapter 3's findings on brigandage on the Yangzi in the Song and the Ming, it would be surprising if Huizhou merchants did

---

[107] Fu Yiling, *Ming Qing shidai shangren*, 68.
[108] Cao Guoqing, "Ming Qing shiqi Jiangxi," 23. Huizhou merchants often settled in Jingdezhen and its ceramic trade for successive generations.
[109] Ibid., 24. [110] Liu Liying, "Yixian shangren," 106.
[111] For example, the Genoese merchants (Lopez, *Commercial Revolution*) and traders in western Japan (Elisonas, "The Inseparable Trinity," 239, makes the point sharply: "By the sixteenth century, seafaring as defined by Goethe's Mephistopheles – 'War, trade, and piracy are an inseparable trinity' – was a time-honoured tradition in the Japanese archipelago").
[112] Li Tao, *Xu changbian*, 461, 11,028. Presumably, the government worried that these Huizhou body guards would practice their skills independently as outright criminals in places and sectors it did not tightly supervise.

not continue to provide such services, along with more conventional private trading, to at least the end of the Song. Certainly, salt smuggling was rife on the river in succeeding centuries.[113] With the establishment of Ming rule and with their return to Yangzhou to work within government salt monopoly operations there from the late fourteenth century, Huizhou merchants emerged in the last third of the fifteenth century as powerful salt merchants and as the pre-eminent regional merchant group in the Yangzi Valley.[114] Becoming eventually the richest and most powerful regional merchant group in all of south China,[115] they also acquired a very different reputation as respectable members of what Chow Kai-wing and others have designated a "scholar-merchant elite (*shishang* 士商)."[116]

Further evidence of a change in the identity of Huizhou merchant families during the Ming also comes from an expansion in the number and location of the villages they came from.[117] Of the ninety-two Huizhou merchants with extant biographies from the Song and Yuan, sixty-four came from seventeen villages in She county (virtually all from wealthy paddy-field villages south and southwest of the county seat), twenty-one from thirteen villages in Xiuning county (virtually half from southeast of the county seat), six from four villages in Wuyuan county, and one from one village in Qimen county. Moving about often in groups and working co-operatively with kinsmen or fellow Huizhou residents, some of these Song and Yuan merchants had taken up residence elsewhere in Huizhou with more available land and better commercial prospects.[118] In the mid and late Ming their counterparts came from hundreds of villages scattered throughout Huizhou, though still primarily from She, Xiuning, and Qimen counties. Relatively few Song Huizhou merchants settled down outside Huizhou, and if they did, they usually returned to Huizhou for retirement and burial.[119]

---

[113] Saeki, *Chūgoku ensei*, 262–85, 345–49, 491–501, 595–650.
[114] Fan Jinmin, "Cantian Dongting," 97–101; Shiba, "Urbanization," 13–48.
[115] Fu Yiling, *Ming Qing shidai shangren*, 107–60; Shiba, *Sōdai shōgyōshi*, 421–35; Terada, *Sansei shōnin*, 231–410.
[116] Tang Lixing, *Shangren*, 107–17; Chow, *Publishing*.
[117] McDermott, *Making*, v. 1, 180–213.
[118] Wang Yuming, "Song Yuan shiqi," 123–28.
[119] Permanent Huizhou emigrants during the Song and Yuan were more likely soldiers than merchants, whose role in paving the way for subsequent Huizhou merchant entry into distant markets merits study.

Furthermore, the number of Huizhou surnames designated rich and powerful merchants increased considerably over the course of the Ming. In the mid sixteenth century, Wang Shizhen had no doubt that two Huizhou surnames (*xing* 姓) merited inclusion in his list of the empire's seventeen richest families with fortunes of over 500,000 taels.[120] A generation later, the Huizhou native Wu Shiqi 吳士奇 concurred, identifying these rich Huizhou surnames as the Wangs 汪 and the Wus (the term "surname" allows for a loose reference to same-surname groups or large and very loosely affiliated lineages) in his far more positive discussion of the empire's richest families. Whereas Wang Shizhen had listed his two Huizhou surnames among disreputable arrivistes like generals and eunuchs, this Huizhou commentator pointedly claimed that the wealth of these Huizhou lineages equaled that of the delta's great scholar-official landed families (that is, like Wang Shizhen's family).[121]

Soon, the 1609 gazetteer for She county expanded this list with six other fortunate Huizhou surnames: the Huangs 黃, the Wus, and the Wangs were the richest of the "big surnames" (*daxing* 大姓), and not far behind were the Chengs 程, the Luos 羅, the Wangs 王, the Baos 鮑, and the Fangs 方.[122] Most of these surname groups, along with others enriched by the salt trade and pawnshops, lived in Huizhou villages astonishingly close to one another, virtually all of them in two locales, the narrow basin bordered by the Fengle and the Fujian rivers in the west of She county and along the Huizhou road eastward to Hangzhou.[123] Merchants in Xiuning county during the Song and Yuan had

---

[120] Wang Shizhen, *Yanzhou shiliao houji*, 36.2a. Zhang Xianqing, *Yan Song zhuan*, 367–429, lists the variety of assets and sources of the exceptional wealth acquired by the mid-sixteenth-century Grand Secretary, Yan Song 嚴嵩. Of the seventeen richest families then, seven were merchants and most of the remaining ten were officials whose chief income source would have been not their formal salary but their official pickings from trade profits (Tang Lixing, *Shangren*, 23).

[121] Wu Shiqi, *Lüzi guan zhengxin bian*, 5.35a. His own family reportedly had more than 100 pawnshops, providing an annual income of 300,000 taels (Tang Lixing, *Shangren*, 22).

[122] *She zhi* (1609), 20, shihuo 1a–3b; *MQHS*, 244, on one Luo merchant, who netted over 800,000 taels from many years of trading in Fujian and southern Jiangxi.

[123] Wang Chongyuan, "Bufen Huizhou Shexian," 11–17, through its survey of this area's more powerful salt merchant families, beginning with the father of Zheng Daotong 鄭道同, the first Huizhou salt merchant son to acquire a metropolitan degree, in 1391, some fifty-seven years before his Shanxi

tended to come from the relatively wealthy villages south of the county seat, but during the fifteenth century, some, like the Wus of Songshan, also came from villages to its west.[124] In Qimen county the Chengs, the Xies 謝, and the Wangs 汪 were recognized as rich and important, and their villages were concentrated in the county's central and southern mountain valleys.[125]

Finally, during the Ming some Huizhou merchants entered burgeoning economic sectors. Aided by a regular income from their dominance of trading in salt, salt certificates, and other large-scale daily commodity markets in the Yangzi valley,[126] an increasing number of Huizhou merchants began financial businesses. They now had the capital to open and run money shops (*qianye* 錢業, *qianpu* 錢鋪, *qianhao* 錢號) and pawnbrokerages (*dianpu* 典鋪, *dangpu* 當鋪) in prosperous towns and cities that stretched the entire length of east China from Beijing to Guangzhou. Sooner than all other regional merchant groups (except perhaps for the Fujian merchants), they operated many relatively simple moneylending businesses far away from home.[127]

As a result of all these commercial and financial changes that tied them down for longer stays away from home, the overwhelming share of Huizhou merchants' wealth – estimated by a knowledgeable delta resident as 90 percent – was by the late sixteenth century being kept outside Huizhou.[128] Active in the delta economy, this capital went into specialized market sectors that its holders favored. For instance, salt trading became the occupation of choice for She and, less so, Xiuning merchants. Pawnbrokering was associated with Xiuning in the Ming and Qing; timber with Xiuning in the Song, Qimen in the Ming, and Wuyuan in the Qing; tea with Qimen in the Qing; and rice with traders from Yi and Wuyuan counties.[129] This apparent shift towards more specialized trading by merchants from these different counties,

---

      equivalent (Wu Zhengfang, *Baiyang yuan*, 19). The Baiyanyuan area, by contrast, tended to house small and middle-scale merchant families, "the class of merchants with a small amount of capital."

[124] Wang Yuming, "'Renfeng ji,'" 108; Brook, "Merchant Network," 197. An exception is Xie Zhaozhe, *Wu za zu*, 4, 108.

[125] For the Xie, see Nakajima, *Mindai gōson*, 115. For the Chengs, Wangs, Lis, and Zhengs, see McDermott, *Making*, v. 1, 239–43; *Qimen xianzhi shizu kao*, 4, 6, and 18–20; *Huizhou qiannian*, v. 3 and v. 4.

[126] *THJ*, 54, 1,143.   [127] Zheng Xiaoruan, "'Xushui,' 'fanbu,'" 112.

[128] Wang Shizhen, *Yanzhou shanren sibu gao*, 61.23a.

[129] Cao Guoqing, "Ming Qing shiqi," 22–27.

however, did not end these merchants' simultaneous practice of risk aversion by investing in a wide range of other goods and services.

The Huizhou Merchants and Other Regional Merchant Groups

In the commercial world of the late Ming only the Shanxi group rivaled Huizhou merchants in wealth and influence. Strikingly, their merchants concentrated on the same types of commodities – salt, grain, timber, metal goods (especially iron), and textiles (especially cotton and silk goods) – but did so in different parts of the country. Whereas Ming merchants from Huizhou focused on markets in central and south China and especially the middle and lower Yangzi Valley, those from Shanxi found most of their markets in north China, in towns far beyond the Great Wall, and also in a few large lower Yangzi Valley cities at the southern end of the Grand Canal, such as Yangzhou, Suzhou, and Hangzhou. Like Huizhou merchants, those of Shanxi from the early Ming benefited from involvement in the administration of the salt monopoly, trading government salt from both the coastal salt flats northeast of Yangzhou and the inland salt ponds within Shanxi. Dominating salt transport and distribution in north China, the Shanxi merchants carved out a dominant position in the delivery of northern border grain supplies for garrison troops and in return the lucrative sale of salt at a highly artificial price in north China's salt consumption areas. Furthermore, they took advantage of their military border connections to dominate trade in a wide variety of goods north of the Great Wall. Trading north and south China's handicraft goods for Mongolian and north Asian furs and metals, they linked these northern land routes to the Grand Canal and thereby formed a north–south delivery chain that at its maximum length outdistanced the Huizhou merchants' salt and rice shipment route up and down the Yangzi. Some Shanxi merchants also ventured into Sichuan, where they competed with Shaanxi traders. Only in pawnbrokering did Huizhou merchants consistently outperform Shanxi merchants in north China's markets during the Ming, and only in the Grand Canal emporium of Linqing did they in the last half of the Ming dominate a large north China market in many goods. Tellingly, pawnbrokers from Huizhou are reported as active in ten Ming provinces including north China, and those from Shanxi in just two, Shanxi itself and Shandong (in the Qing, however, the position of the Huizhou and Shanxi pawnbrokers was reversed).[130]

An alternative contrast of Huizhou merchants with southern rivals like Jiangxi merchants underlines the Huizhou merchants' greater ability to control their southern rather than northern rivals. Huizhou and Jiangxi merchant groups interacted in the same marketing areas of the lower and middle stretches of the Yangzi Valley, but the Jiangxi contingent focused on the cheaper and lower levels of the labor and commodity markets as well as on their volume (for daily consumption goods like rice, tea, paper, mandarin oranges, and bamboo), capital, and services. Like Huizhou's natives many Jiangxi men left their villages to trade throughout the Yangzi Valley and other parts of south China in the sixteenth century.[131] Yet, in the salt, timber, silk, and jewels trades and even in the transport of Jiangxi products like porcelain, tea, and timber, Huizhou merchants dominated. According to the astute observer Wang Shixing 王士性, in the middle and lower stretches of the Yangzi Valley Jiangxi migrants earned their living more often as hired laborers and *declassé* professionals like sojourning geomancers, astrologers, doctor-diviners, and cartwrights than as merchants.[132] Initially, as migrant laborers they stayed for only the winter months, returning home in the spring to farm until, after the next harvest, they left home for another winter on the road. Soon, some of these transients started taking up year-long work alongside the locals, inching up the local social order. First, they worked as peddlers making the rounds at periodic markets. Soon, although most Jiangxi men continued to man the bottom end of the urban labor and distribution markets in these areas, some of the more enterprising ended up like small-scale Huizhou merchants. Establishing successful businesses in neglected corners of southern Hubei, Sichuan, and Hunan provinces, they began with and acquired far less capital than did their Huizhou rivals.[133] Indeed, for centuries Jiangxi merchants reputedly worked as middle-Yangzi subordinates of Huizhou salt merchant cartels.

---

[130] *Dianshang*, 360–61. The eight Ming provinces are Northern Metropolitan, Southern Metropolitan, Henan, Shandong, Zhejiang, Jiangxi, Huguang, and Fujian. Whereas Huizhou pawnbrokers were reportedly "everywhere north of the Yangzi" in the late Ming, by 1795, a century and a half later, they had retreated to just "south of the Yangzi" (Tang Lixing, *Shangren*, 56).
[131] Liang Xiaomin, *Zouma kan shangbang*, 66–74.
[132] Wang Shixing, *Guangzhi yi*, 4, 80.
[133] Wu Shiqi, *Lüzi guan zhengxin bian*, 5.31.9b.

In some southwest provinces the Jiangxi merchants nonetheless predated, outnumbered, and dominated any Huizhou competitors. In Guizhou they constituted the largest contingent of outsider merchants, and in Yunnan 50 to 60 percent of the population (surely an exaggeration) came from the single Jiangxi prefecture of Fuzhou 撫州.[134] In Sichuan Jiangxi migrants usually took up residence in the towns, where they opened shops and markets. By contrast, the migrants from Huguang province from early on in the Ming settled in Sichuan villages, formed lineages, compiled genealogies, and established ancestral halls, as if they had never left their Huguang villages.

In sum, Jiangxi migrants played two contrasting roles in south China's economy, depending on which region they moved to. In the marketplaces of the middle and lower Yangzi Valley they acted subordinate to Huizhou merchants, while in places of southwest China where Huizhou merchants were fewer and weaker, they flourished as traveling merchants. One has to wonder how much of what Jiangxi merchants observed of their Huizhou superiors in the more developed markets of the middle and lower Yangzi they then adapted for their own branches' and lineages' businesses in the upper Yangzi Valley. In other words, merchants from Ming Huizhou proved exceptionally successful as traders and pawnbrokers for many reasons: their relatively early start in commodity and salt trading, their abundant supply of local products in the Song and access to other places' products in the Ming, their proximity to markets in the middle and lower Yangzi, their lineage organization's manpower and cheap capital in the Ming, and eventually their adroit interaction with officialdom.

If men in a poor mountainous prefecture like Huizhou could attain such commercial influence and success, what was there to prevent men in other similarly rugged and disadvantaged parts of the empire like Longyu county in the interior of Zhejiang province and the Dongting islands in Suzhou from doing likewise? Not surprisingly, merchants from Huizhou had contacts with these places either through direct trade or with their merchant groups active in the Yangzi Valley nodes of Yangzhou, Suzhou, Hangzhou, and Nanjing.[135] And one is obliged to wonder how much they taught these regional merchant groups as

---

[134] Wang Shixing, *Guangzhi yi*, 4, 80.
[135] Fujii, "Shin'an shōnin no kenkyū," 36.2, 36–45. Six decades on, Fujii's four-part survey remains essential reading for any student of Huizhou merchants.

well about how to trade, simply by trading profitably with them at quite likely these newcomers' expense.

Huizhou Merchants' Wealth

This collective predominance of late Ming Huizhou merchants over their main competitors virtually assured contemporary fascination with stories about their unprecedented wealth. Indeed, by the late Ming Huizhou merchants were commonly ranked as the dominant regional trading group in the markets of south China, if not the entire empire. In c.1580 Zhang Han showed no hesitation in declaring that "Xiuning and She counties [in Huizhou prefecture] are where those who grasp amazing profits are most numerous."[136]

This wealth, all agree, was mainly acquired outside Huizhou in salt, pawnbrokering, fish, timber, and, to a lesser extent, textile transactions.[137] Generations of Huizhou's merchants, according to Huizhou commentators in 1502 and c.1570, had regularly set off on their annual forays into the Yangzi Valley with expectations of returning by year's end with annual profit rates of 20 percent.[138] Zhang Han put some traders' profit rates far higher: "The best merchants who go to market make several hundred percent profit, those second to them make a hundred percent profit, and the lowest and least talented ones still get ten percent."[139] So widespread was the belief in the extraordinary wealth of salt merchants (and hence of some Huizhou merchants) that by the mid 1620s news of their unmatched wealth – "the richest [merchants] are those who trade in salt and who carry out a commerce more important than that of silks, gold, musk, rubies, textiles and any other merchandise" – reached the ears of Portuguese merchants in Macao and Dutch and other traders in southeast Asia.[140] Whereas Huizhou writers tended to attribute their

---

[136] *She zhi* (1609), 20 shihuo, *passim*; Brook, "On Merchants," 197. Xie Zhaozhe, *Wu zazu*, 4, 108, claims that Shanxi merchants were richer, an exceptional view in Ming writing.
[137] *THJ*, 54, 1,143; Wang Shixing, *Guangzhi yi*, 1, 14.
[138] *Huizhou fuzhi* (1502), 2.39b–40a; Wu Ziyu, *Dazhang shanren ji*, 31.9b.
[139] Brook, "Merchant Network," 197.
[140] Cortes, *Le voyage en Chine*, 258; Meilink-Roelofsz, *Asian Trade*, 76, on how a Chinese merchant in Southeast Asia might acquire in Malacca's commercial circles a reputation for solvency (and thus for being a safe bet), solely on the basis of a rumor that he was a salt merchant.

prefecture's commercial success primarily to hard work and "Confucian discipline," the common perception of Huizhou in popular Ming and Qing fiction was of a prefecture grossly obsessed with the accumulation of wealth and its merchants as natural in their lust for silver as for women.[141]

For confirmation of the great wealth of Huizhou merchants, one need look no further than at Huizhou's village structures surviving from the late Ming. Bridges initially constructed solely with wood were upgraded with masonry, pavilions now lined the shore of garden ponds, paths once layered with mud acquired flat stones suitable for walking, ancestral halls towered over all other village edifices, and walled-in residences rose two or three stories high to protect not just the womenfolk of absentee merchants but also all their other luxuries.

Once admitted into these residences, a guest could be forgiven for thinking he had landed in a refined Suzhou or Songjiang villa. As indicated by surviving wills, family wealth registers, and other private family papers, rooms were graced by numerous pieces of elegant furniture from Suzhou; interior walls hung with fashionable paintings and famous calligraphies from Hangzhou; chests crammed with rare handscrolls from Songjiang; and desks and tables adorned with the finer porcelain of Jingdezhen, the ancient inkstones of Huizhou itself and the softer varieties from Shaoxing, and most delicate rabbit-haired brushes from Huzhou.[142] In the late sixteenth century, the Dai 戴 family of Longfu 隆阜 to the east of Xiuning county seat was particularly fond of flaunting its wealth. When advised to direct their entertainment budget to poor relief, "its members laughed off the suggestion as preposterous."[143]

The recorded Ming response to Huizhou merchants' acquisition and consumption of all these fineries was generally critical, on a variety of grounds. In this whirlwind of material change and moral chaos, as the neo-Confucian master Wang Yangming 王陽明 (1472–1529) warned,

[141] Ōki, *Min Shin bungaku*, 164–67; Zheng Xiaoruan, "Dui Mingdai Huizhou dianshang," 6–10. Many Huizhou locals, sensitive to moralists' carping about their wealth, stressed their mountain area's natural poverty and their modest living conditions as opposed to those down in the delta (where many Huizhou men lived) (Shen Guoyuan, *Liangchao*, 33.6b–8b; *Huizhou fuzhi* (1566), 2.38a–39b, distinguishes the rich portion of Huizhou from the rest).

[142] Wu Renshu, *Pinwei shehua*, 216–25, reveals these trends through an analysis of Huizhou wills and other property lists, drafted between 1475 and 1634.

[143] *Xiuning mingzu zhi*, 3, 551–54; MQHS, 56–57.

a man found it hard to retain his moral bearings and integrity.[144] Some denounced Huizhou merchants as "Huizhou dogs" (*Huigou* 徽狗), as immoral beasts infected with a money madness. Others despised the display of wealth out of fear it would incite envy and disturbances among the less fortunate.[145] Predictably, some mid-Ming scholars expressed sharp disapproval of this blurring of the traditional differences between merchants and scholars, interpreting the transfer of these art objects and social change as a sign of moral decay and dynastic disorder.[146]

Interestingly, these critics, other than suggesting charity to kinsmen and community members, said little about their preferred way to use such money. To a degree that would have surprised earlier social critics, they avoided criticizing the rich Huizhou merchants' disinterest in buying fields.[147] Though this observation appears mainly to concern the lower Yangzi delta where many Huizhou merchants had migrated, the same Ming merchant families showed no interest in acquiring extensive holdings of fields and other Huizhou properties as they had before the Ming. By the late, if not early, sixteenth century, Huizhou's rich families appear to have found local field investment costly, overtaxed, and troublesome to manage.[148] Reportedly, they restricted their Huizhou holdings to between one hundred and two hundred *mu*.[149] Making sure thereby that they had enough land to survive a serious famine, they relied on imports for up to nine months of their annual grain needs.

To probe farther into the life of these men as merchants rather than as lineage members or would-be literati,[150] the Huizhou sources once again prove indispensable. Though fewer of these sources explicitly concern merchants and merchant activities than farmers and farming, they still include a wide variety of manuscripts and imprints that reveal

---

[144] Wang Shouren, *Wang Yangming quanji*, 25, 940–41.
[145] Guo Qitao, *Ritual Opera*, 24, 29, 54, 69–71.
[146] Brook, *The Confusions of Pleasure*. [147] Fujii (3), 92–93.
[148] McDermott, *Making*, v. 1, 176–77, 241–42, 333, 362; *Fengnan zhi*, 6, 385. Land investment in Huizhou did not "revive," as Kishimoto (Nakayama) Mio, *Shindai Chūgoku*, 215–38, and "Shindai zenki Kōnan," 91–96, observed for the late Ming delta.
[149] *Shexi Xi'nan Wushi xianying zhi*, ershisi shizu, 2b.
[150] Over the last half of the Ming merchant biographies tended to highlight their subject's merchant activities more than his putative gentry or scholarly qualities (Zhang Shimin, "Lun Ming zhongqi shangren," 24–27).

the world of Ming merchants both inside and outside Huizhou. The manuscripts range from a few pawnbroker registers, commercial contracts and contract forms to merchant wills and association agreements, in addition to a great number of imprints, including hundreds of genealogies, histories of ancestral-hall construction, merchant manuals for traveling and trading, and even merchant biographies. In sharp contrast to the record of all the other dynasties, a considerable number of these merchant biographies survive from the Ming – over 160 from the collected writings of no fewer than fifty Ming authors. Fortunately for us, nearly half of these biographies come from the brush of one Huizhou scholar-official, Wang Daokun 汪道昆 (who devoted over two-thirds of his 112 biographies to Huizhou merchants).[151]

And yet, on certain commercial and financial topics the Ming record is significantly discreet. The detailed rent account books, collections of contracts, legal case documents, and management prescription books that so enriched volume 1's account of Huizhou village life have few counterparts in all the sources used here for the study of Huizhou merchants and their business practices. Even more disappointing is these sources' silence on merchant dealings with government yamens and officials and on their private negotiations with other regions' merchants. Tight-lipped about their commercial doings, these Ming officials, like the merchants, seem loath to reveal the role of money in their lives. And so, we are obliged, like Huizhou merchants dealing with one another, to tease the aims, tactics, and strategy of these Ming Huizhou merchants from reticent sources intent on persuading us that their commercial and financial success was attributable more to their Confucian morality than to their cunning and guile. Would that pigs had wings!

In exploring how Huizhou men created and used village institutions for their commercial and financial benefit, Chapter 2 will focus on the history of the ancestral hall. Known mainly as the lineage's main place for ancestral worship and moral instruction, this institution in Ming Huizhou also functioned as a credit association or proto-bank that made two kinds of loans, one at high rates of interest to non-hall members to build up the hall's assets for eventual construction and

---

[151] Li Aixian, "Mingdai shangren zhuanji," 68–71; Nie Zhuanyou, "Wang Daokun," 3, 102; Wu Taolong,"Wang Daokun," 70–73.

repair, and another at reduced rates of interest to hall members to provide them with cheap capital. In unraveling this complicated yet common process (at least 6,000 ancestral halls were built in Huizhou between the mid fifteenth and the late nineteenth century), this chapter will investigate the links between ancestral-hall finances, ancestral worship ritual, and "grassroots capitalism."

Chapter 3 will examine Huizhou merchants' efforts to penetrate major market sites in the Yangzi Valley and along the Grand Canal. It will introduce the problems they encountered, such as brigandry when traveling and local protectionism when marketing, and then consider various merchant countermeasures. Ranging from secret security arrangements and bribery to new financial instruments and hired protection or clientage, these merchant responses appear not to have involved any serious effort to forge public or political institutions that would protect merchant interests. Quite likely, the diversity of Huizhou merchant interests obstructed any collective effort leading to one policy or solution. While its shippers may have desired government protection, Huizhou pawnbrokers strove to thwart all government intrusion (the first tax on pawnbrokering dates from 1623). As their credit operations became increasingly enmeshed in commercial deals, pawnbrokers' profits and secrecy aroused greater criticism. Meanwhile, as discussed also in Chapter 4, some wealthy Huizhou merchants carved out a different and dangerous approach to dealing with the government's salt monopoly. Ingeniously adapting a strategy similar to that tried with their ancestral halls, they sought to place themselves inside an authorized institution of the state, the salt monopoly, and then turned the humble salt certification into a financial instrument to their great advantage.

Since these profits fell into relatively few hands, many Huizhou merchants relied on commercial partnerships, formal and informal, to expand their pool of investment capital and the operation of their businesses. Chapter 5 will explore the varieties of these partnerships as well as the solutions these merchants found to common problems of business governance, such as bankruptcy and access to committed investments. Through a series of case studies, Chapter 6 explains how Huizhou merchant lineages, viewed as "house firms," succeeded in the world of Ming business. It explores the development of different types and sizes of commercial organization in response to organizational needs and business opportunities, while also examining the impact of kinship organizations and relationships on their operation.

Finally, Chapter 7 returns to seventeenth-century Huizhou and discusses its political and economic traumas. It will reveal how Huizhou's lineages, especially its merchant lineages and their house firms, suffered severe mid-century challenges from persistent disorder and recession. It will also analyze how Huizhou lineage institutions nonetheless remained dominant over other "village quartet" institutions like the village worship associations and Buddhist establishments. The strongest resistance came from popular cults, which in their many guises survived harsh attacks from orthodox Confucian scholars and thus remained the lineage's strongest institutional rival in Huizhou until the Communist era.

The Conclusion of this volume thus will provide further evidence that Huizhou merchants' commercial and financial operations can be fruitfully studied from within the administrative framework of family and state institutions. Late imperial China's financial and commercial institutions can best be researched only if we reject artificially sharp distinctions, such as public and private, state and society, and state and family, and instead research the actual dynamics of institutions employed by lineages and merchants in their pursuit of profit in villages and markets alike.

2 | Ancestral Halls and Credit
Building, Investing, and Lending

As the lineage during the Ming replaced rival institutions like the village worship association (*she* 社) and became the dominant institution in Huizhou villages, its members commonly sought a permanent center for their performance of ancestral worship rituals and other collective activities. Whereas in the Song and Yuan dynasties they often held ancestral worship and memorial services outside the home at ancestral graves or Buddhist chapels, in mid- and late Ming Huizhou they moved their performance of these ceremonies inside, into a building called an ancestral hall (*citang* 祠堂).

This chapter will discuss this shift, observing how it marked a significant change in not just the religious but also the social and economic life of Huizhou's lineages. Introduced to a world in which lineages were increasingly popular and powerful institutions, the ancestral hall represented more than an extension of previous lineage concerns and a strengthening of lineage presence and power. In Huizhou it often is properly seen as a new and at times alternative form of lineage organization. As discussed in detail in volume 1, many lineages spent decades seeking to defuse intra-lineage conflicts over their charitable landed trusts through management reforms, collective pacts, statute revisions, and new schemes for wealth sharing. After seeing these responses repeatedly rejected by members of discontented branches, some lineage leaders started to propose more radical reforms that would redefine the qualifications for lineage membership. In some cases lineage leaders sought to expand the terms for admission to lineage membership; in other cases they sought to narrow them. Central to these new plans was an ancestral hall, a lineage-led institution that could no longer be assumed to grant membership automatically to all lineage males during their lifetime or afterwards as an ancestor. In trying to reorganize their lineage along less egalitarian and more commercial lines, many lineages and especially their leaders advocated the construction of an ancestral hall with fervor and tenacity.

Ancestral Halls and Credit

In some Huizhou ancestral halls descent alone no longer guaranteed membership, as this traditional principle of determining membership was transformed into membership by descent-plus-investment. As such, these reformed ancestral halls came to represent a meeting point between the lineage order of the early Ming and the heightened commercial imperatives of the mid and late Ming. This merger of village lineage needs and practices with financial and commercial opportunities saw the ancestral hall often replace the landed trust as the key symbolic property of Huizhou lineages and their branches (in fact, many landed trusts were now attached directly to the ancestral hall rather than to the lineage proper or one of its branches). The ancestral hall thus played a crucial role in channeling cheaper credit to its members, in the commercialization of Huizhou village life, and ultimately in the flourishing of Huizhou merchant lineages from the sixteenth to the nineteenth centuries.

Established by lineages, branches, and other kinship groups, ancestral halls had been built in Huizhou since the Song dynasty.[1] Over the course of the succeeding centuries their recorded number would grow at first gradually and later dramatically, from just eleven ancestral halls in 1502 to no fewer than 213 in 1566.[2] The latest comprehensive textual survey by Fang Lishan has turned up textual references to no fewer than 1,193 ancestral halls in Huizhou by the end of the Ming.[3] In Qimen county the growth rate over the sixteenth century was even steeper. Not one ancestral hall was recorded in Qimen's county gazetteer of 1411 or in its section of the prefectural gazetteer of 1502. Come 1566, the new prefectural gazetteer listed twenty-nine for Qimen, and a generation later this county's gazetteer of 1600 mentioned fifty-six – but only after acknowledging that since "every hall, branch, and family has one ... they are too many to be listed in their entirety."[4]

This increase in Huizhou's ancestral halls did not halt in the Ming. In 1718 it was being said of single-lineage villages in Huizhou that

---

[1] McDermott, *Making*, v. 1, 100–7.
[2] *Huizhou fuzhi* (1502), 5.33a–49b; (1566), 21.5b–12b.
[3] Fang Lishan, *Huizhou zongzu citang*, 10–23. Fang lists for the late Tang two ancestral halls, the Northern Song one, the Southern Song sixteen, and the Yuan seven. The Ming ancestral halls far outnumber these figures, as do the post-1500 Ming over the pre-1500 Ming.
[4] *Qimen xianzhi* (1600), 4.50a–52b.

"if it has a descent group, then it has an ancestral hall (*ci* 祠)."[5] Thus, another Huizhou county, Wuyuan, in 1693 had almost as many recorded ancestral halls, 202, as all of Huizhou had boasted in 1566. By 1787 the registered number of Wuyuan's ancestral halls had risen further, to 401, and by 1925 to 619.[6] As a result, the estimate of Liu Miao 劉淼 – that over 6,000 halls were constructed in the six counties of Ming and Qing dynasty Huizhou, mainly after 1520 – is entirely credible and probably is an underestimate.[7]

This change was more than quantitative. The ancestral hall was the major institutional innovation in the Huizhou countryside during the last two centuries of Ming rule. Its predominance among the institutions of village life was particularly evident in villages with large lineages. For, far from being evenly distributed among Huizhou's villages, ancestral halls were often concentrated in large numbers within a single village or in several contiguous villages of a single large lineage. Fang Lishan has located ten or more ancestral halls in no fewer than thirty-one villages by the mid twentieth century.[8] To mention a few such cases: by the late Ming the three villages of the Chengs 程 in Shanhe 善和 in Qimen had no fewer than eleven ancestral halls; the number according to the source rose to fifteen, seventeen or eighteen during the Qing dynasty, so that the locals called the general Shanhe area "the Ancestral Halls Village."[9] By 1775, Jiang Village 江村 in She county had acquired at least thirty ancestral halls; the construction of twenty-three of them supposedly, and quite exceptionally, date from no later than the early Ming, eight more from the sixteenth century, and the rest from the first three-quarters of the eighteenth century. Other villages boasted of as many as seventy-one ancestral halls by the nineteenth century, and a random sample indicates that by the early nineteenth century (see Table 2.1)

---

[5] *SSXT*, 8, 258. Of course, the Chinese character 祠, translated here as a single ancestral hall, can be understood in the plural as well. As this chapter shows, many single lineage villages had far more than one ancestral hall per descent group.
[6] *Wuyuan xianzhi* (1694), 5.30b–35a; (1787), 9.14a–22b.
[7] Liu Miao, "Cong Huizhou Ming Qing jianshe," 21–29. She county alone has twenty-seven Ming ancestral halls and thousands from the Qing (Yan Guifu, *Huizhou lishi dang'an*, 18). Bian Li, "Huizhou de gu citang," 51, puts the total number still standing in Huizhou today (presumably including Wuyuan county) at over 1,000.
[8] Fang Lishan, *Huizhou zongzu citang*, 10–23. This figure seems to be for extant examples, excluding those merely mentioned in Ming–Qing texts.
[9] Yao Pangzao and Mei Wen, "Huizhou gu citang," 16–22, esp. 17.

Table 2.1 *Number of ancestral halls built in a single Huizhou village**

County	Lineage	Village	Number of ancestral halls
1. Yi	Sun	Guzhu	71 (plus 1 apiece in the Outer Village for the Cheng, Bi, and He)**
2.	Wang	Bishan	13
3.	Hu	Xidi	26
4.	Ye	Nanping	11
5. She	Jiang	Jiang Village	71
6.	Luo	Chengkan	14 (15)***
7.	Fang	Lingshan	4
8.	Bao	Tangyue	15
9. Jixi	Cao	Wang Village	11
10.	Xu	Kantou	10
11. Wuyuan	Dong	Yushan	23
12.	Li	Likang	12
13.	Pan	Pan Village	10 (population of 400+ persons)
14.	Pan	Zhifeng	4
15. Qimen	Cheng	Liudu (aka Shanhe)	15, 17, or 18
16.	Xie	Yangyuan	13
17.	Chen	Wentang	12
18.	Wang	Penglong	8 (400+ households and 1,000 persons)
19.	?	Shikang	6 (100+ households and 340 persons)
20.	Chen	Taoyuan	7

* Yao Pangzao and Mei Wen, "Huizhou gu citang," 16–22, esp. 17; Guo Qitao, *Ritual Opera*, 36. In the Guangdong county of Panyu 番禺, lineages with a thousand members likewise crowded their villages with several tens of ancestral halls; smaller lineages of less than a hundred households set up several (Shimizu, *Chūgoku zokusan*, 134). The three figures for the Shanhe Chengs (no. 14) are those separately given in Qimen xiangzhen jianzhi bianxi weiyuanhui, ed., *Qimen xiangzhen jianzhi*, 41 (12); *Qimen xianzhi* (2008), 862 (17); Cheng Biding, Wang Jianshe, et al., *Huizhou wuqian cun*, 224 (18).
** I find the first figure too high. Nonetheless, *Gushe Sunshi jiapu* (1812), 6th *ce*, zumu, 66–78, lists twenty-three ancestral halls for this lineage, at least twelve of which functioned during the Ming and one during the late Song through the Ming.
*** Zhao Huafu, *Huizhou zongzu*, 149–50, specifies fifteen (rather than fourteen), of which two were lineage ancestral halls and thirteen the branch variety; the matter is complicated by the existence of two separate lines, or arguably lineages, that together constituted the Luo lineage of Chengkan. Also, a *c.*200-meter-long row of ancestral halls for the Chengs and Lis constituted what some have called a Museum of Ancestral Halls.

many large Huizhou villages had between ten and twenty ancestral halls, and some of them many more.

The use of so many resources for the construction of so many ancestral halls for use by members of a single lineage in the same settlement area begs many questions, not least why and how were so many separate ancestral halls built by lineage members in the same vicinity. An initial answer emerges from the observation that their growth in numbers occurred when the nature (as well as the roles and organization) of this kind of kinship institution expanded beyond that of a ritual institution performing the ancestral ceremonies prescribed by neo-Confucian scholars. As expected, it was often the site of memorial services and the institution that carried out repairs to ancestral graves.[10] But, from no later than the mid Ming, the ancestral hall also assumed social, educational, and economic roles that put it at the heart of changes in the collective life of large Huizhou kinship groups.

As explained in the 1537 edition of the genealogy of the Xie 謝 lineage in Wangyuan 王源 in Qimen, the ancestral hall provided hall members with a site for the performance not just of their ancestral worship but also of the key rites of passage in their own lives: "The cappings, marriages, funerals, and burial rites are conducted in [the ancestral hall], as if they are being performed at the government offices in Lü [the home area of Confucius]."[11] It was the place where a member's birth and death were recorded in a lineage's registers and where he might undergo a school admission ceremony. It was the courtyard where he heard his elders lecture on lineage rules and customs and listened silently to formal proclamations of the *Sacred Edict of the First Ming Emperor*. It was the gallery where at New Year's and other festivals he might view his ancestors' portraits, their appointment papers to government office, and red-lacquered plaques carved with their lineage's rules.[12]

The events of daily life – and not just banquets for guests or visits by local officials and retired scholar-officials[13] – might also take place in an ancestral hall's courtyards. Young and old would assemble there before work and after work, join meetings there to discuss matters of

---

[10] *Jixi Xiguan Zhangshi zupu*, zongxun, 1a; *Xin'an Bishi zupu*, 2nd *ce*, 17.22a–b.
[11] Zhang Xiaoping, *Huizhou gu citang*, 9.
[12] Such as the large ancestral hall of the Luos at Chengkan in She county.
[13] Zhang Xiaoping, *Huizhou gu citang*, 9; *Xin'an Shuaikou Chengshi cigui xubian*, 1.7b.

Ancestral Halls and Credit 65

common concern, and even attend school classes within its walls.[14] To the dismay of critics, some members stored not only books but also dirty farm tools behind its gate,[15] while others used its courtyard for sun-drying newly harvested grain.[16] Some preferred to use it for their residence, their trading, and, even worse, their exorcisms.[17] Sullied by these vulgar habits, ancestral halls often required a thorough cleaning before they could be used for their ostensibly principal purpose of collective ancestral worship.[18] In sum, the ancestral hall, as prescribed, served as a place where kinsmen could assemble, foster a sense of kinship, be feted and educated, be reminded of their ancestors' contributions and achievements, and perform grand memorial rituals and sacrifices. And, since it was intended to concentrate the worship practices of members whose ancestors had been buried separately over a wide mountainous area, it often ended up located near the center of these villages and thus at the center of their collective life.[19]

Also, it was a kind of lineage law court, where lineages might reproach, shame, and punish their fractious members. As seen in the previous volume, Huizhou lineages during the mid and late Ming commonly suffered from conflicts, sometimes violent, within their ranks or with other lineages. The construction of ancestral halls at this time was partly intended to counter these threats to lineage order. In front of the ancestors' spirit tablets, the lineage head might call forth troublesome members and personally berate them. At times he might enlist members to force recalcitrant members to sign an agreement to mend their ways and work hard to support themselves.[20] Or at other times, like the head of the Zhu family of She county in 1598, he might attempt to shame recalcitrant members by posting "the rules of their ancestral hall" (*cigui* 祠規). He would also print them up for their magistrate's approval and then issue strict bans against members' misbehavior. So closely in the popular mind did these halls become identified with their kinship group that as a rule entry to the building

---

[14] *Shangshan Wushi zongfa guitiao*, 8a.
[15] *Tandu Xiaoli Huangshi zongpu*, 4.8a.
[16] Zhang Xiaoping, *Huizhou gu citang*, 68.
[17] *Xin'an Shuaikou Chengshi cigui xubian*, 1.7b; *Xin'an Bishi zupu*, 2nd *ce*, 17.21a.
[18] *DSGJY*, 3, 20–21, 96; *Jiangcun Hongshi jiapu*, 4th *ce*, 14.2a–3a.
[19] Ma Yonghu, *Hexie youxu*, 27; *Dangxi Jinshi zupu*, 7.15a.
[20] Chen Zhaoxiang, *Wentang xiangyue jiafa*.

itself was restricted to the group's members. Even a kinship group's bondservants were barred entrance; in one case during the performance of ancestral ceremonies they were required to wait in adjoining corridors, and in another case they were to remain outside the hall, unless specifically summoned.[21]

Furthermore, as we shall explain below, not all biological descendants of the honored ancestors were automatically allowed into the hall, since a contribution to the hall was sometimes a condition of membership. Other times, a member's repeated misbehavior inside it – gossiping, laughing, bumping into others, poor posture, lack of attention, and mere absence or late arrival at a ceremony – could lead to the hall's imposition of a punishment and expulsion.[22] The ancestral hall, in other words, functioned as a law court for the lineage. Members were to take their accusations to the county yamen only after the lineage had failed to resolve the problem at the hall. So basic did it become to a lineage's activities and self-perception that expulsion from a lineage was commonly expressed in terms of expulsion from its ancestral hall: "Alive, one is not a member of the lineage; and dead, one is not to enter the ancestral hall [as a spirit tablet]."[23] In short, the ancestral hall, created in the thousands for Huizhou's villages from the mid Ming to the mid Republican period, served as a place of worship, a school, a law court, a registry, a banquet hall, a social center, a barn, a storehouse, a marketplace, and a place for inflicting physical punishment.

According to Chen Keyun and some other scholars, the mid-Ming lineage's adoption of the ancestral hall consolidated its control over its members' activities and their collective property. In their view, lineage members purchased, donated, and bequeathed property to the hall and then took care to have it all officially registered as ancestral hall property. As a result, the ancestral hall, like the charitable landed trust, was used to strengthen the role of the lineage in the life of its members and their collective activities.[24] It institutionalized lineage supervision and governance of its members to an unprecedented degree, demonstrating how a charity had been transformed into a house of penal control.

---

[21] *Shangshan Wushi zongfa guitiao*, 8b; *Xin'an Shuaikou Chengshi cigui xubian*, 1.5b.
[22] Guo, *Ritual Opera*, 47.   [23] *Jinying Zhengshi zongpu*, 8th *ce*, mo, 3a.
[24] Chen Keyun, "Ming Qing Huizhou," 40–45.

A great deal of evidence can be marshaled to support this view, not least the large number of family rule books (*jiagui* 家規) and lineage regulations (*zugui* 族規) that fill genealogies from the sixteenth century onwards. In addition, the government promoted the revival of this Confucian order through its support for community pact (*xiangyue*) groups and its distribution of community pact rulebooks. Often repeating and supporting moral instructions issued by the first Ming emperor, these community pacts contained pages of moral prescriptions about village life and family relationships, all designed to restore a social order that lineage elders feared was threatened by the spread of immoral customs and interminable intra-lineage conflicts.[25] The hall in the eyes of these men was to be a solid base for securing a proper social order and lineage life.

Yet lineage leaders' wishes for tighter control were often frustrated. Just as the proliferation of landed trusts led often to further divisions among a lineage's separate branches and not to any promised harmony, so did the establishment of an increasing number of ancestral halls for usually separate lineage groups often institutionalize and sharpen disagreements among branches and segments. When a comprehensive ancestral hall was constructed for the entire lineage, it could threaten the hegemony of the lineage's already functioning branch-based ancestral halls. The erection of multiple halls allowed eligible lineage members to choose, if they wished, between ancestral halls. They could even decide to construct an ancestral hall that enabled them, as one group of lineage members, to dominate lineage governance and resources at the expense of other members unwilling or unable to join in this ancestral hall's construction project. In other words, what was meant to be an orthodox sign of harmony and order had been turned into a clear sign of internal disagreement and disorder. Arguably, no more devout way could be found to countermand the call for ancestral respect than to build another hall in honor of yet another venerable ancestor.

In analyzing this mid- and late Ming surge in ancestral-hall construction and its consequences for lineage cohesion, this chapter will follow various lineages through the often prolonged process of building their hall. It will first consider the strategies commonly employed by these hall managers to overcome legal obstacles and especially

---

[25] McDermott, "Emperor, Élites, and Commoners," 326–29.

construction-funding shortages. To find this capital, the managers drummed up donations from prospective supporters, formed and funded credit associations to provide their members and others with interest-bearing loans, charged admission fees for the initially temporary and subsequently permanent admission of spirit tablets of members and their ancestors, and, not least, levied post-construction charges for these tablets' continued presence in the hall. While it was usual for these fund-raising efforts to succeed eventually, the arrival of a new ancestral hall represented at least a potential threat to the lineage's previous arrangements. Not only were some lineage members probably ineligible to join since they were not descended from the lineage or branch worthy to be chosen the new hall's principal object of worship, its Prime Ancestor, or Prime Migrant. But also proponents of this new hall, it was feared by other lineage members, would use it to improve the position of their branch or group within the lineage. Just as the charitable landed trust might become an object of dispute among lineage branches in the mid and late Ming (as seen in the fate of the Doushan trust studied in volume 1), so could the arrival of a new ancestral hall prompt great controversy over governance and management of the lineage's resources. In other words, Huizhou's ancestral halls arose in part from the commercial success of their lineages, and their operation was in turn disrupted and threatened by groups within these lineages. By the late Ming the lineage was commonly not just a multi-adumbrated ensemble of branches and segments. In some instances it had also become a multi-stratified ensemble of kinsmen separately affiliated in different ways to different lineage institutions like ancestral halls and landed trusts.

The final section of this chapter will move the discussion on to the ways these halls, once constructed, managed their capital assets profitably. Before construction, they had needed to lend and invest their members' donations with care; after construction, even if they had surplus funds, they needed to amass further funds, if only for future repairs. Hence, before and after its construction, a hall might institutionally function as a "proto-bank" for its members, in that it received and lent their money at interest and at times paid them shares of the profits made from their money. Although it seems not to have received direct deposits from its members, it certainly hosted credit associations which, set up to help finance ancestral worship to the hall's Prime Ancestor, received members' regular contributions. Thus, just as

Huizhou villagers transformed a staid business organization for timber production and ownership into a lively timber futures market, so did they turn a venerable Confucian institution of antiquity, whose operations for ancestral worship had been officially authorized by the government, into a "proto-bank" that in some cases provided members with relatively cheap loans. The multiplicity and ubiquity of the ancestral hall as well as the wealth of sources revealing these activities suggest how central it became not just to lineage life in Huizhou and the loyalty of its members but also potentially to the involvement of these merchant lineages' members in the thriving commercial and financial life of the Yangzi Valley during the second half of the Ming.

Overcoming, or Sidestepping, a Legal Restriction

During the early and mid Ming, two sets of imposing hurdles – one legal and the other financial – impeded the construction of an ancestral hall. At first glance, the legal restrictions on the establishment of an ancestral hall and the use of it for large collective worship of ancient ancestors seem unexpected in a society that emphasized the importance of filial piety. Yet precisely who could perform where what kinds of ancestral worship to which ancestors were issues that Chinese scholars and officials endlessly debated. These matters were tightly wrapped up with questions of relative status and privilege, as sanctioned by the classical Confucian texts and commentaries, centuries of imperial dynasties' practices, and Ming imperial decrees. Certain imperial family members and court officials were privileged, while all others were barred, especially commoners, from performing ancestral worship in such halls.

The early Ming policy was set solidly within this venerable tradition. Whereas the late Northern Song government had relaxed a millennium of these restrictions to allow nonofficial scholars to build their ancestral family shrines, the first Ming emperor had pushed the clock back to confer this privilege only on imperial relatives and very high officials. To the Song government's ban on non-scholar families' having their own detached ancestral hall – they were to use instead a bedchamber (qin 寢) altar within their residence – the early Ming government added several official restrictions on the use of this space for ancestral worship. Commoners were to collectively worship only their two most recent generations of ancestors – their parents and grandparents – during the second month of each season, and were explicitly barred from worshipping their Prime Ancestor. All of these or similar prescriptions had been set out in the *Family Rituals* (*Jiali* 家禮), an influential book attributed to the neo-Confucian scholar-official Zhu Xi (1130–1200). A further restriction insisted that the worshippers be "a very small number of people": "only those who are the successors in the descent line of the Prime Ancestor."[26] In its *Collected Rituals of the Great Ming* (*Da Ming li ji* 大明禮集, compiled in 1370), the Ming government closely adopted Zhu's prescriptions,[27] slightly relaxing one of them in 1384 to allow commoners to worship their great-grandfathers as well.[28]

In 1373 Ming officials were ordered by the first Ming emperor to set up their own family shrine, but to worship no ancestor, including their Prime Ancestor, beyond their fourth previous generation.[29] Furthermore, they could perform these sacrifices only at set times, in the middle month of each season. Perhaps because of these restrictions, few families in the early Ming (just as in the Song and Yuan) chose to set up a family shrine. Not surprisingly, apart from some very highly placed kinship groups, little lineage interest is reported in the first

---

[26] McDermott, *Making*, v. 1, 100–1; Ebrey, *Chu Hsi's Family Rituals*, 167, n. 42. Zhu confesses to self-dissatisfaction with his "overstepping" (*jian* 僭) by performing ancestral rites to his Prime Ancestor. However, he tolerated officials' and commoners' performance of sacrifices to a distant Prime Ancestor at his grave site, but not in an ancestral hall (Inoue, *Chūgoku no sōzoku*, 178–99). Inoue links this view to Zhu's promotion of ancestral worship not by "large communal families" as promoted by Sima Guang 司馬光 and Cheng Yi, but by smaller descent groups (*xiaozong* 小宗). Commoners in such groups, according to Zhu, should sacrifice to their previous four generations (Ebrey, *Chu Hsi's Family Rituals*, 138), a number that excludes their Prime Ancestor.
[27] Xu Yikui, *Da Ming jili*, 6.14a.
[28] Nakajima, *Mindai gōson*, 338. Yuan policy was more tolerant on this point, as it allowed commoners to worship their Prime Ancestor at his grave site. The famous Zheng lineage of Putian 莆田 even included this ancestor's spirit tablet in their family shrine in contravention of government law. Furthermore, as Inoue points out, if the building used for such sacrifices lay alongside the prime ancestor's grave (as would not have been uncommon), then it would have been difficult to prevent his descendants from venerating him at the times (such as Qingming and New Year's) they were venerating their ancestors of two or four generations' standing (Inoue, *Chūgoku no sōzoku*, 166–67).
[29] Chow Kai-wing, *Rise of Confucian Ritualism*, 106.

century of Ming rule for large ancestral halls as well as for collective acts of ancestral worship, particularly of the Prime Ancestor.

At the end of this first century of Ming rule, appeals for a change to these restrictions were voiced in official, but not imperial, circles. In 1476 an official in the Directorate of Education, Zhou Hongmo 周洪謨, sent a memorial to the emperor, requesting that he order all his officials to build their ancestral hall (for worship, once again, of just the four previous generations).[30] Although Zhou's proposals were very conservative – he did not even contemplate the relaxation of a ban on scholar and commoner households' worship of their Prime Ancestor at their annual winter solstice festivities – they failed to win imperial approval.

His voice was nonetheless a quiet harbinger of the avalanche of changes soon to reshape the ancestral hall. Two generations later a memorial from another court official, Xia Yan 夏言, did win another emperor's approval for far more extensive changes, thereby expanding the social composition and number of households legally permitted to engage in large-scale collective performances of ancestral worship. In 1536, after the Jiajing emperor (1507–67; r. 1522–66) had approved Xia Yan's appeals for the destruction of Buddhist temples, Xia reportedly persuaded the same emperor to allow all official and commoner families to perform sacrifices to their Prime Ancestor during both the annual winter solstice and New Year's Day festivities.[31] To justify this change, Xia turned to writings of a founding father of the neo-Confucian movement, Cheng Yi 程頤 (1033–1107), in particular to Cheng's conviction that such ancestral worship was natural to the feelings (*qing* 情) of all men, regardless of their social and legal status: "Men all have ancestors from whom they originate and have no differences in their feelings about them. This ritual ought to penetrate upper and lower [ranks of the population]."[32] Most likely, however, it was neither this neo-Confucian argument nor any consideration of its long-term consequences that prompted this emperor to change the ancient practice. Rather, it was personal frustrations arising from his

---

[30] *Ming shilu* (*fu jiao kanji*), 137.4a.
[31] Xia Yan, *Guizhou zouyi*, 12.18b–22a; and his *Guizhou xiansheng zouyi*, 20.16a–22a for a very similar version. In both texts the memorial is presented as a request, but its placement in both volumes among hundreds of Xia Yan's approved memorials imparts a sense of its full acceptance and legitimacy.
[32] Xia Yan, *Guizhou zouyi*, 12.21b; Inoue, *Chūgoku no sōzoku*, 186–97.

prolonged clash with court officials about his wish to venerate his own ancestors. Adopted from an imperial branch line into the main imperial line in order to succeed the sonless Zhengde emperor (1476–1521; r. 1506–1521), the Jiajing emperor struggled with his court's ritual experts to win permission to worship his natal ancestors in the imperial family's ancestral hall in the palace.[33] His support of Xia's proposal resulted more from his tiffs with his officials than from any considered judgment of this revision's impact on other families and on Chinese society. Even less did it reflect a detailed knowledge of Confucian texts and rites.

Xia Yan, however, was aware that ancestral rites of the sort he envisaged required a fixed site for their performance, and so he appealed to the emperor to allow these same sectors of the population to have and use detached ancestral halls of their own. The officials, he reminded his ruler, had enjoyed this privilege in the pre-imperial past; and now, he argued, they deserved it again:

In the Zhou dynasty and earlier, all [parties] from the Son of Heaven down to the scholar-officials had their own ancestral shrine (*zumiao* 祖廟). Also, each of the commoners (*shuren* 庶人) made offerings in a bedroom. Come the Qin dynasty (221–206 BC), the government brought an end to [the issuance of aristocratic ranks like] marquises and set up prefects; it burned the [Confucian] classics and extinguished learning. This ritual was lost, and therefore no one other than the Son of Heaven dared to have and run a private shrine. The Wei, Jin, and later dynasties began to revive shrine regulations, and allowed all civil and military officials to set up a family shrine, using their official rank to differentiate the number of generations that they sacrificed to. Nonetheless, some reached very eminent positions but still did not run shrines, and it reached the point where some officials who set them up were ashamed of doing so. There was an edict allowing them to set up a shrine, but the mass of officials lacked the willingness to call on the members [i.e. fellow lineage members] to set one up. Eventually an imperial edict sharply censured them – how was it that these ritual teachings alone fell into decline and that [men] were content with the old and accustomed to the normal? Since there are different rites for the old and the recent [ancestors] and since there are different regulations for those with enfeofments and honors, there definitely were some doubts on the matter [of what to do]. But the ritual officials at that time also were not able to give lectures and to demand classical ritual regulations; they were unable to have any definite

---

[33] Geiss, "The Chia-ching Reign, 1522–1566," 443–50.

discussions and to provide the people with a basis to rely on. Therefore, at that time, even if there was an imperial edict, the scholar-officials were dubious about it and afraid of looking back as well as gazing forward. And so, they did not dare to set up [ancestral halls].[34]

Henceforth, at Xia Yan's request, Ming officials were to share a privilege previously restricted mainly to male members of the imperial clan: permission to construct their ancestral hall. Those officials of the top three ranks were allowed to worship members of their five previous generations, and officials of all other ranks just those of the four previous generations. If, furthermore, they sought to worship an even older ancestor than this second change now permitted – such as the Prime Ancestor, whom they were allowed to worship at the winter solstice festival – they were to follow Zhu Xi's advice to make a paper ancestral shrine tablet in this Prime Ancestor's name and then burn it upon completion of the sacrifice.[35] Taken together, Xia's proposals allowed all official households, regardless of their actual official rank, to collectively worship a Prime Ancestor in their own ancestral hall at least once a year.

Yet the change, as Xia recognized, would not end there.[36] Officials of the top three ranks would install fifth-generation ancestors they did not have; and the future descendants of an official, even if they themselves became commoners, would end up keeping tablets of these founding officials permanently in this ancestral hall for communal worship as their Prime Ancestor. Imperial approval of these changes thus would legitimize the establishment and spread of lineage organizations (as seen, for example, in the development of the Shanhe Chengs) for kinship groups with far fewer, if any, officials in their collective past than had the Shanhe Chengs.

Some scholars have argued that Xia Yan's proposal never won the Jiajing emperor's formal approval, as no assent is mentioned or included in the standard court-edited chronicles of Ming history, and as shortly afterwards in 1536 Xia himself acknowledged that he was still waiting for the emperor's response to his proposals.[37] Yet Zhao

---

[34] Xia Yan, *Guizhou zouyi*, 12.22b.
[35] Ibid., 12.22a–25a; Ebrey, *Confucianism and Family Rituals*, 106, 138, 145 on the elderly Zhu Xi's desire for all in general to sacrifice no farther back than four generations (Ebrey, *Chu Hsi's Family Rituals*, 8–9).
[36] Xia Yan, *Guizhou zouyi*, 12.24b.   [37] Ibid., 12.49b–52b.

Huafu 赵华富 and others have observed that the phrase "Assented to" (*cong zhi* 從之) concludes the version of this memorial recorded in a respected collection of abridged historical sources compiled in 1603 by a well-informed scholar in Songjiang prefecture.[38] Furthermore, the knowledgeable and equally orthodox neo-Confucian scholar Guan Zhidao believed that the Jiajing emperor had granted, admittedly in violation of canonical ritual prescriptions, temporary permission to commoner households to "press their sacrifices to go as far back as their Prime Ancestor."[39] Thus substantial evidence in non-court texts supports the claim that the emperor approved the expansion of this privilege to include official families and, if not intentionally, commoner families as well. Even if the Jiajing emperor never formally approved Xia Yan's memorial, some of his Ming subjects certainly thought that he had.

Nonetheless, to focus on Xia Yan and the court only repeats the common Chinese historiographical error of viewing social change in the provinces through the records of the court rather than from the study of local practices, preferably in local records. Not only had lineage members long been worshipping selective ancestors as their Prime Ancestor in local settings and institutions other than an ancestral hall, such as Buddhist chapels, village worship association shrines, and academies (*shuyuan* 書院),[40] but also commoner households in Huizhou had already been worshipping their Prime Ancestor in their own ancestral halls built without government permission for some four or five decades before Xia Yan sent his memorial to the emperor. By no later than the early decades of the fifteenth century, Wang Ti 汪褆 (1490–1530), an ardent advocate of Zhu Xi's School of Principle (*lixue* 理學) in Qimen county, acknowledged, "Men nowadays often set up Prime Ancestor Shrine sacrifices."[41] Thus the impact of Xia Yan's

---

[38] Wang Qi, *Xu wenxian tongkao*, 115.24b–27b.
[39] Guan Zhidao, *Congxian*, 2.4b–5a.
[40] Cheng Minzheng, *Huangdun wenji*, 17.31; McDermott, *Making*, v. 1, 61–62, 87–92.
[41] Wang Ti, *Bo'an ji*, xia, 11a–15a. Such unauthorized action did not trouble him greatly – he simply said, "It is suitable to change ancestral halls dedicated to Prime Ancestors into ancestral halls dedicated to Former Ancestors" and to have a house built separately alongside this hall to house the lineage's senior member, so that he would head the hall and preside at grave sacrifices to the Prime Ancestor. Some of these ancestral halls may well have been revivals of halls destroyed in the Yuan–Ming transition (Xie Chaoyuan, *Houming riji*, 2nd *ce*, *shizu quan mutu*).

reforms seems to have been less to initiate than to legitimize or even neo-Confucianize already existing cultural and intellectual trends, ideas, and practices.[42] In sum, the mid-Ming change in ancestral worship institutions and rituals arguably saw less a government-instigated spread among commoners of the practice of worshipping their Prime Ancestor than a Confucian relabeling and co-opting of an already widespread practice. The government and Confucian officials now wanted to enclose already existing practices within a building that had received government approval and the preferred neo-Confucian name of "ancestral hall" (citang).[43] It is telling that Xia Yan's memorial was seldom, if ever, used by Huizhou lineages to justify their construction of an ancestral hall.[44]

Information on the scale and schedule of the ancestral worship activities within these early Huizhou halls is scant and contradictory. The Wuyuan scholar-official Wang Shunmin 汪舜民 (1478 metropolitan degree) showed little interest in following his fellow county-man Zhu Xi by expressing long before Xia Yan a broad tolerance for the expanded construction and more inclusive use of ancestral halls. He had noticed that both scholars and commoners, particularly at the Cheng surname group's principal shrine in Huangdun 篁墩, were worshipping their earliest ancestors. Rather than being alarmed by this transgression of the dynasty's rules, he approved of their practice, on

---

[42] Chow Kai-wing, *Rise of Confucian Ritualism*, 104; Guo Qitao, *Ritual Opera*, 43–44, mention the innovative 1269 dedication of an ancestral hall to a lineage's Prime Ancestor by the well-known northern neo-Confucian scholar Xu Heng 許衡 (1209–81); but so far I have found no explicit evidence of its influence in Huizhou. More proximate and thus more likely sources of external influence are thirteenth- and fourteenth-century examples mentioned by Inoue, *Chūgoku no sōzoku*, 167–72, of lineages worshipping their Prime Ancestor or Prime Migrant in adjacent Zhejiang province.

[43] Chang Jianhua, *Mingdai zongzu*, 83–95. Under at least the Yuan government a shrine's deity (*miaoshen* 廟神) was sometimes officially registered as the "head" of a family shrine (*Xin'an Dacheng cun Chengshi zhipu*, xia, fulu, 26b); this practice apparently ended or was secularized in the Ming, with the ancestral hall itself registered as the household head.

[44] The Huizhou source most clearly indicating a Xia Yan link to Huizhou institutional reform is the eighteenth-century, not sixteenth-century, source *Yanzhen zhicao* (1737), li ji, 134. Cheng Minzheng, *Huangdun wenji*, 17.10a–21b, describes the New Year and autumn festival worship of Chen Li 陳櫟 by his entire lineage at a shrine built in his honor in 1452, thirty years before Cheng wrote this record. Ebrey, *Confucianism and Family Rituals*, 160–62, recounts discussion of this matter outside Huizhou.

the ground not of human feelings (as expressed by Cheng Yi and Wang Ti), but rather of man's moral duty to his ancestors:

> Some say, "When scholars and commoners sacrifice to their predecessors, the regulations stop them from [sacrificing beyond] their great-great-grandfather. Are they now not transgressing this regulation?" I say, "If the ritual is fine, then righteousness will arise. When men in a rural district died in antiquity, they made sacrifices [to them] at the village worship association. How much more so is this to be done when an ancestor's achievements and a descent group's virtues cannot be forgotten. Those who are the descendants ought to make sacrifices to them out of righteousness (yi 義)." Some also say, "Through its official name the [Huangdun] shrine undertakes worship to the Prime Ancestor of the Chengs, Cheng Shizhong. It is all right to sacrifice to him alone. But now all the other various ancestors are in [the shrine]. Are they not [too] numerous?" I say, "The emperor's collective worship of his imperial ancestors is comprehensively done at the Grand Ancestral Hall. By being done separately [a lineage's rites to its ancestors] cannot be compared to [these imperial rites to the ancestors], and thus their significance is not special."[45]

A generation or two later, the Xiuning scholar Jin Yao 金瑤 begged to differ. In his lineage's genealogy of 1568 he issued a warning to his fellow lineage members not to downplay the importance of the number of generations sacrificed to in their branches' ancestral halls. Jin commoners had long followed the practice of worshipping the four previous generations, as recommended by Zhu Xi in his *Family Rituals*. Yet this number exceeded the three-generation limit prescribed by Ming law. Even if the dynasty's laws could be evaded, Jin warned, it was hard to trick those in the know, including the ghosts and gods (*guishen*) to whom the sacrifices were addressed. As they surely know enough not to accept unauthorized sacrifices, what was the point of offering them?[46]

The thoughts and actions of Wang Ti, a rough contemporary of Jin Yao, prove even more contradictory and confusing on this matter. Wang built a shrine to four ancestors in his own bedroom and also persuaded his kinsmen to build a shrine for collective sacrifices at the start of every year. Yet he still held no set view on the number of previous generations whose spirit tablets he was entitled to have in his ancestral hall. In one composition he favored just two; in another "two, three, four, or five" generations; and in another he opposed

---

[45] Wang Shunmin, *Jinggan xiansheng wenji*, 10.8b–10a.
[46] *Dangxi Jinshi zupu*, 18.13b.

the eventual removal of spirit tablets from the hall for burial outside, seemingly in toleration of the hall's retention of spirit tablets beyond the fourth or fifth generation of deceased members. His principal concern was not with the past and its spirit tablets but with the present and the future, and that meant the inclusion of as many living descendants of the main line as possible in the ritual performances at the hall. His pursuit of this goal thus may have presumed the inclusion of spirit tablets from as many former generations as possible.

From this chaos two conclusions can nonetheless be drawn. Scholar-officials in mid-Ming Huizhou were looking for ways to practice large collective rituals such as they had read about, and some lineages and their branches at chapels and increasingly their own ancestral halls were already worshipping a greater number of ancestors than officially permitted. Thus perhaps one reason why Wang Ti did not discuss an ordinary lineage's worship of the Prime Ancestor and other ancestors was his awareness that regardless of what Huizhou's favorite native son Zhu Xi had prescribed, lineage ritual practices in Huizhou had for generations superseded all this scholarly theorizing and government regulation. Practice had outgrown both prescription and proscription, and ancestral halls were now conceivable and legal for all kinship groups, commoners as well as officials.

The Construction of Ancestral Halls: Issues of Membership

Consequently, the legal, philosophical and political obstacles to the expanded use of the ancestral hall usually mattered less than the financial challenge; that is, the actual cost and financing of its construction. Admittedly, some Huizhou kinship groups relied on the generosity of a single wealthy donor, thereby easily gaining membership for themselves and at least their recent ancestors.[47] But, in the view of a highly knowledgeable native of late Ming Huizhou, Wu Ziyu 吳子玉, collective efforts to raise the necessary building funds from both rich and poor members of a lineage were more common. Humble households reportedly preferred to donate these funds rather than spend them on enlarging their own cramped residences, "so as not to have only rich people gain fame" for their contribution.[48]

---

[47] Zhao Huafu, *Huizhou zongzu*, 155–63, mentions donors anxious to express their gratitude to an ancestor, often the Prime Ancestor.
[48] Wu Ziyu, *Dazhang shanren ji*, 22.14b–16a.

A relatively cheap and common way to construct an ancestral hall was to make it from an already standing building. Reflecting on previous centuries' practice, a Huizhou native in 1758 commented, "Ancestral shrines are in Buddhist monks' temples. Although there is no reference to this in the *Book of Rites* (*Li* 禮), Huizhou has many of them."[49] As many Buddhist temples had been designated "derelict" (*fei* 廢) by the Huizhou yamens in the fourteenth and fifteenth centuries,[50] this type of adaptation would have appeared natural, cheap, and legitimate, especially as few basic architectural differences stood in the way. Xia Yan's concurrent advocacy of ancestral-hall construction and a proscription on Buddhist temples was no accident.

More often, however, the construction of Huizhou's ancestral halls began virtually from scratch. Some halls were very modest, meriting the name of not a hall but simply a prayer altar (*baitai* 拜台). Witness the worship site set up by two She county families on mountain garden land adjoining an ancestral grave site. Collectively owned and managed, this small worship site produced fruit to help pay for its land tax and upkeep.[51] Slightly more ambitious were many other places of ancestral worship. Covering an area no greater than 300 square feet (for example, the Doushan trust's ancestral hall in Shanhe, Qimen county), they were little more than large rooms occupying the rear of a building initially erected or concurrently used for other purposes.[52]

More impressive were detached buildings set up by groups of men through their separate contributions of labor and materials. Although original plans might call for equal shares of ownership among the branches, the actual donation levels might, as we shall see, result in different branches acquiring a different number of shares in the ownership of their shared ancestral hall, a practice that doubtless encouraged the construction of numerous branch and segment halls in Huizhou's villages.[53]

[49] Ye Weiming, *Shexian jinshi zhi*, 8.162a.
[50] *THJ*, jiwai wen, 2,805, discusses the conversion of a chapel into an ancestral hall; McDermott, *Making*, v. 1, 217–22.
[51] *Huizhou qiannian*, v. 4, 346 (1633). The simplicity of the structure is reflected in the simplicity of the punishment promised any encroachment or obstruction of the property: three bushels of Chinese cabbage to be paid to the two families' common expense funds.
[52] Yet their comprehensive lineage ancestral hall, the Tonglun tang, occupies 1,500 square meters (*Qimen xianzhi* (2008), 862).
[53] This practice is related to the common Huizhou merchant practice of forming joint-share commercial partnerships (see Chapters 5 and 6 below).

The Construction of Ancestral Halls 79

As time passed, some ancestral halls for large and wealthy kinship groups ended up far grander. Perhaps the best-known Ming example of the grand ancestral hall is that of the Luos 羅 in Chengkan 呈坎, She county. Its entire surface area is presently no less than 2,875 square meters, including three "courtyards" (*jin* 進) and two large spaces between them.[54] Surrounded by a series of walls two or three stories high, its central courtyard, like that of some other Huizhou ancestral halls, proved capable of holding more than a thousand worshippers.[55] These ancestral halls were far larger and their construction far more costly than the simple adaptations of Buddhist temples.

Table 2.2 *Individual ancestral halls' construction costs**[56]

Lineage	Location	Duration	Cost (taels)
Wu	Wan'an, Xiuning	1611–23	c.2,400–2,600**
Luo	Chengkan, She	1612–19	4,577
Xu	Fangxi, She	7 years	10,000+
Xiang	Guixi, She	c.1616	7,043
		1679–1753: repairs	9,800
		incl. 1703	6,000+
Huang	Tandu	18th century	30,000***
Wang	Zhulin, Xiuning	1761–67	38,230
Zhou	west of city wall, Jixi	1769.4–1776.10	16,800
Jiang	Jiang Village, She	1586–98: repairs	?
		1737–44: repairs	29,190
Hu	Xidi, Yi	1788	6,940+
Bao	Tangyue	late 18th century	3,527

* Zhao Huafu, "Lun Huizhou," 51; and his *Huizhou zongzu*, 155–56; Guo Qitao, *Exorcism*, 695; and his *Ritual Opera*, 35–36; Luo Yinghe, *Miaoshi zhi*, 1, *passim*.
** This includes 1,934 taels collected by 1621.
*** This particular ancestral hall was set up solely for women (*nüci* 女祠).

---

[54] Zhao Huafu, *Huizhou zongzu*, 152. This account has a breakdown of the constituent parts of the hall and their size; yet see the 3,300-odd square meter figure given just for the ancestral hall dedicated to Luo Dongshu (Zhongguo guzhenyou bianjibu, *Guzhen yangxiangguan*, 96).
[55] Zhang Xiaoping, *Huizhou gu citang*, 62–77.
[56] Zhao Huafu, "Lun Huizhou," 51; and his *Huizhou zongzu*, 155–56; Guo Qitao, *Exorcism*, 95; and his *Ritual Opera*, 35–36; Luo Yinghe, *Miaoshi zhi*, 1.

The history of many Huizhou ancestral halls, especially the more expensive, calls into question a set of assumptions common to most modern Chinese discussions of ancestral halls: that membership in an ancestral hall was strictly a matter of biological descent, that membership in it came from membership in the lineage (as identified through inclusion in the descent-line charts of its genealogy and in the ranks of the beneficiaries of its landed trust), and that posthumous membership through representation by a spirit tablet (*shenzhu* 神主), once granted, was permanent. In the rest of this chapter I will show how each of these understandings is at best inadequate, and that membership in an ancestral hall was not automatically permanent, often cost money, sharpened social distinctions between kinsmen, and sometimes came with the fillip of eased access to low-interest loans. Membership entailed contributions both before and after construction, sometimes for the living and at all times for the dead. Thus, from their inception, some ancestral halls functioned, in fact if not in name, as partly voluntary associations, which showered their rewards principally on only their members, identified as descendants of the hall's Prime Ancestor who themselves or whose descendants had crucially also made a donation to the hall on their behalf. The hall's leaders, in light of the intra-lineage quarrels that afflicted many Huizhou lineages at the time, would have wanted members committed to their project, and the surest way to confirm that shared commitment would have been to require shared investment from them.

For signs that membership in these ancestral halls, new or restored, was often not automatic to lineage members, we need merely observe that two of the Ming ancestral halls whose operations we know most about – the Luos of Chengkan and the Chengs of Dongli – charged eligible descendants for the admission of their ancestors' spirit tablets into the hall. Well over two-thirds of the spirit tablets which entered the Luos' ancestral hall upon its opening in c.1616 were admitted on the basis of a donation by a son and/or grandson; that is, the ancestor selected for admission by most donors had been dead for just one or two generations, and yet admission of their spirit tablets still required a prepayment.[57] In one Xiuning lineage in the late sixteenth century

---

[57] Sons alone accounted for 34 percent of all the donors to the Luos' construction; next were grandsons at 13 percent and sons and grandsons giving together at 9 percent.

(reported in 1549 to have close to 3,000 members), half of its households were said to "be afraid of the cost" and so did not attend the services.[58] From its inception, then, the membership of a Huizhou ancestral hall would not necessarily have been the same as that of the lineage as recorded in its genealogy or in the recipient list of annual grants from the lineage's charitable landed trusts.[59]

With membership and its attendant benefits not linked solely to genealogical descent or generational seniority, the benefits of such a hall were also allotted differently from the roughly egalitarian distribution of profits of a traditional charitable landed trust such as the Doushan trust. Distribution was made according not to the number of a lineage's branches or its adult males but to the size of a member's prior investment in the hall as reflected in the number of his portions (*fen* 分) or shares (*gu* 股) in the hall. This principle and practice of making an unequal allocation of the hall's benefits – if only because not all descendants joined the hall and not all members necessarily contributed the same amount of capital – would have probably roughly reflected already existing economic distinctions between members and nonmembers as well as among the hall's members themselves. Thus, although an ancestral hall's resources, ritual, and other practices might resemble those of a lineage trust,[60] their basic organizational principles and operating practices could radically differ. One was a charity generous to all male descendants of a Prime Ancestor with little asked in return, and the other partly a voluntary association whose members claimed descent from a common ancestor and yet – if they wished to become or even remain members – were expected at various times to attend ritual performances and make donations. Viewed from the perspective of the historical development of the ancestral hall, the Huizhou lineage itself was in the mid Ming an institution in transition to becoming a more exclusive and more economically stratified type of kinship institution than had been common earlier in the Ming. Arguably, this change suited the commercial opportunities now eagerly pursued by Huizhou men and some in their kinship groups, as well as the eagerness exhibited by many commoner lineages towards the

---

[58] *Xin'an mingzu zhi*, qian, 53–54; *Xin'an Shuaikou Chengshi cigui xubian*, 3a–b.
[59] Bussotti, "Huizhou Genealogies and Huizhou Lineages," suggests that a donation was required for including a dead or living person's name in a genealogy.
[60] Liu Miao, "Qingdai Qimen Shanhe," 268–74.

construction of a hall previously denied their like. Yet once made, this involvement would have locked them into commitments that in the future they might want to relinquish. The issue of exiting from these kinship groups is never explicitly broached, and any request for a refund would certainly not have been considered.

Pre-construction Fund-Raising

Raising the funds for construction of these halls often required years, if not decades or even centuries, of cajoling lineage members into opening their purses. One Xiuning lineage started plans in the 1270s at the close of the Song dynasty and eventually built their ancestral hall three centuries later in the mid sixteenth century. Between 1447 and 1581 its management on no fewer than nine occasions made purchases of tiny pieces of contiguous land, before judging the site large enough for a hall that could hold all their members (even then the site contained part of an old temple and a shop).[61]

Appeals to improve the family's reputation and social standing were on their own rarely successful in persuading lineage members to donate money for an ancestral hall's construction. Successful fund-raisers found it useful to consider the donor's power and the "face" of his ancestor and himself. Consider how the prospects for the construction fund of the Wus of Wan'an 萬安吳 in Xiuning suddenly improved when some twelve largely fruitless years into the campaign the managers abandoned their original plan to collect the same amount of cash from each adult male member of the lineage. Belatedly but effectively, they devised a new strategy that directly linked the treatment of an ancestor's spirit tablet in the ancestral hall to the amount of money donated by its sponsor, usually a close descendant: each spirit tablet was ranked first grade, second grade, or third grade according to the size of its backer's donation. And so, in the 1610s, 184 members of this Wu lineage made a contribution for the construction of their ancestral hall.[62] While half of them paid three taels of silver, or less, the other half paid enough to distinguish themselves and their ancestors from

---

[61] *Xin'an Shuaikou Chengshi cigui xubian*, 2.2a ff.
[62] *Wan'an Wushi jianci*, 4a–9b. The preference for higher entry charges reflects a concern not just with face or status. Anyone interested in accessing an ancestral hall's funds would clearly be attracted to joining halls with greater funds.

their kinsmen. Annual dividends or rewards would presumably have mirrored these differences.

Another non-egalitarian response to the offer of membership might occur when it was branches rather than individuals who were offered management powers in the new hall. When in 1569 "three big branches" of the Wangs provided labor and materials for the construction of an ancestral hall, their subsequent role in the management of the ancestral hall might reflect already existing differences. Thus, whereas the management of the Wangs' ancestral hall may have been divided into "five equal parts," three were placed in the hands of the single branch that had actually made the greatest contribution to the ancestral hall.[63]

Equally powerful arguments, even if rarely voiced, for making a donation would have been the heady mix of gratitude and guilt that would have troubled many descendants, who had not turned the advantages inherited from their ancestors into a successful career as an official or merchant. Donation at this stage in the construction project was often linked to gaining in return permission to submit an ancestor's spirit tablet to the hall. The chance of thereby meeting their duty of ancestral remembrance and escaping feelings of guilt for their own inadequacies (as well as applying pressure on one's descendants for similarly thoughtful generosity in the future) must have proved too attractive for many men to resist.[64]

Responses to Construction Proposals

Faced with this set of demands from his own branch or lineage, a Huizhou man, assuming he was willing to make a donation to gain a place for his ancestor's spirit tablet in the ancestral hall, had in the mid and late Ming at least three options. He could pay the requisite construction or entry fee either directly, or indirectly by joining a kind of credit association (*hui* 會) that Huizhou men in the Ming commonly set up or participated in, to help them find affordable loans. Second, he might try to alter the price of admission and hold out for a higher or lower price. And third, he might refuse to join this ancestral hall and

---

[63] *Huizhou qiannian*, v. 2, 430; *Chengshi Dongli cidian*, shengxi, 1a, details the admission fees for "all spirit tablets submitted" to the ancestral hall.
[64] Azuma, *Zhu Xi "Jiali"*, 159–203.

look to see if another was available to join (this option doubtless helps to explain the presence in a wealthy village of duplicate halls dedicated to the same ancestor or one of his close descendants).

Each of these options – direct and indirect payment, bargaining, and selective refusal – had its advantages and disadvantages. But in no case was admission financially free; emotionally, it also could inflict a cost, since campaigns to build ancestral halls sometimes aroused deep divisions. As observed in the seemingly endless squabbles of the Shanhe Chengs over timber and forest land in volume 1, a lineage, its branches, and their segments could all have their own ancestral hall and thus compete with one another in parallel worship, fund-raising, and financial activities, their tensions in these efforts all nurtured by already existing conflicts within the lineage.

High-interest rates, loan payment defaults, competition among loan associations, the price of spirit tablets' admission, the ranking and gender of these tablets, and the rivalries among contending lineage halls for members' donations and loyalties, all these issues fueled quarrels among kinsmen. An analysis of first the construction plans and then the administration of certain ancestral halls will reveal how, through their establishment and operation, many Huizhou lineage members laid the basis for a hall's accumulation of capital, funds which from the sixteenth century onward they and other contributing members might borrow.

Payment through Moneylending

To acquire funds for ancestral-hall construction, men in Huizhou commonly set up credit associations, a type of money-sharing institution that had appeared in China by no later than the Tang dynasty.[65] Some of these Huizhou credit associations in the Ming may have originated as grave-protection or graveside worship societies, whose members were expected to take care of ancestral graves and to hold regular sacrifices there, perhaps at the time of the Qingming festival, for their Prime Ancestor or more recently deceased ancestors. These associations' loans would come out of money collected from their

---

[65] Dohi, "Tō Hoku Sō kan," 691–703; Meng Xianshi, *Dunhuang, minjian*; *Huizhou qiannian, v. 3*, 31 (1577); Huizhou Sources (Institute of Economics, CASS, Beijing), 004.1, 004.2, 004.3; Xiong Yuanbao, "Sonraku shakai," 395–418.

individual members, and their annual operating and festival expenses out of the interest each borrower member was expected to pay.[66]

Information on Huizhou credit associations in the Ming dynasty is scant, but it suggests that they would often in principle require each member to commit a certain amount of money every month over the course of a year, in return for a turn to use, as he wished, the total cash payments by his fellow members for one of these months. Often complicated to manage, these credit associations nonetheless found favor with many enterprising Chinese.[67] They tended to set lower interest rates than did the standard moneylenders,[68] they provided a member with a relatively large sum of money at one time for independent use or investment, and they relied on personal ties as much as on the prospect of profit to draw in members with surplus money and then to pressure them to pay back on time. For instance, in 1577 ten Huizhou men formed a credit association that allowed its members to take monthly turns borrowing from the association's capital assets of fifty taels of silver at monthly interest rates of 2 percent.[69] Less often, at least until the sixteenth century, did some credit associations loan their collected capital to non-members or make a collective investment in a business venture that promised annual profits and dividends. Thus an association, whose underlying principles were egalitarian and collective, could through its members' different inputs of capital be transformed into a business that dealt mainly with non-kinsmen and annually brought itself and its individual members commensurately different amounts of profit or dividends.[70]

At times, the leaders of some lineages and branches anxious to build an ancestral hall based their construction-financing plans on this well-known way of raising funds. To cite one 1528 case from Xiuning, fifty-six lineage members, at the prompting of a few leaders, were every

---

[66] Wang Shanghe, *Xiuning Ximen Wangshi zupu*, 2nd *ce*, 11.22a.

[67] Geertz, *The Rotating Credit Association*, indicates the relative complexity and sophistication of credit provision practices of ordinary Chinese, especially in the Yangzi delta, amongst the great variety of Asian loan associations.

[68] The use of a lower rate of interest for kinsmen could have limits – see a loan contract in which one kinsman borrows from another and pays, it seems, no interest for the next three months. But if the loan, just one tael, is not repaid by then, the borrower promises to pay his kinsmen interest in accord with the local practice (*xiangli* 鄉例) (*Huizhou qiannian*, v. 4, 80 (1623)).

[69] Ibid., v. 3, 31.

[70] Joint-share commercial partnerships are discussed in detail in Chapter 5 below.

month or calendar period to donate a set amount of money to the credit association for the eventual aim of constructing an ancestral hall. Through competitive bidding of interest rates each member had in the annual cycle the right to use one month's total sum of donations.[71] While the profits he gained were his alone, any profits accrued by the association would be ploughed back into further investments for the ancestral hall's construction fund.

The operation of these associations sometimes crashed. As seen in what was possibly an archetypical association established for the future construction of an ancestral hall, a few members of a loan-credit association active in either Qimen or Xiuning county during the late sixteenth century brazenly expropriated its wealth for their private benefit and obliged other members to compensate the association for their folly.[72] Initially, some ancestors of the association's members had accumulated a fund of 1,000 taels of silver to construct their lineage's ancestral hall. Judging this sum insufficient, their descendants had decided to designate it "funds for sacrifices" (*jiben* 祭本) and to loan it out to non-lineage members (presumably for higher interest payments than if loaned to kinsmen). The interest thereby accrued would be spent annually on ancestral sacrifices and on dividends distributed to the association's members, in this instance the lineage's three branches.

Towards the close of the sixteenth century, however, the terms for the members' access to these funds were revised. Instead of receiving just dividends based on interest repayments by non-lineage borrowers, the lineage's members pursued an investment strategy potentially more profitable for themselves but certainly more risky for the funds. Henceforth, these "funds for sacrifices" were to be loaned directly to members of the three branches themselves, who promised full repayment with interest to the hall construction fund within three years. The interest payment was to be recorded in three identical registers, one

---

[71] *Xiuning xian shi Wushi zongpu*, fulu, 1.14a–b.
[72] *Wanli jianci pu*. If it is also reasonable to suppose that this fund-raising campaign was to compensate for the losses, then this total figure may well have roughly corresponded to the defaulted loans. The rapidity of the increase in the association's assets is in fact mentioned by this report and would explain the association members' decision to delay construction of their ancestral hall in order to keep investing their capital in such loans, whatever its neo-Confucian diehards might have thought.

held by each of the three contributing branches, and steps were taken to preserve these registers.

For twenty-odd years the members of these branches are reported to have repaid their silver loans at interest, even if some repayments came in other forms of wealth: "When they had silver, they paid back in silver, and when they did not have silver, they paid back with property (ye 業)."[73] Claims of a money shortage were treated leniently. Those without silver and property could work off their debt, in the manner of an indentured laborer, by "using their body to perform hired labor." Nonetheless, the association insisted on its need to investigate any debtor's claim of a shortage of funds, to be assured that the debtor did not "take having to be not-having and deliberately protract his repayment and continue cheating." If this pressure failed, the association then threatened to call on officialdom for support. In most instances, this practice worked, the magistrate applying enough pressure to resolve the matter amicably.

This strategy, however, ran into trouble when it was the offenders who called on official contacts for aid. Two association members defaulted on their loans and resisted all official and social pressure to live up to their promise to repay. Concealing their capital and property, they claimed poverty. Even worse, one of them had a son, the holder of a district degree, tap his official connections to ward off his father's creditors, while the offenders "set up snares to trick orphans and widows and oppressed the entire rural district with their power. They had capital and property but deliberately delayed [repayment] and did not cough up [the money to repay their loans]." The association's other members, learning of the tricks their kinsmen had played on the helpless, of the land they had bought and sold without scruples, and of their profligate use of unrepaid loans to stage a play at a shrine, professed suitable outrage. Collectively, they swore an oath to punish the villains and rescue the fund from perfidy. The three branches in the association then threatened to expel unruly members from the lineage and its (still unbuilt) ancestral hall, to denounce them to the local

---

[73] *Huizhou qiannian*, v. 4, 234 (1627), has a contract in which three men sharing the surname Hong 洪 offer land and rent to aid the Hong lineage in building and repairing an ancestral hall; interestingly, they specify that the donation is for the sacrifice box (*sixia* 祀匣) of a particular individual. Ibid., v. 4, 235 (1627), concerns a separate donation by up to seventeen other Hongs to build a wall of an ancestral hall.

officials, and to have them "spat upon by the members and be banned from entering the ancestral hall." Another ancestral-hall construction committee in 1588 sought to raise funds by fining disobedient lineage members for their infractions of lineage rules.[74]

Regardless of whether such threats were ever carried out, the fund had to recoup its losses, and the rescue here came from relatively wealthy lineage members. Interestingly, although the branches retained considerable political clout in the association, including the power to expel members from the ancestral hall and its fund association, they seem to have lost their economic dominance in the association. Initially, the branch unit had served as the designated conduit for the transfer of any profits from the construction fund to its individual members. But now, some decades after the association had begun, payments into the relief fund for the construction fund's expenses came not from the branches but from separately named individuals (or, I suspect, a group of individuals acting under the name of just one of them). Moreover, the capital holdings of some of these individual, or groups of, investors seem to have become greater than those of their branches in this particular fund. That is, when members, be they itinerant merchants or resident members, were asked to donate 1 percent of their overall capital to rescue the fund, just nine of the thirty-five donors provided three-quarters of the collected 158.5 taels with grants of over five, ten, or in one case fifty taels. If their donation actually represented just 1 percent of their capital assets, then the wealth of these nine donors would have far surpassed not only that of the other twenty-six donors (whose donations ranged between just 0.5 and 0.4 taels of silver) but also that of their branch's total investment in this association. These rich donors (or rich groups of donors) seem, then, to have become the dominant group within the credit association, and presumably they acquired a major voice in determining its operations and response to this crisis.

Finally, the pre-crisis lending arrangement would seem to have been very successful for the members of this construction fund. If we again assume that this 1-percent-of-capital rule did determine the level of their contribution, the total capital assets of these thirty-five donors would have come to at least 15,800 taels, a figure far above the humble initial fund of 1,000 taels that had financed the progress of these

[74] Chen Rui, "Ming Qing shiqi Huizhou zongzu neibu," 166–67.

members' ancestors into commerce in previous generations. Their outstanding success perhaps explains why the rescue effort of the rich members assumed that the association would continue lending its funds and why the original aim of the fund, the construction of an ancestral hall, appears to have retreated into the realm of a distant memory.

Bargaining

Not all proposals for a lineage or branch ancestral hall were welcomed. Members of the Wu lineage of Wan'an effectively demanded a change to their ancestral hall's admission fee. Unexpectedly, perhaps, although the Wus' initial entrance charge faced criticism for being too uniform and too low, the more common complaint about their hall's admission charges was that they were too high, a criticism that would be repeated against the initial efforts of some branches of the Xiang lineage of Guixi 桂溪項氏 in She county to build a comprehensive ancestral hall.[75] Yet, by the close of the sixteenth century, even though more than half of its thirteen branches had built ancestral halls of their own, the lineage still had no ancestral hall specifically dedicated to all its members' collective worship of their shared Prime Ancestor. Thus, beginning in 1595, seven of these branches formed a Prime Ancestor association (*Shizu hui* 始祖會), to fund winter solstice sacrifices to this Prime Ancestor and, ultimately, as in the previous example, the construction of an ancestral shrine in his honor. These founders expected that their association would function as a credit association and that through its shrewd investment and collection of interest payments from its loans it would accumulate enough capital to build an ancestral hall. Funded by an obligatory entry fee, it was managed in rotation by five kinship-based groups (each consisting of

---

[75] Another example concerns the Cheng lineage of Linxi 臨溪 in Xiuning. After compiling a comprehensive genealogy, two or three of the lineage's leaders launched an ancestral-hall construction project by each donating "several strings of cash," earmarked for lending at interest. After twenty-three years (1553–76) of such lending, their capital surpassed a thousand strings of cash. This fund's managers then ordered adult males in the lineage to donate an unspecified amount. Twenty years later, the fund had doubled, presumably aided by profits from loans, enabling construction to begin in 1596 and last until 1600 (Li Weizhen, *Dabi shanfang ji*, 56.8b–9a).

about forty members) who thus took turns handling its funds as well as performing its sacrifices.[76]

This association had several features intended to appeal to the less well-to-do. First, its entry fee, just one *qian* 錢 of silver, was widely affordable. Second, loans issued to association members did not have the usual one-year deadline but could be repaid up to five years later. Third, the annual interest rate was set at just 18 percent, below the 20 or 30 percent market rates commonly practiced by moneylenders then.[77] Fourth, a ten-year management plan allowed for an increase in the association's overall capital, since it tolerated later entrants, so long as they were attached to one of five already existing member groups and supplemented their group's interest payment.[78] And finally, as if to reassure many families new to such practices or aware of past abuses, detailed governance procedures were prescribed to protect their payments. Not only was every transaction to be recorded in five identical account books, but also repayment of the association's loans was to be made by every group a full half-month in advance of the deadline, in order to allow the other groups time to make a close inspection of the funds and transaction records. Violations, especially tardy returns, faced fines ten times greater than an individual's entry fee.[79]

Despite these favorable terms, in 1616 the Xiang lineage's ancestral hall remained unbuilt.[80] Signs of difficulty in launching the association had been evident from the start, or rather from the lack of a start: over ten years passed before the original proposal was acted on. In the end, the scheme's most persistent problem was the lineage members' low level of support and the hall's low capitalization. In all, by 1616 it had collected about twenty-five taels of silver (at the average rate of 0.1 ounce per member), the result in part of its low entry fees. For although the association's total membership of 253 seems an impressive vindication of its implicit strategy to aim for a large membership to broaden its support base within the lineage, this figure is less than half the number of lineage members who paid five times more money to fund

---

[76] *Guixi Xiangshi (Chongbao tang) cipu*, shang, 1b–7a. *Xin'an mingzu zhi*, hou, 542, for a Prime Ancestor worshipped by the village worship association. The outright refusal to pay an equal share of the construction costs, after one has signed an agreement to pay them, could result in the lineage's imposition of a fine, possibly with official backing (*Huizhou qiannian*, v. 2, 430 (1570)).
[77] Ibid., shang, 1b–2a. For "normal" interest rates, see Chapter 4 below.
[78] Ibid., shang, 4a.   [79] Ibid., shang, 3b.   [80] Ibid., shang, 7a–b.

the lineage's purchase of sacrificial fields in 1616.[81] Whatever the reason (distrust, branch loyalty and a wish for access to larger funds being likely culprits), the lineage members' lukewarm response left this association short of funds for the construction and maintenance of a lineage-wide ancestral hall.

Eventually, rescue for this proposal came not from seeking an even wider base among less well-to-do kinsmen or from further or higher contributions imposed on members already enlisted.[82] As with the Wan'an Wangs' "worship association," it came from additional donations by wealthy lineage members who were also the credit association's principal members and supporters. The ancestral hall's construction was eventually completed in 1627, with just nine donors paying nearly three-fifths (that is, 4,347.923 taels) of the total expenditures of 7,043 taels for the construction of the Xiang lineage's comprehensive shrine. Contributions from the other 244 donors ranged from five taels to 100 taels, and accounted for just 20 percent of the total costs. The stark contrast between these figures and those for the association's initial capital assets underline how few of this lineage's members were closely linked to this comprehensive shrine and presumably, then, how many were instead more closely associated with their branch's separate shrine. This preference will be underlined by evidence presented later in this chapter on branch ancestral halls serving as a source of capital for their members, as objects of their investment, and thus a means for increasing their wealth.[83]

Rejection

The most intriguing yet informative account of a rejection of an ancestral-hall project is found in *A Record of the Shrine Matter* (*Miaoshi zhi* 廟事志), a book compiled by Luo Yinghe 羅應鶴 and privately printed for the donors to this shrine's construction in *c.*1620.

---

[81] Ibid., shang, 30a–35b.
[82] In one case reported by Chen Keyun, "Ming Qing Huizhou zuchan," 59, higher charges were demanded from kinsmen, driving them to mortgage their property to fellow kinsmen in order to pay such charges. *Xin'an Shuaikou Chengshi cigui xubian*, 1.3a, reports that the failure of half the lineage's households to contribute as little as three *fen* of silver a year drove up the 174 eventual contributors' annual household charge to two *qian*. Their contributions were then loaned out at interest to pay for sacrificial offerings.
[83] *Guixi Xiangshi (Chongbao tang) cipu*, shang, 7b–13b.

Previously, the Luos of Chengkan in She county had unusually recognized two Prime Ancestors (that is, two brothers who had settled in this area and created separate descent lines),[84] and they had prided themselves on their inclusivity as a "top [village], which other villages envy and emulate."[85] When income and career differences had threatened the lineage's social cohesion in the twelfth and thirteenth centuries, its leaders had taken measures to restore its sense of unity. Fearful of members' emigration, they provided them with grave sites maintained by monks at a temple the lineage had endowed for this purpose (hence, the graves of both Prime Ancestors were located there).[86] They wanted members to stay put, settling on Luo land while alive and under it when dead. In 1498 an ancestral shrine was built for the entire descent group in Huizhou.

By the mid sixteenth century, some of the Luos wanted to end this cosy arrangement. They proposed that another ancestral hall be built to honor a long-dead ancestor, Luo Dongshu 羅東舒, best known for having compiled the lineage's genealogy of 1309. Agreeing that Luo Dongshu was "efficacious" (*ling* 靈), elders of the lineage in c.1540 assembled the lineage, and three of the lineage's five branches (*men* 門) decided to build the proposed hall. Money was raised from the sale of spirit tablets for the donors' relations or ancestors. Yet, about a quarter of the way through the construction, something happened to prevent its completion. "The bedchamber was almost finished. But upon encountering an incident [construction] was halted."[87]

The details of this incident remain today shrouded in a haze of dubious explanations and intentional obfuscation. According to an account by a present-day member of the lineage, the Luos in their construction of the Dongshu Ancestral Hall may well have committed an act of *lèse majesté*. He believes that they may have painted the walls of its back chamber yellow (a color reserved for the emperor) or made use of a fountainhead carved in the form of a fish head that

---

[84] Zhang Xiaoping, *Huizhou gu citang*, 62.
[85] Luo Dongshu, "Zu Dongshu weng," in Luo Yinghe, *Miaoshi zhi*. In its 1143 cadastral land survey the government had acknowledged the Luos as the top lineage in their rural district (ibid.).
[86] McDermott, *Making*, v. 1, 87–89, 154–68.
[87] Luo Yinghe, *Miaoshi zhi*, 7.4a–7b, 8a; Zhang Xiaoping, *Huizhou gu citang*, 49–50.

Rejection

unfortunately resembled a dragon's head (that is, an image reserved for the emperor).[88] Hence, they were obliged to stop construction.

Neither explanation is backed by evidence. Nor is either credible, as one is forced to wonder why seventy years had to pass before this lineage could replace the offensive coat of paint with another of a more acceptable hue or substitute the tabooed dragon fountainhead with one in a less objectionable shape. More revealing of the story behind this incident, even if they remain opaque, are three accounts found in *A Record of the Matter of the Shrine*. According to one of these accounts, during the first construction effort some men one night stole most of the 3,000 logs and a large amount of the stones, tiles, and other building materials that some Luos had purchased to construct this hall. Furthermore, these unidentified "thieves" took the time to destroy the "bedchamber" section of the uncompleted hall. The objections of the hall's unnamed opponents having been aggressively expressed, the project came to a halt. For the next five to six decades no further contribution was made to the ancestral hall's construction fund.[89] No one in the lineage proposed any additional work on this or any other ancestral hall for the next six to seven decades, even though some members had other religious buildings erected in the village.[90] And no one in the village at the time of this incident left a record that clearly identified the culprits and the reasons for their attack on the hall.

One surviving account indirectly attributes the rejection of this construction project to geomantic concerns,[91] another to interference from the lineage's womenfolk.[92] Far clearer is the discussion of another reason for opposing the new hall's construction: its intended exclusivity. First, it is crucial to recognize that the decision of three Luo branches to dedicate a new ancestral hall to their thirteenth-

---

[88] Zhang Xiaoping, *Huizhou gu citang*, 73–74. Ma Yonghu, *Hexie youxu*, 95–96, repeats the error.
[89] Luo Yinghe, *Miaoshi zhi*, 7.4a–7b.   [90] Ibid., 7.8a.   [91] Ibid., 7.4a–8b.
[92] In the early seventeenth century, interest in a Luo Dongshu hall revived, and its proponents dismissed earlier objections to its construction as thoughtless and cowardly: "It was not enlightened to have the ancestors' agreement be shaken by incomplete construction (*daopang* 道傍), and it was not manly (*yong* 勇) for the matter to have been led by the inner courtyard of the house (*weiqiang* 帷牆; literally, curtains)." Precisely what this last remark alludes to – women's pressure on their menfolk to halt construction of a separate women's hall (*nüci* 女祠) for the tablets of both wives and concubines? – is unclear.

generation ancestor, Luo Dongshu,[93] effectively barred the two other Luo branches (*men*) – their ancestors, their living members, and their future generations – from this new hall and its funds right in their home village.[94] Although they still had the 1498 ancestral hall for all branches, this new ancestral hall was clearly intended to keep two of the Luos' five branches out. The fact that most of the Luos who had made a fortune in the Yangzi Valley salt monopoly trade belonged to the three included branches would have only strengthened the two poorer branches' conviction that they were being deliberately excluded from this new center of lineage affairs. Furthermore, this sense of grievance would have been shared with many members of the three branches calling for the new hall, since its proponents had set an entry price – 100 taels of silver – that was bound to restrict membership in the new hall to only the well-to-do of these favored branches. Thus, even if the other two branches had not thwarted the hall's construction, disaffected descendants of Luo Dongshu, who were members of the three branches attempting to redesign the makeup of the lineage, would have certainly felt justified to protest. Whereas concurrent efforts by some lineage members to build other religious structures in the village and even put up a charity house and endow it with 100 *mu* as a charitable trust in order "to bring together those belonging to the lineage" faced no recorded opposition,[95] the proposed construction of a hall for just a portion of the lineage failed, understandably, to win universal approval among the Luos.[96]

The Luos' response to this mid-sixteenth-century crisis was far slower than it had been to the challenges of earlier centuries. For the next two generations the night of trashing appears to have been shrouded in shame and remembered in silence. Not until 1592 were

---

[93] Luo Rusheng, *Chengkan Luoshi zongpu*, 1st *ce*, jiuxu, 1a; Ma Yonghu, *Hexie youxu*, 95.
[94] Ma Yonghu, *Hexie youxu*, observes that descendants of Luo Dongshu belonged to branches with fewer officials.
[95] Lo Rusheng, *Chengkan Luoshi zongpu*, benzu shizu citang chunqiu jitian; Huangshan shi zhengbian wenshi ziliao weiyuan hui, *Huizhou daxing*, 220.
[96] See, below, Chapter 6's discussion of a seemingly similar disagreement in another eminent Huizhou lineage, the Wus of Xi'nan in She county. The issue of identifying the Prime Ancestor was crucial for lineage identity and membership, since the choice decided who could and could not be a lineage's member, particularly when some "modernizing" members of a large and powerful lineage sought to make membership qualifications far stricter.

Rejection

further deposits made to the hall's construction fund, and then in 1606 a lineage member recently retired from office professed anxiety that "the ancestors' spirits were not at peace."[97] With his son he made a donation for construction of the long-delayed hall. Being small, his donation had no impact, until some fellow lineage members appealed to him to head another effort to construct a shrine to Luo Dongshu. Although they acknowledged that "a lineage does not have two shrines just as a garment does not have two collars," these Luos pushed ahead with the construction plan, cautiously. They took steps to soothe any lingering resentment from the past debacle, consciously choosing, for example, to use no remnants of the destroyed hall in the new structure.[98] They also divided the ranks of their critics by defusing past charges of exclusivity: they slashed the controversial entry fee for an ancestor's spirit tablet from 100 to twenty taels of silver. The aim explicitly was to enable "persons of middling wealth" (*zhongren* 中人) and perhaps those with less wealth to meet the payment requirements. In addition, they drew into the project's management team twelve other lineage members who in pairs were delegated the important tasks of handling the finances, managing the materials, and supervising the construction (another influential lineage member was assigned to check the account books).[99] In return for these services, each of these managers was allowed, upon the hall's completion, free admission to the hall of one ancestral spirit tablet of his own choice plus the permanent guarantee of an additional portion of dried pork at the annual lineage festivities for him and his ancestors.

When, five years after commencement, the construction of the ancestral hall complex – consisting of three halls, a bedchamber, two corridors, a screen, a shed, a heavy gate, and a wall around the property – was finished in 1617, the new funding campaign had clearly been a financial success. Virtually all the outlay of 4,577 taels of silver came from spirit tablet admissions charges: 80 percent from newly collected fees and 10 percent from old fees retained from the *c.*1542 fund and

---

[97] Luo Yinghe, *Miaoshi zhi*, 7.8a.
[98] Soon afterwards, the lineage member Luo Renzhong 羅人忠 (1572–1638) had a belvedere, the Baolun ge 寶綸閣, built on the remains of the original rear bedchamber; it was used to store such lineage treasures as copies of the *Sacred Edict of the First Ming Emperor*, official appointment papers, and other imperial presents (Zhang Xiaoping, *Huizhou gu citang*, 60, 74).
[99] Luo Yinghe, *Miaoshi zhi*, 7.8a–b.

Table 2.3 *Funding sources for the construction of the ancestral hall dedicated to Luo Dongshu in Chengkan, She county**

	Taels
Surviving capital and interest from former effort (includes half of the cost in silver of Mt Jiangtong wu 江桐塢)	451.6
Total admission fees for two spirit tablets presented for sacrifices according to the former practice	150
In 1592 Lord Yuande 元德 transacted 30 taels of silver and now finds 70 [more] taels to make it altogether	100
In 1592 Lord Xigu 暘谷 transacted 20 taels of silver to which is now added 80 [more] taels	100
Silver collected from selling spirit boxes (*shendu* 神櫝)	1.55
Admission fees for spirit tablets presented to support sacrifices according to the new practice	3,741
Pinewood and firewood cleared and sold from Mt Jiangtong wu	110
Old materials, trees, branches, and firewood sold for silver by the ancestral hall	140.672
Silver for helping to carry sand from newly presented spirit tablets	56.4
Interest of loans from the ancestral hall	68.01
[Landed] rent supplement of Lord Shijing 仕敬	0.85
Silver collected from the return of the memorial arch	14.065
TOTAL	4,934.147

* Luo Yinghe, *Miaoshi zhi*, 3.1b–2b.

thereafter regularly used for loans. No fewer than 257 tablets were placed on the altar for various ancestors from the sixteenth to the twenty-fifth generations (Luo Dongshu had been in the lineage's thirteenth generation), and the total number of listed donors (overwhelmingly sons and/or grandsons of the person named on an accepted tablet) came to no less than 192.[100] Construction negotiations with fellow lineage members also seem to have been relatively successful, since the building funds were mostly collected within the first two years of the construction to pay the major expenses on time.[101] Furthermore, the collected funds, at least ostensibly, were used solely for the hall's construction costs (construction materials, mainly timber, granite, and

[100] Ibid., 3, *passim*.   [101] Ibid., 3.1a.

Table 2.4 *Revenues and disbursement schedule in the construction of the ancestral hall dedicated to Luo Dongshu in Chengkan, She county**

Year	Revenue (taels)	Disbursement (taels)
1612	1,147.75	710.901
1613	1,644.7	499.401
1614	499.15	1,000.226
1615	260.305	748.632
1616	508.339	587.042
1617	376.938	431.6
1618	32	120.634
1619	23	308.896

* Luo Yinghe, *Miaoshi zhi*, 3.1a–3a.

stone steles purchased in Yi county, accounted for 40 percent, labor costs another 25 percent, and the site and vessels used for ancestral sacrifices almost all the rest).[102]

As we shall see in Chapter 6, the Luos and the Xiangs of Guixi were not the only large and powerful Huizhou lineages to undergo significant constitutional change in their governance at this time through the collective effort to construct a new comprehensive ancestral hall. Their records, especially the Luos', are, however, exceptionally rich in revealing the degree of conflict within major sixteenth-century Huizhou lineages over how to adapt their organization to changing circumstances both within their ranks and in late Ming society. Whereas some members (often grouped into branches) sought to retain their relatively loose traditional organization and practices (what we may consider a Southern Song model of lineage), other members – let us call them "modernizers" – sought to reform the lineage to express actual wealth and power relations to reward and encourage those members successful in the world outside Huizhou as either officials or merchants. This modernizing camp would often represent branch interests and would further the trend towards making Huizhou kinship groups and

[102] Ibid., 3.3a–6a. Compare the greater share for labor expenses recorded in the construction expenditures for the Wangs' ancestral hall in Zhulin, Xiuning: the timber for the Great Hall cost 2,576.52 taels, the stone office's work register 3,109 taels, and the timber work register 3,805.7 taels (Zhao Huafu, "Lun Huizhou," 51).

especially lineages, as represented by their ancestral halls, more exclusive than any of their Song dynasty originators had envisaged. They had proven remarkably successful in overcoming their principal rivals among the "village quartet" of institutions, and now sought to constrain contrary branches and members of their own lineage as well. In short, the ancestral hall, usually interpreted a monumental symbol of lineage unity, was often constructed at great expense and in the face of fierce infighting and bitter memories of the sort described for the Shanhe Chengs in volume 1. The resulting tensions, as we shall find with the Xi'nan Wus in Chapter 6, could be explosive and make the conflicts of the Shanhe Chengs seem child's play.

Post-construction Charges and Activities

Once an ancestral hall was built, it (like the already mentioned grave-sacrifice household) constituted a distinct and legally recognized entity.[103] It held not just the property it stood on but also any fields, other kinds of real estate, and liquid capital acquired by later donations; furthermore, its endowment could increase with revenue acquired from interest-bearing loans to both kinsmen and non-kinsmen. The ancestral hall might also serve as an overseer to credit associations operating under its name and within its framework. Since the ancestral hall and its affiliated associations held funds that it could use as their members wished, it should come as no surprise that in a prefecture as keen on commercial success as was Ming Huizhou such an institution might serve as a fund repository and dispensary (aka a bank) for both the members and nonmembers of its lineage. It brought dividends to its member investors and sometimes provided them relatively cheap loans. The ancestral hall thus could function as a clearing-house and base for the financial activities of its founders (or funders) and their descendants, individually or collectively.

[103] *Huizhou qiannian*, v. 2, 239 (1555); and v. 2, 233 (1563). Yet this type of registration extended older practices of setting up a household under the name of a common deceased ancestor for collectively owned property, even though it and its income belonged possibly to just some rather than all of his descendants (*Jixi Jiqingfang Geshi chongxiu zupu*, 8.1a; Suzuki, "Mindai Kishūfu," 1–29); and also of establishing and registering "a grave sacrifice household" that would maintain ancestral graves and pay their land tax (Zheng Zhenman, "Yingtian," 10–18; *THJ*, 71, 1,462–63).

Management of these resources therefore became an issue, and serious attention was paid to governance through the selection of capable managers and the maintenance of intra-lineage harmony. As seen with the Doushan trust's management history, rules were drawn up in detail to restore order, instil trust, and reduce government intrusion. For instance, every year on the first day of the seventh lunar month each of the three branches (*men*) of the Luo Dongshu hall was to select three experienced and honest members to look after the hall's fields, collect their rent, pay their taxes, manage the sacrifices and rituals at the hall for an entire year, maintain its buildings and walls, and keep its accounts. The hall's grain and cash income were to be counted at the appropriate times, and any surplus remaining after the payment of taxes, ritual performances, and repair costs was to be spent on the purchase of more sacrificial fields and items used in ancestral-hall rituals. As also prescribed in 1545 for the Doushan landed trust in Qimen,[104] the managers, upon completing their business for the year, were to hand over the hall's account books to the next year's managers for inspection during a formal ceremony of ancestral worship.[105]

Instructions issued by a Xiuning lineage, the Chengs of Shuaikou, are particularly detailed about the organization of an ancestral hall's management and the handling of its account books and profits. Claiming that their ancestral hall required centralized management, its leaders agreed to have each of its three branches appoint two honest and talented men to manage the ancestral hall's maintenance and the lineage's graves. In addition, they were to appoint another reliable lineage member to handle the hall's account books for all its silver transactions and to share his records annually at the conclusion of a collective ancestral worship rite involving all three branches:

Every year, when the sacrifices on the thirteenth day of the first month are concluded, the entire membership is to publicly agree to the choice of an honest and trustworthy member from the descendants and to assign him to receive the profits and interests [of the previous year] and to personally write these figures into the registers. He is to hand over these books according to the schedule and cannot cling to sentiment and privately confer them on others and thereby damage our established regulations.[106]

---

[104] *DSGJY*, 13, 15–16.   [105] Luo Yinghe, *Miaoshi zhi*, 3.6a–7a.
[106] *Xin'an mingzu zhi*, qian, 53–54; *Xin'an Shuaikou Chengshi cigui xubian*, 1.9a, 10a.

Remuneration for all this work came in the form of an extra share of the dried portions of pork commonly distributed to all hall members attending the spring and autumn sacrifices. Perhaps because this compensation was inadequate, managers seem to have been prone to lend their ancestral hall's funds to themselves; the Luos of Chengkan warned their managers to avoid this abuse.[107] Such self-denial must have been testing, since managers were expected not just to handle previous donations but also to draw in much new money and then invest it. Much of this additional capital would have come from post-construction payments for the permanent placement of an ancestor's spirit tablet on the hall's altar.

An ancestral hall, once built, often had assets registered under its name or its dedicatee's in government land surveys and household registers.[108] Held usually in the form of real estate (its cash flow was private knowledge), and cash (including money borrowed from it), these assets were acquired either before the construction – as gifts specifically for other purposes – or after it – as the surplus of its building budget and as subsequent donations. The best-known category of such an endowment, "sacrificial fields," annually provided land rents, usually in grain, to meet the cost of the ancestral rites. Yet often a hall's endowment was insufficient for even these ritual purposes, as hall construction and repair costs could readily consume its funds. For instance, out of a construction budget of 4,577.332 taels of silver, the Luos of Chengkan retained just 156.775 taels, or 3.3 percent, all of which was then designated to pay the hall's regular tax levies and any future land purchases.[109] Though their new hall also had sixty *mu* of sacrificial fields, its annual rental income from this small endowment amounted to just 630 cheng of rice (i.e., very roughly, thirty bushels).[110] In short, this ancestral hall had precious little left for the future repairs, extensions, education, and other activities it would be expected to undertake for its members' benefit inside and outside the village.

To deal with this ongoing financial challenge, ancestral-hall managers institutionalized funding practices successfully introduced for the

---

[107] Luo Yinghe, *Miaoshi zhi*, 6.7a.
[108] *Ming Wanli nian yulin ce*, plot no. 2562 in the 17th *du* of She county; *Huizhou qiannian*, v. 3, 241 (1591).
[109] Luo Yinghe, *Miaoshi zhi*, 3.6a.
[110] Ibid., 4.1a–16a. McDermott, *Making*, v. 1, xv–xvi, discusses a *cheng*'s size.

hall's construction: special charges on the continued presence of spirit tablets, the establishment of special credit associations for members, and more commercially minded credit operations for nonmembers. Each of these activities was separate, but overall they show how it was possible, at one extreme, for an ancestral hall to turn itself into an "ancestral bank" drawing increasingly on revenue from outside its membership, or stockholders, to create a multifaceted profit-making institution, even a pawnbrokerage, with interests and investments in the local area. Such an institutional transformation, we shall see, was not speculation.

Permanent Tenure for Ancestral Spirit Tablets

At this juncture, Huizhou custom and Confucian learning provided a solution for the ancestral hall's handling of the ancestors. An ancestral spirit tablet's initial entry, even if paid for, secured it merely a temporary home, since hall managers generally allowed the spirit tablets of the lineage's benefactors and the founder's descendants to remain in the hall for just four generations. Although many lineages would have benefited from the Ming government's extension of the privilege of ancestral-hall construction to any kinship group virtually regardless of their social and legal status, the leaders of these ancestral halls commonly saw no need to extend similarly openhanded benefits to their own kinsmen and dead ancestors. Drawing upon conventional interpretations of the ancient Confucian classic the *Book of Rites*, and the standard *Family Rituals* by Zhu Xi,[111] they restricted the amount of time – four generations – that the spirit tablets of most of their fellow lineage members could stay in the hall before their prescribed removal, usually to a barely distinguishable grave on a distant and inaccessible mountain slope. Thus, once an ancestor became a fifth-generation ancestor, his spirit tablet would be transferred from the hall to his grave or a bedchamber, unless he, or a descendant for him, had made a notable benefaction to the lineage.[112] Past acts of charity, usually to kinsmen, might meet that condition and qualify him for free permanent

---

[111] Zhang Xiaoping, *Huizhou gu citang*, 97–103; Ebrey, *Chu Hsi's Family Rituals*, 20.
[112] *Dangxi Jinshi zupu* (1568), 1.5a; *Renli Cheng Jing'ai tang shishou jiapu*, 1.1b–2a, for a 1504 account.

tenure.[113] So might a sterling reputation for virtue. But the grounds of free permanent tenure most readily mentioned in lineage records were a member's acquisition of an official degree and his appointment to government office.[114]

Therefore the ordinary lineage descendant – a commoner bereft of a career of repeated charity, exemplary virtue, and an official degree or position – usually had just one way to join this club of favored ancestors: a donation to the ancestral hall made by himself or, if he was posthumously fortunate, by his descendants. Otherwise, he faced the prospect of being a victim of social amnesia, of his name surviving only in his lineage's genealogy and of being otherwise excluded from public memory of his name and life. In a prefecture like Huizhou, where countless stone inscriptions, memorial arches, and old buildings proclaimed a lineage's or branch's link to famous individuals, the threat of such social death and exclusion seems to have driven many members to make a donation to at least one ancestral hall for themselves or a dear ancestor. As Rubie Watson has observed on a similar practice in the New Territories area of Hong Kong,

A distinction based on wealth is thus incorporated into the very structure of the lineage's most important collective representation. Viewed from one perspective, the tablets represent the generalized body of all lineage ancestors, whose worship promotes the well-being of the entire lineage. However, if we examine the tablets from another perspective, we find that only a few ancestors are allowed into the hall, a privilege for which they or their immediate descendants pay dearly.[115]

---

[113] Zhang Xiaoping, *Huizhou gu citang*, 96–126. The twelve men who supervised the construction of the Luos' hall were each, in lieu of cash payment, given a ticket enabling them to nominate someone to a permanent membership. See also Freedman, *The Study of Chinese Society*, 273–88, 296–312.

[114] Lin Ji, "Mingdai Huizhou zongzu," 91–93.

[115] Watson, *Inequality among Brothers*, 41. The striking similarity of this Huizhou practice to that in the New Territories near Hong Kong (Ibid., 26–35) belies at least one key difference. In Huizhou a donor's payment for the admission of a spirit tablet at the construction or repair of an ancestral hall did not, as it did in the New Territories, entitle his descendants to free entry for their own spirit tablets; nor does Watson report the same insistence on further payments lest a spirit tablet be removed for burial outside the hall after resting for four generations inside it. Some Huizhou ancestral halls seem particularly costly and elitist despite their rhetoric of inclusivity.

Permanent Tenure for Ancestral Spirit Tablets 103

For ancestors beyond the fourth generation, ancestral-hall membership was definitely not for the needy. To the contrary, it was meant for an exclusive elite within the lineage. Only those "old boys" (or, as we shall see for some Huizhou lineages, some "old girls") who themselves or whose descendants had made a significant contribution to the lineage merited permanent entry. The altars of Huizhou's larger ancestral halls would thus have been crowded with hundreds of spirit tablets of ancestors dead for one to four generations, plus a far more selective senate of those of the more anciently and privileged dead.

The financial donation for a spirit tablet's permanent entry into the hall was made sometimes with land but more commonly with silver,[116] with the required sum varying from lineage to lineage and from hall to hall. It could be as little as one *qian* and as large as 10,000 taels. It could be paid by individuals, households, or associations (*she*, *hui*) composed of lineage members.[117] Physical labor for the ancestral hall is usually not mentioned as a means for gaining permanent entry,[118] quite probably because of its association, at least in the larger lineages, with social inferiority and even bondservitude.

For this permanent admission of a spirit tablet, the managers of some ancestral halls once again devised a varied menu of enticing conditions. Although a donation usually was for just one spirit tablet, some ancestral-hall managers offered prospective donors the option of making a relatively large donation to gain admission for additional tablets. For instance, a donation of up to thirty taels of silver in the mid sixteenth century won "free" additional admission of two other ancestors' spirit tablets to the ancestral hall dedicated to Lord De'an of the Huang 黃 lineage of Tandu 潭渡.[119] In the Qing, the same ancestral hall raised the entry fee per spirit tablet from just three to five taels of silver, still a relatively low fee.[120] Twenty-two of the forty-two listed donors contributed as much as thirty taels – if only to compensate for donors who failed to pay the full set fee.[121]

---

[116] For example, in 1660 two men wishing to fund the admission of an ancestor's spirit tablet into an ancestral hall, donated five taels plus rents from land (valued at twenty-five taels) (Liu Miao, "Chuantong nongcun shehui," 86–87).
[117] Chen Keyun, "Ming Qing Huizhou zuchan," 58.
[118] Two kinship groups, however, which acknowledged such a form of loan repayment from members are discussed below in this chapter and in Chapter 5.
[119] Chen Keyun, "Ming Qing Huizhou zuchan," 59.   [120] Ibid.
[121] Ibid., 58.

Other ancestral halls, operating on the common Chinese assumption that the afterlife functioned like the present world, echoed bureaucratic practice in their handling of spirit tablets for permanent admission. Admitted spirit tablets were ranked in line with the size of the donation. For instance, the Chengs of Dongli required a contribution of 1,000 to 5,000 taels for an ancestor's tablet to be admitted at the top rank. For the second, 600 to 900 taels were needed, 300 to 500 taels for the third, 100 to 200 taels for the fourth, and less than 100 taels for the fifth and lowest.[122]

Sometimes, exemptions to these donation requirements were permitted, if only to honor a lineage member's exemplary loyalty or filial piety. A bondservant in a Huang family of Tandu, for instance, sought to pay the admissions charge for the spirit tablet of his recently deceased master. His funds proving inadequate and his efforts to supplement them all failing, his loyalty nonetheless so impressed the shrine's governors that the members granted his master's tablet permanent admission free of charge.[123]

Such exceptions, however, were few, and permanent admission of a spirit tablet was usually achieved only after its supporters had paid the full charge. In the early seventeenth century, the Luos of Chengkan, for example, specifically identified two ancestors whose supporters needed to pay respectively six and thirteen more taels of silver: "On the day when the payment is sufficient, then and only then do they qualify for admission to receive sacrifices."[124] In many ancestral halls even sons lauded for their filial piety needed heirs capable of paying the admissions charge before they gained permanent admission. Thus we read that in the Xiang lineage's ancestral hall at Guixi a deceased member's spirit tablet would be placed at a particular level on the hall's altar according to the amount his descendants paid. Initially, before the hall introduced a new category, the Great Reward, the admissions charge for all spirit tablets submitted to the shrine was at least 100 taels:

---

[122] *Chengshi Dongli cidian* (1588), jin shenzhu, 1b–2a.
[123] Chen Keyun, "Ming Qing Huizhou zuchan," 59. Nothing is said of why the master's children failed to offer the sum or what the other lineage members thus thought of them, especially in contrast to this loyal bondservant.
[124] Luo Yinghe, *Miaoshi zhi*, 1.23b.

Only when someone had paid in 100 or more taels of funds was [a deceased lineage member] then allowed to be given sacrifices and a mat at the ancestral banquet. This is a rule that has not changed for a thousand years and that has never been altered and violated.[125]

The sole recorded exception to this practice occurred when this hall accepted an initially inadequate donation for a member's spirit tablet with the understanding that it would be used for the hall's money-lending operations until it bore enough interest to pay the full price of admission. And, third, the shine accepted not just the male descendants' spirit tablets but also – contrary to some neo-Confucian prescriptions and classical precedents – those of the wives and mothers of these admitted males. The fee required for a woman's spirit tablet's admission to a separate women's ancestral hall was generally no different from that for a man's to a largely, if not entirely, male hall.[126]

Recurring Fees

Permanent admission of a spirit tablet into an ancestral hall did not end a member's obligation to make further contributions. Before 1559 households of the Cheng lineage of Shuaikou in Xiuning were expected to pay an annual fee of 0.03 tael of silver and a pair of candles, in order to be able to attend ancestral rites at the hall every thirteenth day of the first lunar month. Roughly half of the potential membership refused to pay even this small sum, and so the hall's managers decided to oblige the 174 willing households to pay a higher annual fee of 0.2 taels.[127]

The heirs of those represented by these spirit tablets were also regularly called on to cough up money at particularly auspicious times in their own lives, "to share their happiness." Marriage, remarriage, the birth of the first son, the birth of other sons, a son's admission to school, his capping (a ceremony to celebrate an adolescent male's

---

[125] *Guixi Xiangshi (Chongbao tang) cipu*, xia, 19b.   [126] Ibid.
[127] *Xin'an Shuaikou Chengshi cigui xubian*, 1.3a–b. Greater fees were partly attributed to an unexpectedly large increase in lighting expenses for the halls' memorial services.

coming of age),[128] civil examination success at any level, and especially an official appointment, all in turn provided ancestral halls with opportunities to levy an additional gift from the descendants of their ancestral spirits (presumably, the fortunate member was expected to attribute his good fortune to his ancestors). Few halls in Huizhou seem to have bypassed these opportunities.[129] Since, over time, a single party or descent line might have a spirit tablet in several halls, these levies collectively could have proven burdensome (even though the donor might find the burden relieved by gifts from others on such "happy occasions").

Consider the exceptionally detailed regulations that in 1603 were drafted for such obligatory contributions by the very wealthy Wu lineage of Shangshan in Xiuning for seven types of "happy occasion." The first charge came with a member's capping, when he was finally allowed to step into the hall. In doing so, however, "he had to bring along to the hall his silver," paying from 0.3 to 0.5 tael according to his family's wealth (the destitute were admitted only if extremely filial and sincere). His name, time of birth, and amount of silver payment would then be recorded in the lineage records. Likewise, he had to pay the shrine some money, before he could take a new wife (one to five *qian*) or before his son could take a wife (one tael); presumably, then, if the father were alive, every member's marriage brought in two donations. Failure to pay on time led to levies of, respectively, two or three times the usual charge. Success in the civil service examinations led to an increase in the rates of payment (as well as, paradoxically, the disappearance of any threat of a fine): ten taels of silver for passing the district degree examinations and twenty taels for the provincial degree examinations. Licentiates (*jiansheng* 監生), upon receiving an appointment, paid over five taels for common expenses at the hall, and anyone who arranged the imperial bestowal of an honorific name for a deceased family member had to pay five taels.[130]

In conclusion, we must add that such charges were not unique to the Shangshan Wus. Writing in 1714 about its "set practices" (*dingli* 定例), compilers of the genealogy of the Huangs of Tandu in Xiuning

---

[128] *Jiangcun Hongshi jiapu*, 4th *ce*, 14.3a, specifies different charges for each of the three ranks of capping ceremony carried out in the ancestral hall.
[129] For example, the annual revenue records in the late Ming manuscript, *Tanbin Huangshi shouzhi qingce*.
[130] *Shangshan Wushi zongfa guitiao*, 9b–11b.

provided a list of the occasions when their comprehensive ancestral hall levied charges in silver on members: a member's marriage (five *fen*), his first son's birth (five *fen*), any subsequent son's birth (three *fen*), and any son's capping (three *fen* plus "red chicken [blood] sheets" given for their auspicious color). For entering school, gaining entrance to the National University, succeeding at different levels in the civil service examinations, paying for degrees, and being listed among the successful examination candidates, additional charges were levied at an unspecified level.[131]

Ancestral Halls' Affiliated Associations: A Business within a Charity

An ancestral hall, like many other authorized religious institutions in China, often had affiliated associations set up, as a successor to a pre-construction funding association, to support its and its members' worship activities. The exceptionally detailed records of one such association, the Expansion Association (*Guangyu hui* 光裕會), in She county reveal how an association's moneylending operations could be linked only tangentially to its hall's religious and institutional needs. While this association might accumulate material support for an ancestral hall's repairs and other expenditures, it also could acquire another *raison d'être*. When confronted with the need to hand over its funds to the hall, the members of this association, like those of the already discussed Wangs' "sacrifice association," resisted. Instead of transferring all their assets, they withheld some of them to create a separate fund of money that accrued profits, or dividends, for the members by being annually loaned out to others for repayment at interest. In short, the success of an association's fund-raising could persuade its members to launch an affiliated association operated solely for its members' benefit but within the ambit of a "mother association" and, by extension, its ancestral hall.

As shown in a fascinating study by Xiong Yuanbao,[132] the Expansion Association was set up in 1557 as a credit association to support the performance of rites of worship to a recently deceased ancestor in

---

[131] *Tandu Xiaoli Huang shi zongpu*, 6.28b–29a.
[132] Xiong Yuanbao, "Sōzoku shihon," 437–57.

an ancestral hall established in his honor.[133] It accumulated its assets by collecting regular contributions from its members in five ways: a two *qian* entry charge upon marriage; subsequent annual fees of two *qian* from each member; a donation upon the birth of a son; a donation for each acquisition of an examination degree and official appointment; and fines for a variety of offenses, ranging from absence or poor etiquette at the rites to divulgence of the association's private information to nonmembers and tardy transmission of its announcements to members. In addition, it imposed an annual interest rate of 20 percent on all loans made to its members.

In the association's first twenty-five years, between 1557 and 1581, these arrangements led to a fiftyfold growth in these assets with minimal threat to its expenditures.[134] From the mid 1570s, however, the Expansion Association's expenses rose, due to others' insistence that it make sizeable contributions to the ancestral hall's repair.

Thereafter, this credit association responded to the crisis like a conventional moneylender. From the mid 1570s it sought greater fiscal security by shifting its capital into relatively low-risk investment assets. It began to purchase land, acquire land as collateral from its borrowers, pay annual land taxes, and pay for its official household registration as a separate legal entity. Then, in the early 1580s the rationale for this conservative policy was strengthened by its need to contribute funds first to the repair of its ancestral hall and subsequently to other ancestral-hall construction and repair projects, thereby reducing its own assets considerably. Throughout the rest of its existence, up to its demise in *c*.1664, it survived deaths of its members, attempted theft by lineage members, peasant uprisings, and the turmoil of the Ming–Qing dynastic transition. Furthermore, it continually saw its assets and income consumed by calls for further contributions from its own and other related ancestral halls. As all its members were descendants of the ancestor being honored by the association, as all these descendants

---

[133] This type of association to my mind constitutes a simple Chinese *hui* 會 and is akin to the kind of association designated a "contractual lineage organization" in Zheng Zhenman, *Family Lineage Organization*, 122–42.

[134] An association with the same name is said in a collective association agreement dated 1607 to own burial mounds, a hall house and building, sacrificial fields, a celebratory arch, and additional property (Yan Guifu and Wang Guojian, *Huizhou wenshu dang'an*, 328). Professor Xiong Yuanbao's Expansion Association appears, then, to have acquired additional assets to those he found in his "Sōzoku shihon," 437–57.

were customarily obliged to become members of the association (for them it was close to an involuntary association), and as all its loans were made only to its members, it appears to represent a classic example of a Chinese institution whose collective resources were continually depleted by the demands of family ties and obligations. Deprived of a potential for expansion as a credit association that functioned solely for its contributing members, it certainly could not break free of the ancestral hall, the lineage, or these institutions' members to become an autonomous institution functioning as a collective moneylender on its way to becoming a fully fledged financial institution. In place of that trajectory, it grew poor while some of its members grew richer.

Actually this judgment concerns only part, though the better-recorded part, of the association's history as a moneylender. From at least the 1570s the Yus seem to have been aware of the danger that increased demands from ancestral halls posed to their association's collective assets and income, and we can see its managers thereafter taking steps to secure some autonomy for their assets (they were not fools). In 1588, a year of sharp economic turndown in Huizhou and the rest of eastern China, "the members" withdrew 105 taels from the association's fund. They used it to set up a separate fund affiliated to their association with all its members listed among the new fund's ten separate members. This fund's capital was to be separately lent for profit, apart from the association's regular lending activities to its own members. Though the borrowers are not specified, they most likely were not association members, if only because members of the new lending association already had access to the association's original fund and, more importantly, received annual dividends from this fund's profits. Yet, regardless of whether this money was loaned to non-association kinsmen or to non-kinsmen, it is clear that the association's members had sought to build on its success by hiving off some of the funds of their ancestral worship association to engage in a more strictly commercial enterprise shielded from further calls on its capital by ancestral halls and other lineage groups. Unfortunately, we have no record of how successful this side fund was, as its income and expenditures are not included in the figures given for the Expansion Association. Yet the absence of any such record may well indicate the members' success at concealing these side assets and knowledge of them from other lineage institutions and members. Certainly, the Expansion Association threatened its members with a fine for revealing its private information to nonmembers. This secrecy was most useful in thwarting and then concealing, with government help, efforts by fellow lineage members to steal and sell off its ancestral property in c.1606–7.[135]

This association's history, though short, is important for revealing certain assumptions about financial management common in these low-level financial institutions. Over time these institutions – in this case, the ancestral hall and an attendant credit association – tended, if financially viable, to take on (or be given) a life of their own and to acquire other uses. Both before and after construction their original or ostensible purpose to help in ancestral worship was joined, if not sidelined, by another, more pressing goal to make money for the hall's members and managers. Though security was a priority, the collected capital was seldom allowed to sleep in a silver box. It might be invested in land or repeatedly loaned at interest to suitable parties to accrue sizeable profits. Even when the funds became sufficient for construction, their managers might postpone construction for decades, if only because few wanted to squander these rich sources of revenue by using up these funds for good. Of course, the investment of these funds was never risk-free, but at the very least they provided an administrative position and stable salary to one of the fund's managers obliged to remain in Huizhou away from the "money trees" of the Yangzi delta. In this sense, the situation of these fund managers did not differ greatly from what we saw in volume 1 of the managers of the Doushan and other landed trusts inside Huizhou.[136]

Ancestral Halls and Loans: The Chengs of Dongli

Some Huizhou ancestral halls were not content to serve merely as an umbrella organization for credit associations. As seen in its confidential instructions on how to run an ancestral hall and its ritual activities, *The Sacrificial Rituals of the Shrine of the Chengs of Dongli* (*Chengshi dongli cidian* 程氏東里祠典)[137] provides striking detail on how an

---

[135] Huizhou wenqi zhengli zu, *Ming Qing Huizhou shehui jingji*, v. 1, 566 (1607.2.26). Subsequent violators faced charges of filial impiety and a fine of 100 taels.

[136] Wang Shunmin, *Jinggan xiansheng wenji*, 10.9a; McDermott, *Making*, v. 1, 321–31, 353, 360–61.

[137] *Chengshi Dongli cidian*, sections shengxi 生息, shiji 時祭, jinshenzhu 進神主, yijie 儀節, fenzuo 分胙, and shiwu 什物, contain virtually all the information given above on the Chengs' practices.

ancestral hall might itself function as a credit association, even as a pawnshop, paying for its ancestral worship services and for some members' private expenses. Its funds may have originated from a wish to please and honor the ancestors, but they were used increasingly to create profits for the descendants through their ownership of shares in the hall's income from loans to nonmembers and non-descendants.[138] In short, we see here the formation of a proto-bank out of an association and institution, ostensibly designed, built, and operated solely for the worship of ancestors.

In the Northern Song the Cheng lineage had settled in the Fanchuan 範川 area of Xiuning county, where for most of the next twenty generations its members made a living mainly from farming. In their home village they had set up a hall (*tang* 堂) and for a period in the Ming operated at least one credit association, the Flourishing Virtue Association (*shengde hui* 盛德會). Though they had followed the "old practices for the annual festivities and winter solstice observances," they had never set up spirit tablets in any of their buildings. Instead, as suggested by this description, their social and religious life retained much of the village worship association practices of the Song and Yuan periods.

Yet, by the sixteenth century, some of these Chengs had become interested in Confucian learning and acquired some knowledge of its rituals. In an apparent reference to the Flourishing Virtue Association one member is said to "have wished to build a family shrine to expand the rituals of the sacrifices. But the times and the circumstances did not suit [his plan]. Being modest and humble, he never made it succeed." His son, however, was more enterprising. Capitalizing on his father's efforts, in 1588 he launched a larger campaign to raise funds for an ancestral hall to house its donors' ancestral spirit tablets.[139] While to conventional eyes these efforts bespeak the gentrification of a very minor provincial kinship group – in line with a common reading of late Ming social change – these Chengs had something else in mind.

---

[138] For a detailed discussion of the ancestral hall repair payments expected from hall members (defined as shareholders in the hall) and from the head (*ding* 丁) taxpayers in these shareholder units, see Yan Guifu and Wang Guojian, *Huizhou wenshu dang'an*, 310–11. The charges were also allotted according to the shareholder's landholdings; that is, according to the number of his *mu*, presumably fiscal *mu*, as registered with the local government.

[139] *Chengshi Dongli cidian*, 1588 pref. by Cheng Dexin, 1a.

To ease the transition from the association to the new funding body – the lineage's past experience with the association had been far from happy, since some assets had been diverted to "other uses"[140] – the promoters of the new venture took two steps, one dealing with governance and the other with finances. Firstly, they insisted on full observance of detailed regulations and proper accounting procedures to assure that the managers bore responsibility for preserving any invested capital and its contracts. As such, their rules are reminiscent of the regulations drafted at roughly the same time by many Huizhou lineages to resolve similar concerns over management abuses of their landed trusts.[141] The new rules insisted on the managers' need to retain documentary records, and on the annual appointment of a group of managers assigned to investigate the performance of their predecessors, hunt down debtors, fine violators, and calm members incensed over their potential exclusion from the benefits of this new institution (in this case, membership conferred admission of their spirit tablets to the ancestral hall). The lineage's managers and elders were expected to handle all but the last of these problems; an appeal to local officials was intended to dispel threats of violence from disgruntled lineage members.

To meet all their initial operating and ritual expenses, the new ancestral hall's managers undertook a second, probably controversial, measure. They would rely on funds left in the old association's accounts for the coming year or two, waiting until its poorer members built up enough savings to make an offering to the new funding body and until its richer members had time to adjust their own family's expenses in order to afford a donation. In return, the ancestral hall would compensate the thirty-eight persons who had made a financial commitment to the former association. As not all lineage members had donated to this former association, "one cannot treat them all equally according to one rule. If you do not provide even a small benefit to the families who have given [to the association in the past], then surely they will not be happy. And, is it fair to those who did not give?" Consequently, all thirty-eight donors (and thus members) of this former association were allowed to submit one ancestor's spirit tablet for admission to the hall free of charge. If one such donor died, his sons or wife could submit a name free of charge. Those submitted by

[140] Ibid., shiji, 1b. [141] McDermott, *Making*, v. 1, 310–68.

Ancestral Halls and Loans 113

anyone else required a modest financial contribution, its amount determining which of five ranks it was accorded: the top rank called for ten taels, and the rest in descending order eight, six, four, or two taels. Disagreements over these rules were inevitable. But the managers were exhorted to lead the members to block the entry of those who relied on force and excuses to avoid payment of the admissions charge or repayment of their loan. Those who thereby refused to accept the ranking of their ancestor's spirit tablet were to be reported to local officials for a ruling. Women's spirit tablets, when paid for, were also to be accepted, to be placed on the right, while the men's went on the left.

Asserting that "in the present year we are heading for great profits" (it is 1588, and presumably he is thinking of the land foreclosures that will come his or the ancestral hall's way in this year of great famine and epidemic contagion in Huizhou), the Chengs ran this hall fund along lines that resemble more a business than a traditional ancestral hall. They welcomed spirit tablets from virtually all lineage members, as they sought as wide a field as possible for potential donors and donations (only heirless males, sonless wives, and expelled members were told not to apply).[142] All spirit tablet applicants, except those of successful officials or those judged by the lineage to be "moral worthies" (such as filial sons, obliging grandsons, righteous husbands, and chaste wives), had to pay for membership. And to attract donations, or deposits, to this new fund from lineage members, the fund's founders set up a series of rules that promised to make relatively safe loans, enforce interest-laden repayments, and then distribute profits, in the manner of a bank to its stockholders. Thus the *Sacrificial Rituals'* opening section on "making profits" (*shengxi* 生息) declares, "Hereafter, all presenters of spirit tablets to the ancestral hall are to pay silver upon presentation of the spirit tablets. If this money does not [subsequently] make a profit, then its handlers are never to avoid declaring a financial deficit."

---

[142] These members' spirit tablets were to be lodged in the central hall of the building (*louxia zhongtang* 樓下中堂), to receive separate trays of sacrifices. Five ranks of spirit tablet membership were designated according to five levels of donation: less than 100 taels or without funds, 200 to 300 taels, 300 to 500 taels, 600 to 900 taels, and 1,000 to 5,000 taels. Later on, the "superior rank" was set up for donations of 6,000 to over 10,000 taels.

To acquire the desired profits, the managers imposed a new set of relatively high admission charges ranging generally from 100 to 5,000 taels of silver on virtually all ancestral spirit tablets submitted to the new ancestral hall. The greater the donation, the higher the rank conferred on the submitted tablet. Those paying even more than 5,000 taels – say 6,000 to 10,000 taels – would receive a "super-high" rank, while a potential donor paying only thirty taels would find the members happy to listen to the request so long as he was actually making a generous and sincere deposit. Yet, regardless of the amount deposited, all had to be paid before the hall could accept a spirit tablet and place it in its precincts. One could not, as in some other associations we have introduced, give a small donation and then assume that over time the association's adroit use of it in loans would increase its capital value to the point of gaining the donor an ancestral spirit tablet's permanent entry into the hall. This ancestral hall did not want to act as its would-be members' financial adviser.

Believing that "over the next one or two years spirit tablets will gradually be presented and the profits will gradually increase," the organizers of the hall devised rules on how to turn these deposits of capital into profit-making loans. First, they insisted that they had learned from the failure of the Flourishing Virtue Association to get lineage members to repay their loans: the new hall will "not allow descendants of the branches to receive [any loans]. It is necessary to allow a contract to be set up only for those who have wealth and another surname." As some other Huizhou lineages were willing to admit, the mixture of blood with business often proved highly contentious, if not financially foolhardy.[143] Second, all loans henceforth required collateral in the form of paddy fields (*tian* 田), "lest the money [lent] end up hollow [that is, not repaid]." The ancestral hall will thus become a kind of pawnbrokerage, keeping deposited collateral of land, and drawing its funds at least in part from its lending operations. Third, all loans were to be repaid within a year at an annual interest rate of 30 percent.[144] "If all the capital and interest cannot be collected,

---

[143] E.g., *Xiuning xian shi Wushi zongpu*, fu, 16a, reveals that the credit association of this lineage's grave maintenance association was permanently barred from lending its capital to the members' descendants, since "in many big lineages doing so proves to be the cause of conflict."

[144] As explained in Chapter 4 below, this rate represents the top "standard market rate" permitted by Ming law. Actual annual rates varied greatly, but by the late

then first collect the interest." Former managers who made the unrepaid loans are to co-operate with new managers now assigned to press for their repayment at the same interest rate. Fourth, the profits are to be used first for the seasonal festivities – that is, the regular collective rituals dedicated to the common ancestor in whose honor the ancestral hall was to be built – and the remainder to be accumulated for the construction of the ancestral hall and to be distributed to the members (this practice contrasted with the former association's rough division of silver interest payments into merely separate payments "which lineage members were allowed to press to take for their separate use"). And fifth, the distribution of the dried pork portions usually presented to all attendees at the major lineage ceremonies was also altered. Whereas the hall's organizers admit that according to "moral principle" (*li* 理) one should confer them equally among all the members, they now believed that the people within the lineage were not only too many but also often too incompetent and partial to justify such a standard. Hence they agreed that these ritual meat portions were to be distributed to members according to the position that their spirit tablet had acquired on the hall altar. In other words, the ancestral hall's pork dividend was to be determined by the amount of money that one or one's ancestor had given to the hall. It is as if the member was a depositor who held shares in a bank and regularly received varying dividends from its operation.

These principles for running a profit-making concern were set out only after the heads of this ancestral hall had determined that it was not to loan its money to its own members. Past experience with such practices and associations had shown that some relations simply took advantage of these cheap loans by never repaying them. Or, as in the case of one lineage, the Wus of Shangshan, who made a great fortune by running pawnshops outside Huizhou, members proved particularly adept at reneging on loans from their ancestral hall. An interest rate of 12 percent was so low that borrowing was hard to resist (one only had to loan it on to non-kinsmen at the normal rate of 30 percent to feel rich). Yet failure

sixteenth century lower rates, especially to creditworthy clients, were not uncommon (e.g., the annual 15 to 20 percent rate on loans made by a kinship group in the Huang lineage of Tanbin to its members from 1603 to 1650) (*Tanbin Huangshi shouzhi qingce*). The cash funds of this ancestral memorial association, which also functioned as a loan association, rose fifteenfold in this half century from 1.4 to 22.804 taels.

to repay the capital or the interest became so common that in the late sixteenth century the Wus' ancestral hall felt obliged to establish new rules that required the complete collection of all loans and attendant interest; for five- or ten-year stretches two or three efficient and well-off families in each of the lineage's four branches were to act as managers who annually dunned their branch's debtors and handed over their collected returns to the ancestral hall at New Year's. Deliberate defaults were no longer to be tolerated.[145]

Lest we think that the problem of debt defaults was due to these debtors' or credit associations' attachment to an ancestral hall as opposed to any other institution, let us look at a 1627 list of debts owed a Tunxi 屯溪 pawnbrokerage operating apart from an ancestral hall.[146] Upon the death of its owner and, probably of even greater importance, upon a servant's flight with the account books, the widow was obliged by her in-laws to transfer to them the shop's remaining capital, including its credit from unpaid loans. Members of at least eleven surname groups are listed as owing the pawnshop money. Yet, of these, one group stands out – a group of men with the same surname as the owner – as accounting for roughly half of the shop's borrowers and owing it at least three-quarters of the 2,812.22 taels of silver still unpaid. The shop's transfer of these credits to the lineage's elders seems thus to put them in charge of dunning some of their kinsmen for repayment (the outcome of this challenge is not recorded). Also notable are the absence of interest-rate charges on the loans to these kinsmen, and the size of their loans – up to 1,000 taels of silver – in sharp contrast to the small amounts loaned to non-kinsmen at interest.

Is it surprising, then, that Huizhou pawnshops, other Huizhou banking institutions, and their capital investments were increasingly located outside Huizhou,[147] where their clientele was less likely to share with it a common surname and Prime Ancestor? In other words, the ancestral hall might in later centuries remain a key institution within Huizhou for ordinary lineage members' access to capital and credit at advantageous rates, but the center of financial activity for any successful Huizhou merchant and his lineage would have of necessity moved to elsewhere in the empire. It seems easier, then, to have been a

---

[145] *Shangshan Wushi zongfa guitiao*, 13a–b.
[146] *Huizhou qiannian*, v. 4, 218–20 (1627).
[147] Wang Shizhen, *Yanzhou shanren sibu gao*, 61.23a.

Ancestral Halls and Loans   117

Huizhou merchant than to have been a member of this kind of Huizhou lineage. But, then, the point of this extended account of how ancestral halls found their way to the heart of many a lineage member's economic activities is that such a distinction would have been hard to make and even harder to maintain.

Finally, if only to show how pervasive this ancestral-hall practice of moneylending was, let us return to the collective ancestral hall of certain Cheng lineages at Huangdun in She county, a hall that for centuries had been the object of fierce contention between Cheng and non-Cheng members (who viewed it as a local shrine and not as an ancestral hall). By the end of the Ming the Chengs' push to gain dominance of the hall had progressed far enough to justify an odd relationship between five of its constituent lineage members and the shrine itself. Anxious to encourage other offerings there to their Prime Ancestor, five Cheng lineages in 1629 agreed to make annual offerings of silver to pay for this annual sacrifice. Even though the sums were small, they did so only after being assured that each of them would in return receive 20 percent annual interest for their donations – presumably the Huangdun ancestral hall's interest rate was not lower.[148] Other evidence confirming this use of an ancestral hall as a lending association or proto-bank comes slightly later from Wujiang county, Suzhou, where in the early Qing the list of a lineage's "sacrificial fields" for ancestral worship includes hundreds of taels of silver as assets to be loaned at interest, and from parts of Jiangxi province in 1764.[149] In neither example is the interest rate specified, but the reason for having the ancestral hall make these loans is: ancestral rites.

How did these Dongli Chengs use the loans from their ancestral-hall association? As no specific use is prescribed, proscribed, or described in these Chengs' records, we are forced to consider a range of possibilities in light of additional evidence. First, during the Ming, money was borrowed from such credit institutions by a wide range of Huizhou men for a wide range of purposes. The most instructive example is that of another Huizhou credit association set up in 1639 by fourteen Wangs. Like the Expansion Association, it required a minimal annual fee of 0.5 ounce of silver for membership, allowing the association to

---
[148] *Da Cheng cun Chengshi zhipu*, the last part of the section "Shizhong miao e."
[149] *Wuling Gushi zongpu*, 6th *ce*, jitian zhi, 1b–2a, 3a; Hill Gates, *China's Motor*, 103, unfortunately omits where in Jiangxi.

disburse, at least initially, seven taels annually. From this sum, presumably as a form of payment, it decided to loan its annual heads four taels every year at a 20 percent rate of interest. Defaulting borrowers were obliged to pawn their possessions first with the association and then, three days later, if still unable to repay their loan, with a pawnshop (that presumably was owned or run by the association's kinship group or some of its members).[150] But at the same time this association, on behalf of its members, promised to invest its remaining capital annually in salt monopoly trading in Haiyan county 海鹽 of Jiaxing prefecture. Here we have a group of small-time investors making a collective investment in business that would have been dominated quite possibly by fellow Huizhou families they knew.

Confirmation of this conclusion is found in an unexpected source, a collection of 733 letters sent to the cohead of a Huizhou pawnshop, Fang Yongbin 方用彬 (1542–1608).[151] Though easily dismissed as one of the countless examination failures of sixteenth-century Huizhou, Fang actually lived a busy and diverse life as a merchant. When not at home comanaging the family pawnshop in Yanzhen 岩鎮 market town, he traveled throughout much of eastern China from Beijing to Guangdong, making a living as an art, antiquities, and book dealer, all in order to support himself and his family over several fruitless decades of pursuing examination success and his dream of an official career.

This collection of letters sent to Fang shows him developing and maintaining a close association with at least 352 clients. The great majority of these men were fellow Huizhou natives (including family relations) who were living away from home. Many were based in the Yangzi delta, but overall they wrote to him from fifty-four counties in more than half of the empire's thirteen provinces and two metropolitan areas. Many doubtless had access to other Huizhou pawnbrokers in their actual place of residence. But they turned to Fang Yongbin for loans, presumably because they could rely on Fang Yongbin to keep their financial relationship confidential back in Yanzhen, the Huizhou merchant-gentry-dominated market town where Fang's family was very well known.[152] As revealed in this correspondence, these clients

---

[150] *Huizhou qiannian*, v. 10, 91–101.
[151] Pak Wŏn-ho, *Ming Qing Huizhou*, 123–39. As a collector who engaged in moneylending and pawnbrokering, Fang Yongbin may well have taken art and antiquities as collateral.
[152] Ibid.; *MQHS*, 38.

included not just merchants, artisans, and farmers, but also well-known literati and high officials. Some correspondents specified their intended use of the loan; in addition to paying their living expenses, marriage and funeral costs, legal expenses, and government charges, a few mention use of the money for commercial capital (*shangben* 商本) and loans (*fangkuan* 放款). The loans from Fang Yongbin ranged from a few *qian* to 100 taels of silver, but usually amounted to several taels.[153] In fact, those claiming to need a loan for investment received only small sums, suggesting that in Ming Huizhou, as in the Song and subsequently in the Qing, commercial ventures attracted not just large merchant houses but many small borrower–investors as well.[154]

Some General Remarks on Ancestral Halls

Ancestral halls are religious institutions, and a full account of their impact in Huizhou's villages should consider how their establishment may have affected the power of other institutions or individuals seeking to communicate with the ancestral dead on their own. Ancestral halls essentially brought together a selection of ancestors into one building under the control of their descendants and especially the ritual head of their kinship group. Therefore the operation of these halls with spirit tablets on their altars at the very least challenged, if not undermined, rival claims by local mediums or others about their ability to communicate with a lineage's dead (mediums liked to be associated with village worship associations[155]). Likewise, Buddhist monks would cease to perform the memorial rites for the lineage dead that had been their remit from the lineage. Thanks to the early Ming withdrawal of government patronage for most Buddhist institutions and mid-Ming attacks on their land endowments, many temples would have lacked the resources to resist this push by lineage leaders and their ancestral halls.[156] And, as should be clear from our account of the opposition that some lineage groups posed to some ancestral halls'

---

[153] Chen Chizhao, *Mingdai Huizhou Fangshi*, for the salt merchants Fang Yangeng (v. 1, 487) and Fang Shimo (v. 2, 965). Other merchant borrowers are waiting to be found in this treasure trove of Huizhou financial information. *Dianshang*, 236–47; Wang Shiqing, "Huizhou xue," 12–20.

[154] Huizhou pawnshop practices are discussed in Chapter 4 below, and small commercial investments by ordinary Chinese in Chapters 5 and 6.

[155] McDermott, *Making*, v. 1, 54, 57, 71.   [156] Ibid., v. 1, 213–34.

construction, an ancestral hall could be divisive, allowing some lineage members to redefine membership and redistribute power within a lineage to their own advantage. One important institutional consequence of all this intra-lineage competition (and that described in volume 1) was the large number of ancestral halls common to large, long-established Huizhou lineages. Likewise, there was the growing likelihood that the membership of each of these lineages as represented by its ancestral halls, even its comprehensive ancestral hall, was not identical to that found in its genealogies, grave lists, or lists of descendants actually living in this lineage's village.

Instead, this chapter has focused overwhelmingly on the ancestral halls' financial operations and their expanded role in Huizhou villages at the expense of the other Huizhou institutions in the "village quartet." At first reading this focus may remind the reader of volume 1 of the chameleon-like character of these village institutions so capable of assuming one another's functions without changing their name or goals. Yet in this case we have really one institution, or more precisely only one institution that is officially registered and autonomous. The credit association or proto-bank that operates within an ancestral hall functions therein only with the acceptance (and at the initiative) of the ancestral hall's leaders and at least some of its members; or, to put it more succinctly, it cannot assume the functions of the ancestral hall and stand either independent of it or capture it institutionally. As such, it is embedded within the legitimacy of an institution which ostensibly and legally pursues goals different from profit making and credit building. It is as if we have a bank that is conceived but only half-born; no one has cut its umbilical cord.

It is thus revealing to see how this institution within an institution pursues its own line of development and predictably moves in pursuit of financial profit, demanding, for instance, collateral and thus becoming a pawnshop. But the more common impulse, as it functioned under these institutional constraints, was to become an affiliated association attached to the ancestral hall or even to itself. In directing its new, profit-minded activities through another guise, it thereby acquired protection and a certain degree of legitimacy. But in the end these features did not provide the long-term stability and credibility that were associated with a registered ancestral hall and that were necessary for the successful long-term operation of a financial institution. In later stages of this book we shall return to similar institutional half-births, and observe how Huizhou merchants reduced risks by operating once again from within the refuge of an already legitimate institution like a government monopoly. For Huizhou merchants this kind of camouflage was to prove a highly successful strategy, at least in the short term.

Most obviously, in an era when pawnshops were to be officially registered and were usually located in towns and cities, ancestral halls would have helped to assure that currency circulated down into the countryside and into the hands of ordinary villagers. In addition to thereby satisfying and expanding some of the villagers' demand for credit and commodities, these ancestral halls sometimes provided resident kinsmen with a relatively favorable rate of interest. Even when the focus of their lending may have shifted from kinsmen to non-kinsmen, they would still have provided enterprising local borrowers with some financial support and experience in the usually urban art of "making money from money." Last but not least, their attachment to a semipermanent institution like an ancestral hall would have conferred far greater stability and permanence on their lending relationships than could have ordinarily been expected from autonomous pawnshops and commercial partnerships.

Consequently, what these records reveal about ancestral halls' financial operations are, first, the establishment and provision of "grassroots capitalist" services by kinship organizations in the wake of Buddhist establishments' loss of their endowments and retreat from credit operations, and, second, a tendency for these kinship institutions to evolve into proto-banks pursuing, when necessary, higher returns from non-kinsmen obliged to pay high rates of interest. This experience and training would have served these villagers well, when as prospective merchants and pawnbrokers many left their Huizhou villages in the last half of the Ming to do business in the prosperous and highly competitive markets of the Yangzi Valley.

This positive assessment of ancestral halls' financial activities needs to be muted, however, since this manner of lending, when put in a wider and comparative perspective, still involved potential problems and exposed serious weaknesses in this process of financial development. First, note that the provider of this financial service is not an autonomous institution able to control its funds for clear financial purposes. Embedded in an institution as legitimate as any in late imperial Chinese society, this credit association is not only a family-based institution but also one devoted to ancestral worship and thus potentially more risky than an ordinary bank without such commitments. It was a way to defuse local government worries as well as to blunt some of the social criticism towards its public functioning. What better way to relieve anxiety in government circles than to match this threatening institution, a bank, with the most orthodox and legitimate institution in the entire lineup of Confucian institutions? Second, these halls' maximum capital assets seem in the Ming dynasty to have rarely amounted to more than 10,000 taels (I am assuming that the admission fee paid for most ancestral spirit tablets was well below the maximum fee mentioned above, that of 10,000 taels of silver). In fact, as already noted, the assets held by a pawnshop run by an ancestral hall in eighteenth-century Suzhou are estimated to be only in the hundreds of taels.[157] When set alongside figures compiled by Peng Xinwei and Liu Qiugen for the capitalization of pawnshops elsewhere in the empire, these rough estimates of the total capital assets of ancestral halls in Huizhou and elsewhere place their funds at the middle or lower end of the scale for lending institutions in the Ming.[158] Since these halls tended to have this amount of working capital only for a brief period before using it for construction, their level of capital in most years before and immediately after construction would have usually been lower, sometimes much lower. We are thus dealing here mainly with the world of just low and middle-range finance, having access usually to assets smaller than those of urban pawnshops and other emerging banking institutions in the Ming. This is the world of start-ups, the

---

[157] *Wuling Gushi zongpu*, 6th *ce*, jitian zhi, 1b–2a, 3a. No figures are specified, perhaps because they varied. Yet a credit association established by members of another Suzhou lineage at late eighteenth-century Dongting shan eventually accumulated over 1,000 taels, which when used for loans garnered profits that, among lineage needs, funded ancestral-hall repairs (*Zhengshi shipu*, 8.9a–13a).

[158] Peng Xinwei, *Zhongguo huobi shi*, 741–52; Liu Qiugen, *Zhongguo diandang zhidu shi*, 35. Also, Xie Zhaozhe, *Wu zazu*, 4, 74, attributed 1,000,000 taels to Huizhou's top merchant families and 200,000 to 300,000 taels to its middling merchants. Rowe, *Hankow: Commerce and Society*, 174, assessed the assets of Hankow's native banks at from 2,000 to over 100,000 taels, suggesting that the capital holdings of the larger Ming Huizhou ancestral halls would have fit into the lower end of the credit market in Hankow in the eighteenth and nineteenth centuries. Yet top Huai salt merchant families by the end of the eighteenth century reportedly held tens of millions of taels of silver and the next-level families just several million taels (Fujii, "Shin'an shōnin no kenkyū," 36.3), 76). All these figures require further research.

grass roots of Chinese capitalism, rather than the world of high-risk wheeler-dealing between merchant bankers and salt merchants. And, during the mid Qing at least in Yi county, widely regarded in the Ming as the least commercial and adventuresome of Huizhou's counties, the use of ancestral-hall assets to make loans would be described as a practice of "the old surnames and hereditary families."[159]

Second, the interest rates, even when halved for kinsmen, remained high, and in many cases too high to encourage anything but short-term loans to help borrowers overcome temporary shortages of cash.[160] Against this reasonable view we can consider counterevidence: the ability of kinsmen to acquire larger loans at low rates of interest from a kinsman's pawnbrokerage; their ability to lend the money on to others at the normal market rate and pocket the difference; the likelihood that a small loan from an ancestral hall constituted just a small portion of a prospective merchant's total capital, only some of which was borrowed and had to be repaid; and the expectation of high annual profits (20 percent is mentioned twice) from long-distance trading.[161]

And, third, reflecting these Ming ancestral halls' relatively low level of capital assets, the types of financial services they provided were few and their range narrow. There is no mention of ancestral halls' acceptance of outsiders' capital deposits (as opposed to land as collateral); their transfer of funds to lineage business offices elsewhere; their taking out loans; and their issuance of any bills of exchange, promissory notes, or any other negotiable credit instruments. Likewise, their members do not appear to have engaged in any strategic discussion about how to make their investment capital in this institution work more productively (security seems a priority, with income from the lending capital at times being ploughed into the further purchase of land). Thus the ancestral hall, however important its role in the instruction and involvement of ordinary villagers in money-making activities, was a highly conservative financial institution. Its managers are entrepreneurial mainly in finding new ways to dun its members.

---

[159] *Yi xianzhi* (1871), 3.2a, on the linkage of money associations (*qianhui* 錢會) to such kinship groups' ancestral halls.
[160] For a more pessimistic account of pawnshops in early modern Europe, mainly France, see Laurence Fontaine, *The Moral Economy*.
[161] Wu Ziyu, *Dazhang shanren ji*, 31.9b; *Huizhou fuzhi* (1502), 2.39b–40a, on expected profit rates. See the discussion of pawnshops in Chapter 4 below.

The real entrepreneurial commitment is left to the individual borrowers, whose lenders seem to impose no restriction on the use of these loans, so long as they are repaid in time at interest. No evidence has yet been found in Ming Huizhou sources of an ancestral hall's direct commercial investment, such as has been described for some halls in Hong Kong and Shanxi province in the Qing.[162]

Nonetheless, sometimes these Huizhou halls' indirect involvement in Ming business affairs is made explicit, not only in the use of their loans but also when a humble credit association affiliated to an ancestral hall invested its profits in another Huizhou commercial activity. Witness how in 1639 a group of fourteen Wangs, backed by four additional Wangs serving as "seniors in charge of the oath," agree to set up a credit association that each would head in pairs on an annually rotating basis. Each member was expected to pay in a set amount of silver every year, but be able to borrow from the association four taels during the years he served as a head. Significantly, the association promised to invest the remaining capital annually into the shipment of salt, the monopoly that Huizhou merchants dominated in the middle and lower Yangzi from the middle of the Ming.[163] The annual heads' involvement in the reneging of such a loan, though we have no evidence of its rate of incidence, would undoubtedly have put the borrower under heavy pressure from those closest to him. It also would show how financial activities in the village might be linked to the far greater commercial and financial activities of Huizhou merchants outside their villages. It is these extramural worlds that the rest of this book shall consider, as we leave the world of the village but not the lineage, to understand the risks and rewards that the Yangzi Valley's thriving markets offered Huizhou's more enterprising merchants and officials.

[162] Zelin, "Chinese Business Practice, 774.
[163] *Huizhou qiannian*, v. 10, 91–101.

3 | *The Working World of Huizhou Merchants*
Travel and Trade, Problems and Resolutions

It is time to leave Ming Huizhou and examine the working world of Huizhou merchants outside Huizhou. In recent decades the Ming has been seen as a period of profound economic change, when the command-like economy of its early decades gave way to the more market-based economy of its final decades. The urban dimensions of such studies have often focused on production, usually of high-quality silk textiles in delta cities.[1] This chapter will concentrate instead on the practices of distribution between towns and cities, then, for a wide range of goods and the problems that Huizhou merchants thereby encountered. In assessing the role of Huizhou merchants in these transactions, we will examine how these merchants responded to the persistent obstacles they encountered in delivering and exchanging goods over the dynasty's major roads and its major commercial river, the Yangzi.

To explore the significance of these changes, our analysis will range widely from these merchants' travel and trading environment to their relations with one another, from their trading parties to questions of market governance by Ming officials and institutions, the central and the local. Since it was just these commercial and political dealings that Huizhou merchants and officials seem most keen to exclude from the surviving record, our primary sources will be far less revealing than the rich documentation many of these same merchant lineages compiled and preserved back in their Huizhou villages. We have almost no Huizhou commercial sale contracts, registers, bills, legal rulings, merchant books, and merchant correspondence or writings. Instead, we need to rely on official and military reports, merchant travel guides, some Huizhou merchant biographies, and some private accounts of the fate of these merchants and other Ming travelers in the Yangzi Valley.

As this list of sources suggests, our wider concern with the distribution of goods will have us explore their passage and delivery on land

---

[1] Chen Shiqi, *Mingdai guan shougongye*, 70–106.

and water by a great number of parties, by peddlers, shippers, long-distance merchants, brokers, merchant agents, porters, and even government boats. The focus on transport and trade will naturally introduce questions of risk and danger in the first section as well as in the second, when our concern with obstacles to market transactions will shift from river to land to consider urban obstacles to Huizhou merchants' trading in Suzhou and other delta cities. Here an interest in crime and market security will eventually lead us to examine market governance practices of the mid and late Ming. In an urban marketplace whose practices increasingly became the subject of disputes between outsider merchants and brokers with their local associates, the wealthier outsider merchants appear to have refrained from creating their own public institutions. To gain security for their commercial goods and investments, they turned instead to the long-tested tactic of establishing niches within the offices of an imperial government, that in this instance had supposedly vacated the marketplace.

In short, this chapter introduces us to the discomforts of the merchant world that Huizhou merchants' biographies never cease carping about. Since our story is not of merchant conquest of the marketplace but of his insecure place in what others often imagined was his natural space, we can better understand how and why Huizhou merchants acquired the bulk of their wealth from the extensive web of private contacts they wove in the government's salt monopoly in the Yangzi Valley.

To travel to these rich Yangzi markets down from the thickly forested slopes of Huizhou, merchants had no fewer than five well-recognized routes – two by road and three by water (see Map 1.1). The two most traveled roads out of Huizhou led either due north towards the Yangzi river or northeast towards the city of Hangzhou and the lower Yangzi delta. As usual, travel by mountain river – by the Qingyi river 青弋江 to the north, the Xin'an river 新安江 to the northeast, and the Chang river 昌江 to the south – was far from smooth, with "dangerous rocks and swift waters providing 10,000 knives every foot of the way." Three hundred and sixty waterfalls, by common calculation, closed Huizhou off from the rest of the empire.[2] But, overall, river travel proved cheaper, quicker, and so preferable, especially for those

---

[2] Wang Zhenzhong, *Huizhou shehui wenhua*, 32; Fang Hongjing, *Suyuan cungao*, 17.37a; *FKSFC*, 6.11a, on the surge in river levels that threatened boats on the Xin'an river in the fifth lunar month.

transporting heavy cargo through the mountain valleys of southern Anhui.

Upon arrival downstream in Yangzi Valley ports like Wuhu, Hangzhou, and Jingdezhen, a Huizhou merchant enjoyed easy access to the two most prosperous macro-regions of the empire, those of the lower and middle stretches of the Yangzi Valley. In 1601 a merchant could expect to travel by boat, presumably downstream with the current, as much as 300 to 400 *li* (or, approximately, 100 to 130 miles) in a day, letting him contemplate several long voyages on just the Yangzi every year.[3] Or, he could take advantage of the Yangzi's network of tributaries that offered access to the largest unimpeded expanse of domestic markets in all of Eurasia. The drainage area of the Yangzi river alone was some 468,000 square miles (about two-fifths of present-day China's entire land area). At the mouth of this vast river system traders could also enter the 1,100-mile-long Grand Canal, choosing either to travel north to Beijing or to sail south several hundred miles to Hangzhou and then Ningbo. From this international port they could head northeast to Japan and Korea or southeast along the Chinese coastline to Vietnam nearly another thousand miles away.

With this larger institutional context in mind, of a vibrant commercial economy continually testing and sometimes overwhelming time-sanctioned commercial institutions, we can better appreciate the cunning these merchants needed to reach the deals they traveled so far to transact. In fact, to provide this wider perspective on the operation of Chinese market institutions, our approach here will have to imitate some of their tactics: a close attention to practical details, careful reading of administrative reports, sensitivity to local pressures and customs, and an appreciation of the benefits accruing from an oblique approach to a problem, in order to tease out implicit information about their penetration of markets and attainment of their commercial goals. The same approach will prove equally indispensable in the following chapter's exploration of the Huizhou merchants' success in financial matters.

The Travails of Long-Distance Merchants: Risks on Rivers and Roads

The vibrancy of river traffic along the major trunk routes of the empire has enabled most modern historians to assume that long-distance

---

[3] Guo Hou'an, *Ming shilu jingji ziliao xuanbian*, 586.

travel and trade in premodern China were smooth and uneventful.[4] Yet much of what we find in Ming official and private records suggests otherwise. The major threats faced by Huizhou merchants in the lower and especially middle Yangzi Valley during the Ming stemmed, on the one hand, from the inadequacies of government institutions and representatives and, on the other hand, from pirates, criminal groups, and other local parties on water and land. The waterways and wharves of the Yangzi Valley were, in addition to being the homes of traders, fishermen, and "boat people," the lairs of a fair number of bandits, pirates, and sharpsters. Over the course of the Ming the troubles associated with water travel, as outlined by Tani Toshihito, can appear to have shifted from technical and administrative difficulties on state-run canals (early Ming) to bandit attacks on government vessels on the Yangzi (mid Ming) and eventually to persistent bandit raids on private commercial transport (late Ming).[5] While I suspect this narrative reflects the shifting concerns of our sources as much as actual shifts in types of Ming social disorder, this general description will serve us well in underlining a real surge in both private commerce and reported crime over the last half of the dynasty. Long-distance trade on the Yangzi, as elsewhere, was often the mother of piracy.

As acknowledged in a 1599 encyclopedia's survey of contemporary journeys, "there ought to be an account of the pains and travails for travelers on the roads in the empire." Travelers around the empire, it goes on to detail, faced a great variety of threats, and in every region enterprising merchants had need for prudence:

The mountains and rivers of Ba and Shu [in Sichuan and Guizhou provinces] are dangerous; one has to take precautions against Miao tribesmen, who vanish [at will]. The roads of Shandong province are flat, and one should be careful of its violent horsemen. Shanxi and Shaanxi provinces have precipitous roads. The area outside the entrance to Liaodong is dangerous. The Yellow River has threats from floods. Fujian and Guangdong provinces have difficulties due to their peaks. Guangdong and Guangxi provinces have the poison of biting insects and also disasters from malaria. On the roads there are white-tourniqueted bands [of robbers], and in the boats many assassination incidents. On the roads in Zhejiang and Jiangxi there also are many afflictions. [From] the Central Plain to Yunnan how varied are the

---

[4] Two admirable exceptions are Brook, "Communications and Commerce," 579–707, and Robinson, *Bandits*.
[5] Tanii, "Rotei sho," 415–56.

Risks on the River and Roads 129

difficulties! The Yangzi has distress from [high] winds and waves and from bandits. Hubo has disasters for fishing boats from storms.[6]

At least twenty late Ming stories share this theme of the dangers lurking on the road.[7] Shipping on Ming waterways would have seemed preferable on grounds of cost alone. But, as we shall see, throughout the last two centuries of Ming rule it, too, entailed many risks, not least threats to merchants' safety. Huizhou merchants had to find ways to protect their cargo and themselves from attacks on the very routes where they sought profit.

Early Ming reports of Yangzi pirates and brigands concern attacks on government boats at the mouth of the Yangzi or their links with land-based bandit gangs far upstream, for instance, in modern Hunan and Hubei. In the long stretch from Hengzhou and Changsha to Yuezhou and Wuchang 武昌 groups of non-Han robbers, numbering from 300 to over 2,000 members, reportedly killed Ming officials and military personnel and attacked county seats, thereby fueling unfounded rumors of impending attacks elsewhere.[8] The early Ming government's response, however, remained minimal, as both before and after its move of the capital from Nanjing to Beijing it gave priority to perceived threats along its northern border. Its security policy for the entire Yangzi, its most traveled river, was so focused on its cargo boats' safe delivery of the delta's grain tax that it stationed the bulk of its few Yangzi naval forces and boats along the brief stretch from Nanjing to the Grand Canal.[9] Meanwhile, throughout their first two centuries Ming boatbuilding yards along the Yangzi at Nanjing, Anqing, Jiujiang, and Wuchang, as well as those near the Grand Canal at Qingjiang 清江 in Huainan prefecture 淮南府, seldom met their construction and repair quotas. And, of the boats built, many were too large and flat-bottomed for effective patrolling and fighting on the Yangzi.

The government maintained this low-keyed indifference to a Yangzi defense policy, even after repeated official reports in 1465, 1467, and 1500 that salt smuggling on the river threatened the dynasty's purse

---

[6] Yu Xiangtou, comp., *Wanyong zhengzong*, 21.xia, 24b.
[7] Shao Yiping, *Wenxue yu shangren*, 141–42, 146–153.
[8] Chen Zilong, *Ming jingshi wenbian*, v. 1, 34.5a–6b. Many attacks in this area were reportedly never recorded.
[9] Long Wenbin, comp., *Ming huiyao*, v. 2, 63, 230–31.

and by extension its social order.[10] Particularly during the 1450s and 1460s bands of salt smugglers, often after acquiring military information or training from a government office or a military camp along the Yangzi, traded illicit salt up and down the river between Hubei and Yangzhou, virtually with impunity. Attracting large numbers of army deserters, local renegades, and bandits, these gangs had as many as 200 to 300 boats for their smuggling operations as well as their raids on Yangzi grain boats. The largest gang, consisting of over 2,000 men, once commanded more than a hundred ocean-going boats. Armed with weapons stolen or purchased illegally from garrisons, they and other brigands traded, plundered, and, when necessary, killed on and off the river in its adjacent towns and cities. Government forces, officials in 1436 conceded, were no match for these bandits in number and strength.[11] Indeed, many Ming soldiers regularly plundered salt boats along the river, showing themselves little different from the pirates they were expected to arrest.[12] In 1467 not only did soldiers make use of government boats to smuggle salt in collusion with local brokers, shop owners, and even salt-smuggling gangs in Nanjing and nearby Wujin 武進 county, but also along the Yangzi from Yizhen to Nanjing and from Wuhu through Jiangxi up into Huguang smugglers sacked a variety of settlements. Once bribed, few officials mustered tough resistance.[13]

In the late fifteenth and early sixteenth centuries piracy was reported mainly along the 500-mile stretch between Huangzhou and the river's mouth. Admittedly, some bandits, as in 1510, continued to disrupt Lake Dongting seriously,[14] just as did salt smugglers and other homegrown pirates throughout the valley. In the Chenghua reign era (1465–87) a renegade ex-government slave commandeered enough government vessels in the lower Yangzi to launch a highly successful campaign as a part-time pirate, part-time government suppressor of pirates, and part-time buccaneering trader, until his crisscrossing of the line between government service and independent action grew so flagrant that he suffered execution.[15] Farther up the river, between the

[10] Li Guoxiang et al., *Ming shilu*, 612, 613, 615.
[11] Saeki, *Chūgoku ensei*, 493.
[12] Ibid., 496–99. Eunuchs, working with army leaders, also plundered at the dynasty's expense. Ibid., 492–96.
[13] Ibid., 496, 497.   [14] Li Guoxiang et al., *Ming shilu*, 619.
[15] *Suzhou fuzhi* (1691), 81.17b.

Risks on the River and Roads 131

1480s and 1514, a group of Jiangxi bandits under Xu Jiuling 徐九齡 repeatedly created havoc, pillaging a host of riverside cities between Shanzhou 蘄州 and Taiping 太平 prefectures.[16]

In the first two decades of the sixteenth century, fishermen regularly attacked merchant boats from their lairs on Chongming island at the mouth of the Yangzi.[17] More tellingly, pirate and even land-based gangs from elsewhere started to roam widely on the river. In 1509, for example, a gang of Henan bandits disrupted the river's traffic, boarding boats and even killing a provincial official they unexpectedly encountered on the river. Over the next few years they ransacked towns and cities all the way from Huangzhou down to Zhenjiang, where only an exceptionally robust defense prevented them from entering and causing chaos on also the Grand Canal's southern extension.[18] At about this time riverside residents of Jiangyin 江陰 county in the delta, whenever they saw an itinerant merchant's boat stuck in the water, summoned their group (*dang*) and proceeded to seize the boat and plunder its cargo.[19] Indicative of the continued disorder on the river was the official judgment in 1531 that Jiangxi (and Huguang) robbers on the Yangzi were still "unpacified."[20]

In the mid sixteenth century, disorder intensified in the Yangzi Valley thanks partly to the incursion of Chinese-Japanese pirates (*wakō*). Along the southeast coast these bandits were conducting, in Robert Antony's view, a campaign of piracy "unsurpassed in size and scope anywhere else in the world,"[21] and by the mid 1550s their forays into the delta were threatening many major delta cities.[22] Farther inland, their attacks were fewer, but the chaos seems to have unleashed a great number of small local bandit groups. Denounced as "Japanese pirates," these bands raided some county and prefectural seats as far up the Yangzi as Wuhu. This middle Yangzi port, a lowland base for many Huizhou merchants' operations, was sacked twice.[23]

---

[16] Li Guoxiang et al., *Ming shilu*, 627. [17] *Suzhou fuzhi* (1691), 81.19a.
[18] Li Guoxiang et al., *Ming shilu*, 622, 623, 625, 626. Also see Chen Zilong, *Ming jingshi wenbian*, v. 2, 154 and 190.1a–4b; Robinson, *Bandits*, 19, 149–52; Nishimura, "Riu Roku," 44–86.
[19] Wang Rigen and Cao Bin, *Ming Qing hehaidao*, 27.
[20] Li Guoxiang et al., *Ming shilu*, 630. [21] Antony, *Like Froth*, 19–28.
[22] Geiss, "The Chia-ching reign, 1522–1566," 497–505.
[23] Chen Renxi, *Huang Ming shifa lu*, 45.20a.

In the 1550s these disorders prompted Zhang Shiche 張時徹 (1500–77), the holder of numerous high-ranking provincial posts in security matters, to decry these attacks for having seriously disrupted travelers and merchant traffic on rivers in Jiangxi and elsewhere in central China:[24]

> The scholars and the people all say that bandits along the rivers are acting wildly and that the merchant travelers often suffer their plunder. At night it is hard for them to travel, and so the routes and roads get clogged up (*geng* 梗). Nonetheless, each of the officials assigned to patrol and arrest along the river lives aloft in walled cities and does not supervise the troops and carry out patrols at all. Also they conceal and do not report the situation about the thieves, and so their hollow reports cover over troubles. Upon enquiring [I] have learned that these bandits are residents who hole up along both sides of rivers. They emerge and disappear as migrants coming from all directions and committing crimes. Also there are all sorts of privately held boats that in the daytime take fishing as their occupation. In reality, however, they practice rape and plunder. None of the traveling government troops can arrest and capture them, to the extent that some privately receive monthly cash [payments from the bandits]. Knowingly, they deliberately act wildly and play with the laws.[25]

In the late 1550s, Hu Song 胡松 (1503–66), another official with extensive military experience in the provinces, likewise noted the pirates' damage to Yangzi traffic and trade.[26] Stressing the strategic position of Jiujiang as the Yangzi's point of intersection with Lake Poyang, Hu noted that just as numerous rivers of Huguang, Jiangxi, and Anhui converged at this junction, so did these rivers' brigands and pirates. Gangs of salterns, miner bandits, "sand people" (*sharen* 沙人) from the area around the mouth of the Yangzi, "islet people" (*zhuren* 诸人) from Wuhu and Longtan 龍潭, local minority people (*tumiao* 土苗), and demobilized soldiers fleeing debt collectors, all passed back and forth between river and lake with minimal government supervision. Their work and passage were doubtless aided by their masquerading as merchants, since in this broad area they carried out their raids on merchant boats often from merchant boats they had sequestered. Quite recently, Hu indicates, the threat of Yangzi and Poyang piracy

---

[24] Zhang Shiche, *Zhiyuan bieji*, 5.9a. [25] Ibid., 5.23b–24a.
[26] Chen Zilong, *Ming jingshi wenbian*, v. 3, 246.3a–5a.

had worsened thanks to an influx of bandits from Jiangxi, western Fujian, and northern Guangdong, all intent on plunder.

These raids and consequent appeals to officials forced the Ming to expand its military presence on the river from the mid sixteenth century. Predictably, then, the government increased the number of its officials, soldiers, and boats along the river, and may well have adopted recommendations for the issuance of boat permits for boat owners and local control units (*baojia*).[27] Significantly, it ordered the construction and repair of more suitably sized boats, the establishment of more patrol boat stations and Fishing Tax Offices (*hebosuo* 河泊所) between Lake Poyang and Huangzhou,[28] and the creation by the end of the sixteenth century of nearly sixty sentry stations between Huangzhou and the Yangzi gorges.[29] On this nearly 600-mile passage, government boats were now expected to patrol and protect private travelers. Yet all these underfinanced reforms soon fell victim to continuing banditry on the river in 1576, 1578, and 1589,[30] in confirmation of the already mentioned 1599 survey's view of the Yangzi then as unsafe.[31] At this time just 600-odd soldiers were stationed along the 400-mile stretch between Nanjing and Jiujiang; that is, on average, roughly one soldier every half-mile and one boat every six to ten miles on just one bank of this wide river. At the century's close, actual full-time forces at many Yangzi inland stations reached just a quarter of their official quotas, and any local militia received minimal training,[32] as the government's military presence west of Jiujiang remained even thinner at century's end. No wonder that a late sixteenth-century official concluded that government control of the Yangzi and its traffic in the late sixteenth century "had grown increasingly lax."[33]

Two merchant guidebooks from this period confirm this assessment of trade and travel in the Yangzi Valley, deepening the impression of

---

[27] Zhang Shiche, *Zhiyuan bieji*, 5.9a, 24a–25a, 35b–36a.
[28] Nakamura, *Chūgoku gyogyōshi*, 111–80; Xu Bin, "Ming Qing hebosuo," 65–77; Kawakatsu, *Min Shin kōnōsei*, 284–303; Yin Lingling, *Ming Qing Changjiang*.
[29] Wang Shixing, *Guangzhi yi*, 4, 89–90.
[30] Li Guoxiang et al., *Ming shilu*, 632, 634, 636.
[31] Yu Xiangtou, *Wanyong zhengzong*, 21.xia, 24b.
[32] *Mianyang zhouzhi* (1590), 12.6a–7b; *Anqing fuzhi* (1554), 16, 1,016–23; *Jiujiang fuzhi* (1874), 23.5a–b.
[33] Chen Renxi, *Huang Ming shifa lu*, 44.41b.

minimal government protection and common merchant anxiety about security on the empire's principal commercial river and its many tributaries. Published in Huizhou in 1570 and 1626 mainly for Huizhou merchants, these manuals even specify the relative safety of specific sections of the Yangzi Valley, indicating the routes any sensible merchant would avoid or take.[34]

Within Huizhou the major east–west roads and waterways were usually free of robbers, as were the main river routes between Huizhou and the Yangzi delta (including long stretches of the Qiantang (aka Xin'an) river into the interior of Zhejiang).[35] Also judged safe were daytime travel along much of the Grand Canal trunk route in the delta between Zhenjiang and Ningbo,[36] and even nighttime travel in and out of the prefecture of Huzhou in the southwest corner of the delta (and thus on many Huizhou merchants' road passage to and from Hangzhou).[37] The Huizhou merchants' relatively secure travel access to and from the delta helps explain their continued concentration on its rich markets.

But, by the late Ming, even in Huizhou and the delta, certain routes were judged as risky, some decidedly so.[38] Merchants traveling in Huizhou along the seventy-mile stretch from Chengkan in Xiuning County to Ji Village in the neighboring prefecture of Xuanzhou 宣州 were warned "not to start out [too] early. In the daytime [robbers] size up the situation, and at night they carry out muggings. There are many cases of beatings with heavy staves, and in the winter there are robberies – take care."[39] On the road between Wuhu and Huizhou, merchants, some presumably returning with their earnings and others heading off with silver in their satchels, were warned of trouble every

---

[34] Huang Bian, *Tianxia*; Cheng Chunyu, *Shishang leiyao*. Lufrano, *Honorable Merchants*, 157–76, deals with similar instruction manuals, which though printed during the Qing dynasty were often based on late Ming imprints. Merchant fear of crime and fraud was pervasive in both dynasties and found expression in the new genre of merchant travel books first from the late Ming (Shiba, "Shinkoku," 903–18).

[35] Huang Bian, *Tianxia*, 252.

[36] Ibid., 204 and 232; nonetheless, some locations here were judged dangerous, particularly after poor harvests.

[37] Ibid., 235.

[38] Huizhou itself was not immune to banditry (Guo Yuanzhu, *Qinmin leibian*, 5.8b–9b).

[39] Huang Bian, *Tianxia*, 251–52.

three miles from "demanding ruffians in the early morning, bag snatchers during the day, and robbers at night."[40]

Within the delta, the county seats of Wuxi 無錫 and Wujiang likewise suffered from criminal activities in the late Ming,[41] as the delta's labyrinthine network of canals and rivers offered criminals countless escape routes. By 1607 the marshes along Hangzhou Bay were regularly visited by robbers and thieves, no year passing without residents of four adjacent prefectures suffering raids and plunder. Nighttime bans were imposed on travel in the interior Hangzhou counties of Fuyang 富陽 and Tonglu 桐廬, as well as on fording into Xiaoshan 蕭山 and Zhuji 諸暨 counties in neighboring Shaoxing prefecture.[42] In the 1620s thieves along the Grand Canal, now also to the north of Suzhou, were so numerous that men were advised to boat there only during daylight.[43] For the area south of Suzhou merchant guidebooks gave conflicting advice. One remarked on boats traveling day and night on the Grand Canal between Suzhou and Hangzhou.[44] Yet, another noted that halfway to Hangzhou the sparsely populated marshes stretching from Tangqi 塘栖 to Pingwang 平望 were to be crossed normally only at midday (when the sun was fully up), but never after bad harvests.[45]

By 1629 the attacks from brigands along this vital stretch of Huizhou merchants' passage northward to the Yangzi river had proven so common that merchants halted even their daytime travel.[46] During the late Ming the more heavily traveled routes in the northeast quarter of the delta as well became infested with bandits. Hence merchants were warned to boat between Jiaxing and Songjiang only in the daytime,[47] and north of Suzhou only along the Grand Canal.[48] Late sixteenth- and early seventeenth-century reports tell of local gangsters and brokers taking advantage of salt merchants with impunity on the

---

[40] Ibid., 255.
[41] Huang Xixian, *FuWu xiliie*, 8.1a–b, 21a, 45a, 54a, 66a–b, 69a–70b; He Liangjun, *Siyou*, 35, 323, mentions "a thinning out of [those] Suzhou customs," that cast a baleful influence on neighboring Songjiang.
[42] Jin Zhongshi, *Xunfang guili shiyao*, 15a–b.   [43] Huang Bian, *Tianxia*, 233.
[44] Ibid.   [45] Ibid., 375.   [46] *Xiuning xianzhi* (1693), 1.27a.
[47] Huang Bian, *Tianxia*, 206, 210.
[48] Ibid., 233, 240. Also see the 1583 case in the Shanghai area of a boatman's theft of a Huizhou merchant's silver and the subsequent nighttime seizure and murder of merchants (*MQHS*, 199).

waterways and in the markets of the Yangzi delta.[49] During the late Ming the Yangzhou markets themselves earned a reputation for nourishing thieves and crooks.[50]

Elsewhere, the dangers for merchants generally increased the farther they traveled up the Yangzi away from the delta, and more so in 1626 than in 1570.[51] From Yangzhou to Hunan province, river robbers "raided irregularly and disappeared regularly." Seeking refuge among the numerous islet lairs at both ends of this river route, they profitably pursued the closely associated careers of fishing and piracy.[52] Come nightfall, areas considered safe in the daytime, such as the stretch between Hengzhou 衡州 and Changsha in Hunan, turned dangerous.[53] Merchants were urged to moor their boats at night, or else become easy prey to local bandits. Just off the Yangzi, in the Lake Poyang area of Jiangxi province, robbers were reported to be numerous and murders frequent.[54] The lowlands between Nanchang and Raozhou 饒州 were very risky, particularly after bad harvests.[55] But regardless of a harvest's outcome, the brokers of Raozhou city were declared untrustworthy. Boats they launched to greet visiting merchants were never to be boarded: "One cannot distinguish the good [brokers] from the bad."[56]

Overall, the economic impact of these incidents and of the danger they posed to traders is hard to quantify. Clearly, as two sixteenth-century officials emphasized, these raids and attacks obstructed trade and traffic on the river. Some ships sank, others were sunk, and yet others fell into the hands of these river pirates and marshland bandits. Some voyages were halted, and some cargoes and investments lost. Did some merchant partnerships collapse and some prices for consumers rise? Undoubtedly, and though all these crimes and losses inflicted economic damage on shipowners, traveling merchants, and their investors, the scale of the mass market in these goods and the relatively small size of the cargo on individual vessels or caravans seem to have largely mitigated the economic impact of each incident.[57]

---

[49] Lü Youlong, *Liangzhe chongding cuogui*, 4, esp. 4.58a–68a, 75b–80b. Also McDermott, "Urban Order of Suzhou, 1500–1650."
[50] Wang Rigen and Cao Bin, *Ming Qing hehaidao*, 30.
[51] Brook, "Communications and Commerce," 613.
[52] Huang Bian, *Tianxia*, 190. [53] Ibid., 213. [54] Ibid., 216, 223.
[55] Ibid., 203. [56] Ibid., 227.
[57] Cooper, *Travels of a Pioneer of Commerce*, 118, discusses the absence of formal insurance policies in post-1860s Chongqing in Sichuan: "Their inquiries about Insurance Companies showed that such schemes were not unknown to them, but

The bigger cost to trade, I suggest, would have been psychological and so hard to measure. These raids on merchants and their boats would have fed anxiety about security (so evident in these merchant manuals), a distrust of others and fear of the unknown, and thus a reluctance to invest and send cargoes. As Zhang Shiche and Hu Song noted, the attacks, disruption, and robbery harmed the circulation of merchants and their goods. Even though these disturbances would have benefited other merchants through their creation of artificial scarcities and thus price increases for the remaining goods, these troubles would have obliged Huizhou's itinerant merchants to think twice before undertaking or investing in a long-distance journey. Government disinterest in protecting them and their cargo would have taught them that for protection they would have to rely mainly on their own family's resources and connections, not least in winning officials over to their way of doing business. This defensive response to the challenges they faced on the river would have nurtured the caution they regularly demonstrated in their dealings with others on land and a need to find a safe place within already established state operations on the water and on land.

Traveling Merchants' Recourse, Especially on the Yangzi

While traveling along these risky routes to reach sometimes unwelcoming marketplaces in the Yangzi Valley, Huizhou merchants were nonetheless able to become the dominant commercial group in the Yangzi Valley's commodity and financial markets. Despite personal losses and tragedies as well as being victims of commercial fraud and theft, how were they able to reduce or avoid serious threats to themselves and their cargo boats, to the extent that they could attain and retain that dominance?

> the prevailing idea, expressed without the least reserve, was that with regard to fire and life insurance no insured person's life would be safe, and junks would certainly not reach their destinations, while houses would be burnt most advantageously to the owners – but to the utter ruin of Insurance Companies; and that under Chinese management such schemes would never pay." On reflection, however, some local merchants considered the scheme feasible, so long as Cooper headed this company and could thus assure that British gunboats would support it in a crisis (ibid., 128). They even promised 30,000 taels to start this company under Cooper's name.

Biographers of Huizhou merchants like to attribute these traders' commercial success to their Confucian rectitude and diligence. Pieties aside, clearer insight into Huizhou merchants' practices comes from some sharp criticism made of them and other Chinese merchants by their contemporaries, not least Fu Yan 傅巖, a magistrate of She county, Huizhou, in the late 1630s.[58] His reports on Huizhou merchants' abuses in Huizhou markets make it clear that by the Ming's end, if not much earlier, they had little to learn from other merchants about cunning and deceit. Huizhou merchant guidebooks' sharp criticism of merchant behavior also has little to do with Confucian ethics; it merely reflects a shrewd assessment of Ming commercial practices that Huizhou men had come to adopt and master.

The principal surprise of these merchant guidebooks' anti-merchant barbs, then, is not the behavior they warn of or condemn but that they were written more often than not by Huizhou merchants for Huizhou merchants about Huizhou merchants.[59] And, lest it be thought that these complaints express the views of one set of Huizhou merchants against another, read the roughly contemporaneous critiques of Chinese merchants in general by two European visitors to China (actually, they personally had contact only with southeast coastal traders and were probably mouthing the resentments of bested Portuguese merchants in Macao). In c.1600 the Florentine merchant Francesco Carletti found Chinese merchants "better at [deception] than gypsies" and exceptionally avid for silver,[60] while a Spanish Jesuit shipwrecked along the Guangdong coast, Adriano de las Cortes, declared, "If there exists in the world merchants who are skilled at defrauding and who know how to default, then surely it is these [Chinese]."[61] For learning

---

[58] Fu Yan, *She ji*, 67, 98, 101, 109, 117, 128, 129, to cite just a few examples from this collection of Huizhou announcements and legal case rulings.

[59] Especially in Li Jinde, *Keshang yilan xingmi*, in Huang Bian, *Tianxia*; and Cheng Chunyu, *Shishang leiyao*.

[60] Carletti, *My Voyage*, 152; Boxer, *Fidalgos*, 258. For many Chinese criticisms of merchant theft and duplicity in Chinese, consult Zhang Yingyu, *Dubian xinshu*.

[61] Cortes, *Le voyage en Chine*, 235, 257–59. Chinese views of Western merchants were arguably slightly more appreciative. According to Peter Jackson, *The Mongols and the West*, 294, Chinese had a trope about foreign merchants (to my knowledge it exists only in Western texts): "Chinese merchants have two eyes, Europeans one, and those from the rest of the world none." Its repeated mention in European travel records spanning several centuries by travelers unlikely to have known of one another's texts persuades me to accept this report as credible. In fact, I suspect these foreign records disclose Chinese oral views of

how Huizhou's merchants thrived amidst their fellow masters of cunning, the best starting point surely is the detailed list of recommendations Huizhou merchants' travel books made to those travelers capable of reading Chinese. Alas, few if any European merchants acquired literacy or even oral fluency in Chinese; hence the object and tenor of their complaints seem to change little over the centuries, suggesting that their grievances were those of blind men doomed to learn little from their own and others' experiences, though Chinese merchants and their books contained much to instruct them.

Professed Guidelines

Fortunately, more instructive accounts of Ming Huizhou merchant practices survive in merchant guide books. These manuals' authors, unable to assume government defense of merchants and their cargoes, regularly laced their commercial advice with a strong distrust of others. While these warnings may be read as advice to inexperienced merchant travelers, their anxiety about the dangers of working away from home is so persistent that it seems reasonable to accept them as comments by and about merchants in general in an era of increasing crime and disorder.

At all times, however, we must remember that many of these merchants regularly succeeded, not least in building careers by initiating and fostering ties with others in other places. Their exchange of commodities, to state the obvious, required a minimum of agreement and trust among the traders themselves, if only for future transactions. As one Huizhou merchant lineage member quoting a local saying remarked, life in the countryside relied on power and insults, but a merchant needed a modicum of smooth talk and harmony to trade successfully.[62] Even if the level of trust among non-kinsmen merchants in sixteenth-century China was not high, the level of distrust advised in these Huizhou merchant guidebooks does not constitute the whole story of merchant relations with other merchants in the Ming. As the author of one of these manuals very sensibly remarks, "When traveling

---

foreigners (and foreign gossip about these views) otherwise ignored. Later appearances of this trope or a close variation by João de Barros in 1563 and Andre Pereira, SJ, in Beijing in 1737 are mentioned in Boxer, *João de Barros*, 107, 126 n.24.

[62] *Dangxi Jinshi zupu* (1568), 18.21a.

with companions, one is absolutely to refrain from creating differences with them."⁶³ This same author finishes his advice by reminding his readers to travel with others only after securing their agreement to some sort of commercial partnership, presumably to foster mutual co-operation in any crisis during their trip.

Away from home, a merchant – the counsel here is almost entirely directed to individual merchants – was advised to be wary about virtually every encounter he experienced and every non-kinsman he met. In his daily life, he was to refrain from displaying any sign of wealth: he was to wear drab and old clothing, economize on his food and drink, reside in a modest house, and use old utensils in his kitchen. These anxieties, shaped by lapidary sumptuary regulations in Ming law books, seem to stem from an overriding fear of envy. Wrote one Huizhou merchant:

If others see [wealth], it will result in arousing their thoughts of rebellion. A disregard for others and the overthrow of wealth are almost always due to this. If a close friend sees something in your home, he will perhaps [want to] borrow it. Not only will you then have no way to reject his request with an excuse, but also [your rejection] will invariably arouse his resentment and create a gap between yourself and him.⁶⁴

Thus an itinerant merchant from Huizhou or any other place thought to be affluent was advised above all else to be prudent. He was never to travel at night, taking care to set forth only after the first rays of dawn had lit up the entire morning sky. His planned time of departure, even if daytime, he was to disclose to none of his servants and concubines (whom he should suspect of having colluded with robbers downstream). Once outside his home, he was to make haste and above all find a safe haven for any wealth in his possession: "Do not show your wealth to others. When you get on a boat or climb ashore or put up at an inn or travel in the countryside, you must be extremely careful about the wealth you are carrying with you."⁶⁵

---

⁶³ Yu Xiangtou, *Wanyong zhengzong*, 21.1a. He also advises informing the authorities and acquiring a permit before starting a trip.

⁶⁴ Cheng Chunyu, *Shishang leiyao*, 2.43a, 53b, 55a. Unless noted otherwise, the following account of advice to merchants draws on ibid., 2.43a–45a, 47a–62b; Yu Xiangtou, *Wanyong zhengzong*, 21.1a–5a.

⁶⁵ Cheng Chunyu, *Shishang leiyao*, 2.43a, 53a; Li Jinde, *Keshang yilan xingmi*, 282, in Huang Bian, *Tianxia*.

Traveling by boat, a merchant had to beware of the shipper and the terms of any transport contract. He was to pay the shipper of his cargo only upon its safe arrival and make him compensate for any loss or damage (what today would be known as insurance costs were presumably calculated into the shipowner's overall freight charge).[66] He was to be even more suspicious of the shipper's boatmen. Although in a few parts of the Yangzi Valley – such as northern Jiangxi and perhaps Suzhou – there were "good boatmen," they were judged the exception rather than the rule.[67] Consequently, if on a small boat, he was advised not to poke his head outside the window of his boat cabin: "Be especially afraid that the boatmen will recognize you,"[68] and thereby know that as a traveling merchant you have come to buy goods and so are carrying cash. He was to disregard recommendations made by these same boatmen; they were most likely mouthing what other merchants' agents had paid them to say.[69] Moreover, he was to take steps to prevent them from filching his cargo, particularly during loading and unloading. Creditors might be pressing these boatmen so hard, that in mid voyage they would jump ship and disappear with passengers' goods. In short, "It really is as the proverb says, 'Nine out of ten boatmen are thieves.'"[70]

Fellow passengers on these boats also posed threats. Some boarded a boat deliberately to entice a merchant into gambling away his fortune; others came aboard to poison his food and confuse him, so as to disembark with his goods. In the area between Hangzhou and Suzhou travel at night as ever had its perils, but a boat's passengers might suffer daytime robbery as well. The local custom, whereby merchants were obliged to sit above deck and store their cargo below in the hold, was being abused and had to be countered: "If you don't take care, much will be stolen."[71]

Back ashore, a traveling merchant was to mount his saddle by himself, letting no one near the purse hidden on his body. On the road,

---

[66] Yu Wentai, *Dingqian Chongwenge huizuan shimin*, 16, fen guan sheshi: Gu chuan qi; Niida, *Chūgoku hōseishi*, v. 3, 809; Tong Guanzheng, *Mingdai minshi*, 156–61; and, for the organization of the private boat business for overseas trade, Gipouloux, "Partnerships and Capital Pooling."
[67] Han Dacheng, "Mingdai Huishang," 40; Cheng Chunyu, *Shishang leiyao*, 2.59b; Jin Zhongshi, *Xunfang guili shiyao*, 23b–26b, on incorrigible pilfering by crew and boatmen in northern Zhejiang.
[68] Cheng Chunyu, *Shishang leiyao*, 2.43a.   [69] Ibid., 2.52b.   [70] Ibid., 2.48a.
[71] Ibid., 2.55a.

he was to check the security of his baggage and prevent his porters from deliberately dropping a bag along the way. Staying at an inn for the night, he was "not to take off his underwear – this is the way to protect yourself from the unexpected."[72] At home, even in the heat of summer, he was to keep his house and shop doors locked and windows shut, lest thieves slip in and make off with his belongings.

Three types of people merited a merchant's sharpest suspicion: the poor, fellow merchants, and officialdom. If one's money fell into the hands of a poor man, one had little chance of seeing it again. The same misfortune might befall a merchant when dealing with other merchants. They may not be planning, literally, to rob his money or cargo like the boatmen, and fortunately they did not have the power to punish like an official. But their insincere flattery, their constant boasting of successful deals, and their endless invitations to "safe investments" merited only contemptuous disbelief. If they were not outright liars, they had few scruples about cutting corners with the truth and with everything else: a merchant's word, to state the obvious, was not disinterested fact. Hence, in any commercial transaction, one had to check and measure everything by oneself, just as before loading one's cargo one had to make sure that the hold of the boat was dry, know all the different measures in use along the Yangzi, and be alert to weather changes and harvest conditions.

One was also to be wary of feckless merchants, who "are by nature lazy," and rich merchants, "who invariably rely on others." Even if they do not commit abuses, they will often err in managing their businesses. And so, except when setting prices, one was to guard one's words with other merchants. The wise man lets them talk on, so he could size up their looks, their words, and their outlook before disclosing his own views. Even if such a relationship could escape government notice, it would certainly attract attention and attacks from locals anxious about these intruders' motives. Instead, merchants, either individually or in small groups, were to find their own solutions, leaving moral indignation to the literati and legal action to the ignorant and the desperate.

In all circumstances and at all times officials of whatever rank were to be treated with a complex combination of respect and distrust:

---

[72] Ibid., 2.49a.

Their authority can control others. One cannot, due to their lowly rank, act arrogantly and insult them. If they suffer offence, even though they cannot honor others, they can still dishonor them. If one were to suffer their insults and beatings, how would one wash away the shame? In general, when meeting an official, one must stand up and step back. Being lowly and humble is the lot of us commoners.[73]

Such humility for sure entailed a willingness to collude and, if necessary, bribe. Although none of these merchant guidebooks went so far as to encourage these tactics, the practice was common enough to bear credence when, as we shall see, Ming critics of Huizhou-born officials – with Huizhou merchant relations – denounced Huizhou merchants' resort to collusion and bribery when dealing with obstructive officials over matters like salt deliveries and certificates.[74] Of course, merchants who privately or secretly met with government employees may well have acted less directly, especially if their relationship was long-term. For instance, a low-interest loan to an official or his son would have been the easiest way to strike a deal that brought one great profit and minimal public notice; understandably, many Huizhou merchants found it handy to run a pawnshop or two in delta cities. Short-term or long-term, the guidelines for merchants stressed individual and not collective measures that were intended to attract as little attention as possible to their tactics, strategy, and successes.

Specific Merchant Practices

If, in print, prudence was the main expression of self-interest that Huizhou merchants' would acknowledge, then their actual practices – this chapter will henceforth be concerned largely with the middling and better-off sojourning merchant – demonstrated more flexible strategies of prudence and self-protective incorporation than their critics recognized. Actively, they collaborated with civil and military officials, and made some alliances with other merchants, especially those from Huizhou, all with the aim of gaining a level of security otherwise unavailable from the Ming government and from fellow Chinese.

The self-defense strategies employed by these Huizhou merchants were numerous. They tended to focus on solving specific problems rather than on reforming institutions or on presenting abstract

[73] Ibid., 2.59b.   [74] *Fengnan zhi*, 6, 387.

discussions (such as routinely surround modern Western accounts of Chinese state–merchant relations). For example, a local practice uncongenial to Huizhou merchants would be reconceived and renamed to constitute distinct components, only some of which would be discussed and altered, and so without ostensibly changing the practice they would seek to minimize or end its threat to their commercial interests. Or, an alternative practice would be found, negating or circumventing the impact of the specific practice that had upset some merchants.

Let me be specific: sometimes, when fearful of the dangers entailed in transferring capital over a long distance, a merchant shipped commodities (rather than money) which after their arrival at his destination he would exchange or trade for silver and cash. If this strategy involved shipping something bulky and less easily molten than silver ingots in order to reduce their attraction to robbers, yet more merchants over time resorted to advanced purchase on credit (*maishe* 買賒) and the transfer of money through a private company's bills of credit or remittance notes (*huipiao* 會票). Despite their early origin in China, bills of credit were not as commonly employed in Ming China as in early modern Europe and Japan.[75] The earliest recorded Ming instance of transmitting money over distance "dates to the Yongle era [1403–24]," writes Timothy Brook, "when an agency in the commercial city of Ningbo handled money orders or 'flying money.'"[76] Details of this financial instrument, which was used by a constant stream of traveling merchants in the Songjiang textile trade,[77] emerge from twenty-three remittance notes discovered in 1982 in the Xie 謝 family home in Xiuning county in Huizhou. From 1683 to 1686 individual Xies sent a total of 13,980 taels between Beijing and Suzhou; that is, an average of roughly 600 taels per note. Privately issued, these notes functioned as a kind of paper money for private transactions by private parties, not necessarily merchants but perhaps merely friends and kinsmen. As their use, so far as we know, did not extend to places outside the Yangzi delta other than Beijing, long-distance merchants

---

[75] Faure and Pang, "The Power and Limit of the Private Contract," 57–76. As Totman, *Early Modern Japan*, 158, explains, such conditions prompted Edo merchants to form private trade organizations and seek formal government protection, precisely what in institutional terms did not happen in Ming China.
[76] Brook, *Confusions*, 188–89.
[77] Chen Xuewen, *Ming Qing shehui jingji shi*, 90.

Risks on the River and Roads 145

bound for elsewhere needed to find alternative ways to secure the safe passage of their cargo, their money, and themselves.[78]

Hence, many merchants would have most likely called on whatever informal ties, favors, and connections they and their family could muster with officials. In the early and mid Ming Huizhou merchants would probably often have had better ties with military rather than civil officials, as many Huizhou families could boast of an extended pre-Ming and early Ming service in the military. In pre-Song times they were well known for their military prowess in dynastic transitions,[79] as well as in semi-private commercial matters. And, in the late eleventh century, as noted in Chapter 1, Huizhou men were reported to have formed large bands of men who escorted and guarded salt smugglers.[80]

Subsequently, during the Yuan and early Ming dynasties, far more Huizhou men entered the army than trade or civil officialdom.[81] In the fifteenth century, even before the Yangzi Valley economy revived, some Huizhou merchant families retained close ties with the military, and not just through their grain trade to military leaders along the northern border. Some sons or kinsmen pursued military careers in which they gained appointments at strategic commercial nodes.[82] Consider the case of the Chengs 程 of Shuaidong 率東 in Xiuning county. In the early Ming, portions of this lineage acquired great wealth, only to see much of it confiscated by the government when their head was found guilty of a minor act of corruption. Lying low inside Huizhou, its members revived their fortunes in the second century of Ming rule through military service. No fewer than thirteen of its members secured official appointments in the military, to posts like the Inspectorates of Military Guards Offices in Yangzhou and Nanjing, where they would have been well situated to help with salt monopoly trade inspections in Huainan, the lower Yangzi Valley, and eventually

---

[78] Wang Zongyi and Liu Xuan, "Qingchu," 93–112; Huang Jianhui, "Qingchu shangyong," 1987.1, 3–16; Wang Qingyuan, "Huishang huipiao," 187–94.
[79] McDermott, *Making, v. 1*, 173–74.
[80] Li Tao, *Xu changbian*, 461, 11,028. Presumably, the government worried that these Huizhou bodyguards would practice their skills as outright criminals in places and sectors it did not tightly supervise.
[81] McDermott, *Making, v. 1*, 173–74.
[82] Military official posts, having tripled from 28,000 at the start of the Ming to 81,000 in 1469, outnumbered Ming civil official positions three- to fourfold. Wang Chongyuan, *Ming Qing Huishang*, 50.

coastal Guangdong.[83] How many other Huizhou lineages pursued this entrée into government service is unclear, but the well-attested Song, Yuan, and early Ming links of Huizhou families to military service would have made the job at least as natural to them as their more often recorded civil service appointments.[84]

The valor and thrill of military life also had its attractions for many Huizhou men. Having studied martial arts from local teachers, they tended, as the late sixteenth-century scholar-official Wang Daokun admitted, to be conceited about their military skills.[85] Indeed, during the Ming, Huizhou publishers developed a specialty list in martial arts books, manuals that instructed Huizhou readers how to acquire these skills and perform them competently.[86]

More often as time passed, Huizhou merchants sought, on private terms, close co-operation with civil representatives of the imperial government, especially for transport. Ming law prohibited the private use of government boats to ship private parties and their private goods; it even severely restricted the amount of extra goods an official was allowed to take aboard as his baggage when dispatched on a government boat for government business.[87] Even though the restrictions on merchants boarding or using official or imperial vessels were harsher,[88] the amount of private and consigned cargo on government boats grew over the course of the dynasty, to the extent that one fifteenth-century Shandong magistrate demanded that government goods constitute just most of the cargo on government boats. Slightly later, in the mid-sixteenth century, a court official reported that excessive loading of private shipments onto government boats was even delaying the shipment of government tax grain up to Beijing.[89]

Not surprisingly, travel under government auspices, as when merchants called upon a salt monopoly escort up the Yangzi or used such boats for their other commodities as well, was very attractive. Witness

---

[83] Niu Jianqiang, "Mingdai Huizhou," 74; and *Xiuning mingzu zhi*, 1, 87–90.
[84] McDermott, *Making*, v. 1, 173–75.   [85] *MQHS*, 44.
[86] Wang Zhenzhong, *Qianshan xiyang*, 148–95; Guo Qitao, *Exorcism*, 98; Wang Xiaodong, "Lun Huizhou wushu," 27–31.
[87] Hoshi, "Transportation in the Ming Dynasty," 12–13.
[88] Lei Menglin, *Dulü suoyan*, 139–40; Anon., *Da Minglü zhiyin*, 5, 355–57.
[89] Yu Jideng, *Diangu jiwen*, 13, 235, 241.

a 1646 account of a group of heavily guarded salt monopoly boats sailing inside the delta:

> I met several hundred big salt ships, all as large as grain transport ships ... There were big placards stuck up high with gold lettering saying "Salt Transport Inspectorate." Their merchants were traveling just as if they were government yamen [personnel]; all in their entourage had knives and bows and arrows at their waists, and their own weapons and banners were just the same, in general, as those of government troops.[90]

In the Shandong peninsula, on the eve of the dynasty's collapse, some naval officials colluded with Huizhou merchants to dispatch naval ships to Korea to conduct private trading.[91] Within China the private merchants' expropriation of government ships for their private travel was probably most evident when rich merchants, having purchased a civil service degree,[92] would festoon boats with banners declaring their official title as a tactic for repelling bandit and pirate attacks. This tactic, admittedly, was not absolutely reliable (recall some pirates' accidental attack on the boat of a real official on the Yangzi in 1509), but it must have bought off a great deal of travel trouble for degree purchasers.[93]

Indeed, one is obliged to wonder to what extent Huizhou merchants and their contacts in the military came to establish private arrangements with pirates and brigands along their inland trade routes. How many on the Yangzi followed the lead of the Huizhou native Wang Zhi 汪(王)直 [fl. 1545–59], who became a notorious pirate along the Zhejiang coast?[94] Such a move from one side of the law to the other would have confirmed for domestic waterways the shrewd assessment a sixteenth-century official made about traffic conditions along the southeast coast: "When the market works well, the bandits are all merchants; when the market is prohibited, the merchants become bandits."[95]

---

[90] Yao Tinglin, *Linian ji*, 63; Ho Ping-ti, *Ladder of Success*, 30, 46.
[91] Fu Yiling, *Ming Qing shidai shangren*, 60.
[92] Fujii, "Shin'an shōnin no kenkyū," 36.4, 130; Ho Ping-ti, *Ladder of Success*, 30–33. By the last quarter of the fifteenth century the government had sold several tens of thousands of student-level degrees to finance its operations (Dardess, *Ming County*, 163–64; Long Wenbin, v. 2, 18, 893, and 49, 928–31).
[93] For another instance, see Han Dacheng, *Mingdai shehui jingji*, 194–95.
[94] Geiss, "The Chia-ching reign, 1522–1566," 493–504.
[95] Boyi Chen, "Borders," 92; Antony, *Like Froth*, 24, indicates that many powerful coastal pirate leaders had been merchants and quotes an eighteenth-century official's view: "Pirates and merchants are all the same people: when

Or, did they prefer simply to hire their own guards or pay off the pirates to gain safe passage on the waterways? Certainly, scholars agree that long-distance merchants sometimes hired bodyguards; they disagree only about its date of origin. The great economic historian of China Katō Shigeshi argued that by the mid Ming some boat owners in south China were hiring toughs at so-called "spear agencies" (*biaoju* 鏢局) to safeguard cargo-laden vessels and merchant passengers on long-distance journeys. Chen Guodong and Sōda Hiroshi then examined the term "spear agency" and postponed its origin and first usage to the early Qing. Sōda located evidence of its existence at Linqing, in Shandong, along the Grand Canal in the final decade or two of the seventeenth century.[96]

Terms aside, the practice of using an armed escort for private travel surely originated much earlier in Chinese history, and indeed was in use by the late Northern Song. Not only are practicing archers suggestively depicted alongside goods-laden carts at a central depot for travelers in the celebrated twelfth-century handscroll painting about the Northern Song capital of Kaifeng, *Qingming shanghe tu* 清明上河圖. But also a Northern Song date for the existence if not origin of the use of hired bodyguards is reasonable in light of Liangzhe region salt smugglers' hiring of Huizhou men to escort and guard their illicit trade.[97]

If, however, a merchant ended up unable to make satisfactory protection arrangements with government or private groups, then he would have most likely turned to fellow merchants. As a rule, Huizhou merchants took care to travel with others. Their companions included sons and kinsmen working as branch partners or apprentices in Yangzi port towns, or fellow merchants. In the late fifteenth century, every

---

markets are open, the pirates become merchants, and when markets are closed, the merchants become pirates."

[96] Katō, *Shinagaku*, 127–31, traces the earliest recording of this practice to the sixteenth-century novel *The Plum in the Golden Vase* (see passage on Ximen in Chapter 1). But Sōda, *Hashi*, 334–77, with support from Chen Kuo-tung, prefers an early Qing origin in the Linqing area along the Grand Canal. Also useful is the suggestion by Jing Jia (aka Kei Ka), *Chūgoku bujutsu*, 23–29, that the bodyguard service was eventually, if not initially, a protection racket, in which the Spear Office was run and manned by men in the employ of bandits who raided travelers unwilling to hire the Spear Office for protection during their trip.

[97] Li Tao, *Xu changbian*, 461, 11,028.

year in the first, second, eighth and ninth lunar months several hundred rich delta merchants boarded private vessels that, sailing forth from the Nanjing county of Jiangyin in the company of government salt monopoly boats, could expect privileged protection. Sailing up the Yangzi to the distant interior markets of Hengzhou, Changsha, Nanyang, and Sichuan, they delivered the delta's salt, dried fish, and textiles for products of the middle and upper reaches of the Yangzi, such as raw cotton, charcoal, sesame buns, beans, and especially grain that they annually shipped back to the delta.[98] This protection would have not just won salt boat and salt cargo protection from river bandits; it also would have eased the passage of these salt merchants' other boats, some of their other goods, and attendant boats through customs tax stations as well as their entrée to wharves and marketplaces not always hospitable to outsiders coming to unload their goods and remove local profits.

In sum, during the last two centuries of the Ming, Huizhou merchants traveling on the Yangzi and its direct tributaries regularly faced challenges to their person and cargo. Their response to these threats presumed little institutional help from other parties, especially the government. To assure the safe transport and delivery of their goods, they needed allies among fellow merchants as well as in military and official circles. The high degree of caution merchant manuals advocated was achievable only through private arrangements with other groups along their routes, some of them strangers and others possibly kinsmen. There is no report of merchants organizing their own policing patrols collectively. Stability and safety were ideals they may have shared with officialdom, but their consensus on goals and values, as we shall soon see, could be readily undermined by sharp disagreements on commercial and financial matters.

The Travails of Long-Distance Merchants: Risks in Ming Suzhou

On land, as opposed to water, the Ming government expected to rule without opposition, and nowhere more so than in the large cities where its civil and military officials were stationed in great numbers along

---

[98] Hamashima, *Sōkan shinkō*, 83; Heijdra, "Socio-economic Development," 500–1.

with crowds of their attendants and soldiers. Ostensibly, these forces enabled the government to control important segments of an urban economy, that since at least the Tang dynasty were run as a set of craft and trade associations (*hang* 行) producing for both the state and the market. These associations had commonly sought to encompass all the practitioners of a particular trade or craft within a city, while at the same time a largely distinct system of hostels, shops, and storehouses arose for merchant and artisan visitors, especially those from other regions.[99] Even in the Ming these associations' members would have been locally registered residents (and quite likely natives) of the cities where they practiced their line of craft or trade.[100]

By the mid fifteenth century, these early Ming institutions were losing local control of their craft production and distribution. While some attribute this breakdown to their gross inefficiency and outrageous demands on workmen and merchants and on their overall unsuitability to an economy with a thriving and dominant private sector,[101] other scholars have also paid attention to the pressures exerted on early Ming institutions by the increased number of sojourning merchants in the empire's major cities. Coming from distant locales like Huizhou, these outsider merchants ill fit the traditional model of a trade association member. As ordinary peddlers they could, in the Ming as in the Song, be ignored and not be included in a traditional trade association.[102] But the large outsider merchants of the mid and late Ming, who arrived at a delta port with a quantity and value of goods rarely seen since the Song, were harder to ignore, especially if they arrived regularly with grain this delta city needed to consume. Admittedly, some Ming officials still dismissed them as mere outsiders, believing that just as their commercial profits largely lay beyond state regulation, so naturally did their problems.[103] Nonetheless, as the sixteenth century wore on, that approach made less and less sense. More and more of Huizhou's outsider merchants were settling down in

---

[99] Hu Tieqi, *Ming Qing xiejia*, 58–60.
[100] In the early and mid Ming the large numbers of provincial artisans forced to travel and work in the capital for set periods of time remained registered back home. By the early sixteenth century, when Nanjing had nearly a hundred craft and trade associations (Zhang Xianqing, *Mingdai houqi shehui*, 215), many artisans independently flocked to it and other cities in search of work (no corresponding figure survives on Suzhou artisan associations).
[101] Huang, *Taxation*.   [102] Wei Tian'an, *Songdai xinghui*, 113–18.
[103] *Dianshang*, 345.

large lowland cities of the Yangzi Valley, and over time won admission to and then headship of their trading associations (for instance, the cloth-dyeing trade in Wuhu in the Jiajing reign era).[104]

In Suzhou, a thriving transhipment hub rapidly developing into an industrial and financial center, the commercial thrust was both rapid and comprehensive. Its economy had suffered seriously from early Ming emperors' imposition of heavy land taxes and confiscation. Only in the Chenghua reign era (1465–87) did its prosperity return, with a revival of its craft sector to long-forgotten Southern Song levels of production.[105] The quantity and quality of its products, not least its silk, metal goods, and other handicrafts, gained the appreciation of visitors from as far away as Korea and Flanders. Even its butter won accolades – "the best-tasting in all of China" – from a well-traveled Italian Jesuit.[106]

But for a long time this cultured metropolis, containing by the late Ming some 500,000 people and visited daily by thousands of boats of all sizes, had also held a far less salubrious reputation. In the Southern Song it had been officially judged "hard to govern" and castigated, in contrast to the elegant capital of Hangzhou, as "a rough place."[107] The Ming army's six-month siege and bloody seizure in 1367 had done little to calm local tensions.[108] Apart from the tenures of a few exceptional magistrates and prefects,[109] Ming government control over the city up until the early seventeenth century had proven relatively lax, caricatured well in a local gazetteer's account of the laissez-faire regime of the Zhejiang native Zhu Sheng 朱勝 (prefect 1446–49). Every day,

---

[104] Fujii, "Shin'an shōnin no kenkyū," 36.3, 88–90. Other instances concern prominent salt merchants in Hangzhou, Yangzhou, and nearby Zhenzhou (Huaixi); they presumably represented all salt merchants, not just those from Huizhou.
[105] Wang Qi, *Yupu zaji*, 5, 42.
[106] Ch'oe Pu, *Piao-hai lu jiaozhu*, 55, writing in 1488 at the start of the Ming economy's revival. Golvers, *Rougemont*, 506–7; Fan Jinmin, "Ming Qing shiqi huoyue," 39–46.
[107] Tonami, "Tō Sō jidai," 292–303.
[108] Dryer, "Military origins of Ming rule," 92–94.
[109] The notable exception to this trend was Kuang Zhong, famous for bringing to heel and executing numerous deceitful clerks, unruly soldiers, bully landlords, and other urban troublemakers during an exceptionally long tenure as prefect (1430–42). Marmé, *Suzhou*, 112–15; *GuSu zhi* (1506), 40.25a-ff; *Suzhou fuzhi* (1882), 70.10–12a, 146.129b–130a; Kuang Zhong, *Ming Kuang taishou Longgang gong ZhiSu zhengji quanji*.

we read, he had his yamen clerks present him with documents, had his runners line up and bow to him, and had only serious criminals jailed. Common yamen mispractices he met with a dose of Daoist inaction infused with liberal dashes of wit: "As the clerks are venal, I pass onto them none of my rulings. As the lictors are venal, I don't have anyone beaten with a wooden staff. And, as the jailers are venal, I don't have anyone jailed."[110]

As a result, then, of a general lassitude in urban governance and the delta's broader social and economic changes, the city of Suzhou was by the early sixteenth century nourishing an underbelly of criminal life that lived off its water traffic and that belied the city's other reputation as a comfortable place to live. An increasing number of its youthful emigrants from surrounding villages were forming gangs of "rascals and vagabonds" (*wulai* 無賴). Bereft of a home, family, or legitimate occupation,[111] they aroused widespread concern among Suzhou residents convinced that as representatives of what locals considered the unruly poor – or what James Watson has termed China's huge "bachelor subculture" – they posed a criminal threat to the city's social order.[112] When not loitering in popular sites like Maple Bridge and Chang Gate, taking up lowly, temporary service jobs,[113] and engaging in petty crime, they tended to attach themselves to rich and powerful families, some local and some official, anxious to use them to resolve their own dilemmas.[114] By 1600 no fewer than 300 such urban gangs, each loosely containing several tens of members, were reportedly operating in the cities and towns of just the southern half of the delta.[115] If a long-distance Huizhou merchant could lose hard-won assets in the

---

[110] *Suzhou fuzhi* (1882), 70.12a. From the 1530s many Suzhou prefects lasted in office less than the conventional three years. In the single year 1533 three men in turn held this post; for some years in the turbulent late 1590s and early 1600s the post appears empty. Ibid., 52.37b–38a.

[111] Ueda, "Minmatsu Shincho," 30, note c.

[112] Kawakatsu, *Min Shin kōnōsei*, 265; William Rowe, *Hankow, Conflict and Community*, 217; *Suzhou fuzhi* (1882), 146.41b–42a.

[113] *Suzhou fuzhi* (1882), 68.19a. They had served as granary watchmen and soldiers for Zhang Shicheng 張士誠 in his defense of the city against the first Ming emperor's troops, and in c.1410 the Grand Co-ordinator arrested over a thousand vagabonds in Suzhou and Songjiang prefecture after they rioted (Ibid., 68.19b).

[114] McDermott, "Bondservitude," 675–701; Jiang Liangdong, *ZhenWu lu*, tiaoyi, 2b, 9a, 14b.

[115] Santangelo, "Urban Society," 106.

Risks in Ming Suzhou 153

course of a morning attack on the river, then he could equally see them snatched away by the loose promises of these sharks at an urban wharf or marketplace. And in Ming records, few places seem as vulnerable to such swindling and stealing as Suzhou, especially at night.

Our task here is to examine whether and how these urban crimes created difficulties for Huizhou merchants practicing their trade in Suzhou. We will first identify changes in the incidence of crime in Ming Suzhou and examine the legal and customary obstruction by local commercial organizations to outsider merchants. Next, in the closing sections of this chapter we will discuss the measures taken by Huizhou merchants to defend themselves against all these local threats, legal and illegal, as well as make up for inadequate protection by the government. Finally, we shall explore how and why the collective response of regional merchant groups like those from Huizhou appears to have been so weak to an array of hostile groups – criminals, rival commercial groups, and various parties in unhelpful government offices. In the end, we shall observe how the risks of urban life pushed Huizhou merchants to form private relations with Suzhou's officials and government institutions.

We begin our survey of crime in Suzhou and other big delta cities with a unique register of criminal cases, the *Yanyu gao* 讞獄稿. Compiled by Ying Jia 應檟 in 1531, this record book brings together a series of recent capital-punishment judgments that were made in Suzhou and elsewhere in the lower Yangzi Valley and that in the view of this book's compiler merited judicial review by higher authorities for legal or humanitarian reasons. As such, it provides a narrow and partial window onto the practice of crime and justice in and around Suzhou during the mid Ming. Of its forty-one serious criminal cases reported just from Suzhou and Songjiang prefectures, over half dealt directly with serious theft; that is, theft made serious either by the offender's resort to violence or by his repeated offence.[116] If this low number of serious robberies suggests that theft was not a common form of crime in and around Suzhou in the early sixteenth century, there is no indication that it happened mindlessly or that men stole indiscriminately. One cuckolded friends or acquaintances; one did not rob

---

[116] Ying Jia, *Yanyü gao*, 2. Classification of the crime involved in these cases is sometimes complicated by the same party's involvement in up to three or more offenses, yet this complication is usually offset by the repeat offenders' tendency to commit the same category of crime.

them.[117] Doubtless, face-saving concerns restrained some victims from reporting thieving kinsmen to the court and from seeking compensation through the local court; but, as if to underline overriding family concerns, no domestic servant is charged here with theft despite reports of its occurrence in other contemporary records.[118]

In the Suzhou of the 1520s a thief's preferred target was a stranger and an outsider (like a Huizhou merchant), commonly striking him under the cloak of night.[119] He also showed little discrimination about the type of objects he stole. His eyes and hands might latch onto virtually anything in his victim's house. A tin washbasin, a piece of timber, sheep, chicken, boat, and clothes all passed into his hands (the victims clearly were often not rich),[120] but his principal object of desire was the one most disposable and hardest to trace – money, preferably silver ingots rather than copper coins.[121] Repeat offences were not uncommon, particularly for petty theft, but sporadic.[122] Thus, if some Suzhou residents were supporting their lives through crime, they usually appear to have done so to replace or supplement their income from another kind of job. Precisely what occupation(s) they held is seldom specified. But this compilation's rulings frequently attributed their moral failings to poverty rather than greed, arguing that "although they are not good men, their good hearts have been laid low by loss of employment (ye 業, or property) and by extreme hunger and cold."[123]

Thieves, as any reader of Chinese history and fiction soon learns, like to work in groups. In the delta of the 1520s as many as five men, but more often just three, would do their hit together. They would knock down walls, slip through fences, and break open back doors to force their way into others' houses. They later divvied up the loot amongst themselves, with the head's take (he was usually the mastermind) slightly more.[124] Yet these men do not consciously belong to a gang, or even to a looser collective network of criminals; repeat crimes were committed individually, not collectively.

This conclusion needs serious qualification. The 1531 book includes only serious cases judged worthy of a central-government review for a

---

[117] Ibid., 2.9b, 12b, 14a, 17a.
[118] Nishimura, "Mingdai no doboku," 35, 38–39.
[119] Ying Jia, *Yanyü gao*, 2.13a, 23a, 29a, 36a, 45a, 58b.
[120] Ibid., 2.13a, 40a, 57a.   [121] Ibid., 2.4a, 45a, 58b, 59b.
[122] Ibid., 2.4a, 5b.   [123] Ibid., 2.5a.
[124] Ibid., 2.29a, 36a, 37b, 45a, 51a, 58b.

possible pardon. It is unlikely that professional offenders and gang members, such as the Yangzi pirates we observed, would have won official sympathy for inclusion in this judicial review. Moreover, small criminal gangs had been active in the delta and doubtless Suzhou and other Chinese cities long before the sixteenth century.[125] From as early as the thirteenth century gangs were recognized to be preying regularly on merchants and peasants trying to market their goods in south China.[126] Witness also a more general report of a mid-thirteenth-century official on local bullies' extortion of peasants seeking access to local markets:

In cities everywhere, the profits taken from sales are all monopolized by layabouts (*yushou* 淤手), but no profits are obtained by the hands of the small people in the fields and villages. Everything is produced by field hands and rustic people, with the men working to the utmost at tilling and the women at weaving. But, the profit they get is no more than trifling, while many times more profit ends up with the layabouts. This sort forms groups in the tens and hundreds, who on assembling conceal one another. If it happens that a villager sells goods in the market that have not yet passed through their hands, then a crowd of them rises and attacks him. A mass of hands, going under the name of the Association of Family Undertakings, does the beatings.[127]

In the fifteenth century, as we have seen, bands of salt smugglers coursing the Yangzi river with 200–300 boats and gangs of thieves regularly plundering grain tribute boats were long-standing, if not full-time, groups of criminals.[128] Thus, long before the *Yanyu gao*'s list in 1531 of possibly pardonable crimes, bands of criminals had lived off legal and illegal commerce and assembled around marketplaces in south China, including those in the Suzhou area.[129] Like merchants, they either traveled about (plundering others' shipments on the river) or settled in one market center (enforcing racketeering operations on shops and stalls). In short, mid-Ming criminals, even when targeting just local targets, enjoyed more cohesive levels of organization than the 1531 report suggests.

---

[125] McKnight, *Law and Order*, 283–94; and, of course, the cases of Zhu Qing 朱請, Zhang Xuan 張選, and others in Su Tianjue, *Guochao wenlei*, 69.6b.
[126] *Qingming ji*, xia, 14, 544.   [127] Ibid., xia, 14, 529.
[128] Saeki, *Chūgoku ensei*, 491–506.   [129] *Suzhou fuzhi* (1882), 68.19b.

Nearly a century later, long after highly disruptive pirate attacks on Suzhou city and the wider delta area in the 1550s,[130] recent protests and actions against the government and its tax regime had seriously upset official complacency about the delta residents' natural compliance with dynastic rule. A pair of detailed reports drafted in 1604 by a military commander stationed in Suzhou describe a serious deterioration in the city's order. Nighttime robbery is reported as commonplace, particularly during the cold months. Some thieves continued to leap over fences and bore through walls; others slipped in and out of powerful men's houses without attracting notice. Or in broad daylight they pickpocketed pedestrians and snipped silken coin purses from their owners' sleeves. Their favorite hunting grounds were not just the unpoliced stretches of the city's southeast and northeast quarters, but mainly the densely populated and policed centers of commerce and merchant residences around and outside its western gates. The wealthy quarters near Chang Gate and Yan Gate, and the bustling trading quarters of Maple Bridge, Five Dragon Bridge, Golden Stream Mound, Southern Moat, Northern Moat, Upper New Bridge, and Lower New Bridge, all of them also merchant residential areas, attracted thieves. When chased, the thieves comonly escaped down streets they knew better than their pursuers. Slipping unnoticed into the homes of their protectors (who reportedly were often eminent and official households), they rarely ended up in a magistrate's court.[131]

Over the latter half of the Ming, four qualitative changes in the practice of crime threatened visitors and residents of Suzhou and other delta cities. First, crime, at least recorded urban crime, became more violent. Although the Ming government banned virtually everyone, including soldiers, from carrying a weapon inside a city,[132] the expressive terms "bare sticks" and "staff holders" are attached to descriptions of criminals far more often in the late than in the mid Ming. In fact, by 1615 "bare sticks" were said to "be everywhere and the greatest number is in Suzhou and Changzhou."[133] Second, economic conflicts begot crime more frequently, as when weavers are reported to have robbed from a former employer (though it is hard to believe this is

---

[130] Marmé, *Suzhou*, 221–30.
[131] Jiang Liangdong, *ZhenWu lu*, tiaoyi, tiaochen, 2a–ff; Wu Kuan, *Paoweng jiacang ji*, 38.13b.
[132] Nimick, *Local Administration*, 146.   [133] Xu Sanxing, *Jiaozi liyan*, 2.13a.

the first instance).¹³⁴ Huizhou merchants, as the archetypical rich merchant outsiders, would have been prime targets.¹³⁵

Third, according to this report of Military Commander Jiang Liangdong 姜良棟, criminals were now commonly organized into groups and were operating in gangs called "professional beaters" (*dahang* 打行), composed of a leader and followers drawn from the ranks of part-time government postal station troops:

> There are some men who live near the postal stations and are not registered with officials for labor service charges. Called the Group Heads (*gangtou* 綱頭), they summon bands of unregistered "stick holders" from all directions, and they rear them at home in order to respond to [government] labor service assignments (*fuchai* 服差). The laborers, when their assignment is over, frequently stay at the place of the head of the labor service group who pays for their work with food. When they have a free day, he guides them around the city streets and markets in pickpocketing and snipping off silk purses. At night on the river they break open the holds of ships, or on land they bore through walls, obtain the wealth [therein], and divide it up for their use ... Each Group Head collects and rears unregistered "stick holders," and they are at his house for food and lodging. At dawn they leave the house, and at twilight they go [back] into it. How is it that he does not know what they are doing? He not only greedily plans to encroach on their work pay but also wishes to take a share of the spoils of their thievery without personally participating.

These troops were still part-time criminals, since often they also are engaged in other, more conventional kinds of government labor assignments, such as dragging official boats on the Grand Canal.¹³⁶ The thievery is sometimes actively directed by a boss, and at other times knowingly overlooked by him. But in each reported case the boss, regardless of the degree of his involvement, expected a share of the loot.

Fourth, some gang bosses, as is evident from an early seventeenth-century criminal case from the nearby delta county of Danyang 丹陽,

---

¹³⁴ Qi Biaojia, *Qi Biaojia wengao*, 646-ff.
¹³⁵ See the comments about pawnshop raids in late Ming Suzhou in Chapter 4 below. Also, *Huizhou qiannian*, v. 21, 128 29, reveals the sums of silver reported as stolen from pawnshops in Changshu county, Suzhou, at the end of the seventeenth century – over 200 taels and then over 500 taels in 1693 – were far greater than those reported for Suzhou in the *Yanyü gao* two centuries earlier.
¹³⁶ Jiang Liangdong, *ZhenWu lu*, tiaoyi, 7a, 23a, 23b.

were local traders themselves. As an urban merchant heading a gang of low-class thieves, a certain Zhao Er (fl. 1585–1617) hatched a break-in plot, discussed it with a colleague, contacted other criminals, sent them all off to commit the crime, and then received a share of the loot without having to leave his house. As the host of a criminal lair, he guarded the pickings of another robbery taken by henchmen who apparently had not consulted him (that is, one of his underlings led fellow gang members and other robbers and apparently escaped retaliation for acting independently of his boss's supervision). As a household head, Zhao Er took a young man into his establishment to be his "adopted son" (*yi'nan* 義男), or bondservant, for thirty-two years in his lair of "artful dodgers."[137] And, when he was not busy with crime, his work as a local merchant provided him with many opportunities for a quiet disposal of his share of the booty.

Criminal life in nearby Hangzhou underwent a similar professionalization in the late Ming. The regular members of its gangs are said to have met daily with their boss to share information and discuss their next blackmail job:

Separately they went and hunted out information about local conditions. Once they got an order, those who would die would sometimes be their kinfolk. Sometimes they would present local reports; sometimes they concocted hard-to-refute evidence. They would violently demand wine and food and wealth from people, and if [what they received] was even just slightly insufficient, they would carry out a public beating.[138]

By the 1630s and early 1640s the incidence of crime in Suzhou city by organized gangs and ordinary people had significantly risen. The reports written in 1633–34 by Qi Biaojia 祁彪佳, then the Grand Coordinator for Suzhou and the rest of the northeast quarter of the lower Yangzi delta, make this judgment credible with a wealth of detailed criminal statistics rarely found in premodern Chinese sources. In just six months Qi handled the files of some 1,500 serious crimes, including the review of seventy-seven capital-punishment sentences initially passed between the seventh day of the eleventh lunar month of 1632 and the seventh day of the eleventh lunar month of 1633 (a total of 1,192 men and women in his jails were awaiting execution for

---

[137] McDermott, *Making*, v. 1, 250, for a discussion of *yinan* in Huizhou villages.
[138] *Hangzhou fuzhi* (1579), 19.11a.

unspecified crimes). Theft remained a common problem – over 820 persons were in this area's jails for burglary and at least three of Qi's twenty-two bans in 1633 concerned theft and robbery. Criminal gangs were also reported to be admitting more members and adopting ever more flagrantly outrageous names to frighten their victims into submission. They might be headed by migrants from Shandong who in one case led over fifty men in a particularly violent attack (bows and arrows, knives, and metal spears) on a wealthy pawnbroker's house in Suzhou. Or they might flee south into Zhejiang or north across the Yangzi, escaping their government pursuers.[139] To underline the seriousness of urban crime and his office's resolve to suppress it, Qi in despair ordered the arrest of four Suzhou men. All four were inveterate scoundrels but two were targeted for particular opprobrium for having either murdered a mother or acted like an official to sway others to his majesty. After consulting with "gentry, scholars, and commoners" at the Xuanmiao shrine 玄妙觀 in the center of the city, he had them all publicly executed and their corpses exhibited in the marketplace "to the delight of all."[140]

Eight years later, Qi remained fearful of social disorder. In late 1641 he wrote ominously about the practice of door-to-door extortion in the Lou Gate area of northeast Suzhou,[141] and half a year on he revealed the "bad staves'" illegal dealing with sojourning merchants in the western suburbs:

The entire stretch of land at Maple Bridge is a district where big boats come and go and a place where all things converge. Merchants clutching valuable goods come from afar, all wanting to turn their exceptional objects into profits. Recently I have learned that there are some "bad staves," who view lonely merchants as flesh [to chew on] and rely on the sojourning merchants' (*keshang*) goods to be their profit. If they monopolize the market and carry out trade, they use coercion to buy at reduced prices. They rely on bullying.[142]

In other words, by the late Ming a world of crime and criminals, however defined, had emerged in Suzhou and, by extension, other cities of the delta to pose to long-distance merchants threats as

---

[139] Qi Biaojia, *Qi Biaojia wengao*, 151–56, 601, 626, 627–28, 621, 148.
[140] Ye Shaoyuan, *Qi Zhen*, 2.1a; *Suzhou fuzhi* (1691), 81.45b–46a; Wang Siren, *Qi Zhongmin gong nianpu*, 136.
[141] Huang Xixian, *FuWu xilüe*, 7.21a.   [142] Ibid., 1.70a.

persistent as those that had confronted them on the Yangzi and its tributaries. Theft, common by the mid Ming, had become even more so. The size and organization of criminal groups had grown, and their activities extended from within the city walls of Suzhou to its surrounding countryside and even more distant parts. Most importantly for our purposes, the long-distance merchants, and of course Huizhou merchants in particular, had become a target of attack.[143]

Against this resourceful criminal world, outside merchants seem to have had few Suzhou organizations they could reliably turn to for help. Government protection at all levels remained woefully ineffective. The size of the Suzhou yamen's personnel staff – a total of 1,500 men working in the one prefectural yamen and total of approximately 2,500 others in its two county yamens – underlines the inadequacy of government resources for looking after this city of half a million people and a crowded countryside stretching tens of miles from its walls. In the immediate wake of the mid-sixteenth-century *wakō* invasions of Suzhou, the situation was particularly serious:

> The marketplaces were deserted, all [respectable people] shutting their doors and going into hiding. Those who came from afar were compelled to abandon what they had brought [without compensation] and did not pursue the matter. The leaders all were known by name and native place inside the city and outside it. Yamen underlings and the apprentices of butchers and shopkeepers were all in league with them. Even offspring of good families were often involved.[144]

Though this weak local support for the government was doubtless linked to Suzhou's exceptionally heavy tax quotas, few officials would have predicted that when Suzhou prefecture sought to bolster its defenses against pirates, some of the "martial braves" who had responded to its summons for defense of the city would then spend their daytime rampaging in its streets and their nighttime robbing prisoners in the jails and setting afire government and military offices near Feng Gate.[145] Not surprisingly, then, both city and countryside acquired a reputation for being litigious and poorly ruled. Out of the

---

[143] Liu Shijun, *Wusuo Liu xiansheng*, 487–95. Other legal cases here deal with bandit raids on merchants traveling in the late Ming delta.
[144] Marmé, *Suzhou*, 227–28.
[145] *Suzhou fuzhi* (1691), 81.33a. Some of these braves were eventually arrested on Lake Tai.

several thousand sheets of charges presented to the yamen during every period of court hearings, just one or two ended up being investigated.[146]

And, in the crowded neighborhoods of Suzhou city, crisscrossed by a labyrinth of creeks and alleyways that confounded any policing efforts, the military presence remained weak. A quota of 5,600 troops in five battalions stationed largely at Suzhou's city gates at the start of the Ming soon became a reported 4,480 soldiers.[147] Over the course of the sixteenth century, despite the pirate raids, their number declined, prompting the region's leading military official in c.1607 to call for the government to meet its quota.[148] He even hoped to expand its military protection in order to provide adequate neighborhood patrols and nighttime policing.[149] This official, recognizing the shortage of suitable men, expressed a willingness to find this manpower in the ranks of the local criminal gangs, whose criminal record concealed, he maintained, "good hearts."[150] He blithely ignored reports that soldiers' ranks in Suzhou were infiltrated by "many local criminals and market staff," some of whom had been sentenced to obligatory military service. A couple of decades later its soldiers were condemned by other officials for a long list of crimes, such as extorting extra charges from merchant boats, ignoring the boundary lines of garrisons, and clashing with civilians.[151]

Most often, soldiers without a criminal record stealthily used their army position to form criminal gangs and associations within their garrison. Some became strong enough to dominate their garrison superiors, initiating legal charges against them and even forcing these superiors to leave the garrison.[152] When Qi Biaojia launched a

[146] Huang Xixian, *FuWu xilüe*, 7.31a; the date is 1642. Serious crimes like robbery and murder could be reported any time; less serious crimes and civil plaints were to be submitted on the third, sixth, and ninth day of each of the three ten-day periods that made up a traditional lunar month. Nimick, *Local Administration*, 100, 111.
[147] Marmé, *Suzhou*, 35; *GuSu zhi* (1506), 25.1a–b. Garrisons elsewhere in the prefecture were smaller, except for Taicang (whose garrison troops numbered 11,200 in the early Ming).
[148] *GuSu zhi* (1506), 25.1a–b.
[149] Jiang Liangdong, *ZhenWu lu*, tiaoyi, 7a–11b, and tiaochen, 3a.
[150] Ibid., tiaoyi, 11a.
[151] Qi Biaojia, *Qi Biaojia wengao*, 614. For slightly later bans on soldier misbehavior, see Huang Xixian, *FuWu xilüe*, 4.18a–b.
[152] Qi Biaojia, *Qi Biaojia wengao*, 616.

campaign to arrest disrupters of the Suzhou market, some of the culprits slipped off into these garrisons, to be protected by garrison heads and others with whom they had long before forged close ties.[153] Such was their power that of all the officials informed of their ruse, only one, Qi, is known to have directly countered these criminals. He issued five bans on a wide range of their offenses: the coerced purchase of goods for cheap prices, rape, gambling, theft, prostitution, the spread of false rumors, the murder of innocent commoners under the pretence that they were thieves, and disobedience of their commanders' orders to fight.[154] In 1639 they were still actively committing these crimes, with soldiers on tax delivery boats being described as "often robbers, who carry out raids and kill people."[155]

A large part of these soldiers' grievance derived from their paltry pay,[156] which Suzhou's garrison officials and overseer generals were not above pocketing for themselves.[157] Not surprisingly, the troops spent their time devising ways to secure a living outside the confines of their garrison. Even when they took up manual labor as, for instance, porters,[158] crime could have remained attractive. Suzhou provided an endless array of opportunities, and a nighttime career of crime would have been relatively safe since they quite possibly knew their potential arrestors. Suzhou soldiers, as already noted, had acted as the stormtroops for the first groups of professional beaters, and they retained such ties to escape punishment for their crimes. Sometimes they directly approached rich but weak households (that is, those lacking a degree or close ties to an official household) and pressed them to hand over their property. Other times they closed up a house and then demanded payment before allowing it to be reopened.[159] But perhaps most often, government soldiers in Suzhou posed problems simply by their refusal to catch bandits, knowing from experience that a common reward for making an arrest would be compounded trouble for themselves.[160] Under these circumstances,

---

[153] Ibid.; and Wang Siren, *Qi Zhongmin gong nianpu*, 136.
[154] Huang Xixian, *FuWu xilüe*, 4.18a.   [155] Ye Shaoyuan, *Qi Zhen*, 2.4a.
[156] Jiang Liangdong, *ZhenWu lu*, tiaoyi, 10a–11a.
[157] Ibid., tiaochen, 9b; Qi Biaojia, *Qi Biaojia wengao*, 615.
[158] Cortes, *Le voyage en Chine*, 241, on urban-based soldiers driven by poverty to undertake additional work, like porterage and guarding.
[159] Wang Siren, *Qi Zhongmin gong nianpu*, 136.
[160] Ibid.; Jiang Liangdong, *ZhenWu lu*, tiaoyi, 11b.

even soldiers free of a criminal past or of payoffs from criminals could not have halted the spread of crime.[161]

Furthermore, neighborhood patrols manned by registered commoner households failed at their assignments. As in the countryside, the heads of these households were drafted into labor service units that took turns to patrol their neighborhood's streets at night, arrest criminals, and hand them (female criminals appear few) over to yamen personnel.[162] Local residents' discontent with this arrangement was expressed throughout the sixteenth century, but only at the century's close did the Suzhou government take serious action. In the city's wards it established a total of sixty-one police boxes, each manned by five adult men, explicitly to prevent outbreaks of fire and to arrest criminals.[163] Finally, neighborhood policing units assigned from official *baojia* units often ended up undermanned. Far too few commoners were included in the government's *baojia* membership registers. Not only were immigrants to Suzhou (even if from nearby villages) not registered under their new urban address, but also a strikingly high percentage – three-quarters of the city's registered households – were legally exempt from performing this *baojia* policing duty thanks to their employment by or service for the local or imperial government in other capacities.[164] Consequently, in the damning judgment of a military commissioner in the opening years of the seventeenth century, crime in Suzhou city was virtually uncheckable. The city had become "a metropolis where the shiftless and the rootless types, the gangs with their different speech and different clothing, all put their feet down and secretly settle in."[165] Clichés, yes, but their use here and elsewhere underlines the concern that many late Ming officials shared with locals

---

[161] *GuSu zhi* (1506), 25.1a–b; Jiang Liangdong, *ZhenWu lu*, tiaoyi, 11a, and tiaochen, 3a.
[162] Ibid., tiaoyi, 8a–b.
[163] Ibid., tiaoyi, 1a–2b, 8b–9a. McKnight, *Law and Order*, 283–320, and "Urban Crime," 23–66, describe similar problems and practices in Song dynasty cities.
[164] Jiang Liangdong, *ZhenWu lu*, tiaochen, 2a: "Seventy or eighty percent of [the registered households of] Suzhou city were gentry, licentiates, district degree holders (*shengyuan* 生員), prefects and magistrates, assistant prefects and magistrates, clerks, and those privileged with exemption from *lijia* service." In other words, even in its late Ming rush of commercial and industrial development, Suzhou city remained predominantly a major center of government activity and administration.
[165] Jiang Liangdong, *ZhenWu lu*, 1st *ce*, 2b, and tiaochen, 2a–3a, 9b, 11a, 11b–12a.

about a sharp spike in crime and especially violent, seemingly irrational crime.

Reforms for city policing and security subsequently undertaken at the Grand Co-ordinator's initiative in the early seventeenth century had local garrison soldiers replace the nighttime civilian *baojia* patrols; look after law and order in five specific areas of the city; patrol the city's wall, moat, and canals; and receive better reward and remuneration.[166] Street barricades were commonly erected for regular closure at night, and a nighttime curfew was in effect from the end of the second watch.

But still the city's neighborhood control organization worked fitfully, at best. Its policing units were too loosely co-ordinated, its residences in the poorer areas overrun by a huge mobile population and the large intake of "rascals and vagabonds" (*wulai*).[167] Its patrolmen remained too few, too poorly paid, and, at night, all too often asleep. The increased incidence of crime, particularly theft, prompted the local governments in Suzhou and elsewhere in the delta to expand the size and number of their jails.[168]

Less than three years after these reforms had been implemented, "layabouts in the city amassed into crowds and ransacked from street to street." The initiator of these reforms, still a Grand Co-ordinator, was reduced to rounding up the culprits and having three of them whipped and executed, in order to frighten away their followers and the potential crowds of onlookers.[169] It is clear, then, that although the government's soldiers or policemen, plus those commoners obliged to perform nighttime patrols inside the city, held power over a wide variety of local activities, they could not, particularly at night, assure the city's residents and visitors of secure public space less than half a mile from government offices. Even less could they remove all disruptive parties from canal wharves, creeks, and backstreets, where Huizhou and other outsider merchants arrived and stored their goods, usually in the northwest suburbs along the Grand Canal.

Some communities in the delta took drastic steps, perhaps none more so than the residents of one town fifteen miles southeast of Suzhou city. Already during the Wanli era they had filled up part of

---

[166] Ibid., *passim*.
[167] Ibid., tiaoyi, 1a–14b, and tiaochen, 2a–3a, 9b, 11a, 11b–12a.
[168] Hamashima, "Min Shin," 1–60, esp. 3–16.
[169] Ibid., 1a–2b, 8b–9a; *Wu xianzhi* (1642), 11.44b.

the creek that connected them to trading channels elsewhere, simply to block the robbers' easy entry and escape by boat.[170] Others followed government orders in 1625 to revive the local *baojjia* units. Bolstered with the rules of a community pact, the twelve families in each of these urban units were to take monthly turns reporting on suspicious characters hanging about or coming and going for unclear reasons, the appearance of implements that ought not to be used, and "the unfilial and the unbrotherly." A local military official also warned against abuse of the city's poorer residents by powerful families anxious to guard their houses against fire and by government staff out to extract another levy.[171]

In sum, even if we dismiss the statistics we have on Suzhou crime – I personally see no persuasive reason to do so – other Ming records unquestionably show a heightened concern about crime there over the last century of Ming rule. A sojourning merchant arriving there may have initially expected a place of refuge from the disorders on the Yangzi where the state barely pretended to have a presence. But he would have soon learned of this city's less salubrious side, in which the state tolerated, if not fostered, this disorder and members of its "informal government" were involved in the criminal scene. The consequent spread of fear would have alarmed many merchants and, as we shall see, made them anxious to find ways to protect themselves and their possessions.

The Urban Travails of a Long-Distance Merchant: Market Obstructions and Risks Faced by Merchants in Suzhou

Sojourning merchants were favorite targets for these attacks, partly because they were thought to be rich and partly because their shops and wealth were widely known to enjoy a large tax exemption thanks to a loophole in Ming administrative practice. By law, all households

---

[170] Qi Biaojia, *Qi Biaojia wengao*, 149. Wang Rigen and Cao Bin, *Ming Qing hehaidao*, 19–53, contains many reports of pirate-fishermen attacks on commercial vessels inside the delta in the second half of the Ming and the early Qing. Government control over the delta's labyrinthine waterways was arguably never secure, as the delta's criminal underworld coexisted and spread along with normal shipping operations on these waterways, including the Grand Canal.

[171] *Suzhou fuzhi* (1691), 81.39b–40a.

were to be registered by the government and registered at only one place, typically the place where their parents had been registered and where they would be included in a *lijia* unit for local control. Hence their land and other assets were to be registered and taxed there and only there. The early Ming government assumed that it had severely crippled their movements and numbers, and so apart from a low customs charge and brokerage fee the Ming's rigid tax regime unintentionally released outsider merchants from taxes on their trading profits and wealth away from home. Since Huizhou merchants (and probably other regions' merchants) tended to own no fields in the delta (and precious little back in Huizhou), they were exempt from the delta's onerous land and labor service charges. This loophole survived the imposition of the Single Whip tax reform and sharp criticisms made towards the end of the sixteenth century. And so the arrival then of ever greater numbers of Huizhou merchants in the delta's larger cities proved particularly galling to these cities' taxpaying households. In short, contrary to official rhetoric, traveling merchants in the Ming faced far lower tax levels on their income than did landowners, landlords, and others living off the land in the delta, and by the late sixteenth century the irregular levies imposed on merchants by local governments in Suzhou and elsewhere were too light to abate these resentments.[172]

This animosity in Ming Suzhou was directed against two types of outsider merchants, many from Huizhou: the pawnbrokers and the long-distance traders. Of the two, pawnbrokers were particularly vulnerable to attack, because they were thought to have brought only money to the delta simply to make more money at the delta's expense.[173] Especially when many pawnbrokers closed down their shops for self-protection during severe famines like that of 1588, the pawnshop became a common target of attack in fact as well as in fiction[174] (it was considered a place where thieves could unload their

---

[172] These problems also troubled Hangzhou (Fuma, "Late Ming Urban Reform and the Popular Uprising in Hangzhou," 47–97; Fujii, "Shin'an shōnin no kenkyū," 36.3, 72) and Nanjing (Si-yan Fei, *Negotiating Urban Space*, 222–36).
[173] See Chapter 4 below.
[174] *Dianshang*, 259, 279, 297; Zhou Kongjiao, *Qiuhuang yi*, 9, on harsh punishments for robbers.

loot without being seriously questioned).[175] By the early seventeenth century, these pawnbrokers' tax privilege was being criticized in local officials' reports. The Suzhou prefect Liu Shaoyi in c.1609 claimed that Huizhou pawnshop owners had in the previous year not only escaped land and income taxes but also 70 percent of the other taxes they normally should pay for salt sales and transport.

His successor as prefect submitted an even sharper denunciation of the sojourning merchants' pawnshops, attributing the city's gross inequalities and social discord to the government's failure to tax them adequately:

> When commoner families have real estate (*hengchan* 恒產), they pay taxes on it. The time they spend rushing about to visit government offices [to pay taxes] is very great and, moreover, painful. Yet it is not so at all for a traveler's (*lüren* 旅人) pawnshop. The funds they employ are very considerable, the profits they take in are very abundant, and their operations also are very leisurely. But their names are not written into [government] household registers and maps of landownership (*guaban tu* 挂版圖), and their business does not get caught up in taxes. How is it, then, that they have so many pleasures and to such a great degree? …
>
> At year's end the [commoner landowners] go running about paying taxes, and their funds for tax payments never suffice. Meanwhile, the pawnbrokers sit back, leaning on high pillows, and their income from interest payments doubles their original capital. In short, when interest is again turned into capital, yet again they make interest on it … And so, their yearly taxes barely amount to several taels of silver. Thus, few of the rich houses accumulate property over successive generations, while the pawnbrokers have property (*ye*) for many centuries. In the course of ten years changes [in landownership] are made to the maps of the land registers anywhere from three or four times to as many as six or seven, while [the capital holdings of] the pawnshops, regardless of whether they are small or large, invariably increase. In three years they once get back [from interest payments] the whole amount [of loaned capital].[176]

Despite the pawnshops' wealth and the dynasty's dire finances the tax quota set eventually in 1623 remained surprisingly low.[177] Even in the

---

[175] *Dianshang*, 285, 288.
[176] Liu Shaoyi, *Huangzhu lüe*, 5, 7. Liu implies an annual interest rate of roughly 30 percent, and his "traveler" surely indicates an itinerant merchant.
[177] The annual tax rate was set then at fifty taels for first-rank shops (having capital assets of 10,000 taels or more), forty taels for second-rank shops (having capital assets of 7,000 to 8,000 taels), thirty taels for third-rank (having capital

late seventeenth century, when pawnbrokers routinely and loudly complained of heavy taxes, a Huizhou native acknowledged that Huizhou pawnbrokers were actually paying only a few taels as tax on however "many tens of thousands of taels" they held as capital assets.[178]

Huizhou commodity traders did not suffer the same level of distrust and dislike, yet from the moment of their docking at the wharves of Suzhou and other delta towns and cities they faced numerous obstacles.[179] As long-distance outsider merchants, they had to negotiate with local intermediaries – such as clerks, porters, and brokers. Assigned and hired to facilitate trade, these locals seem equally interested in obstructing transactions by outsider merchants. As locals, some partly and others fully in the employ of local government offices, they are said in the Wanli era and later to have formed gangs and run protection rackets that greatly troubled the city's traders (as well as many of the city's other visitors and residents). Often cloaking their protection charges under the guise of legitimate government levies or customary duties, they acted as members of what I have elsewhere termed "the informal government," consisting of groups operating under the ostensible authority of the formal local government.[180] Whereas their official superiors were assigned by the central government to rule as outsiders over counties and prefectures new to them, these low-ranked, low-paid government employees and hangers-on represented the disreputable face of local government that ordinary residents and visitors to the city were long acquainted with and usually longed to avoid.[181] These yamen employees and hangers-on tended to

assets of 5,000 to 6,000 taels), twenty taels for fourth-rank shops (having capital assets of 3,000 to 4,000 taels) and ten taels for fifth-rank shops (having capital assets of 1,000 to 2,000 taels). Also, note that from 1582, Beijing's two county yamens were allowed to form trade associations (*hang*) for all their pawnshops (as well as textile and grain firms) having 300 to 1,000 taels of capital; less capitalized shops were excluded. Xu Dixin and Wu Chengming, *Zhongguo zibenzhuyi*, v. 1, 135.

[178] Peng Xinwei, *Zhongguo huobi shi*, 745; MQHS, 158; Abe, *Shindai*, 373. Presumably, they paid taxes for any urban real estate registered under their name.

[179] Fan Jinmin, *Fushui jia tianxia*, 313–40, provides much detail on individual Huizhou merchants who traded in Jiangnan, especially Suzhou.

[180] This situation is detailed in McDermott, "Urban Order of Ming Suzhou."

[181] The late imperial broker's job and its structural contradictions bear an uncanny resemblance to the workings of the compradore system that handled foreign

Risks in Ming Suzhou 169

view their yamen position, however lowly, as a license to do as they wished, committing a great variety of largely minor offences, that ranged from overcharging shops and taxpayers and creaming off extra yamen funds to practicing extortion and blackmail on fellow commoners. Pressing legal charges successfully against such entrenched figures was difficult for locals; for outsiders like Huizhou merchants, this recourse would have been far harder.

For these outsiders a persistent minor obstacle was the transport service provided by stevedores and other porters. Coming often from the ranks of lowly soldiers, porters in Suzhou commonly took on their part-time work to supplement their income.[182] By the late Ming, groups of them felt powerful enough to form their own private "guilds of beaters" (*dahang* 打行), or thuggish groups of labor brokers, who, among other things, tended to decide which porters had the prerogative to work in which neighborhood.[183] In monopolizing all porterage work in these "turfs," be it for shifting goods from one boat to another and from boats to warehouses and markets, or for carrying a sedan chair for marriages and a coffin for funerals, they assured that anyone encroaching on their turf and work suffered harsh verbal and physical abuse.[184] Outside Suzhou's northeast gate, for instance, a group of porters monopolized the unloading of

---

traders in Qing China. It is as if Chinese officials' toleration of Western trade was achieved through its extension to Westerners of a system that it had originally designed for the domestic trade and that in fact expected locals to protect local interests with silent government approval.

[182] Cortes, *Le voyage en Chine*, 241. This hired-laborer relationship could be contractual, and thereby impose certain perhaps unexpected responsibilities on the porter, as specified in what is considered a late Ming contract form: "Mr So-and-So, as the man who sets up a written contract for hiring a porter, now takes himself and goes to someone under the name of the sojourning merchant, Mr So-and-So, with a certain amount of such and such goods and is to carry them to such and such a place to hand them over. The three parties [i.e., merchant, porter, and go-between] fix a wage agreement of a certain amount of silver. After he goes on the road, he will look after the goods with total concentration. If there is any delay or loss, then the porter recognizes that he will compensate by repayment. If this man does not arrive [with the goods], then he will be content to use his own silver to pay another to deliver them. Now fearing there is nothing to rely on, we set this contract up as evidence." Niida, *Chūgoku hōseishi kenkyū*, v. 3, 809. Note that this contract allows for prepayment and use of a labor broker, or middleman.

[183] Qi Biaojia, *Qi Biaojia wengao*, 619.

[184] Ueda, "Ryūkako monogatari," 10–22, 30–31.

charcoal from the numerous boats docking there,[185] while two other families extracted payment from porters and boats for the passage of any goods under and over the bridges that they lorded over.[186] By and large, all these informal groups of workers with presumably hereditary jobs carried out "squeeze operations" with considerable autonomy for much of the second half of the Ming. In the 1630s Qi Biaojia speaks of their forming overarching collective associations (*hui*) with names like those of the professional beaters' groups, such as the Wooden Clubs of the Chinese Ilex (*Dongqing bangjian*) and the Reunion of a Hundred Kids (*Baizi tuanyuan* 百子團圓).[187] In the city of Hangzhou, similar turf arrangements prevailed for porters' work from at least the late Ming through the 1660s: "Coroners and others privately set up labor contractors (*batou* 把頭), and divided up the urban quarters. A daily charge for carrying a coffin was extortionately levied and deceitfully coerced, sometimes costing up to several tens of taels of silver. Still [the payments] never satisfied their wishes."[188]

Far more damaging to traveling merchants, however, were local brokers, men who functioned as the main interface between traveling merchants and the local government and other merchants.[189] They

[185] Ibid., 12, 14, 34 n.14 and n.17.   [186] Ibid.
[187] Qi Biaojia, *Qi Biaojia wengao*, 621.
[188] *Renhe xianzhi* (1687), 13.31a. Qing records on this delta custom are far more detailed, presumably because it became controversial. *Jiading xianzhi* (1673), 4, fengsu, reports on private brokers manipulating prices and squeezing both buyers and sellers: "They link up with local thugs and snatch raw cotton from those trading and selling it." *Luodian zhenzhi* (1879), 1, fengsu, reports similar practices for its own market's porters, drummers, sedan chair carriers, and entertainers, each protecting his own turf and pressing charges and threats on any violators. Even when shops wanted goods brought into the town, they had to follow this local labor practice or face trouble, despite official government proscription of the practice in 1681. For further instances, see Fan Shuzhi, *Ming Qing Jiangnan shizhen chuantong de bianqe*, 584–87; Yokoyama Suguru, "Shindai Kōseishō," 49–89. Wood, *Sketches*, 177–78, observes these protectionist practices by coolies in early nineteenth-century Canton: "Regular stands are appointed for these coolies at the corners of particular streets, where they take their turns, regulated by a kind of overseer. They are very tenacious of their right, and fights frequently take place between them and private coolies, who attempt to remove [sic] boxes from home to home, and in some of these engagements serious accidents have occurred from the tremendous blows inflicted by bamboos [which they used to carry boxes and other material]."
[189] For insightful accounts on brokers and marketplace operations in the late Ming and Qing, see the writings of Peng Qiusheng, including his *Dang falü yu shang*

were expected to help a traveling merchant find potential buyers for his goods and then locate someone willing to sell this same merchant goods he wanted to leave with. Consequently, the broker routinely collected trade information, made and received payments, and pushed people to fulfil their promises and complete their contracts. He provided itinerant merchants access to wharves and other merchant trading spots, introduced shippers with goods to local junk operators willing to transport goods to other local sites for sale or resale, and helped to negotiate a market price range for various commodities. He also could be paid to handle taxes for his merchant clients, be asked to extract market entrance fees from market outsiders (sometimes including peasants peddling vegetables), and collect commercial transaction taxes and other charges for the government. And, if that were not enough, he also might be expected to find suitable lodging for a visiting merchant, a warehouse for his cargo, and a reservation on a departing boat. According to Wang Shixin and Hu Tieqiu, the broker could provide such services, since he commonly ran not just a brokerage but also storage depots, hostels, and even shops that made him

---

jingji, 209–17; "Yu Suzhou," 37–91; "Suzhou cheng gongshangye," 83–90; and "Yu shichan," 291–334. Also insightful are Zheng Xiaowen, "Shilun Ming Qing," 43–45; and Watson, *Transport in Transition*, which contains translations of unrivaled firsthand Japanese reports of the late imperial shipping brokerage system, especially in Suzhou, towards the end of its practice. Its account of the financing of this set of services in all likelihood held generally true of lower-level brokers and transactions in the late Ming and the Qing, when Suzhou and not Shanghai was the center of trade and finance in the delta: "The owner of a shipping broker[age] (*dianzhu* 店主) is usually an ex-boatman with a thorough knowledge of the junk industry. He has low capital requirements since he does not carry out any subsidiary undertakings. Small amounts of from twenty to thirty *yuan* can be borrowed from relatives and friends without interest and be quickly repaid. Usually brokers do not borrow from usurers or merchants. On the other hand, they advance small amounts of from four to thirty yuan to boatmen as a means of maintaining close relations. Such short-term, interest-free loans are usually orally contracted. The settlement of these advances is made by subtraction from the transport charge at the time of settling the transport account." Ibid., 38. In at least north China his commission charge was 2 percent of the negotiated sale price. Xu Dixin and Wu Chengming, *Zhongguo zibenzhuyi, v. 1*, 111, claims that to make a loan, one needed to go through an official broker; unless the broker was the go-between or guarantor mentioned in such loans, I confess to having never seen any mention of official brokers in Ming loan contracts; the practice also is not specified in the few Ming laws on contracts.

indispensable to an outsider merchant's success.[190] The growth of commerce and demand for professional services assured that the number of such brokers increased dramatically. Late Ming Yangzhou, to cite just one delta city, had many thousands of these brokers.[191] As Susan Mann showed for Qing China, the growth of these services brought brokers into numerous stages and levels of transactions, as there was "a brokerage for every pocketbook."[192]

And, some feared, in every pocket. For by extending their services beyond simple brokering, these men had incurred strong criticism and faced legal restraints since at least the Song.[193] Indeed, the first Ming emperor so distrusted them and other market middlemen that at the start of his reign (1368–98) he prohibited brokers, the official (*guanya* 官牙) as well as the private variety (*siya* 私牙), from operating in all markets of his empire.[194] He ruled that all trade instead be handled through government-operated or -supervised offices.[195]

Yet his very early Ming ban proved unworkable, leading to his reversal of this policy in 1397. Henceforth, the Ming tolerated brokers, so long as they received an official permit (which every seven years they had to renew at the local yamen for a fee), owned local property that could serve as collateral, recorded every month all their transactions in yamen-issued registers, and annually paid a tax on all their transactions.[196] In the second half of the fifteenth century, a Suzhou

---

[190] Hu Tieqiu, "Ming Qing maoyi," 144–53; Wang Shixin, "Ming Qing shiqi," 20–21.
[191] Han Dacheng, "Mingdai Huishang," 41–42. Figures for registered official brokers in Suzhou survive only from the Qing, and rise from the Kangxi era onward.
[192] Mann, *Local Merchants*, 64–65.
[193] Li Yuanbi, *Zuoyi zizhen*, 7.38a–b, required brokers to deal only in taxed goods and use a contract for any purchase on credit. The local government also banned their obstruction of direct dealings between buyers and sellers, price inflation, and prolongation of sale transactions.
[194] Shen Shixing, (*Wanli*) *Ming huidian*, 35, 255.
[195] Hu Tieqi, *Ming Qing xiejia*, 56.
[196] Xu Pu, *Da Ming huidian* (1503 ed.), 135.14b–16a, for this and other statutes on the market, which, it is claimed here, derive from the *Da Minglü*, itself issued throughout the empire in 1397 (Hu Tieqi, *Ming Qing xiejia*, 57; hence Hu's claim that this revision dates from no later than 1397). The extent to which the broker relied on written contracts for these transactions is unclear, though I suspect the state desired every broker (and his word) to substitute for the written contract and thus prevent a blockage of the law courts with disputes over commercial transactions. In other words, the persistence of the broker in

commoner is thus recorded to have taken "comprehensive charge of merchant capital (*shanggu ziben* 商賈資本) and scattered it to loom workers (*jizhujia* 機杼家)." Yet these requirements for becoming "official brokers" failed to win over some of the previous illegitimate brokers, unregistered newcomers, and some sons of "official brokers," all of whom were now denigrated as "private brokers" (*siya*). Other government bans on arbitrary weight measures, market bullying, price manipulation, and brokers' engagement in their own private sales suffered similar disregard. They were hard to enforce and disrupted markets as much as the "abuses" of private traders and brokers. Private brokers also found it more useful to substitute the official brokers' license fee with private payments to yamen employees.[197]

Unfortunately, no documents survive of actual transactions between a broker and a long-distance Huizhou merchant in Ming Suzhou or elsewhere. But some mid-sixteenth-century letters concerned with Japanese merchants' negotiations with a Chinese broker in the coastal port of Ningbo suggest how an outsider Chinese merchant might have negotiated with an official broker.[198] Each party is seen as deploying its bargaining advantages to win a contract. Upon arrival in Ningbo the Japanese were expected to provide a list of desired goods to a Chinese broker, who in return provided the Japanese with a "tender," or price list, for each requested item. When the broker's prices were judged too high, the Japanese side threatened to approach other brokers for alternative tenders. Nonetheless, much of this correspondence stresses these two parties' favorable past dealings with one another, as the Japanese appear to prefer to retain the same broker, so long as they feel he is not overcharging. They seem, then, at all stages before agreeing to a deal, to have the power to choose their broker.[199]

Chinese commercial exchanges up to our times reflects the state's permanent effort to delegitimize the involvement of another party, like independent lawyers, and thus to monopolize all decision-making and law enforcement in merchant matters.

[197] Huang Xixian, *FuWu xilüe*, 5.62a; Xu Dixin and Wu Chengming, *Zhongguo zibenzhuyi*, v. 1, 63; Qiu Pengsheng, *Dang falü yu shang jingji*, 1–54; Tang Lixing, *Shangren*, 15; Aramiya, "Mindai no gakō ni tsuite ," 848–52.

[198] Oláh, "Brokers, Officials, and Foreign Trade," 31–35. Oddly, nothing is said of how these merchants sold off their Japanese goods.

[199] We, of course, should not dismiss the likelihood that the Ningbo brokers had already collectively agreed to offer identical charges to visiting Japanese merchants, regardless of which broker they approached.

If foreigners, even disruptive foreign merchants like sixteenth-century Japanese, had such leeway in commercial negotiations, we can reasonably make two assumptions. First, Chinese merchants had a similar range of choice in selecting their broker at the start of negotiations, and second, their negotiations often entered second and third stages, when the merchant would bargain the broker's initial prices down to a mutually acceptable level (the seller might have been treated to similar negotiations by contending broker groups). If all this talk failed, then the seller as well as the buyer could approach another broker for an alternative tender or, highly unlikely, leave without a transaction.

The warning of the Hangzhou scholar Xu Sanxing 徐三省 to a merchant – "Only if the broker is practical, widely respected, and honest are you to rely on him" – voices the deep distrust many merchants had for their middleman. Fine brokers, Xu cautioned, are far fewer than the veteran "bare sticks," who linger at important junctions and at wharves in wait for a merchant naïve enough to believe their tales of nearby markets willing to pay inflated prices for his goods. Charging generously for their services, they "lead the duped trader off to empty markets, where they abandon him to a diet of rice gruel in a freezing room."[200]

Such charges against brokers' ethics, however valid, missed two more basic problems with these brokerages: their services were far too many and diverse for a single permit holder to handle adequately, and his multiplying commitments drew him increasingly into conflict with the interests of at least some of his clients. Under such circumstances his conflicting loyalties, not least to his own shops, companies, and loans, inevitably turned him into yet one additional interested party, whom other commercial interests regularly faulted for disguise and deceit.

Consequently, we can discern by the seventeenth century a division of labor taking place in brokerages. Transactions could involve any number of people working for different offices and persons in separate stages of a single complicated transaction. Moreover, a brokerage, official or private, authorized or unauthorized, might consist of more than the single adult party with a permit. It could constitute a family firm, headed by a family head with assistance from his sons, and then

---

[200] Xu Sanxing, *Jiaozi liyan*, 2.13a.

inherited by them as their joint-share partnership. Or the firm could originally be formed as a partnership (in which partners held both ownership and management roles and shared the year's profits or losses), or take the form of a company, financially backed by a partnership of several investors (who would not become involved in managing but would expect an annual share of the profits in terms of dividends). Obviously, family partnerships could form, whenever several sons inherited and did not break up their father's brokerage business. But, taken together, these brokerage groups, family-based or otherwise, could themselves constitute a brokerage guild (*yahang* 牙行) and therefore as brokers be surreptitiously paid to represent local commercial interests opposed to "nonlocal" long-distance merchants' intrusion into the local market.[201] No wonder that the "broker" might be appreciated by some as a Svengali of the marketplace and denounced by many others as a boss of crooks. To make matters worse, a broker had no legal authority to enforce agreements and contracts made under his prompting. Not only did he thus have a need, never authorized by the yamen, to forge close personal ties with local-government underlings, other members of the informal government, in order to assure their aid when buyers failed to pay and sellers failed to hand over their goods. But also, officialdom harbored a constant fear that he would use his central place in all these transactions to set up a fully private office of operations at its expense. Like matchmakers in the marriage market, Ming brokers were destined to be badmouthed by all contracting parties. And, at the same time, it was not uncommon for Suzhou brokers to hold a part-time job concurrently as a clerk or runner in a local yamen, often under another name.[202]

Acting within this competitive arena of conflicting interests, late Ming Suzhou's brokers had acquired a reputation for levying irregular charges, manipulating prices, and so fleecing sojourning merchants.[203]

---

[201] These arrangements represented examples of market manipulation that late imperial officials commonly denounced, probably because they were quite common in delta markets in the late Ming (Zheng Xiaowen, "Shilun Ming Qing yahang," 43–45).

[202] Hong Huanchun, *Ming Qing shi oucun*, 569–70.

[203] Huang Xixian, *FuWu xilüe*, 7.5a, 5.19a, 62a. Ye Shaoyuan, *Qi Zhen*, 2.10a, observes that one of these Hushu customs collectors was a member of the Ming imperial lineage; Kawakatsu, "Minmatsu Shinsho," 75, comments on "turf" practices in Songjiang prefecture in 1580.

By the 1630s, however, some brokerages were actually set up and staffed by "men with knives and staves" who conspired with porters, rascals, and vagrants to manipulate the movement of merchant goods. Criticized for defending only their own interests, they imposed on these itinerant merchants a commission fee of 10 to 20 percent, sometimes under threat of criminal violence.[204] Such collusion of market agents with both criminal and government forces was not restricted to local parties. It would be glaringly evident, as we shall see, in parallel conspiracies, that wealthy Huizhou merchant outsiders plotted with high provincial officials in the late Ming.

Merchant Recourse in Suzhou

The Ming legal code, of course, banned these and other market abuses. All coercive takeovers of a market, price manipulation, unauthorized work by private brokers, the sale of flimsy objects and frail textiles, the making and use of private measures for market transactions, and merchant collusion were from the early years of the dynasty branded crimes in general terms that quite likely pleased local officials.[205] Lacking sufficient resources to enforce these bans regularly, they would have appreciated the legal leeway that the vagueness of these bans afforded them. It let them rule as they saw fit on any specific occasion to achieve the statutes' main if unstated aim of ensuring that merchants continually remained concerned about the yamen's wishes.

Not surprisingly, then, Huizhou merchants, at least up to the late sixteenth century, seem to have preferred seeking recourse outside the law court to pressing charges inside it. And so they resorted to the same kind of nonpolitical and nonviolent tactics they were already deploying to thwart bandit threats on the Yangzi. If a heavy dose of prudence and patience failed to repel "local bullies" from inflicting theft and injury, then merchants might threaten to move elsewhere (just as they took

---

[204] Qi Biaojia, *Qi Biaojia wengao*, 619; and Ueda, "Ryūkako monogatari," 5–7. Similar late Ming complaints about brokers' collaboration with market toughs to extort extra charges (often disguised as taxes) from outside merchants and locals were common in delta counties and market towns, such as Jiading county's Xinjing 新涇 market town in 1636. Shanghai bowuguan tushu ziliaoshi, *Shanghai beike ziliao xuanji*, 82.

[205] *Minglü jijie fuli*, 10.1a, Xu Pu, *Ming huidian* (1502 ed.), 135.14b–16a; Shen Shixing, *Ming huidian* (1587 ed.), 164, 846–47.

steps to avoid dangerous travel routes). This threat was not empty. In the ports of early seventeenth-century Nanjing, where over 20,000 men worked as dockers,[206] some merchants became so exasperated with the imposition of arbitrary levies at two extramural customs stations that they moved their trade upriver to the town of Wuhu.[207] A group of Huizhou silk merchants undertook similar action against crime and corruption in Nanxiang 南翔, a Jiading county market town known for its sericulture trade in mulberry leaves. After years of enduring protection racket squeezes by the town's "professional beaters," these merchants in anger moved their trade elsewhere (possibly to the nearby market town of Luodian 羅店), thereby inflicting long-term damage on Nanxiang's economy.[208] In other delta market towns it was the residents, not just the merchants, who on the town's roads and waterways erected and shut fences they manned to keep robbers out.[209]

In Suzhou city, where the market was far greater, such drastic action probably struck Huizhou merchants as too costly. Through a variety of tactics, ranging from adaptation and negotiation to complaints and appeals, they sought to sidestep or beat their adversaries at their own game. As strongly advised, they showed great caution when hiring a boat for their journeys. They were to travel only on a boat recommended by a long-tested broker, preferably a broker they knew well. They were not to risk their life and cargo by hiring a private broker or a boat for a tiny saving.[210] Only by co-operating with an honest broker could one's business travels and trading succeed.[211]

---

[206] Zhou Lianggong, *Jinling jiangu*, preface, Luo, 366.
[207] Gu Qiyuan, *Kezuo zhuiyu*, 1, 23.
[208] *Jiading xianzhi* (1605), 1.25b–26a. The town eventually revived, but throughout the seventeenth and eighteenth centuries remained plagued by similar problems, as porters and musicians carved up the town's neighborhoods (literally, "privately demarcated land boundaries") for their work. Running essentially "closed shops," they extorted charges for transport, marriages, and funerals. A stele banning the practice was erected in 1686, but to little avail. *Nanxiang zhenzhi* (1807), 12.5a–b; Ueda, "Minmatsu Shinchō," 30, note F. A late Ming instance from Suzhou, when extortionate tax levies drove some sojourning merchants away, is mentioned below in this chapter.
[209] Kawakatsu Mamoru, *Min Shin Kōnan shichin*, 350–89.
[210] Cheng Chunyu, *Shishang leiyao*, 2.46b–47a. Clearly, the outsider merchant here is considered "solitary" and to lack recourse to a collective body like a native-place association.
[211] Adachi, *Min Shin Chūgoku*, 521–50.

Ideally, they might arrange to have the broker become "a dedicated broker"; that is, pay special attention to their work, to the extent of becoming their firm's private agent.[212] But even a well-recommended and trusted broker might grossly overcharge, and so a wise merchant would hold in reserve another reliable broker.[213] Other steps were more forceful, as when a group of Anhui merchants (including some from Huizhou) purchased a Suzhou wharf for their use alone. Able thereafter to avoid arbitrary charges for mooring and unloading their goods,[214] they also escaped mistreatment by unruly crowds of local brokers, porters, and boatmen falsely claiming to represent another long-distance Huizhou merchant. And some Huizhou merchants took the most direct solution: like the Huizhou dye specialist who prospered in the dyeing sector of the textile business at Wuhu they could transform themselves into legitimate "government brokers" and, as already explained, still quietly run their own businesses.[215]

When these tactics did not work and offers of adaptation and cooperation went unheeded, Huizhou merchants, it should be said, were willing to take harsh steps against their adversaries, be they brokers, "bad staves," fellow merchants, or deceitful boat owners.[216] At times, they reportedly inflicted private acts of revenge, made false charges, carried out private arrests, and practiced plunder against men they judged their enemies.[217] Some of their complaints seem justified, as when in 1623 groups of merchants in Suzhou formally reported to

---

[212] Zelin, "Chinese Business Practice," 781, mentions Huizhou merchants' use of this arrangement in Qing dynasty Jingdezhen. The details varied, but the government frowned on brokers' financial involvement (for example, as shareholders) in businesses they were expected to serve rather than own.

[213] Aramiya, *Min Shin toshi*, 305–25.

[214] Long Denggao, *Jiangnan shichang*, 147, for Suzhou, Hangzhou, and even You 攸 county, Hunan province. In Yangzhou, the Xie 謝 lineage of Qimen had from the late fifteenth century already acquired its own wharf, and held on to it up to the early seventeenth century. McDermott, *Making*, v. 1, 262, n.86.

[215] *THJ*, 35, 634–35. Wang Tingyuan and Wang Shihua, *Huishang*, 240–46, has much on Huizhou merchants working as textile brokers in delta market towns in the late Ming and early Qing.

[216] Wang Yajun, *Ming Qing Huishang*, covers Huizhou merchants' litigation cases but despite its title contains precious little Ming dynasty information on Huizhou merchants. The same problem afflicts Fan Jinmin's otherwise informative *Ming Qing shangshi jiufen*.

[217] Jin Zhongshi, *Xunfang guili shiyao*, 12a–33a, provides a rich survey of such abuses of the legal system in northern Zhejiang at the start of the seventeenth century.

officials that yamen underlings were forcing them to sell their goods at much-reduced prices. In the recorded Ming instances of 1623 and 1634 these angry merchants numbered, respectively, no fewer than thirteen and thirty-four.[218] They presented their complaints to the Changshu county yamen, whose head official's subsequent bans on these and other marketing abuses were carved into stone steles placed in a public site in the city.[219] Shipowners and other merchants selling a variety of products ranging from silk cloth to oil and timber could henceforth point to these local officials' public rulings as legal precedents to protect them and their goods from mistreatment by subsequent local officials, their underlings, and other offending parties in local markets.[220]

Predictably, it is only from the 1680s, four decades after the Ming's demise, that Huizhou merchants are explicitly listed as appellants in these inscribed complaints about Suzhou market abuses.[221] Quite possibly, some individual Huizhou merchants had been involved in the earlier legal complaints of 1623 and 1624, if only because Huizhou merchants tended to play a dominant role in all the varieties of trade the appellants of these claims are said have to practiced. Encouraging this speculation is a stele set up in Huizhou itself to declare prefectural restrictions on levies imposed on merchants, especially in Yan market town, where two merchants litigated against official abuses.[222] Of wider significance is a strain of contemporary criticism about the obstinacy of Huizhou merchants. The highly informed scholars Wang Shixing of Taizhou 台州 and Gu Yanwu of Suzhou both faulted Huizhou merchants with being stubborn and litigious,[223] and the late Ming scholar-official Li Weizhen 李維楨 complained that "rich Huizhou merchants are bold in conducting private vendettas, not giving up

---

[218] Jiangsu sheng bowuguan, *Jiangsu sheng Ming Qing*, 74.
[219] By contrast, a stele declaring mid-sixteenth-century administrative revisions in the Hangzhou salt administration was set up with co-operation between the local salt office and the reforms' advocate, the eminent Huizhou salt merchant Cheng Zhengkui. *THJ*, 47, 990.
[220] *MQSZ*, 4, 193–96. No merchant criticism of officials' misdeeds is recorded here.
[221] Ibid., 4, 186, on pawnbrokers with a Huizhou household register. Quite likely they were involved in the 1656 stele's ban as well.
[222] *Huizhou fuzhi* (1699), 8.53b–54b.
[223] Wang Shixing, *Guangzhi yi*, 2, 34; and *MQHS*, 54.

when they failed [at the first effort], and skilled at currying favor with the authorities."[224]

Confirming this criticism of Huizhou merchants as interested in resorting to legal threats and pressure is a recently published assortment of legal claim forms included in a sixteenth-century legal handbook.[225] Compiled by a "pettifogger" apparently from Wuyuan county in Huizhou, this manuscript – until recently, the sole surviving copy of this text – shows how merchants at times pressed charges against a wide range of marketplace characters we know all too well: the scheming brokers, the shop owners failing to pay on time for the goods purchased from an "outsider merchant," the slippery middlemen deceiving both buyer and seller, the irresponsible boat owner damaging his customers' cargo, the thieving "bad sticks" buying another merchant's salt on credit and failing to pay on time, and the porter disappearing with the loads he was assigned to carry. This manuscript includes forms for pressing charges against virtually the entire list of rascals and misdemeanors we found to have been common in Ming Suzhou's markets, a reminder of how pervasive were the problems that obstructed outsiders seeking smooth access to markets in the Yangzi Valley.

Yet, as if to add a cunning sting to this reading, no form is included in this book of complaint forms for charging yamen personnel with a crime or abuse, such as were denounced in late Ming Suzhou's stone steles. No yamen position or figure in either the formal or informal government is even mentioned. Although Huizhou merchants are shown to have turned to local courts for compensation or protection from fellow commoners, such as their clients and fellow merchants, they did so cautiously and selectively. They normally did not press charges against officials, government representatives, or their direct subordinates for legal misconduct or abuses. Compensation from such quarters would have been hard to

---

[224] *THJ*, v. 2, 45, 950; Tang Lixing, *Shangren*, 78–79; Pak Wŏn-ho, *Ming Qing Huizhou Fangshi*, 135.
[225] Xiao Taoyuan juefei shanren, *Erbi kenqi*, hu, 23–29. Fuma Susumu here dates the manuscript and its information to between 1500 and 1569; its Huizhou connection is evident in several passages which mention Huizhou or describe a prefecture like Huizhou. The manuscript's present storage in the Wuyuan County Library strengthens the likelihood of its contents' link to Huizhou.

obtain, and legal demand for it a waste of time and money, that could easily backfire.[226]

Native-Place Associations: A Resolution?

The institutional solution to the protection of merchants and their interests might seem, then, to have been the establishment of a merchant institution – normally called a native-place association (*huiguan*) or public place (*gongsuo* 公所) – that was oriented to the interests of sojourning merchants. But that is precisely what did *not* happen in late Ming Suzhou. Admittedly, well over 2,000 of these institutions were built in some 300 different sites in late Ming and Qing China, mainly in the Qing and in the Yangzi Valley.[227] But, until the eighteenth century, few Huizhou merchants promoted or associated with them. Even native-place associations established by other merchant groups in the Ming did not gain the prominence they assumed in the Qing as centers of commercial interest.

The creation of native-place associations, as they won neither inclusion nor approval in Ming and Qing legal codes and statutes, would have needed local-government approval.[228] Usually, they were proposed, built and joined by sojourning males – not just merchants but also artisans, examination candidates, officials, and other traveling natives – from the same county, prefecture, or province, who while living together in this association's lodge agreed to help one another adapt to their new circumstances far from home. Membership conferred certain benefits: a place to live, regular exchange with other members of information on trade and local conditions, collective worship of a popular deity from their home area or the ancestral father of their trade, and, most importantly, security for themselves and their goods. Membership would also qualify them for others' charity, medical help, a decent coffin, and a respectable burial. The irony that those who might want to set up such a local institution as a native-place association in a nonnative place might be supported by lineages which

---

[226] Yang Lien-sheng, "Government Control," 40, mentions the post-Taiping judgment of the experienced official Wang Shiduo (1802–89) that although merchants were crafty and crooked, the only social group less rebellious were the urban literati (who nonetheless tended to be "obstinate and inflexible").
[227] Belsky, *Localities*, 35–36; his 2,000-plus figure omits the hundreds in Beijing.
[228] Miles, *Upriver Journeys*, 121.

had replaced their communal village institutions back home in Huizhou was lost on contemporaries. Huizhou sojourners tended not to broadcast their problems back home to others, and few Yangzi delta natives showed an interest in social life elsewhere. Nonetheless, the establishment of native-place associations and public places has been taken to highlight the adoption of new local commitments and identities by Chinese commercial and occupational groups active in long-distance trade and in making a heightened demand for accommodation, warehouses, and other services.[229]

Clearly, the construction of these establishments in the Ming could have solved some of the problems faced by traveling merchants in distant cities, not least the obstruction and controls of market brokers,[230] and could have also given them some collective protection from other hostile parties in their new settlement. But Ming sources on native-place associations pay strikingly little attention to the commercial concerns and activities – such as their imposition of a price or price range on their members and thus the local market and their power to represent the merchant community from their area or in their particular trade in dealings with the government – that would greatly concern native-place establishments in the Qing dynasty.[231] Quite likely, these Ming associations gained their social respectability and official legitimacy from including and serving many men not engaged in trade, such as officials and examination students.

In fact, the slow development of mercantile native-place and public-place institutions in both Ming Beijing and Suzhou is emblematic of the social and political resistance to the establishment then of institutions solely or mainly for itinerant merchants. At no point in the Ming is it possible to certify that most of the native- and public-place institutions established in Ming Beijing catered principally for merchants and were concerned principally with mercantile affairs. In function if not in name, these associations emerged in Ming Beijing at local shrines or

---

[229] Shiba, *Chūgoku toshi shi*, 135–52.
[230] Tang Lixing, *Shangren*, 88, rightly links merchant support for the native-place association with their opposition to local brokers' protectionist practices.
[231] Zelin, "Chinese Business Practice," 783, specifies this economic role as serving "their members' desire to safeguard profits by restricting competition among themselves and between themselves and non-members ... by limiting membership, regulating apprenticeships, controlling the size and location of workshops, and setting product standards and prices."

inns. One Beijing contender for the first such lodge is the Shrine for Two Loyal Men (*Erzhong si* 二忠祠), set up in 1376 to honor two Song loyalists from Ji'an 吉安 county, Jiangxi; not long afterwards it was transformed into a native-place association for visitors from this county.[232] A slightly later instance is the house for Wuhu natives set up in the 1420s by a court official who, upon leaving his post, donated his Beijing residence to serve as an inn (*lüshe* 旅社) for fellow Wuhu natives visiting the capital. Two other native-place associations from the Jiangxi county of Fuliang and all of Guangdong province were also set up in Beijing during the Yongle reign (1403–24).[233]

In the last half of the Ming, such Beijing institutions became more secular and autonomous. They tended to stress their non-merchant character and membership, and none more so than the native-place association set up for She county, the wealthiest and most commercial of Huizhou's six counties. The She native-place association in Beijing was built in the early 1560s by men intent, as their rules made clear, on establishing a capital residence for Huizhou examination degree holders and aspirants and officials like themselves, and *not* for merchants (even though many of these official-donors came from lineages and in some cases families long involved in commerce).[234] This native-place association, we read in a mid-eighteenth-century record, "has been set up solely for metropolitan examination candidates (*gongche* 公車, literally provincial degree holders) and others taking examinations in the capital. Sojourning merchants doing trade (*maoyi keshang* 貿易客商) have their own travel lodges. They cannot reside at the native-place association and park their goods there. It would not be in accord with [the association's] *original* aims."[235]

---

[232] This view was first presented by the exceptionally knowledgeable scholar of Chinese merchant practices Negishi Tadashi, in his *Chūgoku no girudo*. This shrine was from 1408 used for official performances of memorial rites to these two neo-Confucian heroes. Yet the claim that the shrine was established in the early Ming for solely Ji'an natives is based on Qing, not Ming, records. Masui, *Chūgoku no gin*, 138.

[233] Belsky, *Localities*, 24, 27.

[234] Li Linqi and Liang Renzhi, *Huishang huiguan*, v. 1, 144–50.

[235] Xu Shining and Xu Zeng, *Chongxu Shexian huiguan lu*, 31, italics added. Xu Chengyao, *Sheshi yitan*, 10, 345, dates this native-place association's repair to 1564–65. Ibid., 11, 357, says it was built at the same time as a charitable-trust shrine established to handle the burial of She county natives in Beijing. Terada Takanobu, "Beijing Shexian huiguan," 29, dates the opening of this She county lodge to 1563. Wang Tingyuan, "Lun Huizhou shangbang," 44, claims a

Other native-place associations in Ming Beijing had strikingly similar aspirations. Having initially been associated more with shrines than with officials and scholars, they had become bastions of a capital officialdom intent on securing its social exclusivity. Frequented neither by merchants and modest officials nor by groups of artisans and other travelers, they tended to serve only the upper stream of official and gentry culture (even though some undoubtedly had merchants in their family, past and present).[236] And in Qing Beijing that tone of official elite membership did not fade, as by the close of the nineteenth century just 14 percent of its hundreds of native-place associations and public-place associations catered solely for merchants.[237] In sum, these Beijing institutions, whatever policy they had on merchant membership in the Qing, were set up in the Ming for use primarily, if not solely, by officials and aspiring officials. Funded and managed in Ming Beijing as private concerns, they retained their official elitist character.[238]

Down south, in a thriving commercial metropolis like Ming Suzhou, the story was yet more complex. Ming sources say nothing about what to us today appears the most obvious direct solution to the Huizhou merchants' problems of long-term protection, accommodation, storage, and representation in any Suzhou town or city – the acquisition of a collectively owned and used place of their own like a native-place association's lodge. The silence initially seems baffling in light of their concurrent ingenious transformation of village institutions like the ancestral hall and introduction of timber options, quite probably because these successes were undertaken with kinsmen for kinsmen in villages they controlled and had not required the support of a wider collective prefectural or county network (as implied by an institution operating for "Huizhou" or She county merchants).[239] It is even more baffling when one recognizes

similar social restriction held true for the Xiuning native-place association in Beijing; I have not yet confirmed this claim.
[236] Shen Defu, *Wanli yehuo bian*, 24, 608–09.
[237] Belsky, *Localities*, 91–92, in confirmation of He Bingdi's point about the coexistence of two separate types of native place association, the official and the predominantly mercantile (*Zhongguo huiguan shilun*, 120–22). In 1712 Cantonese merchants erected their own native-place association in Beijing apart from an older association there dominated by Cantonese scholar-officials.
[238] Belsky, *Localities*, 31, 59–60. Indeed, the late imperial native-place associations may well have been modeled on institutions set up by earlier dynasties to house provincial officials visiting and serving in the capital.
[239] More simply, Huizhou merchants would have been loath to put in writing any account of their winning ways with officials.

that, first, in the late Ming, one native-place association and one public place were set up in Suzhou's prefectural seat by sojourners from, respectively, Guangdong and Zhangzhou prefecture in Fujian;[240] that, second, cotton cloth merchants from three Suzhou counties had as early as 1466 built a hall for themselves in Linqing along the Grand Canal; and that, third, Ming Huizhou merchants themselves had established native-place associations elsewhere, two in Beijing (one for tea merchants, one for officials) and one in a backwater market town of western Hunan,[241] and one public place, albeit obliquely, in the Suzhou county seat of Changshu 常熟. It is as if in Suzhou city Huizhou merchants were obligingly following their own travel manual's advice that when dealing with an official, they were to "stand up and step back. Being lowly and humble is the lot of us commoners." Was this strategy, apparently followed in the imperial capital of Beijing, sensible for them also in a commercial center like Suzhou city? Are we, then, left to conclude that the absence of an institutional solution to the Huizhou merchants' problem in Suzhou was what these merchants quietly wanted?

Let us begin by examining what Huizhou merchants actually did to find a secure place for themselves and their goods in Suzhou, both in the prefectural seat and in its Changshu county seat. Some found brokers able to help them out for short visits,[242] and other Huizhou merchants interested in longer stays and even in setting up a branch of their commercial house purchased a Suzhou home for themselves and their relations,[243] or, as in earlier imperial dynasties, lived in a residential establishment with others who shared their business interests.[244]

---

[240] Fan Jinmin, *Ming Qing Jiangnan shangye*, 286.
[241] *MQHS*, 122; the deity worshipped in this association was Guandi.
[242] Later reports of this service come from *c.*1940 Suzhou (Watson, *Transport*, 20–21) and mid Qing Chongqing in Sichuan (Tanii, "Shindai chūki," 140).
[243] Long Denggao, *Jiangnan shichang*, 144. Studies of the major families in Suzhou city during the Ming remain strikingly few, but Inoue Tōru's pioneering list of the families which built ancestral shrines in Ming Suzhou contains no Huizhou migrant (*Chūgoku no sōzoku to kokka*, 144–90). Until the government in 1600 allowed salt merchants' sons to enter the examinations from their actual place of residence in Hangzhou rather than from their registered home county in Huizhou, few Huizhou migrants would have been encouraged to think of their delta residence as home. Even fewer delta residents would have thought of them as locals.
[244] To cite a few examples, in Southern Song Hangzhou a neighborhood near the West Lake (Wu Zimu, *Mengliang lu*, 13, 239); in Ming Nanjing (*MQHS*, 164), and in Ming Hangzhou and Kaifeng (*FKSFC*, 198, and Chapter 6 below).

In other words, although these recorded instances are few, they suggest that when it came to settling into another community where their presence was not always welcomed, Huizhou merchants individually adopted in Suzhou city the same cautious, understated, and well-funded approach that enabled them to survive the difficulties they encountered in their travels and trading elsewhere.

This assessment is confirmed by the background history of the sole Huizhou native-place association or public-place lodge erected in Suzhou prefecture during the Ming. Its establishment, at an unspecified Ming date, in the county seat of Changshu was achieved and recorded in the most guarded manner. Neither its name – Plum Garden Public Place (*meiyuan gongsuo* 梅園公所) – nor that of its attached Keeping Benevolence Alive Hall (*Cunren tang* 存仁堂) – indicates even the slightest connection with Anhui or Huizhou or the use of this structure to house merchants and their goods.[245] Furthermore, this establishment was situated not in Shantang 山塘, Chang Gate 閶門, or any of the other bustling commercial quarters in Suzhou's prefectural seat, but instead at the bottom of the northern side of a small hill in a neighboring county seat. So humble and cramped was this hall and adjacent garden site that these buildings and garden escape mention in Changshu county's otherwise very detailed gazetteers. Their bland names and this public place's ostensible functions as a hospital for the sick, a cemetery for the deceased, and a warehouse for corpses and coffins to be shipped back home to Huizhou by a monk custodian – all inauspicious features – would, I suspect, have persuaded most Chinese to restrain their natural curiosity about this establishment and walk pass it without turning an eye.

Predictably, then, the sole surviving notice of this Plum Garden and its Keeping Benevolence Alive Hall comes in a stone inscription dated as late as 1802, a century and a half after the Ming dynasty had ended. This reticence on the part of the merchants and other visitors from Huizhou and their discouragement of local interest in their "garden" accord well with this chapter's earlier account of the physical and other threats that faced long-distance merchants in Suzhou: "As a residence for outsiders [or traveling merchants], it attracted bullying (*keju zhaowu* 客居招侮)."[246] In sum, the rough ways of both the rivers

---

[245] *MQSZ*, 349.
[246] Ibid. Also Aramiya, *Min Shin toshi*, 210–38, links the establishment of this Changshu public place to a history of arbitrary government levies on merchants here. The expression *keju* could also be translated as "resident outsiders."

and the delta's marketplace seem to have pursued Huizhou merchants ashore to the doors of this urban lodge in a county seat.

Indeed, what is most notable about the merchant native-place associations and public places in the Ming emporium of Suzhou is their scarcity for travelers from virtually every part of the empire (see Table 3.1) and especially for those from Huizhou (see Table 3.2). Furthermore, those readers looking for a large imposing merchant structure in Ming Suzhou, Hangzhou, or Linqing with the swagger of a rich European guildhall or even the imposing scale of a Chinese native-place association building in nineteenth-century Shanghai and Guangzhou need to gaze elsewhere.[247] It is no surprise, then, that we have so few Ming records of what went on or was discussed in these Ming native-place associations,[248] and that far fewer pre-1880 histories of native-place associations or public places exist in Chinese than do late imperial histories of its temples, shrines, and academies.[249] Thanks to their wealth these men drew enough attention from government and locals, and they preferred not to attract any more by constructing a "guest house" that would have closely identified them as rich outsiders.

This conclusion seems reasonable for Ming Suzhou, but only if we add two significant caveats. First, if government and Huizhou merchants' practice elsewhere in the delta's larger cities can serve as a guide, the government may have resorted to a personal rather than institutional solution to some Huizhou merchants' needs. In Yangzhou and Hangzhou, salt merchants had a Libationer (*jijiu* 祭酒) serve as their formal head for the communication of their wishes and needs to

---

Fan Jinmin, "Cantian Dongting biandi hui," 100; Jiang Hong, *Suzhou cidian*, 1,058–59; Hong Huanchun, *Ming Qing shi oucun*, 571–72. Those built in the prefectural seat of Suzhou from the Wanli era on were for natives of, separately, Fujian, Guangdong, and the Guangdong county of Dongwan; that in Changshu county was apparently for all Huizhou male natives. At the establishment of the Hangzhou silk merchants' native place association in Suzhou, its founders proclaimed the end of rental costs, fear of bandits and robbers, and serious damage from dampness and heat. Long Denggao, *Jiangnan shichang*, 153.

[247] Goodman, *Native Place, City, and Nation*, 18–21.
[248] Li Weizhen, *Dami shanfang ji*, 15.27b, reports a discussion in the She native-place association in Beijing about the never-realized compilation of a supplement to the celebrated mid-Ming collection of historical writing by Huizhou natives, the *Xin'an wenxian zhi*.
[249] Li Linqi and Liang Renzhi, *Huishang*, v. 1, 5, claims knowledge of some fifty titles for Huizhou native-place associations.

Table 3.1 Non-Huizhou native-place associations and public places in Suzhou prefecture during the Yuan and Ming dynasties

Name	Location	Membership / Donors	Date of Initial Construction	Source
Wujun jiye gongsuo 吳君機業公所	Huaqiao Belvedere 花橋閣	silk weaving	1295	SZSZ, v.3, 449
Datie gongsuo 打鐵公所	Laujun Hall 老君堂, Northern Garden	iron making	Ming Wanli reign (1573–1620)	Ibid.
Lingnan huiguan 嶺南會館	west of Shantang Bridge, outside Changmen Gate, Tiger Hill	Guangzhou officials and merchants	Ming Wanli reign	Ibid., v.3, 446
Dongguan huiguan 東莞會館	Shantang Street, outside Changmen Gate, Suzhou city	merchants from Dongguan county, Guangdong	1625	Ibid.
Sanxian(shan) huiguan 三仙(山)會館	Xu Gate, Wannian Bridge, Big Road, Suzhou city	fruit/flower merchants of Fuzhou (esp. Putian 莆田), Fujian	Ming Wanli reign	Ibid., SZSZ, v.3, 446
Zaiguan huiguan 在官會館	Bantang 半塘, in the western suburbs of Suzhou city	unspecified	1625	Gu Lu, Tongqiao 88

Table 3.2 *Huizhou native-place associations and public places in Suzhou prefecture during the Ming and Qing dynasties*

Name	Location	Membership	Date of Initial Construction	Source
Huijun huiguan 徽郡會館	in front of Provincial Military Intendant's Office, Suzhou city	Huizhou oil, dates, and mulberry paper merchants	1770	Fan 287; SZSZ, v.3, 448
Anhui huiguan 安徽會館	Nanxianzi 南顯子 Alley, Suzhou city	Anhui officials and merchants	1866–67	Fan 287; SZSZ, v.3, 448
Xin'an huiguan 新安會館	Shantang 山塘 Street, outside Changmen Gate	Huizhou merchants	unspecified	Fan 287; SZSZ, v.3, 448.
Xin'an huiguan 新安會館	36 Wan Nanxianzi Alley	Cloth merchants of She county, Huizhou	Qianlong era (1736–95)	Ibid.
Hui Ning huiguan 徽甯會館	Shengze 盛澤 market town, Wujiang county	Huizhou and Ningguofu 甯國府 merchants	1809	Fan 287
Huizhou huiguan 徽州會館	Tongli 同里 market town, Wujiang county	unspecified	end of Qing	Fan 287
Meiyuan gongsuo 梅園公所	Changshu county seat	Hui[zhou] natives	Ming	*Ming Qing*, 349
Huizhou huiguan 徽州會館	Jiading county, Nanxiang 南翔 town	Huizhou merchants	end of Tongzhi era (1862–74)	Fan 288

Tables 3.1, 3.2 source notes: Fan Jinmin, *Ming Qing Jiangnan shangye de fazhan*, 286–87; Gu Lu, *Tongqiao yizhuo lu*, 88; Suzhou lishi bowuguan et al., *Ming Qing Suzhou gongshangye beike ji* 349; SZSZ. The first two places listed in Table 3.1 may well have been craft guilds. Table 3.2's Anhui huiguan, Xinan huiguan, and Huizhou huiguan in Suzhou city have possibly been confused with one another for the obvious reason that th-y all can or do refer to the same place, Huizhou. A recent dictionary on past and present Suzhou, *Suzhou cidian* (Suzhou: Suzhou daxue, 1999): 1058–59, has a shorter list of Suzhou prefecture's native associations and public places that confirms most, but not all, of the information in these two tables.

the local government (upriver in Wuhu it was the indigo dyeing association that had a Huizhou merchant serve as its Libationer). The qualifications for this position are clear: great wealth, a high level of credit, and considerable social standing (at times, sons succeeded their father to this position). The appointment process, however, is murky. A few sources suggest that the power of appointment lay in the hands of the top local official, while another suggests that real power lay with the appointee's fellow traders, who would decide on their favorite candidate and recommend him to the local government for its formal approval and appointment (this second process seems more likely, as it echoes a pre-1400 alternative Ming government route to official appointment and ensures shared merchant responsibility for subsequent mistakes in this office's administration, thereby reducing the officials' own culpability). Either way, the appointed party was expected to lead all the association's members as Libationer in collective worship festivities and toast making at public rituals, and, most importantly, to help his fellow merchants negotiate their legal and financial problems among themselves, their creditors, and the local government.[250] Part-official, part-merchant, part-lawyer, part-financial adviser, and, I suspect, part-banker and investor in his fellow traders' concerns, this senior figure tended to hold on to the post until his old age, ceding the post, if all went well, to his similarly well-endowed son. Such a position, if well handled, would have reduced

[250] For the "head merchant" (*zongshang* 總商) post in the Qing salt monopoly delivery system, the terms of service are described in greater detail: the thirty "head merchants" – initially thirty and by the eighteenth century's end sixteen, including four "Big Heads" – were chosen for the Liang Huai salt consumption region. Each head merchant was likewise chosen for his financial and social position among the salt merchants (his wealth was usually judged in terms of his number of salt certificates and his place within his merchant syndicate); in the sixteenth century his seat and prominence at Yangzhou salt merchants' meetings were determined by his relative wealth (*THJ*, 34, 759). He also served as the leader and guarantor of a large, unspecified number of far smaller subordinate salt merchants (*sanshang* 散商), whose salt certificate fees, delivery expenses, and other government charges he would annually pay the government in advance and be subsequently compensated for by these subordinate merchants. He also would split with his merchant followers any funds presented him by a salt official for profitable investment; they were likewise to pay him the expected profits. He also shared with officials the task of checking the salt reserves in government store holds. In other words, he functioned half as a merchant and half as an official. Saeki, *Shindai ensei*, 241–47; Lin Zhenhan, *Yanzheng cidian*, 17 strokes, page 11.

the government's need and merchants' demand for a native-place association or public place. But it clearly met the needs of resident and regular sojourning merchants more than those of either the struggling merchant newcomers or short-stay itinerants in search of accommodation and security for their persons and goods. At this point, the social and class differences between the different kinds of Huizhou merchants would have mattered, obliging the more fortunate of these ordinary merchants to rely on kinship or surname ties to help them through troubles in a "foreign city." The less fortunate had to fend for themselves, somehow.

That somehow (though the evidence is less than conclusive) can be found in the suggestion of several scholars that religious institutions or inns would have served these merchants' needs.[251] The erection of the Huizhou native-place association in early Qing Hankou they have linked to a religious institutional model[252] – the ancestral hall,[253] Buddhist temple,[254] popular cult shrine, or neo-Confucian academy. Shiba Yoshinobu's wider research has confirmed the wisdom of this approach for earlier periods as well. He traced the early Ming origins of the Ji'an native-place association of this Jiangxi county in Beijing to an earlier Beijing shrine for Jiangxi worthies, and he also located a base of operations for Ming Huizhou merchants in Suzhou in a temple set up in 1379 just one mile southeast of the prefectural seat for worship of

[251] The emphasis placed by Hu Tieqiu, *Ming Qing xiejia*, on inns, innkeepers, and warehouse owners, and their close ties to powerful provincial groups throughout the Ming and Qing dynasties supports this claim. His evidence of their power comes from Tibet, northwest China, and Nanjing, but so far not Suzhou.

[252] Peng Zeyi, *Qingdai gongshang*, 150, shows the allocation of space in the eventual Huizhou native-place association in Suzhou to the worship of Zhu Xi, a decision doubtless made to reflect Huizhou merchants' self-image and increase their moral credit in Suzhou. The attraction of Huizhou merchants to shrines dedicated to this neo-Confucian sage is mentioned also in Tang Lixing, *Shangren*, 36.

[253] Rowe, *Hankow*: Commerce and Society, 255, stresses Huizhou merchants' use of the ancestral-hall model for new Hankou commercial native-place associations, quoting one of the founders of an early Qing Huizhou native-place association there that "all provincial groups at Hankow adopt the title 'ancestral temple' as a pretext for founding their *hui-kuan* [sic], thereby implying a covert aspect to such organizations."

[254] Wang Zhenzhong, "Ming Qing yi lai," 81–118, shows the use of a Buddhist temple and chapel, or at least their names, to cloak Huizhou merchants' use of a Hankou site and building by their native-place association.

the popular Huizhou cult deity, the Five Penetrations (*Wutong* 五通).[255] Yet no evidence explicitly shows Huizhou merchant attachment to or involvement in this shrine or this cult's subsequent Suzhou base of operations, the Lengqie temple 楞伽寺 at Mt Shangfang 上方山 three miles southwest of Suzhou city. In the fifteenth century, this suburban temple started to attract Wutong devotees from throughout the delta, promising them untold riches in return for their contributions. If the receipt they received for their original sacrifice did not wrinkle after a few days, the faithful confidently believed that they could proceed to make their anticipated loans with the money supposedly coming from Wutong. A year later, they shared their rich returns with the deity, by giving him a suitable sum of silver plus interest. This cult's obsession with money and interest and its appeal to merchants are obvious. Far less clear here is its link to Huizhou merchants, individually or collectively. In fact, no Ming source I know of about this shrine explicitly refers to Huizhou merchants as its devotees, though individual Huizhou merchants surely numbered among the shrine's clientele.[256]

We can, then, tentatively conclude that Ming Huizhou merchants in the prefectural seat of Suzhou had no officially acknowledged establishment called a native-place association but probably relied on a dual strategy: the better-off and better-connected turned to the head of their trade association to plead their cause, while the less fortunate and more credulous relied on another kind of institution, perhaps an inn,[257]

---

[255] Shiba, *Sōdai Kōnan keizaishi*, 326, 333, 400–2, esp. n.16, and 505–6. His essay, "Sōdai no toshika o kangaeru," 4, points out that the pre-sixteenth-century merchants' reliance on religious buildings makes it hard to estimate the number of buildings actually functioning as local-place associations in Song and Ming times. Goodman, *Native Place*, 91–92, comments knowledgeably on the early sojourning merchants and artisans' practice of establishing their associations as "religious corporations." Such a link may well have existed in Ming Suzhou; witness a Suzhou shrine, one of many dedicated to the notorious Five Penetrations cult native to Huizhou, which had been established with images brought there by its monk caretaker from Wuyuan county in Huizhou (*Wu xianzhi* [1642], 21.17b). Likewise, a Fujian merchant was crucial in the establishment in 1613 of a second Suzhou city shrine to the goddess Tianfei 天妃 (*Wu xianzhi* [1642], 21.14a).

[256] Von Glahn, *Sinister Way*, 220–32, Cai Limin, *Suzhou minsu*, 146–51; Tang Bin, *Tang Qian'an ji*, shang, 4–5, yishu, 9.

[257] Hu Tieqi, *Ming Qing xiejia*. Long Denggao, *Jiangnan shichang*, 143, tells of a well-traveled Huizhou merchant who ended up dying in a Suzhou inn (*lüdi* 旅邸) in c.1580. For an introductory study of both government and private inns in the Ming and Qing dynasties, see Song Lizhong, *Xianya yu fuhua*, 247–74, esp.

Native-Place Associations: A Resolution? 193

a shrine, or a temple like the Lengqie,[258] where they met not officials but one another. Here they felt safe and comfortable, surrounded by fellow merchants and travelers from Huizhou, some of whom may have even been their kinsmen.[259] Mention of a strictly "commercial center" for Huizhou merchants in Ming Suzhou, however, remains moot and probably irrelevant. More importantly, we know even less about what, if anything, might have happened at such places than on Suzhou's streets at certain festivals.

The reluctance or inability of Huizhou and Shanxi merchants to establish a single institution for themselves may well have reflected internal differences in their own ranks that they were careful to keep out of the historical record. But, almost regardless of their intentions, neither merchant group established for itself a native-place or public-place association in Suzhou city for well over a century after the Ming's fall. Long after tens of other regional merchant guilds had established their association's lodge in Suzhou, only then did the two most powerful regional merchant groups in the Ming and Qing choose to do likewise.[260] The breakthrough date for Huizhou in Suzhou city appears to be 1770, with enlargements to the association's hall following in 1773 and 1795,[261] and with four additional Huizhou-linked native-place associations built there by the end of the nineteenth century.[262] Over time – a long time – as the number of commercial travelers from a county or prefecture increased during the Qing dynasty, and as they introduced the goods and trades associated with their native county or prefecture, the number of these native-place associations in the delta towns and cities steadily expanded, just as their commercial constituency and character eventually prevailed.[263]

253–68. Private inns in larger delta cities were commonly regarded as coarse and uncomfortable, even though their service improved during the Ming.
[258] Shiba, *Sōdai Kōnan keizaishi*, 400–2, esp. n.16.
[259] Huizhou merchants' cultish devotion to the god Wutong was undoubtedly fueled by this anxiety over threats to the preservation of their silver (von Glahn, "The Enchantment of Wealth").
[260] Fan Jinmin, *Ming Qing Jiangnan shangye*, 287, with another for all of Anhui. Peng Zeyi, *Qingdai gongshang hangye*, 149–50, dates the first construction of the Huizhou native-place lodge in Suzhou to 1770, full payment of its construction costs came later, in 1773.
[261] Jiang Hong, *Suzhou cidian*, 1,061.
[262] Fan Jinmin, *Ming Qing Jiangnan shangye*, 287 ff.
[263] The precise process of raising funds to build these native-place associations and public places is rarely clear. Even if donated "seed money" from one or more

The Qing, unlike the Ming, even set up detention centers in the delta's growing number of market towns to detain those charged or found guilty there of either serious or petty crime.[264]

If, then, the long-term evolution of native-place associations towards a relatively independent merchant organization and membership, towards becoming sites of Huizhou commercial groups and interests, seems to have been glacial,[265] it would be wise not to stress its impact on the financial and commercial well-being of Huizhou merchants. After some trouble in the turmoil of the mid-seventeenth-century dynastic transition these same Huizhou commercial interests flourished outside Huizhou up to the nineteenth century.[266]

If, then, Huizhou merchants had an unnamed home base in or around Suzhou city, they were decidedly hesitant about announcing it and discussing in public their collective situation in this large city. To assure their safe return to the imagined comforts of home, they would have had to take private responsibility for protecting themselves and their assets. This approach called for considerable caution and a strong suspicion of the world beyond their front door; in short, a stance in accord with the approach recommended in their merchant manuals

individuals might have been loaned out at interest repeatedly to raise construction funds (in the manner of the ancestral hall), the income these institutions acquired from loans after their construction would have been quite small (and so any capital used for loans would appear to have also been insignificant). In one more indication of the priority that Huizhou merchants gave to kinship ties when dealing with money, they used the ancestral hall for making money far more regularly than they did any putative or real merchant institution. Negishi Tadashi, *Chūgoku no girudo*, 183–84, 189–92, 310–12.

[264] Ōta Izuru, *Chūgoku kinsei*, 54–87. Within the western half of Suzhou city, these measures entailed the narrowing (from six to three meters in width) of the nine trunk canals and reduction in the number of side canals, changes that would have impeded criminals' escape in this part of the city (the eastern part of the city changed far less, some sections even reversing these narrowing trends. Takamura, *Chūgoku no toshi*, 60–65.

[265] He Bingdi, *Zhongguo huiguan shilun*, 18, argues that the oldest surviving set of native-place association regulations, those of c.1560 for the She county native-place lodge in Beijing, deals only with private merchants and mentions not a single official. By contrast, the trade associations (*hang*) of the pre-Ming by and large functioned as state-established institutions to help the government collect taxes and other levies from wealthy merchants often thought to have escaped the government's tax net.

[266] Fan Jinmin, *Fushui jia tianxia*, 313–40, shows that the growth of Huizhou merchants' urban philanthropy in the delta was negligible during the Ming and directed overwhelmingly towards their own Huizhou community.

and strongly in favor of private solutions to their problems, be they public or private. In the following subsection, I wish to consider each of these realms separately, to suggest how Huizhou merchants made their way in the Ming world in order to gain and preserve wealth and power, a kind of political power that arguably to their satisfaction presumed no formal public recognition by the government.

Private Resolutions to Public and Private Problems: From Co-operation to Collusion and on to Corruption

Our discussion of merchant–official relations will be instructed by the observation of the great French sinologist Jacques Gernet on the pre-modern Chinese state's role as "the great organizer of society and territory." While acknowledging the Chinese political elite's insistence on the primacy of social and political order, Gernet wrote,

The only [domestic] problem for the Chinese state, in the course of its long history, was to prevent the development of powers other than its own, such as that of the merchants, the armies, the religious communities, and to prevent dangerous splits at the top. It is this which explains the constant effort to devise mechanisms and arrangements capable of preventing the development of parallel powers, not only outside the central state power, but also within it.[267]

Gernet's insight, that the threat to central-government power might lie as much within the state as outside it, helps to clarify the range of official and merchant interactions in the late Ming. On the one hand, officials could as private individuals or as government representatives practice predatory levies on merchants. Most notoriously, the Grand Secretary Yan Song 嚴嵩 (1480–1565) robbed wealthy individuals and families through threats and abuses of power.[268] Abetted by a clever Huizhou native he hired officially as his private secretary (and unofficially as his bribe collector), Yan accumulated one of the greatest official fortunes in the dynasty, only to have it confiscated upon his decease.[269] More commonly and legitimately, officials levied arbitrary taxes on merchants in various lines (*hang*) of trade or by annually targeting a few wealthy merchants to sell their goods cheaply to the

---
[267] Gernet, "Introduction," xxxii.
[268] Goodrich and Fang, eds., *Dictionary of Ming Biography*, v. 2, 1586–91.
[269] Shen Defu, *Wanli Yehuo bian*, 8, 214.

government through a traditional practice euphemistically termed "harmonious purchase" (*hemai* 和買).[270]

A more nuanced government way to profit from merchants involved investment instead of taxation. Quite reasonably, some officials recognized that a more productive way of increasing their office's funds was simply to invest in a merchant with a record of success. Known as "giving merchants money to make profits" (*fashang shengxi* 發商生息), this practice of investing government money in a private business for government profit obliged the private business to return, at an agreed time, the invested principal and an agreed dividend (or interest) out of the profits resulting from his deals. Viewed by some scholars as an informal form of taxation (it would have been difficult for a merchant to plead failure), this mixed public–private investment practice is commonly believed to date from the reign of the Yongzheng emperor (r. 1724–35), nearly a century after the Ming.[271] Yet a pre-Ming origin is conceivable due to a Song government office practice from 1072 of delivering money to a pawnshop expected to make profits from it for the office. In this Song practice the pawnshop was a government pawnshop – not, as in the eighteenth century, a private one. But conceivably, when government pawnshops in the Ming disappeared, this practice may have been altered to rely on private pawnshops in acknowledgment of their ascendance in the brokerage business.[272]

In all these cases the active party was the official or government office and as such is presented as co-operation or, at worst, collusion. But, once the merchant became the more active party in the merchant–official relationship, such arrangements fell under suspicion of corruption. Such cases commonly occurred when Beijing moneylenders,

---

[270] Tang Wenji, *16–18 shiji Zhongguo shangye*, 249–56, for Beijing and Nanjing, and Aramiya, *Min Shin toshi*, for Nanjing, Beijing, Suzhou, and Changshu. The actual burden of these imposts is usually hard to measure; Chinese and Japanese historians have tended to accord them greater economic and political significance than have Western historians.

[271] Yang Lien-sheng, "Government Control," 39; Saeki, *Shindai ensei*, 243–47; Zelin, *Magistrate's Tael*, 281–84; and her "Chinese Business Practice," 783.

[272] This Song practice had underfunded government military schools (*wuxue* 武學) and military arsenals send their limited holdings of money to a prefectural office or government pawnshop (*didangsuo* 抵當所) to be loaned at interest for these military institutions (the monthly interest rate, at least in Qing times, varied from 1 to 2 percent). Liu Qiugen, *Zhongguo diandang zhidu shi*, 100; Wang Wenshu, *Songdai jiedai*, 156–72.

having lent money to officials, followed them to provincial appointments, where they proceeded to forget such debts, once their indebted officials introduced them to lucrative deals in the provinces.[273] Or, when as in Suzhou in 1601 a tax-collecting official was able to borrow money at advantageous rates from wealthy Suzhou moneylenders anxious to avoid heavy government levies. These "big households" (*dahu* 大戶) would have almost certainly included Huizhou pawnbrokers.[274]

Fortunately for modern historians, the silence that usually concealed such instances of co-operation and collusion between Huizhou merchants and Ming officials sometimes broke down, to reveal details of Huizhou merchant corruption. Huizhou merchants had a reputation for currying favor with officials, for seeking out their friendship through common literati interests such as poetry and wine drinking, and in some places for serving as their friendly moneylender. Conscious that market collusion was taking place, and not only among merchants, some Ming officials noisily aired their concerns. Complaints against fellow officials and merchants may have simply been their latest vindictive moves in the late Ming's endless game of political chess; but at the very least their information indicates what kinds of merchant machinations were credible to Ming officials and many other late Ming cognoscenti of political gossip.

Three major Wanli-era incidents stand out, all occurring in places where many Huizhou merchants traded and resided – Linqing, Huizhou, and Suzhou – and resulting from the emperor's decision in 1596 to dispatch his agents to impose levies in the provinces on whatever revenue source they found ripe for plunder (that is, the infamous tax-collection campaign inaccurately termed the "tax from opening the mines" (*kaikuang zhi shui* 開礦之稅)).[275] All three cases reveal how Huizhou merchants actively chose to mediate their dealings with official members of the imperial government through powerful

---

[273] Han Dacheng, *Mingdai shehui jingji*, 195–97.
[274] Shen Shixing, *Cijian tang ji*, 40.11a–12b. See also the case of the highly regarded Huizhou salt merchant Wang Quan 王全 (d. 1554), who attracted investment funds from scholar-officials appreciative of his opposition to eunuchs. *THJ*, 45, 950; and, Fujii, "Shin'an shōnin no kenkyū," 36.3, 71–73, for this and four other instances of officials investing in Huizhou merchants' business ventures.
[275] Guo Hou'an, *Ming shilu jingji ziliao xuanbian*, 524–26; and Wang Chunyu and Du Wanyan, *Mingdai huanguan*, 128–32.

nonofficial intermediaries like eunuchs, special emissaries, and private agents. Huizhou's merchants appear as easy targets, vulnerable not just to official charges of corruption, but also to merchant protest in public. In fact, when all three scandals were resolved by the emperor's belated recognition of his emissaries' misdeeds and confiscation of their property, compensation to these merchant victims is mentioned, if at all, only as an afterthought. It certainly was not comprehensive.

In the first of these cases the eunuch Chen Zeng 陳增 took revenge on a Shandong magistrate for claiming that he, Chen, was exploiting local laborers to open government-owned lead mines in Shandong, while simultaneously pocketing most of the profits for himself. Chen responded with a flood of abusive countercharges, the most coherent being that his critic, a native of Huizhou, was a kinsman of certain Huizhou merchants who had called on their fellow lineage member, this official, to promote their own plan to develop the government's lead mines for themselves and not the dynasty.[276]

The second incident involved a vendetta led by a certain Cheng Shouxun 程守訓, a "market rascal" discovered and adopted by Chen Zeng.[277] This native of Huizhou knew many secrets of his home area, some of which he fed to his new "father" along with suggestions on how to increase government tax revenues from mining. As he proceeded to travel about the Jiang Huai 江淮 region as an imperial delegate charged to investigate families "who had not followed the

---

[276] Li Weizhen, *Dami shanfang ji*, 64.34a–42b, esp. 34b–37a, names Wu Hongdao 吳弘道, Wu Shilai 吳時來, Wu Pang 吳滂, and Wu Shifeng 吳時俸 as the men whom Cheng Shouxun denounced for bribing Wu Zongyao. He also describes Wu Shifeng as "a pre-eminent merchant with a great number of assets." Wu Zongyao was a native of Bei'an 北岸 Village in the north of She county, while the four other Wus came from the west of the county (where Xi'nan is located). The kinship links of Wu Zongyao's family to the Wus of Xi'nan are mentioned in ibid., 64.37a; and in Li Dou, *Yangzhou huafang lu*, 13, 282, both of which designate the Bei'an and Xi'nan Wus as "men of the [same] descent group" (*zongren* 宗人). *Fengnan zhi*, 6, 316, names Wu Shifeng as one of the Xi'nan Wus who received an honorary degree after his family donated 300,000 taels of silver to the Ming court to help fund its military support for Korea in resisting the Japanese invasion. The *Xin'an Shexi Xi'nan shipu* (1602 ed.) lists Wu Pang (24b), Wu Shilai (59b), and Wu Shifeng (59b) as members of, respectively, the 23th, 24th, and 24th generations. For more discussion of this famous lineage, see Chapter 6 below.

[277] Liu Shijun, *Wu suo Liu xiansheng juguan shuijing*, 2, 496; Shen Defu, *Wanli Yehuo bian*, 6, 175–76, and 16, 427; Wei Jianlin, *Mingdai huanguan*, 344–45; Guo Hou'an, *Ming shilu jingji*, 586–87.

law and others who had hidden away valuable treasures," he targeted certain Huizhou merchants whom he despised. After being rebuffed by thieves in Suzhou, he returned to his native Huizhou "letting people first divulge secrets about others even slightly well off, whom he then punished harshly to extract lies [to continue his vendetta]." To the outrage of many, he set up a huge mansion in Huizhou's prefectural seat, at whose gates he had the temerity to erect two memorial arches on which he had his name inscribed above those of high provincial officials. Before his eventual arrest for rapacious robbery, he had reportedly brought down several salt merchant families, looted 400,000 taels for himself, and forced more than several thousand other Huizhou men, including salt merchants, to fall to their knees before him, plead for their lives, and hand over huge gifts of silver.[278]

A third incident, probably the best-known of the three, concerns Suzhou, where the eunuch Sun Long 孫隆 arrived in 1601 as an imperial agent authorized to collect a special new tax for the court. A Huizhou pawnbroker there, in addition to supplying Sun with gifts, bribed an assistant of Sun to ensure that some of Suzhou's market riffraff would collect the special tax. Once appointed, these men "kept their watch on the major waterways and roadways, where they openly plundered goods from traveling merchants (*xingshang* 行商)." In response to local sentiment, Sun "levied only the traveling merchants and not the resident merchants." For a time, "people's hearts began to settle down," until the traveling merchants deliberately avoided Suzhou and its waterways. Not only did the tax collectors' revenue from these arbitrary levies fail to meet the official quota, but also Suzhou's residents soon found their income declining. Their feelings towards Sun turned sour, especially when he imposed a separate levy on the owners of silk-weaving looms in the city, and crowds of ordinary protestors from Suzhou city and the surrounding countryside started to protest in public against Ming misrule.[279] They attacked first the residence of the tax-collecting official Wang (or Huang) Jianjie 王(黃)建節 and then the homes of the "big households," who had reportedly loaned him money as a kickback for

---

[278] Gu Yingtai, *Mingshi jishi benmo*, v. 3, 1,009–17; Ding Yi, *Mingdai tewu zhengzhi*, 206, 212–13, 226.
[279] Guo Hou'an, *Ming shilu jingji*, 590–91.

exempting their goods, but not the peasants' chickens and vegetables, from the new taxes.[280]

These cases concern extreme situations which did not bring Huizhou merchants into direct contact with court officials (for that level of involvement we shall have to wait until the Mt Huang disaster of the 1620s, when one of Huizhou's wealthiest families would suffer grievously at the hands of court leaders). Nonetheless, these three smaller-scale cases help explain why, in the latter half of the Ming, Huizhou merchants rarely sought the limelight. As outsiders, they preserved a public reticence that helped to keep the government and its representatives at bay. When She county suffered a sudden land tax increase, it was not they but Huizhou's office holders and degree holders who in 1578 had the temerity to hold a public protest and demonstration (admittedly, some of their lineage or family members probably were merchants).[281] By contrast, the merchants chose to oblige their superiors and refrained from pressing any request for the public establishment of native-place associations in the delta cities and market towns where they resided as sojourners. Not for them the moral outrages of the Donglin 東林 scholars against Ming misrule, nor some late Ming intellectuals' courageous critiques of social and economic abuses. Nor even the efforts of some merchants from elsewhere in Suzhou to set up in public stone steles inscribed with government bans on arbitrary attacks on merchants and their market activities by brokers, yamen underlings, and "bare sticks."[282]

During the Ming, however, they practiced a policy of making private arrangements, often involving collusion, to achieve at least a partial resolution of their problems. Instead of fighting to escape the government's clutches, they aimed at embedding themselves within the administration of one of its offices. Nowhere was this strategy more evident and successful than in their activities in the Ming's salt monopoly, not in the sale of salt but in a highly speculative investment contest that they played with Ming eunuchs and officials. Some rich Huizhou merchants won this Yangzhou financial match, acquiring by the early seventeenth century a legitimacy, wealth, and security far greater than

---

[280] Shen Shixing, *Cijian tang ji*, 40.11a–12b. *Suzhou fuzhi* (1691), 81.36a–b, mentions the alternative surname Huang.
[281] Fuma, "Shilun Mingmo Huizhoufu," 271–90.
[282] Peng Qiusheng, "Yu Suzhou jingshang," 37–91; and his "Ming Qing shidai Suzhou," 83–90.

Native-Place Associations: A Resolution?

they could have acquired and retained through conducting merely commodity trading in the Yangzi Valley. It is this half-hidden duel, shrouded in guile and deceit, that the next chapter investigates as further evidence of how these Huizhou merchants struggled to find a protected niche in Ming financial administration that they could twist to their lucrative long-term advantage.

In sum, if there was "a Huizhou merchant way" of working outside Huizhou, it was for top merchants, whenever possible, to run business operations from within the private halls of officialdom and out of the back corridors of power. Or, to put it more concretely, it was to take their commercial assets and their financial skills and deploy these within organizations of safe government monopolies, next military officials, and then civil officials. They thereby could meet the dual goal of gaining the dynasty's stamp of approval and winning enough earnings to please the ancestors and relations who back home awaited every New Year's for the dispensation of their latest dividends.

4 | Huizhou Merchants and Their Financial Institutions

As the secular expansion of long-distance trade took root in the Yangzi Valley during the second half of the fifteenth century, the commercial economy of central and south China increasingly functioned on credit, driven to ever higher levels by the circulation of huge sums of imported silver and by the Ming government's monetization of basic tax payments. Two kinds of merchants, moneychangers, and pawnbrokers (aka, to some scholars, merchant bankers) (*dianshang* 典商), predominated in this invigorated financial world, operating, respectively, money exchange shops (*qian hao, qianpu, qianye*) and pawnshops (*dianpu, dangpu*). The extended pre-Ming history of both of these institutions plus the slimness of their historical record makes it impossible to demonstrate, as some have argued for the medieval West, a line of institutional evolution from the money shop to the pawnshop. Instead, the work of these two types of financial institution overlapped as late as the Ming, even though right up to the twentieth century the pawnshop by all accounts played the far more significant role in the late imperial Chinese economy.

Discussions of Huizhou merchants' role in the financial institutions of the Ming economy have thus naturally concentrated on the pawnshop, arguing that profits from these businesses were a major source of the capital that their Huizhou owners invested in other businesses in the Yangzi delta and the Grand Canal area. This scholarly focus on the privately run secular pawnshop is particularly appropriate, since by the mid Ming this kind of pawnshop had become the predominant type of Chinese pawnshop, often operating under a Huizhou merchant's management. In fact, more often than not, the Huizhou merchant and pawnbroker (or perhaps money shop owner) were closely linked, if not identical, parties. Dealing in a wide variety of goods, from salt and textiles to tea and timber, they turned to opening pawnshops in the same town or area where they had migrated or set up agents to trade their commodities. The pawnshop was an obvious place to park their money, especially as repeated government closure of temples, defrocking of monks, and confiscation of monastic endowments had since the 1390s greatly weakened competition from temple pawnshops. In the institutional vacuum brought about by the demise of this millennium-old Buddhist rival, the secular pawnshop moved forward with little opposition or competition, offering credit not just to merchants but also to ordinary people in much of east China from the fifteenth century. A century later its impact there was pervasive, profoundly influencing both urban and rural transactions in credit and even handicraft production.

Past studies on the rise of these private secular pawnshops have also revealed their centrality in the delta's financial life and in Huizhou merchants' financial activities there. Such findings have been crucial in highlighting the distinctive evolution of China's financial institutions, but this insight has come at a cost. It has distracted financial historians from studying another type of Ming financial activity and institution that arguably was more important for the Ming economy in general and far more profitable for Huizhou merchants in particular than were pawnbrokering or moneychanging, namely these same merchants' repeated speculation in the intricacies of Ming government salt monopoly transactions and administrative practices. The first half of this chapter seeks to reverse this historiographical neglect and show how Huizhou merchants' deep involvement in the Ming salt monopoly became concerned with much more than salt. The discussion then will move onto the money shop and pawnshop operations at the opposite, the lower, end of the hierarchy of credit institutions associated with Huizhou merchants in the Ming, as we gain a comprehensive view of the changes in credit institutions and arrangements that proved vital to the success of Huizhou merchants outside Huizhou.

The Ming Salt Monopoly

By all accounts the Ming salt monopoly administration of the production and distribution of salt was a monument to poor co-ordination and to all varieties of cupidity.[1] To start with, it lacked a head office and a head administrator, and was simultaneously run by no fewer than six salt distribution commissions and eight salt distribution

---

[1] Huang, *Taxation*, 189–224.

superintendancies, all of them handling the personnel, prices, delivery deadlines, penalties, and needs of distinct salt-consumption areas scattered about the country.[2] Although the originators of this patchwork of institutions delegated great unilateral powers solely to the emperor and the Minister of Revenue, they set up a remarkably makeshift set of offices and practices to implement their decisions.[3] The government supervised hereditarily incarcerated men in the production of salt in a few, mainly coastal, areas, and then selected and assigned merchants to deliver this salt to designated areas for sale at highly inflated prices to its advantage.

Intended to be simple and straightforward, the administrative arrangements for salt production and distribution were designed as a grain–labor–salt barter scheme. But over time they became increasingly complicated and inefficient, with none of the involved parties, including the government, incentivized to introduce, or locate resources for, better methods of salt production. If production had been small and profits minimal, these drawbacks would not have mattered. But as the scale of salt production and trade surpassed that of all other Ming products except grain,[4] the cumulative inefficiencies of this Ming government arrangement must have seriously damaged government revenue.[5]

The functioning of this salt monopoly was established on a set of highly questionable assumptions. First, its creators, the founding emperor and a set of his officials, assumed that bartering practices suitable to a primitive rural market could be transposed to handle complex transactions in a vast empire with a long history of commercial activity. While the government may have thereby been able to administer its monopoly cheaply, it is hard to call its administration efficient or effective. Its detachment from close involvement or supervision in the production and distribution of "its" salt opened the door

---

[2] Ibid., 189–91.   [3] Ibid., 200–01.
[4] Saeki, *Chūgoku ensei*, 374, reports a 1614 claim that most of the dynasty's cash revenue came from salt, as much as 60 percent by one contemporary estimate. But, Huang, *Taxation*, undermines such claims, if only because the Ming had poor accounting practices and highly erratic annual cash income totals (see Table 14, pp. 216 and 274, for an estimated basic central-government cash income in 1614 of 2,000,00 taels and an actual cash income twice that figure).
[5] Ibid., and, Puk, *Rise*.

to unregulated production and distribution, or smuggling, on a scale that eventually led to significant tax losses.[6]

Second, the same creators and their successors assumed the stable functioning of a rough balance between the amount of salt produced by government saltern workers and the amount of salt redeemed by salt merchants using government-issued certificates (*yin* 引) to acquire salt to distribute around the empire. Yet this balancing act very soon broke down. Inadequate government planning and financing drove most of the involved parties to find alternative ways to produce, distribute, and sell salt. Already in 1435 total accumulated salt tax arrears in just the Lianghuai 兩淮 area surpassed 700,000 *yin* of salt, roughly equivalent to this area's annual salt production quota.[7]

By the mid fifteenth century, the breakdown had become systemic, in that the working practices of parties at all levels of production, distribution, and administration seriously diverged from the official script. From its start the Ming government had failed to provide transport facilities for its operating agencies, who thus were obliged to rely on private merchants to distribute "its" salt.[8] The saltern households, paid by the government for at least the first Ming century with increasingly worthless paper money, frequently abandoned their hereditary labor duties; if they did not abscond completely, they regularly failed to meet their production quota, since they preferred to produce salt privately for better-paying smugglers, some of them Huizhou merchants.[9] Patrols drafted by the government to police production regularly colluded with saltern households to sell off salt privately and thus illegally, even while they were also paid by the same government to capture and submit an annual quota of contraband salt.[10] Furthermore, the officials appointed to run the operations for the government rarely had the time to master the monopoly's administrative practices and procedures. Inexperienced and appointed for short tenures, they also were often too few to handle all the work properly; for instance, the staff of the Lianghuai regional commission consisted of about sixty officials and a hundred-plus runners and other lowly functionaries, all scattered about in different offices at the rate of about one official per office.[11] As a result, actual management of production and distribution

[6] Saeki, *Chūgoku ensei*, 376–404.   [7] Puk, *Rise*, 52.
[8] Huang, *Taxation*, 193.
[9] Ibid., 195; Saeki, *Chūgoku ensei*, 384–86, 491–92; *MQHS*, 63.
[10] Huang, *Taxation*, 198.   [11] Ibid., 197.

often fell into the hands of private local parties with their own agendas (which frequently included smuggling).[12] And, in accord with the dynasty's general political culture, the court itself showed blatant disregard for the long-term well-being of this monopoly, as it – or rather, different Ming emperors – tended to view the salt monopoly office as a personal "piggy bank" with unlimited cash reserves to be smashed and raided at imperial will.[13]

Nonetheless, as the Ming government itself accumulated heavy debts from the rising cost of running itself and the imperial household and from its brainless military ventures along the northern border, its offices usually remained underfinanced.[14] Ostensibly to help them find further funding, over the course of the fifteenth and sixteenth centuries no fewer than thirty eunuchs, the powerful bosses at the court as well as the underlings they despatched to provincial salt monopoly offices, acted to impose yet another level of supervision, or extortion, on salt monopoly administrative centers like Yangzhou. When an enterprising merchant wished to buy new salt certificates but found them oversubscribed, he would find that a well-placed bribe to a eunuch or official would lead to the overissuing of that year's quota of new salt certificates to both buyer's and seller's considerable profit (in the mid Ming it was estimated that some 200,000 salt certificates, the equivalent of approximately 80,000,000 catties (*jin* 斤) of salt, were being annually handled illicitly by eunuchs and private merchants along the Yangzi).[15] By retaining merchant payments for salt certificates these eunuchs grew fabulously rich. The more cunning sent some of their pickings on to the palace in Beijing, where they eventually rose high in the ranks of eunuch administration, regardless of the chaos they left behind in their provincial offices.[16] Between 1486 and 1626 over twenty of these high-ranked eunuchs altogether acquired 2,000,000 salt certificates, which brought them great wealth when subsequently sold or exchanged for a commensurate amount of salt and silver.[17] And so, even though the Ming government's excessive issue of salt certificates can be seen as a cunning indirect way for it to impose heavy

---

[12] Saeki, *Chūgoku ensei*, 392–403; Huang, *Taxation*, 191–92, 196–97.
[13] Huang, *Taxation*, 222: "The salt monopoly never became a public service, but remained only a source of government revenue."
[14] Ibid., 194, on the clumsy procedures for issuing salt certificates.
[15] *Fengnan zhi*, 6, 387; Luo Zhuandong, *Chang Jiang*, 341.
[16] Huang, *Taxation*, 211–12.   [17] Luo Zhuandong, *Chang Jiang*, 341.

taxes on salt merchants without increasing its administrative costs, the actual enforcement of this clever idea fell often into the hands of eunuchs with their own agendas. As a result, in Ming official circles the salt monopoly became a byword not just for Huizhou merchant wealth but also for merchant, eunuch, and official corruption.[18]

Thus Ray Huang's damning judgment – "It was perhaps in its management of the salt monopoly that the Ming government demonstrated most clearly its ineptitude in business management" – remains as valid an understatement today as it was when he first issued it in 1974.[19] Yet, in a manner we have come to expect from historians of central-government financial administration, Huang neglected to recognize that the purpose of the arrangements he denounces were not just business-related, at least in the modern sense. These "abuses" unintentionally created opportunities for private provincial parties to profit at government expense. Huizhou salt merchants, in particular, would find golden – or more precisely silver – opportunities to run profitable businesses in and around salt monopoly transactions. What was an administrative swamp for the government proved to be virtually a silver mine for those Huizhou merchants willing to adapt their operations to the needs and wishes of this peculiar political, not business, institution. What had begun as a clever Ming government tactic for indirect taxation wound up, in the hands of cleverer merchants, as a means to get great wealth from ultimately the public purse.

In reaching a roughly similar conclusion that the salt monopoly was a highly profitable sphere of commercial trading for Huizhou and other regional merchant groups during the Ming, past students have by and large assumed that these Huizhou merchants' profits from the salt monopoly came predominantly from their authorized sale of government salt.[20] They have continually pointed to a basic mid-Ming reform of the early Ming salt distribution system that lightened the burden for merchants, especially Huizhou merchants, since it allowed different merchants for the first time to perform the two different stages of a job that previously had had to be performed by the same merchant. Following this administrative reform, the Huizhou merchant

---

[18] *MQHS*, 39, indicates that Huizhou salt merchants often came from the ranks of Huizhou's gentry families and great lineages; Huang, *Taxation*, 221.
[19] Huang, *Taxation*, 189.
[20] This view permeates most research on Huizhou merchants and the Ming salt monopoly. Even Saeki, *Chūgoku ensei*, seems vulnerable to this charge.

was allowed to focus on the more lucrative stage of the delivery work; that is, in the lower and middle Yangzi Valley, where he happened to be busily setting up his wharves, shops, and business networks in other trades. The boost he acquired from his improved position in the salt monopoly administration would have profound consequences for his market dominance in other commodity and money markets in the Yangzi Valley.

In the first century of managing their supposed "command economy" the Ming rulers had sought to solve some basic military, fiscal, and transportation problems at their merchants' expense. For at least the first fifty years of the dynasty these problems were particularly acute in north China, where both the agricultural and commercial economies were barely capable of sustaining the civilian population. The relocation in 1419 of the capital and much of its population from Nanjing in the southeast to Beijing in the northeast only worsened the north's perennial food shortage problems and strained a rickety infrastructure for grain transport.[21] Using forced labor, the Ming restored the canal section to Beijing with some success. But the establishment of Nine Defense Areas along the porous northern borders in the 1420s imposed yet further strains on transport beyond Beijing, as now huge numbers of government troops – by the century's end about 300,000 men[22] – were permanently stationed in these out-of-the-way garrisons and had to be fed. After failing to get these border soldiers to till the soil to feed themselves, the government resorted to a solution of Song dynasty origin.[23] It coupled a requirement of grain deliveries to these northern border garrisons with official permission to undertake the highly lucrative sale of salt to civilian consumers in the prosperous Yangzi Valley. Ingeniously simple in design and cheap to administer, this solution shifted the government's problem into the hands of private merchants rich enough to complete these two interlinked government jobs – the task of delivering grain to the northern garrisons, which upon completion qualified (and obliged) the same grain

---

[21] Hok-lam Chan, "The Chien-wen, Yung-ho, Hung-hsi, and Hsuan-te reigns, 1399–1435," 251–57.
[22] Mote, "The Cheng-hua and Hung-chih reigns, 1465–1505," 373.
[23] Chien, *Salt and State*. The Ming characteristically altered this Song practice by exerting more control on the merchants: it banned their use of any money, metal or paper, in the transaction.

transporter to distribute and sell a fixed amount of government salt to other areas of the empire specified by the appropriate salt commission office.

The first stage's grain transport from the lower Yangzi delta to a northern garrison area – for instance, from Yangzhou to the frontier Shanxi walled city of Taiyuan – was a round trip of nearly 1,200 miles. As this stage's work brought few, if any, immediate profits, its expenses were largely borne by merchants out of their delayed share of profits from the second stage's round trip of another 1,200 miles between two commercial centers of the lower and middle Yangzi Valley such as Yangzhou and Wuchang. Thus political, economic, and transport needs were all to be met by an integrated 2,400-mile-long travel scheme that would satisfy diverse interests – official and merchant, regional and imperial, military and economic – and yet be led and even performed by a single party under strict government supervision. The fact that salt merchants, upon selling the Yangzhou salt for great profit in Wuchang, could fill their ships with goods from the middle Yangzi for profitable sale back in the lower Yangzi markets only made them more eager to sign up for this deal. The bitter afflictions of Yangzi river travel described in the previous chapter would have been assuaged by the provision of this sweetener of a very lucrative return voyage.

Such was the political and economic scaffolding on which the fledgling Ming cobbled together a plan to graft the devastated economy of north China onto the relative affluence of south China. Huizhou merchants – and virtually any other well-funded merchant willing to do the job – were thus expected to transport government-acquired grain to the Ming frontier garrisons, and only upon their return to the salt production area of Huai'an and Yangzhou could they pick up a corresponding amount of government salt that they were to transport to and sell at other specific sites. Huizhou salt merchants by and large were assigned to sell their salt in the two most profitable of the eleven Ming salt consumption areas, Lianghuai and Liangzhe 兩浙, in the lower and middle Yangzi Valley and Zhejiang province.[24]

Even though these benefits persisted for government and merchants alike over the fifteenth century reliable figures are very few, but in the Liangzhe area government charges in grain on merchants seeking to acquire a salt certificate rose arguably as much as 50 percent between

---

[24] Puk, *Rise*, 29–30, Table 1.1 and Map. 1.1.

1370 and 1436[25] – it took little time for both parties to start faulting and abusing the arrangement. For all their promise of high rewards, these arrangements, on reflection, imposed on long-distance traders heavy costs that were inescapable. Each round trip of some 2,400 miles was meant to take no less than two years, but often it was two or three times longer. Also, it required so much capital investment that only rich merchants ventured to participate directly in this transport scheme. Two or more years of logging up expenses without a centime of compensation was not the kind of deal that Huizhou merchants were accustomed to sign up to.[26]

By the mid fifteenth century, not surprisingly, the early Ming arrangement was fraying at more than its edges. The government, while still trying to steel-wall its command economy against market forces it could not control, suffered the consequences of imperial overreach, of claiming power the dynasty could never efficiently manage and yet continued to presume was its to use and expand. At the same time, it repeatedly initiated policies that undercut the value of its own long-term needs as well as the interest of its merchant partners' investments. It tolerated falls in salt production and eunuch interference in salt administration, and also engaged in vain and costly military ventures.[27] It issued excessive supplies of paper money and failed to mint sizeable amounts of new copper cash or allow for the legal use of silver. Starved thereby of sound coinage and reliable currency, Ming merchants, ordinary consumers, and even some government offices felt obliged to violate the dynasty's laws by completing their salt transactions with privately exchanged silver ingots. Meanwhile, the Ming government was hesitant to sponsor large-scale exploration of silver and copper mines, out of fear of promoting social unrest by miners and out of knowledge that recent dynasties had failed to find large new deposits of these metals. Furthermore, in its eyes a scheme that exploited merchants had the moral benefit of preventing men empowered by wealth alone from assuming greater social and political power.

Nonetheless, the Ming government's command over its "command economy" seriously deteriorated over time. If it wanted merchants to

[25] MQHS, 54–55. [26] Huang, Taxation, 194.
[27] Wang Chunyu and Du Wanyan, Mingdai huanguan, 133–61, probes eunuch intrusion in salt monopoly operations but not their relations with Huizhou merchants.

buy salt certificates and so improve its revenues, it seemingly would have to pay more attention to their interests. Yet it was the salt merchants, almost certainly those from Huizhou, who against engrained Ming official distrust of silver and merchants found a solution – a highly remunerative solution – to their problems by introducing greater flexibility into the financing of grain deliveries to the frontier.

The key to the radical improvement in merchant profits is usually taken to be the new distribution policy decided in 1492 by the then head of the Board of Finance, Ye Qi 葉淇. Salt merchants, along with the head Grand Secretary Xu Pu 徐溥 are said to have persuaded Ye to decouple the century-old barter arrangement by allowing for payment in silver for salt certificates and by decoupling the two steps of the delivery process.[28] No longer did Huizhou salt merchants have to deliver grain to the northern border garrisons. Now they could use silver to pay transporters to deliver grain for them to the frontier, purchase these certificates from the grain transporters upon their return from the frontier delivery, or pay the government directly in silver for the amount of salt certificates required for them to carry out the Yangzi salt transport stage of the work. Partially in 1489 and comprehensively in 1492, it carried out these procedural reforms that simplified the administrative process and replaced a form of merchant labor service requirement with a silver payment. It thus allowed merchants, particularly Huizhou merchants, to focus solely on the far more profitable second-step work of selling salt in the Yangzi Valley, without needing to do the first-step grain delivery in the north. This introduction of silver into this powerful government monopoly helped to stimulate the circulation of all kinds of other goods in the public and especially the private economy, if only because upon returning from the middle Yangzi Huizhou merchants' boats invariably carried products of this area for the towns and cities of the delta.

Predictably, this policy change aroused considerable controversy among official circles and some overlooked merchant groups, and it soon was temporarily reversed to improve military defense against a

---

[28] Saeki, *Chūgoku ensei*, 463–69; Puk, *Rise*, 70; Xue Yingqi, *Xianzhang lu*, 41.12b; Fujii, "Shin'an shōnin no kenkyū," 36.2, 35–36; Lei Li, *Huangchao lieqing ji*, 32.40b, indicates that Ye Qi made the proposal at the prompting of senior Grand Secretary Xu Pu, a fellow 1456 recipient of the metropolitan degree (Goodrich and Fang, *Dictionary of Ming Biography*, v. 1, 599).

potential Mongol invasion.[29] Yet, in the long term – certainly from the start of the Jiajing reign era (1522–66) – this reform became the dominant state policy, not just because some Huizhou families had successfully colluded with a high official. Huizhou merchants appear to have been cunning enough to assure that their reform's change of the means of payment from grain to silver, at an agreed rate of 0.3 to 0.4 tael of silver for each salt certificate and its corresponding amount of salt, was bound to increase state revenues (and increase it in a much more handy and mobile form of currency).[30]

The 1492 reform not only achieved its promised revenue expansion for the state but also had a profound impact on the regional division of labor in the salt monopoly, on border defense and regional integration, and on the role of Huizhou merchants in the overall Ming economy. Whereas northern regional merchants from Shanxi and Shaanxi would henceforth tend to dominate the grain trade of north China as frontier merchants (*bianshang* 邊商), Huizhou merchants, along with some enterprising Shanxi and Shaanxi merchants, became its "interior merchants" (*neishang* 內商), centering their operations in the more profitable lower and middle stretches of the Yangzi Valley, particularly in Yangzhou. Their presence in Yangzhou salt merchant circles for sure dates back to the start of the Ming and earlier,[31] but their numbers then were fewer than those from Shanxi and Shaanxi. Accounting even in the sixteenth century for less than a tenth of all the empire's salt merchants,[32] they nonetheless became the powerful linchpins who often bought the frontier merchants' salt certificates and then shipped and sold the salt itself onto Jiangxi and Huguang merchants, the so-called "river merchants" (*shuishang* 水商). As a result, they acquired virtually monopoly control over these smaller traders, dispatching them to deliver and sell salt for them in counties lower down the marketing hierarchy of the middle Yangzi Valley.[33]

[29] Saeki, *Chūgoku ensei*, 471–73.
[30] Wang Tingyuan and Wang Shihua, *Huishang*, 57.
[31] Ibid., 55, for two powerful early Ming Huizhou salt merchants, one from Wuyuan and the other from She county. For Huizhou involvement in the Song salt monopoly see Chapter 1 above.
[32] Saeki, *Chūgoku ensei*, 475.
[33] Ibid., 290–91; *Jiangdu xianzhi* (1811), 12.3a, names the major post-1492 migrant families to Yangzhou: "The Liang 梁 of Sanyuan 三原, the Yan 閻 of Shanxi, the Liu 劉 of Fengzhou 縫州 in Shanxi and of Lanzhou 蘭州 in Gansu, the Qiao 喬 and Gao 高 families of Pingyang 平陽 in Shanxi, the Zhang 張 and

The consequences of this policy decision did not escape the notice of Li Mengyang 李夢陽 (1473–1529), a bright young bureau director in the Ministry of Revenue. Writing in c.1506 about the salt monopoly office administration at the turn of the century, he criticized the salt delivery reform for fostering corruption between salt merchants and officials. Not only "did salt merchants now have wealth equal to that of princes and marquises," but also they were using this wealth to win regulatory favors from officials. As a result, officials in the salt monopoly "were accumulating in one day millions of taels for themselves. Their wealth was sufficient to check the great merchants ... Virtually all the merchants from all directions were emerging from [these officials'] gates."[34]

Meanwhile, certain Huizhou salt merchants, many of them surnamed Huang, Wang, Cheng, and Fang,[35] greatly profited from this enlarged and emboldened network of collusion. Often the offspring of Huizhou's great lineages and gentry families, they came to dominate the salt trade as well as many associated commodity markets in the Yangzi valley during the second half of the Ming. In fact, within two generations of the 1492 reform other regional merchant groups were acutely aware that they were being directly and indirectly controlled by Huizhou merchants. With few alternative customers for their salt certificates, the frontier merchants often felt obliged to sell on their certificates to rich Huizhou merchants, who predictably beat down the initial selling price. The river merchants likewise had no choice but to deal with salt merchants from Huizhou on disadvantageous terms, since the bulk of salt certificates and salt reserves were in the hands of Huizhou merchants.[36] Needless to say, these Huizhou merchants did not rely on local brokers to negotiate these deals.

Guo 郭 of Jingyang 涇陽 (i.e., Xi'an fu 西安府), the Shen 申 of Xi'anfu, the Zhang of Lintong 臨潼 (in Xi'anfu), and the Dai 戴 of Shandong's Dengzhoufu 登州府, as well as various surnames from Huizhou, such as the Chengs 程, Wangs 汪, Fangs 方, and Wus 吳. All of these surname groups moved to Yangzhou in the mid Ming." As Saeki, *Chūgoku ensei*, 471, says, this move coincided with the government's conferral of the examination privilege on the sons of salt families living in Yangzhou, by which time these families would have had time to settle into Yangzhou.

[34] Fujii, "Shin'an shōnin no kenkyū," 36.4, 131.
[35] Zhang Haipeng and Wang Tingyuan, *Huishang yanjiu*, 39.
[36] On the frontier and river merchants' opposition to the interior merchants, see Puk, *Rise*, 70–71.

For sure, these changes in salt monopoly administration empowered and enriched these interior merchants. But over the last half of the Ming even greater fortunes were made by Huizhou merchants in the salt monopoly from their sale not so much of commodities like salt and timber as of salt certificates, pieces of paper that have only recently begun to receive the scholarly attention they merit. Studies by David Faure and Puk Wing-kin, in particular, have made it clear that the Ming salt merchants acquired significant income by creating and running a highly speculative and profitable market in this humble but essential item of their trade.[37] As Puk has demonstrated, the salt certificate became a financial instrument that enriched many Huizhou merchants, especially its more successful salt merchants. By 1617 their pre-eminence in the private but flourishing market for these salt certificates was such that a deeply indebted Ming government, unable to redeem all the certificates it had issued, conferred on these certificate-holding salt merchants official recognition and status as hereditary members of salt merchant syndicates. Dominated largely by Huizhou's salt merchant elite, these merchant groups would control the highly rewarding Yangzi Valley salt trade until the mid nineteenth century, outlasting the Ming's demise by two centuries.[38]

In telling the why and the how of this remarkable tale of fortunes built up on unfulfilled promises and unrelenting fears, the next section will reveal how, by embedding themselves within the government salt monopoly, Huizhou merchants succeeded in accumulating an exceptionally large amount of salt certificates and capital and thereby also secured their privileged place in the late imperial economic order. Even in a dynasty well known for its high levels of intrigue and mismanagement, few tales of corruption and collusion rival this particular story for the opacity of its operations and the extent of its impact on the ascendance of Huizhou merchants to a highly privileged position in the salt trade and in the commercial economy of the Yangzi Valley. Although at this remove in time and place it is difficult to unravel all the layers of merchant deception and official camouflage around this story (the main salt merchant villains are never named), fortunately for us there survive some denunciations of these salt merchant practices by a few officials, outraged by their fellow officials' surreptitious surrender to eunuchs and merchants. It is their reports and memorials that

[37] Ibid., 95–96; Faure, *China and Capitalism*, 22–24.   [38] Puk, *Rise*, 85–109.

reveal for us the serial abuses of salt monopoly trading and investment speculation that enriched many Huizhou merchant families.

This opaque tale of some Huizhou merchants' cornering a substantial share of the market in salt certificates (and by extension salt) is perhaps best conceived of as a fencing match. Imagine that just one of the fencers, supposedly representing the government, is in view, if barely, through a matt screen. His actions, though possibly prescribed by offstage parties, are at least discernible, whereas his opponent's (that is, the merchant's) moves are far more furtive, discernible solely through the tense quivers of the visible tip of his foil. And, when we read a string of government declarations and official denunciations issued over the course of the fifteenth and sixteenth centuries, we usually end up not knowing for sure whether their announcements are, to complete the metaphor, the government's (or official's) thrusting responses to a salt merchant's advances, its efforts to keep on supporting the camouflage of nonexistent administrative policy (when all it had was a clever means of extracting a great deal of money from merchants whose wealth it sought to limit), or themselves pre-emptive lances at merchant moves they seriously feared. The government may have thought its bans on salt certificate abuses were one step ahead of these certificate holders' moves, but most likely it lagged by many steps. To that extent, these matches add up to an extended series of "cat-and-dog-like" skirmishes that suggest the otherwise invisible tactics and deals we might expect officials to have struck with late Ming merchants in Hangzhou, Suzhou, and other big delta cities.

For the government and the salt merchants the principal issue was how much each side could skim off the profits from transactions in salt certificates. By common understanding, from the Yongle era (1403–24) onward salt merchants were to acquire half of all the profits involved in the trading of salt.[39] In the fifteenth and sixteenth centuries, the trade in salt certificates can be understood as the merchants' main gambit to acquire an even larger share of this honeypot, at a time when many officials and eunuchs were anxious to do likewise for themselves and their government, often in that order. The ensuing clashes provided enough backstage drama to fill countless scripts of official denunciations of merchant rule breaking and merchant tales of diligence justly rewarded.

---

[39] *Ming shilu*, Shezong, 515.5b–6a.

Salt Certificates and Their Financial History

At the upper levels of Ming dynasty finance, fifteenth- and sixteenth-century innovations in credit arrangements conferred great significance on the salt certificate.[40] Issued by the Ming salt monopoly administration from 1371 onwards, this paper certificate was initially expected to serve four functions. Most basically, it was a unit of weight that indicated the amount of salt a certificate holder was to receive upon exchange of the certificate with a government office; one *yin* normally was considered 200 catties (*jin* 斤) of salt in weight.[41] Second, it was a piece of government-issued paper that permitted its holder to acquire or sell this commensurate amount of salt. Third, it served as a travel permit for any merchants traveling with salt or other goods more than 100 *li*, or roughly thirty-three miles, from his home area. And, as a salt merchant was obliged by the nature of his job to travel from a salt production site to often distant and disparate sites of salt consumption, it also came to function as a requisite receipt at various inspection and commercial tax payment points in his delivery of grain to northern frontier garrisons and of salt to middle-Yangzi ports. Hence, all merchants involved in the early Ming salt monopoly's delivery work needed this humble piece of paper to perform legally both stages of their transporting and trading work under government supervision.

Questions naturally arose over which party had the power to issue or transfer these certificates. From its start the dynasty severely restricted what uses other parties made of these pieces of paper. It issued outright bans on lending, pawning, and especially selling any of them. Admittedly, as was almost the norm in Ming financial history, the first party to break out of such an official straightjacket proved to be the same government that issued the ban, as when in 1404 and later it linked the value of certain salt certificates to the value of its paper money, in a desperate effort to revive its depreciated paper currency. First in the capital and then in the provinces ordinary people asked the government to give them these certificates in place of its paper money, and then started using them to handle their dealings with the government.[42] Later, in the fifteenth century, the government sometimes bartered them for grain and money to relieve famine-stricken

---

[40] Faure, *China and Capitalism*; Puk, *Rise*.   [41] Puk, *Rise*, 55.
[42] Saeki, *Chūgoku ensei*, 439.

commoners or soldiers.[43] In the early sixteenth century, eunuchs even used them to pay private parties for the silk thread they sent to the imperial silk factories.[44] As the salt merchants bought and retained an increasingly large stock of salt certificates, some of them traded, pawned, paid bills with, and sold them, at least when conducting private deals with fellow salt merchants and others. In other words, both the government and these merchants had surreptitiously hit on an alternative form of paper currency that they wanted to use in the private commercial economy. As with all "crypto-currencies" not automatically exchangeable for precious metals or widely cashable currencies, the use of these certificates depended heavily on the level of trust others had in their users. Since few trusted the Ming government and its currency more than the Huizhou merchants and their salt, these unauthorized uses of the salt certificate did not seriously threaten their transferability among merchants.

Nonetheless, the bulk of Ming officials regarded this additional fifth function of the salt certificate as anathema. Having designed a monopoly to run at minimal cost to the dynasty, they were loath to allow these certificates to gain a monetary power that they themselves could not control (especially when by the 1420s the government's own fiat currency of paper money had plummeted to less than 2 percent of its stated value) and that would thereby directly enrich merchants rather than themselves.[45] The government's reissue of these bans in 1424 and 1483 reflected its awareness of the ongoing popularity of private, albeit illicit, transactions with these certificates and its own need to reassert its ban against a rising tide of violations.[46] For the rest of the dynasty it never legitimized these lucrative practices by salt merchants; nor, however, did it halt them.

Soon, this aversion to the actual practices of the private market in certificates confronted a problem that even the Chinese government could not ignore: death and its impact on a salt merchant's unused salt certificates. In theory, unredeemed certificates did not exist, since every year the amount redeemed was to equal the total amount produced. But not only did the saltern households' production often fail to match their production quota but also the revenue-hungry government itself often issued and sold more certificates than it knew it could exchange

---

[43] Ibid., 442.   [44] Ibid., 495–96.
[45] Von Glahn, *Fountain of Fortune*, 70–82.   [46] Puk, *Rise*, 34–35.

for its fixed salt quota. In other words, the government deliberately created more certificates than its offices could legally redeem. In no way did the law acknowledge that a salt certificate holder might be left in the lurch or, worse, die with certificates unredeemed.

Since the government refused to amend the law to solve the problem it had created, the heirs understandably took the law into their own hands by practicing fraud. They often camouflaged the father's death or simply acted in his place, faking his name and even calligraphy to ensure that they could redeem his salt certificates. For a century emperors and officials turned a blind eye to the practice, until in 1488 the Hongzhi emperor (r. 1488–1505) allowed direct heirs to petition the government to request an exception to the law in order to allow for inheritance of this form of property. Then, in 1503, he simplified this revision by requiring the heirs merely to notify the government of their household head's decease.[47] By this time, we can be sure that many merchants had become accustomed to deceiving the government and that many fraudulent certificates were circulating privately in a legal limbo.

The underlying problem of a mismatch between supply and demand was also complicated by the fact that some certificate holders – their purchasers as well as their heirs – preferred not to redeem them, at least as quickly as the government wanted. Believing their certificates' value would rise over time, they held on to these assets and eventually, despite the ban, started to pawn and sell them privately to cash in on any perceived increase in their market value. They were anxious to ensure that profits ostensibly destined solely for the government's coffers would come their way as well. This difficulty, which thanks to government controls over production, price, and schedule was not supposed to happen, probably worsened over time, because production setbacks increased, because the government's issues of certificates also expanded disproportionately, and because the merchants began to corner the market for salt certificates in ways that created a private market largely among themselves, eunuchs, and officials and thus disrupted government price regulations.

At all times the government theoretically had the political authority to renege completely on its debt and declare all these troublesome certificates worthless. Yet, when faced with the prospect of this

[47] Ibid., 33–35.

monopoly's financial collapse, it – or rather the eunuchs and officials who shared the top administration of the salt monopoly and the illicit and semi-licit profits raked from it – knew well enough to refrain from punishing these new paymasters, doubtless fearing that a financial collapse of the paymasters would damage their own well-being as well.[48] If Huizhou merchants would not invest in these certificates, then what other merchant group in south China would have had the funds to do so at the prices these government representatives were used to charging? The resulting damage to themselves would have been more than collateral.

Hence for the next two centuries the government sought, with varying success, to renege only selectively on its debt through a series of self-serving edicts. For instance, in 1429 it decreed different redemption policies for salt certificates issued before 1402 and for those issued afterwards. The early batch were declared redeemable only for a small amount of paper money and not salt, and holders of the post-1402 variety were told to cash in their certificates as soon as possible. In 1480 the government, facing an even greater number of unredeemed certificates, extended this selective reneging programme: those certificates issued before 1450 were declared redeemable only for paper money and those issued after 1450 could be redeemed at a rate favorable to the government or used to acquire salt from other production areas, or their holders could just do as normal and wait many years until it was their turn to redeem them for salt at Lianghuai. By 1489 this policy's failure was self-evident: some 5,000,000 certificates remained unredeemed and were not simply resting in their holders' chests.

Next, in 1490, the government made its rules even more draconian: all certificates issued more than thirty-five years previously – that is pre-1455 – were now declared defunct and unredeemable, while those issued since 1455 all faced annual depreciation in their redeemable-in-salt value. Their paper value would last just thirty-five years (presumably, the length of a salt merchant's career), and so those holding the more recent batch were under pressure to redeem them with the government as soon as possible.[49] In this case the government was probably bluffing. The number of unredeemed (mostly post-1455) salt certificates in private hands already in the previous year exceeded

---

[48] Wang Chunyu and Du Wanyan, *Mingdai huanguan*, 133–61.
[49] Puk, *Rise*, 45–46.

5,000,000,[50] and its readily available funds could pay nowhere near the redemption value of even a small portion of these certificates. And yet, through their partial reneging on the original terms of these certificates' purchase, officials threatened to halt the salt merchants' practice of hoarding, presumably to assert their own official clout in this duel of clashing fraudsters.

From 1492, once silver became an acceptable medium of exchange to supplement and replace the grain–labor–salt barter scheme of the first half of the dynasty, the situation changed. From then until the early seventeenth century, the government adjusted its monopoly over salt and salt certificates largely through changes in regulations that superficially were just administrative measures. It introduced new categories, new weights, and new exchange values for some old categories of salt and salt certificates ("regular," "surplus," and "reserve stock"),[51] all with the real aim of raising new silver taxes that would enrich the government (or its eunuch deputies) at the expense of merchants trying to redeem their salt certificates. Specifically, the government designated a part (usually 20 percent) of every year's salt quota production as "surplus" and made it redeemable only at a higher cost than the remainder of the salt quota (the other 80 or so percent) and limited it solely to holders of salt certificates. Furthermore, it offered saltern households more money for any salt they produced over their quota, out of a desperate hope to acquire more salt, including that already being sold as contraband. From 1522 on, this "surplus-salt silver" levy provided between a quarter and a half of the dynasty's annual revenues in silver (that from just the Lianghuai consumption area accounted for 600,000 taels; that is, 15 percent of the dynasty's annual revenue in silver). Although this levy succeeded in expanding the government's revenues, it did not alter the underlying problems of salt administration. In violation of centuries-old laws more merchants than ever before were dealing directly with the saltern households. They were willing to offer purchase prices higher than the government's, simply to shorten the time they were forced to wait when applying through government-prescribed channels.[52]

Probably to undercut this growing practice, in 1561 the government introduced a special "river salt certificate" for those who bought its newly introduced "surplus salt." Those who paid an extra fee for this

[50] Ibid., 42.   [51] Ibid., 40.   [52] Ibid., 126.

certificate were entitled to jump the queue of waiting salt merchants, shortcut the usual weighing and clearing procedures for purchased salt, and escape the need to sell their salt certificates cheaply to those who had hitherto dominated the interior market in salt. Needless to say, this policy change aroused strong opposition from those interior merchants who were still waiting for the government to deliver commensurate salt in return for salt certificates they had submitted several years earlier. A group of these interior merchants, consisting mainly of Huizhou salt merchants, expressed outrage at the inequity of the new arrangement. They were convinced that the government was intruding on highly profitable deals for frontier merchant certificates that they tightly controlled, and so they sought to drum up support for their opposition from allies in official ranks. These allies dutifully denounced this new arrangement for arbitrarily hastening the delivery of salt for some merchants at the expense of others. Some interior merchants even complained that their waiting time had now doubled, imposing expenses they could not afford, especially as they no longer had profits from their control of the frontier merchants' certificates. This reform lasted for seventeen years, inflaming the already tense relationship between the interior and frontier merchants. As each merchant group continued to feel poorly treated by this tax arrangement (the interior merchants for a time even refused to buy the now overpriced frontier merchants' salt certificates), they barely talked with one another. To quote Puk Wing-kin,

Lacking the capital to pay the surplus-salt silver, as well as connections in and familiarity with the Yangzhou milieu, [the frontier merchants] became easy targets for usury and fraud. The feud between frontier and interior merchants had reached a point where violent assaults erupted on the streets and even during official hearings.[53]

Subsequent official reforms repeatedly sought to halt the blockage of the salt and the hoarding of the salt certificates, but they all failed. The government increasingly focused on simply increasing its taxes from salt, especially with its introduction of a tax that aimed at raising more salt-surplus tax more quickly from unredeemed certificates. This step, like virtually all previous government measures, was short-term and provisional, essentially allowing it to grab hold of taxes that would

[53] Ibid., 70–72, 73.

have most likely come its way eventually.[54] In fact, by 1614 it had started to impose this pay-in-advance tax on all unredeemed salt certificates, as its options for finding future revenue sources had narrowed considerably.

Although we lack a series of clear annual figures for the number of salt certificates issued over time, a few surviving figures indicate the alarming scale of the government's debt problem: for instance, whereas the annual quota for salt certificates for sale in 1484 was 700,000 for Lianghuai and 440,000 for Liangzhe, the number actually issued and sold by the government that same year for these two areas totaled nearly 50 percent more; that is, respectively, 1,020,000 and 740,000 salt certificates. As this pattern persisted despite official and merchant criticisms, the government became caught in a vise largely of its own making, between selling the certificates to satisfy its short-term revenue needs and clinging to them due to its long-term commitment to maintain the market value of these pieces of paper. Government policy veered back and forth. Market anomalies, sharp price fluctuations, and merchant manipulation led to the increasing concentration of these certificates in the hands of a small number of interior salt merchants. By the early seventeenth century, the more wealthy salt merchants, mostly from Huizhou, had so outfoxed rival merchant groups, distracted government officials, and incompetent eunuchs that the Huizhou salt merchants, somewhat to their fright, held the dominant hand in the operation of the salt monopoly as the government's creditors.

While up in Beijing the Wanli emperor (r. 1573–1620) still refused to meet his officials and thus impeded any collaborative policy decisions on salt administration and other matters, down in Yangzhou eunuch managers were busy playing havoc with the salt monopoly's budget, not least by letting groups of salt merchants there dominate the market in salt certificates. As the mountain of unredeemed certificates piled up and as the government redemption policy often prioritized the more recently issued certificates over the older variety, well-heeled merchants ignored the government denunciations of "hoarding" and increasingly cornered the market in all forms of salt certificates. Empowered by this market control, these "powerful interior [Huizhou] merchants" pushed the purchase price of a frontier merchant's salt certificate down to a fifth of its official sale price, and then proceeded to

[54] Ibid., 86–87.

sell off their newly acquired certificates to less fortunate interior or water merchants at three times the official price. These supremely wealthy Huizhou salt merchants had outwitted the government by turning its monopoly into theirs.

By 1615 government salt monopoly finances had worsened. Revenues from the Lianghuai salt tax and salt certificate sales had dropped dramatically, even while their interior merchant holders were very lucratively expanding their own holdings of the certificates through private purchases. For example, the official price that year for a Huainan certificate was 0.85 tael, but the interior merchants were knocking it down by 80 percent when buying frontier merchants' certificates on the black market. Then, in 1616, we read from one official's report, "The hoarders of the certificates annually get great profits from Lianghuai, [where] the 680,000 salt certificates in Huainan cost 0.85 taels apiece and the 220,000 certificates in Huaibei cost 1.30 tales apiece. And, of the 900,000 certificates annually redeemed, the hoarders have cleverly earned 864,000 taels from the state coffers!" In other words, "the hoarders" (*tunhu* 囤戶) – identified here as "the powerful among the interior [that is, Huizhou] merchants" – were annually earning from these transactions alone 40 percent more than the government did from its own sale of "surplus salt."[55]

As a result, a backlog of unredeemed salt certificates had accumulated so thickly that if the government were to redeem them as promised, it would have consumed all its salt monopoly income for the next eight years, during which it would have been unable to redeem any of its more recently issued certificates (numbering now in the millions for the two major salt consumption areas served by Huizhou merchants). With its back to the wall and threatened with closure of its normal business operations, the Ming government was stymied. Its old tactics of confiscation, heavy fines, and arrest would no longer work, not least because the sums were so great that fewer merchants could independently afford to risk any investment in its operations. These rich merchants, meanwhile, were now able to manipulate the demand for certificates, to the extent that they could greatly influence the government's sale price for the certificates and eventually even the salt consumer's purchase price.

---

[55] Ibid., 88–100. Speculative sales broke out among these same merchants over changes in the government's prices for salt certificates.

Thus, in 1616 and 1617, the government, deeper than ever in debt to these rascals, decided to rewrite the rules of the salt monopoly's administration. Without fanfare the top official in Yangzhou met with the top salt merchants, and a deal was struck, privately. Instead of reneging on their debt completely, or making new paper certificates to replace the old or forcing the merchants to buy them in return for promises of future silver payments for all the past borrowing, the Ming government decided to rewrite its salt monopoly rules fundamentally. It would reimburse its creditors with an exclusive political privilege.[56] Henceforth, the salt merchants would, in theory, negotiate with the government not as individual salt merchants (or any privately formed commercial partnership), but as newly formed syndicates of creditor salt merchants chosen for each syndicate by the government. So long as these syndicates annually paid the government a silver-based salt tax, it would sell its salt certificates solely to them. As a result, those merchants who had cornered the market – identified as "the powerful among the interior merchants," and thus mainly from Huizhou[57] – were now elevated into elite groups of salt traders assured of regular sales and thus regularly high profits from trading in the most profitable mass commodity in the world's largest domestic market. They also had secured a permanently hereditary government post and thus hereditary official status, a privilege that few ordinary Ming civil officials would have ever contemplated as a feasible goal for themselves and their descendants.

Having gained renown as bodyguards for smugglers of salt in the eleventh century, merchants from Huizhou had come a long way. Already by the twelfth century they had graduated to trading salt and grain on their own. Then, by the late fifteenth century they had collectively become the most powerful commercial force in the Yangzi Valley's salt trade. By the second half of the sixteenth century they had by and large bested their rivals in the salt monopoly as a whole, and now in the early seventeenth century they had elevated themselves to become permanent purveyors of His Imperial Highness's salt and, by extension, any credit based on it.[58] They had done this off the scene, virtually outside the official Veritable Records, and certainly not in the records of the places they traded in. We know of their salt monopoly

---

[56] Ibid., 99.   [57] Ibid., 88–89.
[58] Faure, *China and Capitalism*, 22–24; Puk, *Rise*.

dealings principally through privately published denunciations by their official rivals, anthologies of important official writings, and a small number of salt merchant biographies privately published in Huizhou decades after the events described.

This tale of a prolonged contest between state and salt merchant over pieces of paper and silver constitutes a significant, if long-neglected, chapter in the history of the Ming economy. Pieced together from a variety of court records, salt official reports, local gazetteers, and the pioneering research of several East Asian scholars, notably Puk Wing-kin and David Faure, it reveals indirectly the specific tactics cunningly deployed by Huizhou merchants to outwit their government. Transparency in commercial and financial dealings was a strong card of neither party. And so we can probably infer that in this match of wits "the powerful among the interior merchants" had employed strategies we have seen practiced elsewhere by those known as "Huizhou merchants": risk-aversion (as in the Huizhou timber trade), the pooling of resources for multiple-party ownership (as in their joint-share partnerships), the frequent and quick resale of shares (as in their timber and rice sales), a stress at times on market share and a concomitant need to hoard goods or shares (as in village worship society conflicts), the holding of shares in numerous ventures (as with spirit tablets in multiple ancestral halls), the reliance on people already well known to them as kinsmen and fellow locals, the use of novel financial instruments like salt certificates for collateral in other business investment (such as pawnshops), and their struggle in volatile markets to create safe niches in government-administered offices or agencies from which they could profitably operate their other businesses in salt certificates as well as in timber, tea, and pawnshops. If the government could not protect them adequately as independent merchants, then they might find an authorized place within it from which to pursue their own commercial and financial interests. In other words, they sought to carry out in a government office a set of maneuvers arguably akin to those they had used in their transformation of authorized ancestral halls into credit institutions.

By the early decades of the seventeenth century, the capitalization and profit level of the Lianghuai and Liangzhe salt markets had soared far beyond anyone's expectations. According to estimates made by the knowledgeable Song Yingxing 宋應星 (c.1600–?), during the late Ming 30,000,000 taels were annually invested in the Yangzhou salt monopoly trade by private merchants, leading to annual profit returns of 9,000,000 taels. Higher than "the wholesale gross [profits] of over 7,000,000 taels" separately estimated by two scholars for the salt monopoly in 1723,[59] this late Ming estimate is likewise a gross-profit figure. Song himself whittled it down by subtracting 3,000,000 taels for necessary operating expenses and 1,000,000 taels for taxes, leaving the Yangzhou salt merchants with 5,000,000 taels of net profit in the Wanli era (that is, an annual net profit rate of 17 percent on investment).[60] And, even if this late Ming figure of 5,000,000 taels ends up after further subtractions (such as bribes, agreements, and other parties' shares in the trade), to approximate the 3,500,000 taels recently estimated as the salt monopoly's net profit in 1723, these Ming merchants' profits would have been large enough to fund a great number of salt merchant investments in other economic activities, and not just the entertainments, buildings, and pleasures mentioned by Song himself. As this estimated level of returns on capital investments appears to exclude their profits from speculative salt certificate dealings and from Huizhou merchants' salt trading in Hangzhou and the empire's other salt trading centers, the salt monopoly might justifiably be considered the monopoly of some Huizhou merchants rather than of the Ming dynasty. And so the merchant policy of "standing up and stepping back [in the presence of officials], of remaining lowly and humble," may have had its political costs. But such modesty harvested very immodest economic gains, and suggests the cunning and rapacity of these Huizhou merchants in private markets, like pawnbrokerages and many commodities, where they need not have regularly worried about the government.

Pawnshops

If the salt certificate is the Ming Huizhou merchants' major addition to the short list of Chinese financial instruments, then pawnshops are their main contribution to the late imperial development of financial institutions. As one of their number observed in the mid sixteenth century, whereas the Suzhou and Songjiang area (*Dongwu* 東吳) had silk and cotton and the Yangzhou and Huai area had salt, Huizhou,

---

[59] Finnane, *Yangzhou*, 125, drawing on Wang Fangzhong, "Qingdai qianqi," 37.
[60] Song Yingxing, *Yeyi lunqi, tantian silian shi*, yanzheng yi, 35.

Pawnshops

with its unfertile soil, had its "interest and dividends" (*ziqian* 子錢); that is, its credit institutions, or pawnshops.[61] The Huizhou contribution lay not in creating this institution – that innovation had been accomplished by Buddhist temples a thousand years earlier – but in helping it spread and become an essential part of the credit economy of late imperial China.[62]

This predominance of Huizhou pawnshops in the Ming credit sector is evident in their share of the tax quotas for pawnshops and their location at most of the major Ming commercial centers. A 1623 list of regional pawnshop tax quotas (the first such tax in Chinese history) ranks Huizhou second-highest along with the three delta prefectures of Suzhou, Songjiang, and Changzhou (Tables 4.1, 4.2, 4.3). But Huizhou was not the only place where Huizhou merchants kept their silver. And so, if we add to Huizhou's quota those of prefectures and provinces where Huizhou pawnshops predominated – the entire

Table 4.1 *Special pawnbrokerage tax levy quotas for specific provinces and metropolitan areas, 1623*

Province/MA	Tax quota (taels)
Zhejiang	25,000
Fujian	20,000
Henan	20,000
Huguang	20,000
Jiangxi	15,000
Guangdong	10,000
Shaanxi	10,000
Shandong	10,000
Sichuan	10,000
Shanxi	5,000
Guangxi	3,000
Yunnan	3,000
Subtotal	151,000
Northern Metropolitan Area	15,300
Southern Metropolitan Area	29,009
TOTAL	195,309

[61] *Dianshang*, 271. [62] McDermott, *Making*, v. 1, 92–94.

Table 4.2 *Pawnbrokerage tax levy quotas for specific prefectures in the Northern Metropolitan Area, 1623*

Prefecture	Tax quota (taels)
Baoding	4,000
Daming	2,500
Zhending	2,500
Hejian	2,000
Shuntian	2,000
Guangping	1,200
Yongping	1,000
Shunde	100
Subtotal	15,300

Southern Metropolitan Area, Zhejiang, Huguang (the Hankou area), Jiangxi, and Shandong (the Linqing area) (see Tables 4.1, 4.2, 4.3) – Huizhou pawnshop owners would at the minimum account for over half of the empire-wide pawnshop tax levy. Even if Huizhou pawnshop owners did not by extension have a similarly high share of the empire's silver in their hands, they collectively ranked as the merchant group with the greatest share of this silver.

This pre-eminence dates from the sixteenth century, when they expanded their operations beyond Huizhou. Ever since the eleventh century, a few pawnshops had been run by Huizhou natives within their prefecture, but only from the mid Ming do they become quite common there, even in some villages. Slightly later, they expanded into virtually every major and minor marketing center in the Yangzi delta, along the middle and lower stretches of the Yangzi river, and on the Grand Canal. Moreover, in certain delta prefectures they gained a decided predominance: Changzhou, Yangzhou (where their main contenders were from Shanxi and Shaanxi provinces) and Nanjing (where by the late Ming only the Fujianese rivaled them in ownership of the city's 500 pawnshops).[63] In the provincial capital, Hangzhou, at least ten of them qualified for inclusion among "the rich of Hangzhou,"[64] a group celebrated for financing the city's defense against the *wakō*. Slightly to the north in Nanxiong, Huizhou's merchants invested their

[63] Wang Shihua, "Ming Qing Huizhou dianshang," 62.   [64] *Dianshang*, 280.

Table 4.3 *Pawnbrokerage tax levy quotas for specific prefectures in the Southern Metropolitan Area, 1623*

Prefecture	Tax quota (taels)
Yangzhou	4,180
Huizhou	3,000
Changzhou	3,000
Songjiang	3,000
Suzhou	3,000
Zhenjiang	2,000
Ningguo	1,500
Luzhou	1,500
Fengyang	1,500
Huai'an	1,180
Anqing	1,000
Chizhou	1,000
Yingtian	849
Taiping	600
Xuzhou	600
Chuzhou	400
Hezhou	300
Guangde	400
Subtotal	29,009

Tables 4.1, 4.2, 4.3 source notes: tabulated in 1623 at the order of the power-hungry eunuch Wei Zhongxian 魏忠賢 to support a Ming military buildup at the border, these figures indicate the parts of China that the government thought had the largest holdings of silver ingots (*Dianshang*, 307, Table 6.4, based on Lin Meiling, *Wan Ming Liaoxiang*, 64, 68, drawing upon Chen Renxi, *Huang Ming shifa lu*).

profits from this town's flourishing sericulture transactions not in paddy fields but in the more lucrative pawnbrokering sector.[65] The northeast quarter of the delta proved particularly attractive to pawnshops. In its coastal market town of Yuanhua their number rose from one in 1556 to fourteen or fifteen in 1610, a sign of an expanding reliance then on pawnshops and credit in this textile production area.[66]

The city of Suzhou also strongly attracted them at this time, serving in the view of a high official there as an "external storehouse"

[65] Ibid.   [66] Von Glahn, *Fountain of Fortune*, 173–74; *Dianshang*, 279–80.

(*waicang* 外藏) for their capital and commodities outside Huizhou.[67] Despite high entry costs (estimated at between 10,000 and 30,000 taels[68]), many Huizhou merchants set up pawnshops there, the larger holding assets of 10,000 or more taels and the smaller 5,000 or 6,000 taels (data from specific shops confirm these figures).[69] In the nearby Suzhou county seat of Changshu (where a Huizhou "public-place" association opened in the Ming), most of the eighteen pawnshops in the mid seventeenth century were owned by Huizhou merchants; by the century's end these shops numbered thirty-seven, most of them still in the hands of Huizhou merchants.[70]

In other towns and cities of the lower and middle Yangzi Valley, Huizhou pawnshops secured at least a foothold from the early sixteenth century. These additional sites were as varied and dispersed as, to name just a few, Yangzhou, Yizhen 儀鎮, Qingpu 清浦 (on the Yangzi opposite Nanjing), Wuhu, Datong 大通 Market Town (in Chizhou 池州), Tanggou 唐溝 Market Town (in southern Anhui), Anqing, Jiujiang, Huangzhou, Guangji 廣濟 county in Huangzhou, Hankou, and northern Hubei (Xiangyang 襄陽 prefecture and Jiyang 棘陽 county).[71] Within much of Jiangxi as well, Huizhou pawnbrokers gained a powerful share of the market. For five or six successive years during the 1630s, for instance, each of the five Huizhou pawnshops in the prefectural seat of Fuzhou annually earned profits of 3,000 to 4,000 taels; no mention is made of Jiangxi-run alternatives.[72] Along the Grand Canal Huizhou pawnshops spread north to Linqing (where

---

[67] Liu Qiugen, *Zhongguo diandang zhidu shi*, 349, no. 1187.
[68] These figures omit the considerable cost of adapting the interior of a building to the special requirements of a pawnshop (Wang Shihua, "Ming Qing Huizhou dianshang," 67).
[69] Ibid.; *Dianshang*, 214–18. Ibid., 299, tells of a young Huizhou native planning to open a Suzhou pawnshop with several thousand taels being warned by an experienced pawnbroker that 10,000 taels was a more realistic starting sum.
[70] Fan Jinmin and Xia Weizhong, "Ming Qing Huizhou," 2; and, for the history of a more than three-century pawnshop practice that lasted into the 1920s in Changshu county, Suzhou prefecture, see Wang Zhenzhong, "*Wang Zuofu tongnian aihuanlu*," 115–17. Chen Xuewen, "Huishang yu Jiadingxian jingji," 149–55; and "Suzhou de shangye," 160; Qu Yanbin, *Zhongguo diandang xue*, 50. MQHS, 158, indicates that no fewer than several tens of Huizhou families were pawnbrokers in Changshu county, all with little capital; Fujii, "Shin'an shōnin no kenkyū," 36.2, 45–46; Zheng and Zhou, *Shiwu-shiba shiji*, 159.
[71] Nanda T 1377 Ming Wanli 16 (1578); *Chengshi fenjia shu*; *Huizhou qiannian*, v. 8, 285; Fujii, "Shin'an shōnin no kenkyū," 36.2, 46–47.
[72] Ai Qianzi, *Tian yongzi ji*, 6.30a–31a.

Huizhou merchants owned most of the several hundred pawnshops in the early seventeenth century[73] and on to Beijing (where one Huizhou pawnbroker had by the end of the Ming reportedly accumulated several million taels from several tens of pawnshops).[74] In short, Huizhou pawnbrokers operated in virtually every important commercial center in the eastern half of China from Beijing down to Ningbo, and thus some of them were exceptionally well placed to profit from major commercial transactions.

This mid- and late Ming expansion appears to have followed two general strategies. First, success in one city commonly persuaded pawnshop owners, usually one or several families in a joint-share partnership,[75] to open branches either in the same city or elsewhere in the delta and in places as far north as Beijing and Linqing in Shandong or as far south as Fujian and Guangdong.[76] For instance, one late sixteenth-century Huizhou merchant owned eighteen pawnshops in just the single delta county of Jiangyin, while slightly later another Huizhou merchant had several tens of shops in Beijing,[77] and yet another over a hundred shops in the delta prefecture of Huzhou.[78] A major attraction of this distribution policy would have clearly been its facilitation of supervision. But for those who had several available sons or capable relations, an alternative (and not necessarily contradictory) policy of setting up pawnshops in different delta towns or Yangzi ports would have made sense. It reduced the risk of direct competition among one's shops by diversifying one's investment into different urban markets. It would also have let a Huizhou merchant pursue profits in the markets each town was considered most

---

[73] Qi Yangkun and Chen Jun, "Ming Qing shiqi," 146.
[74] Ibid. During the Qing, despite the decline in the number of Huizhou pawnbrokers in north China, the Huizhou dialect reportedly became the common means for oral communication among pawnbrokers in Beijing (Zheng and Zhou, *Shiwu-shiba*, 95).
[75] Zheng and Zhou, *Shiwu-shiba*, 69, 254; Cao Lin, *Mingdai shangren*, 130, telling of brothers, a father and son, and four men with three different surnames opening pawnshops outside Huizhou. Note also the employee who deposited 800 taels of his own silver in his master's pawnshop holdings. To at least this minimal extent, some larger pawnshops had deposits and depositors, in addition to partners.
[76] *MQHS*, 160 (Linqing), 163 (Guangzhou, where they were decimated in the Manchu conquest); Wang Shihua; "Ming Qing Huizhou dianshang," 63 (Beijing and the northeast).
[77] Zhang Xianqing, *Mingdai houqi*, 185–86.   [78] *THJ*, 52, 1096–97.

productive at: salt in Yangzhou, cotton textiles in Songjiang, silk thread and textiles in Suzhou and Huzhou, porcelain in Jingde zhen, etc.

Over time, certain Huizhou pawnshop practices, ranging from the type and treatment of collateral to the policy on pawn redemption and especially the rate of interest, enabled Huizhou pawnshops to build up a dominant share of this credit market and distinguish them from their competitors. Although some of these practices varied from region to region, others came over time to constitute a distinctive set of Huizhou pawnshop lending practices applied in locations as diverse as Fuzhou (Jiangxi), Suzhou, and Beijing. First, the pawns that Huizhou pawnbrokers accepted were very diverse, ranging from jade, other jewels, and artworks to furs, real estate, textiles, and clothing, including both old clothes and court attire (no mention is made of human pawns).[79] The conditions for these loans confirm these merchants' reputation as greedy. They commonly gave low evaluations to pawns: no more than 50 percent of presumed resale value was their general rate of payment to the borrower (an observation confirmed in reports from Beijing (1605) and late Ming Fuzhou and Jiangxi).[80] In early seventeenth-century Suzhou, the rate apparently was more generous, though only when grain was abundant: the 70 percent evaluation rate in normal years fell to as low as 30 percent in poor-harvest years (after some crop failures they refused to lend starving locals any money or grain, presumably judging them unlikely to survive long enough to repay).[81] The treatment of the pawn was equally hard-hearted: the pawnshop rejected all responsibility for any collateral left in its care,[82] a stance made even more dubious by the absence of any identification of the pawned object on all surviving pawn slips issued to the borrowers. Huizhou merchants were also known, at least in the Jiangxi prefecture of Fuzhou, for shortening the time span a debtor legally had to redeem his pawn, from the legal minimum period of two years to just ten months.[83] Thereafter, the pawn belonged fully to the

---

[79] Zheng and Zhou, *Shiwu-shiba*, 159.
[80] Liu Qiugen, *Zhongguo diandang zhidu shi*, 270, no. 905 – this low basis for assessing the level of a loan was accompanied by an annual interest payment of 20 to 30 percent; and Qi Yangkun and Chen Jun, "Ming Qing shiqi," 145.
[81] Wang Tingyuan, "Huishang yu Shanghai," 14–15.
[82] Yan Guifu and Wang Jianguo, *Huizhou*, 290–91, 297.   [83] *Dianshang*, 322.

pawnshop, and could be redeemed by the creditor, if at all, only at full cost. And, to add salt to the wound, interest was levied on the first day of the month, while pawned goods could be redeemed only on the fifteenth. No wonder the Jiangxi native reporting these practices claimed that the people of Fuzhou suffered more from pawnshops than from the bandits (and resulting government levies) then plundering much of the empire.[84] Or, that long before their heyday, Huizhou merchants were being denounced in the 1480s for having snatched much of Songjiang's wealth or were ejected from a delta market town by the county magistrate a few years later.[85] With their interest rates and trading tactics fueling locals' enmity,[86] the pawnshops were not surprisingly targeted for attack by hungry locals in urban protests, the real as well as the fictional.[87]

This antagonism seems to have been fueled by complaints about capital shortage and an intensively competitive demand for capital from throughout society, even though Huizhou pawnshops' interest rates in the delta fell and stabilized over the course of the Ming, at least until the dynasty's chaotic final years. Whereas the early Ming government decreed a maximum monthly interest rate of 3 percent and a maximum cumulative interest repayment (for the next thirty-three or more lunar months) of 100 percent[88] – these figures remained in government statutes up to the early twentieth century – the actual rate imposed by Huizhou pawnbrokers and other lenders during the first century of Ming rule was often much higher. The government routinely mishandled the economy, not least with a daft currency policy that banned the use of silver while insisting on the use of its copper coins and its increasingly worthless paper money. Under these circumstances, borrowers commonly paid interest rates higher than those legally tolerated by the dynasty.

From 1435, however, the Ming government began to permit some use of silver ingots and copper cash for certain tax payments and government disbursements, a policy shift that, once it was confirmed

---

[84] Ai Qianzi, *Tian yongzi ji*, 6.30a–31a.
[85] Fu Yiling, *Ming Qing shidai shangren*, 69; and Wu Ren'an, *Ming Qing Jiangnan wangzu*, 234.
[86] *Dianshang*, 254, 279, 297.
[87] E.g., ibid., 279, 297 in Suzhou, its Wujiang county seat, and the market town of Zhouzhuang.
[88] *Minglü jijie fuli*, 9.1a.

by similar currency changes in other government policies, led to greater stability in both the money supply and market prices. Although for loans there was no single or fixed "market rate," custom, the law, the import of foreign silver, and overall market expansion resulted in the Yangzi delta in a long-term reduction of annual interest rates. The evidence of this change is itself rich and varied, ranging from general descriptions of pawnshop rates, several pawnshop account registers, interest rates for private loans, and reports that Huizhou pawnshops in particular offered relatively low rates that frequently fluctuated between 20 and 30 percent and that sometimes dipped even lower.

To be specific: during the sixteenth century, a Huizhou pawnbroker's annual interest rate for a loan in silver reportedly dropped in the Shaoxing county of Xinchang 新昌 from a steady 50 percent to one fluctuating between 30 and 50 percent, and even lower in the Suzhou county of Wujiang 吳江, to between 20 and 50 percent.[89] If we compare these figures to others reported from outside the delta in the mid sixteenth century, their relative cheapness is notable: the 60 percent customary in the Baoding 保定 area of Hebei, the 50 percent common in the Jiangxi county of Qianshan 鉛山, the very common rates of 30 to 40 percent in coastal areas of the southeast a century later, and the 30 percent in the Jiangxi prefecture of Fuzhou.[90] Before that report, we learn of one mid-sixteenth-century Huizhou merchant who in the delta market town of Jingkou 京口 offered rates of 20 percent in place of the 30 percent customarily demanded; not surprisingly, his reduced rates are said to have won him the town's respect and much profit.[91] By the dynasty's end the general annual interest rate in some delta cities had fallen even further.[92] In Nanjing and Huzhou, some Huizhou pawnbrokers, flush with huge caches of capital, offered annual rates as low as 10 percent, in contrast, for example, to the 30 to 40 percent rates levied by their biggest rivals there, the Fujianese

---

[89] Zhang Xianqing, *Mingdai houqi*, 189.
[90] Golvers, *Rougemont*, 572, 585–86; *Dianshang*, 325; Yang Lien-sheng, *Money and Credit*, 98.
[91] Wu Ziyu, *Dazhang shanren ji*, 48.8b.
[92] MQHS, 160–61, tells of a Huizhou merchant who ignored the customary spring-to-autumn interest rate in Lishui 溧水 county (in Jiangning 江寧 prefecture) of 100 percent for families of limited means (*xiahu* 下戶) to offer them loans at just 10 percent.

merchants who had previously displaced the Nanjing pawnbrokers in their hometown.[93]

Second, this attested decline in the pawnshops' interest rate in at least some of the delta's cities during the Ming is supported by a parallel and yet more comprehensive set of data on Huizhou personal loans in general dating from the three centuries that followed the Ming. According to research conducted on over 2,000 extant Huizhou loan contracts by the Chinese scholar Wu Bingkun 吳秉坤, the interest rate in the Qing dynasty's first fifty years hovered at about 20 percent, and thus was in line with the figure commonly found in more general abstract discussions of interest rates in Huizhou during the Ming and Qing periods (see Table 4.4). In fact, additional evidence from Wu's survey suggests that the subsequent span of average and median interest rates up to the 1930s changed astonishingly little.[94] From the Manchu conquest up to the post-World War II period the average annual rate of interest on loans in Huizhou, when tabulated in fifty-year stretches, was about 20 percent.

As this general rate was specified in contracts under all sorts of economic conditions, we may sensibly question whether it ever in practice retained such a consistency and universality over so long a time. Not only did some Huizhou pawnshops usually alter their interest rates in response to general market conditions,[95] but also the actual rate specified in these contracts for sure did change in line with all the harsh economic and political changes in Huizhou during these centuries. There were recurrent food shortages and economic crises as well as highly destructive invasions by Taiping rebels in the mid nineteenth century and the Japanese invasion of Anhui from 1936 to 1945. In short, although Wu's important batch of Qing contracts is far from ideal for our purposes, enough other textual evidence survives on late imperial Huizhou pawnshops and private lenders to indicate that their

---

[93] Xie Guozhen, *Mingdai shehui jingji*, v. 2, 200; Wang Shihua, "Ming Qing Huizhou dianshang," 65; *THJ*, v. 1, 19, 413, and v. 3, 61, 1, 266–67; *MQHS*, 293–94 (by the mid nineteenth century some monthly interest rates in Jiangsu pawnshops were just 2 percent).

[94] Wu Bingkun, *Qing zhi Minguo*, especially Preface 2. This conclusion has been greatly strengthened by the seminal work of three Chinese scholars on the history of Chinese interest rates from 1660 to c.1950: Chen Zhiwu, Peng Kaixiang, and Yuan Weipeng, "Qingchu zhi ershi shiji qianqi zhongguo lishuai shi chutan." Unfortunately, no similar work has been done on the far fewer extant Ming loan contracts.

[95] *Dianshang*, 328–29.

Table 4.4 *Huizhou loan contracts' interest rates: lowest, highest, average, and median*

Statistical Index	Explicit interest rate							Converted interest rate						
	Pre-1750	1750–1800	1800–1850	1850–1900	1900–1937	Post-1937		Pre-1750	1750–1800	1800–1850	1850–1900	1900–1937	Post-1937
Lowest interest rate	10	5	8.3	5	0	10		6.22	6.29	2.27	2.37	0.76	3.89
Highest interest rate	40	36	40	36	36	540		40	48.48	64.02	132.5	346.13	655.56
Average interest rate	21.35	21.21	20.49	21.06	18.97	58.73		17.77	21.29	22.12	25.35	20.34	61.73
Median number	24	24	20	20	20	20		16.64	19.93	21.07	22.35	16.56	43.65
Standard difference	6.87	5.54	4.57	3.82	3.74	80.7		6.98	9.12	8.93	12.93	23.02	80.58
Sample number	45	60	185	448	632	90		39	95	342	300	243	96

loans regularly came with annual interest rates in the general range of 20 to 30 percent.[96] To that extent, we can say that interest-rate changes associated with the spread of Huizhou merchants and their pawnshops in the delta during the last century of the Ming appear to have proven remarkably long-lasting, even in Huizhou itself.

In a recent set of comments on China's premodern economy, the economic historians Jean-Paul Rosenthal and R. Bin Wong have raised doubts about the suitability of using any of this data on pawnshops and personal loans to understand the workings of the premodern Chinese commercial economy in general. Seeking to disprove the conventional wisdom that premodern China's interest rates were prohibitively high, they have argued that modern Chinese economic historians have invalidly compared two different kinds of interest rates, the pawnshop or personal loan rates in China and the commercial credit rates in Western Europe, and thus reached an untenable conclusion that it was these high interest rates that kept the Chinese commercial economy from growing as fast as the Western European. Making much use of an 8 percent per annum rate they found for one commercial credit loan dating from nineteenth-century China, they claim that earlier Chinese commercial interest rates would have fallen within this range and thus have posed far less of an obstacle to commercial development than was previously thought. They also speculate that Chinese merchants resorted to a great variety of credit sources still unknown to modern researchers, some of which they then suggest in a survey of the variety of Chinese private, commercial, and public debt practices before the arrival of Western banks and their cheaper rates in the mid nineteenth century.

This critique has been most welcome for clarifying key assumptions in previous analyses. Yet as a critique it is flawed on two counts. First, it ignores an important early seventeenth-century Chinese discussion of commercial credit interest rates that essentially refutes their claim of a distinction then between personal and commercial rates of interest. In his book (*Keshang yilan xingmi* 客商一覽醒迷, 1630) written for Huizhou merchants, the outspoken Fujianese merchant Li Jinde 李晉德 refers to personal and commercial credit rates as separate categories of loans. Yet whatever Li's grounds for categorizing these

---

[96] For example see, the findings in Chen Zhiwu, Peng Kaixiang, and Yuan Weipeng, "Qingchu zhi ershi shiji qianqi Zhongguo lilüshi chutan."

two types of interest rates, he fixes the commercial interest rate at the same, or roughly the same, level as the personal loan rate. In prescribing interest rates for commerce equal to those practiced by Huizhou pawnbrokers for noncommercial loans, he thus was actually putting his commercial interest rate at a level at least three times higher than the common rate in early modern Western Europe:

> For engaging in trade (*jingying maoyi* 經營貿易) and for making private loans (*fang sizhai* 放私債), only take an interest of 20 or 30 percent. This is the ordinary take, for which there is no resentment [!]. If you want 70 or 80 percent interest, then even though it approaches the [purchase] cost of the piece, it is all right (*ke* 可). It is hard to regard it as a permanent [rate].[97]

Yet, as Wong and Rosenthal seem to acknowledge, this distinction between a commercial and a personal interest rate, however desirable in the abstract, is hardly relevant to pre-nineteenth-century Chinese business practice when Chinese banks were rudimentary organizations. Like private businesses in general, they operated on highly personal arrangements between creditors and debtors (remember the close personal ties observed in Chapter 2 between Fang Yongbin and many of his 300-odd clients). Consequently, Ming China had at most an emerging commercial credit market, one that seldom enabled capital-short merchants to get loans from credit institutions at rates significantly lower than those available for noncommercial purposes (also recall that in the Ming dynasty people who engaged in commerce did not constitute a distinct legal status group or possibly even a distinct occupation or social status group[98]). As we shall see in the next two chapters, late imperial Chinese merchants in search of capital or investment tended to opt for commercial partnerships rather than loans, as such arrangements offered them capital far more cheaply, even if it enabled others to intrude into their business operations.

If, then, all the explicit evidence on Huizhou interest rates lets us conclude that by the early seventeenth century pawnshop interest rates in Yangzi delta towns and cities had both fallen and stabilized at around the 20 percent per annum level, the benefits to the economy as a whole and to delta and Huizhou residents, merchants, and clients would in theory have been considerable. Let me mention just a few.

[97] Li Jinde, *Keshang yilan, xingmi*, 310, as reported in Brook, *Confusions*, 216.
[98] For a discussion of this point, see Chapter 1 above.

Pawnshops

First, any drop in the general interest rate for non-kinsmen outside Huizhou would have most likely put downward pressure on the already lower interest rate often offered kinsmen, especially inside Huizhou.[99] Second, it would have reduced the required level of profit margins expected of all merchants and – given the lower borrowing rates and costs among kinsmen – Huizhou merchants in particular, thus making their commercial success more likely. As already noted, in 1502 and *c*.1570 two Huizhou residents in turn observed that Huizhou's ordinary merchants expected from their annual trading trips earnings of 20 percent, the same rate commonly levied as the lower band of the fluctuating rates in their delta pawnshops.[100] Third, a lower rate would have encouraged Huizhou borrowers to undertake more risks in long-distance trade, with returns, potentially, commensurately higher. And fourth, it allowed a greater number of traders with limited capital assets to take on higher levels of debt, thus further lubricating the circulation of capital among small-time savers and buyers.

However reasonable and even logical these suppositions seem to us today, they are hard to find expressed in Ming sources either as theory or as confirmed fact. For sure, the attested fall in interest rates was accompanied by more and more reports that Huizhou merchants were delving farther and farther into the outreaches of southwest China, just as the personal wealth of Huizhou merchants soared in these years, with surviving wills of individual pawnbrokers revealing that their valuables in metal amounted to as much as 790,000 taels.[101] On the

---

[99] For instance, between 1604 and 1650 a 20 percent rate was regularly collected from fellow kinsmen in a credit association of the Tanbin Huangs (*Tanbin Huangshi shouzhi qingce*) and a 12 percent rate imposed by the Chengs of Huili in Xiuning on a daughter-in-law (Nanjing University, History Department, Nanda, T 1377). Yet note the prevalence of a 30 percent annual rate of interest posited in late sixteenth-century hypothetical cases presented in Cheng Dawei, *Suanfa zuanyao jiaoshi*, 121, 124 (one listed case, however, has a 27 percent annual rate of interest). Liu Qiugen, *Zhongguo diandang*, 217–35, lists actual and prescribed rates of interest, useful so long as one remembers the real world of poor harvests, family ties, and threats which often forced lenders to fit their rate to each request's circumstances.

[100] Wu Ziyu, *Dazhang shanren ji*, 31.9b; *Huizhou fuzhi* (1502), 2.39b–40a.

[101] Wang Yuming, "Ming Qing fenjia kuishu," 101. Their listed pawnshop assets alone ranged between 6,000 and 11,461 taels, yet note that pawnbrokers often owned more than one shop. This type of arrangement probably helps to explain how one Huizhou pawnbroker in Jiangyin county was able to offer 175,000

other hand, it is equally evident that the benefits accrued by these pawnshops were not passed on to all their clients equally. For the delta's numerous poor, any reductions in interest rates were parceled out ever so stingily, since interest rates, even when generally reduced, were not identical for all customers. An "old custom" of pawnshops in the delta prefecture of Huzhou in the late seventeenth century – and thus dating back at least a generation or two to the end of the Ming – prescribed three monthly rates of interest according to the amount of silver borrowed: 3 percent for loans under one tael, as opposed to 2 percent for those between one and ten taels, and just 1.5 percent for those over ten taels (the variety of interest rates reported for other places in the delta during the late Ming thus possibly reflects not competition among different pawnbrokers but the different rates generally set for different types of clients, such as the new and untested versus the old and tested (credit, as ever, creating credit) or for members of different socioeconomic groups.[102] The poor, whose possessions by definition were less valuable collateral than those of the wealthy, were largely restricted to borrowing smaller, yet more costly, loans. If, as supposed above, generally lower interest rates had the benefit of making loans financially conceivable for a larger number of people, they ironically had the downside of drawing an ever greater number of people into the pawnbroker's and moneylender's snare.

That trap would have most likely been painful for anyone caught in its web. At a time when men might borrow up to 60 percent of their capital for a commercial venture,[103] a delta resident's loan from a pawnshop at even the relatively light annual rate of 20 percent could have easily become a very alloyed blessing, particularly when repayment was seldom as straightforward as it can seem to scholars of written contracts. Underhanded tricks, as reported from the mid-seventeenth-century Shanghai area, were common: "In general, when one is borrowing ten taels, [the lenders] break off [from the ingot] some of the

---

taels for a pro-Ming defense of the city against the Manchu invaders (*MQHS*, 286).
[102] *Huzhou fuzhi* (1884), 77.37b, and 97.24a–b, as in Yang Lien-sheng, *Money and Credit*, 98. The famous literatus Li Yu corroborates this understanding more generally, when he observed in the early Qing that the 30 percent annual rate common for one- or two-tael loans fell to 20-odd percent for larger loans (*Dianshang*, 325).
[103] Li Le, *Jianwen zaji*, 9, 745; Zhang Xianqing, *Mingdai houqi*, 194.

profit for themselves, so that just nine taels actually end up in one's hand. When one assesses its [silver] value, one finds it is worth no more than 8.3 taels [of high-quality silver]."[104] Forced nonetheless to pay back a full ten taels plus interest, the interest-rate reduction we have discussed above would have lost much of its attraction to these ordinary families. If they proved unable to pay back the full amount demanded by their creditors, they might face beatings, death, and even incineration of their corpse. Back in Huizhou, default on a loan would have cashiered their chance for future loans and thus their hopes for a merchant career. A borrower there might be jailed for defaulting on just a few taels: at one time in the late sixteenth century, the Huizhou prefectural jail housed several tens of small debtors.[105]

The economic situation for small debtors in the delta was particularly perilous, since most people had few material resources to draw upon. Not only did they tend to be tenant households already paying half of their annual rice crop over to their landlord, but also as part-time workers in the delta's cotton and silk industries they commonly came under the control of pawnbrokers. As explained in the description of sericulture work in the Chongde 崇德 (aka Shimen 石門) county gazetteer of 1611, these workers had aimed to supplement their rice income by performing home-based jobs, but they ended up having to borrow equipment from no one other than pawnbrokers (functioning here also as local silk merchants):

The most profitable crops here are silk and grain. Although silk is the more profitable of the two, it is a gamble for the poor to raise silkworms and produce cocoons. All their sericulture equipment is borrowed from pawnshops. As the months go by, the bitter work dims the eyes and turns the hair white; finally the silk is reeled just before the year is brought to a close. [At the end of the year] public and private debts are settled at the silk market.[106]

Shortly before, another Shimen county magistrate in 1607–9 denounced the same pawnshops' cruel fleecing of the local peasants: "Pawnshops' expenses are slight, and their revenues large. When they deal with peasants, they squeeze out of them their last drop of blood, and leave them, as before, empty-pocketed."[107] Although another

[104] Ye Mengzhu, *Yueshi bian*, 6, 137.
[105] Fang Hongjing, *Suyuan cungao*, 13.32b, where several tens of men held in jail had collective debts of just 100-odd taels.
[106] Tanaka, "Rural Handicraft in Jiangnan," 82.   [107] Ibid.

Shimen official had previously argued that pawnshops were overall a positive addition to the local economy since they provided cash and credit to ordinary people with few alternative outlets,[108] it really is no surprise that, as seen in the previous chapter, few Suzhou residents shared this rosy view of their neighborhood pawnbroker or moneylender.

Pawnshops and Profits

All commentators agree that Huizhou merchants' pawnshops were profitable – many claim they were very profitable – and yet the actual profit rates observable in pawnshop account records show great annual variations and occasional losses and, according to a recent study, an average annual net profit level of about 10 percent, far lower than the general figures given so far as standard rates of interest.[109] The scarcity of sources obscures the reasons for these variations and this relatively low return level. But the likelihood of many defaults plus consequent reluctance of pawnshops to loan their silver would appear to be a likely explanation, even though Huizhou pawnshops in some places seem to have actively targeted a wider range of clientele than was previously welcomed in pawnshop dealings.

Let us begin by examining a few surviving records of actual pawnshop operations. Usually located in the informative, if idealized, prefaces of Huizhou merchants' wills or in separate registers, these accounts indicate that pawnshop profits could be considerable – a threefold increase in capital assets, for instance, in less than two decades, or a twentyfold increase in less than four decades. In the first of these wills, Zhu Shirong 朱世荣, an impoverished member of a Xiuning lineage proud of its scholar-official pedigree,[110] had to leave home at the age of eleven with the aim of succeeding as a merchant. Twelve years later he returned home and with funds earned from his years of labor away he could afford a marriage. His bride then promptly died, and upon marrying another woman he sold off some of her clothing and family servant(s), presumably parts of her dowry, for a mere 15.4 taels. In the next three years he transformed these

---

[108] MQHS, 155–56; Gu Qiyuan, Kezuo zuiyu, 5, 162–63, including the view of the Huizhou native and official Fang Hongjing.
[109] Dianshang, 329–31.   [110] Xiuning mingzu zhi, 3, 526–30.

Pawnshops and Profits

start-up funds into over 130 taels of profit (plus the cost of supporting himself and his family), that with the aid of a nephew as his partner he then used to set up and run for ten years a pawnshop in the backwater county of Chao 巢 in northern Anhui.

For ten years he endured the archetypically long hours and painful journeys on foot and in the snow that any self-respecting self-made Chinese businessman was expected to experience on his way up the rungs of the Huizhou wealth ladder. As a result, he earned enough to afford not only to marry off all five of his children properly but also to join a commercial partnership at a copper forge in Wuhu. Even so, after three years of hard work and smooth running of this business, he was stunned to see his shop closed up by the government and himself and his partners forced to split up their assets (no reason is given). Nonetheless, with these funds he engaged with his brothers in a copper goods shop at Wuhu and with another family, the Xu 許, in two shops selling copper and tin goods in Suzhou. In the 1620s, at the age of sixty-eight he drafted a will for silver assets of 2,791.662 taels plus some annual paddy field rents. Clearly, for this man pawnbrokering was, as he intended, a means for collecting the funds needed to launch his business career (quite possibly he had acquired the confidence to do this by spending his apprentice years in a pawnshop). As an adult, he worked in several places and invested in shops in at least two places, as he was making the best of his humble beginnings and a late start in most of his businesses.[111]

A more revealing account of the practice of pawnbrokering is found in the 1588 will of another Xiuning native and merchant, Cheng Yujing 程宇敬; it itemized the value in silver of his liquid assets in various places. While this list explicitly omits virtually all his real-estate holdings (no separate register survives), it does contain all his commercial assets and something more: Cheng took the time to insert in his will the amount of his inheritance valued in silver as of 1570 and, even more helpfully, an annual summary of his business revenue, expenditures, and net liquid assets in silver for most of the years between 1577 and 1588. Starting with 8,637.618 taels when he became independent of his brothers in 1570, he started his career three times richer than Zhu Shirong had been at the conclusion of his. Cheng's fortune also increased nearly threefold under his individual

---

[111] *Tianqi Weinan Zhu Shirong fenjia pu*, preface.

care: his net liquid assets rose to 14,067.95 taels in 1577 and then to 23,649.9 taels in 1588.

How was such financial growth possible? According to both Zhu Shirong's and Cheng Yujing's autobiographical prefaces to their wills, the explanation for their success was simple: hard work and no play. From his youth Zhu had worked diligently as a merchant traveling the 200 or 300 miles between the county seats of Jiangpu 江浦 (on the northern bank of the Yangzi opposite Nanjing) and Wuhu and the market town of Datong in Wuhu county. The sole party he was willing to mention as sharing responsibility for his success was his wife. She ran the family at home, while he busied himself making money for it elsewhere.

Though this explanation describes well a common division of labor in Chinese families, a more credible explanation of his business success is found in two rich sets of figures that Cheng also placed in his will: a virtually year-by-year breakdown of profits earned by his family business between 1577 and 1588 and next a breakdown of his assets as of 1588. Consider first the increases in capital assets and their annual net rates of increase (Table 4.5).

With annual profit levels fluctuating so greatly, this business needed to manage its assets cautiously. As we might expect, diversification characterized its core decisions on capital holdings, commodity specialization, and most obviously location. During his lifetime Cheng Yujing expanded his business operations to six sites – Wuhu, Datong, Tanggou, Yizhen, Longping 龍平, and Liuhe 六合 – and set up shops

Table 4.5 *Capital assets of Cheng Yujing and annual net rate of increase*

Total	Capital assets (taels)	Annual net rate of increase
1570	8,637.618	–
1577	4,069.95	c.7.0%
1578	14,687.17	9.5%
1579	14,690.39	2.8%
1581	16,632.61	17.2%
1582	18,015.75	11%
1583	21,194.339	19%
1584–87	21,752.9	c.0.3%
1588	23,649.9	8.02%

(*dian*) or outlets in the first four. This policy was risky, potentially destructive. But as he was seeking to expand his business market area and potential customer base, he chose locations all conveniently located along or close to the Yangzi for its vibrant river trade.

Diversification also marked the firm's decision to store assets other than silver, such as salt and textile goods. These stocks may simply have been pawns accumulated in running a pawnshop. Nonetheless, these goods were two of the most readily exchangeable products of the time (grain, a degradable product, accounted for less than 0.1 percent of the value of Cheng Yujing's listed assets), thus enabling the firm to unload its moveable assets relatively quickly, if and when it needed money. Furthermore, these stored commodities differed from shop to shop, with each shop or outlet tending to store one type of product in large amounts for specialized trading: salt in Yizhen, Wuhu, and Datong, and cotton cloth in Wuhu (five varieties), Tanggou, and the two eastern Hubei outlets. The storage of a particularly large amount of salt at Datong Market Town suggests that this store retained close ties with Yizhen; that is, a Yangzi river salt trade center very close to Yangzhou where the firm also kept some salt and other property. But, overall, this house firm took care to keep its batteries of eggs in several scattered baskets.

A policy of risk avoidance seems also to have guided the firm's financial management. No institution is listed as its creditor. Its sole recorded links to external financial activities, other than its pawned loans, were its participation in two mutual-credit associations, for a total of merely 19.5 taels. Internal – that is, kinship-based – loans were also few and given to individuals: fewer than 15 percent of the approximately 315 clients that Cheng Yujing lists as his debtors (owing 4,285.24 taels – an average of 13.6 taels per client, who by and large were not big borrowers) – held his surname. Caution alone keeps us from considering these Chengs as unrelated debtors, since on the two instances when Cheng Yujing loaned money to a relation, he listed their debts separately from those of his other clients and specified the rate of interest levied on them (including a lower rate of 12 percent for a daughter-in-law).

An even clearer sign of his firm's caution is its branches' retention of two-thirds of all their silver holdings for the practice of pawnbrokering, and yet as of 1588 they committed less than half of this fund to loans. In other words, the annual variations in the firm's profits may reflect variations not just in the local economy's performance and the returns from loans and investments but also in these branches' willingness to invest their funds in the economic opportunities or pawns offered to them. They made considerable profit per loan, but ever so conservatively.[112] Finding reliable borrowers appears to have been harder than most writers on Chinese pawnshops have assumed, and so an average net revenue of about 10 percent is more easily understood, at least in this case. Complaints about Huizhou merchants' failure to reinvest their profits in their new places of residence – as would be directed against some in Linqing in the early Qing[113] – appears to have ignored the underlying reasons: pawnshops all too seldom found enough reliable borrowers. Capital preservation was a higher priority than profit maximization. Interest in making loans to relieve food shortages was a very distant concern.

Who, then, determined and managed a pawnshop's lending policy and ran these pawnshop branches? Cheng Yujing's will presents him as actively involved in managing his business up until his retirement in 1588. It is likely, then, that he set the overall policy and that, after he had given equal shares of his estate's assets to his three sons in 1577, he and the three sons separately ran one branch apiece of the family firm (a similar practice was followed by Zhu Shirong with his sons). Except for the father and one son, they would have lived separately (a supposition strengthened by the differences in the expenses each son annually reported for himself between 1577 and 1588 and the separate funds given to one son for looking after the parents). Such decentralized management would also have fit well with the disparate locations of the firm's branches, since as of 1588 two-thirds of the firm's total liquid assets were located in branches away from its main shop in Wuhu.

Furthermore, Cheng Yujing's cautious supervision of his firm's assets seems to have kept him from adopting a practice favored by

---

[112] Strictly speaking, the rates of profit and capital increase do not represent the interest rates on the loans and pawns made by this firm, since not all its capital was lent out at any time. If the share of the assets actually loaned was as low as I have suggested above, then the actual lending rate would have been close to double that of the figures listed here as annual rates of net profit. The 1579 and 1584–87 rates would remain low but could perhaps be explained by a default on other loans during these years.

[113] *Dianshang*, 289. The mention of this abuse in a novel suggests it was a general practice.

some Huizhou merchants: the hiring of "talented and worthy men," not their sons but other kinsmen and even non-kinsmen, to manage their shops.[114] Skilled at accounting, these managers would annually notify the absentee owner of their revenues. Their remuneration was determined on the basis of their intake that year (from a fifth to a half of the profits), or on the basis of a set pay, or a fixed dividend, for the owner in each particular year (that is, the manager would be renting the capital and shop from their owner and pay him a mutually agreed share of the revenues).

A very detailed account of this practice is found in the 1629 will of a member of another Xiuning lineage, the Chengs of Shuaidong. One family group in this lineage owned a group of seven pawnshops, or pawnshop branches, one in Huizhou and six, like the previous Chengs' branches, located in towns and cities along the Yangzi: Anqing, Jiujiang, Guangji, Huangzhou, and Huguang. One member of this family, when writing his will in 1629, made it clear that he had contracted others – his younger brothers, partners, or hired employees – to manage these pawnshops for him, paying them either a set wage or set share of the proceeds made from their management of his capital.[115] As if he were lending them his money, they would pay him and other shareholders in the pawnshop partnership an annually predetermined rate of return on the pawnshop's capital under their management. As this 1629 will shows, these annual rates of profit for the owner could change from year to year, apparently according to these parties' forecast of business conditions and expectations or need of capital. As a result, those who actually ran the business took as their pay any profits above and beyond the amount promised the shop's owners (the shop's capital was to remain untouched). In short, this arrangement sharply distinguished ownership from management and rewarded the manager for his annual performance (in the manner of both "commenda" commercial partnerships and fixed-rent tenancy contracts which let a tenant retain all of a harvest above a preset figure).[116]

After Cheng Yujing conferred on his three surviving sons equal shares of his estate in 1577, these different shares' expenditures – just

---

[114] This practice is mentioned in *MQHS*, 156, 163; and in Chapters 5 and 6 below.
[115] Wang Chongyuan, "Huizhou diandang," 47.
[116] The practice continued in Republican China (Köll, *From Cotton Mill to Business Empire*, 130; Shiroyama, "Companies in Debt," 300).

as we might expect if the sons lived apart and thus had separate living and operation expenses – varied annually and among themselves. The annual rate of profit for these shares correspondingly varied greatly from year to year, but not *among* the three sons' shares of the shops' total annual profits (which remained virtually identical and equal). A single party – if not the father, then a management office – would appear to have been managing all three shares of the family property that the father had set up out of his estate during all these twelve years. Since the annual rate of profit varied so greatly and was for many years far below that which could be gained by even limited lending operations at the normal 20 to 30 percent rate of interest,[117] it seems more likely that the father, not a management office, had made such arrangements with his sons over their "sons' shares." While conceivably he may have retained personal control over other pots of unused capital, the harmonization of the sons' profits from interest payments makes it more likely that their payment arrangements functioned along lines of the model we shall soon discuss as a sleeping joint-share partnership (though it could have originated as a normal Chinese family practice that had the sons pool all their income and receive equal shares from it). In this form of commercial partnership the investors were anxious to minimize their liability for the potential troubles of their firm, and so reduced evidence of their management and investment involvement in the firm, to the extent of accepting a fixed rate of dividend rather akin to a loan or bond than to the varying returns on stock or shareholdings.

To their dominance of the grain, timber, fish, tea, and salt markets, Huizhou merchants in the Ming thus added a lucrative and multileveled business in loans and pawnshop transactions. Their offer of relatively cheap credit in the last third of the Ming gained them at first a foothold and later a long-term place in the financial economy of cities and market towns in the delta. However much the people there disliked them, they needed them. Huizhou merchants appear to have provided competition to other trading groups and often cheaper interest rates to at least their safe clients. And, by the close of the sixteenth century, they had become an accepted, if not admired, part of economic life in

---

[117] The latter condition would seem the more important factor, as Wang Chongyuan, "Huizhou diandang," 44, indicates that reliance on a manager need not imply use of a fixed annual dividend.

many delta villages and even more so in towns and cities of the delta, along the Yangzi river and the Grand Canal, and increasingly in the hinterlands of Anhui, Shandong, Hubei, and Hunan provinces.[118] As these house firms set up pawnshop branches in disparate places, families like the Chengs naturally stopped living in one collective residence and sent their sons to manage their branches separately.

As mentioned above and as detailed in the next two chapters, Huizhou merchant families commonly sought to link their pawnshops up with one another and, more significantly, with trade they conducted collectively with their kinsmen. With one group's financial clout backing up another's commercial operations, these kinship groups expanded their sources and supplies of capital as well as the amount of profit gained from both lending and trading. They formed with kinsmen and even non-kinsmen commercial partnerships that served as substitute for cheap commercial loans and that bound partners more tightly to one another in collective financial and commercial ventures. The capital accrued from speculative salt monopoly investments, the risk-avoidance strategy of the pawnshop, the revenues clawed from trade, and the generous lending policy of ancestral halls and fellow kinsmen underpinned the economic expansion of the sixteenth and early seventeenth centuries.

Conclusion

Clearly, the salt monopoly and the pawnshops that Huizhou merchants established and operated during the Ming differed radically in the sources and amounts of their capital holdings, their clientele, their administrative practices, and their relation to the government. The salt monopoly certificates, though ostensibly a part of the government salt monopoly administration, also functioned as a privately held financial instrument for a very private speculative market created by government policies and funded by wealth expropriated from an artificially constructed market in salt, the most commonly consumed commodity at the time. The merchant participants in both the salt and salt certificate markets were frequently Huizhou merchants, who sought not just proximity to the officials and eunuchs managing the salt monopoly offices but also a niche within this government monopoly from which

---

[118] Zhang Xianqing, *Mingdai houqi*, 197–99, for pro-pawnshop views.

they would function as "official merchants" (*guanshang* 官商) in salt.[119] In seeking to "piggyback" their way onto the workings of this government monopoly, they sought a security for their person and goods that otherwise was difficult to assure on the river, roads, and some marketplaces of this time.

By contrast, the second financial institution in which Huizhou merchants became deeply involved was the pawnshop. Here they initially faced competition not just from other secular and privately held pawnshops but also from Buddhist temples', Confucian ancestral halls', and other religious establishments' lending associations. Commonly operated in eastern China by outsider merchants, up to 1623 these pawnshops escaped virtually all taxes on their lending profits and principals. Although they dealt with far smaller amounts than did the usual salt market speculators, they served a wide variety of clients, including ordinary urban residents and poor peasants. And so, even if not as profitable as the trade in salt and salt certificates, they dealt with a much wider and deeper market of customers. As a result, they gleaned from a multitude of transactions enough profit to back their owners' further expansion into a chain of other pawnshops and commodity trades like timber, textiles, and fish. Their lending practices, apparently in sharp contrast to those of the speculators in salt certificates, appear to have been very conservative (except arguably when indulging their kinsmen's demands for loans). Another key difference from the salt certificate manipulators was their shops' publicness and thus their vulnerability to popular attack by crowds of would-be customers outraged by their closure during food crises when the demand for their capital ran highest.

These differences in the Ming between the worlds of salt merchants and of pawnbrokers ran deep, but not deep enough to prevent links between them. The most obvious link, as exemplified by a host of individuals and families in the salt monopoly trade, was their simultaneous investment in both worlds and especially the use of their salt trade and salt certificates' profits to finance the opening of new pawnshops usually in the Yangzi Valley and along the Grand Canal. Their pawnshops were often a chain of pawnshops, sometimes located in the same town (to permit closer supervision and reduce the threat of serial defaulters). But these salt merchants also made loans to other

---

[119] Finnane, *Yangzhou*, 264.

pawnshop owners they trusted or invested in their shops as partners. Either way, they helped circulate the profits garnered in the salt monopoly.

Another fruitful way of thinking about the relations between these types of financial institutions is to recognize that they reflect the exceptional range of Huizhou merchants' involvement in the Ming economy and thus the exceptional diversity of occupations within their own ranks. Whenever late Ming and Qing commentators treated them as one uniform group of super-rich merchants, Huizhou natives liked to blunt these denunciations by stressing the very different levels of income and consumption among their prefecture's merchant families, even to the extent of thinking of them and their income level in three categories – top, middling, and lower (*shang* 上, *zhong* 中, *xia* 下). If we attach to this crude schema the type of work done by these merchants, Huizhou's salt merchants can be seen to have constituted the top group, the pawnbrokers and high-profit commodity traders (for example in timber, textiles, and dried fish) the middling, and the numerous peddlers who dealt in a variety of goods the lower ranks. Membership of these groups was definitely not fixed, and even though the gaps between them widened greatly over the last half of the Ming, many wealthy merchants then, as their biographies make clear, began their merchant life as peddlers, working their way up to at least the second rank of the merchants' ladder of success.

In other words, the success of these Huizhou merchant groups created different communities of merchants which worked in different markets at often different levels of capitalization, with different degrees of credit, and of course different relations with the government. The ascent that most Huizhou merchants sought, of a career that rose in turn from being a traveling merchant to pawnbrokering and eventually dealing as a salt merchant, constitutes the narrative of many Huizhou merchant hagiographies and the dream life of many others. As the next two chapters will show, this career passage actually tolerated many versions of commercial and financial arrangements. But, if at all levels they found commercial partnerships, usually with kinsmen, to be crucial for their success, so then at the uppermost levels of commerce and finance the salt merchants also found maintenance of good ties with the government, even the central government, essential for the continued health and ascent of their house firm.

5 | *Huizhou Merchants and Commercial Partnerships*

The family (*jia* 家) is the kinship group that throughout Chinese history has consistently served as the basic unit for economic organization in commerce as well as in agriculture.[1] In the Ming dynasty, Huizhou merchant houses regularly followed this unit's traditional principles and practices of shared labor, capital, and management, all the while recognizing their vulnerability. In addition to recurrent risks of poor security, price manipulation, and capital shortages discussed in the previous chapters, they had to face the virtual inevitability of the family's breakup and thus the dismemberment of its businesses and its assets. Upon its head's death a male heir could call for his share of this wealth, thereby terminating his family's potential growth into a larger kinship group with its promise of greater security and collective prosperity.[2]

For handling these problems of family division, the family did have some recourse to dynastic law, which presumed such a practice. For virtually all the other problems a business would encounter, including funding and security, the family and other kinship forms in late imperial times received only minimal direct institutional support from their government. The Ming dynasty, like the Song and Yuan before it and the Qing after it, had no commercial code and no commercial statutes. It also had precious few laws or ordinances useful for establishing, operating, or protecting a business, other than those written to help people engage in any type of economic activity, be it agriculture, fishing, hunting, trade, or finance. Commercial organizations, in other words, were to be treated not as a distinct type of economic unit but as parts of kinship or family units, as they almost always were in practice. Why provide such support and legitimize such institutions, when doing

---

[1] Ebrey, "Conceptions," 219–45; Goetzmann and Köll, "The History of Corporate Ownership," 151.
[2] Freedman, *Chinese Lineage and Society*, 44–45; Wolf and Huang, *Marriage and Adoption*, 57–69.

so would give them and their wealthy members an independence and legitimacy that might endanger the government-ordained order? The government could engage with merchants, even invest in their pawnshops and other ventures; but why would it want to waste time, energy, and money on creating a body of law, regulations, and privileges solely to handle commercial matters and conflicts that could be more easily treated as problems of household law (and thus most likely be resolved outside the law court, probably to the pleasure of all parties)? Such legal autonomy for merchants would invariably increase the likelihood of yamen representatives becoming entangled in the thankless task of disentangling family quarrels from wasps' nests of envy and resentment. At worst, it would set up a distinct body of legal statuses and privileges that would provide the rich with yet another lode of loopholes for hiding and protecting their wealth at the government's expense. And, if the government's investment in profitable businesses like pawnshops suggests its willingness to act like a commercial partner in an otherwise private business, it did not need a set of laws to privilege itself at the expense of fellow private investors. It seems thus to have turned a blind eye to trespassing any conventional distinctions between private and public parties, and few merchants objected. Interestingly, neither side expressed a strong interest in the use of either private or government contracts for commercial partnerships. References to their use for commercial transactions become common only in the second half of the Ming, and even then their use may have remained a minor practice. As was shown in volume 1, Huizhou residents tended to view contracts as being as useful for initiating and focusing disagreements as for reaching long-standing agreements. Consequently, it may be preferable to think of these commercial partnerships as based more on common understandings of commercial commitments than on written contracts, especially when the partners were close kin.

Indeed, Huizhou men likewise preferred to think and act around all these legal and economic obstacles, by making the most of whatever institutional resources they or their families had. Reports of their formation of family firms only beg the question of what kind of family organization is being considered. In addition to a stem-family cycle, such as experienced by the Zhangs of Xiuning,[3] they had potential

---

[3] Yang Guozhen, *Ming Qing tudi qiyue*, 225–30.

recourse to other Ming models of family organization previously introduced – a large communal family, a lineage, a branch, a segment, or one headed by a uxorilocal son-in-law. Furthermore, even an elementary nuclear family could, as seen already with the charitable landed trust, simultaneously exist and function as part of a larger kinship unit, such as a branch or lineage. Admittedly, the family that researchers might identify on a business organization chart as "small" might never develop into a large family with a large family firm. But it could link its own commercial activities with other businesses formed by fellow lineage members and thus participate as a family firm in a larger commercial organization without any obvious expansion in their operations' staff.

In other words, there was no necessary contradiction between the fact that Huizhou was celebrated, on the one hand, for its hundreds of eminent merchant lineages and their large business operations and, on the other hand, for a multitude of small merchants who ran tiny family businesses often as peddlers. The spectrum of its family-based commercial operations ranged from a single merchant peddling his family's goods from market to market, to a trading house owned and run by two or three generations of direct descendants within one narrow descent line, to a sizeable interregional trading firm manned by many lineage members and backed by funding from families within the lineage. To a large extent, the success of many Huizhou merchants lay in their forging partnerships, usually with kinsmen, out of all these varieties of commercial life and organization.[4]

To describe and explain in detail how this transformation of business and kinship organization took place in Ming China – how a type of commercial partnership was married to a lineage framework limited in its claims on its members' assets and yet often generous to its members in the distribution of its trust's income – is not easy. The relevant Ming records are few, their data and details are inadequate, and the modern scholarship is sparse. Yet, when read together with some earlier and later sources, the Ming records show how, by expanding the scale of the functioning kinship group and thereby enhancing the accessible supply of labor and capital, Huizhou lineage

---

[4] Xu Dixin and Wu Chengming, *Zhongguo zibenzhuyi, v. 1*, 102–3, tells of how a senior relative's word of approval guaranteed juniors in his Huizhou lineage financial backing from others.

organizations helped to transform not just the concept and organization of the "family firm" but also the scale and scope of its impact on Chinese life.[5] Indeed, the sixteenth-century transformation of Huizhou kinship organizations that is described in this and the previous volume – the growth of large kinship groups around common ownership of some property, their collective worship of a common set of ancestors, their virtual subjection if not replacement of rival religious institutions in Huizhou villages, and their encompassment of largely independent and even fractious branches and segments – set the stage for this upgrade in the organization and operation of relatively large-scale commercial houses in south China during the latter half of Ming.

As a result, forms of commercial partnerships commonly vulnerable to the whims of short-term commitments acquired a greater possibility for long-term stability, wider sources of investment, larger amounts of capital, and greater institutional strength. Just as lineage ancestral halls and even their pawnshops helped to compensate for some inadequacies of the private banking system, so did lineage-financed and -staffed commercial partnerships meet the needs of an increasingly commercialized economy – one that relied on regular long-distance transactions of mass commodities – for higher levels of investment and greater organizational stability. A Huizhou merchant in search of a large supply of capital would have found no cheaper aid than a kinsman's capital presented as a bid for shares in a commercial partnership. Governance of commercial partnerships, their different modes of operation, and their different distribution of profits thus become central to our analysis of Huizhou merchants' activities and success during the Ming and Qing.

Models of Commercial Partnerships

As most Ming Huizhou merchant families lacked direct and cheap access to the great amount of capital circulating in salt monopoly transactions, they tended to reply primarily on various types of commercial partnership to help fund their commercial ventures. The evidence for this broad claim is not just the sudden increase in the late

---

[5] There is no evidence that the Chens 陳 of De'an 德安 county in the tenth and eleventh centuries (McDermott, *Making, v. 1*, 124–33) engaged in trade as a lineage, branch, or individual family investors; the same holds for all other known large communal families.

Ming of reports on commercial partnerships.[6] But also there was a shortage of attractive and viable alternatives for someone anxious to find capital or invest the little he or she had in nonagricultural assets. Recall the limited variety of institutions that accepted even small deposits of cash, the prohibitively high rate of interest imposed by pawnshops and other lenders (but for some ancestral halls to their members), the thriftiness of many working men, and a commonly perceived need to expand one's farming income. Consider the limited availability of attractive investment opportunities outside one's personal network of connections, the high degree of commercialization and thus great demand for credit, and the restriction of readily available Ming currency to just clumsy copper coins and silver ingots. And, when faced with the likely and unappealing alternative source of capital – an inescapable annual obligation to make 20 or even 30 percent interest payments to lenders whom one did not know and who did nothing else for one's business than sit and wait for the next instalment of interest payment – a merchant in need of capital would have easily concluded that involving one or more kinsmen as partners in a business venture made both common and economic sense. Partnership also made great sense in another way: through a commercial partnership the capital-short merchant would share his risks as well as profits and, crucially, escape all legal obligation to repay his partner if the business faltered. Also, it attracted investors bound to him by more than the cash nexus and thus more amenable to his subsequent appeals for their patience and understanding during difficult times.

If we adopt the perspective of the investor, then comments on Chinese commercial partnerships by an experienced British lawyer in late nineteenth-century Hong Kong merit close attention, particularly his claim on its attraction to Chinese "men and women of all classes":

Hence it is that the innate desire to re-invest even small savings forthwith in a profitable way, led, in the absence of savings banks, to the practice now universal throughout all the larger cities of China to invest money in shops and trading concerns of all descriptions with the understanding that the lender receive a certain percentage on the annual net profits of the business, as shown by the annual balance sheet made out by general custom, after stock-taking, at the end of every year. Domestic servants, male and female,

---

[6] Liu Qiugen, *Zhongguo gudai hehuo*, 186–243, contains numerous sources on Chinese commercial partnerships.

employés in Government offices or houses of business, artisans and small farmers, men and women of all classes are thus most commonly dormant partners to a gradually increasing extent in business or industrial undertakings. Business men, also, find it affording useful information or help, to invest surplus funds of their own business, on the basis of dormant partnership, in parallel or competing shops or firms. Persons who thus invest their savings frequently also arrange, when the amount at stake is large, to get a trusty relative employed in the business in which they are dormant partners, so that he, while earning his own wages as servant, salesman or accountant, may keep the dormant partner informed as to the stability or solvency of the concern, or check the correctness of the annual dividend allotted.

To satisfy their need for capital and nonfamily staffing, Chinese developed commercial partnership models as alternatives to the one-, two-, or three-generation family firm. Our late nineteenth-century British commentator observed with self-conscious exaggeration that Chinese have made use of "floating capital on the basis of partnership and joint-stock associations since the time when our ancestors were still squatting in the bush."[7] More recent research has concluded that Chinese forms of partnership began possibly from as early as the eighth century BC and the commercial variety certainly by no later than the second century BC.[8]

The known varieties of commercial partnership in China followed different guidelines for the sharing of capital, management, or labor. These arrangements fall along a spectrum of variations in, first, the degree to which they distinguished between the investor–owner and the manager; second, the actual roles these parties adopted to operate the partnership; and third, their adaptability to investor management from afar. Consequently, three basic varieties of commercial partnership – "commenda" (*weituo* 委托, *fuben* 副本), agency (*jingshang* 經商),

---

[7] Anon., *Commercial Law*, 6.
[8] Hino, "Tō Sō jidai no gōhon," 485–98; Liu Qiugen, *Zhongguo gudai hehuo*, 90–91, 157–85; *MQHS*, 81, 549–53, where the calculation errors of a mathematics manual are corrected. Von Glahn, *Economic History of China*, 109–13, shows a Han origin, but Zhang Qiujian, *Suanjing*, xia, 389, and Shiba, *Chūgoku shakai keizai shi yōgokai*, 205, prefer a Tang dynasty origin. Liu Xufeng, "Jindai Huanan chuantong shehui," 244–60, reviews past scholarship on the origins of premodern companies (*gongsi* 公司). A man might rely upon capable bondservants to conduct trade for him, or co-operate with a brother to run a firm, whereby one brother in Luzhou 瀘州 sent (not sold) commodities to the other in Nanjing (Cao Lin, *Mingdai shangren*, 114).

and joint-share (*heben* 合本, *hegu* 合股) – can be discerned. Despite the paucity of the sources these three varieties merit particular attention, as they were all used by Huizhou merchants in the Ming. The following account of these partnerships will provide an evolutionary analysis of their late imperial development. To compensate for the likely assumptions in this deceptively smooth and rationalistic account, this chapter will conclude with consideration of the broader religious and cultural context in which these commercial partnerships took shape and operated.

The identification and focus on these three types of Chinese commercial partnership will almost inevitably arouse debate. The Chinese record, at least as so far studied, contains no commercial code, no clear legal guidelines, and no official and unofficial comparisons or even general discussions of the varieties of commercial partnerships practiced in late imperial times. This choice arises from my reading of a wide range of relevant late imperial sources and differs from those schemes recently proposed by some Chinese scholars. In place of their choices that tend to stress sources of funds and adopt a relatively ad hoc, unstructured approach,[9] the choice presented here is supported by a clarification of these three types' implicit principles and by empirical evidence.[10] Nonetheless, this selection, especially the first category, commenda, is still vulnerable to three kinds of criticism – historiographic, terminological, and empirical – each of which needs to be directly addressed before we proceed to the main task of this chapter: a historical survey of the evolution of late imperial China's different types of commercial partnership.

First, the historiographic charge against the category of commenda is that no actual or model commenda contract survives in China from before the late nineteenth century and thus from before the introduction of modern Western notions and practices to East Asian commerce. This recognition of the inadequacies of the Chinese record on

---

[9] The persistent interest in sources of capital rather than in methods of its deployment probably stems from Fujii Hiroshi's pioneering study of Huizhou merchants (Fujii, "Shin'an shōnin no kenkyū," 36.3, 67). Fujii's category of entrusted (*weituo* 委托) capital, which actually encompasses many of the examples used in this chapter, has usually been used uncritically rather than analyzed.

[10] This evidence largely concerns commercial activities, but *Dianshang*, 299–302, 319–21, shows also the relevance of these types of partnership to Ming pawn brokerages.

commercial practice is welcomed, but it does not prevent us from also recognizing the similarity of certain Chinese commercial practices to one another within China and to those found elsewhere which historians over the past century have come to designate a commenda type of commercial partnership. Furthermore, the terminological complaint observes that, not surprisingly, no such term as "commenda" (or its Arabic and Hebrew parent) can be found in the Chinese historical record to describe any type of Chinese commercial partnership. Once again, this charge is true, but we are presumably interested more in describing and accounting for actual practices than in uncritically reproducing terms, especially as it is unlikely that these non-Chinese terms would have had the same meaning in Ming China as they acquired elsewhere in Eurasia. The most suitable Chinese expression for commenda is probably *weituo* (literally, to entrust), a term that in fact some recent Chinese studies have used to categorize all the long-distance commercial partnerships that I by contrast prefer to distinguish historically and analytically. And finally, there is the sensitive matter of some scholars' questionable use of the term "commenda" to support claims for which there is no concrete evidence, namely the claim that China learned this practice from non-Chinese, Islamic or European merchants. As we shall see in detail below, the only evidence of such a flow of influence is weak and circumstantial (arguably, the flow of influence could have been in the opposite direction). In other words, it is quite sensible to focus on Chinese and non-Chinese reports of Chinese commercial partnerships as shaped primarily if not entirely by Chinese conditions within China and not dependent on foreign influences, even while leaving open the possibility of external sources of change. To leave this final issue open and to acknowledge the earlier Chinese contributions to this discussion, I will attach quotation marks to the category of commenda, so that it reads as "commenda."

In analyzing the long-term evolution of "commenda," agency, and joint-share partnerships, I aim to indicate recurrent differences in their duration, the number of their partners and other participants, their practices for distributing profits and losses, and, when possible, their typical level of capital investment. The analysis will also assess the solutions each type of partnership offered for recurrent problems of financing, management, and personnel. By thereby clarifying the operational practices of what became the most popular type of Huizhou commercial partnership – the joint-share partnership – it will identify key advantages that Huizhou merchants enjoyed in their competition with those merchants, often of other regions, who relied on usually smaller, and simpler, varieties of partnership. Precisely how matters of scale and kinship affected Huizhou merchants' use of the joint-share partnership model to create commercial networks will be explored in detail in the next chapter, as here we will concentrate on describing and explaining the evolution of key differences in these three most common modes of commercial partnership from the Song through the Qing dynasties.[11]

From early on, some Chinese investors pooled their capital together in farmland, urban property, a resident shop, a business, or other type of jointly owned property. More temporary joint investments in specific commercial ventures also appeared early on, allowing one party to supply the land, shop, business, property, or other form of capital in return for another's provision of management skills and labor.[12] In one variety of this kind of arrangement the investor(s) provided capital to a manager who was dispatched as an itinerant partner to use this capital (or its equivalent in commodities) to conduct distant business transactions that would eventually profit both parties. Viewed in terms of traditional Chinese categories for merchants, it had one or more "resident merchants" establish a partnership, whereby he or they would invest in a long-distance business venture undertaken for a year or more by an experienced "travelling merchant," usually another party. Upon this merchant's return, he would repay the investing "resident" partner(s) the original capital investment plus no less than half of the profits he had garnered in the empire's distant marketplaces or in overseas ports; the rest of the profits he pocketed for himself. Assuming a sharp distinction between owner and manager, the terms of such "commenda" partnerships had the investor(s) provide all the financial capital and the itinerant partner his managerial capital; that is, his skills, experience, time, labor, connections, and perhaps other

---

[11] The focus here on the differences between these partnership models should not prevent us from noticing that these models could be combined and practiced by the same party, in that the investing partner in a "commenda" partnership or an agency partnership could, of course, be involved separately in a joint-share partnership, just as there was nothing to prevent the traveling merchant in a "commenda" partnership or the agent in an agency partnership from being engaged in or financed by a joint-share partnership for his part in a "commenda."

[12] Hino and Kusano, "Tō Sō jidai no gohon," 486–98.

nonmonetary resources. While this arrangement did not bar the investing partner from establishing a general strategy for the venture (for example, the type of cargo, travel destinations, profit levels, and local contacts), it did prevent him from micromanaging its day-to-day operations, simply because he did not join his traveling-merchant partner for the duration of his trip.[13] In compensation, however, the investor was able to postpone payment of the manager, until the manager had handed over to him all the profits. He thus could avoid advance payments and so devote all his capital to the business venture (and to the purchase of its commodities) before rewarding his manager for his services. His own eventual profits would thus have been proportionately greater.

As a mid-eighteenth-century commentator recognized, this form of commercial partnership left an investor vulnerable to the wiles and foibles of the merchant he had engaged:

One entrusts [a contracted traveling merchant] with much capital, lets him do the buying and selling, and allows him to go anywhere. Sometimes after one year they close the books, or sometimes after half a year they hand over the accounts. Yet, it is difficult to examine and check whether there are profits or not. That is, if [the traveling merchant] gets great profits, the good ones will hand over no more than 50 or 60 percent of them. If they are not good ones, they will completely encroach on [the capital], practice deceit, and so provide no compensation at all. It can get so bad that some of them love gambling and having a good time so much that all the capital is wasted and in the end blown away and not returned to its original owner. How could it not be considered a loss of wealth for the owner?[14]

As is clear from this passage, the traveling merchant received the investor's capital without the burdens normally assumed by someone borrowing another's money. While the investor's profits might far surpass those acquired from a simple loan, his manager, unlike the defaulting borrower, was under no absolute obligation to return the capital entrusted to him or to pay any interest on his use of it. Any loss of the venture's capital would thus be solely at the expense of the investor(s). What would have encouraged the merchant to work hard

---

[13] The earliest, and still useful, discussion of Chinese "commenda" arrangements is Shiba, *Sōdai shōgyōshi*, 441–51.

[14] Hu Wei, *Zhijia lüe*, 3.26b, is quoting an eighteenth-century man from Lanxi 蘭西 county in the Zhejiang interior, who reportedly observed this practice while residing in the county seat.

for these investors (though admittedly not as hard as he would have for himself alone) would have been his contract's fixed-share terms for the venture's profits. Like a tenant sharecropper on a farm, he would in theory attain greater profits for himself the more time, skill, and intelligence he committed to his work.[15]

Thus the working terms of a "commenda" partnership required, as indeed our eighteenth-century source warns, that the traveling merchant be chosen for his diligence, skill, and honesty. If such a good man were found – it clearly made sense to choose someone known and trusted, like a relation, adopted son, fellow villager, or close friend – this kind of highly personal partnership could have worked within the common understanding of the practice of long-distance trade in Song, Yuan, and Ming China. On the one hand, there would be a fifty–fifty share (or up to 60 or 70 percent in the investor's favor) in profits potentially high enough to outdo the 30 percent interest rate regularly imposed on loans; hence the itinerant merchant did not want to work for a fixed cash payment as if he were a mere hired laborer, and thus, in Song legal terms, a servant to the investor(s). And, on the other hand, there would be a complementary sharing of different kinds of risks and drawbacks: the merchant (along with his crew) had to endure prolonged absence from home and constant exposure to physical danger, while the investors had to face, until the merchant's successful return, the possibility of suffering the total loss of their capital without compensation. Interestingly, although the economic terms of this arrangement – the investor's 50 percent take of the profits in the Northern Song became 70 percent in the one known instance from the Southern Song (one wonders if he therefore assumed some new risks, like making use of his own boat) – may not have improved for the traveling merchant during the Song, his social status did. In the mid eleventh century, an itinerant merchant, managing a commercial venture with funds provided entirely by others, tended to be regarded as his master's hired hand and thus as his servant or retainer; in this arrangement "commenda" can be seen as a form of loan,[16] or as an alternative to

---

[15] With so much riding on the manager's performance, "commenda" arrangements conceivably involved the investors' seizure of his family members as hostages along with the family's assets, until he returned with the requisite profits (see note 123 below).

[16] Anhui bowuguan, *Ming Qing Huizhou shehui jingji ziliao congbian*, v. 1, 580, includes a loan contract in which five parties lend an equal amount of money to

long-term hired labor.[17] But a century or so later his "master" (that is, the investing partner), while still requiring a close personal, if less unequal, relationship, presumed less of him, possibly because he, the investor, ended up with a larger share of the profits.[18]

By their nature these "commenda" partnerships were usually for a single round-trip venture, not just for the contracting parties but also for any contacts and transactions made by the manager in distant markets during his journey. To the best of my knowledge, no Chinese source indicates that they were intended to function as tests or seeds for larger, more complex commercial operations. Yet common sense suggests that some merchants would have taken this approach, especially for domestic voyages. Having tested their manager's profit-making plan to their satisfaction, they would have wanted to repeat the arrangement several times for mutual advantage.

Other merchants, their ears open to latest news of market demands in distant places and anxious for a more regular arrangement, would have preferred to sign up trading representatives in the places judged most profitable and promising. Yet the manager, having learned where lucrative markets were located, would have been sorely tempted to use this knowledge and his share of the profits to make more profits for himself. Either he would turn himself into an investor in his or others'

---

another party for a specific commercial use, specifying that party's obligation to pay them annually a set percentage (8 percent) of their initial total capital outlay; nothing is mentioned of any journey, termination date, or profit sharing, but its terms suggest how this practice might eventually have led investors into lending money to, or investing in, an itinerant merchant's return-trip venture on commenda-like terms.

[17] The "commenda" partnership can be seen as a means of hiring someone without imposing servitude, the legal status that Song and Ming law specified for long-term hired laborers. On the latter, see Oyama, "Min Shin jidai," 249–74.

[18] Despite the likelihood that a manager's success in one "commenda" venture would have attracted competitive offers for his services, no evidence so far confirms a link between his improved status and his acquiring more than one investor in any of his trading ventures. Yet the issue merits further study. Certainly, the trading goods taken on board by members of the crew may well, like those of the captain, have been paid for by loans from friends and relations and sold at different ports along the ship's journey inland or overseas. Under such arrangements a single boat on a single long-distance voyage would have been the home simultaneously to a considerable number of different "commenda" arrangements (see the loose arrangements allowed a traveler on an overseas voyage in the late Ming short story included in Ling Mengchu, *Slapping the Table in Amazement*, 16–20).

voyages, especially if, as an investor, he could expect a 50 or 70 percent share of the profits for himself. Or, if he wished to settle in one of these lucrative markets, he might set himself up there as an experienced local agent for his unadventurous investors, whose interest in his distant dealings had been piqued by news of his success. Such distant agents, rural as well as urban, were already by the twelfth century regularly purchasing and storing up local products like linen cloth for their employer's annual collection. Under a long-term contractual understanding these agents worked on commission, taking a portion of the profits from the local transactions and relying on funds issued by the merchant directly and possibly indirectly. At least initially, a local innkeeper, shop manager, or broker could assume this extra job with minimal extra work. An innkeeper, in addition to having storehouses, could find his new partner's customers among his regular lodgers and clientele, just as a shop manager and local broker could in the course of their regular duties introduce their customers to the goods of their distant partner.[19]

The advantages of this type of agency partnership, as opposed to the "commenda" arrangement, were obvious: it required minimal capital outlay and expenditure, demanded less commitment from both parties, posed fewer risks, and potentially lasted longer and thus required less time for rearranging and managing. The investor and his agent would each operate somewhat independently, if only because almost certainly this type of agency partnership would have provided each partner with just a part of his income. It certainly did not bar them from establishing additional businesses and forming partnerships with other parties; it could also occur with traveling merchants themselves working within a "commenda" arrangement. Such looseness in business arrangements would have had particular appeal to merchants and agents testing out a possible long-term partnership or when the merchant postponed making a more permanent commitment until he could be confident of the agent performing his work profitably. In the end, both parties would have realized that these advantages probably stemmed as much from the investor's shortage of capital and suitable staff as from his desire for flexibility. In other words, come an economic crisis, this institutional flexibility could become institutional instability. Or, come

---

[19] Hong Mai, *Yijian zhi*, kui, 5, 1,254; Liu Qiugen, *Zhongguo diandang zhidu shi*, 90–91, 103, no. 4.

an expansion of the business when the investor had sufficient funds and had built up his own trusted full-time staff, an agency partnership would have lost its initial advantages. Not expected, then, to be permanent or even long-term, this kind of partnership, like that of the "commenda" variety, would possibly end up giving way to more settled arrangements.

While this successful development of the agent's work led sometimes to the establishment of branch offices manned by full-time hired workers, it also encouraged investors to establish a more settled type of commercial partnership that simply required of all participants a commitment of capital: what is called a joint(-share) partnership in both China and Europe. Chinese investors, regardless of whether or not they became actively engaged in the management of a business, would supply capital to form a commercial partnership whose profits and losses they would share according to the relative amount of their capital investment (hence their investment was usually identified as a number of parts (*fen* 分) or shares (*gu* 股) and accordingly rewarded). Contrary, at least until recently, to the conventional wisdom in Chinese historical circles, this practice dates back to far before the Ming and may have been influenced by foreign merchant groups like the highly successful Sogdian merchants active in north China.[20] By no later than the early twelfth century in the Yangzi Valley, joint-share commercial partnerships had evolved into a variety of organizational forms, such as joint-capital partnerships (*liancai heben* 聯財合本), associations of partners (*jiuhe huoban* 糾合夥伴), and associations of those in the same trade but without joint-capital investments (*fei liancai heben er jiuji tonghang* 非聯財合本而糾集同行).[21]

No further distinctions are made in extant Song sources between these three kinds of business association. Indeed, the first and third may well be different terms for the same kind of arrangement. But the first seems to have become popular to a wide spectrum of investors, quite likely because its arrangements were more readily adapted to the

---

[20] La Vaissière, *Sogdian Traders*, 24–32, and 147.
[21] Xu Song, *Song huiyao*, shihuo, 16.1b; my thanks to Prof. Zhao Dongmei 赵冬梅 for suggesting this translation, as preferable to another acceptable translation of the phrase 同行 as "co-travelers." For more detail, see McDermott and Shiba, "Economic Change in China, 960–1279," 402–5. Liu Qiugen, "Shi dao Shisi shiji," 109–22, includes many multiparty partnerships, some involving the government, among his joint-share partnerships.

circumstances and wishes of prospective partners than would have been a single family's firm. These joint-share partnerships could be flexible about the minimal level of investment – witness the several hundred copper coins that every family along the southeast coast from Zhejiang to Guangdong is said to have "leaked," or invested, in overseas voyages to Japan in the early thirteenth century.[22] They allowed an experienced traveling merchant to invest in his own return ventures to places he had found profitable or to settle in one place and then direct for as long as he wished the activities of his appointed managers or partners' activities in these promising markets, possibly on different terms for different ventures. Likewise, they allowed the various investors of a partnership to put different amounts of capital in a business venture (ranging, for example, from ten to 100,000 strings of copper cash) and also to invest simultaneously in other business ventures, probably out of a wish to spread their own exposure to risk (there was no explicit practice or even notion of insurance policies or limited liability). And investments, at least in the Southern Song, could be made in virtually any type of currency, in copper cash, precious metals like gold and silver, salt vouchers, paper money, or monk certificates.[23] From the mid fifteenth century, the overwhelming preference was for silver investments, though in Ming and Qing Shanxi a share in the firm and thus its profits was sometimes awarded to the firm's accountant after many years of fine work.[24] Overall, one cannot but be impressed by the breadth of the social strata investing in these commercial deals. Knowledge of banks and moneymaking appear to have been much more widely diffused in this culture and society than in early modern Western Europe, where it often remained in the hands and heads of a small capitalist class working in banks.

In the Yuan dynasty, virtually all we know of commercial partnerships concerns the practice of "commenda," or rather a Mongol government adaptation of its Southern Song version: "The Yuan government, in providing boats and capital, selected individuals to go abroad to trade for it in sundry goods. As for the profits thereby obtained, the government [that is, the investor] took 70 percent for

---

[22] Bao Hui, *Bizhou gao lüe*, 1.17a–b.
[23] Xu Song, *Song huiyao*, shihuo, 70.102a–b; Hino, "Sōdai chōseiko," 228–31.
[24] Shi Tao and Li Zhifang, "Chanquan," 125.

Models of Commercial Partnerships

itself and gave the merchants [that is, the hired hands] 30 percent."[25] These favored merchants were predominantly Muslims from Western Turkistan, plus some Uighurs, Persians, Armenians, Jews, and Syriac Christians engaged in trade primarily with Inner Asia, Persia, and, out of the Fujian port of Quanzhou, Southeast Asia. Conducted for the imperial family or individual princely houses, this trade was primarily a government-sponsored trade in foreign and Chinese luxury goods, that thus was both highly capitalized and profitable for those with good political connections. Han Chinese private trading for the court and officialdom continued, but Han merchants appear to have been at best minor participants in these Mongol–Muslim trading ventures. Any putative Middle East influence on Chinese "commenda" practices in the Song would have strengthened during the Yuan.[26]

During the Ming these three types of Song commercial partnerships – "commenda," agency, and joint-share partnership – continued to be formed.[27] With the restoration of Han Confucian official rule the practice of "commenda" partnerships reverted to being primarily, if not entirely, a private merchants' institution. Furthermore, thanks to a strict government ban for two centuries on private parties' direct engagement in overseas trade,[28] it would have differed radically from Yuan practice in being overwhelmingly concerned with the domestic market and more commonly having multiple investors, rather than a single one.[29] Its popularity varied from region to region, though not on

---

[25] Allsen, "Princes," 117–19; Endicott-West, "Merchant Associations," 127–54; Xiu Xiaobo, *Yuandai de semu shangren*, 21–40; Liu Qiugen, *Zhongguo gudai hehuo*, 172–73; Schurmann, *Economic Structure*, 222.

[26] For the possible Muslim Influence on China, see Çizakça, *A Comparative Evolution of Business Partnerships*; and Udowitch, *Partnership and Profit*.

[27] Liu Qiugen, "Mingdai gong shangye," 58–64, introduces the first and third of these kinds of commercial partnerships and distinguishes those forms of partnerships which use hired managers (this might constitute his version and understanding of agency partnerships) from those contractual arrangements which had coinvestors work as comanagers. His latest study of commercial partnerships, *Zhongguo gudai hehuo*, shows, in my view, an advance on his earlier articles, with its overall schema of three kinds of commercial partnership distinguished by their use of capital and management: joint-share partnerships, "commenda," and a mixture of the two (no mention is made of the agency variety).

[28] Wills, "Relations with Maritime Europeans, 1514–1662," 333–75.

[29] Sixteenth- and seventeenth-century European merchants engaged in trade in East Asian waters made use of a variety of commercial and financial practices in Macao and Japan (e.g., bottomry, *respondencia* bonds) (Boxer, *Fidalgos*,

the rough north–south or east–west divides commonly employed by Ming historians today to denote regional economic differences. By no later than the sixteenth and seventeenth centuries, the "commenda" partnership had become the most common form of commercial partnership among at least two, if not three, important regional merchant groups. In Shanxi (and Shaanxi) province the terms of the "commenda" arrangement most widely used had one party supply the capital for a business venture, while a host of others provided its labor and management.[30] "With those who have capital and those who lack it all able to make a living from it, the rich do not hide their wealth privately in their families. They scatter it completely among their employees," many of whom were, if not members of an investor's family, then fellow residents of his rural district.[31] Yet, by the 1560s some Shanxi merchants took to the road to find suitable partners along the empire's northern border:

With large amounts of capital they arrive in market towns and walled cities. They hand over their capital to local merchants with whom they join as friends to operate businesses for profit. Each privately sets up contracts, whereby the one who donates the capital (*ziben* 資本) counts up the profits and the one who personally does the transport and receives [the investment] gets a certain portion of the profits.[32]

The merchants of Sanyuan 三原 county in neighboring Shaanxi province also acquired a reputation for engaging in long-distance "commenda"

119–21, 281). While Chinese merchants engaged in overseas trade may have had different ways of raising large sums of capital on the basis of their vessels with or without cargo, the possible impact of Western practices on Huizhou and other Chinese domestic-market merchants remains to be explored. The fact that some Huizhou merchants engaged in overseas trading to Japan (where for decades they would have interacted and traded with Western merchants) encourages me to suspect that some may have experimented with these novel forms of finance for foreign or coastal trade.

[30] A Ming Chinese variant practiced in the Shanxi prefectures of Pingyang 平陽, Ze 澤, and Lu 潞, had "one party provide the capital and the others together do business with it" (Wang Shixing, *Guangzhi yi*, 3, 61–62). Unfortunately, Wang Shixing comments little on the precise division of profits and dividends, as he seems more interested in these employees' reputation for probity than in their employer's financial organization, "commenda" or otherwise.

[31] Shen Sixiao, *Jin lu*, 3. Joint-share partnerships also won favor among Shanxi men, including a fifteenth-century official (Terada, "Sansi Kōshu," 127–40); shares were transferable and inheritable.

[32] Chen Zilong, *Ming jingshi wenbian*, v. 5, 359, 3,876.

trading of northern commodities to the lower Yangzi delta, until they accumulated enough capital to shift into the salt monopoly trade.[33]

Down south in the Suzhou area, merchant families native to the pair of Dongting islands in Lake Tai likewise tended to separate investors sharply from managers: "In general, men who practice trade invariably never have their own capital. Often many receive capital from a rich house, and by permanent custom they recognize a thirty–seventy split of the profits, whereby the investor gets 70 percent and those providing labor 30 percent."[34] The continuation of the investors' 70 percent share of the profits since Song times probably reflects the strong hand of investors benefiting arguably from the already noted decline in the interest rate on pawnbrokerage loans in this area from 50 to no more than 30 percent for the well-to-do; it also provides one reason why "commenda" arrangements remained popular with some investors here.[35]

Finally, "commenda" arrangements were common in long-distance Ming trade along the southeast coast. On boats owned by one or more men, investors entrusted the boat's captain with goods for sale at selected destinations on a two-way voyage. Overall, such managers in Ming coastal domestic trade commonly benefited from a higher share of profits than in the Song: 50 percent or more. The figure could even be higher if the captain was also the boat's owner (who, if a third party not directly involved in the partnership, might acquire as much as 20 percent of the profits). Interestingly, the crew on these "commenda" voyages would also often engage in their own "peddling," since in return for their on-board labor they were remunerated with free cargo space in the hold. Through storing and then buying and selling their load of goods at each port they visited, they had numerous opportunities to engage in their own "commenda" agreements.[36]

These observations on "commenda" have equal, if not greater, validity for Chinese, mainly Fujianese, merchants trading overseas in

---

[33] Fan Jinmin, *Fushui jia tianxia*, 331.
[34] Wang Weide, *Linwu minfeng*, 7.10a–b.
[35] Gui Zhuang, *Gui Zhuang ji*, v. 2, 6, 425, initially seems to be describing the practice of "commenda" partnerships, whereby in c.1669 rich Dongting merchants conferred funds on poor merchants who ran the business for them. But he makes no mention of their division of profits, thereby leaving open the possibility that the managers were hired by the merchants.
[36] Zhang Wei and Tang Zi, "Ming Qing haiwai maoyi," 35–41.

the Indonesian archipelago and probably elsewhere in Southeast Asia. As researched by François Gipouloux, the shipowner, who often consisted of many parties,

> had enough capital to build the ship and recruit the crew. He solicits the merchants who will take part in the voyage overseas, assembles the cargo, and launches the expedition. But, in other cases, he is content to let out the vessel to a merchant who will organize the expedition overseas, and to charge a commission on all the commercial operations carried out.

The partners could consist not simply of the joint-share owners of the boat but also those merchants who, often as trustworthy relations, adopted sons, indentured bondservants, and close friends, rented part of the boat for their cargo and their persons (or representatives) during a "commenda" voyage. If the owner let the boat to other merchants for an overseas voyage, he usually expected a quarter of all the profits, which then would be subdivided among the co-owners according to their number of co-ownership shares.[37]

Dutch and Portuguese records on Chinese "commenda" in the Indonesian archipelago are particularly rich for the sixteenth and seventeenth centuries.[38] According to M.A.P. Meilink-Roelofsz,

> The entire overseas trade of the Chinese [there] was carried on almost exclusively in the form of commenda and only very few of the merchants on the Chinese junks were traveling to the Indonesian Archipelago with their own goods and capital. The money-lenders and suppliers of goods who remained behind in China derived huge profits from this commenda trade. The nearer the foreign ports were to China, the smaller were the risks and the expenses and the larger the profits.[39]

---

[37] Gipouloux, "Partnerships and Capital Pooling," 3–5.
[38] Zhang Wei and Tang Zi, "Ming Qing haiwai maoyi," 35–41. Evidence of a kind of "commenda" in Northeast Asia comes from a 1639 report on Huizhou merchants who colluded with government officials to send Ming navy vessels on a private commercial voyage from the coastal Shandong prefecture of Dengzhou 登州 to Korea to trade Chinese silk cloth, cotton textiles, and mercury for Korean ginseng. These merchants provided the cash backing and got 70 percent of the profits, while the boats' owners (i.e., government officials) ended up with 30 percent of the profits plus a portion for the payment for accompanying military guardsmen (Fu Yiling, *Ming Qing shidai shangren*, 60).
[39] Meilink-Roelofsz, *Asian Trade*, 265. Her assessment is based on a thorough knowledge of the Dutch archives, but makes no use of Chinese sources.

Every year usually eight large Chinese boats holding 300 or more men arrived at Malacca, laden with a great variety of Chinese manufactured and processed goods to sell for a relatively narrow range of local spices and other natural resources they would take back north, mainly to China. In addition, "At the beginning of the seventeenth century, 300 ships left the Fujian port of Yuegang every year. The merchants operate overseas and trade with forty-seven countries in an area stretching from Manila to Nagasaki, Siam, Banten, and Patani, from Champa (present central and southern Vietnam) to the Sulu archipelago."[40]

For most other areas of Ming China the sources are too few to support such forthright pronouncements on the relative popularity of the different types of commercial partnerships, even though associations requiring all members to make cash outlays were commonly formed for virtually every kind of social activity.[41] While some Ming manuscripts and imprints record Huizhou merchants' formation of "commenda" partnerships,[42] far more common are references to their and other parties' resort to joint-share commercial partnerships for pawnshops, transport, commodity trading, handicraft sales, shops, lumber, and mining.[43]

Ming evidence of the general preponderance of the joint-share partnership model, especially the cash-based variety, is extensive. Be it their relatively frequent mention in merchant biographies, the repeated inclusion of a joint-share partnership contract form (and none for "commenda" or agency) in popular encyclopedias and form-writing books from Huizhou,[44] or the thousands of already discussed Huizhou contracts that specify the shares of different parties in future timber crops,[45] Ming sources show how attractive this relatively flexible and well-established form of commercial investment was in Huizhou trading circles during the sixteenth and seventeenth centuries. Such a preference over "commenda" partnerships made considerable sense in

---

[40] Gipouloux, "Partnerships and Capital Pooling," 2.
[41] A form of partnerships was used in even the arcane world of book collecting (McDermott, *Social History*, 155–63).
[42] *MQHS*, 76–80; and Fan Jinmin, *Fushui jia tianxia*, 331.
[43] Liu Qiugen, *Zhongguo gudai hehuo*, 189–244; Satoi, "Shindai kōgyō," 32–50, discusses use of commercial partnerships in mining in southwest China.
[44] Imabori, *Chūgoku hōken*, 659–62.
[45] Liang Mingwu et al., "Ming Qing Huishang mucai," 63–67.

Ming Huizhou, since its merchants were themselves emigrating to the markets of the Yangzi Valley to profit more directly from the trade. Their separate merchant bases in the Yangzi Valley could have concurrently funded some "commenda" ventures to other markets or have had agents work for them in other places; one might even hypothesize that a young Huizhou merchant not instructed by his father into the intricacies of commercial partnership might work first as the manager in a "commenda" scheme and later on the basis of such experience move on to become involved in an agency arrangement and then a joint-share partnership as an active partner. But they would likely have done so, in the "commenda"-style case, within an overall framework of these families' joint-share arrangements and, in the agency case, would have done so most likely on a provisional, trial basis before establishing a longer-term base for a joint-share partnership.[46]

One minor variety of joint-share partnership merits a brief mention at this stage, if only as a contrast to Huizhou merchants' use of commercial partnerships. Some joint-share partnerships relied not, as was normal, on cash investment but on the participants' input of their labor. For example, sometimes Chinese workers adopted the organizational model used by the simple kind of credit association described above in Chapter 2 to collectively own and manage a mine. Whereas in this credit-association example, members without funds could pay fines with their labor rather than their silver, in the case of certain mines in southwest China during the Qing dynasty capital-poor but labor-rich individuals were all expected to input equal amounts of labor into the opening and running of a mine. In return they might expect that as coinvestors they would subsequently all in turn acquire all or part of the profits made by the venture over equal periods of time. This ideal of economic equality was in some cases linked to an egalitarian scheme of governance, that allowed individual workers to

---

[46] The joint-share partnership is also reported from Suzhou and Guangzhou by no later than, respectively, the mid sixteenth century and the early seventeenth (Fan Jinmin, *Ming Qing shangshi jiufen*, 19–20). Xu Dixin and Wu Chengming, *Zhongguo zibenzhuyi*, v. 1, 657, finds its use in the late Ming shipbuilding industry for sand boats in Yangzi delta towns and cities like Taicang, Congming, Changshu, Jiangyin, Tongzhou, and Taizhou. During the Qing it was used in a wide variety of industries and places: Yunnan (ibid., 501–6), Shandong (527–28), Beijing coal (537–39), and iron production in Daoguan, Hunan (465). Zelin, *Merchants of Zigong*, 31–49, recognizes its prevalence in the exploration of salt wells in Zigong, Sichuan.

participate in the firm's decisions on management as well.[47] Another possible example of this type of business arrangement concerns some Chinese shops and their workers in the relatively poor northwest province of Xinjiang. According to N.V. Bogoiavlenskii, a late nineteenth-century Russian consul there, ordinary Chinese in Xinjiang enjoyed entering all kinds of commercial partnerships. Although he does not specify the precise type or terms of their partnerships, he does indicate their social equality by contrasting them with the Russian practice of hired labor and its sharp distinction between owners and workers. In the Chinese companies he writes about, "each worker feels that he is the owner."[48] Here the workers, I suspect, may have invested some capital as well as their labor, presumably in roughly equal amounts; hence the survival of social equality in these economic arrangements.

The mining example and, in my view, probably that of the Xinjiang shops represent one kind of late imperial joint-share partnership, whose concern with social and economic equality would have tended to limit their capital holdings and their duration.[49] In fact, their stress on equal inputs and equal rewards reads as if they wish to apply family-based business models to non-kinsman-based businesses. Yet, to the best of my knowledge, no joint-share partnership of this kind has been found in the Huizhou sources to have succeeded as a business, especially for an extended period of time. Both the mining and shop examples clearly required their members not to move about like a Huizhou long-distance merchant, and their operating principles would have made it hard to establish a trading firm, harder to manage it, and very hard, if not impossible, to manage it from afar. The fictive family

---

[47] Wang Tai Peng, *The Origins of Kongsi*, 4–6.

[48] Bogoiavlenskii, *Changcheng wai de Zhongguo xibu diqu*, 160. Unfortunately, he does not indicate whether these northern workers also invested money in their joint venture. These comments on north China accord with the claim of Wang Tai Peng, *The Origins of the Kongsi*, about the egalitarian nature of Chinese commercial partnerships, often based on credit association (*hui*) financing, for mines and maritime trade in south China and Southeast Asia. For a similar practice in Ming Fujian, see Liu Qiugen, *Zhongguo gudai hehuo*, 310–11.

[49] Most Chinese mines were small-scale and scattered, and their production unpredictable and irregular; deep digging was uncommon until modern times (Golas, "Mining," 278–88). Poorly funded mines, like those described by Wang Tai Peng, tended to have a short life span.

ties in their arrangements underline the strains involved in operating such businesses for a long time.

Indeed, the most important contributions that Huizhou merchants made to the joint-share type of commercial partnership – their linkage of its practices to their lineage organization and resources – would have tended to make relations among partners distinctly unequal, though not along strictly genealogical lines. Huizhou merchants took advantage of the size and flexibility of both the lineage institution and the joint-share partnership arrangements to attract more investors. Ordinary joint-share commercial partnerships in the late Ming consisted of as many as several tens of members,[50] and included not just merchants and officials but also village farmers and even a merchant's own bondservant.[51] Far more significantly, they allowed their various partners to invest different amounts of capital at different times and to share the profits on the basis of the amount of their capital investment and time as partners.[52] Hence, despite talk of the partners being equal, this ideal eventually gave way to a tolerance of unequal investments, unequal assignments in the managerial hierarchy, different numbers of financial supporters backing each of the partners with their capital,[53] and eventually a very complex financial organization hard to manage to the equal satisfaction of every partner. At the same time, some of these lineage-linked joint-share commercial partnerships enjoyed greater stability and longevity than in the past.[54]

This last point, to the best of my knowledge, is not mentioned by Ming commentators, but a comparison of Song and Ming practice suggests that it may well have played a role in attracting investment to joint-share partnerships. The few recorded instances of Song joint-

---

[50] *MQHS*, 74; *Shuaidong Chengshi zupu* (1563 ed.), 4.17a; and *THJ*, 61, 1,266, for ten persons, all relations, investing 300 strings of cash apiece in a "commenda" partnership, that had one Cheng do the trading in Huzhou. Imabori, *Chūgoku hōken*, 664–65; and Akuno, "Shina ni okeru Raimukoi kō no kenkyū," 731–822, both give a wide-ranging treatment of this sorely neglected topic.

[51] *MQHS*, 78. In one venture a Huizhou merchant unwittingly received a sizeable investment of 500 taels from one of his own bondservants.

[52] Cheng Dawei, *Suanfa zuanyao jiaoshi*, 119–23.

[53] Liu Qiugen and Xie Xiuli, "Huishang shanggongye shangye," 83.

[54] The number of partners may also have increased not just to reduce risks but also in response to business cycles usually not discernible today (the higher the point in a business cycle, the more investors, small or big, presumably engaged in the market).

Models of Commercial Partnerships

share partnerships, while tending to last longer than their "commenda" counterparts, typically had a life span of just a few years; none, as far as I can discern, lasted longer than ten or more years.[55] In the Ming, short-term joint-share partnership contracts, specifying an annual review but no termination date, were common enough to be reprinted in five popular encyclopedias and anthologies of social and business letter-forms from the late Ming.[56] But, at least in the latter half of the Ming, some commercial partnerships survived far longer, apparently avoiding the partition of family property that ordinarily followed the decease of the family's head.[57] Certainly, no Song

---

[55] McDermott and Shiba, "Economic Change in Sung China, 960–1279," 403–04; Qin Guan, *Huaihai ji jianzhu*, 33, 1,081.

[56] The contract form reads: "The men setting up this contract, Mr. So-and-So and Mr. So-and-So, have seen that wealth is born out of partnership, and business results lie in human actions. Therefore, the two men agree to combine their capital and seek for profit. It is proper to rely on a middleman to see one another [literally, So-and-So]. Each issues forth a certain amount of silver to be capital. With a shared sense of purpose we will pluck up the courage and will manage plans to practice business. The profits and money which we acquire, we will each year face-to-face count up and make clear. We will measure the portions (*liangfen* 量分) for family expenses but will retain the capital, regarding [this procedure] as a plan to have the source [of wealth] not dry up. Each will on his own provide for his personal expenses, and is not allowed to break up and use (*chedong* 扯动) this silver and to confuse the registers' accounts. Therefore, we in particular drink blood and fix an oath, so as to form one peaceful group. The pains and the pleasures we receive will be equal, and we will take care not to persist in conflict and enmity. One cannot accumulate for oneself and enrich oneself [alone]. If anyone violates this agreement, may the gods and men together bring death upon him. Now, fearing there is nothing to depend on, we set up this partnership contract (*heyue* 合约) in two identical copies to be used as evidence later on" (Niida, "Gen Ming jidai no mura no keiyaku (1)," 780, in his *Chūgoku hōsei shi kenkyū*, v. 3). Also, Yang Guozhen, "Ming Qing yi lai 'heben' jingying," 2, lists five imprint titles with this form of contract. Note the contract's silence about possible resort to law and courts and about the distribution of profits or losses (presumably according to a partner's number of shares). Indeed, little mention is made in Ming records of any regular practice of ploughing profits back into a business's operations, though strong evidence of commercial growth suggests that some businesses planned for the expansion of their operations and presumably some reinvestment.

[57] Zhou Shengchun and Chen Qingqing, "Jiazu shanghao quancheng," 34–43, introduces the case of an eighteenth-century Huizhou ink-making family. Its business survived family divisions right up to the mid twentieth century, as the heads of the first two generations monetarized the value of all family property and then equally divided it among the sons, so that just two of them (and their descendants) inherited equal shares in the family ink business and the other sons acquired commensurately valuable pieces of other family property. By essentially

counterparts rival in longevity a number of business partnerships in later centuries, such as the more than two-century partnership (*hehuo* 合夥) set up by two Huizhou merchants for a cloth shop in late Ming or early Qing Suzhou,[58] the Wanquan Tang 完全堂 Drug Shop (which was owned by just the Le 樂 family from the Yongle reign (1403–24) to 1755 and thereafter to the twentieth century by the Le and the Suo 索 families together), and the Southern Goods Store (*Nanhuo pu* 南貨鋪) which opened in Suzhou during the Wanli reign (1573–1620) and was still operating there nearly two and a half centuries later.[59] Quite likely, such extended durations were exceptional, though some historians have rightly observed a growing tendency for commercial businesses to survive their founder's death in the hands of heirs with alienable shares of ownership and oversight.[60] Indeed, these examples point to the likelihood that compared to early dynasties' business practices, Ming contractual arrangements, while remaining adaptable to changing circumstances, acquired a greater degree of stability that would have proven attractive to many investors, especially when these same investors had set up distant business branches to carry out routine long-distance trading for the partnership.[61] In short, a Huizhou merchant or investor could put as much money as he wished into as many partnerships as his capital allowed for as long as he wished, so long as he had the money and persuaded others to join his ventures and let him join theirs.[62] His difficulties arose when he overstretched his funds, thereafter trying to shift capital from one investment to another without his partners' knowledge or permission.

> dividing ownership of this business into shares and separating this ownership from management of the business, this ink business remained in the hands of these two branches for roughly a century and a half. While it is not clear how common this practice was in other Huizhou families, the merchant Hong Dagong wrote a will in 1642 that established a charitable trust composed of commercial enterprises that he wished to escape any family property division (see pages 279–80 below).

[58] Xu Feng'en, *Liuxian waishi*, 3–5. This partnership was sealed by over two centuries of marriage ties between the two merchant families.
[59] Zhang Zhongmin, *Jiannan de bianqian*, 11; Qian Yong, *Lüyuan conghua*, v. 2, 24, 640–41.
[60] Zhou Shengchun and Chen Qianqian, "Jiazu shanghao quancheng," 34–43.
[61] Chapter 6 discusses a lineage branch's formation of a commercial network bridging the middle and lower Yangzi Valley.
[62] The emphasis here falls on the investment of capital rather than, as in a "commenda" partnership, on the investment of both capital and labor (or management).

Lineages and Commercial Partnerships

This use of the shared-capital commercial partnership in Ming Huizhou would have been strengthened by the ability of Huizhou merchants to redefine and recompose the notions of the "house firm" and "partnership" through their use of kinship groups larger than the stem family or a loose set of relations (no suggestion is ever made that commission agents in the Song, themselves often the owners of inns and storehouses, were lineage members or even kinsmen of their traveling-merchant employer). A study, then, of how Huizhou merchants made use of this partnership form will reveal how wider kinship, and indeed lineage, ties profoundly shaped the organization of their and other Chinese family firms.

Let me clarify this claim by stating first what a lineage did not do in joint-share partnerships in Ming Huizhou and then indicate the different relations its members had to a joint-share partnership, landed trust, or ancestral hall functioning within their lineage. First, a Ming Huizhou lineage rarely, if ever, formed, constituted, owned, or managed a "house firm" in the manner of the large communal family. We shall find an early Qing lineage that engaged in urban and rural real-estate transactions as well as moneylending and shop rentals.[63] But there is no evidence that this lineage or any other institution it may have formed made a commercial partnership with another party or that it itself constituted a commercial house. In fact, the active agent in all these economic activities was not the lineage per se but its ancestral hall, which we have seen was a distinct legal and economic entity separately registered as a household in the government's household registers. Second, the ancestral hall and two other institutions closely and commonly associated with a lineage – the landed trust and the commercial partnership – were all corporate bodies, which bought land, sold grain and timber, and lent money at interest to both kinsmen and non-kinsmen, as well as regularly transacted goods and shared profits with their members as dividends. The first two, however, differed crucially from the third, a commercial partnership, in that they were not to sell their land and were expected to use at least part of their profits to fund ancestral worship and other lineage activities.

---

[63] See the discussion of the Shuangshan Wang lineage of Wuyuan county in Chapter 7 below.

Another key difference often lay in the nature of their membership: unlike the position of a partner in a commercial partnership, their membership and its attendant rewards derived from their attested claim to a blood tie; that is, from the members' sharing a male ancestor. Members of a landed trust and ancestral hall, as we have seen, sometimes mortgaged or used their expected rewards from their membership as collateral for loans, and descendants of a hall's Prime Ancestor were often obliged to donate money to gain membership for themselves and a deceased ancestor's spirit tablet; but they could not withdraw from and sell their membership per se. A partner in a joint-share partnership, however, could do just that: so long as he met the contractual conditions of the partnership, he could get rid of and sell his share just as he had bought it. Consequently, unlike a landed trust but like an ancestral hall built with contributions from a selection of lineage members, members of a joint-share partnership were allowed to own different amounts of shares and thus receive different amounts of dividend from the collective net profits. As seen in the sale of timber shares, joint-share partners were rarely obliged to sell shares only to kinsmen. Of course, a partner wishing to sell his shares might need the approval of his partners to do so (one might even conclude that the great popularity of timber-share contracts and agreements strongly indicates the pervasiveness of this practice of joint-share arrangements in Huizhou's commercial sphere). But such a transaction did not violate the common understanding of the relatively wide range of options (and risks) held by a commercial partner as opposed to the holder of a membership in a landed trust or ancestral hall. In sum, just as the multiplicity of ancestral halls allowed a lineage's members greater choice than a landed trust in choosing their coinvestors, so did the joint-share partnership permit a lineage member even greater leeway in the selection of his partners and in the activities he backed with his capital.

Thus lineage members (not their lineage) who formed a joint-share partnership among themselves would not, as in the large communal family model, be obliged to take on all their fellow lineage members as staff due to their common descent from a Prime Ancestor. In an era of unlimited liability, an employment policy of so limited discretion and discrimination would have been financial folly. By instead selecting partners and staff from among suitable well-funded kinsmen, joint-share partners could give greater weight to a member's skill or the size of his investment over, say, a partner's seniority. And of course, the shared partnership, at least initially, required a continuing financial investment and commitment from all partners, whereas no such demand was made of the beneficiaries of a landed trust or even an ancestral hall. It was voluntary and autonomous enough to attract even non-kinsmen as members.

Consequently, as already seen in volume 1's extended discussion of the Shanhe Chengs and their landed trust, a Huizhou lineage in Ming circles, commercial as well as agricultural, is best considered not as a tightly controlled unit whose members followed the commands of its heads and managers. Rather, it functioned as a coalition of highly competitive smaller groups – branches, segments, alliances of only some members of these branches or segments, or a circle of cousins – each of which had its resources and command structure, under the aegis of a larger kinship group like a lineage with far from comprehensive economic and juridical powers. The active number of such groups and their relative power relations were not fixed. As they united and dissolved, grew and expanded, and assumed some independence, segments, branches, and partnerships could influence the nature and functions of the lineage from within it. These groups, especially the branches and segments, could build their own ancestral halls and acquire considerable ritual independence from the comprehensive lineage, but they still could have access and recourse, when desired, to the lineage's ancestral-hall ceremonies.[64]

The extent of this prolonged process in the commercialization of kinship ties and a lineage's assets is evident in the policy adopted by one independent-minded Huizhou family towards the close of the Ming. This family sought to carve out for itself, presently as a stem family and in the future potentially as a much larger kinship unit, a collective existence primarily as a family firm rather than as a family farm. In the culmination of his family's collective shift from agricultural to commercial concerns, a certain Hong Dagong 洪大功 established in 1642 a commercially oriented business-based trust for his own heirs and descendants. In his will he deliberately chose to endow his heirs not with paddy fields alone or with paddy fields and forested mountain land – like the Shanhe Chengs' trust – but with just

---

[64] Faure, *China and Capitalism*, 37–40; and, the cases discussed in Chapter 6 below.

businesses and other market-oriented property. Previously, in the mid Ming, the members of this old Huizhou family had changed their occupation from "ploughing and reading" to growing trees and trading timber. Then in the late Ming the young Hong Dagong had been sent by his father to diversify the family's business activities by trading in textiles, probably cotton cloth, in Yushan 玉山 county in Jiangxi province. Having succeeded in this assignment, Dagong then had his own two sons and a son in-law take up this trade – "Each created a Yushan shop (*dian*) and carried on my ambitions."

When, as an old man, he drew up his will, he allocated his property along lines that reflected the basic structural changes that had shaped the recent past of not just his family but also the Huizhou economy as a whole. In place, then, of the former practice of trying to hold the family together through a commonly owned landed trust, he ordered collective ownership for just those resources of his that were more closely linked to commerce and the market. Whereas he bequeathed his sons equal portions of all his paddy fields, dry land, garden plots, and houses – the kinds of property that the Hongs had separately held before they became interested in commerce – he at the same time insisted that his mountain land, mills, tea plantations, kilns, and of course his grave sites serve as part of this indivisible trust for his male offspring and their descendants. In an even bigger change from early Ming practice in Huizhou, he designated that the family's textile shops and businesses also be retained as collectively held family property for all his descendants. Thus he wanted his descendants to retain their collective identity and ownership through the more lucrative market-oriented property rather than either through agricultural land as had been bequeathed by Fan Zhongyan 范仲淹 in mid-eleventh-century Suzhou or through a combination of forested mountain land and agricultural land as reconstituted by Cheng Doushan and then revived by Cheng Chang in Huizhou's own Qimen county.[65] In short, the family's corporate wealth had become a hereditary joint-share commercial partnership consisting of a range of businesses that would have distributed their commercial profits to the founder's descendants; it was intended to survive the father's death and subsequent threats to its

---

[65] McDermott, *Making*, v. 1, 133–39, 235–368; *Shunzhi shiyi nian Hongxing jiu shu*. The precise locations of this property and the Hong family's homestead within Huizhou are unclear.

existence as corporate family property. Meanwhile, the lineage was to continue operating outside these constitutional changes to one of its member families keen to build up its own permanent shared assets as a segment or branch within it.

Even if in David Faure's words "the lineage was certainly not a business company,"[66] its members could, as kinsmen, belong to and operate a large number of commercial organizations, especially joint-share commercial partnerships at least in Huizhou. Not only did such use of lineage ties satisfy the government's requirement from 1531 that only kinsmen (*qinzu* 親族) could become commercial partners in the salt trade without its explicit approval.[67] But also these connections could provide a partnership with the means to reduce its operating expenses, to attract a larger circle of kinsmen investors at cheaper rates of borrowing, and to draw in more people to staff the partnership's offices and carry out its tasks. Thus they might establish a private means for resolving risks in capital transfer and credit extension over long distances.[68]

The first of these benefits can be explained by reference to Ronald Coase's classic analysis of firms and their business practices. In a seminal essay on business economics Coase argued that a private firm is intended by its founders to reduce their reliance on the market. Since all market activities incur transaction costs, men commonly set up a firm to reduce or eliminate their engagement in those business activities that are judged to cost them less outside the market than inside it: the search for information on prices and quality selection, the subsequent bargaining and negotiating for this information and the desired goods and services, the payment of transaction taxes, and eventually the policing and administrative enforcement of any decision. When it determines that these activities are handled more efficiently outside the market, the firm tries to bring as many as possible of these essential exercises and transactions within its own house, so that a vertical integration of its management and command structure will help it acquire cheaply and efficiently the information it needs to participate

---

[66] Faure, "The Lineage as Business Company," 371.
[67] Liu Qiugen, *Zhongguo gudai hehuo*, 192.
[68] Note the importance of kinsmen in the key sources of Huizhou merchant capital – lineage members' investments and loans, inheritance from father and other ancestors, and wife's dowry – identified in Fujii, "Shin'an shōnin no kenkyū," 36.3, 66–78.

in the market. Thus, in place of drafting a great number of separate contracts for each party in each of its transactions, the firm can draft a modicum of contracts and so enter and exit the market at relatively limited cost and risk.[69]

Now, in this description of the firm's activities, replace "firm" with "house" or "family," and the import of these wider kinship ties becomes self-evident. If we conceive of large Huizhou kinship groups – that is, the branches more so than the lineages – as a potential ensemble of firms, then what Coase said of the business firm's relationship to the market – "firms will emerge to organize what would otherwise be market transactions whenever their costs are less than the costs of carrying out the transactions through the market"[70] – becomes relevant to our comprehension of the actual operation of Huizhou house firms and their dependence on kinship relations.[71] These kinship ties provided a loose institutional alternative to the market in a variety of transaction activities, most notably in accumulating capital, staffing firms, and distributing goods and services. Hence, within the operation of Huizhou prefecture's own economy there naturally was a paradox long ago observed by Shiba Yoshinobu: Huizhou produced many merchants and goods for markets but had far fewer markets and market towns than its wealth and production level would have suggested.[72] And outside Huizhou, the Huizhou merchant would have found help in solving many of the problems that plagued the traveling merchant away from home. Where better in these distant towns and cities to find a "home-away-from-home" than in a building rented or owned by a group of kinsmen?[73] Or, to find help from kinsmen in the form of needed boats and carts, long-distance co-travelers, long-term storehouses and short-term residences, easier access to cheaper credit, up-to-date information on market conditions, and even a reduction of the customary market entry charges imposed on newcomers – what else could one expect of a fellow lineage member who was serving as a

---

[69] Ibid. [70] Coase, *The Firm*, esp. 7.
[71] Chen and Myers, "Coping with Transaction Costs," 317–41. As already noted, the absence of such institutions for Huizhou merchants until the late sixteenth century and their remaining scarcity for another century highlight an important difference between Ming and mid-Qing commercial practice.
[72] Shiba, "Urbanization," 41.
[73] Shiba, *Sōdai Kōnan keizaishi*, 283, n.31 (Hangzhou) and 313, n.129 (Yangzhou).

broker in a Yangzi river port like Wuhu?[74] Market evasion made even more sense, when the actual marketplace for an outsider like the long-distance Huizhou merchant might be as unwelcoming as those seen in Chapter 3.

Qing dynasty Chinese observers of the expansion of Huizhou merchant activities coined the adage, "Wherever one finds a Huizhou man, one finds a market." Yet these merchants' ability to rely on extended kinship ties actually made it more likely that when an eminent Huizhou merchant operated in the larger towns and cities of the Yangzi during the latter half of the Ming, his lineage ties and wealth might help him avoid the market and certain of its transaction costs. As a well-placed merchant outsider, he was capable of avoiding the market's vicissitudes or at least of dealing with them on advantageous terms. Surely it was this ability to stand at times apart from and indeed above the dusty marketplace and its objectionable fray that helped major Huizhou merchants retain their protected profits and gain the allure, at least in their own eyes, of being "a Confucian scholar-merchant (*rushang* 儒商)."

Business Problems and Lineage Solutions

In theory, a larger pool of kinsmen eligible for membership and a longer financial commitment from them would have tended to increase the availability of capital funding for a firm and thus to have eased its shortage of capital as well as the insecurity of its investments. Recall the relatively cheap interest rates offered by Huizhou lineages' ancestral halls – a category of funding source that would for merchants and other members of larger lineages have encompassed numerous halls in their village, plus a shared-surname ancestral hall for all "common-descent" members possibly in another location. Yet, as ancestral hall loans alone would have rarely provided their recipients with enough capital for large-scale trading ventures, ambitious lineage members regularly turned as well to better-off kinsmen for loans to support their commercial ventures.[75] That is, fellow lineage and branch members invested in a variety of one another's commercial activities, with the understanding that investment in such commercial partnerships would be safer than those made in partnerships with non-kinsmen.

[74] Fujii, "Shin'an shōnin no kenkyū," 36.3, 85–86.   [75] Ibid., 65–78.

To realize this larger body of potential investors and a longer duration for their investments in a "lineage partnership," partners would ideally have known from custom or contract the terms of their access to the funds of the partnership and the extent of their shared liability for any losses. For instance, in helping to clarify the answer to the first of these questions, David Faure has sensibly warned us away from presuming that late imperial investors and merchants knew the precise amount of capital assets active in their partnerships. The clear distinction that one finds in Ming and Qing merchants' contract forms between a partner's personal and business expenses, he argues, is not found in the Qing and Republican business account books that he has examined.[76] While practice on this point probably varied according to place, type of trade, and local accounting customs,[77] at least two Ming Huizhou sources, a 1588 will and a 1613 contract with an attached list of actual profits and expenses for the designated heirs in years leading up to 1613, demonstrate without doubt the use in late Ming Huizhou merchants' records of accounting practices that made distinctions that Faure rightly warns not to assume.[78]

[76] Faure, *China and Capitalism*, 36–37.
[77] Gardella, "Squaring Accounts," 317–39. Whelan, *The Pawnshop in China*, 42–46, mentions seven types of ledgers used by pawnshops.
[78] The first piece of evidence, the 1588 will introduced in Chapter 4 above, shows each son of the Huizhou pawnbroker Cheng Yujing operating his own branch of the family business. In listing all his assets Cheng Yujing separately listed each son's annual expenses for several years and then broke down this general category of expenses into, on the one hand, those incurred by each son and, on the other hand, those incurred by or for holders of each son's share. The precise source from which these figures derived is not specified, but their inclusion in this will suggests that Huizhou family firms made the kind of distinction that Faure says he did not find in late imperial documents (from elsewhere than Huizhou). A second Huizhou source illustrates the practice of allotting the sharing of losses as well as profits in even a short-term joint-share partnership. Dated 1613, this contract, plus an attached list of the apportioned profits and expenses, concerns a commercial partnership that involved non-kinsmen in a short-term commercial venture. As such, it has greater import for revealing the general practice of securing trust and damage compensation among partners through the drafting of a business contract. This contract and its subsequently composed appendix together show how five partners carried out in a clear and orderly manner their contract's original provisions for protecting their profits from unintended operating costs. Together they had bought and cleared some trees in Qimen county, only to see some of their prospective profit vanish during the trees' passage by river to Yangzhou. Not only were some trees lost to strong winds, high tide, and rough waves along the Yangzi, but also the investors had been obliged to undertake an additional loan, pay more commercial taxes, and incur

More troublesome, both to the practice of commercial partnerships and to our understanding of their operation in the Ming, are two matters of crucial interest to anyone forming a commercial partnership: the extent of a partner's financial liability (especially in cases of bankruptcy) and a partner's access to his funds invested in the partnership. Huizhou practices of timber land purchasing and trading indicate a sharing of liability among partners for any losses and their easy exchange of ownership shares in this sector of the economy.[79] Yet Ming legal sources and even private records rarely, if ever, address either of these topics directly enough to give a general statement on bankruptcy arrangements and financial practices of commercial partnerships.

For further instruction on these vital matters we presently have little recourse but to look at later, nineteenth-century texts that describe Chinese commercial practices and their legal standing. Ming and Qing legal codes, building on earlier Tang dynasty codes and practice, threatened punishment for lenders in default, and a harsher, more graded revision of this punishment appeared as a statute in the *Collected Statutes of the Ming* (*Ming huidian* 明會典).[80] But, to the best of my knowledge, no Chinese legal text from the Tang through the Ming ever specified the extent of liability in cases of commercial bankruptcy. In fact, it is probably easier to fix the meaning of the most nebulous concepts of a Daoist philosophical text than to determine the precise degree of liability for partners in a bankrupt partnership as prescribed or described in legal codes alone or in actual practice during the Ming or any earlier dynasty. Chinese creditors, as we have seen with moneylenders in Hunan in the Southern Song, might run their own jails, to

---

more expenses due to delays. The resulting contract (which is intended to determine the graded responsibility for the losses and the graded distribution of the profits) specifies that these additional costs were to be deducted from the gross profit made in the sale of the timber. The resulting net profit for twelve shares was to be allocated to the investing parties in line with the five, four, one, one, and one shares they separately held from their original investments (*MQHS*, 264). Thus, by the late Ming, if not long before, some commercial partnership contracts specified ways for determining the investing parties' liability. More importantly, this 1613 contract shows how such contract conditions were actually enforced. Once again, how such transactions were recorded in account books is not clear, but surely the actual practice matters more than the manner of recording, even in an account book.

[79] McDermott, *Making*, v. 1, 387–95, 421–26.
[80] Shen Shixing, *Ming huidian*, 164, 864.

frighten debtors into repayment. But other than punishing acts of cruelty by creditors, Ming law stayed clear of making pronouncements on the handling of bankruptcy cases. It seems to have regarded bankruptcy as a debt like any other: to be repaid, but on terms to be worked out by the parties involved without resort to brutality.[81] The real punishment, most officials doubtless thought, would come from the damage done to a merchant's reputation and from the likelihood that he and his descendants would never again have access to credit unless they repaid the debt, probably at interest.

From the late eighteenth century we have later Chinese observations on commercial bankruptcy, in all cases involving the heavy insolvency of several Guangdong trading houses to foreign, mainly British, merchant houses.[82] Liability was held to proceed from the remaining assets of the bankrupt house to those of the commercial house that replaced it in its group of merchant houses or *hong* (aka *hang*), and then to those of the entire *hong* itself. To help resolve any member's bankruptcy these *hong* would eventually create their own separate funds out of commission charges levied on all transactions by these merchant houses.

In turning, then, to late Qing observations, one British and one Chinese, for further clarification on commercial partnerships and practices, my aim is primarily to determine the range of possible degrees of liability and access that would have faced partners in a Ming commercial partnership. The Briton's description of the pressures exerted on a debtor by creditors *in extremis* echoes the point of the Song legal case from Hunan: creditors will pursue their debtors outside the courts in whatever ways they judge effective. It is hard to think that Ming practice was markedly different from such earlier or later practice. Yet both of these late Qing sources, after all their learned explanations, conclude that the answer to any questions of liability depended usually on the specific circumstances of each case and that resolution particularly of partnership debts and bankruptcy almost always was reached through unreported, out-of-court negotiations between the private parties concerned. This uncertainty would have often stemmed from

---

[81] Fan Jinmin, *Ming Qing shangshi jiufen*, surveys a great variety of legal disputes over business matters, dating overwhelmingly from the Qing dynasty and ranging from fraud and failure to bill payments to brand stealing and shipment damages. Interestingly, bankruptcy is rarely, if ever, mentioned.
[82] Ch'en Kuo-tung, *Insolvency*, 178–80; Grant, *Chinese Cornerstone*.

Business Problems and Lineage Solutions 287

the importance given to noncontractual or nonlegal ties for determining a partner's share in his firm's debts and for directing the pressures he would have felt to bear part of that burden. In other words, a merchant's success in noncommercial relationships would have mattered almost as much as his failure in a commercial venture. Thus, although contracts and general practice might stipulate that liability was determined by the relative size of a partner's investment in the failed venture, the same kinship ties that were often judged vital for forming partnerships might understandably determine the allotment of a partner's actual share in a partnership's debts and losses, if and when it went into bankruptcy.

The clearest statement of this understanding and practice comes from the same late nineteenth-century British observer of Chinese commercial practice, whose views on the popularity and prevalence of commercial partnerships in China were mentioned earlier in this chapter. Once again, due to the acuteness of his insight and to the absence of any alternative Ming commentary, his observations on liability in commercial partnerships merit mention:

persons so investing their money in any legitimate business undertaking are not held responsible by Chinese commercial law for liabilities incurred by the firm to which they lend their funds, nor are they known to outsiders or held responsible by the law in case of insolvency except merely to the extent of their funds actually invested, for the recovery of which they have a right to sue the actual partners. The Chinese law, in fact, treats as responsible only those partners of a firm who are the actual unpaid managers, or those in whose name or under whose orders the business is conducted. But such general partners, who actually, either in person or by their agents, manage a business, are held by Chinese law jointly and severally responsible with their property, person and life, for all the liabilities of their business concern.[83]

---

[83] Anon., *Commercial Law*, 6. No such case is reported in extant sources from Ming Huizhou, but by the early seventeenth century a similar custom arose there in cases not of bankruptcy but of unexpected death. As explained by a She county magistrate of the mid 1630s, people in Huizhou would try to blame their relation's death on others, "to the extent of amassing and plundering [the accused person's home]. Unrelated kinsmen also rely on this to profiteer and raise lawsuits and extort and swindle." In the 1630s, punishments slightly reduced the incidence of this "custom" (Fu Yan, *She ji*, 5, 54), but the custom was alive well into the twentieth century (Cochran et al., *One Day in China*,

Slightly later, a Chinese commentary on Anhui (and thus Huizhou) practices for handling debt largely confirms this view, going so far as to assert the infinite duration of these parties' debt until they had fully repaid it:

> In the past our country has had no time limit for the repayment of debts. A proverb says, "A man dies but not his debts. A father's debts, the sons repay." This is virtually what society publicly recognizes, so much so that if the debtor has no wealth, he then prepares to set up a "prosperity ticket" (*xinglong piao* 興隆票). Even several decades later, the creditor is allowed to demand compensation. There is no so-called "diminishment due to time."[84]

The Anhui commentator about Huizhou customary law on debt significantly qualifies the generalizations of his contemporary British observer. First, a contracted transaction often involved a guarantor, whom a frustrated creditor would invariably turn to for help in forcing the debtor to live up to his repayment obligation and, if that failed, to make this payment himself.[85] A guarantor's sole recourse in this situation was to make direct appeals or threats to the debtor and his family and to initiate a lawsuit against them.[86] Second, while the one or two persons in overall charge of an enterprise's management commonly

---

22–25). Marriage ties between lineages nourished not just alliances and partnerships, but also vendettas.

[84] *Anhui sheng xianzheng diaochaju*, 71–72, 85. A "prosperity ticket" would seem to be the debtor's written reconfirmation of his obligation, when he has the funds in the future, to meet his creditor's demands. This information, it must be said, is neither comprehensive nor necessarily valid for all of Huizhou, since the answers to the survey's questions tend to be listed under the categories "the majority practice" or "the minority practice," with specific counties and prefectures usually mentioned for each of these two kinds of response. The answers attributed explicitly to any Huizhou county are few, and so the composite picture presented here amounts to less a clear and comprehensive summary of Huizhou practice than a series of insights into how Huizhou men in certain Huizhou counties resolved problems that faced partnerships everywhere: management, shareholder power, and dissolution. They deserve mention here, not only because they represent the best general account we have of Huizhou's commercial partnerships, but also because they show how Huizhou men in their partnerships addressed problems of investment management and control – such as the termination of ownership, the use and transfer of shares, the identity of one's partners, and the partners' knowledge of one another's operations – that they would surely have encountered in Huizhou and elsewhere during the Ming.

[85] Ibid., 79, 80. Though liable to ongoing interest-rate charges for all of the debtor's unrepaid loan, the guarantor was free of any liability for interest levied on the debtor's unpaid interest charges (ibid., 76).

[86] Ibid., 81, 82.

Business Problems and Lineage Solutions 289

held sole responsibility for the outcome of an enterprise's activities, management of its affairs was handled collectively by several persons or subdivided among distinct individuals, each assigned specific tasks.[87] Third, some owners, regardless of the formal distinctions between them and their managers, became deeply involved in their managers' work.[88] And, last but far from least, liability in Chinese eyes cannot be assessed merely in terms of contractual responsibility. Men become involved with one another's affairs, it is claimed, through kinship or acquaintance. "Their relationship completely relies on friendly sentiments and cannot be entirely wrapped up in [terms of formal] responsibilities."[89] In other words, in pressing for repayment, a creditor might feel both obliged and entitled to extend the scope of liability beyond the restricted sphere specified in the contract.

To the British commentator, this informal notion of limited liability for all but managing partners seemed reasonable, indeed eminently French, until he felt the need to mention certain complications. Just as small investors "generally select for their investments business concerns the responsible partners of which belong to families or clans well known and accessible to the investor, so that, in cases of fraud, the latter may fall back for compensation on the families or clans concerned,"[90] so might claimants in cases of bankruptcy stretch their claims for compensation beyond the managing partner:

According to Chinese law the responsibility of a general active partner in a firm does not end with the extent of the personal assets, nor is there any distinction of a man's property from that of his wife or sons, but the responsibility extends, if a partner's personal property or that of his immediate family is insufficient to cover his abilities, to the property and persons of his father, of his brothers, of his uncles and if necessary even farther. All the members of a class [i.e., kinship group] are, in theory and in practice, solidarily [sic] responsible with their persons and goods for the liabilities of any one of them. The creditors of a partnership concern need not rest satisfied with prosecuting the actual managing partner but may even set him aside if he has no wealthy clan behind him and proceed, on the ground of this law of mutual solidarity, against several or all of the other general partners and their clans. This terrible power being exercised in the form of the harshest criminal proceedings, it is manifest that *the consciousness of eventually bringing whole families or clans into the clutches of the criminal*

---

[87] Ibid., 128.   [88] Ibid., 137.   [89] Ibid.   [90] Anon., *Commercial Law*, 6.

law makes the position of a partner in China a far more serious concern than anywhere else in the world.[91]

This extended process of seeking redemption from, in turn, the active manager, his immediate family, his fellow clan (or lineage) members, the more active partners, their immediate family, and eventually even their clan (or lineage) members, and then the less active partners, their immediate families, and their clan (or lineage) members, surely gave commercial partners sufficient reason to think more than twice about becoming partners. If they chose to join a partnership, then they would have had good reason to downplay their role in the active management of businesses held by their partnership and thus be extra careful in choosing the actual manager. Eventually, creditors, threatening reprisals, would press their demands on all of these parties without calling on the local yamen for help:

an arrangement [is] made between the creditors and the bankrupt's family and clan to pay a certain percentage in satisfaction of all claims, whereupon the bankrupt, having become the debtor of his clan, has to work the rest of his life to clear off his liabilities to his clan till its members are satisfied.[92]

The few cases of bankruptcy eventually reported to the yamen were motivated by the creditor's despairing desire for revenge, for a furious unleashing of the full wrath of the state against his slippery debtor.[93]

Although this observer claims that creditors have pressed their claims in this manner since the Yuan dynasty, he provides no evidence. Several modern historians have, however, noted the late imperial use of a type of

---

[91] Ibid., 7, italics added; Niida, *Shina mibunhō shi*, 225–36.
[92] Anon., *Commercial Law*, 10. The details of the creditors' recourse read like a chapter from a Chinese novel (ibid., 8–9).
[93] Ibid., 8–10, gives a graphic account of such vengeance. In late imperial law a debtor's relatives extended to an astonishing genealogical distance from him. In Ming times they encompassed those relations living with the guilty party, "relatives of the third degree of mourning or closer, maternal grandparents, grandsons in the female line (*waisun* 外孫), wife's parents, sons-in-law, wives of maternal grandfathers, husband's brothers and brother's wives." Reduced penalties were promised to relatives of four or more degrees' distance, as well as other relatives (Jiang Yonglin, *Great Ming Code*, lxxiii). Likewise, in the Qing, a criminal's coresidents, relatives of the third degree or above, maternal grandparents, children of daughters, wives' parents, sons-in-law, wives of sons' sons, a husband's brothers, or brothers' wives were all legally protected from punishment for concealing him from government arrest (Jones, *Great Qing Code*, 66).

commercial partnership actually mentioned by the British observer: the dormant, or sleeping, partnership (*yinming hehuo* 陰名合夥), that reduced a commercial partner's degree of liability. According to this custom, an investor who did not directly manage the firm and who received no pay from the firm for any work for it (apart from his dividends as a stockholder) did not qualify as an active partner and thus usually escaped all liability beyond his invested capital. Faced with such a division of fiscal liability, an investor would have understandably taken care before involving himself in the active management of his commercial partnerships. To the extent that he spread his investment risks, he would have been expected to acquire mainly sleeping partnerships in a variety of commercial partnerships. In fact, since kinsmen investors in Huizhou commonly formed a group holding under the name of a common deceased ancestor, the partners in a commercial partnership may well have not known the identity of all the sleeping partners in their partnership; that is, all the names of the persons represented by a known dormant party in the partnership. Such an arrangement would then have resembled the opaque conditions of shareholding noticed in volume 1 for shareholders on Huizhou's timber land.[94]

In sum, we have investments made in the shares of commercial partnerships without recourse to a commercial law code and a legitimate public institution like a stock exchange. Bereft of the intermediary services of banking or capital experts, these investors, big and small, put their money into partnerships whose coinvestors, owners, or managers they almost certainly knew but did not necessarily inform of their investment. A very active and equally private market for capital was conducted outside the supervision and regulation of the government or any neutral party, as the commercial economy and the range of its activities had shot far ahead of either the private or the public institutional infrastructure that a great number of private parties had cobbled together to enable these financial transactions. Such investments would certainly have been regarded as risky, thus compelling prospective partners to be doubly cautious about precisely to whom they entrusted their money and under what terms of private regulation and supervision their commercial partnership would have to operate. If one then was forced to determine an investment only after assessing a

[94] McDermott, *Making*, v. 1, 387–90.

man's moral character as "honest and frugal," as in fact family instruction books often advised,[95] then one had to take extra care that one's investment and potential liability did not suffer from one's absence from direct management, from others' nepotistic appointments, and from another partner's wilful neglect of the bottom line.[96]

The second issue that faced a commercial partner – what access, if any, did he retain over funds he had invested in the partnership? – likewise finds no ready answer in Ming legal texts. Although sale contracts of timber shares manifest minimal concern for other shareholders' transactions with their shares, Ming Huizhou land sale contracts regularly confirm the commonsense belief that any commercial partner would have been concerned with fending off threats to his already invested capital. Indeed, even in the contracts for timber share transactions, buyers repeatedly inserted the seller's denial of any previous sale of this land and his willingness to assume responsibility for all subsequent complications arising from other parties' complaints about the sale.

Exceptionally, then, for studies of Ming commercial partnership, our best Ming guide to clarifying the degree of access a partner had to his investments is an account register for an actual dye shop partnership. Active between 1591 and 1603, this partnership dealt in calendared cotton textiles woven most likely in the northeast quarter of the Yangzi delta. As revealed by recent research, the terms of this shop's partnership were remarkably open to changes in membership as well as sources and flows of capital. Two men of different surnames (quite likely Huizhou men) had founded the partnership with respectively 930 and 563 taels of silver in 1591. Within two years their firm's capital had increased fourfold, mainly drawn from three other partners bearing the surname of one of the founding partners (in some cases they were family members). Over the next twelve years two of these new partners kept their funds in the partnership, but the other left with

---

[95] For example, Ebrey, *Family and Property*, 301.
[96] Kirby, "China Unincorporated," 46; Théry, *Les sociétés de commerce*, 2, 119–29. Théry also claims that both active and sleeping types of joint-share partnerships "have existed since time immemorial" (ibid., 2), but unfortunately provides no pre-twentieth-century evidence. Gardella, "Contracting Business Partnerships," 334–35, questions the viability of this type of sleeping partnership, once it involved more than two partners. Nonetheless, the British observer testifies to its popularity in the late Qing.

his capital after four years to be succeeded by another whose capital stayed for just as long. A sixth partner appeared in 1599, and stayed until 1603. By this time, when the partnership ended, the financial base of the shop's operations had been transformed. Whereas in 1593 the shop's operating capital consisted of two-thirds of the partners' own capital investments and the remaining third of loans they had secured from relations, pawnshops, and credit associations, in 1603 these proportions for the shop's different sources for its assets had been reversed.[97] Total capital had doubled since 1593, but a partner's share was just half that of the partnership's loans from relations, pawnshops, and credit associations.

This account book also appears to confirm some of our earlier reflections on the division of responsibility in Chinese commercial partnerships. The five to six partners clearly fall into two distinct types, the active and the less active (aka "dormant") partners. Initially, the two founders were active partners. But swiftly the larger investor took charge and made key decisions by himself. He seems to have enjoyed considerable executive leeway in the partnership's acceptance of new capital investment, the withdrawal of capital for expenses, the use and payment of profits, any reinvestment of profits, and the withdrawal of a partner from the partnership. In fact, this chief manager's array of powers would have made him the sole figure responsible for independently handling most of the adversities that might strike this small shop and partnership. The sole matter he seems not to have controlled is his fellow founding partner's withdrawal from the partnership (the stated reasons were his father's death and his wish to practice business on his own). At this point, the account book ends, along with the partnership.[98]

For understanding the rules and practices behind all these decisions, the most useful guide once again is the late Qing government survey of economic customs in Anhui province, as this volume details the conditions under which a partner in a joint-share partnership, like the founding partner mentioned above, had access to his investment during its commitment period.[99] By and large, the reported practices represent a balance between the often contradictory desires for stability

---

[97] Fan Jinmin, "Mingdai Huishang randian," 2–4.
[98] Liu Qiugen and Xie Xiuli, "Ming Qing Huishang shanggongye," 79–87.
[99] *Anhui sheng xianzheng diaochaju*, 127–33.

and flexibility, for the interests of the partnership, and for the interests of its individual members. On the one hand, the shares of a Huizhou partnership, right up to its termination, were regarded as the corporate and collective property of the partners. A partner who acquired his shares and thus partnership solely through purchase with silver could not withdraw his capital and shares at will;[100] he needed prior approval of his partners. The price of his shares was generally assessed at their current market value, though in the Huizhou county of Jixi he would be paid for them, at least by the other partners, at their original price.[101] As if to prevent the abuses sometimes reported of a lineage member's unauthorized private mortgage or sale of his annual share of income from a charitable landed trust or a co-owner's share of timber mountain land,[102] a partner was also barred from using his shares in a partnership as collateral or credit for other investments (for example in a Ponzi-like loan or investment scheme) without the permission of his fellow partners. In other words, any additional partnerships he entered needed separate funding or his outstanding partners' awareness and tolerance of his risky venture (or skulduggery).

To enforce these restrictions, at least in She and Xiuning counties, each partner had the right to examine the partnership's account books and its other documents at an appropriate time (though not the right to examine his fellow partners' private accounts and papers). Proper checking and rechecking of account books had ranked high among the prescriptions set by Cheng Chang to restore trust and order among his Shanhe kinsmen in the Doushan landed trust,[103] and so we are not surprised to learn that shareholders in She and Xiuning counties as well were allowed to check the account books of their commercial partnership at the end of a year or at the end of any of the three periods (*jie* 節) that comprised the accounting year. Such checking or closing of the books was usually done by the partners themselves; in Xiuning a partner was even barred from delegating this task to another party, presumably to prevent him from evading responsibility for permitting duplicity or to discourage subsequent charges that others had fiddled the books. In Shanhe the Chengs had avoided this problem by having a representative of each branch check the books and then having the

---

[100] Ibid., 127. He could not acquire shares through labor or on credit.
[101] Ibid., 131–32. [102] McDermott, *Making, v. 1*, Chapter 6.
[103] Ibid., 329–30; McDermott, "Private Non-commercial Publishing," 215–23.

results of the check, including the figures, made known collectively to all the other members.

A related matter, the retention of an emergency exit for one's capital after it was invested in a joint-share commercial partnership, is seldom discussed in Ming Huizhou imprints, contracts, or other manuscripts. Yet it receives a thorough treatment in this same late Qing survey of Huizhou's commercial customs and management practices, supporting some scholars' claim that Huizhou's partners enjoyed remarkable fluidity and freedom in withdrawing money.[104] Although all partners were restricted from withdrawing money from one partnership for reinvestment, for example as collateral in a separate business venture, they still worried about the length of the commitment of their own and their copartners' capital to the partnership. The common contractual rules in Huizhou called on partners at the formation of their partnership to fix the date and terms for renewing or terminating the partnership and thus for a partner's authorized power to sell off his shares for a profit or loss. In addition, a partner secured a limited safety exit for himself by having the power to withdraw from the partnership at any time after its inception, if and only if all his fellow partners agreed to its dissolution. Such dissolution might occur due to an unexpected crisis for a partner. But death alone did not end a partnership. At a partner's death his heirs were expected to succeed to his share in the partnership, and thus acquire a claim on its profits as well as liability for its losses.[105] If a partner anxious to leave a partnership was frustrated by these rules and by the opposition of his copartners, he might persist in asking for an initially uncontracted withdrawal from the partnership in the hope that he might win these partners' approval for his leaving it at a future date. In most of Anhui province a partner could broach this possibility with his fellow shareholders at the halfway point in the contracted period of the partnership. In Xiuning and Wuyuan counties such an approved withdrawal would be arranged at the end or start of the calendar year after the annual or period review and the closing of the partnership's account books.[106] Presumably, the other partners'

---

[104] Liu Qiugen and Xie Xiuli, "Ming Qing Huishang shanggongye," 85.
[105] For a Ming example of how a partner nursed his deceased copartner's investment for an orphaned son, see Liang Mingwu et al., "Ming Qing Huishang mucai," 64.
[106] *Anhui sheng xianzheng diaochaju*, 130b–133a. The heir was responsible for all obligations and debts incurred by his benefactor while a partner.

approval would come only after they had been compensated by the withdrawing partner (perhaps by his offering them his shares at a favorable price).

These practices recorded for the late Qing almost certainly would have grown out of problems that had confronted earlier Huizhou merchants and investors in the course of doing business. The precise date of origin for these customs, in the Ming or Qing dynasty, is unclear. But at the very least these customs indicate that a partner's unanticipated or hurried exit from his financial commitment in Ming times was conceivable, that it might well have been difficult but under certain conditions was allowed, at a cost. With a partner's consequent need to retain good relations with copartners and fulfill obligations to them, he would have found it sensible and profitable to build their partnerships on close kinship ties and obligations, if only to minimize the likelihood of any shocks to their collective commercial venture.

Personnel Problems and Lineage Solutions

The operation of a commercial partnership depended heavily on staff to oversee and develop the partnership's trading or moneylending.[107] While many a late Qing firm's employees might be expected to have invested in the firm and thus to have simultaneously been its investors, co-owners, and workers, no Ming source indicates how common such a practice was, especially in larger business operations.[108] These employees, like the partners themselves, were often the investors' and managers' sons, brothers, nephews, and fellow lineage members; that is, persons they knew, trusted, could easily control, and could expect to be loyal and honest. When these kinsmen proved insufficient or unsuitable, the managers and owners tended to rely on another group of trustworthy males, their own or their lineage's bondservants. Having usually been domestic rather than field servants, these bondservants came to hold in family businesses a great variety of positions. Some

[107] MQHS, 181, on Huizhou timber merchants selling timber in Hangzhou and Songjiang.
[108] Liang Mingwu et al., "Ming Qing Huishang mucai," 65, quoting the Russian observer Nicolai Viacheslavich Bogoiavlenskii on late Qing Chinese merchants operating beyond the Great Wall. Such an arrangement would have helped preserve the family-like nature of most smaller Chinese businesses heavily dependent on cheap or free family labor.

Personnel Problems and Lineage Solutions 297

worked in shops and markets as local agents with considerable autonomy, while others did less demanding work as office or manual help. Numbering as many as several tens of "household guests" (menxia ke 門下客), some of them would be assigned to mundane jobs for little, if any, pay beyond their bed and board. A third pool of potential personnel consisted of other Huizhou natives, who shared the dialect, customs, social networks, and quite possibly a marriage tie with their employer. These fellow countrymen could provide everything from manual labor to commercial information and contacts.[109]

The number of such employees naturally varied from merchant house to merchant house. In 1640 the Xiuning native Jin Sheng wrote that big merchant families from She and Xiuning counties "brought along relations and acquaintances (qinqi zhijiao 親戚知交) to their trading places, thereby enabling hundreds and even thousands of families to stay alive."[110] But the only example I know of that even slightly approaches this claimed scale – the Xus 許 of Wuyuan with forty or more pawnshops and 2,000 employees in many parts of Jiangsu and Zhejiang provinces – dates from the nineteenth century.[111] According to Usui Sachiko, his staff, as well as that of other large firms, consisted of four groups.[112] Delegated managers ran branch outfits, when necessary with some of their own funds. Deputies interacted with government institutions and officials on behalf of the business, collected information for it, and helped the managers supervise the accountants. The accountants managed each shop, and were in charge of the sales (including peddling) and handling revenues. And shop employees were often hired to help with business in branch outlets.

In Ming times the staff usually would have been far smaller, at most in the low hundreds (with the owners of a large string of pawnshops) and most often in the low tens. Meanwhile, most merchant firms, as already noted, had a handful of staff in addition to the head's immediate family. Indeed, Adachi Keiji, after reading the seventy-two stories about Ming merchants in the late Ming imprint *The Book of Swindles* (Dupian xinshu 杜騙新書), observed that none of the traveling or

[109] Ibid., 192. Chinese investors, as mentioned above in this chapter, liked to have a relation become an employee of any company they invested heavily in, just to remain aware of any changes in the company's condition.
[110] Jin Sheng, *Jin taishi ji*, 4.9a.   [111] Tang Lixing, "Lun Huishang," 151–52.
[112] Usui, *Kishū shōnin*, 94–95.

resident merchants in this book, including those from Huizhou, had an accompanying staff of more than one or two and that most of these merchants seem to have been operating on their own.[113] In the early Qing the very knowledgeable historian Gu Yanwu qualifies that overall assessment by acknowledging the different practice for the very wealthy Huizhou merchants:

> If a big Huizhou merchant has several hundred thousand [taels of silver], he would have assistants, and several men would work helping his ears and eyes. These men are all paid and are not his private possessions (*busi* 不私). Therefore, there is no doubt that with their work they can gain good fortune from big merchants. In the future, if when they count up the interest and profits there is a great surplus, then [these] deputies will separate themselves [from the big merchant] and become merchants on their own. Therefore, a big merchant does not have the strength of [just] a single person.[114]

Furthermore, a big merchant had more than one outlet for his goods – the late Ming Huizhou merchant Luo Yuanlin 羅元林 had branch shops (*fenhao* 分號) in over a hundred places,[115] and consequently many openings for his kinsmen.

In these relatively large firms, usually located outside Huizhou, the personnel in the late Ming would have consisted of four groups, as described by Fujii Hiroshi (Usui Sachiko's account differs slightly, perhaps because she is interested primarily in the Qing and her focus fell on a house firm's branch outlets and Fujii's on its main base of operation). At the top under the head's supervision was the chief administrative assistant – literally, "the one in charge of the counting" (*zhangji* 掌計).[116] Far more than just an accountant or bookkeeper, he usually was a highly trusted second-in-command, who administered the business's daily affairs, often in the absence of its owners. He legally borrowed money under their name, defended the business from threats, and sometimes decided even the business's general strategy, and thus he could be held liable for the business's failings. Over time his success in fostering others' wealth might bring him considerable

---

[113] Adachi, *Min Shin Chūgoku*, 547–48.
[114] Gu Yanwu, *Zhaoyu zhi*, 11, Huizhoufu.   [115] *MQHS*, 244.
[116] Fujii, "Shin'an shōnin no kenkyū," 36.3, 78–80. A monthly clearing of their books was done, at least by larger Huizhou merchants (Jiang Shounan, "Lanxi Huizhou," 926–29), while the Southern Goods Store in Suzhou, set up in the late Ming by an immigrant from Ningbo, closed its accounts both daily and annually (Qian Yong, *Lüyuan conghua*, v. 2, 24, 640–41).

wealth, letting him, as Gu Yanwu claimed for one case, turn the 1,000 taels he accumulated in Yangzhou as an accountant into a huge personal fortune of tens of thousands of taels from his trading as a salt merchant.[117] In a large organization he would be assisted by one or two general managers, who like him had no capital of their own invested in the business.

At the next lower level were specially designated departmental heads, who made their trading decisions either separately or by consensus through a majority decision. Farther down the organizational hierarchy were a great variety of caretaker and managerial jobs, ranging from looking after storehouses and boats to the multiple tasks of a branch agent handling a considerable sum of the business's money in separate towns and cities. At the bottom were an even greater number of manual laborers engaged for portage, transport, security, and other physical services.

The scale of these operations could grow considerably, once a firm set up agents and offices in key locations to deal in particular goods. Long-distance trade encouraged the establishment of multiple offices if only because of the need to store goods, the chance to practice trade at different ports along the way, and the availability of kinsmen to act as agent middlemen in a distant market (and so reduce reliance on local brokers). Sometimes, a family firm also established separately financed kinsmen at the endpoints of long-distance trading routes, such as Huizhou merchants trading Shandong raw cotton to kinsmen in the Shanghai area for its woven thread and textiles.[118] Or, in dealing with less disparate locations, such as delta towns and different cities, these merchants sometimes set up an identical set of general rules for money-lending by their separate shops:

> Wang Tongbao and various juniors made a pact (*yue* 約) to live in different counties and not to manipulate interest rates, not to mix up the good loans with the bad ones, not to go after small amounts when collecting interest, not to invest in ventures promising excessive profits, and not to collect extra amounts by calculating [interest] by the day.[119]

---

[117] *SSXT*, 28, 996; Wang Tingyuan,"Huishang congye renyuan," 119–25.
[118] Fujii, "Shin'an shōnin no kenkyū," 36.3, 82; and, the cases discussed in Chapter 6 below.
[119] Wang Daokun, *Fumo*, 4.46b; Fujii, "Shin'an shōnin no kenkyū," 36.3, 81.

Within these branch offices away from the firm's base site, the top non-partner staff consisted of managers, whose overall responsibility for their branch's well-being sometimes had them make up for cash shortages with their own capital. Their sheer distance from the firm's head, based either in a Yangzi Valley city or back in Huizhou, would have conferred on these branch office heads considerable autonomy in running their daily operations.[120] Next were assistants (*fushou* 副手), who supported the managers by supervising the accounts, collecting market information, and handling all dealings with government offices. A third level consisted of shop managers, assigned to handle all the transactions at the shop where they were based. Finally, there were the shop employees, hired as clerks, floor boys, apprentices, and messengers for various tasks. Even at this shop-floor level, though less so than at the upper levels, one might find kinsmen employed for jobs and training.

Retaining the loyalty of such a large workforce, even if composed of kinsmen or family bondservants, was not easy. Stories of staff members absconding with their Huizhou master's cash were common.[121] By contrast, Shanxi merchants became legendary for their incorruptibility and for never reneging on loans. They reportedly worked decades to repay their creditors, even if the father who had died on the road had bequeathed them only his coffin and debts. "Wealthy investors vied with one another to get such persons to be their staff members (*huoji* 夥計), saying that 'If these persons did not forget [the debts of their father] when he was dead, how could they want to forget [their own debts] while they were alive?'"[122] This degree of Shanxi merchants' integrity, despite the claims of their eulogists, was not natural. Rather, it resulted from a strict regime of "rewards and punishments" for employees and their families, encouraged by the preference in Shanxi for "commenda"-type partnerships. For whenever a Shanxi merchant received others' funding and went on his trading travels, he was reputed to have been obliged to leave his wife and children behind as hostages in his investors' care. Regaining them required repayment at whatever cost.[123]

---

[120] Ibid., 84.   [121] Ibid., 83–4, 86.
[122] Shen Sixiao, *Jinlu*, 3; Wang Shixing, *Guangzhi yi*, 3, 61–62.
[123] "When a man is appointed to a post at one of the branch offices, his family is taken charge of by the bank, and held as security for fidelity and good behavior. At his post, the employee may send no letter to his family, except an open one through his master; he receives no pay salary of any kind whilst away; officials

Personnel Problems and Lineage Solutions 301

In Huizhou, where family-run joint partnerships were far more common than "commenda" arrangements and where the staff were often kinsmen, the controls were usually more indirect. In place of demanding some financial or human collateral, the heads of Huizhou commercial families tended to mix the arts of persuasion, rewarding, and punishing, such as we have seen in volume 1 practiced by, among many others, the Shanhe Chengs of Qimen for their own lineage members and field servants. The father might have one son devote his time at home to examination study, while he himself spent most of his time on the road with his other sons.[124] From various accounts, the father seems to have rarely refrained from sharing his wisdom, often thickly larding his talk with Confucian nostrums about family life. Moral behavior was to be learned, as much as were the Confucian classics, from experienced teachers.

Shop employees most likely would have normally worked and lived as apprentices in the shop and thus have been under the constant surveillance and ready control of their boss. The boss's favorite tactic, or rather the one most recorded, was moral instruction. Calls for filial piety, obedience, and righteousness filled the advice he provided regularly in heavy doses to apprentices and young employees. By seeking to inculcate in their staff as well as their families a deep sense of loyalty and compliance, Huizhou merchants acquired a reputation for being "Confucian merchants." Violations of a firm's rules and practices were treated severely. In a commercial world where insurance was unavailable, a

are entertained, clothing is purchased as required, and sundry expenses are incurred, and every item is met with the bank's money, the strictest account being kept of all expenditure on behalf of the individual. A man holds his appointment for three years, and then returns to his employer's house, taking with him the account of the money expended during his term; he is duly searched, and the clothing he has purchased undergoes examination. Should it happen, after examination, that the accounts, etc., are satisfactory, and the affairs of the bank have been prospering during the man's tenure of office, he is handsomely rewarded, and is allowed to join his family, who are immediately released. If, on the other hand, business has not prospered under the man's management, and he has presented an unsatisfactory account, clothing and everything are retained, and the family are held in bondage until a suitable fine is paid, or the man himself may be imprisoned." H. Neville and H. Bell's Section, *Report of the Mission to China*, 245–46. Yang, *Money and Credit in China*, 83–84, cites a 1892 report by T.W. Wright of the Chinese Maritime Customs with the same views, suggesting the origin of the Blackburn report's account. So far, I have found no Chinese text that confirms either claim.

[124] Cao Lin, *Mingdai shangren shangye*, 121–22.

firm's reputation for strict integrity was its best passport to affordable credit. Failure to handle money properly or repay a debt on time besmirched one's record, persuading Huizhou moneylenders and investors to close ranks and reject offenders' future loan requests.[125]

Yet threats of punishments needed to be balanced with the promise of rewards. Hence a common way that Huizhou merchants had for nourishing and retaining their employees' loyalty was better remuneration. The normal pay scheme had partners receive dividends, ordinary employees a salary, and agents commission fees. Employees who demonstrated exceptional loyalty and turned in stellar job performances were sometimes rewarded with a share in the business's reported profits for one year; yet Huizhou merchant houses, unlike some Shanxi firms, rarely rewarded their managers with a permanent share in their firm's business profits.[126] Their salary, as Gu Yanwu observed, sometimes funded their own advance into the ranks of merchants, but a surprising number of those who became Huizhou merchants seem to have come up through the ranks of a family business.

What, though, of the employees at the lowest level of the firm's hierarchy in its agency offices outside Huizhou – say, the porters, the storehouse guards, the boatmen, and any local salesmen? Flexibility in hiring and firing at this level was especially desirable, and job pressure as well as the axe surely fell regularly on non-kinsmen staff in the less important jobs. Sixteenth-century Ming law allowed employers, commoners as well as official households, to hire and fire seasonal or short-term laborers,[127] and we have no reason to think that Huizhou merchants dispensed with such support in dealing with non-kinsmen employees.

Yet it is very difficult to find confirmation of this claim in Ming or even Qing sources on workers in the trades that Huizhou merchants prospered in, such as timber, grain, and tea. And so a Republican-period report, despite its late date, on employers' treatment of workers in the timber trade merits some attention. According to the interwar Japanese specialist on Chinese business practices Yoneda Yūtarō, branch and shop employees in Chinese timber firms of the early twentieth century often moonlighted by simultaneously operating side

[125] Ibid., 3, 61–62; Terada Takanobu, *Sansei shōnin*, 266–67.
[126] Zhang Zhengming, *Chengxiong shangjie*, 155–56. Such relative generosity by Shanxi merchants reflected the relative power of accountants, or general managers, in Shanxi partnerships (which often were "commenda" operations).
[127] Oyama, "Min Shin jidai," 250, quoting a 1587 memorial.

businesses for themselves without notifying their employer and gaining his permission. Prompted in part by their low salaries, these employees relied on their local experience, presence at the lumberyard, and inside knowledge of the timber trade to serve as independent advisers, salesmen, middlemen, and guarantors to their employer's customers at virtually every step in the process of selling them timber. It was as if these firms had taken in local brokers who continued to provide their traditional services in a new setting.

Thus they introduced their employer's customers to other suppliers and wholesalers. They themselves dealt in recycled timber, buying their employer's old planks, poles, tracks, and beams and selling them on to workplaces making any number of wooden products. In fact, some ran these side-shops themselves (or relied on a manager they hired) to manufacture products out of wood purchased at reduced rates from their employer's lumber firm. They also on the side arranged the sale to their employer's customers of other construction materials like tiles. And from all these transactions they acquired commission fees or profits for themselves, not for their employer. Thus, in the years leading up to the time when they had learned enough of the firm's business and earned enough to break off and become independent operators of their own firm, they ran their own business operations, as Gu Yanwu suggested, within the protective umbrella-like organization of their own employer's firm (whose potential loss from this arrangement – assuming that he knew of its existence – was presumably countered by the low wages he could afford to pay such employees).[128] The resemblance to rich Huizhou merchants' predilection for running their businesses under the wing of or out of a government salt office is not accidental. Contrary, then, to many of our modern Western assumptions about business organization and practices, Huizhou firms would have hired some non-kinsmen on terms designed to prevent them from becoming tightly integrated into a family firm. The firms did not want these non-kinsmen to learn too much about their employer's family business. As a result, such employees would be allowed, even expected, to run their own businesses while in the employment of a larger firm. The employees' goal, of course, was

---

[128] Yoneda, *Shina no shōnin seikatsu*, 52–61. Yamane, ed., Rinji Taiwan Kyūkan Chōsakai, comp., *Shindai keiyaku*, 82, for a contract drafted in Taiwan in 1904 that explicitly bans this practice of "private trading" by a firm's manager.

commonly understood to have always been to go independent and set up their own business, so that they could parley their experience, contacts, investments, and capital into the establishment of their own timber firm, even if it nominally remained inside another.

In sum, as we have seen in salt merchants' speculative purchases of salt and salt permits and in other merchants' interactions with local government officials, the aim was to run a private business from within an already functioning legitimate private business, thereby "piggybacking" their way to profits without bearing transaction and office costs normally associated with operating a business. In such cases, Huizhou merchants were concerned less with creating and building institutions than with transforming those already existing from within, exploiting them for their own uses, and making it appear as if nothing had changed. In that sense they were only doing with others' business organizations what they or others had already done to their own lineages' ancestral halls back home in the villages of Huizhou.

Some Chinese Characteristics of Chinese Commercial Partnerships

So far, this chapter has represented these late imperial Chinese forms of commercial partnership as a set of institutions evolving in line with economic reasoning to satisfy the economic needs of long-distance traders in a commercializing economy. This path of economic rationality emphasized not just efficient problem solving but also the solution of problems with minimal recourse to the encompassing social and cultural resources of this admittedly commercial society. The Chinese state would seem irrelevant, as would claims of a noneconomic rationality.

I wish to complicate this late imperial story by recalling certain neglected features of Chinese commercial partnership practice that for sure played a part in the overall development of these forms and rules. My aim is less to be thorough and comprehensive than to probe the power and pull of what are more customary than legal supports for protecting commercial partnerships and investments. The first two features are shaped by a concern to reduce risk and the third by a way of thinking normally unrelated to the practice of business.

First, observations made above by two Westerners and one modern Chinese on commercial partnerships in late Qing China have highlighted the relatively egalitarian nature of commercial partnerships based on the association (*hui*) model, enabling us to speculate that participation in commercial partnership was more accessible to ordinary Chinese with a little surplus cash to invest than in Europe, where commercial investment was usually the concern of a distinct and small class of well-to-do capitalist investors. I have reservations about this claim, not only because of my findings about the high levels of inequality within the operation of these Chinese partnership schemes, but also because of the terms of the comparison. Our key concern in making such a comparison should be openness or accessibility, not equality. Neither European nor Chinese partnerships in these centuries were truly public, equal, and open to all comers with the appropriate levels of cash. Kinship ties, close friendship, common regional origins, and reliable recommendations – that is, matters already determined – mattered greatly in these simple arrangements, as is clear from a close reading of the comments of our British attorney in Hong Kong or even the already noted employment practices of the major regional merchant groups.

Second, this chapter has consistently presumed a sharp public-versus-private distinction in the forms of commercial partnership, with no role for the state and its representatives. This assumption is unrealistic and questionable, in light of what we have learned of not just the unequal nature of any merchant's relation to Ming officialdom but also their interaction in a large delta city like Suzhou. In fact, the two main forms of commercial partnership we have considered, joint-share partnership and "commenda," would have tolerated and encompassed a combination of private and public interests. Although one can imagine a merchant commending money to a friendly government office to help him achieve certain business goals, this act would have been considered tantamount to a bribe and thus have made both parties liable to charges of corruption. The marriage of official and merchant interests in the opposite direction, as we have seen in a previous chapter's discussion of private business relations with government officials and offices, saw a government official or office depositing its money in the hands of a merchant expected to work with it as a partner in a commercial venture. The frequency of such partnerships is hard to determine, but it is wise not to omit them from any overall account of the world of Ming commerce.

Third, the world of commercial partnership, as presented here, is a totally secular affair. In late imperial China that assumption did not always hold, not only because ancestral halls, as seen above in Chapter 1, mixed the business of loans with ancestral-worship religious practices, but also because Buddhist and folk notions of reincarnation supported the traditional Chinese insistence that a debt had to be repaid, if not by the debtor, then by his family and heirs.[129] As expressed in over a hundred folktales and novels, this common belief would have had countless Chinese over the past two millennia expect that a man who died in debt would suffer reincarnation at a lower rank in the order of creation. As a fish or domestic animal (ox, horse, donkey, or pig) in his creditor's household, he would pay off his debt through labor and/or by being eventually chopped up and consumed by his owner (that is, cannibalism, by one remove). Some Tang dynasty stories along such lines have the creditor turn down purchase bids of a lower-order animal by the debtor's heirs and family, underlining how debts were not erased by death and that debt bondage remained a distinct possibility for the unredeemed debtor in his or her next life. Although this notion appears in famous Ming and Qing novels like the *Shuihu zhuan* 水滸傳 (*The Outlaws of the Marsh*) and *Rulin waishi* 儒林外史 (*The Scholars*), the notions of debt and debt collection seem by then to have become secularized. In later centuries it more often than not proved a subject for humor in this life rather than for fear of what might be awaiting a renegade debtor in his afterlife.[130]

Conclusion

In this chapter I have tried to describe how late imperial Chinese merchants established a flexible yet reliable institutional framework that provided access to cheap capital investments and that clarified financial responsibilities and liabilities for investors and managers. It has surveyed the history of three types of commercial partnerships – "commenda," agency, and joint-share – common in late imperial times. Instead of searching for their origins, it has been concerned with the changing practices of these three types of business funding and organization and their relative prevalence at certain times and in certain places since the Song dynasty. The joint-share partnership was found to be the most common form of commercial partnership

---

[129] Fukuda, "Chikurui shōsai-tan," 69–86. This Buddhist-inspired understanding seems to reflect temples' anxiety over their client–borrowers' defaults.
[130] Wang Zhenzhong, "Shexian Ming Qing Huizhou," 34–43, relates the Qing dynasty tale of two Yangzhou salt merchants who, having separately fled their creditors, meet up by chance in a Yangzhou drum tower. One has enough capital to pay off the other's debts, and so loans it to him – at an interest rate high enough to score a profit – even when in flight from his own creditors.

practiced in Ming and Qing Huizhou, helping its long-distance merchants acquire requisite capital and personnel and operate under contractual practices that facilitated their dominance in many markets of the Yangzi Valley. The analysis has emphasized these merchants' regular reliance on kinship ties to support the relocation of the base of their commercial work outside Huizhou into Yangzi delta towns and markets. Government-backed institutions did not satisfactorily secure these merchants' routes of transport, provide sufficient supplies of capital for lending, or establish secure credit institutions despite the providential import of huge supplies of foreign silver that greatly promoted trade and enriched both merchants and the government.

Commercial partnerships nonetheless often suffered from inadequate capitalization and from the short-term duration of their loans and their partners' investments. For solutions to these problems Huizhou merchants turned to kinsmen, to fund and to manage their pursuit of profits throughout the empire. In particular, Huizhou merchants turned to fellow lineage members to acquire partners, borrow capital, manage and work in market-oriented businesses, and, if fortunate, secure wealth from speculation and then from hereditary privileges in the government's salt monopoly trade. They also, as tightly knit kinship groups within lineages, established for themselves joint-share commercial partnerships, that brought greater and longer stability to their commercial activities and engaged a greater number of kinsmen as staff and as investors. The lineage itself was seldom a business, but many of its members were active in establishing, investing in, and running many different businesses with fellow kinsmen. For Huizhou's merchants it provided an ample source of capital and an unrivaled source of trustworthy staff and laborers.

Yet how, in practice, did these general rules and principles of commercial and financial partnerships work as "house firms"? What type of family organization and which kinship ties mattered most in their business operations, especially in establishing commercial networks? How, if at all, did these "house firms" avoid the troubles that so divided Huizhou lineages over their collective landholdings? And, perhaps most importantly, how did they retain their kinship basis in a highly competitive commercial world whose economic imperatives would have ordinarily ripped apart the lineage framework? These are some of the issues that the following chapter will address through three case studies of Huizhou merchant lineages.

6 | *Huizhou House Firms*
The Binds of Kinship and Commerce

Ever since Fujii Hiroshi's seminal studies, scholars have attributed the notable success of Huizhou merchants to their reliance on kinship ties and institutions, especially lineages. These kinship institutions vary greatly in size and complexity, ranging from the simple nuclear household and stem family to large communal families (*dajia* 大家) and lineages (*zu* 族). Within lineages, mention has been made of branches (*fang* 房, *men* 門), segments (*zhi* 支), and lineage trusts (*yizhuang* 義莊), while some lineages sought to expand their connections with larger kinship-related groups such as descent groups (*zong* 宗) and common-surname (*tongxing* 同姓) alliances.

Strangely, despite the wealth of Ming comment on these Huizhou kinship institutions, modern scholars have tended to accept these lineages' inflated self-assessment at face value. They have seldom probed into these general claims to determine precisely which of these kinship institititions, which kinship ties, and which forms of lineage organization were crucial for these merchants' success at different stages in their commercial development. This scholarly reluctance is even odder, since we should not presume that these kinship institutions, having emerged from and been shaped by a largely agricultural society, were all automatically and equally useful to that same society's commercial development. Nor can we presume that a government which had stubbornly restricted the ancestral-hall privilege to a tiny portion of just its officialdom would have welcomed the appearance of these institutions in the commercial sector.

In addressing these issues, this chapter will be alert to the diversity of both these kinship institutions and kinship ties, that Huizhou families adapted for their needs. As was evident in the development of the ancestral hall, the actual operation of these institutions and kinship ties was not fixed in stone. Members of Huizhou lineages routinely adopted and adapted certain ideas and forms of organization to suit their own needs in partnerships as well as in simple family businesses.

To explore this flexibility and variety in Huizhou commercial organizations, this chapter will adopt an overarching concept of the "house firm" (aka "family firm") (*hao* 號, *tang* 堂), understood in light of two of the numerous definitions for the word "house" in the *Oxford English Dictionary* – "a place of business, *transf.*, a business establishment, a mercantile firm" and "a family linking ancestors and descendants; a lineage, a race, especially one having a continuity of residence, of exalted rank, or high renown."

Within the wide embrace of this concept we shall investigate three common types of "house firm" – the multigenerational joint-house firm, the branch-based partnership firm, and the multi-segment syndicate firm,[1] with each of these having a different kinship framework and set of commitments. In traditional Chinese kinship terms, the first two types fit comfortably within the categories of, respectively, the large stem-house firm (*jia*) and the multi-branch (*fang*) house firm. The third type, the multi-segment firm, seems to fit within the notion of the multi-branch (*fang*) house firm, but does so only far more loosely within a very large lineage (*dazu* 大族) that allowed its segments much more freedom to make commercial arrangements with other segments within its branch, other branches, and non-lineage members. In large part these types differ according to intrinsic differences in the size and complexity of their membership, capital assets, staff, organizational structure, corporate governance, geographical stretch, market network, and official ties. Even so, what will be striking is the central role in all three types of house firm of a small unit of usually two or at most four generations in any larger unit's overall commercial success. Hence, we have the only apparent contradiction of a very large and powerful lineage containing a great number of small "house firms" actively engaged in commercial ventures, sometimes co-operatively and sometimes not.

In all three of these types of house firm, members commonly took part in long-term strategy formation and daily administration. Although a house firm might be expected, like the Chinese nuclear household or family, to break up eventually, a dynastic imperative

---

[1] This selection of "house firm" types is based on my judgment of their typicality and relevance to this chapter's analysis. It does not preclude the existence of other house firm types.

pervaded the aims and activities of all these firm types, as members regardless of type sought to transmit their skills, assets, and management practices to future generations. The relation between these types of house firm can be seen as sequential, from smaller to bigger, with the simplest type of multigenerational house firm growing into a multi-branch firm, which might eventually expand into a multi-segment, multiregional syndicate of house firms set up and owned by members of a very large lineage. Such indeed is the trajectory suggested by the order of their treatment in this chapter. Yet there was no certainty that the smaller and simpler type directly evolved over time or organically into a larger, more complicated type. Indeed, individual members of a house firm which was participating in a relatively complex partnership arrangement, might simultaneously enjoy a simpler set of commercial commitments with another kinsman or non-kinsman party; or, thanks to the short life of many commercial partnerships in Ming China, it might withdraw from a larger and more complex form of house firm to join one smaller. Indeed, a secondary aim of this chapter is to show how expanding kinship organizations helped house firms negotiate these transitions and how they handled their attendant problems of ownership and management. The problems that arise in such a commercial context will seem familiar to those conversant with the previous volume's observations on the land trust model's toleration of its members' formation of and participation simultaneously in a wide variety of other property and kinship arrangements.[2]

Likewise, the first two of these three types of house firm – the multigenerational house firm and the branch-based partnership firm – could operate either independently, or concurrently within what was an even larger, umbrella-type organization like the multi-segment syndicate firm. When encompassed and enveloped within this larger organization, the smaller house firms need not have functioned as the metaphorical assembly of "Chinese boxes," each operating within one or more larger boxes, partly because they were different types of arrangement and partly because the fit was looser than suggested by the "Chinese boxes" metaphor. A member of a "large joint-house firm" might retain its own web of kinship-based commercial ventures

[2] McDermott, *Making*, v. 1, 20–24, 138–39, 166–68.

and commitments and so enjoy a three-dimensional complexity of commercial memberships and commitments that two-dimensional charts of this firm's organizational structure fail to capture. And, if the smallest of these three types of family firm can have such a level of complexity, then the larger and more loosely encompassing type of the multi-branch and multiregional "house firm" would naturally have been more complex, not least because their goals of dynastic stability were frequently threatened by conflicts over succession to their headship.

Ideally, this chapter on kinship and commerce would study the commercial records of these differently sized kinship units, in order first to determine their different trading strategies and practices and then, if possible, to compare and relate their profitability and durability to their form of commercial partnership. More precisely, this chapter should study account books and business contracts to discover changes in Huizhou merchants' methods of managing their assets and adjusting their kinship organizations.

Unfortunately, that approach is not feasible here. No single source or collection of sources discloses the detailed development of a Huizhou house firm in the Ming, in the way that *The Family Agreements* in volume 1 clarified the long-term evolution of the landed trust lineage. More importantly, apart from the handful of private commercial statistics and pawnshop record books already introduced, Ming sources provide very few reliable figures on the finances of private businesses. Bereft of instructive figures about matters as basic as budgets, investments, revenues, and profits, we have no choice but to base our extended analysis of case studies of family firms and their management practices on mainly nonquantitative evidence. Consequently, our first case study will address the problem of how to form and run an expanding family firm, the second the problem of how to expand and maintain a multi-branch family firm beyond its Huizhou base, and the third the problem of how to run a business empire consisting of numerous branches containing a large number of segment-based house firms operating over a great expanse of space, largely but not entirely under the umbrella of a very large and loosely organized lineage.

This approach, however much it will disappoint students of Huizhou merchant finances, will eventually garner some key insights. It will reveal about Huizhou merchants what the analysis of both quantitative and qualitative sources about landed trusts seldom revealed about the Shanhe Chengs – the dynamics of a family member's personal and segment, as opposed to branch and lineage, relationships and their impact on a lineage's or branch's asset management and fortune creation. In using case studies to explore the impact of various kinship ties and units on the formation and operation of "house firms," this chapter will thus identify and investigate the key kinship relationships in most house firms – father–son, grandfather–grandson, uncle–nephew, and brother–brother – and then examine the way these ties were used by usually smaller families and their heads to form and operate their commercial organizations. These ties will also be seen as the points at which tensions within a house firm clashed, tearing at its operation and survival, virtually regardless of its size.

Next, this chapter will analyze how members of a large branch of a famous lineage actually built on such understandings of branch ties to form and develop a house firm's commercial network. These branch-based firms, usually staffed by members of their own branch or segment, conducted regular long-distance trade with one another, thereby helping to integrate previously distinct processes of production, distribution, and consumption in two of Ming China's most prosperous macro-regions, the middle and lower Yangzi Valley. Such success, however, posed a threat to the long-term stability of these branches' network arrangements, and their struggle to preserve the links between their growth as a lineage and as a house firm, between their development of new lineage branches and their founding of new commercial outposts, shall be studied to test the long-term suitability of a lineage framework for conducting long-distance trade.

Finally, this chapter will analyze a case in which relations between men in different branches of a lineage broke down. It will consider how an eminently successful merchant within one large and wealthy Huizhou salt merchant branch came under attack from an embittered kinsman in another branch and how this intra-lineage dispute played out in both family and court politics. It also will focus on this wealthy merchant's distancing of his family firm from his own branch by appointing personally adopted sons and other non-lineage members to top managerial positions in his multiregional trading network. Such a way of hiring, even if requisite for the success of a salt merchant lineage's highly capitalized ventures, would have gone against the grain of a Huizhou commercial group's more ordinary hiring and management practices. And so, when these family clashes and hiring practices became entangled in wider political struggles at the court as in the famous Mt Huang disaster of 1626–27, the fallout would highlight fault lines in branch and other relations within the commercial operations of a large Huizhou merchant lineage by the late Ming. It will also lay bare the organizational and operational limits in Huizhou to the development of a private, multi-surname commercial syndicate in long-distance networks in late imperial times.

Each of the three remaining sections of this chapter will thus concentrate on the commercial success of one Huizhou kinship group and its most prominent form of commercial organization. It will consider the commercial and financial history of these three lineages – the Fangs of Yuetan 瀹潭方氏, the Chengs of Taitang 泰塘程氏, and the Wus of Xi'nan 溪南吳氏. All three of these lineages claimed a pre-Song ancestry in Huizhou; all were located in She or Xiuning county, Ming Huizhou's two richest and most commercialized counties; and all became wealthy by trading outside Huizhou, often through involvement in the government's salt monopoly.

Yet, in order to highlight the diversity and complexity of their and other families' paths to commercial fortune during the Ming, these three kinship groups have been chosen primarily for their differences – in membership size, capital resources, geographical span, variety of commodities, market locations, scale of success, nature of internal organization, and proximity to the government and its representatives. The sequence chosen for treating these lineages is intended to reveal microeconomic processes by which Huizhou's business organizations were formed and managed and how these changed over the course of the Ming. The evolution of their commercial activity and organization – from itinerant peddler to residential dealer, from struggling retailer to dominant wholesaler, from selling timber and grain to investing in cloth weaving and salt trading, and from dealing in mass-market transactions of commodities to running pawnshops and bribing officials – is, to repeat, not intended to demonstrate an organic evolutionary process linking these different types of commercial and family organization. Instead, it will show how the structure of these commercial units and of the Ming economy in general expanded, diversified, and matured during the last two centuries of Ming rule, in ways that allow these three different house firms to encompass and hold, loosely but respectively, different functions and features of the three ranks of merchants and merchant businesses – the top, the middling, and the low-level – loosely sketched in Chapter 1. Here, we are mainly interested in the multiple uses these merchants made of certain kinship ties and institutions – in their immediate family or branch or larger kinship units – to create, build up, operate, and, in one particular case, tear apart the bonds of commerce and kinship in a house firm of great complexity.

The Fangs of Yuetan: Family Successes and Lineage Weaknesses in Regional Businesses

The commercial history of the Fangs of Yuetan, a lineage whose ancestors first settled in this mountainous corner of She county in the tenth century, is of considerable interest to the historian of premodern Chinese business organization. In addition to revealing the distinctive roles of the family (*jia*), the branch (*fang*), and the lineage (*zu*) in the establishment and practice of business, it highlights the relative importance of these kinship organizations – of the branch over the lineage and of the family over the branch – in the overall operation of a mid-Ming business. In the 1550s this Fang lineage consisted of more than a thousand adult males in six scattered branches (*men*).[3] Yet only one of these branches, previously the poorest, had by then broken through to commercial success. Numbering at any single time no more than thirty households (*hu* 戶),[4] it retained a noticeable independence from the other branches. Not only did its members continue to live apart from other Fang branches in the area of Huizhou where they had dwelled since the early Southern Song,[5] but also the members of the four generations of this branch described in some forty biographies by

---

[3] *FKSFC*, 110, 111.
[4] Ibid., 110. Their migration to Huizhou probably was prompted by the Fang La rebellion, which a few years earlier had killed off many families, driven the fortunate into flight into the mountain uplands, and left much land open for seizure and resettlement. The term "household" here is the tax-bearing unit registered by the government and so liable to local government service assignments. It loosely corresponded to the "family" (*jia*).
[5] Ibid., 89–90.

Fang Chengxun 方承訓 appear to have formed few commercial partnerships with persons outside their branch. Indeed, the institutions these men ended up creating for their branch or entire lineage – an ancestral hall, a charitable landed trust, and a genealogy – emerged only after they themselves had grown rich from trade, as this lineage's growth came out of the prior enrichment of just some of its members.

Their commercial success, like that of members of the other lineages discussed in this chapter, was achieved primarily outside Huizhou. It resulted from management and financial arrangements created and implemented by largely independent households rather than by their branch and especially their lineage. When one member of their branch sought donations from its members to set up a separate ancestral hall for the branch, he may have boldly declared, "The entire branch is one family."[6] But the stubborn resistance of many branch members to a full donation – they begged poverty and forced three or four very rich members to pay for half the costs and then grudgingly paid varying amounts themselves[7] – underlines how few of this branch's members held this expansive view of their branch and indicates that this man spoke so only rhetorically. The members' business organizations and their day-to-day operations remained resolutely based on relatively small and intimate family groups.

Thus, of these three Huizhou types of kinship organization, it was small "family units" – those that fall comfortably within the parameters of the traditional "mourning grades for agnatic kinsmen" group (*wufu* 五服)[8] – that most frequently set up and managed the Fangs' businesses and that bore responsibility for their fate and held powers of ownership, management, and wealth transfer. In all twenty-one instances when the amount of money (or more precisely silver) earned by a Fang is specified, this fortune-maker is said, as if it were a mantra, to have thereby raised his family (*qijia* 起家) in the world.[9] Regardless of the scale of these Fang members' earnings – which escalated from 500 to several tens of thousands of taels over the span of four generations – no Fang branch or lineage organization is ever said to have had a natural or rightful claim to any part of their wealth. A man's commercial earnings were intended for the use of his tightly knit family

---

[6] Ibid., 197–98.   [7] Ibid., 110.
[8] Ebrey, *Chu Hsi's Family Rituals*, 86–97, esp. 90.
[9] FKSFC, 140, 144–45, 154, 160–61, 171.

and for whatever commercial arrangements it, and neither the lineage nor the branch, made for itself. Any profits that ended up in the hands of the branch or lineage came as donations from a family or family member for the construction of schools, bridges, houses, and ancestral halls, or for the performance of ancestral worship.

Just as telling was what happened when a family lost its members' earnings and assets. When bills could not be paid, the family, but not the branch nor the lineage, went bankrupt and fell afoul of creditors. It was specifically the head and descendants of a bankrupt family whom the creditors and indeed other relations first held responsible for compensation. Creditors revealed their understanding of this "common sense" by converging first at the home, and not the ancestral hall, of the crestfallen merchant and his family. Later on, of course, if this approach did not work, they might well seek recourse from rich relations. But, until then, they sought compensation from the debtor and his heirs, not his lineage and lineage relations.[10]

Management of a family's capital and operations likewise remained tightly within its own members' control, the most remarkable example being the transmission of one Fang Tingke 方廷珂's business interests within his line of descent for four successive generations. Retiring from his business in his sixties, Fang Tingke placed its management in the hands of his sole surviving son, Fan Qi 方起.[11] This son, acting as the caretaker of both of his deceased brother's sons, thus took charge of his father's entire estate, estimated at 10,000 taels. After increasing that sum four- or fivefold, at about the age of forty he handed over his business interests to his son, Fang Sui 方歲,[12] who later on at roughly the same age handed on the management of the family business to one of his own sons under his loose supervision.[13] Ownership and management thus were transmitted for three successive generations.

How, then, did such a family build up a family business? Like many, perhaps most, successful Huizhou merchant families, the Fangs started with very few economic and political resources. Struggling to scratch a living out of the rocky slopes around them, they initially had been barely capable of feeding themselves with sufficient grain and vegetables in good years; in bad years they had scrounged to find enough fish, firewood, fruit, and nuts to hang on until the next grain harvest. However convenient was their access to the Xin'an river and its

---

[10] Ibid., 151–52.   [11] Ibid., 179.   [12] Ibid., 185–86.   [13] Ibid., 194.

passage to the markets of the Yangzi delta, only rarely did they produce items for elsewhere. They were mountain farmers with few products to offer the outside world and thus with few means to acquire that outside world's own products.

The Fangs suffered from political impotence as well. In the five centuries leading up to the Ming their sole metropolitan degree holder had risen no higher in officialdom than to prefect. Thereafter, two or three handfuls of Fangs acquired honorary admissions to the National University, brief appointments to provincial county posts in times of dynastic disturbance, and some district studentships held by members anxious to climb the bureaucratic hierarchy to work and live elsewhere.[14] Consequently, they appear to have held no important sub-bureaucratic appointments outside their village, while within it the lineage organization that had emerged by the Yuan dynasty was little more than an occasional ritual group with few resources other than prayers and goodwill to help its members handle more pressing problems of food shortages and heavy taxes in the first half of the Ming.

The solution for these Fangs, like the answer to our question, lay elsewhere. In the latter half of the fifteenth century they turned to trade outside Huizhou, initially with reluctance but eventually with enthusiasm. In their eyes they were turning their back on the respectable profession of farming to take up the risky and disreputable occupation of a merchant. Though their first efforts at trading may have been merely slack-season ventures into the markets of nearby prefectures,[15] they soon realized the wisdom, if not the virtue, of the change. Long-term earnings from even these adventures surged – in one case reaching ten times more than the value of an ordinary Huizhou family's property. In particular, long-distance trade in the lucrative markets of the Yangzi Valley promised members of this branch far more gratifying returns than a life of toil on the land and even in a local shop. "I want to be a long-distance merchant," sighed one early sixteenth-century Fang, "and get double the cash." For the rest of his life, however, he was stuck trading cloth in the interior of Zhejiang province, in a backward county seat where "night and day these thoughts went around his head. He would think about them, and then look up, to find nothing."[16]

---

[14] *Xin'an mingzu zhi*, qian, 116–18. [15] *FKSFC*, 181. [16] Ibid., 171–72.

Most of the Fangs discussed here found a more rewarding escape from the mountain enclosures of Anhui and Zhejiang by pursuing a life of commerce farther away, in the Yangzi delta and especially Kaifeng, the capital of Henan province north of the Yangzi. Their initial flight from upland poverty and its unfulfilled dreams can be traced, for the Fangs as for many other humble Huizhou lineages, to the success of their founding peddler.[17] Fang Chengxun's biography of Fang Tingke is a rags-to-riches tale of how a late fifteenth-century peddler traded his way up the commercial ladder to become an early sixteenth-century merchant-investor with considerable wealth for himself and his descendants. In describing how his capital expanded over the course of his career, from virtually nothing to several hundred, then a thousand, and eventually ten thousand taels,[18] it presents an archetypal account – minus the domestic ministration of a virtuous wife – of the different stages in a poor Huizhou man's ascent into the towers of wealth.

As a twenty-year-old Huizhou peddler, he started with little support but for a small loan, a sharp aversion to farming, two strong legs, and considerable pluck, all concentrated on realizing the dream of making himself and his family rich. In the next twenty years he traded first in a nearby county, then throughout the Yangzi delta, the Huai region, and once even north of the Yellow River. Repeatedly, his travels met with rebuffs in the marketplace. Twice he was able to repay loans totaling fifty taels, but the derisory net profits for his family garnered merely the scorn of his neighbors. Then, unexpectedly, at the age of forty he struck it rich. Able now to afford to borrow twice as much, he turned this expanded capital into the basis of his family's fortune:

> Within three years he obtained several hundred taels as profit for the family. He then returned and built a house. The remainder was less than 100 taels, and again he borrowed 100 taels to make up for [what had been spent on the house]. He then traded solely in Kaifeng and no longer traveled and moved about. Within several years he made a fortune of 1,000 taels. Within several more years his fortune reached 10,000 taels. At this time he was sixty-nine years old.

---

[17] My interest in the Fangs and in this source was sparked by Wang Zhenzhong's fine pioneering study in his *Huizhou shehui huashi tanwei*, 20–92.

[18] This detailed information about the varying fortune of twenty-one families in a large kinship group over three generations has, I believe, no counterpart in data about the changing size of the assets of the separate members of this or another lineage or large kinship group.

Having risen to the heights of a respected resident merchant who was investing in Kaifeng's commerce, this former peddler eventually returned to Huizhou, where he reputedly died the richest man in the countryside west of She county's seat.[19]

We see Fang Tingke progress from farming fields in his home village to peddling goods in urban markets, follow his transformation from an ordinary resident merchant into an established merchant-investor operating an expanding family firm far from the Huizhou hills, and learn of his eventual return to die the richest resident of his still poor homestead. Yet how was this transformation of his economic circumstances possible for him, when it was not for many other aspiring families, like the Zhangs mentioned in the previous chapter? On this vital point his posthumous biography provides minimal explicit instruction, since it discloses little specific information about how this man, his kinsmen, and their descendants made their commercial fortunes and then held on to and even expanded them over the course of their lifetimes. Virtually nothing is said about the actual commercial transactions and decisions that were essential to Fang Tingke's success in business – what gave him his crucial breakthrough, what he traded in, what strategies for purchase and investment he pursued, what margins of profit he attained, under what terms he traded with others, and what investments he made with his profits. Of his descendants' and relations' commercial activities we fortunately learn a little more: some traded raw cotton, cotton cloth, or linen textiles; others "miscellaneous goods"; others salt; a few wine; and many took up the practice of moneylending. But for all of them, very little else is revealed of their actual business work. These biographies fail even to pose, let alone answer, the obvious question: how could this group of ill-educated villagers make money in a large metropolis like Kaifeng, where they encountered rich and polished merchants from Shanxi, Shaanxi, Beijing, and the rest of north China in a fierce competition for profits?[20] Their in-house biographer Fang Chengxun consistently prefers to stress the high reputation they enjoyed in Kaifeng's commercial circles, the charitable works they performed at home, and the harmony they achieved with kinsmen in business operations. In short, Fang often writes the lives of his ancestral merchants as if they were Confucian scholars like himself.

[19] FKSFC, 140, 185, 186. [20] Ibid., 145.

Paradoxically, it is Fang Chengxun's Confucian interest in kinship relationships that provides useful information, if not on the way Fang Tingke first acquired his wealth in the markets and yamens, then on the ways that he and others organized themselves and used their wealth to accumulate more of it. The Fangs are described as pursuing two different kinds of management for their family firms – one based on the often hierarchical father–son relationship and the other on more collaborative brother–brother relationships. Both approaches were for a time commercially successful, both sought expansion through the formation of close ties with other kinsmen, and both remained resolutely focused on their family rather than on branch and lineage relationships and resources. Yet these individual Fangs' commercial and financial arrangements, the dynamics of their key relationships, their preference for dealing with one family generation over another, and their ability to institutionalize long-term commercial success differed considerably, especially in dealing with the basic organizational problems of management and succession to a family's headship and wealth.

In running his family firm, Fang Tingke appears to have, deliberately or otherwise, followed certain practices so regularly that they merit being considered general guidelines for his management policy of using a relatively narrow range of kinship ties to set up and run his business firm. When we identify the Fangs he brought to Kaifeng, those he traded with there, and those he loaned or gave some of his capital to for trading there, it becomes clear that he did not involve members of his own and older generations in the lineage in close business ties, especially in the management of his operations. He conceivably borrowed some capital from them for his early commercial forays and received investments from them for his later business ventures: a brother who stayed at home in Huizhou "shared his funds with his [unnamed] relations in trading,"[21] and his brothers (as well as some other kinsmen of his generation) attained levels of wealth not readily attainable in Huizhou from agriculture alone.[22] Of course, he may have simply divided up the family property to be outright gifts or have reached an agreement with them that they would take care of the

---

[21] Ibid., 91.
[22] While they may have invested in or practiced forestry, there is no record that Fang Tingke was involved in such business.

family property at home while he carved out his separate career elsewhere. Yet, whatever the grounds of their understanding, Fang Tingke left home to travel and trade, while his brothers stayed at home, took care of the family's few fields, gained power over local affairs, and did not become directly involved in Fang Tingke's commercial life and decisions.[23] A similar detachment appears to have characterized his relationship to Fang Xin 方信, the sole branch member of his generation who followed him to Kaifeng.[24] Though Fang Xin practiced business there for a decade, no record even suggests a link with Fang Tingke. In short, Fang Tingke strove to be – or at least is depicted as – a self-made man, a patriarch who was not particularly brotherly.

In forging business ties with kinsmen Fang Tingke seems, then, to have actively followed a second unstated guideline: do business with members of only the junior generations of one's branch. Even then, he was selective, as business loans, informal trading partnerships ("he did trading with [So-and-So]"), and gifts are explicitly mentioned only for his two sons, three of his grandsons, two or more of his nephews, and one grand-nephew.[25] In fact, these four kinship relationships – plus that of the brother-to-brother relation – account for the great majority of business relationships explicitly mentioned in Fang Chengxun's biographies. By contrast – and this is Fang Tingke's third unstated guideline – even in the bustling metropolis of Kaifeng he and virtually all of his kinsmen seem to have refrained from forging close business ties with other surname groups, including those from Huizhou. They may well have entered short-term business relations with same-surname Huizhou merchants outside Huizhou (as, for example, in the salt trade, which required much capital). Yet just one of the forty-one surviving biographies of these Fangs mentions a tie-up with merchants of a different surname.[26]

---

[23] Ibid., 40–41, 91.
[24] After spending his twenties in Kaifeng and acquiring desultory profits, he returned to Huizhou "to look after the ancestral graves." After initially working as a yamen clerk, he turned again to trade, but centered it within Huizhou (ibid., 145).
[25] That is, Fang Taiyi, Fang Jingren, Fang Qi, Fang Shiyong, and Fang Jingong, as well as Fang Xi and Fang Sui.
[26] *FKSFC*, 105, in which the family head delegates managerial responsibility to four heirs, who in turn worked with men of "miscellaneous surnames" to revive a family firm. Another possible case (ibid., 166), in which Fang Zuo, a merchant active in north China and based in Kaifeng, retained close ties with two Huizhou

This extraction of certain principles that guided the Fangs' practice of business relationships – what represents, in effect, the common sense of the founder of a family firm – describes for a family firm a three- or four-generation life cycle, whereby its capital assets grew along with its labor (from one to roughly fifteen members), until the death of the family head led to the division of the family and its assets into separate one- or two-generation units again. The intergenerational and intra-generational tensions that commonly lead to such breakups in Chinese families are well recorded in the sinological literature for family ownership of landed property, but far less for family businesses.[27] Within such firms we thus want to see how such tensions arose and were played out, especially if the members as sojourning merchants might engage in independent decisions on volatile commercial transactions that directly affected their sons, brothers, and nephews. The following examination of these business relations for Fang Tingke and later of his fellow branch members will show how these key family relationships shaped and structured business activities, enabling them sometimes to become more flexible and resilient than in landed trusts. Although in the end Fang Tingke and his heirs still could not prevent self-destructive actions similar to those that so disrupted the Shanhe Chengs' management of their rural properties, he nonetheless laid the institutional basis for the creation of larger family organizations that became deeply engaged in commerce.

Key Family Relationships

The father–son relationship, even when one allows for the conventional obligation of a son to profess a deep debt to his parents, was presented as crucial to the career of nearly all the merchants discussed in Fang Chengxun's biographies.[28] Initially, the father often was too busy away from home to pay attention to his children, sons included;

---

men, a Wang 汪 and a Bao 鮑, all his life, reveals, unfortunately, nothing of their business relationship.

[27] An exception is Sui-lun Wong, "The Chinese Family Firm: A Model," 327–40, which argues for four stages in the developmental cycle for certain kinds of Chinese family business: emergent, centralized, segmented, and disintegrative. Although all the family firms and business families discussed in this chapter emerged and eventually broke up, I do not see, perhaps because of the shortage of sources, how their histories sensibly fit into Wong's second and third stages.

[28] A clear exception, of course, is Fang Tingke's shadowy father.

and those who stayed away for years on end were said upon return not to recognize their own sons.[29] When the sons were in their early adolescence, however, the father's attitude would change. He often took responsibility for training them in his business activities, managing their collective revenues, and overseeing their business performance. When deceased, he often loomed over their decisions, not least because he had bequeathed them an equal share in his still-functioning business or in his estate. In addition to this seed capital, he often from the grave influenced their business practices by past instruction or ongoing example.

This type of family business arrangement,[30] in which the son worked with his father and gradually emerged from direct paternal supervision, is evident in an account of two generations of Fangs at work in the salt trade. When already forty years of age, Fang Tianbin 方天斌 decided to abandon farming for trading and went off with his son Fang Zhen 方震 to Hangzhou, "a place where merchants congregate with satchels of salt." The account continues:

> The rich merchants of Xiuning county and Fang Tianbin shared quarters and relied on services from [Fang Zhen]. They greatly marveled at him, as with his father he traded in salt and earned for his family 1,000 taels of silver. The son then took over for his father, and the property increasingly grew. He expanded the base capital and the interest it generated, earning the family 10,000 taels. In general, none of the resident salt merchants in Hangzhou matched Fang Zhen.[31]

Hyperbole aside, this text provides a classic description of that key point in the father–son business relationship when the father decides to hand over the general management of the family business to the next generation. In most cases, the son must earn his promotion, principally by earning additional money for the family business. He does so first under his father's orders, then under his supervision, and eventually, usually when the father has reached fifty or sixty years of age or died, on a loose rein or even independently. However, the father, even after his withdrawal from active management, often kept an eye on the finances, checking the overall figures – as opposed to the transaction details – in the business's account books. The importance accorded to a business's account books in stories about the power balance in a

---

[29] MQHS, 46, 51.   [30] FKSFC, 177.   [31] Ibid.

father–son relationship (note that no mention is made of granaries and store holds) indicates that the business capital of the Fangs was by and large monetarized. Interestingly, these biographies never refer to the practice of hoarding. Instead, they repeatedly refer to "profits" and "interest" (*ziqian* 子钱), suggesting that this family's capital was seldom allowed to sleep. Rather, it was expected to breed more and more capital through investment in other businesses or in direct loans to others.

The immersion of two or three generations of males in this collective effort obviously gave the father (and grandfather) many opportunities to compare the skills and commitment of the sons (and grandsons) to the family enterprise. At the very least, he could observe whose incompetence would most likely strike at the heart of his life's work, and then he could reflect on how best to thwart or minimize the foreseeable damage. Inevitably, preferences for one or two sons emerged, especially in delegating responsibility for the business while still alive in old age. Fang Tinggui 方廷貴 (*c.*1469–1558) relied on the youngest two of his four sons, and especially his last son, to help him manage the business,[32] while Fang Xin favored his eldest son, giving him a purse of several hundred taels of silver and letting him handle the firm's finances with only light supervision.[33] Since all the sons eventually would have an equal share in the ownership of the father's business, this favoritism was essentially an aging father's desperate effort to control his business in the face of his sons' growing maturity and his own approaching demise. His intrusion, if anything, may have mollified the tensions among the brothers, since some Fangs were praised for ignoring their father's unconventional wish that they divide the family property.[34]

Relations between a grandfather and a grandson in the management of a business are commented on only infrequently in Fang Chengxun's biographies, but for Fang Tingke (as indeed for the Shanhe Chengs in volume 1) the relationship assumed considerable importance. He had just one surviving son, and though he reared his orphaned nephews, he showed particular favor and attention to his sole grandson, the son of his sole surviving son. Fang Tingke took him to Kaifeng, where he introduced him to his merchant friends (who knew well enough to extol his talents), set him on his path to commercial success, and then

[32] Ibid., 140.   [33] Ibid., 147–48.   [34] Ibid., 147.

Key Family Relationships 325

doted on his accomplishments: "Fang Tingke was very fond of his grandson Fang Sui, saying, 'He does not reduce my enterprise (*ye*) in Kaifeng.'"[35]

Relations with family orphans, as just noted, receive some comment, as an uncle often assumed responsibility for orphaned nephews, treating them "as if they were his sons."[36] Some uncles engaged nephews in their business, as when Fang Tingke took his nephews Fang Jingren 方景仁, Fang Jingyong 方景用, and Fang Taiyi 方太乙 to Kaifeng to introduce them to the life of a merchant, even to "trade along with them."[37] The financial dimensions of such a relationship usually escape comment, but in one instance an uncle anxious to support his nephew took the highly unusual step of mortgaging "permanent property" (that is, inalienable land) to support the needy nephew.[38] The problems in such relationships receive no mention, but the relative frequency of their appearance in Fang Chengxun's accounts of family heads' financial relationships suggests that this was a common way for men to fulfill (and thus terminate) their brotherly responsibilities. While it may also suggest that they had washed themselves clean of their deceased brother's business commitments, disentangling themselves from his debts and their ongoing interest charges would alas have not been so easy.

Unlike the other family relationships already considered, business relations between brothers would by definition exclude the active participation of a father or senior figure. Constituting a single family, these male offspring of the same father pooled their inherited and otherwise acquired wealth and also shared their income. They might distribute work and profits flexibly, with some brothers arranging to work at commerce and others at something else,[39] or with one brother simply refusing to acquire personal property and perhaps directing some of his earnings to his wife's needy parents.[40] Far more commonly, however, brothers who were engaged in the same business shared equally in its work and its rewards for as long as they remained together and constituted the family firm (I suspect that any written guarantee for the continuation of such shared work would have been their father's last will rather than a document they drew up themselves).

---

[35] Ibid., 194. [36] Ibid., 179, 203–4. [37] Ibid., 97, 143, 144.
[38] Ibid., 154–155. [39] Ibid., 158. [40] Ibid., 155, 158, 172.

Three brothers – Fang Taiqi 方太齊, Fang Taili 方太禮, and the early deceased Fang Taide 方太德 – won a reputation for achieving this ideal arrangement of shared business work: "They were very close, they loved to trade, and they shared their revenues and expenses."[41] Their collaboration in work began no later than in their adolescence, when they all farmed in the family's fields and worked to pay off their father's debts. Their willingness to co-operate survived their initial ventures into trade as well. At about the age of twenty, the two eldest brothers (the third was soon to die) abandoned Huizhou for Kaifeng, where it was soon reported that "none could surpass" these brothers in the trade of "miscellaneous lines of goods (zahang 雜行)" and then cotton.[42] In the view of their biographer, "they topped the various markets of Kaifeng." Yet, in light of these brothers' eventual breakup, it is notable that they acquired their reputation as successful merchants in distinct lines of business. The younger brother soon branched off into moneylending; his modest lifestyle supposedly so successfully convinced others of his integrity that aspiring borrowers were attracted to him even though his annual interest rate for loans was double the 20 percent offered by rivals in Kaifeng.[43]

What eventually led to the breakdown of these brothers' co-operation is not stated. But a common point of tension in the brother–brother relationship in business seems to have been practices that violated expectations of an equal sharing of profits and compensation for work expenses. This problem is alluded to less by criticism of the violation of this ideal than by the frequent absence of any praise of its realization, as if not very many brothers actually attained the ideal. Thus several sets of brothers – but far from the majority – are praised for not taking any unreported share from the profits they made as merchants, for working different markets but sharing their profits equally, for not hesitating to hand over their profits, or for "delighting in halving" their trading profits with each other.[44] The establishment of separate residences and thus separate long-term expenses for brothers – such as when one brother went off to another town to tap a new market for the family business – would probably have hastened the breakup of many such shared businesses.

---

[41] Ibid., 152. Other examples include Fang Jingdi 方景迪 and his younger brother Fang Xuan 方選 (ibid., 171–72).
[42] Ibid., 151.   [43] Ibid., 147.   [44] Ibid., 147, 149, 166, 177.

Fang family divisions led to the breakup of their family businesses, and, not surprisingly, some Fangs then went into business with close cousins rather than with brothers. Usually, they came to an agreement to trade with one another in Kaifeng.[45] But in one case, they agreed to pool their resources and actually trade in different areas. Fang Zuo 方作, who initially "did not work at the livelihood and enterprises of the family members," ended up forming an alliance with a cousin who agreed with him that they would not trespass on one another's market area.[46] Such terms would surely have been demanded by some Fangs when a fellow lineage and especially branch member, earning thousands and then tens of thousands of silver taels, threatened to extend his business into a kinsman's area. The mention of these numbers in published biographies suggests that this information was already common knowledge in a tightly knit community, whose members could see whose gate was newly painted, whose house had been enlarged, and whose recent marriage festivities and burial processions had been lavish.

It was not only the breakdown of relations between brotherly families or short-lived agreements between cousins that posed problems for the Fangs as they entered their third generation of trading. Over time, Fang Tingke's descendants, including grandsons and great-grandsons, came to prefer the settled and profitable comfort of a moneylender's life to the physical risks and potentially greater profits of long-distance trading. Some Fangs set up permanently in Kaifeng, where they took pride in the apparently important place they came to occupy in the city's merchant community. Other Fang merchants in Kaifeng spent their free time socializing in the circles of imperial princes and scholar-officials, some of whom were members of famous Huizhou lineages.[47] Others preferred to retire to the village homestead in Huizhou, where they devoted their urban earnings to the pleasures of a supposed gentry lifestyle and sometimes the creation of more profits from local money-lending.[48] While some doggedly sought out success in the official examination system (one spent 400 taels of silver in Beijing to master the proper standard calligraphy script required of examination candidates),[49] most recognized the wisdom in the warning one family elder imparted to a junior with high-flying aspirations: their family simply

[45] Ibid., 154–155, 175, 204.   [46] Ibid., 166.   [47] Ibid.
[48] Ibid., 91, 139–140, 141, 144–45, 194.   [49] Ibid., 151, 160–61, 175.

lacked the resources to support the requisite education, and any future family head needed to focus on immediate family responsibilities.[50] As a result, most Fangs of this branch in the first half of the sixteenth century avoided the lure of the examinations and instead clung to their now well-tested recipe for commercial success. If anything, financial services, in the form of moneylending (no mention is made of a pawnshop), gained in popularity, and one family of Fang moneylenders back in Yuetan lived off others' interest payments for at least three successive generations.[51]

Also, few Fangs strove to open and develop new markets for goods or moneylending outside Kaifeng and Huizhou. Even less impressive is the failure of those who tried to establish branches or enterprises that outlasted their stay in a new place. Some, like Fang Shiqing 方時清 (1510–81), during the middle of the sixteenth century, traveled widely through the southeast quarter of the country. Whereas his father had gone no farther than neighboring Yanzhou 嚴州, he traded first in Kaifeng, next in Nanjing, then in Fujian, and eventually in Hangzhou.[52] Even so, he nowhere set up a branch or independent base from where he traded regularly with his relations in Huizhou, Kaifeng, or any of their urban settlements.

Likewise, in the three Yangzi delta destinations that particularly attracted the Fangs – Songjiang, Suzhou, and Hangzhou – no long-term trading branch was ever established. These prefectures and their cities, located conveniently for journeys between Huizhou and Kaifeng, contained markets richer and more readily accessible than those in other parts of the empire. Moreover, textile weavers in the Songjiang area required imports of raw cotton, such as were harvested in the countryside around Kaifeng and traded in its markets.[53] Some Fangs brought the goods of the south to Kaifeng,[54] but there is no evidence that they enjoyed anywhere near equal success in transporting northern products in the opposite direction and in selling them in the delta. In fact, it is the Fangs' failure to break into the lower Yangzi delta market and to establish a long-lasting base there that ended up restricting the location of their major success to Kaifeng and thus made it very difficult, if not impossible, for them to expand into the middle Yangzi Valley as well.

[50] Ibid., 156–57.　[51] Ibid., 176.　[52] Ibid., 175.
[53] Fujii, "Shin'an shōnin no kenkyū," 36.1, 11–12.　[54] *FKSFC*, 166.

Key Family Relationships 329

The reasons for this failure in the lower Yangzi delta are doubtless many, with inexperience, shortages of capital, few local contacts in Yangzhou's salt trade and the lower Yangzi delta's textile trade, and the sharp competition among merchants in these places probably ranking high among them. When we look at specific cases, references to this failure and its causes are at best veiled. For instance, when, in old age, Fang Taili shifted his trading operations from Kaifeng to Songjiang, one might have thought that he would have taken advantage of his brother's reputed dominance in the Kaifeng cotton market to establish strong trading links with him in the cotton business. But, whatever trading ties he did set up in Kaifeng came to an end upon his retirement to Huizhou. His sole son had died, and his relations in Kaifeng and Huizhou sent no one in his place. Indeed, while in Songjiang he appears to have lost close contact and perhaps even had a falling out with his Kaifeng relations. When at his sixtieth birthday his Songjiang neighbors toasted him with drinks and gifts in their effort to forge ties with him, his family back in Kaifeng, his biographer pointedly notes, sent no one to extend their congratulations.[55]

In Suzhou, the Fangs' problem seems to have been less a breakdown in relations between brothers or kinsmen than a failure to build up local contacts and their belated arrival in this intensively competitive and highly prosperous commercial center. In the early sixteenth century, Fang Jingdi spent a long time in Suzhou (and in Songjiang), but a cultural gap between his sense of thrift and the locals' worship of luxury is said, though the logic is hard to discern, to have made his stay relatively unprofitable.[56] Only in the mid sixteenth century did some Fangs make a serious concerted effort to gain a foothold in this demanding market. Three of them, in their twenties and thirties, began to trade in Suzhou together, but they too enjoyed no success. After two of the brothers died, the survivor, Fang Yongxi 方永希 (1508–52), was forced by his poverty to move on to Kaifeng. There he made some money, but never gained wealth.[57]

In Hangzhou, a few Fangs did experience success in one trade but were never able to expand on it commercially or geographically. To them, as well as to many other Huizhou lineages, Hangzhou was probably the most attractive of all the lower Yangzi delta cities in which to settle. Some traded there, not too successfully, on their way

---

[55] Ibid., 151, 154–55. [56] Ibid., 158. [57] Ibid., 160.

to making a fortune in Kaifeng.⁵⁸ A few acquired considerable wealth in Hangzhou after some years in the salt trade.⁵⁹ Others even ended up there for much of their commercial life after doing some trading in Kaifeng and the Huai area.⁶⁰ But none ever opened a business in Hangzhou that linked up successfully with Fangs trading elsewhere, especially those in Kaifeng. In short, Hangzhou seems to have been the place where the Fangs went primarily to have a good time, even if it meant losing business.

Witness the three-generation experience of Fang Lu 方錄, Fang Xin, and Fang Liangcai 方良材. Something of a wastrel when young, Fang Lu left Huizhou and, instead of heading for the markets of Kaifeng where his uncle was known to be making his fortune, he "traveled on the rivers and lakes" of south China. Like many such wanderers before him, he ended up at Hangzhou, where he set up a wine business that, to the astonishment of all, proved an immediate hit. Within two years of opening, his shop had attracted hundreds of wine lovers from throughout the Yangzi delta, the rest of eastern China, and even as far up the Yangzi Valley as Sichuan. Sales reached several thousand taels of silver in the first year alone, and for the rest of his life it remained a highly profitable business. Annual profits came to 500 taels of silver, and the shop continued to prosper under his son and, for a time, under his grandson.

Yet at no time did the profits of this business entice Fang Lu, Fang Xin, or Fang Liangcai to trade their wine actively elsewhere or have their Kaifeng relations join them in Hangzhou or other places in this business. People visited the shop from far and near, but no fan of the wine is ever said to have set up a branch in his hometown. Although the need for a great deal of extra capital and the lack of legal protection from counterfeiting rivals may explain this passivity, the reasons discernible from their biographies appear to have been personal. The founder of this wine shop, Fang Lu, was far less interested in pursuing commercial profits and market expansion than in gaining physical immortality, and so he threw his profits – "thousands and tens of thousands of taels of silver he spent without unhappiness" – into research on the tempering of metals. As the pleasures of drink, even

---

[58] Ibid., 139–40.
[59] For instance, Fang Zhen and his father, as already mentioned.
[60] Ibid., 203–4.

his own drink, seem not to have satisfied him, he spent a vast amount of money in an all-consuming quest for the perfect drug of immortality. Soon, his Hangzhou home was attracting not trading relations or partners but Daoists and would-be immortals: "He was interested in alchemy, in becoming a Daoist immortal, and in flying up high with wings. Daoists from throughout the empire converged on his shop, and they tried to make elixirs. For forty-odd years he experimented, [but] he never got anything."[61] One senses in this concluding comment the frustration of a disappointed heir–accountant getting the better of a supposedly disinterested literatus's appreciation of the family's favorite eccentric.

His son Fang Xin continued in the same vocation and avocation. Initially, he remained affluent, earning several thousand taels of silver for his family. But, eventually, his profits fell victim to the cost of his Daoist research and to competition from imitation wines by rival wine houses, which profited not as his partners but as counterfeiters. The grandson would for a time carry on the family business in Hangzhou, even earning 1,000 taels for his family. But aware of the frustrations in this trade and not sharing his father's and grandfather's belief in a pill of immortality, Fang Liangcai left the pleasures of Hangzhou for the profits of Kaifeng. Soon after joining his relations there, he ended up making twice as much money as he had from wine.[62] So ended a three-generation effort to create and maintain a thriving business in Hangzhou, at the end of which, according to Fang Chengxun, "they put out the fires, and there was nothing to get. Their goals had become as [transient] as the wind."[63]

What role, then, did the lineage play in all these businesses of the Fangs? As a formal institution, it had at best a minor role in the establishment and management of the Fangs' businesses. It was too poor and too poorly organized to take an active, independent role in such commercial activities at this time. The same was by and large true for the practice of charity. Whereas "several tens of lineage members" are said to have individually practiced charity by the mid sixteenth century,[64] the lineage itself was more the beneficiary than the benefactor of charity, as when it received a successful merchant member's donation of fields or money for the construction of a bridge, a school, or an ancestral hall. Moreover, these structures started to appear for

[61] Ibid., 180–81.   [62] Ibid., 197–98.   [63] Ibid., 162.   [64] Ibid., 197–98.

the Fangs only in the sixteenth century, and only from the mid sixteenth century did their lineage have enough funds to lend money to some members of its ancestral hall (and also threaten to deny loans to those who misbehaved at its ancestral ceremonies).[65]

If, however, we put aside the notion of the lineage as described in a Huizhou genealogy, with its well-defined kinship positions, roles, benefits, and duties, and adopt a vaguer understanding of a Huizhou lineage as a loose collection of kinsmen drawn together by affective ties, some common interests, a shared claim to the same "Prime Ancestor," and often a common base of residence, then such a large and loose kinship group drawn from a lineage can be seen to have played a vital part in identifying the span of people who financed and staffed some Fang businesses up to at least the end of the sixteenth century. Such a large and loose group drawn from lineage members often acquired its active form from kinship relationships shaped by debts and obligations between rich and powerful patrons and their poorer and weaker client kinsmen. Trust also played a part, and so the more intimate kinship ties, such as between members of the same branch and especially segment, assumed considerable significance in relations between lineage members. Overall, the line of credit for a flourishing house firm ran eventually not from senior to junior generations within a tightly structured and well-funded organization, but from wealthy individuals to needy, skilled, trustworthy, and favored kinsmen seemingly almost regardless of age and generation.

Thus an individual member would receive rice grants during famines and interest-free loans in hard times not from his lineage but from a successful lineage member.[66] In normal times as well, it was the wealthy merchant who might provide support for a kinsman's fledgling business, such as Fang Tingke was said to have done after striking it rich in Kaifeng:

In general, those descendants in the lineage who were even slightly accustomed to trading all went to Kaifeng and traded goods. He brought them along and aided (ji 濟) several hundred families, all of whom raised 1,000 taels of silver for their families. All was due to his kindness ... and he benefited the entire lineage (quanzu 全族).[67]

---

[65] Ibid., 24.2b–4a. [66] Ibid., 186. [67] Ibid., 179.

Key Family Relationships 333

The precise nature of this aid – a loan, a gift, a job, an apprenticeship, a partnership, or just a recommendation – is left unclear, quite possibly because it encompassed all these and other types of assistance. But whatever the nature of the aid, Fang Tingke helped a substantial number of his lineage members make money through trading in a distant city.

Nor was he the only Fang to have done so. His son Fang Qi 方起, in an extended discussion of his charity to lineage members, is said to have "assisted" (*zuo* 佐) nearly two hundred merchants, "each of whom exhausted his abilities" in making use of this aid.[68] For a member of a slightly later generation, the nature of the aid is made more explicit: after Fang Liangcai had succeeded in Kaifeng, he is said to have loaned money to many in the lineage.[69] Furthermore, the expectations that the Fangs in Kaifeng had to bear from their relations back in Yuetan were enormous, as when in the 1550s the wealthiest members of these groups were pressured into paying most of the construction expenses for both their branch and lineage ancestral halls in Huizhou.[70]

The opportunities for privately determined loan links among branch or lineage members were countless, partly because of the huge income disparity between the few rich Fangs and the great majority of their poorer branch or lineage relations. According to Fang Chengxun, the very affluent members of the branch of Fang Tingke in his own lifetime accounted for less than 10 percent (that is, one or two) of its thirty households; those next in affluence 10 percent (that is, three households), and those of the lowest grade of affluence 20 percent (that is, six households); in other words, over half of the household members of this relatively rich branch of the Yuetan Fangs were judged poor or close to poor.[71] Within the lineage, the groupings were not very different, with the least well off representing 50 percent, the next rank 30 percent, and the best off 10 to 20 percent.[72]

These figures on wealth distribution can easily be interpreted to suggest a sharply lopsided division between a few very wealthy patron lenders and a host of kinsmen who were client borrowers in straight and simple lines of financial dependence. Actually, as more and more Fangs were reported to have earned more than 1,000 or 10,000 taels

[68] Ibid., 185–86.   [69] Ibid., 197–98.   [70] Ibid., 88–89.   [71] Ibid., 110.
[72] Ibid., 110–11.

for their families, these cash relations in all likelihood became far more complex and intermeshed than in Fang Tingke's time, when with 10,000 taels he was the lineage's only big earner and when he followed slightly different moneylending guidelines. These wealthy merchant families needed to find safe but productive havens for their capital. Commonly choosing to put it into moneylending and commerce rather than into land, they needed men they could trust as honest and competent borrowers (as well as employees). For these successful Fang families, their lineage, or more precisely their branch, provided a sensible outlet and solution to this problem of how to invest their profits safely and profitably. The lineage's poorer members, especially when not employed in fellow members' far-off branch establishments, wanted capital for their own commercial ventures, and so there emerged among the Fang lineage's kinsmen a web of economic and social debts that is mentioned only randomly among the Fangs' biographies as good deeds. Thus, concurrent with the three-generation succession of moneylenders among Fang Tingke's and Fang Pu 方朴's descendants,[73] there were the cousins who lent one another money,[74] the widows who loaned cash to neighbors and others in the rural district, the grandmothers who loaned cash at interest to poor wives in the lineage, and the ancestral hall and village worship association, which enjoyed lending its endowment money at interest to members for reportedly great profit.[75]

A strong mid-Ming trend towards greater autonomy for smaller kinship units – as opposed to the large communal family model of shared residence and shared wealth in the tenth century – was thus matched by an unprecedented opportunity for cross-investment by families in their kinsmen's business activities. Lineage relations, if not the lineage institution itself, thereby acquired far greater substance in commercial matters than they had enjoyed in the early Ming, as now relations of intimacy outside the immediate family might be forged by the pressing need of many Fangs and other merchants for silver in order to prosper from many other Huizhou merchants' push for commercial expansion. And, within the Fang lineage of Yuetan, it tended to be branch relations, which played a vital role in helping to finance business ventures by their kinsmen. How often these financial linkups constituted actual commercial

[73] Ibid., 176.   [74] Ibid., 154–55.   [75] Ibid., 111, 140.

partnerships is unclear. But if their commercial partnerships anywhere approximated the number of persons that Fang Tingke and Fang Qi are said to have aided financially, then in most of these commercial partnerships this founding father and son would have surely been no more than dormant partners. The apparent disregard already noted for age and generation in the dispensation of such loans may actually cloak a more complicated web of debt-related ties than the blood ties found in genealogical charts. The sheer number of persons this father and son are said to have helped indicates that most recipients were not of their branch. If we had records of their mutual loans and debts over time, we might discover the existence of a "financial branch" alternative to the smaller family units of the branch, that the Fang Chengxun biographies emphasize as the basic units for Fang family businesses.

Finally, there is little sign that individual Fangs or their branches regularly sought to engage with non-kinsmen in commercial activities or organizations. One member of the branch retired at the age of forty, delegating his business management to "four heirs, who along with various [unnamed] surnames repaired the enterprise and kept it alive."[76] As these heirs traveled to Xuzhou 徐州 in northern Jiangsu province as well as to north China, it is clear that these Fangs formed a multiple-surname trading group that traveled far from home and quite possibly set up interlinking commercial ties among themselves. While the Fangs' coresidence with other merchants in Hangzhou or close association with them in Kaifeng almost certainly entailed some financial dealings among them, the record on these activities is sealed. Instead, we have small family units, less so their branch, and even less so their lineage, at the heart of Huizhou merchant groups and activities, as during the mid Ming it rose from poverty to wealth over the course of three generations. The practice of long-distance trade by kinsmen with one another would work best when fellow branch members settled in different places from which they would carry out regular trade in local products. Such arrangements required a higher level of wealth and commercial organization, such as that achieved not by the Fangs of Yuetan but also by branches in other Huizhou lineages, such as the Chengs of Taitang.

---

[76] Ibid., 105.

The Chengs of Taitang: Lineage Organization and Market Networks in Multiregional Business

Like the Fangs of Yuetan, the Chengs of Taitang became important Huizhou merchants in the sixteenth century without trading Huizhou products and without simultaneously pursuing success in the official examinations. But, unlike the Fangs, some Chengs had already, in the late fourteenth century, become rich both as landlords and as merchants. Moreover, in contrast to the Fang merchants' overwhelming concentration in Kaifeng and reliance on its Grand Canal trade, the Taitang Chengs took up long-term residence as merchants in a variety of towns and cities in the lower and middle Yangzi Valley. These advantages laid the basis for succeeding, far more than the Fangs, at forming a long-term commercial network along the Yangzi river, the principal and most profitable artery for private trade during the latter half of the Ming. The span and stretch of the Taitang Chengs' commercial activities highlight the achievement of some Huizhou lineage branches not only at getting their members to engage in shared commercial ventures but also at integrating markets in different sectors and distant regions of the sixteenth-century economy in the Yangzi Valley.

Thanks largely to the inclusion of an exceptionally informative celebration of these Chengs' success in their 1598 genealogy, we can analyze in considerable detail the Yangzi Valley trading network of the Taitang Chengs.[77] This account of the Taitang Chengs' long-distance trade shows how these Chengs acquired and retained considerable wealth by exchanging the salt, textiles, and other manufactured products of the Yangzi delta for raw materials of the middle Yangzi, such as minerals, grain, and timber. Their domination of this long-distance marketing network thus linked their fortune to the two most prosperous macro-regions of the Yangzi Valley in the regular trade of basic commodities, but also connected key sectors of the Yangzi Valley's commercial economy – the grain of Hubei and Hunan and the cotton and silk textiles of the Yangzi delta – that hitherto had functioned by and large separately from one another. In describing how these economic sectors – agricultural, commercial, and financial – were integrated vertically and horizontally, this genealogy's celebration of the

---

[77] The following account of the trade network draws mainly on Cheng Yizhi, *Cheng dian*, 23.1a–4a.

Taitang Chengs' success reveals basic shifts in the focus of their investments and marketing. A family whose wealth had originally derived from landownership increasingly grew rich from trade in mass commodities like salt and textiles, and eventually moved into financial operations like pawnbrokering and moneylending. The social and economic transformation of the livelihood of the Taitang Chengs during the first two centuries of the Ming would thus encapsulate many of the changes experienced concurrently by other Huizhou lineages as well as by the macro-economy of Huizhou and the middle and lower stretches of the Yangzi Valley.

The gradual integration of these Chengs' complex and expanding commercial network in the Yangzi Valley was greatly influenced by kinship ties within their large and highly articulated lineage organization. Branch affiliation in particular greatly determined the directions in which these Chengs migrated and the choice of the towns and cities they eventually settled in throughout the middle and lower Yangzi Valley. The initial success of this commercial expansion by means of branch migration, however, prompted serious concern back in Huizhou over the possibility of the disintegration of both their lineage and this commercial network. Consequently, the emergence of long-distance trading networks pushed this and presumably other similarly challenged Huizhou lineages to develop the means to tighten their kinship ties through shared commercial exchange and investment. Commercial and lineage expansion, they sought to demonstrate, could coincide so long as members of the lineage and especially its dominant branch remained involved in a host of ritual and other collective activities centered at their common ancestral hall back in their Huizhou homestead of Taitang.

In short, this section will first discuss the economic features of the Chengs' trading network, then analyze key dimensions of their branch and lineage kinship organizations, and finally show how their successful adaptation to resettlement in the middle Yangzi Valley uplands may have in the long run threatened the survival of the close trading network they had built up on kinship ties. The development of the Taitang Chengs, as befit a far larger lineage than the Fangs of Yuetan, elevated the links between commerce and kinship to a higher and more complex level of interaction not uncommon among the more successful Huizhou merchant lineages in the latter half of the Ming. Lineage ties here thus mattered more to these Chengs than to the Fangs, yet again branch and close family ties mattered more than other kinship relations in the practice of business, especially commercial partnerships.

The Cheng lineage's attainment of this commercial success had come neither easily nor quickly. Their Prime Ancestor had moved to a mountainous area some sixteen miles south of the Xiuning county seat in 1125, and for the next two to three centuries his descendants, like their contemporary Fangs of Yuetan, had eked out a living in the three villages they came to inhabit. Sometimes they fished, hunted, and practiced forestry, but by and large they conducted "slash-and-burn" farming on the least promising slopes and practiced settled agriculture elsewhere. Of the roughly "10,000 *mu*" in their mountain valley area, just 40 percent was permanently arable. For a population that in the mid sixteenth century numbered in the thousands,[78] this arable-land figure translated into fewer than four *mu* of poor-quality land per Cheng. And, since at least some of this land was rented out to others, the Chengs' economic situation was bleak. More to the point, in their own eyes it was turning bleaker. An increasing share of their tenancies' annual harvests, they complained, was ending up in the hands of their tenants. As a result, in the sixteenth century, it cost more to buy a farm plot's tenancy – so their lament went – than its ownership.

Nonagricultural income, even after the Chengs had planted mountain orchards, remained insignificant; they had few trees to cut and no mines to dig, and the gains from hunting and fishing barely provided basic subsistence. Their only marketable product, tea, had a low level of production and a flavor disparaged even by ignorant locals. The limited contact the Taitang Chengs had with outside markets, some said, kept most of them happy and honest; more realistically, these benefits locked them into poverty. "At the time [that is, in the early Ming] there was no family which had stored up a thousand taels of silver. If a family perhaps had a hundred taels of low-grade silver, then acquaintances in neighboring villages would vie to come and gaze at it. This was the extent of their simplicity."[79] Faced with these unpromising prospects, some ambitious Taitang Chengs claimed that they had no choice but to engage in trade. A past family tradition of official service and Confucian learning, seldom very successful, offered the majority of them little help out of this dire situation.

[78] Ibid., 20.1a–b, 2b.   [79] Ibid., 23.1b.

But what could they trade, and where? The Taitang Chengs needed to find a commercial staple that was essential to the livelihood of a great number of consumers, that had relatively reliable levels of production and profits, that could be linked with other products on the same trading routes, and that they could ship about the Yangzi Valley. Only then could they break out of their subsistence standard of living and gain some of the profits then circulating as silver in the lowlands of the empire.

The principal answer to their needs was salt. Beginning in the first half of the fifteenth century, some Taitang Chengs secured a foothold in the state monopoly selling this basic commodity for daily consumption. How they gained this foothold is not clarified, but within three generations they had established a reputation for cunning and caution in what was often a volatile market. Production and initial sales of this product were concentrated in the Yangzhou area, as were the loading of the transport boats and the inspection of their cargoes (salt boats headed for Jiangxi and Huguang provinces needed to undergo investigation in Nanjing and Jiujiang as well). With each of these huge vessels holding up to several tens of thousands of small batches of salt produced in the flatlands east of Yangzhou, the cargo of just one of these boats was worth from 1,000 to as much as 3,000 taels of silver. Moreover, the number of ships in these ports was so great – "their masts and sails resemble a forest" – that merchants and officials could identify the salt boats and their owners from afar merely from the distinctive "house banners" flapping atop their masts. With their ship's flags publicizing a firm's name (hao 號) – those from the Taitang Chengs all contained the character tai, as in the names Taixing 太興 and Ritai 日太 – these merchants established contact points at various ports along the lower and middle stretches of the Yangzi river and some of its tributaries.

Success in the salt trade provided other benefits for the Taitang Chengs. The official backing they won for the delivery of this daily necessity would have won them and their cargoes some official protection from the pirates/fishermen who preyed on Yangzi river traffic throughout the sixteenth century.[80] Moreover, as authorized salt merchants with automatic access to designated wharves and markets, they would have found it easier to introduce additional products into local

---

[80] See Chapter 3's discussion of Yangzi river security.

markets otherwise difficult to penetrate. Thus they bought textiles in Songjiang, Suzhou, and Hangzhou, and then sailed forth to sell them in towns and cities along the middle stretches of the Yangzi river – Jiujiang in Jiangxi province, Wuhu in south Anhui province, and Longping 竜平, Xingguo 兴国, Tongshan 通山, and Wuchang in modern Hubei province. Cotton cloth woven in Songjiang they sold not just in all parts of neighboring Suzhou prefecture but also beyond the delta in Wuhu and Longping along the Yangzi. Silk thread, woven silk gauze, and twilled thin silk from Suzhou and Hangzhou they sold in Tongshan, and indigo dye produced in the delta they transported to as far away as north China, to the areas of Youzhou 幽州 and Yanzhou 燕州 (aka Beijing). In general, in large urban centers like Wuchang with highly articulated markets they specialized in just one or two items, while in smaller places they dealt in a variety of goods. Such out-of-the-way places included the markets, towns, and cities that lined the forested banks of the Fuchi 富池 river in southern Hubei, an area once but no longer famed for its mineral deposits. Leaving the Yangzi at the market town of Fuchi, some Taitang Chengs sailed their cargo southward up a mountain valley for twenty miles to the Xingguo prefectural seat, then another twenty miles to Pai 排 [aka 牌] Market, and finally yet another forty miles deeper into the mountains of Tongshan county to its county seat. There they sold salt and other goods of the Yangzi delta and in return bought these places' local products – raw cotton, tong tree oil, hemp, coal, husked rice, timber, and firewood – before selling them downstream for other goods.

The Taitang Chengs' participation in this long-distance trade that constituted the lifeblood of Yangzi river commerce in the latter half of the Ming nonetheless differed from that of many other Huizhou merchants trading along the Yangzi in two respects. First, the grain shipments that are thought to have constituted the bulk of the upriver exchange for downriver salt and textiles appear to have occupied only limited space in the Chengs' boats. Second, the Chengs attained an exceptional degree of spatial and vertical integration of their markets through the nearly institutionalized regularity of their transactions in the Yangzi delta and southern Hubei. At both ends of their trading network's main line of transport they annually bought and sold outside prefectural and county seats, by entering into local market towns and penetrating, at least in the delta, even into villages. In the Suzhou and Songjiang (Wu Song 吴松) area in the northeast quarter of the delta they set up "letting-out" arrangements for textile production in villages, where they sold raw cotton material in village – presumably periodic – markets (*cunxu* 村虛) and in return bought cotton cloth woven by the villagers that they sold elsewhere, in the delta and the lower and middle Yangzi Valley. Their vertical integration of this textile manufacture – linking the raw cotton of southern Hubei with the skilled weavers of rural Suzhou and Songjiang to make cotton goods for distribution throughout the lower and middle Yangzi Valley – enabled them to establish direct control over all stages in the distribution of this cloth. By contrast, they sought, at most, indirect control over most of the means of this cloth's production (for example, the weaving machinery and the cotton fields themselves). Aware from their Huizhou experience of the limited returns from landownership, the high costs of attendant labor service charges, and the greater profits from pawnshops, they sought to spread their financial control over virtually all the other stages in the process of producing cotton cloth without having to deal with all the complications of land tax, rent collection, and tenant control that came with landownership in the northeast corner of the delta. Thus, in villages in the same Suzhou and Songjiang area where they let out raw cotton, some Taitang Chengs operated pawnbroker outlets, while in the delta's big cities of Suzhou and Nanjing others set up pawnshops (*dianpu* 典鋪). They lent their "base capital" at interest in expectation of regular repayments from their customers (at least until the *wakō* invasions disrupted businesses in the eastern delta in the early 1550s). Meanwhile, in southern Hubei, at the opposite end of their main line of trade, yet other Taitang Chengs were selling textiles and running pawnshops, lending capital at monthly or yearly rates of interest in Tongshan county and trading in salt in Pai Market Town. Thus the Taitang Chengs' investment in the economy of the lower and middle Yangzi Valley's commercial economy encompassed a great variety of interconnected commercial goods and distribution services, but increasingly it was directed towards financial operations that enabled them to invest their profits in whatever promised attractive and reliable returns.

The establishment and spread of the Taitang Chengs' commercial and financial operations in the Yangzi Valley during the sixteenth century appear so reasonable and inevitable that it comes as a surprise to read that their own involvement in this trade may have originated from merely exploratory ventures by adventuresome ancestors. In the late Yuan and early Ming, for example, some Taitang Chengs had emigrated to Yangzhou, Huai'an, Hangzhou, Nanjing, and Songjiang, only to disappear thereafter from the lineage's records.[81] Likewise, a century later some Taitang Chengs in the early fifteenth century traveled up the Yangzi Valley as far as Changsha, Yuezhou, and Chengtian prefectures in modern Hunan province; of them and their descendants as well, we also hear nothing more. But, by no later than the mid sixteenth century such trading trips had turned into regular annual tours between the delta and southern Hubei (e.g., Pai Market in Xingguo prefecture[82]). "Some use their wealth to trade (yi 易). Then, turning once again, they go off in the four directions, where they trade and again do business. Thereupon, they have the goods they trade in, return to these places, in what is every year a regular affair."[83] In fact, by this time some Chengs were residing permanently in the delta and southern Hubei, carrying out a wide variety of local as well as long-distance transactions with one another at the opposite ends of this 600-mile trading route. The Cheng genealogy's account of its lineage members' trading practices leaves no doubt that in all of these marketing areas some Chengs settled down as resident traders and others traveled among them as both local and long-distance merchants.

The formation of this Hubei/Hunan–Yangzi delta network for regular long-distance trading in the mid and late Ming has long been recognized as a major development in the commercial economy of south China. Some have argued that the high volume of its transactions saw ordinary private goods like grain and textiles replace government and luxury items as the principal products in regular long-distance trade.[84] Others have stressed that it thus laid the basis for much subsequent transport of private goods between these two vital areas of the Yangzi Valley economy.[85] And yet others have held that it made private transport merchants, especially those from Huizhou, an increasingly wealthy and powerful group in the Yangzi Valley's economy and society.[86] Even though these claims neglect to note that government salt made up a significant portion of the commercial goods

---

[81] Cheng Yizhi, *Cheng dian*, 2.shang, 2a–11a.   [82] Ibid., 12.16b.
[83] Ibid., 23.2b, 18b.
[84] Rowe, "Approaches to Modern Chinese Social History."
[85] Terada, *Sanshi Shōnin*, 89; Fujii, "Shin'an shōnin no kenkyū," 36.1, 19–21, 25–26, and 36.2, 33–37.
[86] Zhang Haipeng and Wang Tingyuan, *Huishang yanjiu*, 129–45.

shipped upstream, they have considerable validity, when seen as post facto consequences from a macroeconomic perspective. Yet, when seen from the perspective of those actually engaged at the time in the formation of this market network, the institutionalization of this Yangzi Valley trade would have grown out of far less grand intentions and would have held another meaning for its creators. In other words, these steps that led towards the integration of the lower and middle Yangzi Valley economy were intended to solve other problems faced by merchants in rapidly changing and competitive markets. Flush with profits from the prosperous salt trade between Yangzhou and Wuchang, these merchants were anxious to avoid sinking their profits into overpriced and overtaxed land. They needed to identify relatively safe commercial activities for the investment of their increasing supplies of capital. These reliable harbors they found in mass-market products like grain, textiles, timber, paper, other wood products, and soy sauce, products whose markets their salt profits let them dominate even though they were mainly produced outside Huizhou. All these commodities presented relatively few risks for sixteenth-century Huizhou merchants understandably anxious to protect profits they made in a region whose situation they initially knew little about and whose transportation security they often had good reason to doubt. In other words, the history of the Taitang Chengs parallels much of the market expansion by Huizhou merchants in the lower and middle Yangzi Valley and thus promises to reveal a great deal about underlying regional economic changes and relationships of the late Ming.

To understand the part these Chengs and other Huizhou merchants played in the economic integration of the Yangzi Valley's two most thriving macro-regions, we need to shift our concerns away from the goods these merchants circulated, the credit they provided, and the market sites they visited. More relevant now to an understanding of the issue of market development are simple questions of personnel: which Chengs did the trading, and trading with whom? Descent lines, migration lists, and long-term kinship affiliation as recorded in the Taitang Chengs' genealogy show that all these markets visited by the Taitang Chengs fell largely under the influence of distinct yet close kinship groups within their lineage. Not only did just one of the three large branches of Taitang Chengs dominate this trade between the lower and middle sections of the Yangzi Valley. But also each of the four segments in this branch dominated just one of the Taitang

Chengs' four major trading sites there. Furthermore, these segments' establishment of their dominance over a particular market area and at times its specialized goods and services emerged from a two-pronged strategy by the leaders of this Taitang Cheng branch for expanding its wealth and influence both inside and outside Huizhou.

In other words, this branch's commercial activities away from Huizhou, in contrast to those of the Fangs, need to be understood at least until the middle of the sixteenth century as the fulfillment of its early Ming leaders' strategy for protecting and expanding their landed and commercial interests at home and away. Whereas Fang Tingke and his descendants initially seem to be using commercial success outside Huizhou in part to build up a local base superior to that of rival richer branches or segments within their lineage at home, some Taitang Chengs developed their arsenal of wealth and power in a more carefully structured manner from within their home base. Beginning in the fourteenth century as local power men, they transformed their military prowess into landownership. As powerful landlords in their district, they then expanded into the risky but highly profitable world of long-distance trade outside Huizhou. This commercial expansion, which would have introduced these Taitang Chengs to the cultural as well as commercial riches of the Yangzi Valley, led to some of them unexpectedly pursuing their passions for Daoism, Buddhism, and eventually literary culture. As some sixteenth-century members of the family then sought to succeed in these new spheres, the Chengs, regardless of their poor performance in the examinations and limited representation in officialdom, were judged by one of their biographers to be "heading towards being civilized" (zhi wen 之文).[87]

This civilizing process, however real in Huizhou, was far less evident in those segments of the branch and lineage active elsewhere. Far more segmented and layered an organization than ever before, this dominant branch of the Taitang Chengs was confronted with a structural problem similar to that of the descendants of Fang Tingke: how to balance their branch's needs at home with those elsewhere. Yet the Taitang Chengs' relationship with "elsewhere" was triangular rather than dyadic. They had kinship and commercial commitments in Huizhou, southern Hubei and the Yangzi delta, especially Yangzhou. Seeking to bridge all of these very different trading and social worlds, different

---

[87] Wu Ziyu, *Dazhang shanren ji*, 44.12a.

generations of Chengs during the Ming would respond differently to these opportunities and responsibilities. By the end of the sixteenth century, the contradictions in these relationships became intense and complicated enough to require our separate discussion of them under concepts more precise than that of "civilized."

The successful mid-Ming merchants of the Taitang Chengs traced their origins to Cheng Junzuo 程均佐 (active 1340s–1370s) and Cheng Shenyou 程神祐 (1323–1374), both members of the Tianrui 天瑞 segment of the Kezhou 可周 branch of the Taitang Chengs. These two brothers rose to military and economic prominence in Huizhou during the three bloody decades of the Yuan–Ming transition. When contending armies and bandit gangs were decimating much of Huizhou and its population, the elder of these brothers, Cheng Junzuo, raised local militia in support of dynastic forces, first the Yuan and later the Ming. The latter display of loyalty won him an appointment by the new Ming government to the post of sheriff in neighboring Qimen county. But as he would soon suffer banishment to a frontier area during one of the first Ming emperor's recurrent purges of officialdom, it was his younger brother, Cheng Shenyou, who made a more lasting improvement to his descendants' fortunes. For while the elder brother was leading troops and while Xiuning landowners were fleeing bloody battles and abandoning their fields to wasteland, Cheng Shenyou deftly managed to acquire (one is tempted to say, seize[88]) a thousand *mu* of local fields. This surge in his property holdings eventually had him invited to the Ming imperial palace in Nanjing and, like his brother, win a local appointment from the new government, in his case the headship of a rural district. But unlike his brother and many other Huizhou survivors of the Ming conquest, he succeeded in passing on his official appointment (as tax collector in his rural district) as well as his wealth to his son and grandson. In fact, he elevated his village and his branch in it from being the poorest to the richest of the Taitang Chengs' three villages and branches. His landholdings thereby laid a basis for the wealth acquired from their trading network by at least the next three generations of his descendants.

Like the founding brothers, members of the branch's subsequent generations would divide their spheres of action into a home base with landed wealth and an outside world with commercial activities

---

[88] McDermott, *Making*, v. 1, 175–77.

(officialdom took a distant backseat). At home in Taitang, Cheng Jingshi 程靖师 (1349–c.1374), Cheng Shengde 程胜得, and the adopted son Wang Lian 汪簾 would in a direct line of descent from Cheng Shenyou succeed one another as head of the family and its landed property inside Huizhou.[89] Twice the descendants of this line would divide the family property, and once adopt Wang Lian to continue the family line. But thanks to resolute leadership, astute land management, and fortunate marriage alliances they are said to have avoided destructive parcelization and diminution of the family's landholdings.[90] The family property even survived Wang Lian's unexpected return to his natal descent line, as the Taitang Chengs thwarted his removal of any of their original property by forcibly seizing it back from him and his natal family. In sum, landownership remained an important part of the local wealth of Cheng Shenyou's descendants and would have helped to fund the extension of their commercial activities beyond Huizhou to the lowlands of the Yangzi Valley. The land shortage that reportedly drove so many Huizhou men to emigrate as petty merchants undoubtedly restricted these Chengs as well. But it was not the hunger or even the poverty that troubled their less fortunate kinsmen or the Fangs of Yuetan. Rather it would have been a shortage of reasonable opportunities for further investment in a local economy, whose soaring land prices in the mid Ming would have helped to make external commercial operations and their promise of high returns appear less speculative and far more attractive investments in the long run.[91]

In the commercial world of the lower and middle Yangzi Valley, descendants of Cheng Shenyou and Cheng Junzuo were instrumental in establishing and developing four market areas crucial to their own descendants' expansion. As explained by the experienced editor and author Cheng Yizhi 程一枝, the Taitang Chengs' participation in each of these markets was initiated by a separate member of the Taitang lineage and/or his descendants and then carried on up to at least the end of the sixteenth century. By then, members of these descent lines had settled in these market areas, where they established a prosperous base for trade (Table 6.1).[92]

[89] Yan Guifu and Wang Guojian, *Huizhou wenshu dang'an*, 335–36.
[90] Cheng Yizhi, *Chengdian*, 16.1a–3b.   [91] Ibid., 16.2b–3b.
[92] Cheng Renshou, ibid., 2, shang.35a, 12.9b, 23.3a; Cheng Daode, ibid., 23.3a; Cheng Wenbian, ibid., 2 xia.62a, 12.16b, 23.3a; and Cheng Junzuo, ibid., 23.3a.

Table 6.1 External market bases of the Taitang Chengs during the early Ming

Market base initiator	Birth and death dates	Generation	Location	Business
Descendants of Cheng Renshou 程仁壽	1363–c.1433 or c.1439	13th	Suzhou–Songjiang	pawnbrokering
Cheng Daode 程道得	1382–c.1434	14th	Yangzhou	Salt
Branch of Cheng Junzuo 程均佐	Early Ming	After 13th	Xingguozhou, Tongshan	Wood products
Cheng Wenbian 程文編	1460–c.1518	17th	Xingguozhou, Pai Market	Salt

The first, second, and fourth of these groups descended from Cheng Shenyou and used his wealth for three kinds of commercial activity that required considerable outlays of capital from the start: dealing in salt, dealing in timber, and pawnbrokering. Cheng Shenyou's son Cheng Renshou became wealthy by trading commodities (most likely, textiles) in the lower Yangzi delta – he was the first in the lineage recorded to have done so. His descendants continued this commercial success, some by shifting to pawnbrokering: "The various grandsons of Cheng Renshou therefore often practiced pawnbrokering in various rural areas in Suzhou and Songjiang (Wu Song 吴松)."[93] His nephew, Cheng Daode, the beneficiary of his own father's land inheritance from Cheng Shenyou, would achieve an even more significant breakthrough for the Taitang Chengs' future as traders: he became involved in the salt trade, thereby generating the profits that financed much of the rest of the Chengs' commerce with the middle Yangzi.

Towards the close of the fifteenth century, several other descendants of Cheng Shenyou, led by Cheng Wenbian, entered the then booming Yangzi salt trade. Insisting that the land-poor Chengs had to trade themselves out of poverty, he and his brothers for thirty years shipped salt and wine from the Yangzi delta to markets mainly in Hubei and Hunan. When he first arrived at Pai Market Town in Xingguo Prefecture, he reportedly sighed, "Here one can accumulate and sell." Making a profit of 2,000 taels of silver in the course of a year, he made plans to accumulate salt and subsequently sell it for his kinsmen. "At this place they forged friendly relations with one another and formed a settlement. Cheng Wenbian really guided them there. By accumulating satchels of salt, they attained wealth."[94] Other descendants of Cheng Junzuo settled in the same county of this prefecture to trade in the lumber industry, quite possibly laying the basis for Cheng Wenbian's commercial success there in the early sixteenth century. But regardless of who came first and so helped the other's later business operations, Cheng Wenbian's salt cargoes would have satisfied his relations' need for a product with a local demand as strong and as steady as that for their lumber downstream in the Yangzi Valley. Their two products of salt and timber thus formed the basis of a regular exchange cycle between kinsmen in the delta and southern Hubei.

[93] Ibid., 23.3a.   [94] Ibid., 12.16b; Wu Ziyu, *Dazhang shanren ji*, 44.11a–b.

Table 6.1's dates underline how early – two or three generations before many other Huizhou groups like the Fangs – the Taitang Chengs had turned to developing external market bases and contacts, first on both sides of the lower Yangzi delta and then in the uplands of southern Hubei in the middle Yangzi. It also indicates that these bases were established and dominated by two distinct descent lines among the descendants of Cheng Shenyou. Lured by the promise of commercial opportunities and fearful of their declining agricultural income at home in Huizhou, members of these two lines would continue to migrate from Taitang and would keep their branch and their segments within it involved at both ends of this trading network up to at least the late sixteenth century. By then there had emerged distinctive cultures among the Taitang Chengs that reflected differences in the needs of these regional markets and in the wealth of these kinsmen (those descended from Cheng Shenyou were richer and more likely to be involved in more capital-intensive businesses like the salt trade and moneylending).

The Taitang migrants to the delta were far outnumbered by those to Xingguo prefecture in southern Hubei. Of the more than 134 Taitang Chengs reported to have shifted their formal lineage residence out of Huizhou during the Ming,[95] nearly three-quarters moved to the middle Yangzi Valley, overwhelmingly during the final decades of the fifteenth century and the first half of the sixteenth century. At least half of all recorded Cheng emigrants from Taitang moved to Xingguo prefecture, mainly to its Tongshan county and Pai Market (which, as a thriving crossroads, became known as "Cheng Market").[96]

These recorded Taitang migrants to Xingguo prefecture all belonged to one of either two kinship groupings of Chengs formed in Huizhou in the early fourteenth century. Subsequently, these kinship groupings subdivided. The Taitang Cheng immigrants to these Xingguo sites were members of nine such segments (zhi) or sub-segments (pai 派), but just one or two of these segments predominated at the two most popular of these settlements.[97] At Pai Market over two-thirds of the recorded immigrants belonged to the Cheng Renshou segment, in confirmation of the claim of the genealogy's compiler that descendants

---

[95] Cheng Yizhi, Cheng dian, 2, shang and xia.
[96] Wu Ziyu, Dazhang shanren ji, 44.11b.
[97] From biographies in Cheng Yizhi, Cheng dian, 2, shang and xia.

of Cheng Wenbian, himself a descendant of Cheng Renshou, had settled there. In Tongshan county, two segments of one Taitang branch paired up to account for 40 percent of the immigrants, and two others separately represented another 35 percent. And, when more closely examined, the Taitang Chengs' settlements in the Fuchi river valley were probably most affected by more intimate kinship ties than the formal ties of a segment or branch, since most of these settlers joined or were joined by their sons, nephews, close cousins, or most likely a brother or two. However ignorant these immigrants may have been of the specific economic conditions facing them at their destination, they would have recognized the benefit of traveling and settling down with kinsmen they already knew and could trust.

Their adaptation to Xingguo, and indeed to their other destinations in the Yangzi Valley and north China, seems to have been socially successful as well. In Xingguo some of the migrants married local women, some received an education at its state school, others were buried in its hills, and yet others in its Pai Market Town are said to have acquired a reputation for virtue and righteousness. A Huizhou merchant surnamed Cheng is even mentioned as a 1591 donor of land to the county school of Tongshan.[98] But by and large, they showed no interest in official titles, examination degrees, or Confucian gentry culture.

On this point the difference from their kinsmen back in Huizhou and the lower Yangzi delta could not have been greater. The Taitang Chengs who were active as salt merchants in Yangzhou sought to present themselves as civilized scholar-merchants, acquiring the patina of a Confucian education in their youth and perhaps an official title (almost certainly purchased) in their adulthood. They regularly returned home to Taitang, where they saw to the care of ancestral graves, the compilation of genealogies, and the dispensation of charity to kinsmen. Whereas other salt merchants are commonly criticized for their greed and crimes, these Taitang Chengs are placed above the fray of commercial life as men with proper breeding and education. They sought to be appreciated as "Confucian scholar-merchants."[99]

A knowledgeable late sixteenth-century member of the lineage who resided in Huizhou attributed this growing difference among the Taitang immigrant groups to the regional character of the different places

[98] *Tongshan xianzhi* (1868), 8.5a.   [99] *THJ*, 48, 1,025–26.

they or their recent ancestors had settled in and adapted to. Those settling in Huguang sites like Xingguo, he claimed, had become stingy, those in the Suzhou area smooth and sophisticated, and those in the Beijing area prone to be passionate and lose their temper.[100] Lineage members staying in Taitang, who tended to view themselves as living a simple life with few desires, would have had as much trouble understanding their relations as recognizing themselves in Ming fiction's stereotypical representations of Huizhou merchants as men as loose with women as they were close with silver.[101]

Behind this member's notice of the emergence of distinct subcultures within the lineage there lay a sense of anxiety about the lineage's future. Like his brothers and nephews and many other contemporaries in the salt trade, Cheng Wenbian and one of his sons retired to Huizhou to live the life of a wealthy landlord, who supervised the work of field workers and dispensed charity to Taitang kinsmen.[102] But many of his descendants and close relations who moved to Xingguo did not. Accounting for the great majority of Taitang emigrants, these Chengs were still being directed to on average one new market site in Xingguo county per generation, thereby reducing the direct competition among them. Yet, as these Chengs succeeded economically and socially in their Hubei milieu and as their absences from Huizhou grew longer and longer, those Taitang Chengs based back in Huizhou or even Yangzhou faced a conundrum. For the smooth running of their trading network they depended on the co-operation of the increasing number of distant relations who had shifted their formal lineage affiliation from Taitang to Xingguo. What could be done to retain their links to Taitang and their submission to the lineage's heads back there? Especially, what could be done to foster closer ties among all its members and to institutionalize their long-term commercial commitments to one another, when unlike earlier generations of itinerant Chengs (and also the Fangs of Yuetan) fewer and fewer of their successful merchants were returning to Huizhou to enjoy the aging fruits of their labors, gain burial in lineage grounds, and most importantly bequeath their commercial estate to sons who remained fellow residents of this "home village"?

[100] Cheng Yizhi, *Cheng dian*, 23.2b–3a.
[101] Ling Mengchu, *Erke paian jingqi*, v. 2, 28, 519–33; 37, 658–73; Cyril Birch, *Stories from a Ming Collection*, 45–96.
[102] Cheng Yizhi, *Cheng dian*, 12.16b–17a, 18b–19a.

Perhaps, though, the greatest threats to their continued co-operation in long-distance trade emerged in the "civilizing process" taking place in the Huizhou mountain settlement of Taitang. Over the course of the first two centuries of Ming rule, the lineage in Taitang had become far more self-conscious of its organization and its self-governance. Its size, despite the apparent failure of nearly a third of its members to produce heirs,[103] had grown beyond recognition. Between the mid fifteenth century and the late sixteenth its registered membership had risen from 196 males in the sixteenth generation to 301 in the seventeenth, 431 in the eighteenth, 521 in the nineteenth and 335 in the still emerging twentieth.[104] The Renshou branch (*fang*) alone had expanded dramatically from one male to fifty males over six generations up to 1545.[105]

The lineage's organization at home had also become far more formal and complicated. Although it had lost the sole copy of its genealogy to military fires in the Yuan–Ming transition,[106] in 1545 it had a fresh genealogy compiled from its surviving records. This new genealogy contained clear, and for the pre-Ming era probably abbreviated, descent lines, but little else.[107] Then in 1598 the Taitang Chengs published a far more ambitious and comprehensive record of their history, the *Cheng dian* 程典, that in parts assumed the role of a genealogy of record for all the Cheng lineages in Huizhou. It notes the years when these other lineages completed the compilation of their separate genealogies and when some of them performed collective Cheng ancestral rites. On its own, the Taitang Cheng lineage had over time adopted a more organized approach to the practice of these rites and the maintenance of their ancestors' graves. In 1423 its members had agreed to look after these graves.[108] Then, at the relatively early date of 1481 they built an ancestral hall and subsequently had it repaired in 1537 and 1578.[109] The lineage made use of this hall's construction to establish its lending operations,[110] and some of its members composed a set of rules regulating its annual collective rituals and some of its

---

[103] Ibid., 2.xia, 11a. Many of these Chengs without a reported heir had probably failed in their commercial ventures and so stopped reporting back to a home base that no longer provided support.
[104] Ibid., 2.shang, 98a.
[105] *Shizhong Chengshi Taitang zupu* (1545), 3.42a ff, 3.73 ff.
[106] Cheng Yizhi, *Cheng dian*, postface by Cheng Can, 10b.
[107] That is, *Shizhong Chengshi Taitang zupu* (1545).
[108] Cheng Yizhi, *Cheng dian*, 6.shang, 47b.
[109] Ibid., 6.shang, 71a; and, 6.xia, 31a, 75a. [110] Ibid., 24.2a.

customs.[111] All that is missing from this list of elite family activities is a record of their examination degrees. And yet, if we can trust the complacent tone of the compiler of their 1598 genealogy in his discussion of the Taitang Chengs' marriage alliances,[112] their failure in the examination halls seems not to have damaged their prospects in the ongoing Huizhou family game of racking up social prestige by forging closer ties with ever more powerful families through marriage. The Taitang Chengs' wealth had perhaps kept them eligible and desirable in the marriage market of Xiuning.

The Cheng lineage in Taitang, in short, was fully engaged in running itself, and when it thought about its external affairs, it thought mainly about the towns and cities in the delta where many of its members lived and made profits for themselves and anyone back home in Taitang who had invested in them. The matters of a county seat and market town in southern Hubei would have mattered to an important branch of the lineage, but they too would have been focused primarily on their investments in the delta.

The problem faced, then, by the Taitang Chengs – how to retain a branch-based exchange network in the face of their branches' separate paths to success – was not the problem that confronted the even larger and richer Wus of Xi'nan in She county during the latter half of the Ming. Instead, it was how to replace a set of relatively loose institutional practices that had proven remarkably successful in the first two centuries of Ming rule with a pair of seemingly contradictory goals that called simultaneously for consolidation of power and organization within the lineage and for consolidating external ties with other Wu surname groups both inside and outside Huizhou. This two-pronged policy sought by one powerful segment within one branch saw certain powerful and wealthy Wus tie their external future not to colonizing Wus from their own She county villages but to same-surname groups with only tangential ties to the Xi'nan Wus. Their clash with kinsmen was played out with the language and moves not of a company boardroom but of a Confucian-based kinship group: the ownership and management of graves, ancestral halls, and genealogies, matters central to the controversies that disrupted Huizhou villages and their institutions in the first two centuries of the Ming. In this case, they represent efforts by a very ambitious group within the dominant

---

[111] Ibid., 24.1a ff.   [112] Ibid., 8.lun.

branch of the Xi'nan Wus to take advantage of their position as one of the empire's wealthiest salt merchant house firms, all with the implicit aims of establishing dominance in their home base of Xi'nan and forming a burgeoning network of close connections elsewhere in the lower and middle stretches of the Yangzi Valley. The tension would persist throughout the second half of the Ming, when this group of Xi'nan Wus became fabulously wealthy, when many other Xi'nan Wus became rich, and when tensions between segments and others within the lineage erupted into one of the greatest scandals of the late Ming, the Mt Huang disaster.

The Wus of Xi'nan: The Dynastic Cycle of Imperial Syndicates

During the second half of the Ming the Xi'nan Wu lineage of She county became one of the richest merchant lineages in the entire empire thanks largely to its members' success in the salt monopoly in Yangzhou and the Yangzi Valley. Though they had first participated in this government monopoly in the twelfth century, they did so in great numbers only from the late fifteenth century, when the scale of their wealth, individual as well as collective, began to expand enormously along with their ways of consuming it. Whereas at the end of the fifteenth century a Xi'nan Wu was regarded as rich when he had several tens of thousands of taels,[113] in the sixteenth century such conventional standards for assessing a male's wealth were upgraded to stress the size of his collection of women (a hundred concubines in the case of the highly successful Wu Gongjin) or houses (a Wu merchant reportedly owned "ten large buildings, twenty celebrated halls and belvederes, and twenty-four famous halls and courtyards").[114]

By the sixteenth century's end a Wu family member's wealth was judged in terms of how much he could afford to give away, as when some Wus in the 1570s donated to the government 200,000 taels (to relieve famines and natural disasters elsewhere) and other Wus gave 300,000 taels in 1595 (to help the Ming repel the Japanese invasion of Korea and rebuild three large palace buildings recently destroyed by

---

[113] *Fengnan zhi*, 6, 369–70 (Wu Yougui 吳有貴).
[114] Ibid., 5,316; and a certain Wu Yunfu 吳允复 (1555–1624) reportedly had over 100 concubines (Dong Jian, *Ziran*, 27).

fire).[115] So rich had some Wus become that in 1618 one of them paid 1,700 taels for a tenth of an acre of dry land in their village area (a year later he sold it on to another Wu for 1,870 taels),[116] all at a time when a similarly sized plot of productive Huizhou paddy field usually cost less than a mere twentieth of these prices.[117] Tellingly, none of these estimates of the Xi'nan Wus' collective wealth were made in terms of their landholdings. No wonder, then, that at roughly this time a knowledgeable member, Wu Shiqi 吳士奇, ranked his lineage, conceived collectively in the most general terms, as one of the wealthiest kinship groups in the empire.[118]

The Wus' acquisition of their Ming fortunes from involvement in the Ming salt monopoly, as we now know, begs many questions, not least the two that shall most concern us in this section: their role in its administration and its impact on their own lineage's organization and operation back in Huizhou. First, they attained a wide range of trading positions dispersed throughout the various levels of this monopoly's distribution organization. At its lower levels, especially in the mid Ming, some Wus worked alone as itinerant peddlers,[119] without borrowed capital,[120] and even refusing to take on debt.[121] Wu Zhengeng (1482–1541), born lame and orphaned when young, typified this type of resourceful, if singular, Wu entrepreneur. Having no brothers

---

[115] *Fengnan zhi*, 5,316; Zhao Chengzhong, "Huangshan yuanan," 30. After the first gift, two Wus, both sons of the donor Wu Shouli, acquired official status and appointments. Two decades later, these two sons, joined by a brother, led their kinsmen in making a second donation, that gained for five kinsmen (including one apiece of their sons) official status and position. Dan Qu, *Liang Huai yanfa zhi* (1806 ed.), 21.4a, mentions donations by four other Wus in 1588.

[116] *Huizhou qiannian*, v. 9, 448–49. A site with the same registration name and number measured 0.45 fiscal *mu* in 1618 and 0.398 fiscal *mu* in 1619; it was sold for 3,788 taels in 1618 – that is, at a rate of more than 4,800 taels per fiscal *mu* of dry land. The most obvious explanation of these extraordinary prices is the great fascination that Huizhou men, educated or not, had with geomancy and its supposed impact on their fate and fortunes (*THJ*, 42, 894, and 47, 1,000).

[117] McDermott, *Making*, v. 1, 271, Table 4.5.

[118] Wu Shiqi, *Lüzi guan zhengxin bian*, 5.35b–36a.

[119] E.g., *Fengnan zhi*, 6,372, on Wu Zhengfang, who was reportedly gifted at speculating. Also, the remarkable case of Wu Ke 吳柯, who traded well into his sixties in Linqing, Hangzhou, Suzhou, and Qingyuan Market Town in Jiangxi, increasing his capital from ten taels to over a thousand (ibid., 6,378).

[120] Ibid., 6,374.   [121] Ibid., 6,372.

or immediate family to travel with and rely on, he nonetheless made a living as a peddler along the roads and on the lakes of central China, where he died in a salt boat as a minor salt merchant.[122]

Yet at the opposite level of success in salt dealings the Wus built up a formidable record, which their sources highlight. During the latter half of the Ming no fewer than six Wus held the head post of Libationer in the Yangzhou salt merchants' group.[123] In addition to enlisting salt merchants into joint ventures (including commercial partnerships), enforcing their agreements and resolving their disputes, the holders of this powerful and prestigious semiofficial post represented salt merchants collectively in negotiations with government offices in Yangzhou.[124] The Wus' pre-eminence survived the government's reform of the salt monopoly administration, when they were included in the cartel of seven salt merchant syndicates established in 1617 on government orders (overall, the Wu surname group was rivaled in this rearrangement only by Wang 汪 and Cheng surname groups, also from Huizhou).[125]

With these sources of wealth located outside Huizhou, the Xi'nan Wus understandably emigrated during the Ming in great numbers, some permanently, like the Taitang Chengs. From the mid Ming many of their males spent much of their adolescence and some of their adult

---

[122] Ibid.

[123] Ibid., 6,378 (Wu Shouli; Wu Honglu, 1540–1617); *THJ*, 53, 1,120 (Wu Zhengzhong and his elder brother) and 37, 808–11. This term was also used then for "the man in charge of the vessels" in ancestral worship sacrifices (ibid., 51, 1,074, and 57, 1,193).

[124] The source of this figure's authority and legitimacy is hard to determine and in fact may have varied according to location and trade. While unusually rich, experienced, and successful in the salt monopoly trade, the holder of this Yangzhou position clearly needed the approval of both the important salt merchants and the Yangzhou salt office. Being the head of a wealthy salt-trading family like the Wus was a useful qualification, yet the process of selection seems less direct government appointment than a nudging search for consensus among all concerned parties, merchant and yamen (in Hangzhou, the yamen may have had the greater say). Yet some merchant heads set policies that government officers implemented, and some powerful Wus in Yangzhou seem to have chosen their own successor, another Wu, presumably after negotiating this selection through a variety of deals (*Fengnan zhi*, 6,378). On another occasion two Wu brothers were in turn made heads supposedly on the basis of their independent-minded action to correct administrative abuses and rigorously apply the law and punishments (ibid.).

[125] Puk, *Rise*, Tables 5.1 and 5.2, 145–46.

years outside Huizhou. An increasing number did so permanently from the twentieth generation onward; that is, from roughly the final decades of the fifteenth century, when twenty-one Wus are recorded to have moved away for good (the total for the eight previous generations from the twelfth to the nineteenth had been just seventeen).[126]

Interestingly, these permanent migrants initially settled down in many dispersed destinations (sixty-two places throughout the eastern half of China). Their top nine destinations were Hangzhou (sixteen Wu migrants), Yangzhou (fourteen), Gucheng 谷城 (seven), Linqing (seven), Hanyang garrison (*wei*) (five), Guaixi (five), Guidefu (five), Yizhen (four), and Wuweishou (three). Some of these Wus, like the Taitang Chengs, made a living trading regularly between the middle and lower Yangzi Valley,[127] traveling between delta sites like Songjiang and Nanjing and markets out west in Hubei–Hunan and possibly as far away as Sichuan.[128] Others sojourned at Grand Canal ports all the way from Hangzhou to Linqing in Shandong and on to Beijing. Yet others traded for generations in the smaller markets of north China,[129] and some even spread their sails farther afield, heading northwest into the river valleys of Shanxi or eastward onto the "Eastern Sea."[130] To cite one well-recorded case, a late Ming Wu family firm had men working in its employment in places as disparate as Huizhou, the lower Yangzi delta and Zhejiang (Liangzhe), Yangzhou, Huainan, Beijing, and Tianjin 天津.[131]

Over time a preference for the lower Yangzi delta, the center of the late Ming economy and the salt monopoly trade, became discernible. Whereas before *c*.1500 the Wus' most popular destinations by far were, like the Taitang Chengs', off in the middle Yangzi, at the Xiangyang garrison, and at Gucheng county in Hubei, from the twenty-first generation Yangzhou and its surrounding area begin to be recorded with far greater frequency. Yet only from the twenty-second generation

---

[126] The numbers on Wu migrants derive from information found under the individual Wus listed in their 1602 genealogy.
[127] *Fengnan zhi*, 6, 387. Others practiced lending money inside and outside Huizhou, some succeeding far beyond their expectations (ibid., 6, 383).
[128] Ibid., 6, 354, 355–56, 356, 378. In the late sixteenth century, one Wu died in Sichuan; his involvement in trade there is not made explicit, but his family certainly traded (ibid., 6,380).
[129] Ibid., 6,387.   [130] Ibid., 6, 355–56, 356.
[131] Cheng Yansheng, *Tianqi Huangshan dayu ji*, 43, 49, 50.

are delta cities very commonly listed as destinations,[132] thereby enabling certain quarters (*fang* 坊) of Yangzhou city to become Xi'nan Wu neighborhoods by the eighteenth century (in the way that parts of southern Hubei became virtual colonies for the Taitang Chengs in the late Ming).[133] Nonetheless, no single delta location, even Yangzhou, attained overwhelming domination, and one does not find evidence of their involvement, like the Taitang Chengs, in establishing a regular exchange of goods between the middle and lower Yangzi Valley.

With so many members heading to so many places, the Wus would have found it hard to impose control from a base in Huizhou. Furthermore, that Huizhou base was far from unitary. Until the construction of a "large descent-line ancestral hall" (*dazong ci* 大宗祠) in 1547 the Xi'nan Wus did not build a lineage-wide ancestral hall or one dedicated to its Prime Ancestor or another early ancestral figure.[134] Hitherto (and subsequently), all Ming ancestral halls of the Wus – by 1600 they numbered eight – were built and dedicated by members of one small segment of the lineage to their own more recent ancestors. Wu lineage members admittedly had an "Old House Shrine" (*laowu ci* 老屋祠) for lineage-wide ceremonies, especially rites dedicated to their Prime Ancestor Wu Guang 吳光. But this building was simply Wu Guang's own former residence, and his descendants' use of it did not indicate their success in transforming themselves into a well-organized lineage during the Ming. And so, before 1547, members of virtually all branches and indeed segments of the Xi'nan Wu lineage had no ancestral hall at which they all might assemble, make offerings, and collectively celebrate. At most they had this "Old House Shrine," which by no later than the mid Ming was too small to hold them all for these ceremonies.

---

[132] My rough dating of a generation's emigration relies on dates given for the examination successes by other members of the same generation.
[133] Li Dou, *Yangzhou huafang lu*, 13,296.
[134] *Fengnan zhi*, 2,257–58, and 5,316, 2,257; yet see ibid., 5,316, for mention of this ancestral hall in relation to a 1594 donation. Of the nineteen ancestral halls known to have been built in Xi'nan from the tenth to the twentieth centuries, as many as eight were built in the Ming between c.1505 and 1630, the first in c.1505, the second in 1519, another in either the Zhengde or Jiajing reign, another in the mid sixteenth century, another before 1594, another possibly in the late sixteenth century, another in 1586, and the last no later than 1628.

At first sight, the lineage's branches (*pai*) appear much stronger, having emerged quite early upon the mid-eleventh-century termination of the Wus' "large communal family" arrangements.[135] Their memberships were even described in the thirteenth century as "increasingly numerous."[136] Their power over three institutions that are usually understood to constitute a lineage's collective life and to fall under its administration – the ancestral graves, genealogy, and ancestral hall – grew considerably at the lineage's expense. In 1405, after a series of complaints about lineage members' trespassing on ancestral grave sites, some lineage members set up a pact (*yue*) that banned all trespassing on these sites. Ten years later, after this ban had been repeatedly flouted, the heads of the Xi'nan Wus' branches agreed that henceforth each segment and branch (*zhipai* 支派) was to manage its own ancestral graves. Genealogies likewise suffered some lineage disinterest and detachment; at least six Ming compilations were routinely disparaged for inaccuracy and incompleteness even with Ming entries, as the lineage did not closely supervise the editorial work. Towards the end of the sixteenth century, Wang Daokun (whose mother was a Xi'nan Wu) understandably claimed that among the Xi'nan Wus the primary focus of their kinship relations and affiliation was the branch and not the lineage.[137] Each branch (*men*), he (and she) argued, separately handled its ancestral-worship rituals and other collective ceremonies.[138]

Yet the actual situation of the Xi'nan Wu branches was far more complicated than Wang let on. No branch, and for that matter no segment or sub-segment group, is recorded to have had a charitable landed trust, suggesting a lack of institutional commitment on the part of those seemingly empowered to lead. As already seen, management of the ancestral graves shifted from the lineage to the branches, but initially none of the branches was anxious to assume responsibility for the graves of the first six or seven generations (who were not literally members of these branches, all subsequently formed). And the sole surviving Ming genealogy (that of 1602) shows, in addition to an idiosyncratic understanding of standard lineage terms such as *zong*,

---

[135] *THJ*, 64, 1,332–34.   [136] *Fengnan zhi*, 6,368–69.
[137] *THJ*, 64, 1,332–34. The sole extant Ming edition (1602) suffers similar deficiencies.
[138] Ibid., 71, 1,462–63. Wang Daokun was very knowledgeable about sixteenth-century Huizhou in general and the Xi'nan Wus in particular (his mother had been born into an important Xi'nan Wu family).

fang, pai, and *men,* a rather confusing type of organization, in which segments appear to be accorded more importance than branches (individual male Wus are grouped under the name of an ancestor with an identical branch founder but are constantly subdivided into segments whose relationships are unclear). Thus, as we might expect from a very uneven distribution of wealth among these branches and segments, the Xi'nan Wus appear to have functioned very loosely as a kinship organization. Their low-keyed handling of lineage and branch affairs suggests a large kinship group far from the unified organization disparaged by their rivals for its excessive wealth.

The evidence about the Wus' way of doing business points to the same conclusion. Despite their greater numbers and wealth, these Wus functioned in business like the Fangs of Yuetan: their members usually formed house firms out of small groups of close relations, usually of no larger or wider kinship links than those of the traditional Confucian mourning-rites group (*wufu*). Biographies of individual Wus consistently linked them not with distant biological progenitors (as do biographies of the Yuetan Fangs and especially the Taitang Chengs), but with far more recent "wealth progenitor" kinsmen, usually a father or grandfather.[139] As with the Fangs, the most important kinship relationship to these Wu merchants, then, was the father–son relationship, probably because it was critical to the survival of a house firm in the eventual transmission of its management and ownership powers from one generation to another.

This loose lineage and branch organization was also reflected in the Wus' (and many other Huizhou lineages') pattern of running their house firms. Young Wus would typically follow six to eight years of education in a lineage or village school with an adolescence on the road. They would spend years journeying as apprentices to their father or grandfather, while family matters at home were left to a wife,[140] or even an elder sister (*zi* 姊).[141] Sometimes, the son would quickly assume some responsibility for the family's commercial affairs,[142] perhaps even prompting a father to acknowledge, proudly and encouragingly, his son's superior managerial skills.[143] More often, the son

---

[139] For a singular exception, in which the biographer links the origins of the family's present wealth to the collective efforts of the seven or eight preceding generations, see *Fengnan zhi,* 6,380.
[140] Ibid., 6,377–78.   [141] Ibid., 6,383.   [142] Ibid., 6,372.
[143] Ibid., 6,387. For similar admiration from uncles, see ibid., 6,372.

had to wait until his elder, usually the father, grew tired of his own work and travels. At that point the elder sometimes divided up his business wealth with them and gave them ownership shares; more often, in line with Ming law and general practice, he handed over to his juniors only the reins of management until he died.[144]

Heavy managerial responsibilities would then fall on the firm's operating head, chosen usually by a family's senior generation (typically including the father or, in larger joint family-like commercial operations, a grandfather or even a group of elders). At home the grandfather head (as with the Shanhe Chengs) might call on a grandson to help him supervise a drive to collect funds to build an ancestral hall,[145] or to look after the family and its affairs at home, while two Wus from an older generation continued to manage the family's businesses in Yangzhou and the capital.[146] In even larger house firms the summons to lead might come from a group of elders, who showed no hesitation in determining the career of a Wu lineage junior.[147] But, if only because of short life spans, the order to the young man seems most often to have come directly from the father rather than grandfather, as when the eighteen-year-old Wu Zizhong 吳自重 was told to assume the governance of family matters at home.[148] Behind all of this senior control lay, I suspect, not only the elders' judgment that the young were far too inexperienced to manage the firm's network of connections and commitments, but also the younger-generation members' awareness that they needed these elders' financial and social capital to succeed in the highly capitalized salt trade.[149]

Though successful Wu merchants attracted offers of capital and service from non-kinsmen,[150] offers of capital and support from close

---

[144] Ibid., 6,369–70, 380.
[145] Ibid., 6,351. See another case of a man praised for his making plans to make a living as well as managing the lineage with diligence (ibid., 6, 374).
[146] Ibid., 6,359.   [147] Fang Hongjing, *Suyuan cungao*, 13.32a.
[148] *Fengnan zhi*, 6,372.
[149] Ibid., 6,379, tells of a Huizhou merchant launching his career with inherited wealth, while *THJ*, 53, 1,119–21, tells of a land-based merchant who gave profits acquired from long-distance salt and grain trade in Huaiyin and Kaifeng to brothers engaged in ocean trade.
[150] *Fengnan zhi*, 6,381, and 6,376, which tells of three non-Wu admirers requesting one Wu merchant to join them in trading in a northern part of present Jiangsu province. Another Wu used capital from non-kinsmen merchants, with whom he set up a commercial partnership based on a mutual-aid and credit association, itself modeled on a celebrated eleventh-century community pact (*THJ*, 47, 997).

kin were more appreciated. Support from uncles was particularly valued, as when one uncle acting as a surrogate father took along his nephew to do the trading,[151] looked after his finances for a time,[152] or helped him escape the clutches of the law (by hiding him in a boat that skirted off to Suzhou away from charges of fraud back in Zhejiang).[153] Praise is often accorded brothers who sacrificed to keep their family firm afloat, sharing the profits equally and co-operating even when living and working apart: "They were one mind and one force, ministering to one another like the hands and feet."[154]

Hence, violations of proper relations among close kin received particularly harsh criticism, as when a late sixteenth-century Wu, having been cheated by elder brothers of an equal share to his father's estate, then entrusted over 4,000 taels of his inheritance to an uncle (i.e., his mother's elder brother), who proceeded to waste it and, even after litigation, repaid just 200 taels.[155] Hints of similar abuses are evident in, paradoxically, not criticism but praise. Individual Wus were lavishly extolled by their mid- and late Ming biographers for either their performance of simple virtues – as if they were not normal or as if the deceased had achieved nothing notable – or their avoidance of certain vices – as if these abuses were normal. Men are thus lauded for getting on harmoniously with others, keeping the affairs of a house in order and having all its juniors and seniors follow its rules;[156] for acting kindly to bondservants and not making much of generational and age differences;[157] for not being crafty and deceptive;[158] for not bad-mouthing others;[159] for not speaking disrespectfully, not expressing anger, and not acting violently to others;[160] for not practicing greed in dealing with others;[161] or, in the village, for not coddling up to the powerful when deciding what is right and wrong.[162] In short, despite

---

Proposals for a commercial partnership might be presented in the most unbusinesslike terms: one prospective investor said he was happy to hand over his capital for investment in a Wu's salt trade transactions, so long as this Wu merchant agreed to meet his investor for "high-minded discussions" (*gaoyi* 高議), presumably a euphemism for insider-trading news and other private information on Yangzi Valley markets (*Fengnan zhi*, 6, 376.).

[151] Ibid., 6,376; THJ, 47, 997.   [152] *Fengnan zhi*, 6,378.   [153] Ibid., 6,380.
[154] Ibid.   [155] Ibid., 6,383.
[156] Ibid., 6,369–70. Typically, Wu Yugui is praised for sympathizing with the needy after a bad harvest.
[157] Ibid., 6,368–69.   [158] Ibid., 6,379.   [159] Ibid., 6,372.   [160] Ibid.
[161] Ibid., 6,380.   [162] Ibid., 6,382.

The Wus of Xi'nan

their relative wealth and size, these Xi'nan Wus in their commercial ventures were wrapped up in highly personalized relationships common to house firms far smaller in staff numbers and the range of their operations.

Fortunately for us, the Ming house firm whose operation methods we know most about seems to have been set up and run by a twenty-second-generation Xi'nan Wu in the late sixteenth century.[163] As the third son of a salt merchant, Wu Mianxue 吳勉學 had followed his father into the family business, until he grew bored with its routine and won release from direct paternal control by being adopted by a sonless uncle and soon thereafter inheriting his estate. He then combined earnings from his salt merchant days with this large inheritance (including a sizeable book collection) to launch a commercial publishing house (*shuli* 書隸) that he named the Study That Takes Antiquity as Its Teacher (*shigu zhai* 師古齋). Between 1572 and 1610 it became the most prolific of all Ming commercial publishers, issuing in Huizhou and Nanjing more than 300 titles, many of them already standard best sellers and medical works that it repackaged into collecteana (*congshu* 叢書).[164]

To achieve this impressive publishing list, the firm followed highly flexible management and workforce policies. Even while expanding production, Wu Mianxue kept the staff small and varied its members' tasks and numbers from title to title, often making use of only a small circle of close family members. Sometimes he had his sons and grandsons do the editing. Sometimes he provided the capital and asked them, or others, to do the collating. Sometimes he would reverse this arrangement, doing only the collating himself. And sometimes he would handle all the printing and marketing arrangements (but not the actual carving and printing) and share the editing.[165] On one occasion, after purchasing the carved woodblocks for most of an edition of Sima Guang's *Zizhi tongjian* 資治通鑒 from the Huizhou scholar-official Zhang Yigui 張一桂, he reduced his involvement to mainly printing and marketing. And on other occasions he paid for and managed the production of certain titles, only to sell the woodblocks later on to

---

[163] McDermott, "How to Succeed Commercially as a Huizhou Publisher," 388–99; also *Xin'an Shexi Xi'nan shipu* (1602), 84b.
[164] Zhao Jishi, *Jiyuan jisuo ji*, 11,909.
[165] Fang Weibao and Wang Yingze, *Huizhou gu keshu*, 55.

others.[166] His son would inherit the family firm, carry on successfully printing the titles that had won it fame, and eventually sell off some of its woodblocks to other publishers (who had their name carved into the woodblocks to replace Wu Mianxue's as the edition's collator or compiler). In sum, this house firm lasted just two generations in the same family's hands and when sold off passed into the hands of non-kinsmen to continue as a strictly commercial venture.

Wu's publishing practices – an interest in expensive editions and comprehensive compendia of texts, a preference for books with a relatively large literati demand, the involvement of other kinsmen in his publications and his involvement in theirs, and a publication list that did not seek to rock any authority's boat – all indicate a man experienced in the arts of reducing or buying off competition and co-opting rivals and potential troublemakers. In other words, he can be seen as deploying in the world of commercial publishing some of the tactics he and his ancestors would have naturally learned from their years of trading in the mass market for salt: play to one's strengths (capital, control over the supply of the commodity, and connections in Nanjing's and Huizhou's markets) and avoid potentially risky diversions (such as experimenting with new genres and opening up new markets elsewhere). It is also possible to see these skills as extensions of the political and social lessons that the Wus would have collectively learned from their lineage's and families' much older experience in forming extensive alliances with Huizhou locals, mainly kinsmen, to dominate their village in the highly competitive Huizhou countryside. To that extent, the political success of the Wu lineage in dominating Xi'nan would have helped to lay the basis for Wu Mianxue's exceptional success as a commercial publisher. One is forced to wonder if those of his kinsmen who served as Libationer in Yangzhou and Hangzhou salt merchant circles likewise drew upon their family's experiences in the Huizhou countryside.

The Long-Lasting House Firm, as a Business and as a Kinship Group

Small-scale operations, organizational flexibility, and unadventuresome taste seem then to have characterized this and probably other

---

[166] Xu Xuelin, *Huizhou keshu*, 84–88.

successful house firms of the Xi'nan Wus. Yet the very looseness of this lineage's or even its branches' control over their members assured a diversity in the form of its members' organizations, especially those small-scale units which survived for three or more generations to become significantly wealthier and larger house firms. The trajectory of one such Xi'nan Wu group located within its dominant branch shows how such a segment could evolve over six generations from the late fifteenth century to the early seventeenth into another type of house firm – far richer, larger, and more politically active – and how it could seek to translate its wealth and power into extensive reforms in lineage arrangements back home in Xi'nan.[167]

The founding father of this segment was Wu Zuren 吳祖仁 (twentieth generation), in many ways an archetypical early Ming founder of a trading dynasty. Starting off with mainly his wife's dowry (it could only have been small), he peddled his way to riches in the Yangzi Valley. Overcoming unspecified dangers and obstacles during his travels in the delta, he eventually acquired enough capital to arrange his brothers' marriages and to help them in their trading. As a result, his family's property was considered "prominent in the entire rural district." His sole son, Wu Chongshu 吳崇恕 (twenty-first generation) climbed another rung or two up the ladder of commercial success by concentrating on commodity trading in the northeast quarter of the delta (probably textiles) as well as in Shandong (probably including Linqing). As his trading prospered, his own earnings reportedly came to surpass the size of the fortune bequeathed him by his ancestors. The career of his son Wu Shangyang 吳尚瑩 (twenty-second generation) marked the family's first significant entry into both the world of Confucian education and the salt trade at Yangzhou.

His own son Wu Zhengxue 吳正學 (twenty-third generation) got no farther into officialdom than a brief stay at the National University, but he achieved far greater success in the salt trade than had his ancestors. He even distributed his earnings of some 100,000 taels among his younger brothers, thus helping to assure that his sons' generation would be three times larger than his generation (that is, male offspring in the twenty-fourth generation numbered twenty-nine sons, representing a nearly threefold increase in the lineage's male membership).

[167] Zheng Zhenman, "Yangtian," 10–18; plus *Xin'an Shexi Xi'nan Wushi shipu* (1602 ed.), 40b–42a.

In this next generation, Wu Guangyue 吳光岳 followed his father and elder brothers into the Yangzhou salt business, making sure that his own sons all mastered the family business and "the art of the abacus." The eldest of these three sons, Wu Gongjin (twenty-fifth generation, 1555–1624), extended the firm's success in salt trading and assured that his sons and grandsons all acquired the education increasingly considered desirable for success in this line of business. His high standing in Yangzhou's salt circles was confirmed when the salt merchants there backed his promotion to the post of Libationer. In short, over the course of six generations this segment of Xi'nan Wus had formed a family business that had mounted the commercial ladder of success from peddler to typical house firm to top salt merchant, all the time not acquiring the examination degrees that many judged essential for a family's success. In fact, the Xi'nan Wus' top success in the Ming examination circus would end up as their most dangerous member in one of the great scandals of the late Ming.

At no time is the means of this salt monopoly success ever described or divulged. Indeed, the lineage's own sources discuss this success principally as a "modernizing" challenge to the inward-looking practices of the lineage and most of its branches. The twenty-fifth generation of this segment of the Xi'nan Wus had thirty-seven males in the late sixteenth century, thus outnumbering the membership of Yuetan Fangs' predominant branch at its largest size. More significantly, this group pushed for a two-pronged set of "modernizing reforms": greater lineage centralization at the expense of other segments and the expansion of its links to other Wus in Huizhou and beyond. At this time these aims were not novel, as these men were doubtless made aware of such centralizing moves by the increasing popularity of ancestral halls throughout Huizhou and the rest of south China. Also, in Huizhou, Yangzhou, and other cities they would have encountered other Wus, with whom they quite likely would have desired to cultivate closer ties. Just as efforts to expand connections to powerful people outside one's place of residence would have been part of the common sense of men who spent most of their life away from home in search of profitable deals,[168] so were these goals of lineage reform commonly espoused by powerful groups within the highly competitive world of Ming Huizhou

---

[168] See Chapter 3's account of Huizhou merchants' collusion and corruption scandals.

lineages. Even the terms with which they practiced their lineage politics – graves, genealogies, ancestral halls, and landownership – constituted the lingua franca of Huizhou's village politics.

First, in 1547 four of this segment's members, greatly enriched by three generations of salt monopoly profits, called out for the construction of a "large descent-line ancestral hall (*dazong ci*)." They deliberately signaled their wish for this hall to have a much wider and more inclusive membership, by dedicating it not to a recent ancestor (as had been common with the previous ancestral halls) but to the Xi'nan Wus' commonly accepted Prime Ancestor, Wu Guang, plus two other of its ancestral sages, Wu Xiaowei 吳少微 (the first Wu to have moved into Huizhou prefecture (in neighboring Xiuning county) in the late Tang) and to Zhou Taibo 周泰伯.[169] This hall proved popular enough to last until the twentieth century, doubtless because it opened its doors to all Xi'nan Wus, many of them excluded from the village's other ancestral halls except for the "Old House." In other words, this segment spearheaded its branch's move to lead the lineage.

Second, this same segment started to act like the textbook lineage. It succeeded in buying and owning part or all of the grave sites of the first eight generations of the Xi'nan Wu males (and some of their wives) back to Wu Guang and claimed both the right and the responsibility to maintain their upkeep. In 1405 the Xi'nan Wu lineage had discovered that despite their setting up grave guardians in 1388, lineage and non-lineage members had encroached on and sold off ancestral grave sites, including Wu Guang's. After further encroachments on its burial sites, the lineage in 1415 let three of its branches dig a total of eight graves at four of its sites but banned any transfer and further sale of these sites' plots and other land. A century and a half later, upon noting a bondservant's transgression of this pact, it sold off in 1541 all but two other grave sites at Wu Guang's burial place and then in 1581 it sold off about half of Wu Guang's own grave. The buyer in both instances was the very segment anxious to set up the lineage's comprehensive ancestral hall, known commonly as the Zhou Taibo Ancestral Hall. In 1562 this hall, having assumed tax responsibility for the grave sites of the first eight generations of Xi'nan Wus, donated sixteen *mu* of fields to "a grave sacrifice household (*muji hu* 墓祭户)," essentially a legal trust that henceforth was to pay these graves' and fields' taxes

---

[169] *Fengnan zhi*, 2, 257; Zheng Zhenman, "Yangtian," 13.

from its fields' annual rents.[170] Having acquired these graves and thus the control of access to the Xi'nan Wus' most venerable ancestors, this segment strengthened its claim to be the leader of most branches and lineage members. Third, the same segment also was intimately involved in the editing of the lineage's genealogy of 1514. Since the 1514 edition does not survive, this segment's impact on compilation practices is evident mainly from surviving prefaces of this and other editions which reveal a protracted debate among the Xi'nan Wus about their proper line of descent and thus their genealogies' contents and their memberships.

This 1514 genealogy's compilers took a very expansive view of the lineage's membership and the identity of its Prime Ancestor. In the mid thirteenth century, the influential neo-Confucian scholar Cheng Yuanfeng 程元風 (1200–1269) of She county first cast doubt on the Xi'nan Wus' belief that they descended from the mid-ninth-century figure Wu Guang.[171] Thereafter, some prefaces to the 1321 genealogy shared his skepticism, while others in the succeeding 1371, 1397, and 1486 genealogies reclaimed Wu Guang as their Prime Ancestor. Then the 1514 preface radically cast doubt on this conventional wisdom,[172] asserting that the Xi'nan Wus' actual Prime Ancestor was a certain Zhou Taibo and that the supposed Prime Ancestor, Wu Guang, was merely their Prime Migrant, "the man who first moved to Xi'nan."

To many Xi'nan Wus these changes would have seemed unwarranted, and the new choice for Prime Ancestor highly arbitrary.[173] The new Prime Ancestor was not even surnamed Wu; he was simply the first king of the very ancient Kingdom of Wu 吳, from which the

---

[170] *Shexi Xi'nan Wushi xianyang zhipu*, *shizu*, 7a–17a; second generation 11b (1644), third generation 4a (1572), fourth generation 4a (1581), fifth generation 6b (1581), sixth generation 2b (1572), seventh generation 9a (1589), eighth generation 11a (1581). The date given for each generation indicates the earliest-found confirmation of the Zhou Taibo (or Comprehensive) Ancestral Hall as owner of the members' grave site in the attached documentation, even though this ancestral hall's land purchases in 1547 or 1581 surely contained these grave sites.

[171] *Xin'an Shexi Xi'nan Wushi shipu* (1747 ed.), 1325 preface by Wu Mu 吳沐.

[172] Ibid. (1602 ed.), prefaces section.

[173] This branch's arrogance surely aroused hostility among other branches, and may well be related to the 1572 destruction by one Xin'an Wu faction of three stone steles set up by another faction (*Shexi Xi'nan Wushi xianyang zhipu*, qishi zu bi, 10a–b). This incident attracted much attention, including a county magistrate's ruling and a detailed written report, apparently no longer extant.

surname Wu supposedly derived.[174] He had lived more than 2,000 years earlier at the start of the Zhou dynasty (eleventh century BC–BC 222). He had no personal connection with Xi'nan, She county, or anywhere else in Huizhou. And, though known to most other Wu lineages in Huizhou, he was just part of their surname's ancient history and not their lineages' apical Prime Ancestor. The most common Prime Ancestor for Huizhou Wus, as reported in two late Ming historical surveys of Huizhou lineages, was the late Tang official Wu Xiaowei, supposedly the first of Zhou Taibo's descendants to have moved to Huizhou in the late Tang.[175]

But that very arbitrariness made Taibo attractive to some other Xi'nan Wus. Indeed, the practice of compiling "same-surname genealogies" (*tongpu* 通譜) was, according to Gu Yanwu, very common in seventeenth-century China, "invariably with the aim of setting up cliques for their selfish interests."[176] A descent line that traced back not just half a millennium to 860 but two and a half millennia earlier to the tenth century BC vastly expanded the Xi'nan Wus' prospects as a great lineage, if only because it greatly enlarged the ranks of their potential membership. Forget the extended history of the Wus in Huizhou, for by adopting and acting on the ancient concepts of a descent line (*zong*) and same-surname linkage, these Xi'nan Wus could adopt Taibo as their Prime Ancestor and thereby open their lineage/ branch hall to include men surnamed Wu outside the Xi'nan Wus' traditional descent line. In rethinking their lineage's history and meaning these Wus were thinking big. They could now form meaningful ties, real or fictive, with other Wu lineages, so long as they all were willing to consider Zhou Taibo as their shared Prime Ancestor. Having a common ancestor, especially one so apical and royal, enabled different Wu lineages and families to find a shared interest, perform collective ancestral rituals, and even form business ties with one another. They essentially could establish and carry out a loose alliance, in which

---

[174] *Xin'an Shexi Xi'nan Wushi shipu* (1602 ed.), prefaces, 1515 preface; *Xin'an Shexi Xi'nan Wushi shipu* (1747 ed.), 1325 preface by Wu Mu.

[175] *Xin'an mingzu zhi*, hou, 366–415; and *Xiuning mingzu zhi*, 3, 401–96. The Xi'nan Wus do not appear in the first attempted survey of Huizhou's lineages by the Yuan figure Chen Dingyu (*Xin'an liuxian mingzu zhi*, shang, 36).

[176] Gu Yanwu, *Rizhi lu jishi*, 23, 809, 811. The custom of forming same-surname alliances was more common in north rather than south China, where kinship alliances were commonly based on lineage ties.

they could deal with one another as "brothers" or "relations" in the manner described for the Fangs and Chengs. The fact that these newcomers would have probably sided with their welcoming patron and thus strengthened this segment's position within the Xi'nan Wu lineage went without saying.

Nor was mention made of the potentially great number of these new lineage members. The line of descent from Zhou Taibo, as recorded in a special "outer genealogy" (*waipu* 外譜) section of the Xi'nan Wus' genealogy of 1602, includes Wus from throughout the lower and middle Yangze Valley, from Zhejiang, Hunan, Jiangxi, and Anhui provinces. In theory, this scheme would have greatly increased the number of other Wus eligible, in accord with neo-Confucian practice, for sharing ancestral worship and for forming close ties in these very same parts of the empire where the Xi'nan Wus were heavily involved in the salt trade. In other words, in Ming Huizhou a commercial lineage group was anxious to form alliances not simply with those in their own county or prefecture (in the manner of the popular cults and their shrines in the Song or even of the early lineage groups in the Yuan and early Ming) but also with others in distant parts of the empire where their own members may have migrated or found people surnamed Wu with whom they would have wished to deal regularly. Hence the lineage, a form of organization commonly criticized by modern Chinese as highly exclusive and restrictive, was to be transformed here by some of these sixteenth-century Wus into an institution flexible enough to admit same-surname parties interested in pursuing collective interests on grounds hard for the Ming government to criticize. Once again, Ming Huizhou men had found ways to circumvent seemingly insurmountable obstacles to their practice of trade, all within acceptable Confucian institutions and without need for native-place associations.

To these men there was no irreconcilable contradiction between these different policies of centralized power at home and expansion abroad. They were trying to create a much stronger, more centralized lineage for their development of a network of same-surname groups outside their village and its lineages as well as to make their home base of kinsmen more attractive to a potential network of allies elsewhere.

What, then, is the significance of this wealthy segment's involvement in these institutional changes? Clearly, they wanted an ancestral hall, ostensibly not just for themselves but also for all men bearing their surname inside and outside Huizhou (they possibly were legitimizing already-existing trade and other links). And, as these reformers were full-time salt merchants mainly based in Yangzhou, it is hard to avoid concluding that they wanted this at least partly to expand their commercial network and even their access to these other Wus' capital (recall the use of ancestral-hall funds for relatively cheap loans, and the push by some ancestral halls for donations from new members wishing to enjoy the "effectiveness" (*ling* 靈) of the hall's ancestors).

And yet not all Xi'nan Wus were of a like mind. While they did not oppose their lineage's replacement of their village worship association as their village's most powerful institution, they were not yet willing to give up their distinct territorial identity for an empire-building myth of fictitious descent ties. Hence, I suspect, we have their repeated reference to other Wus by the place of their residence, the admission in one seventeenth-century biography that this scheme had never been carried out, and the 1602 genealogy's inclusion of the pre-Wu Guang ancestors in a special "outer genealogy." The "reformers," however, had different ideas. They wished to extend their success in ways that few of their forebears had carefully considered. Though that vision now became the theoretical basis for forming an empire-wide network of shared kinship and interests – that is, a syndicate of Wus – so far no genealogy I have examined for a Wu lineage in Yangzhou, Huizhou or elsewhere confirms the formal establishment of such a wide linkup.

The Mt Huang Disaster

To understand how a large syndicate house firm operated, we turn at last to the most ill-fated segment of the Xi'nan Wus in Ming times. By the 1620s this house firm was well into its fourth generation of success as salt merchants. Begun by Wu Shouli 吳守禮 and expanded by his son Wu Shizuo 吳時佐, this segment was affiliated with the Shijian Ancestral Hall 師儉祠 (commonly called the Two Gate Ancestral Hall 兩門祠).[177] By the late sixteenth century the family firm, headed by Wu Yangchun 吳養春 (1543–1626) had become very wealthy.[178] The dispersal of his enterprises throughout the eastern half of central

---

[177] *Fengnan zhi*, 2,258 and 5,316.
[178] Ibid., 6,358–59 (biography of Wu Yangdu). This brother of Wu Yangchun, while his father was busy in Beijing and grandfather in Yangzhou, supervised administration of the family at home and subsequently took little part in the

China confirms that at least one Wu house firm spread its business investments and operations far beyond the salt merchant hothouse of Yangzhou by marrying its private wealth to the emoluments of government office.

The private and public resources that Wu Yangchun thereby marshaled to run his firm's network were exceptionally large and diverse.[179] First, he (and it) boasted considerable wealth, inherited and personally acquired. The heir to at least two generations of great wealth from the salt trade, he himself ran a very successful business, based on salt and timber, that stretched seven hundred miles from Huizhou and Hangzhou in the south to Beijing and Tianjin in the north. In between, he had men looking after his interests in Nanjing, Hangzhou, Yangzhou, the Huai region, and Linqing. At home in Huizhou he "occupied" no fewer than 2,400 *mu* of mountain land on Mt Huang, whose timber had over the years enriched him to the tune of several hundred thousand taels. And, when one adds his landed property outside Huizhou to his liquid assets – assessed incompletely in 1627 at over 936,000 taels[180] – his total assets would have far exceeded 1,000,000 taels and thus, according to an estimate of 1609, qualified him and his family for admission into the richest merchant circles of late Ming Huizhou.[181]

Second, he and his entourage enjoyed very close ties with the Ming government. Not only did he work as a merchant in the government's salt monopoly trade, and not only did several fellow Xi'nan Wu salt merchants gain appointment as Libationer in Yangzhou and Hangzhou, but also he was an official thanks to his grandfather's sizeable donation to the Ming government. In 1594 Wu Shouli gave it 300,000 taels (officially to help repel the Japanese invasion of Korea and repair three imperial palaces seriously damaged by recent fires); in return he received an official title and appointment, as did five of his descendants, including Wu Yangchun.[182] The salt merchant Wu Yangchun

operation of the house firm. He reportedly showed little interest in property matters.

[179] This account of the Mt Huang disaster draws upon Cheng Yansheng, *Tianqi Huangshan dayu ji*, 43, 49, 50; *Fengnan zhi*, 10,580–82; and Yang Liwei et al., *Huizhou daxing*, 153–55.
[180] Shen Guoyuan, *Liangchao congxin lu*, 31.12a–b.
[181] *She zhi* (1609), 20, *huozhi*, 1a–3a.
[182] *Fengnan zhi*, 5,316. Apart from the son Wu Shiwei (who, and whose heirs, acquired no degree), the pattern of the distribution of these degrees suggests

thus became an official (*guan*) with all the attendant privileges, his official position, like that of one brother, being the titular post of Secretary of the Palace of Art (*wenyi dian zhongshe ren* 文藝殿中舍人).[183] Such a prestigious title conferred scant authority in dynastic matters. But one member of the Wu lineage,[184] Wu Kongjia 吳孔嘉 (1587–1667), who was quite close to Wu Yangchun, did rise swiftly to high official power through conventional means. Having passed the local and the provincial examinations, he gained the metropolitan examination degree in 1625. Ranked third in the palace exams, he won a highly prestigious appointment to a committee of officials entrusted with the sensitive task of compiling a history of the present and two previous reigns.

Wu Kongjia enjoyed this uncommon official success largely due to the largesse and patronage of Wu Yangchun. Wu Kongjia, when young, had lost his father, and thereafter he and his widowed mother had received living and education support from Wu Yangchun in the manner of a rich uncle caring for a needy nephew. In addition, Wu Kongjia's very high rank in the palace exams was secured through his patron Wu Yangchun's payment of 50,000 taels to the eunuch boss Wei Zhongxian 魏忠賢, then dominating both the inner and outer courts in Beijing and pushing to spread his power throughout the country. Wu Kongjia may have reciprocated his Huizhou patron at home by becoming a supporter of the She county native-place hall in Beijing, by requesting the court to set up special examination registers for Huizhou merchants in Hangzhou, and by writing a preface for the collected writings of an ancestor of Wu Yangchun.[185] And when he was appointed to a high editorial post on the court's committee to draft parts of sources used eventually for the dynasty's history, it must have

---

that a degree was intended for each son of Wu Shouli, or, if a son was deceased, to one of his own sons or, if necessary, grandsons. The grant of one of these degrees to Wu Xiyuan in the Wu Zuren segment, however, suggests a close tie between these two groups of kinsmen despite their membership in different ancestral halls (ibid.).

[183] Ibid.; *Xin'an Shexi Xi'nan Wushi shipu* (1602), 42a–b, 59a.
[184] Ibid., 84b, Wu Kongjia, 24th generation; 59a, Wu Yangchun, 25th generation.
[185] *SSXT*, 10,346; *Fengnan zhi*, 6,283. The preface was for collected writings of Wu Shouhuai (c.1523–c.1587), the granduncle of Wu Yangchun's father (1603, 58b), a serial exam failure and a literati-collector who borrowed regularly from the pawnbroker-literatus Fang Yongbin (Chen Chizhao, *Mingdai Huizhou Fangshi*, v. 1, 423, and v. 2, 625–26).

seemed as if the Xi'nan Wus had reached the pinnacle of Ming social and political success. But Wu Kongjia's willingness to become Wei Zhongxian's adopted son, signaling a shift of his allegiance and alliance, should have set off alarm bells down in Huizhou. The stage was set for when Wu Kongjia had to choose between his two patrons, his would-be uncle or his adopted father in a battle between his lineage and political obligations.

Third, Wu Yangchun enjoyed extensive connections in other official and cultural circles. In forging ties with court officials and local gentry, he adopted the wealthy scholar-official practice of setting set up a private publishing studio that printed books he could distribute to his scholarly friends (between 1589 and 1616 it had issued at least seven titles).[186] And, although he was denounced for barring others from collecting firewood on his Mt Huang land, Wu Yangchun nonetheless kept good ties with local literati by supporting monks on Mt Huang. In particular, he helped the Buddhist monk Pumen 普門, a favorite of Huizhou's literati and gentry, open up Mt Huang's paths and peaks for the construction of Buddhist temples. Eventually, he contributed to one such temple's construction.[187]

Fourth, to help him manage this commercial and political network he kept a group of agents and "sons," or "men" (nanzi 男子), at least twelve of whom we know by name. Four of these twelve were registered fellow Xi'nan Wu lineage members, and one had commended himself (touxia 投下) to Wu Yangchun and become his bondservant. Quite different were those "sons" like Cheng Menggeng 程夢庚 (aka Cheng Menglong 程夢龍). Described in official reports as a briber of officials in Huizhou and Yangzhou, Cheng was also a member of a very wealthy family in a distinguished Xiuning lineage.[188] He had studied long enough to become a licentiate, his elder brother had become a high court official in the Chancellory, and his father had served as the Deputy Director of the Court of Imperial Entertainments (Guanglu si 光祿寺), and in 1626, when making his Beijing bribery rounds for Wu Yangchun, Cheng Menggeng himself had made contact with as eminent an official as the notorious Grand Secretary Feng

---

[186] Xu Xuelin, Huizhou keshu, 70–73. These highly orthodox titles included the complete works of Zhu Xi and general anthologies of orthodox Confucian and literati writings.
[187] Min Linsi, Huangshan zhi dingben, 2.67b–68a.
[188] Wang Yuming, "Ming Qing fenjia kuishu," 94, 96–97.

The Mt Huang Disaster

Chuan 馮銓.[189] In addition to benefiting from all their father's official connections, Cheng Menggeng and his three brothers inherited several pawnshops and total liquid assets of over 790,000 taels of silver (a sum nearly equal to the total sum of all the other estates listed in a recent survey of twenty pawnbroker wills drawn up between 1588 and 1894). In short, Cheng Menggeng was as rich and as well-connected an agent and fixer as Wu Yangchun could have wanted. The reach of his bribes through Ming officialdom shows how high this segment of the Xi'nan Wus had risen and how widely and deeply its wealth and connections cut through the ranks of Huizhou's commercial and Beijing's political elite. Adoption had long been a way for unrelated males to bind themselves into very close ties, and Wu Yangchun (like Wei Zhongxian) seems to have employed it widely to spread and secure his commercial entanglements. Though not a member of the segment or even the branch of Xi'nan Wus which had dreamt up the expansion scheme of a grand Wu alliance, Wu Yangchun clearly had similar ambitions for his family.

Finally, when Wu Yangchun was seriously challenged, he showed few reservations about using his resources to defend himself and eliminate his opponents. To the extent we can trust the reams of malicious gossip about him in contemporary writings, it seems that his downfall resulted from a vicious domestic quarrel first with a younger brother, Wu Yangze 吳養澤, over family property and then with other family members, that transgressed those relationships – "father–son" and uncle–nephew – considered significant in other Huizhou lineages' commercial success. When this younger brother Wu Yangze pressed legal charges against Wu Yangchun for his unequal division of the family estate, Wu Yangchun counterattacked ruthlessly. In addition to using his fortune to win this case in the courts, he reportedly had others kill off this brother, poison his seven year-old son, and seize several tens of thousands of taels of his wealth.[190] He also is said to have had others kill off another relation, taking care to conceal his involvement.[191] To these domestic crimes, he added a more public infraction: his illegal occupation of 2,400 *mu* of Mt Huang and its forests and the removal of them from government land registers.

---

[189] Zhao Chengzhong, "Huangshan yuanan," 31. Wu Yangchun's grandfather Wu Shouli 吳守禮 had held an honorary appointment at the Court of Imperial Entertainments. Hummel, *Eminent Chinese, v. 1*, 240–41, on Feng Chuan.
[190] Cheng Yansheng, *Tianqi Huangshan*, 44.   [191] Ibid.

His family had for generations held property on Mt Huang – not for nothing did the Wus call it "family property" (*jiachan* 家產) – and without authorization he had hired men to fell its timber for huge profits.[192]

When news reached Wu Yangchun, still active in his eighties, that officials were once again considering the government's confiscation of trees from Mt Huang for use in rebuilding imperial palaces, he set his network in motion. He dispatched a family servant, Wu Wenjie 吳文節, to Beijing with instructions to his representatives there to nip this idea in the bud. Stopping at Tianjin to pick up his kinsman, Wu Junshi 吳君實, Wu Wenjie proceeded to Beijing, armed with 30,000 taels to provide his master's representatives in Beijing with sufficient funds to halt any move against his interests.

At this point in a drama worthy of Shakespeare, things started to go seriously awry for Wu Yangchun and the Xi'nan Wus. For, when Wu Yangchun's agent Wu Wenjie arrived at the Beijing home of the lineage's rising star Wu Kongjia, he was met by a bête noir of his master. Wu Rong 吳榮 was a discredited bondservant and ex-business associate (*huoji* 夥計) of Wu Kongjia's deceased father. A few years earlier he had been jailed at Wu Yangchun's insistence for embezzlement of his ex-master's property and abuse of a concubine, charges apparently drummed up by Wu Yangchun to shut him up and prevent him from identifying Wu Yangchun as his master's murderer. Yet, somehow, Wu Rong had weaseled his way out of prison, and when he saw Wu Wenjie ready to ply his trade of bribery in Beijing, his desire for revenge intensified. Privately, he "spat out" to Wu Kongjia startling revelations about his surrogate father Wu Yangchun, claiming that Wu Yangchun's aid to Wu Kongjia and his mother had been a fraud and intended simply to disguise his involvement in the death – nay, murder – of Wu Kongjia's father.

Wu Kongjia was highly susceptible to such claims, as he had long been troubled by his father's early death. When young, he had sought refuge from family difficulties in a Mt Huang temple, where in six years of solitary study he had never spoken to others. The monks remembered him principally for brushing onto the walls of his room and into the pages of his notebooks a single Chinese character, that for "death" (*si* 死).[193]

---

[192] Ibid., 13–14, 41–42, 44; Zhao Chengzhong, "Huangshan yuanan," 30–33.
[193] Cheng Yansheng, *Tianqi Huangshan*, 35.

And when he passed the palace examinations so handsomely in 1625, he was drawn into the web of the eunuch boss Wei Zhongxian, who soon promoted him and formally adopted him as his "son." Thus, in the second half of 1626, the revelation to Wu Kongjia that Wu Yangchun had reportedly murdered his father steeled his decision to pass on the charge of murder to his new "father," along with other charges that the evil Wu Yangchun had bribed officials to shelve an earlier official's report calling for government confiscation of half of his (that is, Wu Yangchun's) Mt Huang property, that he held huge stocks of timber from this illicit Mt Huang property, and that he was still bribing officials to get his way in official deliberations, most recently through agents based in Beijing.[194] This news unleashed a series of court attacks on Wu Yangchun, that Wu Kongjia doubtless knew would damage not only Wu Yangchun but also his family, branch, and lineage, all of them dependent on good relations with the Ming government for their wealth. Yet so fierce was his hatred and remorse, that whatever the cost to himself, his family, and his lineage, the filial son Wu Kongjia now acted to wreak revenge on his duplicitous patron.

In the sixth lunar month of 1626 the emperor passed judgment on all the reports Wei Zhongxian had privately passed on to him about these Huizhou matters: he ordered the arrest of Wu Yangchun, two of his sons, and no fewer than twelve accomplices implicated by the charges; the seizure of an estimated 300,000 taels of past profits from the sale of Mt Huang timber; and the return to government registers and ownership of some 2,400 fiscal *mu* of forested land that Wu Yangchun had occupied on Mt Huang.[195] Three months later Wu Yangchun himself was arrested. Thinking that he still could buy his way out of his troubles, he arrived in Beijing little realizing that he would instead be thrown into jail, brutally cross-questioned and tortured, and treated as a supporter of Wei Zhongxian's archenemy, the Donglin 東林 faction.[196]

Wei Zhongxian's subsequent dispatch of two government delegations to Huizhou, however, proved a gross political misjudgment, with disastrous consequences for all parties, including the Xi'nan Wus.

---

[194] Ibid., 11–14.   [195] Ibid., 16–17.
[196] Ibid., 15–21. Wu Yangchun had committed the unforgiveable offense of establishing in Huizhou a private academy, just when Wei Zhongxian was ordering the destruction of all such private educational establishments throughout the empire.

Late in 1626 these Beijing interrogators and their entourages arrived in Huizhou, where in confiscating Wu Yangchun's wealth and digging up further incriminating evidence against him, they acted as if they were reclaiming not just Mt Huang but the entire prefecture. In the last lunar month of 1626, Lü Xiawen 呂下問, Wei Zhongxian's lackey as Director in the Ministry of Public Works, received an order to press the Wus for over 300,000 taels, an additional 600,000 taels, and the arrest of eight men. Claiming powers to search wherever they wished, they barged into the homes of Huizhou families unconnected with Wu Yangchun's crimes and activities. They raped and plundered with impunity, demanding from the prefecture 20,000 taels as surcharges. Soon, the delegated representatives of this eunuch tyrant found themselves attacked on the streets and chased out of the prefecture by huge mobs composed of far more surname groups than just the Wus.[197]

Initially, Wei Zhongxian's raiders plundered some 6,000 taels from Wu Yangchun's sons,[198] recovered 85,000 additional taels estimated to be Wu Yangchun's long-term profits from illicit sales of Mt Huang timber and from the value of the confiscated sites,[199] and took some of the Wu family's salt trade profits held in Huizhou.[200] But they so mishandled the auction of the confiscated forest land on Mt Huang – one bidder at the auction purchased far more of Wu Yangchun's confiscated acreage than officially allowed[201] – that an official sent after Wei Zhongxian's downfall and death recommended the return of any unsold land to the family of Wu Yangchun as compensation for its losses.[202] There is no evidence that such a request was ever carried out. But the new magistrate of She county (exceptionally, a native of another Huizhou county) successfully petitioned for the return to the Wus of 320,000 taels plus 57,000 more taels as compensation for their losses.

Meanwhile, with the death of the Tianqi emperor and subsequently the enforced suicide of Wei Zhongxian in Beijing in 1627, Wu Kongjia lost his court patrons and official appointment. Demoted to the status of "commoner," he returned in disgrace to Xi'nan, where he passed the remaining forty years of his life mainly in a garden owned by another member of the lineage. During the Manchu conquest of Huizhou he earned the gratitude of some kinsmen by twice leaving this seclusion to

[197] Ibid., 22–28.   [198] *Yanzhen zhicao*, 126.   [199] Ibid., 124.
[200] Ibid., 126.   [201] Ibid., 123.   [202] Ibid., 127.

persuade conquering commanders to bypass Xi'nan and not distress several hundreds of its women. Nonetheless, after he died, some fellow Wus barred the admission of his spirit tablet into their ancestral hall, thus forcing other Wus to build a separate shrine for their offerings to him.[203]

Wu Yangchun's bête noir Wu Rong faced an even more unsettled end. Initially shielded by a gentry family in the Beijing area, he was hounded out by a Yangzhou official, who had him arrested and secretly returned to Yangzhou for cross-questioning. When Wu Rong made no effort to conceal his whole story, this official spent two successive nights writing up a report on his crimes. Who would have guessed that before this report had left the Yangzhou yamen, orders would arrive from the Ministry of Justice in Beijing to have Wu Rong return to the capital for yet more questioning? Wu Rong was thus sent off, to a fate unmentioned in the Chinese record.[204]

So much for the high-stakes political drama and the family tragedy. Collusion here has progressed to outright corruption, involving the highest ranks of Ming commercial and political life. Yet what interests us most about this tale is less its immoral incandescence than its revelations about Wu Yangchun's network and its operations. As one of the wealthiest Wus of his generation, he had no fewer than fourteen agents and managers, identified in official reports as his "sons," working for him in the capital and in salt-producing sites scattered about east China from Hangzhou northward – including Yangzhou, Huai, and Tianjin.[205] For a time in 1626 some of these men left their offices to seek refuge from Wei Zhongxian's men in seaside towns. But normally, apart from looking after Wu Yangchun's business interests, they are depicted as working as his "bag men"; that is, as the deliverers of his money from one site to another, usually to bribe officials, to smooth the advance of his business interests.

We have also seen how at home the Wus for long tolerated a very loose form of lineage and branch management, in which house firms

---

[203] *Fengnan zhi*, 10,587; Dong Jian, *Ziran*, 33. Another possible public act by Wu Kongjia to recover respect from his lineage came in 1633, when a lineage member named Wu Kongjia donated one tael to protect the grave site of an eighth-generation member of the Xi'nan Wus (*Shexi Xi'nan Wushi xianyang zhipu, bashi zu*, 13b).
[204] Zhao Chengzhong, "Huangshan yuanan," 33.
[205] Shen Guoyuan, *Liangchao congxin lu*, 33.7b.

carved out their fortunes without direct supervision by their branch or lineage. Left out of this analysis, of course, is whatever cross-funding was made by members of other Xi'nan Wus' segments, branches, or house firms. But such channeling of capital would probably have occurred more often after certain centralizing reforms had been undertaken within the Wus by more wealthy members in search of further capital as well as a secure base from which to court new members, including those with just a common-surname connection. Not all these reforms lasted. By no later than 1602 earlier efforts to count the lineage's generations from Zhou Taibo had ceased and been replaced with the pre-sixteenth-century practice of counting from their now reconfirmed Prime Ancestor Wu Guang; even so, its editors accorded the "outer genealogy," with the pre-Wu Guang descent line back to Zhou Taibo, pride of place at the start of the 1602 genealogy.

The Wus who survived the domestic and dynastic debacles of the 1620s–1640s lived on into the Qing, eking out a far more "cramped" life.[206] Not long after the fall of the Ming a certain Wu Erxiang 吳爾襄 tried to revive the family's fortune by trading in Jiangxi and then in Hankou, where he was appointed Libationer for the salt trade. By the century's end, when the Qing had restored the salt monopoly and certain families like the Wus had retained their hereditary rights to membership in salt trade syndicates, some Wus eventually resumed their privileged place in Yangzhou's salt monopoly trading. But, more than in the Ming, an increasing number of Wus, like the Taitang Chengs, the Shanhe Chengs, and many other Huizhou lineages, left their home village in Huizhou for good.[207] Unlike these two Cheng lineages, the Xi'nan Wus won more examination degrees in the Qing dynasty than in the Ming, and some even enjoyed official careers at court.[208] Nonetheless, the focus of the Xi'nan Wus' economic activities remained down in Yangzhou and other rich towns and cities of the Yangzi delta, where they settled permanently and where their profits by and large remained. Even though the place where they lived and worked gradually came to mean more to them than the place where their ancestors had been buried centuries ago, they and their commercial descendants were still known as Xi'nan Wus and Huizhou merchants. Less involved in lineage matters than ever before, their own

[206] Zheng Zhenman, "Yangtian," 11.   [207] *Fengnan zhi*, 10,586–87.
[208] Ibid., 5, 309–13.

organizational changes down in Yangzhou had little impact on lineage matters and organization back in Huizhou. Yet they retained their formal ties to their lineage's ancestral village and its halls, and they operated as house firms composed overwhelmingly of Xi'nan Wu members. Wu Yangchun's hiring practices seem to have died with him.

The Xi'nan Wus had retreated from center stage. But the scars of this tragedy lingered on, and the Wus' abiding sense of a great loss was captured in a series of paintings of the "family property," Mt Huang, by the Huizhou monk Hongren 弘仁 (1610–63). Even at this distance in time Hongren's sparse landscapes of Mt Huang reveal the depths of loss the Wus felt, especially after the damage of the Mt Huang disaster was compounded by the collapse of Ming China to the Manchu invaders in 1644. For a long time the mountain scenery of Mt Huang had been imagined in writing and painting as a Daoist paradise or Buddhist refuge, its forested slopes, lofty peaks, and circling clouds all floating far above the dusty world. Hongren's paintings of Mt Huang – after 1644 he became a close friend of several Wus, stayed several times in a Xi'nan temple the Wus had supported, examined the remains of their celebrated art collections, and painted at their request scenes of their Mt Huang "family property" – banish these Ming fantasies. Devoid of color and nature, his wintry mindscapes of Mt Huang's rocks and cliffs, of bare geometric forms with little surface detail, tell us that something terrible and final has happened to this scene. People have vanished from its treeless slopes. Its few remaining huts are empty even of furniture. The survivors, wherever they have fled, may feel a sense of release. But they surely were fortunate in no longer having to live in this bleak place. More sharply than any written document, these paintings pose the painful question, how had the history of Huizhou led to this?[209]

Conclusion

From these three cases, so different in scale, capital, and staffing, several clear conclusions can be drawn. First, all talk of a single Huizhou way of organizing business, of "a Huizhou model" for commerce and finance, needs to be shelved. Despite sharing a central role in the trade of several highly profitable commodities, especially salt and

---

[209] McDermott, "Chinese Mountain," 163–64.

timber, Huizhou house firms did not follow a single trajectory to either success or failure. Not only did merchant lineages follow distinctive trajectories, but also the separate house firms within any specific lineage developed distinctly, thus making it hard, if not impossible, for us today to reach any overall assessment of a single lineage's financial and commercial condition at any single time. To that extent, the house firms studied here are like the charitable landed trusts, whose rise and fall need not have indicated the overall general condition of the lineage within which they were held.

Second, like the charitable landed trusts, these house firms nonetheless provide deep shafts of light onto the workings and problems of often secretive organizations. For despite all the talk of merchant lineages, these house firms, even the more wealthy and long-lasting, usually remained composed of small-scale units, highly flexible in organizing their membership and determining and managing their commitments. Although they preferred to hire within their families and lineages, by the end of the Ming some of the larger firms had drawn under their wing useful non-kinsmen to do important work. Adoption, marriage, and same-surname alliances were doubtless effective means of looking beyond the lineage for new "family members" (*jiaren* 家人), but at this stage they had not become a new norm for these firms' development of networks and interests outside Huizhou.

Third, certain groups, branches and especially segments came to dominate a large firm's business successes, and their impact on the home lineage's organization and noncommercial activities naturally grew, either to expand their power within the lineage and its institutions or to control their relations with other groups judged worthy of an alliance. This strategy drew on the same kinship and economic concerns that defined the management of the charitable landed estate in the first volume, as village practices helped to shape, if not define, the ways these Huizhou men did business in distant markets. They may no longer have lived in their home village, but they for sure did not leave its practices and problems behind, even when trading and acting at the highest levels for the highest stakes.

And finally, it remains necessary to mention certain problems that the great success of many Huizhou merchants created or did not solve for their lineages and kinsmen: the great inequality among lineage members, the difficulty of creating large staffs with full-time commitment to a house firm that was not of their segment or branch, the weakening of meaningful ties among kinsmen due to the expansion of their separate business commitments down in the Yangzi Valley, and the highly unsettled situation of these merchants and their ambivalent attitude to the state. Like moths to a candle, they were drawn to work for the late imperial government by the promise of great rewards. Preserving those rewards required extreme care if the flame of the candle was not to burn them and extinguish them in the end. Such a fate for merchants, we might conclude, was common sense to experienced officials, in yet another instance in which the life patterns of some merchants and officials came to overlap in an increasingly commercial society. The late Ming merchant manual's injunction that merchants should step back when dealing with officials surely helps explain why we sometimes need to explore poetry and paintings rather than letters and memoirs to understand the haunted response of those house firms which dared to ignore the wisdom of this warning.

7 Conclusion

The Mt Huang disaster marked the beginning, not the end, of Huizhou's troubles in the seventeenth century. The two remaining decades of Ming rule and their succession by the invading Qing forces saw a turbulent reversal of its commercial and financial expansion in the previous century and a half. Huizhou, however steep the mountains around it, was not free from harvest failures and the disorders of the valleys and plains. Even before news of the fall of Beijing to peasant rebels and then of the Manchu invasion and conquest destroyed its peace in the mid 1640s, a string of poor harvests over the previous decade had severely damaged its residents' sense of well-being. While these economic setbacks and the ensuing turmoil in the Ming–Qing transition did not match the scale of death and destruction inflicted during the Yuan–Ming transition of the mid fourteenth century[1] – Huizhou's buildings and infrastructure survived the Ming–Qing transition largely intact – the devastation was enough to persuade many of Huizhou's perceptive residents that more than the name and ethnicity of the dynasty had changed. Although the Qing forces needed more than four decades to impose their rule, an era of Huizhou's history, they sensed, had ended at mid-century.[2]

In the previous century and a half, many of Huizhou's lineages and their members had accumulated considerable wealth. By speculating, moneylending, and trading, sometimes at grave risk to themselves and their cargoes, they had overcome poverty at home, dominated many of the lower and middle Yangzi Valley's commodity markets, and become the richest regional merchant group in south, and probably all, China. They also had outwitted their rivals in pawnbrokering and salt permit sales in the eastern third of the empire. Such rapid success may have persuaded some late Ming Huizhou merchants to avoid the travel and

---

[1] McDermott, *Making*, v. 1, 171–73, 344, Table 5.1; *DSGJY*, 5, 93.
[2] Wakeman, *Great Enterprise*, v. 1, 312.

travails their ancestors had endured in setting up and running their house firms. But in the seventeenth and even eighteenth centuries, most Huizhou merchants retained the imaginative resilience that had enabled them in the Ming to transform venerable institutions like the ancestral hall and the lineage itself into institutions more suited to their commercial and financial needs. Bereft of institutions like banks that might lend them substantial capital, they had turned to kinsmen and kinship organizations to form commercial partnerships to finance their business ventures. Whereas they showed little hesitation in manipulating village Confucian institutions to their wishes, they made similarly bold deals with officials and government institutions, only after they had secured overwhelming predominance, as in their early seventeenth-century conflicts over salt certificates.

Yet even then they restricted their demands to their trading position and wealth, not to a say in politics. However rich they were as salt merchants, they were still barred from formally participating in the major policy decisions that determined how this vast empire was ruled and that directly affected their wealth and investments. Like other Chinese subjects, they could appeal to government officials for a policy reconsideration, but they never acquired the power to make the decision. While they rarely failed to seize market opportunities to pursue their interest even at government expense, they showed little inclination to challenge government institutions and laws directly, especially if outside the confines of their job. In short, they sought refuge within the embrace of two of the most legitimate institutions of late imperial society, the government and the lineage. In particular, these wealthy traders and moneylenders often sought safety in government offices, where their services were sought after by officials, some of whom were in debt or otherwise beholden to them. Likewise, they would have surreptitiously used family and kinsmen officials to represent their interests, though such influence was also vulnerable to criticism in the highly charged politics of the late Ming. They also used the lineage to help organize their pursuit of profit, to provide staff and capital, to control markets, and to carve out safe passages for their goods and themselves in a world that distrusted them as much as they distrusted it. As a result, thanks to selective aid from the government in its salt monopoly, some of these men became the wealthiest merchants in Ming China, and transformed much of commercial life in central and southern China.

The aim of this concluding chapter, then, is to assess the impact of all these late Ming economic changes and the turbulence of the Ming–Qing transition on Huizhou society itself. The focus will fall once again on the "village quartet," those four kinds of institutions we found active in Huizhou villages from the early Song to the mid Ming – the village worship association, the Buddhist temples and Daoist shrines, the countless popular cults, and the large kinship organizations now overwhelmingly made up of lineages. Even if certain lineages like the Shanhe Chengs or the Xi'nan Wus suffered serious damage from these turbulent changes, the lineage as an institution had by 1700 risen to unprecedented prominence in Huizhou society, not least because it and its ancestral halls were considered vital for a local economy and social order damaged by decades of disturbances in the second half of the seventeenth century. An overall assessment of the relative power of the village quartet's separate institutions in the early Qing (1644–1911) will then necessarily follow a survey of Huizhou's overall military, economic, and social situation between the collapse of the 1630s and the recovery of the early 1700s. Its lineages were not as powerful as they liked to present themselves.

From the gray ashes of peace few survivors called for a new order. Exhausted voices of the defeated instead sought to reform Huizhou's lineages and other village institutions along stricter neo-Confucian lines. The Huizhou economy and society that a generation later emerged from this dynastic catastrophe would be poorer, weaker, and not necessarily wiser. Its lineage institutions, however, would overall emerge stronger and their role more central in the lives of their members by the mid Qing. They would live on, surviving even the Taiping Army's brutal occupation of Huizhou in the mid nineteenth century, and persist well into the twentieth century as essential to the life of both men and women in this prefecture.

In a seventeenth-century Huizhou capable of producing less than half of its grain needs, a grain shortage had immediately dire consequences. As the member of an eminent lineage acknowledged in the late sixteenth century,

> The grain in the fields cannot suffice half a year's food [needs], and in general [Huizhou] relies on supplies from outside. From Zhexi and Jiangxi [the grain vessels] enter shallow clear water and climb against the torrent. When the rain falls in torrents, a vessel's [loadable] cargo is no more than 100 bushels. Normally [the shipments] only go by rafts. Even in a bumper harvest the rice

price is three times that in other prefectures. If there is a slight thriftiness [or shortage], then the price soars beyond calculation. [As] a house of 1,000 taels has no rice stored up, there is no use talking about the situation of the poor.[3]

The deadly impact of a series of severe grain shortages on Huizhou's population during the last decade of the Ming and the first decade of the Qing thus came as no surprise to locals. The severe drought of 1636 did much more than reduce the local harvest. It so lowered the level of Huizhou's waterways that shipments of grain relief were sharply disrupted. As fear of an impending famine spread, "local hooligans" plundered grain boats and granaries. Frightened landlords secured the locks to their store holds. Beleaguered officials called vainly for help. Prices rose prohibitively. And much of the populace fell into prolonged hunger, if not outright famine: this food crisis, at least in She county, persisted for over two years. Members of the local elite started to organize their communities for self-defense against local troublemakers.[4] But one cannot fail to note what Joanna Handlin Smith observed of the Yangzi delta's famine-relief efforts at this time – the relative insignificance of private merchant grain supplies.[5] Their absence in grain relief despite their reported dominance in this market in the Yangzi Valley can be explained in part by the breakdown in grain delivery lines due to famines and insurrections in normal rice-surplus areas of the middle Yangzi and frequent bandit interruptions of rice delivery boats in the lower Yangzi area. Nonetheless, their retreat from the grain market is noticeable in this home area of great grain merchants.

In 1639, in the late summer and fall of 1640,[6] and most relentlessly in 1641 the twin scourges of drought and famine struck all six counties of the prefecture. In 1641, the third successive year of serious grain shortages throughout the prefecture, bandits blocked rice shipments.[7] Once again rice prices surged: an adult's minimum daily rice needs reportedly cost more than 0.4 tael (one report puts the figure at a full tael). With public and private agencies in Huizhou overwhelmed by the scale of the demand for food, some residents were driven to practice

---

[3] Li Weizhen, *Dabi shanfang ji*, 56.23b.
[4] Jin Sheng, *Jin Taishi ji*, 3.12a–13c, 6.20a, 8.35a–42b; *Yi xianzhi* (1825), 11.44a; *Wuyuan xianzhi* (1757), 38.4a; Fu Yan, *She ji*, juan 6 and 8.
[5] Smith, *Art of Doing Good*, 284.   [6] *Yi xianzhi* (1825), 11.14a.
[7] Huang Xixian, *FuWu xilüe*, 6.1a, 8.50a, 52a, 60a.

cannibalism on the already fallen. Others collapsed to their knees, and in their despair and delusion scraped the earth – they thought it resembled flour – and mixed this "Guanyin 觀音 flour" with weeds to bake buns. Within days they too were dead.[8] In the following year famine, along with an epidemic, again struck She county.[9]

In 1646 Qimen's shortage was alleviated by special deliveries of grain from neighboring She, Yi, and Shili 石埭 counties, but many still died of hunger.[10] Wuyuan, meanwhile, was suffering another severe drought. In 1647 famine again struck all six Huizhou counties. Prices in Xiuning and Wuyuan soared – an adult's daily rice needs there cost respectively 0.6 tael and 0.8 tael – as their roads became littered with corpses.[11] Wuyuan then suffered a famine in 1648, an epidemic in 1650, and a flood in 1651.[12] In 1652 all six counties once again suffered famine. Thereafter in the 1650s, their fate somewhat diverged: Wuyuan's wheat and barley crops were damaged by hail showers in 1653, She suffered another drought and famine in 1654, some of Xiuning's fields and houses were wrecked by mountain floods in 1655, and the rest of Huizhou returned to producing thin harvests.[13]

These two mid-century decades of natural disasters and poor crops inflicted great material damage and loss of life not just in Huizhou. Geoffrey Parker in his epic study *Global Crisis* presents overwhelming evidence that in the mid seventeenth century identical climate problems afflicted not just many other parts of China but also many other parts of the northern hemisphere. Parker links China's problems to problems of drought and cold in the northern hemisphere during the Little Ice Age and attributes this climate change to reversals in the surface air pressure in the eastern Pacific equatorial area, a phenomenon known today as the El Niño effect. Instead of taking place at the historically normal incidence rate of just once every five years, the air pressure

---

[8] Jin Sheng, *Jin Taishi ji*, 6.20a, 6.25a; *She xianzhi* (1690), 1.14b–15a; *Huizhou fuzhi* (1699), 18.34b–35a; *Qimen xianzhi* (1683), 1.10b; (1873), 36.7a; Peng Chao, "Xiuning Chengshi zhichanpu," 66; *Wuyuan xianzhi* (1757), 38.4a. Guanyin is a Buddhist deity of mercy.
[9] Jin Sheng, *Jin Taishi ji*, 6.20a; *Fengnan zhi*, 10, 595; *She xianzhi* (1690), 1.15a; *Huizhou fuzhi* (1699), 18.34b.
[10] *Qimen xianzhi* (1873), 36.7b.
[11] *Huizhou fuzhi* (1699), 18.35a–b; *Wuyuan xianzhi* (1757), 1.34b.
[12] *Wuyuan xianzhi* (1757), 1.34b and 38.4b.
[13] *Huizhou fuzhi* (1699), 18.35a–b; *Fengnan zhi*, 10, 595; *Xiuning xianzhi* (1693), 8.6a.

Conclusion   389

reversal in the El Niño phenomenon occurred nine times in the fifteen years between 1638 and 1652.[14] While Parker's explanation may on first reading seem far too technical and deterministic, this meteorological change in the past has usually wrought havoc on agricultural production in China and elsewhere. It actually helps explain overpopulated Huizhou's dire crop record during these years. "For those farming 1,000 feet or more above sea level [as would have been the case throughout Huizhou], a fall of 0.5 degree C in mean summer temperatures increased the chance of two consecutive harvest failures by 100-fold." The global cold persisted, so deeply that between 1666 and 1679 nine of the fourteen summers were either cool or exceptionally cool.[15]

No less painful for Huizhou, in the early 1640s and in the following two decades, was a series of disorders, mainly military, which arose in large part from the catastrophic failure of the Ming government to protect its borders and maintain stability. In the second and third lunar months of 1641 the countryside of Xiuning and Qimen counties was greatly disturbed by the incursion of several hundred "big robbers" from Shili county in neighboring Chizhou 池州 prefecture. After attacking the gentry-style village of Zhengjia wu 鄭家塢, and torching two of its storehouses and killing many of its men and women, these bandits moved on to Qimen county, where they continued their onslaught until stopped by outraged local forces.[16] This unexpected invasion was soon followed by an even stranger military incursion, a sign, if needed, that the fading Ming world was out of kilter. In the third lunar month of 1643 bands of troops arrived in Qimen, claiming to have marched from distant Guizhou province in order to support the threatened dynasty.[17] Suspicions about their claims and intentions arose, however, due to their lack of official papers, their irregular route of arrival via Jiangxi, and their telltale Hubei–Hunanese accents. Soon, their behavior – the occupation of civilian homes, the murder of tens of

---

[14] Parker, *Global Crisis*, 14, 125–29, and 136 (Table 18).
[15] Ibid., 18, 144, 146.
[16] Huang Xixian, *FuWu xilüe*, 6.1a, 7a; *Xiuning mingzu zhi*, 3, 546.
[17] Reliable news of the last Ming emperor's death on the nineteenth day of the third lunar month reached Nanjing in the middle of the fourth lunar month. It reached elsewhere in the delta about two weeks later (Kishimoto, *Min Shin kōtai*, 143–57). Qing troops arrived in Huizhou in the sixth intercalary lunar month of 1645 (*Wuyuan xianzhi* (1755), 1.34a).

civilians, and the rape of hundreds of their women – confirmed the locals' worst suspicions. The Qimen militia retaliated, killing some and driving the rest of these bandits up into the mountains to return to a life of undisguised brigandry.[18]

The next two uprisings in 1645 were also exceptional, in that they erupted from within Huizhou and involved hundreds, if not thousands, of bondservants. After centuries of apparent submission and quietude, these "base people" rebelled against their masters in various villages. Claiming that the recent collapse of the Ming had invalidated their dynasty-stamped servitude contracts, they demanded "a rectification of their station" (zheng mingfen 正名分). Their masters, bolstered by government support, forgot their own rivalries to reject the bondservants' demands and suppress their protest. In a rare surviving document from this rebellion, one of the bondservant (dipu 地僕) rebels pleads amnesty by pinning the blame for the troubles on three henchmen. He claims to have been fatally misled by these leaders into setting houses on fire and attacking others with a sword. They had seduced him into their ranks, plundering landlords' houses, calling for disorder, and cutting down several tens of his master's trees to build a fort, presumably to thwart an expected counterattack.[19] The masters' victory, however real, proved incomplete.[20] In a prefecture where a slight alteration in the social distinctions between master and servant had long been enough to arouse a bitter quarrel,[21] the suppression of these rebellions left long-simmering resentments and unspoken fears of a relapse into chaos. In response to reports of bondservant insolence,[22] Huizhou's rich families are in the early Qing said – surely with a fist of salt – to "no longer dare to rear bondservants (nu 奴)."[23]

Thus much of the Ming regime for bondservants survived well into the Qing. As before, in 1659 an owner was willing to turn to the local courts to punish rebellious bondservants he accused of stealing and selling his trees and firewood.[24] Not only do we have reports of

---

[18] Zhao Jishi, Ji yuan ji suoji, 11, 921, 926–27; Jin Sheng, Jin Taishi ji, 2.12a–b.
[19] Huizhou qiannian, v. 11, 11–13.
[20] Zhongguo renmin daxue Qingshi yanjiuso et al., Kang Yong Qian shiqi, v. 1, 504–7; Zurndorfer, Change and Continuity, 225–45; Jiang Taixin, "Lun Qingdai Huizhou tudi maimai," 1,079–86.
[21] Huizhou fuzhi (1699), 2.fengsu, 69b.   [22] Qimen xianzhi (1673), 1.25b.
[23] Fan Shuzhi, "Ming Qing de nupu," 72; Huizhou fuzhi (1699), 2.69b.
[24] Huizhou qiannian, v. 1, 52 (1659).

grainless masters selling off a fourteen-year-old (*sui*) maidservant doubtless ripe for marriage.[25] But also in the early Qing a Huizhou man, faced with starvation or servitude, surrendered himself to a Xie ancestral hall, consenting to become its bondservant and committing his wife and descendants to the same fate. A contract drawn up in 1671 even refers to the "Huizhou custom," whereby if you farm another's land, live in his house, and are buried on his land, then for generations you submit to give labor service as a bondservant (*zhuangpu*).[26] And at century's end we read of how the purchase of just a half of a one-sixteenth share in a bondservant tenants' house (*huopu zhuangji*) – five rooms on two stories – assures this buyer of bondservant service from the house's residents at future New Year and end-of-year celebrations, capping ceremonies, marriages, and burial sacrifices.[27] As late as 1923 a report on Huizhou's hereditary-servant system (*shepu zhi* 世僕制) noted that they still provided a wide variety of services to their masters ranging from farming and making wine to sweeping and service in the family's major ceremonies.[28]

Over the next three decades these local insurrections in Huizhou also became a battlefield for foreign and domestic invaders. Within its boundaries, troops, the dynastic as well as the rebel, engaged in no fewer than four major military campaigns. The first of these began with the arrival of Qing troops in the sixth lunar month of 1645. Twice in the next few months, in the plains and in the mountains, these Qing forces overwhelmed loyalist Southern Ming troops fighting to restore the Ming.[29] Two years of relative peace ensued, only to be disrupted in 1648 when mountain bandit gangs smashed through the city wall of Qimen and ransacked its buildings.[30] Later that year, as the Southern Ming leaders retreated, worse trouble came from its disgruntled soldiers. Unpaid, they came upriver from Jiangxi in search of Huizhou's fabled wealth and supposed store holds of grain. In Qimen they

---

[25] Ibid., *v. 21*, 22 (1649).
[26] Ibid., *v. 21*, 68. Ibid., 86 (1680), includes a reprimand of a bondservant and his daughter for having claimed that she can move on as she wished.
[27] Ibid., *v. 21*, 108 (1691).
[28] Shi Beisheng, *Zhongguo minshi*, 6th bian, 2 lei, p. 21; these hereditary servants could not be sold or mortgaged off.
[29] Zhao Jishi, *Ji yuan ji suoji*, 9, 912–13; *Jixi xianzhi* (1810), 6, 106; *Fengnan zhi*, 10, 587; *Xiuning Jinshi zupu* (1748), second *ce*, jia–zhuan 3, 15a–16a.
[30] *Qimen xianzhi* (1683), 5.22b.

ransacked city and countryside alike, before proceeding to search out another hoard to plunder.[31]

In this political vacuum, other military groups disrupted whatever remained of Huizhou's order in 1653, 1656, and especially 1659.[32] Unruly Qing soldiers, after plundering Qimen's countryside, enlisted locals to smash its city wall and raze hundreds of residences.[33] They next raced to the seat of Xiuning, where a terrified populace crouched behind locked city gates until rescued by local soldiers. Two years later in 1661, disorder struck Huizhou again from Jiangxi. Bandits from Fuliang 浮梁 county made their way upstream into western Huizhou, once again inducing Huizhou's own malcontents to join them, this time in successfully sacking the county seat of Xiuning.[34]

In 1669 other rebels disrupted Huizhou from within the prefecture,[35] but far more damaging were the roving Fujianese bandits who in 1674 and 1675 followed the well-trodden path for brigands invading from Jiangxi. Allowed into Qimen city by a soldier in the employ of the Qing, they proceeded to slaughter countless soldiers and civilians during the month or so they occupied the city. "Qimen was turned into a pit, in which the old and the young were piled up [as corpses], as [the brigands] hunted the mountains for precious metals and coins. Ever since antiquity Qimen had never suffered anything comparable to the cruelty of this conflagration." Remembering the horrors of the mid thirteenth century's Yuan–Ming transition, one wonders if this view needs qualification. But of this dynastic transition's own horrors, no one should doubt. "When Qing troops arrived, the bandits fled off in the dark, and throughout the night the cries of the victims could be heard."[36] These bandits cut their way through Xiuning, She, and Jixi counties (where the magistrate fled their advance), until they were repelled in the ninth lunar month of 1674 by specially dispatched Qing forces.[37]

After all these disruptions Huizhou's wealth was estimated at the end of the seventeenth century to be just a tenth of what it had been in

---

[31] Ibid., 5.22b–23a, 27b.
[32] Dong Jian, *Ziran*, 138; and *She xianzhi* (1771), 3.4b.
[33] *Qimen xianzhi* (1683), 5.23a; (1827), 1.25a, 26a.
[34] *Xiuning xianzhi* (1693), 1.29a–30b, 7.110b.   [35] Dong Jian, *Ziran*, 138.
[36] *Qimen xianzhi* (1873), 36.8a.
[37] *Jixi xianzhi* (1810), 6, 106, 1.31a–b; Ling Yingqiu, *Shaxi jilüe*, 2.26; *Huizhou fuzhi* (1873), 16.21.65a. Bandits came also from Fujian (ibid., 16.2.42a).

Conclusion 393

the late Ming.[38] A hyperbole, but all contemporaries agree that the human and material cost to Huizhou from all these natural and human disasters was enormous. Already in the chaotic final decade of the Ming, according to Jin Sheng, three-quarters of Huizhou's merchants had lost assets.[39] "Every Huizhou person," he later wrote in 1643, "has suffered,"[40] a claim that held especially true for those Huizhou merchants massacred in the peasant uprisings in Hubei, Beijing, and north China in the early and mid 1640s.[41] In c.1664 poor families in Huizhou were pawning their clothes for rice or money, just to scrape by.[42] Its prefect that year reported that while many of its wealthy were busy trading elsewhere, most of those staying at home owned no land and were often driven by poverty to pawn their clothing for basic necessities.[43] A severe shortage of silver further blighted the hopes for a commercial recovery.[44] By century's end, south China's (and by extension Huizhou's) late Ming preponderance in pawnbrokering and in retention of silver holdings had ended; in 1695 three of the five provinces with the most registered pawnshops were located in north China and collectively accounted for more than half of the empire's 7,695 shops. The Northern Metropolitan circuit alone had 2,266

---

[38] *Huizhou fuzhi* (1699), 2.67b and 68a.   [39] Jin Sheng, *Jin taishi ji*, 5.21a.
[40] Ibid., 5.2b and 6.20a, for a claim that in the previous decade four-fifths of its residents had suffered loss of property north of the Yangzi. In 1642, at the start of this endless tragedy, Jin put the Huizhou victims at half of its population (ibid., 8.9b).
[41] *Dianshang*, 258–61, 288. In Linqing they had once accounted for almost all the pawnbrokers. But after the Qing conquest they were reduced to less than half; many locals assumed their place.
[42] Ibid., 272. An apparently unique document listing the landholdings of all landowners in a *lijia* unit in Qimen county in 1655 (*Qimen xian xinzhang qingong shouzhuang*) suggests considerable hardship and inequality in landownership: of this unit's 677 fiscal *mu*, over half was owned by just six of the unit's eighteen registered households. The top landowning household in this unit (itself dominated numerically by Wus 吴) held 18.3 percent of the total land. The average landholding household held 37.6 *mu*, and the median household 43.5 *mu* (nothing is said of tenancy, bondservitude, or multiple ownership). In short, a bare subsistence livelihood from agriculture alone appears just viable for most families in good harvest years; in the many bad harvest years of the early Qing, the situation for most households must have been dire. The push to emigrate would not have abated, even if the external markets' demand had.
[43] Fu Yiling, *Ming Qing shidai shangren*, 61.
[44] Kishimoto, *Shindai Chūgoku*, 239–89.

shops.⁴⁵ The eventual restoration of order did not signify a restoration of Huizhou's prominence in that new Qing order.

Surveying Huizhou's situation c.1681, the She county native Hong Yutu 洪玉圖 lamented, "Recently, year after year crops have not grown, and many are increasingly impoverished. In the aftermath of the military conflagrations, [Huizhou's supplies] have day by day become increasingly insufficient. Furthermore, labor service charges have become heavy, and the people increasingly cannot feel at ease." Its people, he pessimistically adds, have become less disciplined and less determined to succeed, its fine handicraft products have been reduced to just tea and ink sticks (its famous inkstones and paper were no longer obtainable), and its people understandably have started to leave the area for good: "In the past merchants sometimes settled down alone outside Huizhou, but now they go off with their wives and children. In the past merchants returned home once every few years, but now they go off, abandoning their mounds and graves."⁴⁶ Or, if these emigrants did return regularly, they did so as the richer and dominant party, whose support became vital not just for Huizhou lineages' ongoing involvement in the culture and economy of the lower Yangzi delta but also for the upkeep of their local ancestral graves and the education of their members for the civil service examinations. Huizhou-based lineages would continue to participate in commercial networks through branches established elsewhere, but often as the poorer cousins.⁴⁷

The 1699 gazetteer for She county concurred with this downbeat assessment, stating that ever since the expulsion of the Fujianese rebels in 1675, "the people in She county have become poorer by the day."⁴⁸ And, in a 1699 review of overall conditions in Huizhou, the Xiuning

---

⁴⁵ Abe Takeo, *Shindai shi no kenkyū*, 372–73, provides a breakdown by province: Zhili: 2,266 (29.4 percent), Jiangsu: 1507 (19.6 percent), Anhui: 304 (4 percent), Zhejiang: 559 (7.3 percent), Jiangxi: 38 (.05 percent), Hubei: 111 (1.4 percent), Hunan: 42 (0.5 percent), Fujian: 95 (1.2 percent), Shandong: 516 (6.7 percent), Shanxi: 1,281 (16.6 percent), Henan: 237 (3.1 percent,), Shaanxi: 200 (2.6 percent), Gansu: 406 (5.3 percent), Guangdong: 130 (1.7 percent), and Guangxi: 3 (0.01 percent). The number of registered pawnshops rose to 18,075 in 1751 and 23,139 in 1812. Liu Qiugen, "Ming Qing Minguo shiqi," 68–69.
⁴⁶ Hong Yutu, *Shewen*, 1a, 5b–6b, 10b; *SSXT*, 21, 717.
⁴⁷ Xu Maoming, "Qingdai Hui Su liangdi," 25–35.
⁴⁸ *She xianzhi* (1690), 1.15b–16a; Di Tunjian, Zhou Xiaoguang, and Bian Li, *Huizhou wenhua shi*, 541.

native Zhao Jishi 趙吉石 concluded that twenty-five years after order had been restored, the prefecture had not yet recovered its sense of well-being.[49] Everywhere, even in his own lineage's village, he saw ghostly reminders of a vibrant past:

> Where my father [and others] had congregated, there had once been a market (shi 市). Now it is wilderness (ye 野). The road by which people came and went on their carts and horses was spanned by a stone bridge that had been restored by my great-grandfather Guanglu 光祿 when it had fallen into disrepair. That was some fifty-odd years ago. Now [once again] it is damaged and tilting. Although this bridge is no more than ten spans long, the currents of the streams in this valley have increased, and the foamy crest of waves often flows several feet above it.[50]

No repairs are promised.

Meanwhile, the returns from trade, the prefecture's lifeline in the Ming, were endangered by a far harsher tax regime for merchants along the Huizhou merchants' most traveled routes in the Yangzi Valley. Whereas for most of the Ming the entire Yangzi had only two customs stations that collected commercial taxes (at Nanjing and Jiujiang), by 1685 the Qing government had set up five others, at Wuhu, Wuchang, Ganzhou 贛州, Jingzhou 荊州, and Guizhou 夔州. By the mid eighteenth century, the customs duties collected at these six Yangzi customs stations were nearly 100,000 taels annually. In short, the Yangzi customs stations' revenue had risen from a mere 8 percent in the Ming to, in the mid eighteenth century, 85 percent of all customs revenues collected along the Grand Canal.[51]

Landlord income would likewise have been reduced by the spread within Huizhou of the "one field, two masters" (yitian liangzhu 一田兩主) form of land tenure. In this arrangement the tenant could independently sell his tenancy and even contract a third party to till the land for him for an annual rent payment from the main rice crop.[52] Later on in the eighteenth century, timber production would be seriously threatened by the encroachment of "shed people" (pengmin 棚民) on Huizhou's forested uplands. Prevented from settling in crowded

---

[49] Huizhou fuzhi (1699), 1.78b. [50] Zhao Jishi, Ji yuan ji suoji, 11, gulao zaji.
[51] Zhou Xiaoguang, Huizhou wenhua shi, 541.
[52] Huizhou qiannian, v. 21, 51 (1659), 109 (1692), 133 (1694). It was practiced on most Huizhou fields by the late eighteenth century (Yan Guifu and Wang Guojian, Huizhou wenshu dang'an, 326).

villages, these immigrants were forced to settle on mountain slopes, where they scratched out a living. However, their upland farming caused widespread soil erosion, mud avalanches, and many other environmental problems for the alarmed villagers below. No wonder that the prefectural gazetteer of 1699 would conclude, "Whereas the rich eat three times a day, the poor eat only twice. For food they eat only rice porridge, and when guests arrive, they do not make rice for them."[53]

Some lineages, such as the Shanhe Chengs of Qimen county, suffered sharply from these natural and human disasters as well as from the economic downturn.[54] In the annual rent collection figures that we have for five years between 1597 and 1716, the Chengs' Doushan trust never collected more than a quarter of its annual quota of paddy field rice rents. So complete was the collapse of this once stable portion of the trust's revenue, that its recorded return in 1716 totaled less than a tenth of the 3,000 *cheng* (roughly 120 to 150 bushels) estimated in 1656 to be the trust's initial fixed paddy field rent quota.[55] Its mountain timber revenue also suffered from members' continued violations of old and new trust pacts, which left more Qimen mountains bare and drove more tenants into flight.[56] As a result, the trust hobbled on, providing minimal benefit for its members.

Predictably, by 1682 as much as 70 percent of the membership of this lineage's Renshan Branch (*Renshan men* 仁山門) (which included all the Doushan trust's members) had disappeared from Qimen for good.[57]

---

[53] *Huizhou fuzhi* (1699), 2.fengsu, 68a.
[54] Other impoverished lineages included the once fabulously rich pawnbrokers the Wus of Shangshan (ibid., 11, 902), and the Xus of Xiuning (Xu Xianzu, *Xiuning Futan zhi* (1722), 3, 288). In the early eighteenth century these Xus calculated that they had lost more than half of their late Ming fortune during the dynastic turmoil. Their very rich households had in the late Ming numbered more than ten, but in 1722, 80–90 percent of the Xus' houses were empty; their family and ancestral properties were being encroached on and robbed.
[55] McDermott, *Making*, v. 1, 344, Table 5.1; *DSGJY*, 5, 93.
[56] *DSGJY*, 5, 92–93.
[57] *Shanhe Chengshi Renshan men zhipu* (1682), fanli, 1a. No fewer than twenty-two members of the twenty-sixth to thirtieth generations of the Guishan Branch of the Shanhe Chengs emigrated. In 1682 many Shanhe Chengs were residing in Jixia 暨夏 Market Town, HuGuang province; others were living in the Guazhou and Yangzhou (瓜楊) area. In 1694 one member spoke of the Shanhe emigrants moving to both south and north of the Yangzi, as well as to HuGuang province, to Yangzhou, Luzhou 廬州 (in the north of present Anhui province), and Chahe

Already by the second half of the sixteenth century some Shanhe Chengs engaged in trade far from Huizhou. Witness the case of the lifelong merchant Cheng Shenbao 程神保, a member of the fourth branch who seems to have spent much of his life away from home.[58] Taking to the road with his father at an early age, he traveled to Shandong and soon acquired all the necessary skills of a successful merchant. He subsequently traded in Xiajiang 峽江 county in Jiangxi, in Fujian, in the Huai–Yangzhou area, in the Hubei–Hunan area (Chu 楚), and in Kaifeng. By the time he was active in Hubei–Hunan, he had accumulated 700 taels (most of which he used to help others). At one stage, apparently towards the end of his career, he formed a commercial partnership with two of his kinsmen,[59] each of whom gave him 100 taels for his work as merchant. Over the course of ten years he paid them a steady stream of dividends, that eventually reached the same 100 tael sum each of them had added to his own pot of capital in this simple partnership. What was notable about this partnership was Cheng Shenbao's eventual inability to retain use of one of his investors' capital when called upon to return it.

At the time of the Ming's collapse many senior members of this lineage were trading far from home in places like Yangzhou, the site of a notorious Manchu massacre.[60] Meanwhile, those who stayed in Shanhe interacted with one another less often as a lineage: "The lineage's assemblies are infrequent. There is a schedule for sacrifices and sweeping [of the graves], but there is only one meeting a year. The meeting lasts several days, and afterwards they promptly separate and

岔河鎮 Market Town in Huai'an 淮安 in northern Jiangsu (*Chengshi zhipu fanli*, 1b).
[58] Li Weizhen, *Dabi shanfang ji*, 73.11a–b.
[59] One of these Cheng Ling is called 子揚 here by his literary name (ibid.; *DSGJY*, 254) and listed as a signatory to three Shanhe Cheng pacts (1547, 1570, 1575; ibid., 86, 88, and 89) drafted to resolve mountain-land disputes. As McDermott, *Making*, v. 1, 340–42, shows, the seventy-five-year old Cheng Ling in 1571 ran into trouble with his sons over his handling of their expected inheritance; the omission of all reference to commercial assets in the documents that passed between father and sons suggests either his duplicity with these heirs or his transfer by then of his capital funds into Huizhou landownership shares and their annual grain rents. His listed assets mention only these rents, while among his listed debts the only possible reference to this Cheng Shenbao arrangement was credit he had given out (no collateral is mentioned).
[60] Anon., *Huizhou huishe zonglu*, 4th juan, 29a.

depart."[61] Only in the final decades of the Qing dynasty are there signs of a revival by one of this lineage's segments.[62]

The drastic decline in a lineage's membership had serious repercussions on its societies and institutions, especially those that depended on the rotation of staff positions and management powers among its separate branches. Price increases in the early Qing increased the burden on often impoverished survivors, further threatening the continuation of these arrangements and lineage co-operation.[63] In this instance the experience of the Shanhe Chengs (as well as that of the Xi'nan Wus) seems not to have been representative of Huizhou lineages in general. In fact, even if they were already in the late sixteenth century anxious enough to register with the government all their common landed property (including tenanted fields, other sacrificial fields and garden land, burial sites and mounds) as permanent lineage property never to be alienated, they seem more worried about their future prospects in the face of their and their members' serious commercial losses during the 1640s and 1650s.[64] Most Huizhou lineages appear to have retained far more social, political, and economic power than did their institutional rivals in Huizhou villages. Reports composed by returnees in the early eighteenth century, as well as local gazetteer assessments written throughout the Qing, stress the continuing centrality of Huizhou's lineage institutions to the concerns and activities of its residents,[65] to the

---

[61] Ibid., 2nd *ce*, 31b. Throughout the Qing they acquired no metropolitan degree and only two provincial degrees (Bian Li, *Ming Qing Huizhou*, 56). Their lower degrees – twenty-five district degrees, five tribute student (*gongsheng*) degrees, and thirty-three studentships at the National University (*taixuesheng* 太學生) – were acquired by members of the twenty-seventh to thirty-fifth generations; they led to just one recorded official position, that of a lowly county schoolteacher (*Qimen Shanhe Chengshi Renshan menzhi xiu zongpu* (1907), 19.7b, referring to Cheng Cheng in the twenty-eighth generation). At least some of these lower degrees would have been purchased.
[62] The Shanhe Chengs are included only in the second of two lists (one for 1690 and the other for the late nineteenth century) of Cheng lineages, which took obligatory turns as manager of the Cheng Lingxi Shrine in Huangdun (*Huangdun shizhongci gong sipu*, 3b).
[63] Anon., *Huizhou huishe zonglu*, 1st juan, 31b–32a, dated 1652.
[64] For instance, the encroachment of one lineage on another's grave mountain during the Ming–Qing transition (Anhui sheng bowuguan, *Ming Qing Huizhou shehui jingji ziliao congbian*, v. 1, 567).
[65] Guo, *Ritual Opera*, 9; *Xiuning xianzhi* (1693), 1.64b; (1815), 1.38a; *She xianzhi* (1690), 2.fengsu, 7a; *Qimen xianzhi* (1827), 5.2b–3a.

extent that in 1718 Huizhou villages were still thought to hold just one surname group.[66]

In the case of commoner or less well-educated kinship groups, the lineages sometimes established their own security associations or made security alliances with a few other lineages in their area. Formed for military protection during the chaotic years of the Ming–Qing transition, these security associations were doubtless kept alive by their lineages' continuing security needs during the first four decades of Qing rule. Thereafter, they seem to have assumed a wide range of nonmilitary duties as well, in some cases until the 1950s.[67]

Among the better-educated lineages such a guiding role was held by "culture associations" (wenhui 文會), run by degree holders along the lines of the "Culture Group's" (Siwen hui 斯文會) rule over the Doushan trust of the Shanhe Chengs during the late Ming and early Qing.[68] Even so, such informal groups of local self-rule acting as intermediaries between the countryside and the county government acknowledged the primary position of the lineage. All quarrels in the countryside, we read in an early nineteenth-century account, were first and foremost adjudicated by lineages. Only after lineages had failed to resolve a conflict was first a village's "culture association" and then, if necessary, the yamen called in to settle the dispute: "[Government-established units for local control like] the *lijia*, community pact, urban neighborhood units, and *baojia* have absolutely no authority in these matters."[69]

Economically, despite the permanent departure of many rich merchants and their families from Huizhou and the relative decline of Huizhou's influence on the Qing as opposed to the Ming economy, many lineages still expanded their wealth and property share both outside and inside Huizhou. In place of just the Huangs, Wangs, Wus, Chengs, and Fangs who had dominated the salt monopoly in the Ming, there appears a larger group of Huizhou salt merchants

---

[66] MQHS, 57. [67] Wang Zhenzhong, "Ming Qing yilai Huizhou," 17–102.
[68] McDermott, Making, v. 1, 353–59.
[69] SSXT, 18, 602; Tang Lixing and Zhang Xiangfeng, "Guojia minchong," 59. As late as 1950 a multi-surname village like Lianhua in Qimen had five work associations (gonghui 工會) and literary associations (wenhui 文會). One of these, consisting of four surnames, had 9.6 *mu*; another, the Pufu Temple Association, was formed by nine surnames (the most powerful being the Wus), and had twenty-odd *mu* with rent.

sharing the profits of the salt monopoly. The She county gazetteer of 1936 in fact lists fourteen lineages that flourished in the Qing salt monopoly: the Jiangs of Jiang Village 江村江, the Wus of Fengxi 豐溪吳 (aka Xi'nan), the Wus of Chengtang 澄塘吳, the Huangs of Tandu 潭渡黃, the Chengs of Lingshan 嶺山程, the Wangs of Choushu 稠墅汪 and the Wangs of Qiankou 潛口汪, the Xus of Fuxi 傅溪徐, the Zhengs of Zheng Village 鄭村鄭, the Xus of Tangmo 唐模許, the Caos of Xiong Village 雄村曹, the Songs of Shangfeng 上豐宋, the Baos of Tangyue 棠樾鮑, and the Yes of Lantian 藍田葉.[70] Certainly, some powerful and well-connected She county lineages like the Tangyue Baos and the Tangmo Xus did grow more wealthy, a fact reflected in the greater amount of money a mid- or late Qing (rather than late Ming) Huizhou family like theirs needed to be considered rich.[71]

Lineage dominance in landownership also grew. If mid-twentieth-century commentators are even half-correct about Huizhou lineages' collective dominance of Huizhou's land economy,[72] then at some point in the Qing many other lineages must also have secured that local position of landed power. Precisely how they gained that wealth is suggested by the combination of traditional and innovative practices pursued by the Wangs of Shuanglin 雙林王, a relatively minor lineage in Wuyuan county. Beginning c.1630 with just 103 *cheng*, the annual revenue of this lineage's charitable trust expanded seventyfold to 7,560.5 *cheng* in 1776. The trust's growth over a century and a half came from its ownership of not just paddy fields but also city shops (which by 1784 totaled twelve), a commercial type of real estate and revenue uncommon in Ming trusts. Moreover, by 1796 these mixed assets had risen in value to 1,902.564 taels,[73] which the ancestral hall was allowed for specific purposes (for the hall, its school, related temple and shrine, and matters of common concern to trust members) to loan at interest to trust members. In

---

[70] *Shexian zhi* (1937), 1. fengtu, 6a.
[71] Finnane, *Yangzhou*, 124–27; Chang, *Court on Horseback*, 223–27; Wu Yulian, *Luxurious Networks*; Xu Dixin and Wu Chengming, *Zhongguo zibenzhuyi*, v. 1, 105–6.
[72] Lineage corporate land in Huizhou accounted for 14.32 percent of the total land registered in Huizhou in 1949 (Guo, *Ritual Opera*, 31), a figure far higher than I can imagine on the basis of Ming fish-scale registers listings and other Ming sources.
[73] *Shuanglin Wangshi zhipu* (1860), 11, lici zongce.

short, this hall had become an urban landlord cautiously engaged in lending money.[74]

Elsewhere in Huizhou, we have a report of an ancestral hall providing small loans, in 1694, to non-kinsmen, such as their bondservants (*zhuangpu*).[75] Other ancestral halls proved more adventuresome, as they developed complex economic operations and ritual performances for their lending and investing. For example, by the early nineteenth century, half of the ritual land attached to an ancestral hall of one large She county lineage consisted of land mortgaged to the hall by impoverished lineage members in order to win the admission of their ancestors' spirit tablets before the same hall rented this land back to these poor households as its tenants.[76] Within some ancestral halls as well, complicated rituals took root, allowing for some lineages to rank and place spirit tablets on the altar according not to generational descent but to the amount of money donated to secure their tablets' admission. Some lineages even graded the size of donations by nine ranks, in explicit imitation of the nine-rank (*jiupin* 九品) system of officialdom, in order to designate status differences and altar placements among the ancestral hall's spirit tablets.[77]

Strengthened by these political and economic resources as well as by their members' desperate resourcefulness, Huizhou lineages and their Confucian supporters in the Qing often advocated policies to restrict the activities of other religious institutions in their midst.[78] Overall, their stance was stricter than in the past,[79] but the severity varied according to the type of rival institution. Village worship associations, for instance, escaped their harsh criticism, if only because they appear neither to have questioned lineage dominance nor to have reorganized themselves to reverse their decline.[80] For instance, in Wuyuan county in 1700, one villager bemoaned that his village's village worship association had no altar or other site for performing its prayers and

---

[74] Ibid., zongce, 1b. The ancestral-hall managers' tasks are detailed in *Jiangcun Hongshi jiapu* (1730), 14.1 ff.
[75] *Huizhou qiannian*, v. 21, 136.   [76] Guo, *Ritual Opera*, 31.
[77] *Jixi Nanguan Jingxu tang Xushi zongpu* (1889), 9.6a–10b, 10.38a–41b.
[78] Goossaert and Palmer, *Religious Question*, 19–42.
[79] A harsh but far from unique example is the late Ming jeremiad against threats posed to lineage power by a group of mediums, Buddhist monks, Daoist priests, and women (*Xiuning Yeshi zupu* (1631), 6, baoshi, 31b).
[80] *Chengyang sanzhi*, 7, 646–47, details how the village worship association fit into a single-lineage village; McDermott, *Making*, v. 1, 180–213.

sacrifices. "It doesn't even drive rats away [from the fields and granaries], and if it does not do that, then what is a village worship association for?" Its inactivity and poor facilities the villagers blamed on its lack of funds.[81]

Its inactivity, however, appears to have been more than a matter of funds, as the political flexibility and economic adaptability of the Zhusheng Association, the village worship association briefly introduced in volume 1, is nothing short of startling.[82] Having begun its life as a three-village (and three-lineage) alliance in 1602, this association survived the turmoil of the latter half of the seventeenth century as well as the nightmares of the Taiping rebels' occupation of Huizhou in the mid nineteenth century, to carry on its festivals and other acts of collective worship for two lineages up to the late 1940s, a lifespan longer than the Qing dynasty's.[83]

Throughout its three-century history, the organizational structure of the Zhusheng Association remained stable, despite membership changes and financial crises.[84] After flourishing in the first two decades of Qing rule, it was impoverished by a tax increase from c.1670 and by a prolonged stagnation in farm rent income over the last third of the seventeenth century. Recovery remained slow even in the opening decades of the next century.[85] Its survival depended on cutting costs (at first it halted play performances but kept its banquets, until some members criticized this preference as self-indulgent and displeasing to the gods). It also for a time raised annual membership fees, and after protracted trouble collecting its grain rents decided to diversify its, and its members', sources of revenue.[86] It turned membership into

---

[81] Zhan Yuanxiang, *Weizhai riji*, 199–200.
[82] Shibuya, "Min Shin jidai," 59.1, 103–34, and 59.2–3, 93–129.
[83] This association in Futan with thirty-two households taking annual turns to head its activities survived a sharp early Qing decline in the lineage's wealth (Xu Xianzu, *Xiuning Futan zhi* (1722), 3, 288).
[84] From the 1670s members began to withdraw. Ultimately, just one lineage dominated the alliance but never, in three centuries, did the association unravel.
[85] Kishimoto, *Shindai Chūgoku*, 153–57; Kuroda, "What Prices Can Tell Us," 105–7, for a price table for Tunxi market town in the late eighteenth century.
[86] The grain rent actually collected annually between 1638 and 1800 usually amounted to 60 to 80 percent of the total rent quota for all holdings (Shibuya, "Min Shin jidai," 59.2–3, 116). Zhang Yuyi notes that actual rents paid in Huizhou during the seventeenth and eighteenth centuries usually reached no more than 70 to 90 percent of their quota; from the eighteenth century on, the percentage dropped further (see his *Ming Qing Huizhou tudi*, 141–62, 163–92).

transferable shares (gu 股), that by no later than 1738 it and its members were selling to others,[87] and from 1759 it allowed its head to lend its cash profits from the sale of grain rents to rich people willing to pay regular interest. Although this lending was initially intended to fund repairs needed after a fire damaged the association's shrine and images,[88] this new arrangement lasted long after these repairs were done. It certainly made the post of headship more attractive.[89] These changes underline how much the commercial practices of Huizhou's lineages shaped the activities of the other village institutions that centuries earlier had rivaled their power.

Buddhist institutions, as seen in the previous volume, had been the favorite bogey of Confucian scholars and government officials alike in the Ming. Having lost land and been deprived of some of their traditional role in funeral rituals, they also found their heads appointed by local groups, who claimed to represent lineages. The monks themselves might try to develop their temple's numinous "dragon pool" into a popular pilgrimage site, but in the late sixteenth century they faced intrusion by outside groups of other monks and "local ruffians" seeking to secure their share of this new enterprise's proceeds.[90] Protection from these rivals comes from other local groups, including lineages, local sub-bureaucratic rural post holders (yuezheng 約正, baojia ren 保甲人), and minor degree holders.

---

[87] This practice would have been adopted relatively late by the Zhusheng Association. In Jiang Village it was adopted by 1526 (Chengyang sanzhi, 6.1a, where an initial total of twenty-four shares was reduced to sixteen). McDermott, Making, v. 1, 369–429, describes the practice of dividing mountain landholdings into ownership shares.

[88] Shibuya, "Min Shin jidai," 59.2–3, 121. After a 1757 fire, the association stopped sponsoring banquets for sixteen years.

[89] A household's withdrawal or absence from the association did not automatically deprive it of its right to membership, even if it missed its scheduled turn as head. Rather, a family's membership position (often encompassing more than one actual household) was expected to pass from one generation to the next within the family and would be held in abeyance until the family's return to the village, when it might eventually renew its membership and serve again as association head. Also, the individual party acting as the head of a village worship association could in at least one case transfer his management powers, as he wished, to another in the association (Huizhou qiannian, v. 21, 68 (1671)).

[90] Cheng Wenju, Yangshan sheng, 5.1a–6b. McDermott, Making, v. 1, 222–23, recounts similar scuffles between monks and locals over another potentially numinous grave site.

Although Buddhist temples seemed less threatening to Huizhou lineages bolstered by their wealth and numerous ancestral halls, Confucian-minded men in late Ming and Qing Huizhou reflexively continued to disparage Buddhist establishments and teachings. Huizhou's temples and monasteries they judged to be small and poor in contrast to its ancestral halls and even the Yangzi delta's temples. Buddhist teachings they likewise rejected as passé and inconsequential: "Nowadays, by and large, those who chat about Meditation (*chan* 禪) and talk of Buddhism are extremely few; they are not at all worth taking seriously."[91] Hence, by *c*.1800, a Huizhou Confucian scholar could confidently deny the relevance of Buddhists and Daoists to the concerns of Huizhou and its people:

> The customs of Huizhou pay no respect to the teachings of Buddha and Laozi. The monks and Daoist priests are used solely for exorcisms and sacrifices and for community ritual services for the living and the dead (*zhai jiao* 齋醮). They receive no respect and trust, no reverence and offerings.[92]

The Wus of Mingzhou 茗洲吳, to cite just one lineage example, barred their members from becoming Buddhist monks and Daoist priests and from turning to these clerics when ill. A sick lineage member was to summon a good doctor (*liangyi* 良醫); if instead he persisted in summoning a cleric and let him set up an altar for prayers and rituals, his fellow lineage members were to upbraid him and deprive him of his customary portion of pork at one of that year's festivities.[93] Indeed, in more recent centuries some lineages not only literally bought monks and housed them as religious specialists in a lineage-run temple but also considered and treated them as bondservants with specific obligations to provide funeral services. As lineage dependents these monks held a decidedly low social status.[94]

This antagonism to Buddhism no longer, as in the Ming, needed to be whipped up by the government. So common and pervasive was it in Huizhou's Confucian circles that some scholars revived the ancient charge that Buddhism had defiled China's classical culture. Buddhism, they asserted, had introduced to China such supposedly unknown objects as statues and images and thereby deluded its people. Hence Huizhou's most famous private academy decided in the late

---

[91] *Huizhou fuzhi* (1699), 2.66b.   [92] *SSXT*, 18, 607.
[93] Wu Di, *Mingzhou Wushi jiadian*, 1, 20, 22.
[94] Lagerwey, "Village Religion," 305–59.

seventeenth century to destroy its long-standing statues of Zhu Xi and his father Zhu Song 朱松 and to replace them with wooden spirit tablets.[95]

Towards popular cults, Huizhou scholars' antagonism was more sharply expressed, especially by district degree holders and unemployed scholars; it is hard not to attribute their critical stance to a wish to acquire a social distinction denied them by their failure in the civil service examinations. These cults might seem to be rather weak threats to the Confucian order, since, but for a few notable exceptions like Zhang Xun 張巡, Cheng Lingxi 程靈洗, and Wang Hua 汪華, many lacked strong institutional support and arrangements. Also, their popularity, once again with these and a few other notable exceptions, fluctuated greatly over time. Nonetheless, it was this very instability that fostered a deep concern about their uncontrollability. And so, during the Qing, they replaced Buddhism as the principal object of orthodox Confucians' social criticism.

The cults said to be popular in early Qing Huizhou had a bewildering variety of origins and practices, belying all efforts to squeeze them into a single category like "lewd cults" and to extirpate them from Huizhou life. Some were distinctly local, such as those worshipping Zhang Cishan 張祠山 and Xie Xu 謝緒, both of whom were thought to govern the waterways, and the Two Green Dragons who were associated with a Buddhist temple set up near Mingzhou in the Ming dynasty. Other gods were regional, like Wutong 五通, whose cult was so vile that reportedly "even bad Daoists and evil shamans wanted to vomit when they learned of its practices" (later in the Qing it would be tamed).[96] And others were so nationally renowned and government-approved, that they were included in the Qing dynasty's official pantheon of gods acceptable for official worship throughout the empire – Guanyin; the City God; the Buddhist god Dicang 地藏, the worship of whom had long been considered a filial practice in the Wu area; the Dongyue 東嶽 God of Mt Tai 泰山; Zhenwu 鎮武, the Martial Warrior considered the patron god of the Ming dynasty and closely associated with Mt Qiyun in Huizhou; and Zhang Tianshi 張天師, the

[95] *She xianzhi* (1937), 16.39a–40a.
[96] Von Glahn, "Enchantment of Wealth," 651–714.

founder of the Daoist religion.[97] In short, the world of popular cults in Huizhou drew support from a variety of social and political worlds so disparate that a uniform Confucian or government policy towards them was hard to formulate and enforce.

The policy for treating these cults proposed by *The Family Code of the Wu Family of Mingzhou* (*Mingzhou Wushi jiadian* 茗洲吳氏家典), an influential book written and published in eighteenth-century Huizhou, was nonetheless harshly antagonistic. Combining bans, substitutions, and reforms, it sought to make the local populace's religious institutions, ritual performances, and values more akin to those of orthodox neo-Confucianism.[98] Thus the Xiuning degree holder Wu Di 吳翟, who oversaw the final editing of this book, denounced all these cults as dangerous. He also urged his lineage to reject all "lewd" sacrifices except for those associated with festivals explicitly approved by the *Collected Statutes of the Qing Dynasty* (*Qing huidian* 清會典) – the end-of-the-year sacrifices to the Stove God, the rural district's exorcisms on the Qingming Day and on the first day of the tenth lunar month, and the village worship

---

[97] Wu Di, *Mingzhou Wushi*, 7, 288–94.
[98] Usually, a set of family instructions like *The Family Code* can be considered relevant to just a few lineages and certainly not to an entire prefecture. But such caution is not justified for this title. Judged by Guo Qingtao (*Ritual Opera*, 29) as probably the most detailed of all sets of ritual regulations drafted in Qing Huizhou, it was completed by the prefectural school student Wu Di (d. 1736) in 1713 partly as a critique of his Xiuning lineage's improper practices and partly as a comprehensive guide for conversion to orthodox Confucian ritual practices for readers both inside and outside his lineage. The book's ideas and details derive from the personal experiences of several generations of Wus, their study of the main Confucian ritual texts, and their experience in performing them. Wu Di acknowledged his debt to these ancestors for their learning and their compilation of the manuscript he completed; doubtless he was also influenced by his time as a lecturer at a local Confucian academy. For the final editing and collating he relied on fifty-three of his kinsmen and sixty-seven members of his local Confucian academy (who bore twenty-one distinct surnames) (Wu Di, *Mingzhou Wushi*, 11–13). At least four editions were published upon its completion (1713, 1727, 1733, 1735), the last apparently outside the lineage and thus with non-lineage funds to meet readers' demands (ibid., Editor's Introduction, 1–11). More than a century later it won praise in print for changing its readers' behavior and for setting a model for the proper performance of Confucian ritual in Huizhou (Chen Rui, "Ming Qing shiqi," 60). *The Family Code* clearly had an authorship and readership far larger than, respectively, one man and one lineage.

association's annual fall and spring festivities in honor of the tutelary gods of the earth and grains.[99]

To replace the unacceptable cults and sacrifices, Wu Di and his Huizhou supporters proposed the observance of a long and regular schedule of Confucian family and lineage rituals. Drawing heavily from Confucian and neo-Confucian ritual classics like the *Book of Rites* and Zhu Xi's *Family Rituals*, as well as from the *Collected Statutes of the Qing Dynasty* and gentry family instruction manuals, *The Family Code* laid out in considerable detail how to perform a wide variety of family and lineage rituals. In addition to prescribing the movements for participants in the now traditional family rituals of capping, marriage, burial, and mourning, it told families anxious to be respectable which seasonal festivals and lineage celebrations they should observe and how to perform their ceremonies properly.

For Wu Di's own lineage, the proposed shift towards orthodox ritual practice was a major headache, since the identity of its Prime Ancestor and the proper place for this ancestor's spirit tablet had serious implications for the lineage's structure, ritual activities, and now its social position. As seen in volume 1, the person from whom all Mingzhou Wus had traditionally traced their descent was not the standard "he" but a particular "she."[100] The concubine of a ninth-century Wu, this Ms Cheng had for some eight centuries been honored as their Prime Ancestor and her spirit tablet had been accorded pride of place on the altar of the Mingzhou Wus' ancestral hall. Every year at fixed dates hundreds of males in this self-professedly patrilineal descent group assembled at this hall to make collective offerings and worship her as the foundress, or rather founder, of their lineage. Henceforth, this practice was to stop. She was to be demoted, her spirit tablet removed from the ancestral hall to a shrine set up at her grave, and its central place of honor on the altar as Prime Ancestor taken by that of a much younger ancestor, a late thirteenth-century official previously considered just the lineage's Prime Migrant. So ended a set of ritual practices in this village and lineage of eight centuries' standing, when confronted with a staunch proponent of neo-Confucian orthodoxy.[101]

---

[99] Wu Di, *Mingzhou Wushi*, 7, 282.   [100] McDermott, *Making*, v. 1, 68–73.
[101] Wu Di, *Mingzhou Wushi*, Editor's Introduction, 3, 1, 24, and, 6, 240–41. Simultaneously, the spirit tablets of all concubines were ordered out of the ancestral hall (ibid., 2, 32).

In carrying out these reforms, Wu Di encountered many obstacles. Not only were most adult lineage members working far from their village and thus hard to control, but also those who stayed in Huizhou had a depressing record of neglecting these canonical prescriptions and the knowledgeable advice of their learned kinsmen. As a result, the Mingzhou Wus had long ago stopped performing certain traditional family rituals, such as the capping ceremony for younger male members.[102] And their performance of other collective "Confucian" rituals often violated Confucian norms and forms of propriety. Their marriage ceremonies, for instance, commonly included plays and musical performances, mixed men and women, and allowed them to act "like animals" in "what is known by vulgar custom as 'the raucous room' (naofang 鬧房)"; that is, the lewd bantering of the married couple in their wedding bed by a group of intrusive friends and relations.[103] Though the lineage's funeral performances were thought to have become more proper since the Ming, sometimes the ancestors were formally notified of a lineage member's death not by the son of the deceased but by his nephew or, even worse, by someone pretending to be the son.[104] Some spirit tablets were placed out of genealogical order on the altar of the ancestral hall,[105] and sometimes they were disrespectfully treated or even inappropriately worshipped by younger members, ignorant of their elders' tablet misplacements and their past appointment of lineage heads on grounds other than the proper generational order of descent. Most regrettably, despite the construction of an ancestral hall for the entire lineage in the mid sixteenth century, lineage members continued to prefer to worship, apart from Ms Cheng, just their recent ancestors.[106]

Consequently, the proposed changes to lineage ritual, structure, and management entailed a thoroughgoing reform of lineage members' customs, as much in their daily life as in their ritual performances. Henceforth, juniors were to address their seniors by their proper formal name; accept in silence their criticism, even when invalid; and spend their own time largely in reading Confucian books for the official examinations. They were to refrain from engaging privately

---

[102] Ibid., 3, 63.
[103] Ibid., 4, 81. This practice originated long before this report, and long outlasted it (Van Gulik, *Sexual Life*, 104–5).
[104] Wu Di, *Mingzhou Wushi*, 5, 116.   [105] Ibid., 5, 122–24.
[106] Ibid., 1, 26–28.

in social intercourse under the pretence of protecting and helping the village; from gambling and living without gainful employment; and from having contact with "chess boards, another board game known as 'double six' (*shuangliu* 雙六), disorderly ballads, and [playing with] insects and birds." Any disobedient male, if he continued to ignore his elders' censure and to learn nothing from beatings, was to be reported to the officials and expelled from the lineage through removal of his name from its genealogy.

Women were made to suffer even tighter and more comprehensive controls over their daily life and movements:

Unless they have a good reason, [women] cannot go out. At night they are to travel with candles; if they have no candles, then they are to stop. If they are lewd, one should promptly get rid of them. If there are any who are jealous and have a long tongue, for the time being reproach them. If they do not go along, then get rid of them."

They were strictly forbidden to play cards and watch plays, have contact with female purveyors of religion, and use Buddhist or Daoist ceremonies at funerals.

But to what extent were these and similar injunctions adopted and imposed in Qing Huizhou? One general account of early nineteenth-century Huizhou provides an answer admirably clear and direct. Lineage institutions, we learn, so dominated the villages and towns of this prefecture that they by and large excluded rival cults and their religious institutions:

The fact that Huizhou especially has no cults (*jiaomen* 教門) is also due to the residence of lineages here, not only in the villages where it is difficult [for cults] to reside alongside lineages but also in the cities and markets where the various great surname groups have settled on pieces of land that they have portioned up [amongst themselves]. None of the so-called "Halls of the Master of Heaven" (*Tianzhu tang* 天主堂; that is, Roman Catholic churches) and temples for ceremonies and visits is allowed to be built here. Therefore, some members of these cults, when they come to Huizhou to trade, have no place to congregate and assemble. It is then hard for them to stop here for long.[107]

Buddhist and Daoist establishments, though still standing, were also said to be insignificant structures: "They are nothing more than huts

---

[107] *SSXT*, 18, 607.

where people donate boiled water for tea and shrines where they present incense. If you seek awesome and resplendent places, the so-called 'palaces of Buddha and Laozi,' there are absolutely none of them here."[108] Some Qing village records support these descriptions, suggesting that lineage institutions now overwhelmed any Buddhist, Daoist, or other religious institutions that had once challenged lineage dominance. Witness the situation in Jiang Village of She county: in 1775 in "this kingdom of Zhu Xi's School of the Way," this village catchment area had just one Daoist shrine (of late Ming vintage) and four Buddhist establishments (only one of which was functioning), but thirty separate ancestral halls, mostly built before the Qing and thus in operation for over a century before this report.[109]

Such claims, it must be said, exaggerate lineage domination. Other evidence suggests only qualified hegemony, in which other religious institutions held some power thanks to their continued presence in many villages, their use by villagers for certain rituals, their hold on the values and beliefs of ordinary villagers, and even their institutional arrangements. For instance, the Jiang Village figures that attest to the weakness of Buddhist and Daoist establishments need to be read against others – such as those from Shaxi[110] – that suggest that lineage institutions, however predominant, did not eliminate all other religious, even Buddhist, institutions and associations in their midst. Indeed, a mid-eighteenth-century Wuyuan gazetteer marveled at the ability of Buddhist temples in Huizhou to survive so much attack and destruction.[111]

Furthermore, while we might accept the early nineteenth-century report of lineage predominance, we must challenge first its sharp distinction between Buddhist temples and ancestral halls and thus the validity of simple comparisons between the total number of ancestral halls and those of other religious, especially Buddhist, establishments. According to an earlier 1758 report written by a Huizhou native about an ancestral hall built by sixteen lineages, the distinction between these rival establishments was often moot: "The ancestral shrine (*zumiao* 族廟) is in a Buddhist monks' temple. Although there

---

[108] Ibid. [109] *Chengyang sanzhi*, 8.1a–6a, 9b–12b.
[110] Ling Yingqiu, *Shaxi jilüe*, provides a strong counterinstance, but the data in other surviving Huizhou village gazetteers generally indicate a preponderance, but not overwhelming dominance, of ancestral halls over temples and shrines in single-lineage villages.
[111] *Wuyuan xianzhi* (1757), 38.8b–9a.

is no reference to this in the *Book of Rites* (*Li* 禮), there are many of these in Huizhou." This commentator proceeds to mention two well-known historical precedents of mixing Buddhist temples with secular structures. But he stresses that this 1758 Huizhou case is special, since its donors are concerned primarily with their ancestors' well-being rather than with their personal afterlife. Their filial piety justifies this mixing of institutional types: "The descendants push to admire their deceased ancestors, and they wish to incur good fortune for them from the Buddha. Moreover, they make prayers and offerings for an entire area's people. Thoughts of benevolence and filial piety – it can be known that these do not violate righteousness." Just as moneylending and ancestral worship coexisted amicably in the establishment and operation of ancestral halls, so, then, could a lineage's commitment to filial piety justify its aid for repair of a Buddhist temple complex in which its ancestral shrine was sited.[112]

Hence, as some excellent work by John Lagerwey on Huizhou religious culture has demonstrated, villagers' values, customs, and commitments to local religious institutions and religious cults remained very strong.[113] Admittedly, Confucian scholars tended to dominate the performance of funeral rituals in well-educated households, or so one is led to believe from repeated claims that Huizhou lineages adhered to Zhu Xi's *Family Rituals*.[114] Yet some Confucian-minded lineages allowed monks to perform some rituals at the actual funerals or read sutras to help the soul of the deceased reach the underworld safely.[115] And a minority of lineages clung to traditional practices, allowing monks to perform funeral observances in their village with funds acquired from annual membership fees and land rents of Buddhist associations (*fohui* 佛會).[116] In sum, Buddhist monks may have generally yielded to Confucian scholars in death and memorial rituals, but they and their services were still available and called upon.[117]

---

[112] Ye Weiming, *Shexian*, 8.162a.
[113] Lagerwey, "Ethnographic Introduction."
[114] *Fengnan zhi*, 1, 257; *Chengyang sanzhi*, 6, 645; Ling Yingqiu, *Shaxi jilüe*, 642; Xu Xianzu, *Xiuning futan zhi*, 3, 286.
[115] Xu Xianzu, *Xiuning futan zhi*, 3, 288; *Fengnan zhi*, 1, 257; *Chengyang sanzhi*, 6, 645–46.
[116] Chen Keyun, "Ming Qing Huizhou zongzu," 49.
[117] Huang Laisheng and Chen Liyun, "Shuma cun," 158–81, cites a temple in Shuma Village with limited tasks and powers.

In the observance of other non-Confucian rituals and observances, Wu Di's ban on lewd sacrifices was even less heeded. A 1718 agreement between six Huizhou men shows how simple it was for six lineage members to form a credit association to build up funds to create a tutelary-god worship association (even easier and cheaper than an ancestral hall in the Ming):

Each man paid out one item (*jian* 件) of rice for a total amount of six items, that from 1705 to 1718 the tutelary-god association loaned out for interest. It now takes the capital and the accumulated interest to buy nearly two hillocks of fields to set up a tutelary-god worship association for which this land will permanently provide supplies for sacrifices.[118]

In other words, small groups of males with small funds established and ran disparaged religious associations without need for approval from the government and, in this case, their lineage leaders.

And so, throughout the Qing dynasty, Huizhou festivals dedicated to local deities like Wang Hua, Zhang Xun, and Cheng Lingxi continued to be lavishly funded. Daoist exorcisms remained regular events in Huizhou villages, and popular cults to local deities flourished both as collective festivals and in more private acts of worship.[119] The social world as well as the imagination of most Huizhou residents remained resolutely wrapped up with a set of religious practices that survived the lineages' attacks on rival religious institutions.

Perhaps the most notable of these religious associations were the "Five Sectors" groups, who worked with the urban and rural "protection associations" to worship gods and carry out exorcisms that were to shield villages and lineages from disease, disorder, and other misfortune.[120] Different deities reportedly flourished from county to county: in the late nineteenth century, Yi county was the home of a particularly large cult of the Tang military hero Zhang Xun, while She county reportedly favored the worship of the Eighth Elder (*Ba laoye* 八老爺), Xiuning the Ninth Minister (*Jiuxiang gong* 九相公), and Qimen the Seventh Dragon King (*Qilong wang* 七龍王) and the Eighth Dragon King (*Balong wang* 八龍王).[121] State support was conferred on deities

---

[118] Yan Guifu and Wang Guojian, *Huizhou wenshu dang'an*, 386. The size of a *jian* is unclear.
[119] *Yi xianzhi* (1813–24), 3.2a; (1868), 3.2b; Guo Qitao, *Exorcism and Money*.
[120] Wang Zhenzhong, "Ming Qing yilai Huizhou," 17–102.
[121] Wang Zhun, *Han Chu erxi Wangshi jiasheng* (1910), 2, wenxian, 5b. The Seventh Dragon King was also called Lord Shuang 爽公, the Eight Dragon King Lord Jun 俊公, and the young son of these kings the Ninth Minister.

celebrated for their dynastic loyalty, and Huizhou's famous Song dynasty neo-Confucian philosopher Zhu Xi, whose thought provided intellectual ballast to Manchu rule, received widespread veneration as a god (*shen*) as much as a sage (*sheng*).[122] Itinerant Huizhou merchants worshipped him as their occupation's deity in some of their native-place associations, as the gap between official thought, or Confucianism, and commercial values (in recent decades sometimes called secularization) narrowed, even though the government still expressed support for agricultural deities judged capable of protecting harvests.

And so some Huizhou Confucians' claims to have eliminated popular cults and their ritual alternatives especially for physical well-being, burials, and funerals grossly exaggerated their prowess. In the villages of Huizhou, local-place gods and cults may have been less public and prominent, but they remained at least as testimony to the community's and lineage's shared history. Witness the fate of efforts to suppress worship of the widely venerated deity Dutian 都天, the cult of the Tang hero Zhang Xun, whose death at the hands of rebels in the eighth century won him a wide range of admirers both inside and outside Huizhou. A model of pure loyalty, he became a cult figure for avoiding epidemics as well as defending the well-being of Huizhou merchants in their travels during the very late Ming and the Qing. His close association with itinerant merchants from Huizhou was particularly strong in delta cities frequented by salt merchants and others actively engaged in silver transactions from the mid Qing. Worshipped in many temples in Zhenjiang, Zhenzhou, and Yangzhou, he was considered a Huizhou variant of the universally popular deity Guandi 關帝, the god of dynastic loyalty, and also a more subdued version of the Wutong deity. His admirers in places like Nanjing and Zhenjiang were all traders, who relied on the cult's local funds to protect them from tax levies. In Nanjing an annual three-day lantern festival was held by Huizhou timber merchants in the god's honor, while in Zhenjiang a great fair was held, its proceeds providing some merchants with most of their annual profits.[123]

And within Huizhou this god won staunch supporters as well as severe critics. One arch Confucian scholar there gained fame for his attack on this cult's activities:

---

[122] Tao Mingxian, "Zhang wang," 144–64.
[123] Zhu Xiaotian, "Jindai Jiangnan miaohui," 58–65; Wang Zhenzhong, "Ming Qing Huainan," 27–32, 64; Gan Xi, *Baixia suoyan*, 7, 74–75.

Cheng Guxue 程古雪 urged people to desist on grounds of moral principle (*li*). Members of his lineage did not heed him. Furthermore they set up a shrine to the Dutian Deity just to the right of the ancestral hall of the ancestor Wang (*Wangzu* 王祖). Greatly incensed by this, Cheng went and had the shrine's base brought down, personally smashing its spirit tablet (*zhu*) and casting it deep into a pond.[124]

His written denunciation of the custom aroused the anger of a crowd of locals, who only after a long time quieted down; they did not rebuild the shrine.

So passed the lull before the storm. When a relation of Cheng's became seriously sick, the relation invited monks (*seng*) to come and sacrifice to Dutian. They arrived and started performing rituals aimed at curing the sick. Wielding staves and swords during their "wild wanderings" into the women's quarters (*neishi* 内室), even after their patient had died, they drove Cheng to apoplexy. He grabbed hold of the figure of Dutian these monks held and smashed it to the ground, earning an accolade from a local twentieth-century scholar. The cult and its popular impieties, however, long survived his tirades:

This matter was very difficult. During the Kangxi (1662–1722) and Qianlong (1736–95) reign eras a district degree holder (*shusheng* 書生) of an entire rural district could violate a crowd's anger and destroy the authority of a god. He had not the slightest fear at all. It was even more remarkable than the destruction of the shrine of the Wutong god by Tang Bin 唐斌 in Suzhou. That Huizhou (She) customs today are still like this is even more lamentable.[125]

It is almost as if we are reading a Song scholar's denunciation of the foibles of the ignorant masses.

Finally, how does one estimate the degree of acceptance accorded orthodox Confucian values and beliefs in Qing Huizhou? According to research by Cynthia Brokaw and Chow Kai-wing, the tragic downfall of the Ming dynasty encouraged social critics of the early Qing to search for orthodox Confucian certainties, such as those promulgated and supposedly practiced in the early Ming.[126] Social order was the principal concern of these early Qing writers, and their means of

[124] *SSXT*, 3, 88.   [125] Ibid.; von Glahn, *Sinister Way*, 236–46.
[126] Brokaw, *Ledgers*, 157–236, esp. 187; Chow Kai-wing, *Rise of Confucian Ritualism*, 129–60. Van Gulik, *Sexual Life*, 333–35, mentions that some officials sought such changes to "lewd customs."

achieving and maintaining this goal within the given hierarchy entailed the setting and enforcement of different rules for people in different roles within Qing society. The harmony arising from these parties' fulfillment of their reciprocal duties would, it was thought, enable China to avoid a relapse into the moral decay of the late Ming and the destructive chaos of the early Qing. It would also assure a vital role for the educated elite, if only because in a properly ordered world they would naturally hold the highest status and responsibility and provide models of proper behavior. The strength of this consensus lies in the varied social status of its proponents: the scholar-officials and their major thinkers studied by Chow and the moderately literate and educated studied by Brokaw.

Huizhou counterparts to these views can be found not only in *The Family Code of the Wu Family of Mingzhou* but also among the writings of a wide spectrum of educated and non-educated men in the mid Qing. The most famous Huizhou figure who adopted such a stance was the neo-Confucian thinker Ling Tingkan 凌廷堪 (1757–1809). Reared and educated in Huizhou, he taught for a time at its most celebrated academy. Towards the close of his life his writings attracted attention for their stress on the centrality of ritual in Confucian learning. In his view, moral principle, the key concept of orthodox neo-Confucian thought, was lodged in ritual and could be neither found nor learned outside it.[127] A moral social order thus required action based on prescribed canonical forms of gesture and moral behavior, with the aim of laying a stable basis for the development of better human relations with nature, mankind in general, and the moral self.[128] Predictably, the orthodoxy associated with the state-based examinations and the writings of the Song thinkers, the Cheng brothers and Zhu Xi won increasing favor among local scholars as the key to achieving the goal of social harmony.[129] And there arose a local cult, a male version of the chaste-widow culture already popular in Huizhou, that showed great esteem for very old men of all social ranks.

---

[127] Ling Tingkan, *Ling Tingkan quanji, v. 1*, 13–18; Zhang Shouan, *Yili dai li*, 76–117.

[128] For an idealistic depiction of how lineage rule would lead to such a society, see Liu Boshan, "Ming Qing Huizhou zongzu yu xiangcun shehui de wending," 179–202.

[129] Zhu Changrong, "Qingchu Cheng Zhu," 152–76.

Feasts were held in their honor, and public honors conferred for their services to the public good.[130]

Lower down on the social scale, but equally committed to the importance of Confucian ritual, were many ritual specialists (*lisheng* 禮生). These Huizhou men made an itinerant living by imparting to ignorant families and villages elsewhere in central and south China what they had learned of the arcane proprieties of Confucian ritual from their experience in Huizhou.[131] Like their commercial counterparts, the Huizhou merchants, they made their way to out-of-the-way parts of the country, spreading knowledge of ritual and related institutions (surely their activities spurred on the adoption elsewhere of the Huizhou practice of financing ancestral-hall construction and operation as a credit association). Such associations, at least in the surviving record, were formed far more often in the Qing than in the late Ming, but their aims remained the same over time. Kinship or very close friendship was the key to determining membership. Credit associations often had a specific welfare purpose for their members (such as aid for funeral or marriage expenses), management duties rotated among the members, cash disbursements were small, and grain sometimes replaced money as the membership charge.[132]

An even wider representation of educated Huizhou society was involved in the establishment of a "Confucian Village" in the Huangdun 篁墩 area of She county in Huizhou in the early eighteenth century. After generations of government indifference and Cheng lineage hostility, some She county students, officials, gentry, and higher-level government officers co-operated to induce some Chengs to sell off land in Huangdun. In thereby supposedly recovering some graves of Zhu Xi's family and a site for the eventual construction of a Three Masters shrine in honor of Zhu Xi, Cheng Hao, and Cheng Yi, these neo-Confucian enthusiasts gave concrete meaning to the prefecture's frequent boast of its close historical ties to the founding fathers of the philosophical orthodoxy of the Ming and Qing governments.[133]

---

[130] Zhang Xu, "Shang xing er xia xiao," 198–208.
[131] Liu Yonghua, *Confucian Rituals and Chinese Villagers*; Wang Zhenzhong, *Ming Qing yilai Huizhou*, 138–81; Zhang Xiaoping, *Huizhou gu citang*, 137–38, mentions their Ming roots and the diversity of their lineage duties.
[132] Xiong Yuanbao, *Shindai Kishu*, 124–28.
[133] Zhao Pang, *Cheng Zhu Queli zhi*. These trends permeated the Qing government's stress on orthodoxy and some Confucian scholars' advocacy of "simple learning" (*puxue* 樸學) (Inoue, *Min Shin gakujitsu*, 192–286, 315–84).

The fly in this orthodox ointment, as Cynthia Brokaw recognized, would be the undeniable importance of a cash economy to the well-being of men and women in southeast China, including Huizhou.[134] Commerce, supported by an obsessive concern with silver, continued to be attacked by some Confucian scholars for fostering excessive human desires and rewarding materialistic impulses that threaten social stability and solidarity. But most early Qing officials showed no wish to reverse the spread of this area's highly commercialized economy. If men in places like the Yangzi delta thus retained an ambivalence towards this form of wealth and made certain allowances "for inescapable social and economic changes,"[135] how much more ambivalent was the response of equally conservative commentators in Huizhou! Its educated families, so dependent on commercial profits for their livelihood, continued in the Qing to stress the happy marriage of their Confucian values and learning with their trading occupation, even though transactions by and for Huizhou lineages increasingly dealt only in silver (cult associations often dealt, by contrast, in units of grain). These lineages' collective silence about obvious contradictions between their commitments is not surprising, so long as ancestral halls and ritual continued to be commonly enmeshed in financial concerns and transactions to no one's serious distress.

In Qing dynasty Huizhou greater lineage dominance may well have left rival village institutions less vibrant and autonomous than during the early and mid Ming. But calls for the moral and social orthodoxy associated with the lineage order did not prevent at least some lineage members from continuing to make complex and diverse responses to social and cultural changes, even in as arch a site of neo-Confucian orthodoxy as Huangdun. Huizhou scholars' reverence for Huangdun's Song sages might owe as much to the popular religious imagination as to the classical texts and their Song philosophical interpreters. For example, the two early eighteenth-century students who strove to establish a Huangdun shrine for the Three Masters acknowledged that their inspiration for this shrine had come in part from dreams, in which they had met not just a yellow-robed spirit who resembled Zhu Xi, but also two deceased women of Zhu's family and an elderly resident of Huangdun.[136]

---

[134] Brokaw, *Ledgers*, 161, 173, 207–16.
[135] Ibid., 215; von Glahn, *Fountain of Fortune*, 215–24.
[136] Zhao Pang, *Cheng Zhu Queli zhi*, 101–3; *She xianzhi* (1771), 2, 4.6a. None of the active proponents of the neo-Confucian Village of Huangdun was surnamed Cheng.

Moreover, the actual membership of lineage alliances at Huangdun did not necessarily follow the orthodox social rules. Despite a requirement of common Cheng ancestry, some members of the Huangdun shrine alliance dedicated to Cheng Lingxi turned out not to be Chengs of the same descent line: in the doubling of the shrine's membership from over eighty in 1690 to over 150 in 1745, some segments were admitted due to fraudulent genealogies, gullible elders, and a general wish not to upset previous private arrangements.[137] Within Huangdun itself another lineage pressed the validity of its own presence: by 1739 nineteen Huang lineages had collectively acquired ritual fields there to preserve their ancestral graves, construct their own Huangdun ancestral hall, restore the original name of the village (at least in Huang lineage records), and advance their cause against the Chengs in their unending competition for glory and legitimacy.[138]

And back in Qimen county, the Shanhe Chengs themselves, despite all their economic troubles and lineage quarrels, proved resilient in fostering new and smaller organizations that mixed religious and commercial commitments. Totaling no fewer than twenty-nine over the course of the Qing, these credit associations seem to have far outnumbered their Ming predecessors. They consisted of a total of 534 memberships, which men could hold either fully or partly (most were divisible by inheritance), enter and leave fairly freely (admission charges and annual fees were standard), and buy and sell among their kinsmen. These credit associations were dedicated not just to lending cheap money (to kinsmen and non-kinsmen alike), but also to worshipping deities. Lineage leaders bemoaned their own members' disinterest in Confucian studies and, correspondingly, "their paying respect only to the teachings of Buddha and Laozi," phrases readily understood as a shorthand for any mixture of these religions and popular religious cults.[139] The names of the deities actually worshipped by

---

[137] *Huangdun shizhong cigong jibu*, 1a, 5a–b, 9a.
[138] *Xin'an Huangshi Huangdun muci jitian ji*.
[139] Liu Miao, "Qingdai Qimen," 8 (1993.10), 256–66, and 9 (1994.11), 268–74; and "Qingdai Huizhou de 'hui' yu 'huiji'," 235–40 (Liu numbers these associations at thirty-three). Xiong Yuanbao, *Shindai Kishū*, 122. Another Qimen village, consisting mainly of Wus, in 1655 reported the presence of at least nine religious associations (their landholdings, collectively totaling less than 2 percent of the village area's registered fiscal acreage, were tiny compared to holdings registered for different branches of these Wus) (*Qimen xian xinzhang qingong shouzhuang*). Financial accounts and rules for at least

these religious associations include Dizang, Zhang Xun, Wenchang, and Cheng Shizhong, popular gods whose names capped these associations' names and whose festivals brought members together to make offerings on behalf of their ancestors.

What say did a lineage have in the practices and finances of the cults its members belonged to? The sheer number and variety of these cults and lineages prevent a single answer. Even when some leaders of a powerful lineage like the Xiuning Jin in 1699 funded ancestral-hall repairs by appropriating three years of rent revenues from religious associations its members belonged to, their dominance was nowhere as assured as we might presume. First, these associations were described as "within the lineage" (zuzhong 族中), and thus did not include many other religious associations (like the Dutian cult) that were not lineage-associated and thus harder for lineages to control.[140] Second, the confiscated property of these associations had an annual grain income worth about 140 taels, a sum that suggests that considerable landed resources remained in the hands of these lineage-based associations.[141]

In sum, the economic conflicts, political and social jockeying, and ingenious adaptation of local customs and institutions in both Huizhou village life and merchant work throughout the Ming persisted well into the Qing. Within the framework of a lineage-dominated society that enveloped but did not eliminate the village's institutional alternatives, a great number of lineage members held a variety of religious views and institutional commitments that they saw as benefiting themselves and their kinship group, be it a small family, a branch, or a lineage. Those anxious to throttle these impulses and remove "unorthodox" religious practices by and large had to wait until the revolutions of the twentieth century to see their wish fulfilled.

---

fourteen Shanhe Chengs' associations survive for the years between 1644 and 1834 in the Huizhou sources collection of the Institute of History of CASS in Beijing (Yan Guifu and Wang Guojian, *Huizhou wenshu dang'an*, 126); so far, I have been unable to examine them.

[140] *Xiuning Jinshi zupu* (1748), second *ce*, 13th juan, frames 28 and 86–88. Even though the project had been first proposed in 1675, its lineage leaders took over twenty-five years to raise from members just half of the required repair funds. Doubtless out of frustration, these leaders without consultation declared their seizure of these associations' collective rental income.

[141] Von Glahn, *Fountain of Fortune*, 211–15, 244–45, 255; Kishimoto, *Shindai Chūgoku*, 151–57, for delta land prices in Tunxi, Xiuning, in the late eighteenth century, see Kuroda, "What Prices Can Tell Us," 105–7.

In 1700 these dramatic changes lay in the future, unknown and unimagined. Meanwhile, Huizhou merchants flourished, as did their commercial practices and financial institutions in the Yangzi Valley's cities, where so many of them increasingly lived, worked, and were buried.

Bibliography

Abbreviations

CASS = Chinese Academy of Social Sciences, Beijing

Dianshang = Wang Yuming 王裕明, *Ming Qing Huizhou dianshang yanjiu* 明清徽州典商研究 (Beijing, Renmin, 2014).

DSGJY = *Doushan gong jiayi jiaozhu* 竇山公家議校注 by Cheng Chang 程昌, revised by Cheng Fang 程钫, Zhou Shaoquan 周绍泉 and Zhao Yaguang 赵亚光, eds. (Hefei: Huangshan shushe, 1993).

FKSFC = Fang Chengxun 方承訓, *Fang Kuishan fu chu ji* 方鄈邖复初集 (Wanli ed.) (*SKQSCM*).

MQHS = Zhang Haipeng 张海鹏 and Wang Tingyuan 王廷元, comp., *Ming Qing Huishang ziliao xuanbian* 明清徽商资料选编 (Hefei: Huangshan shushe, 1985).

MQSZ = Suzhou lishi bowuguan 苏州历史博物馆, et al., comp., *Ming Qing Suzhou gongshangye beike ji* 明清苏州工商业碑刻集 (Nanjing: Jiangsu renmin, 1981).

Nanda T = Nanjing University, History Department, Huizhou Sources, Tunxi Rare Books Bookstore (the number written on each of these documents is specified in each use here).

Qingming ji = Zhongguo shehui kexue yuan lishi yanjiusuo Song Liao Jin Yuan shi yanjiushi 中国社会科学院歷史研究所宋遼金元史研究室, comp., *(Minggong shupan) Qingming ji* (名公書判)清明集 (Beijing: Zhonghua, 1987).

SBCK = *Sibu congkan*

SBCKXB = *Sibu congkan xubu*

SKQSCM = *Siku quanshu cunmu (congshu)*

SKQSZB = *Siku quanshu zhenben (congshu)*

SSXT = Xu Chengyao 許承堯, *Sheshi xiantan* 歙事閑譚 (Hefei: Huangshan shushe, 2001).

SZSZ = *Suzhou shizhi* (Nanjing: Jiangsu renmin, 1993).

THJ = Wang Daokun 汪道昆*Taihan ji* 太函集 (Hefei: Huangshan shushe, 2004).

XXSKQS = *Xuxiu Siku quanshu*

Huizhou Sources: Collections

Huizhou Sources, Anhui Provincial Library, Rare Books Room.
Huizhou Sources, Institute of Economics, CASS, Beijing
Huizhou Sources, Institute of History, CASS, Beijing.
Huizhou Sources, Nanjing University, History Department.
Huizhou Sources, Shanghai Municipal Library, Rare Books Room.
Huizhou wenqi zhengli zu 徽州文契整理組, comp, *Ming Qing Huizhou shehui jingji ziliao congbian* 明清徽州社会经济资料从编, *v. 1* (Beijing: Shehui kexue, 1988).
Ming Qing Huizhou shehui jingji ziliao congbian 明清徽州社會經濟資料從編, *v. 2* (Beijing: Shehui kexue, 1990).
Liu Boshan 刘伯山, comp., *Huizhou wenshu* 徽州文書 (Guilin: Guangxi shifan daxue), *vv. 1–10* (2005), *vv. 11–20* (2006), *vv. 21–30* (2009).
Zhou Shaoquan 周绍泉 et al., comp., *Huizhou qiannian qiyue wenshu* 徽州千年契约文书 (Shijia zhuang: Huashan wenyi, 1991–93; identified throughout as *Huizhou qiannian*).

Other Primary Sources

Ai Qianzi 艾千子, *Tian yongzi ji* 天慵子集 (Taipei: Yiwen yinshuguan, 1970).
Anhui sheng xianzheng diaocha ju minshi xiguan wenti dang'an 安徽省憲政調查局民事習慣問題檔案 (National Library of China, manuscript).
Anon., *Chengshi pubian* 程氏譜辨 (undated manuscript in Anhui Provincial Library).
Anon., *Da Minglü zhiyin* 大明律直引 (1526 ed.).
Anon., comp., *Huizhou huishe zonglu* 徽州會社綜錄 (manuscript compilation in Xiamen University, Huizhou Documents Collection).
Anon., *Xinbian shiwen leiju qizha qingqian* 新編事文類聚啓箚青錢 (c.1450 ed., Naikaku bunko copy).
Anqing fuzhi 安慶府志 (1554).
Bao Hui 包恢, *Bizhou gao lüe* 敝帚藁略 (SKQSZB ed.).
Cao Sixuan 曹嗣軒, comp., *Xiuning mingzu zhi* 休寧名族志 (Hefei: Huangshan shushe, 2007).
Changshu xianzhi 常熟縣志 (1539).
Chen Dingyu 陈定宇, comp., *Xin'an liuxian mingzu zhi* 新安六县名族志 (v. 1 of *Huizhou mingzu zhi* 徽州名族志) (Beijing: Quanguo tushuguan wenxian suowei fuzhi zhongxin, 2003).
Chen Longzheng 陳龍正, *Jiting quanshu* 幾亭全書 (1665 ed.).

Chen Qidi 陳其弟, annot., *Wuzhong xiaozhi congkan* 吳中小志叢刊 (Yangzhou: Guangling shushe, 2004).
Chen Renxi 陳仁錫, *Huang Ming shifa lu* 皇明世法錄 (Taipei: Xuesheng, 1965).
Chen Zhaoxiang 陳昭祥, *Wentang xiangyue jiafa* 文堂鄉約家法 (1572 pref., reprt. 1638).
Chen Zilong 陳子龍, comp., *Ming jingshi wenbian* 明经世文编 (Beijing: Zhonghua, 1962, reprt. 1987).
Cheng Chunyu 程春宇, comp., *Shishang leiyao* 士商類要 (1626 pref.).
Cheng Dawei 程大位, *Suanfa zuanyao jiaoshi* 算法纂要校释 (1591 pref.) (Hefei: Anhui jiaoyu, 1986).
Cheng Minzheng 程敏政, *Huangdun wenji* 篁墩文集 (SKQSZB ed.).
 Xin'an wenxian zhi 新安文獻志 (Hefei: Huangshan shushe, 2005).
Cheng Tong 程曈, *Xin'an xuexi lu* 新安學系錄 (Hefei: Huangshan shushe, 2006).
Cheng Wenju 程文舉, *Yangshan sheng* 仰山乘 (Taipei: Mingwen shuju, 1980).
Cheng Yizhi 程一枝, *Cheng dian* 程典 (1598 ed.).
Chengshi Dongli cidian 程氏東裡祠典 (1588 pref., late Ming manuscript, National Library of China).
Chengshi shipu zhengzong 程氏世譜正宗 (1812 manuscript copy).
Chengshi zhichan bu 程氏支產簿 (CASS, Beijing, Institute of Economics, Huizhou Sources).
Chengyang sanzhi 橙陽散志 (1809 ed., Tōyō Bunko copy).
Choe Po 崔溥, *Piao-hai lu jiaozhu* 漂海录校注, ed. Pu Yuangao (Shanghai: Shanghai shudian, 2013).
Adriano de las Cortes, SJ, *Le voyage en Chine d'Adriano de las Cortes, S.J.*, trans. Pascale Girard and Juliette Monbeig (Paris: Chandeigne, 2001).
Da Chengcun Chengshi zhipu 大程村程氏支譜 (1740, manuscript copy at National Diet Library).
Dai Tingming 戴廷明 and Cheng Shangkuan 程尚寬, comp., *Xin'an mingzu zhi* 新安名族志 (Hefei: Huangshan shushe, 2004).
Dan Qu 單渠, *Liang Huai yanfa zhi* 兩淮鹽法志 (1806 ed.).
Dangxi Jinshi zupu 珰溪金氏族譜 (1568).
Fang Hongjing 方弘靜, *Suyuan cungao* 素園存稿 (SKQSCM ed.).
Fengnan zhi 豐南志 (c.1944) (Shanghai: Jiangsu guji, 1992).
Fu Yan 傅巖, *She ji* 歙紀 (Hefei: Huangshan shushe, 2007).
Gan Xi 甘熙, *Baixia suoyan* 白下瑣言 *Baixia suoyan* (Nanjing: Nanjing chubanshe, 2007).

Gu Qiyuan 顧啓元, *Kezuo zuiyu* 客座贅語, as part of a dual publication entitled Lu Can 陸粲, *Gengsi bian* 庚巳編, and Gu Qiyuan, *Kezuo zuiyu* (Beijing: Zhonghua, 1987).

Gu Su zhi 姑蘇志 (1506).

Gu Yanwu 顧炎武, *Rizhi lu jishi* 日知錄集釋 (Changsha: Yuelu shushe, 1994).

Zhaoyu zhi 肇域志 (Shanghai: Guji, 2004).

Guan Zhidao 管志道, *Congxian weisu yi* 從先維俗議 (Tai Kun xianzhe yishu).

Gui Youguang 歸有光, *Zhenchuan xiansheng ji* 震川先生集 (Shanghai: Guji, 1981).

Gui Zhuang 歸莊, *Gui Zhuang ji* 歸莊集 (Shanghai: Guji, 1984).

Guishan Chengshi zhipu 桂山程氏支譜 (1694 ed.).

Guixi Xiangshi (Chongbao tang) cipu 桂溪項氏(崇报堂)祠譜 (1761 ed.).

Guo Hou'an 郭厚安, comp., *Ming shilu jingji ziliao xuanbian* 明實錄經濟資料選編 (Beijing: Zhongguo shehui kexue, 1989).

Guo Yuanzhu 郭元柱, *Qinmin leibian zhaichao* 親民類編摘抄 (pref. 1586, 1588; Shidō bunko copy).

Gushe Sunshi jiapu 古筑孫氏家譜 (1812).

Hangzhou fuzhi 杭州府志 (1579).

He Liangjun 何良俊, *Siyou zhai congshuo* 四友齋叢說 (Beijing: Zhonghua, 1983).

He Qiaoyuan 何喬遠, *Mingshan cang* 名山藏 (1640 ed., Taipei: Chengwen, 1971).

Hong Mai 洪邁, *Yijian zhi* 夷堅志 (Beijing: Zhonghua, 1981).

Hong Yutu 洪玉圖, *Shewen* 歙問 (Zhaodai congshu jicheng ed.).

Hu Wei 胡煒, *Zhijia lüe* 治家略 (pref. 1739).

Huang Bian 黃汴, *Tianxia shuilu lucheng* 天下水陸路程 et al., ed. by Yang Zhengtai 楊正泰 (Taiyuan: Shanxi renmin, 2003).

Huang Xingzeng 黃省曾, *Wufeng lu* 吳風錄 (CSJC ed.).

Huang Xixian 黃希憲, *Fu Wu xilüe* 撫吳檄略 (Naikaku bunko copy).

Huang Xuanbao 黃玄豹, comp., *Tandu Huangshi zupu* 潭渡黃氏族譜 (1731).

Huang Zongxi (aka Huang Tsung-hsi) 黃宗羲, *Ming Wenhai* 明文海 (Beijing: Zhonghua, 1987).

Huangdun shizhongci gong sipu 黄墩世忠祠公祀簿 (CASS, Beijing, Institute of Economics, Huizhou Sources, no. 119).

Huangshan zhi dingben 黃山志定本 (1667).

Huizhou fuzhi 徽州府志 (1502).

Huizhou fuzhi (1566).

Huizhou fuzhi (1699).

Huizhou fuzhi (1827).

Huzhou fuzhi (1884).

Bibliography

Jiading xianzhi 嘉定縣志 (1605).
Jiading xianzhi (1673).
Jiang Liangdong 姜良棟, *ZhenWu lu* 鎮吳錄 (Naikaku bunko copy).
Jiangcun Hongshi jiapu 江村洪氏家譜 (1730).
Jiangdu xianzhi 江都縣志 (1811).
Jiangsu sheng bowuguan 江苏省博物馆, comp., *Jiangsu sheng Ming Qing yilai beike ziliao xuan ji* 江苏省明清以来碑刻资料选集 (Beijing: Shenghuo, Dushu, Xinzhi sanlian shudian, 1959).
Jin Sheng 金聲, *Jin taishi ji* 金太史集 (Qiankun zhengqi ji ed.) (Taipei: Huanqiu shuju,1966).
Jin Zhongshi 金忠士, *Xunfang guili shiyao* 巡方規吏十要 (Naikaku bunko copy, 1607 pref.).
Jinying Zhengshi zongpu 錦營鄭氏宗譜 (1821).
Jiujiang fuzhi 九江府志 (1874).
Jixi Jiqingfang Geshi chongxiu zupu 績谿積慶坊葛氏重修族譜 (1565).
Jixi Nanguan Jingxu tang Xushi zongpu 績溪南關驚敘堂許氏宗譜 (1889).
Jixi Xiguan Zhangshi zupu 績溪西關章氏族譜 (Ming ed.).
Jixi xianzhi 績溪縣志 (1810).
Kuang Zhong 況鐘, *Ming Kuang taishou Longgang gong ZhiSu zhengji quanji* 明況太守龍岡公治蘇政績全集 (1764 ed.).
Lei Li 雷禮, comp., *Huangchao lieqing ji* 國朝列卿紀 (Taipei: Chengwen, 1970).
Lei Menglin 雷夢麟, comp., *Dulü suoyan* 讀律瑣言 (1565 ed.).
Li Dou 李斗, *Yangzhou huafang lu* 揚州畫舫錄 (Beijing: Zhonghua, 1960).
Li Guoxiang 李国祥 et al., comp., *Ming shilu leixuan, Hubei shiliao juan* 明实录类选, 湖北史料卷 (Wuhan: Wuhan, 1991).
Li Jinde 李晉德, *Keshang yilan xingmi* 客商一覽醒迷, in Huang Bian, *Tianxia shuilu lucheng* 天下水陸路程 et al., ed. by Yang Zhengtai 楊正泰 (Taiyuan: Shanxi renmin, 2003).
Li Le 李樂, *Jianwen zaji* 見聞雜記 (Shanghai: Guji, 1986).
Li Tao 李燾, *Xu Zizhi tongjian changbian* 續資治通鑑長編 (Beijing: Zhonghua, 1993).
Li Weizhen 李維楨, *Dabi shanfang ji* 大泌山房集 (Beiping Library Rare Books Microfilm Collection, 1600 ed.).
Li Xianting 李獻廷, *Guangyang zaji* 廣陽雜記 (Beijing: Zhonghua, 1957; 3rd ed., 1997).
Li Yuanbi 李元弼, *Zuoyi zizhen* 作邑自箴 (SBCKXB ed.).
Lin Xiyuan 林希元, *Lin Ciya xiansheng wenji* 林次崖先生文集 (1759 reprt. of late Ming ed.).
Ling Mengchu 凌蒙初, *Erke paian jingqi* 二刻拍案惊奇 (Beijing: Renmin wenxue, 1996).

Ling Tingkan 凌廷堪, *Ling Tingkan quanji* 凌廷堪全集 (Hefei: Huangshan shushe, 2009).
Ling Yingqiu 凌應秋, *Shaxi jilüe* 沙溪集略 (1759) (Shanghai: Jiangsu guji, 1992).
Liu Ruoyu 劉若愚, *Zhuozhong zhi* 酌中志 (CSJC ed.).
Liu Shaoyi 劉少彝, *Huangzhu lüe* 荒著略 (CSJCXB ed.).
Liu Shijun 劉時俊, *Wu suo Liu xiansheng juguan shuijing* 勿所劉先生居官水鏡 (late Wanli ed.).
Long Wenbin 龍文彬, comp., *Ming huiyao* 明會要, 2 vols (Beijing: Zhonghua, 1956).
Lu Wengui 陸文圭, *Qiangdong leigao* 牆東類稿 (SKQSZB ed.).
Lü Youlong 呂猶龍, *Liangzhe chongding cuogui* 兩浙重訂鹺規 (1711).
Luo Rusheng 羅汝聲, comp., *Chengkan Luoshi zongpu* 呈坎羅氏宗譜 (1507 ed.).
Luo Yinghe 羅應鶴, *Miaoshi zhi* 廟事志 (Wanli ed.).
Luodian zhenzhi 羅店鎮志 (1879).
Mianyang zhouzhi 沔陽州志 (1590).
Min Linsi 閔麟嗣, *Huangshan zhi dingben* 黃山志定本 (Taipei: Wenhai, 1975).
Ming shi 明史 (Beijing: Zhonghua, 1974).
Ming shilu (fu jiao kanji) 明實錄 (附校勘記) (Nan'gang: Zhongyang yanjiu yuan lishi yuyan yanjiusuo, 1964).
Ming Wanli nian yulin ce 明萬曆年魚鱗冊 (Nanjing University, History Department, Huizhou Sources).
Minglü jijie fuli 明律集解附例 (Taibei: Chengwen, 1969).
Nanxiang zhenzhi 南翔鎮志 (1807; reprt. 1924).
Qi Biaojia 祁彪佳, *Qi Biaojia wengao* 祁彪佳文稿 (Beijing: Shumu wenxian, 1991).
Qian Yong 錢泳, *Lüyuan conghua* 履園叢話 (2nd ed., Beijing: Zhonghua, 1997).
Qimen Shanhe Chengshi Renshan menzhi xiu zongpu 祁門善和程氏仁山門支修宗譜 (1907).
Qimen xian xinzhang qingong shouzhuang 祁門縣新丈親供首狀 (no. 563266, Shanghai Library, Rare Books Room).
Qimen xiangzhen jianzhi bianzuan weiyuanhui 祁門鄉鎮簡志編纂委員會, ed., *Qimen xiangzhen jianzhi* 祁門鄉鎮簡志 (Qimen: Qimen County Government, 1989).
Qimen xianzhi 祁門縣志 (1600).
Qimen xianzhi (1683).
Qimen xianzhi (1873).
Qimen xianzhi (Hefei: Huangshan shushe, 2008).
Qimen xianzhi shizu kao 祁門縣志氏族考 (1942).

Qin Guan 秦觀, *Huaihai ji* 淮海集 (SBBY ed.).
Qingdai riji huichao 清代日记汇抄, ed. by Shanghai renmin chubanshe 上海人民出版社 (Shanghai: Renmin, 1982).
Qingjiang xianzhi 清江縣志 (1642).
Qiu Jun 邱濬, *Chongbian Qiongtai gao* 重編瓊臺稿 (SKQSZB ed.).
Renhe xianzhi 仁和縣志 (1687).
Renli Cheng Jing'ai tang shishou jiapu 仁里程敬爱堂世守家譜 (1829).
Shanghai bowuguan tushu ziliaoshi 上海博物馆图书资料室, comp., *Shanghai beike ziliao xuanji* 上海碑刻资料选集 (Shanghai: Shanghai renmin, 2000).
Shangshan Wushi jiapu 商山吳氏家譜 (Ming manuscript, Shanghai Library).
Shangshan Wushi zongfa guitiao 商山吳氏宗法規條 (1603 pref., Ming manuscript, National Library of China).
Shanhe Chengshi Renshan menzhi pu 善和程氏仁山門支譜 (1682).
She xianzhi 歙縣志 (1690).
She xianzhi (1771).
She xianzhi (1937).
She zhi 歙志 (1609).
Shen Defu 沈德符, *Wanli Yehuo bian* 萬曆野獲編 (2nd ed., Beijing: Zhonghua, 1980).
Shen Guoyuan 沈國元, *Liangchao congxin lu* 兩朝從信錄 (Taibei: Jinghua, 1968).
Shen Qiqian 沈起潜, *Xianyuan zashuo* 莧園雜說 (1826) (Siku weishou jikan).
Shen Shixing 申时行, *Cijian tang ji* 賜閒堂集 (1616 pref.).
    comp., *(Wanli) Ming huidian (*萬曆*)*明會典 (Beijing: Zhonghua, 1959, reprt. 1980).
Shen Sixiao 沈思孝, *Jin lu* 晉錄 (CSJC ed.).
Shen Yao 沈尧, *Luofan lou wenji* 落帆樓文集 (CSJCXB ed.).
Shen Zhou 沈周, *Shitian zaji* 石田雜記 (CSJC ed.).
Shexi Xi'nan Wushi xianying zhi 歙西溪南吳氏先瑩志 (1635 orig. ed., 1689 update, Tōyō bunka kenkyūjo copy).
Shexian shizheng ce 歙縣實征冊 (Nanjing University, History Department, Huizhou Sources, She: 社 460/809).
Shizhong Chengshi Taitang zupu 世忠程氏泰塘族譜 (1545).
Shuaidong Chengshi zupu 率東程氏族譜 (*c*.1563 ed.).
Shuanglin Wangshi zhipu 雙林王氏支譜 (1860).
Shunzhi shiyi nian Hongxing jiu shu 順治十一年洪姓闔書 (CASS, Beijing, Institute of Economics, Huizhou Sources, no. 374).
Song Yingxing 宋應星, *Yeyi lunqi, tantian silian shi* 野議 論氣 談天; 思憐詩 (Shanghai: Renmin, 1976).

Su Tianjue 蘇天爵, comp., *Guochao wenlei* 國朝文類 (SBZK ed.).
Sun Zhilu 孫之騄, *Ershen yelu* 二申野錄 (1721 ed.).
Suzhou fuzhi 蘇州府志 (1691).
Suzhou fuzhi (1882).
Suzhou lishi bowuguan 蘇州历史博物馆 et al., comp., *Ming Qing Suzhou gongshang ye beike* 明请蘇州工商业碑刻 (Nanjing: Jiangsu renmin, 1981).
Tanbin Huangshi shouzhi qingce 譚濱黃氏收支清冊 (Anhui Provincial Library, Rare Books Room).
Tandu Xiaoli Huangshi zongpu 譚渡孝里黃氏宗譜 (1731 pref.).
Tang Bin 湯斌, *Tang Qian'an ji* 湯潛菴集 (1701 ed.).
Tianqi Weinan Zhu Shirong fenjia pu 天启朱世荣分家譜 (Shanghai Library, Rare Books Division).
Tongshan xianzhi 通山縣志 (1868).
Tuncun zhi 屯村志, 313–38, in *Tongli zhi (liang zhong)* 同里志(兩重) (Yangzhou: Guangling shushe, 2011).
Wan'an Wushi jianci 萬安吳氏建祠 (1611 pref.) (Huizhou Sources, Institute of History, CASS, Beijing).
Wang Daokun 汪道昆, *Fumo* 副墨4 (Wanli ed.).
Wang Junyuan 王濬原, *Wangshi jiacheng* 王氏家乘 (manuscript, 1769 and 1913 prefaces).
Wang Qi 王錡, *Yupu zaji* 寓圃雜記 (Beijing: Zhonghua, 1984).
 comp., *Xu Wenxian tongkao* 續文獻通考 (Wanli ed. reprt., Hangzhou: Zhejiang guji, 1988).
Wang Shanghe 汪尚和, *Xiuning Ximen Wangshi zupu* 休寧西門汪氏族譜 (1527),
Wang Shixing 王士性, *Guangzhi yi* 廣志繹 (Beijing: Zhonghua, 1981).
Wang Shizhen 王世貞, *Yanzhou shanren sibu gao* 弇州山人四部稿 (Taipei: Weiwen tushu, 1976).
 Yanzhou shiliao houji 弇州史料後集 (1614 ed.).
Wang Shunmin 汪舜民, *Jinggan xiansheng wenji* 靜軒先生文集 (XXSKQS ed.).
Wang Siren 王思任, comp., *Qi Zhongmin gong nianpu* 祁忠敏公年譜 (Taipei: Taiwan yinhang, 1969; v. 279 of Taiwan wenxian congkan).
Wang Ti 汪禔, *Bo'an ji* 檗菴集 (SKQSCM ed.).
Wang Weide 王維德, *Linwu minfeng* 林屋民風 (SKQSCM ed.).
Wang Yangming 王陽明, *Wang Yangming quanji* 王陽明全集 (Shanghai: Guji, 1997).
Wang Zhun 汪准, *Han Chu erxi Wangshi jiacheng* 韓楚二溪汪氏家乘 (1910 ed.).
Wanli Jianci pu 萬歷建祠譜 (CASS, Beijing, Institute of History, Huizhou Sources: 534/7727; this title and number seem not to be included in

Huizhou wenshu leimu (2000), the catalogue of this institute's collection of Huizhou sources).

Wu Di 吳翟, *Mingzhou Wushi jiadian* 茗洲吳氏家典 (1733) (Hefei: Huangshan shushe, 2003).

Wu Kuan 吳寬, *Paoweng jiacang ji* 匏翁家藏集 (SBCK ed.).

Wu Shiqi 吳士奇, *Lüzi guan zhengxin bian* 綠滋館征信編 (SKQSCM ed.).

Wu xianzhi 吳縣志 (1642).

Wu Zimu 吳自牧, *Mengliang lu* 夢梁錄 (Taibei: Guting shuwu, 1975).

Wu Ziyu 吳子玉, *Dazhang shanren ji* 大障山人集 (SKQSCM ed.).

Xiuning Mingzhou Wushi jiaji 休寧茗洲吳氏家記 (1584) (manuscript copy, Tōyō bunka kenkyūjo).

Wuling Gushi zongpu 武陵顧氏宗譜 (1774 ed.).

Wuyuan xianzhi 婺源縣志 (1694).

Wuyuan xianzhi (1757).

Wuyuan xianzhi (1787).

Xia Yan 夏言, *Guizhou xiansheng zouyi* 桂洲先生奏議 (Beiping Rare Books Microfilm Collection, 1541 ed.).

Guizhou zouyi 桂洲奏議 (1541 ed., Naikaku bunko copy).

Xiao Taoyuan juefei shanren 小桃園覺非山人, comp., *Erbi kenqi* 珥筆肯綮 (Beijing: Shehui kexue wenxian, 2012; in Lidai zhenxi sifa wenxian series).

Xie Chaoyuan 謝朝元, *Houming riji* 厚銘日記 (1621–27 ed.; National Library of China copy).

Xie Zhaozhe 謝肇淛, *Wu za zu* 五雜組 (Shanghai: Zhonghua, 1959).

Xin'an Bishi zupu 新安畢氏族譜 (1509).

Xin'an Chengshi zhupu huitong 新安程氏諸譜會通 (1450–52).

Xin'an Da Chengcun Chengshi zhipu 新安大程村程氏支譜 (1740).

Xin'an Huangshi Huangdun muci jitian ji 新安黃氏黃墩墓祠祭田紀 (1739 pref.).

Xin'an Shexi Xi'nan shipu 新安歙西溪南世譜 (1602).

Xin'an Shexi Xi'nan Wushi shipu 新安歙西溪南吳氏世譜 (undated manuscript copy, post-1572, Shanghai Library).

Xin'an Shexi Xi'nan Wushi shipu 新安歙西溪南吳氏世譜 (1747 ed., Shanghai Library).

Xin'an Shuaikou Chengshi cigui xubian 新安率口程氏祠規續編 (1678 pref., Shanghai Library).

Xin'an Wangshi chongxiu bagong pu 新安汪氏重修八公譜 (1535).

Xin'an Xiuning Wenchang Jinshi shipu 新安休寧文昌金氏世譜 (*c.*1550) (CASS, Beijing, Institute of History, Huizhou Sources).

Xin'an zhi 新安志 (1175; Hefei: Huangshan shushe, 2008 reprt.).

Xiuning Jinshi zupu 休寧金氏族譜 (1748).

Xiuning mingzu zhi 休宁名族志 (Hefei: Huangshan shushe, 2004).

Xiuning xianzhi 休寧縣志 (1693).
Xiuning xian shi Wushi zongpu 休寧縣市吳氏宗譜 (1528 ed., Shanghai Municipal Library).
Xiuning Yeshi zupu 休寧葉氏族譜 (1631).
Xu Feng'en 許奉恩, *Liuxian waishi* 留仙外史 (Hangzhou: Zhejiang guji, 1989).
Xu Pu 徐溥, comp., *(Zhengde) Da Ming huidian* (正德)明會典 (Beiping Library Rare Books Microfilm Collection, 1503 ed.).
Xu Sanxing 徐三省, *Jiaozi liyan* 教子俚言 (1615 pref.).
Xu Shining 徐世寧 and Xu Zeng 楊熷, comp., *Chongxu Shexian huiguan lu* 重續歙縣會館錄 (1834 ed.) (reprtd., Hong Kong: Dadong tushu gongsi, 1977).
Xu Song 徐松, comp., *Song huiyao jigao* 宋會要輯稿 (Taibei: Shijie, 1969).
Xu Xianzu 許顯祖, *Xiuning Futan zhi* 休寧孚潭志 (1722).
Xu Yikui 徐一夔, *DaMing jili* 大明集禮 (SKQSZB ed.).
Xue Yingqi 薛應旂, *Xianchang lu* 憲章錄 (reprt. 1574 ed., Beijing: Quanguo tushuguan wenxian suowei fuzhi zhongxin, 1988).
Yanzhen zhicao 岩鎮志草 (1737) (Shanghai: Jiangsu guji, 1992).
Yao Tingxiao 姚廷遘, *Linian ji* 历年记, in Shanghai renmin chubanshe 上海人民出版社, ed., *Qingdai riji huichao* 清代日记汇抄 (Shanghai: Renmin, 1982).
Ye Mengzhu 葉夢珠, *Yueshi bian* 閱世編 (Shanghai: Guji, 1982).
Ye Quan 叶权, *Xianbo bian* 贤博编 (Beijing: Jiangsu renmin, 1981, in the *Mingshi ziliao congkan* 明史資料丛刊 series, 1).
Ye Shaoyuan 葉紹袁, *QiZhen jiwen lu* 啓禎記聞錄 (Taipei: Taiwan yinhang, Zhonghua shuju, 1968).
Ye Weiming 葉為銘, comp., *Shexian jinshi zhi* 歙縣金石志 (Taipei: Xin wenfeng, 1984).
Yi xian xuzhi 黟縣續志 (1825).
Yi xian zhi 黟縣志 (1812).
Yi xian zhi (1871).
Ying Jia 應檟, comp., *Yanyü gao* 讞獄稿 (Tianjin: Tianjin guji shudian, 1981).
Yu Jideng 余繼登, *Diangu jiwen* 典故紀聞 (Beijing: Zhonghua, 1985).
Yu Wenbao 俞文豹, *Chuiqian lu quanbian* 吹劍錄全編 (Shanghai: Gudian wenxue, 1958).
Yu Wentai 余文台, *(Dingqian Chongwenge huizuan) Shimin wanyong zhengzong bu qiuren quanbian* (鼎鋟崇文閣彙纂)士民萬用正宗不求人全編 (1609).
Yu Xiangtou 余象斗, comp., *(Xinke tianxia simin bianlan santai) Wanyong zhengzong* (新刻天下四民便覽三台)萬用正宗 (1599).

Zhan Yuanxiang 詹元相, *Weizhai riji* 畏齋日記, in Zhongguo shehui kexueyuan lishi yanjiusuo Qingshi yanjiushi 中国社会科学院历史研究所清史研究室, ed., *Qingshi ziliao* 清史资料, series 4 (Beijing: Zhonghua, 1983).

Zhang Qiujian 張丘建, *Suanjing* 算經, in Qian Baozong 錢寶琮, ed., *Suanjing shishu* 算經十書, v. 2 (Beijing: Zhonghua, 1963).

Zhang Shiche 張時徹, *Zhiyuan bieji* 芝園別集 (Naikaku bunko copy).

Zhang Yingyu 張應俞, *Dubian xinshu* 杜騙新書 (Shanghai: Guji, 1992).

Zhao Jishi 趙吉士, *Ji yuanji so ji* 寄園寄所寄 (Hefei: Huangshan shushe, 2008).

Zhao Pang 張滂, *Huangdun Cheng Zhu queli zhi* 黃墩程朱闕里志 (1771 ed.).

Zhengshi shipu 鄭氏世譜 (1792 ed.).

Zhonglin hexiu Chengshi zhipu 中林合修程氏支譜 (1906 ed.).

Secondary Sources

Abe Takeo 安部健夫, *Shindai shi no kenkyū* 清代史の研究 (Tokyo: Sōbunsha, 1971).

Adachi Keiji 足立啓二, *Min Shin Chūgoku no keizai kōzō* 明清中国の経済構造 (Tokyo: Kyūko Shoin, 2012).

Akuno Tatsuoi 稲野達夫, "Shina ni okeru Raimukoi (kōkai) no kenkyū 支那における賴母子講 (合会)の研究," 731–822, in *Tōa Dōbun shoin daigaku Tōa chōsa hōkokusho, Showa jūroku nendo* 東亜同文書院大学東亜調査報告書・昭和十六年度 (Tokyo: Minritsu insatsu kabushiki kaisha, 1942).

Thomas J. Allsen, "Princes and Their Partners, 1200–1260," *Asia Major* 2.2 (1989), 83–126.

Anon., *The Commercial Law Affecting Chinese, with Special Reference to Partnership, Registration, and Bankruptcy Law in Hongkong* (Hong Kong: China Mail Office, 1882).

Antony, Robert J., *Like Froth Floating on the Sea* (Berkeley: Center of Chinese Studies, University of California Center for Chinese Studies, 2008).

Aramiya Manabu 新宮学, *Min Shin toshi shōgyōshi no kenkyū* 明清都市商業史の研究 (Tokyo: Kyūko shoin, 2017).

"Mindai no gakō ni tsuite 明代の牙行について," 841–60, in Mindaishi kenkyūkai Mindaishi ronsō henshū iinkai, 明代史研究会明代史論叢編集委員会, ed., *Yamane Yukio kyōju taikyū kinen Mindaishi ronsō* 山根幸夫教授退休記念明代史論叢 (Tokyo: Kyūko shoin, 1990).

"Mingmo Qingchu Suzhoufu Changshuxian de tongye zuzhi yu Huizhou shangren 明末请初苏州府常熟县的同业组织与徽州商人," *Jiang Huai luntan* 江淮论坛1996.2, 93–96.

Azuma Jūji 吾妻重二, *Zhu Xi "Jiali" shizheng yanjiu* 朱熹《家禮》實證研究 (Shanghai: Huadong shifan daxue chubanshe, 2012).

Marianne Bastid, "The Structure of the Financial Institutions of the State in the Late Qing," 51–79, in Stuart R. Schram, ed., *The Scope of State Power in China* (London and Hong Kong: School of Oriental and African Studies and The Chinese University Press, 1985).

Beattie, Hilary J., *Land and Lineage in China: A Study of T'ung-Ch'eng County, Anhwei, in the Ming and Ch'ing Dynasties* (Cambridge: Cambridge University Press, 1979).

Richard Belsky, *Localities at the Center: Native Place, Space, and Power in Late Imperial Beijing* (Cambridge, MA: Harvard University Asia Center, 2005).

Bi Minzhi 毕民智, "Huizhou nüci chukao 徽州女祠初考," *Huizhou shehui kexue* 徽州社会科学 1996.2, 45–50.

Bian Li 卞利, "Huizhou de gu citang 徽州的古祠堂," *Xungen* 寻根 2004.2, 50–55.

Ming Qing Huizhou shehui yanjiu 明清徽州社会研究 (Hefei: Anhui daxue, 2004).

"Ming Qing shiqi Huizhou de xiangyue jianlun 明清时期徽州的乡约简论," *Anhui daxue xuebao* 安徽大学学报26.6 (Nov. 2002), 34–40.

Cyril Birch, trans., *Stories from a Ming Collection: Translations of Chinese Stories Published in the Seventeenth Century* (London: Bodley Head, 1958).

Nicolai Viacheslavich Bogoiavlenskii (尼・维・鲍戈亚夫连斯基), *Changcheng wai de Zhongguo xibu diqu: qi jin xi zhuangkuang ji Eguo chenmin de diwei* 长城外的中国西部地区：其今昔状况及俄国臣民的地位 (Beijing: Shangwu, 1980) (trans. *Zapadnyi zastennyi Kitai, ego proshioe, nastoishchee sostoianie i polozhenie v nem russkikh poddannykh* St Petersburg: Tip. A.S. Suvorina, 1906).

Charles R. Boxer, *Fidalgos in the Far East, 1550–1770* (2nd ed., Hong Kong and London: Oxford University Press, 1968).

João de Barros: Portuguese Humanist and Historian of Asia (New Delhi: Concept Publishing Company, 1981).

Cynthia J. Brokaw, "Empire of Texts: Book Production, Book Distribution, and Book Culture in Late Imperial China," 187–235, in Joseph P. McDermott and Peter Burke, eds., *The Book Worlds of East Asia and Europe* (Hong Kong: Hong Kong University Press, 2015).

The Ledgers of Merit and Demerit: Social Change and Moral Order in Late Imperial China (Princeton: Princeton University Press, 1991).

Timothy Brook. "Communications and Commerce," 579–707, in Frederick W. Mote and Denis Twitchett, eds., *The Cambridge History of China*,

v. 8, the Ming Dynasty, 1368–1644, pt. 2 (Cambridge: Cambridge University Press, 1998).

The Confusions of Pleasure (Berkeley: University of California Press, 1998).

"The Merchant Network in Sixteenth-Century Ming China: A Discussion and Translation of Chang Han's 'On Merchants'," Journal of the Economic and Social History of the Orient 24.1 (1981), 165–214.

Michela Bussotti, "Huizhou Genealogies and Huizhou Lineages," paper presented at Cambridge EFEO Workshop on Local Primary Sources, Cambridge University Library, September 2016.

Michela Bussotti, and Jean-Pierre Drège, eds., Imprimer sans profit? Le livre non commercial dans la Chine impériale (Geneva: Droz, 2015).

Cai Limin 蔡利民, Suzhou minsu 苏州民俗 (Suzhou: Suzhou daxue, 2000).

Francesco Carletti, trans. Herbert Weinstock, My Voyage around the World (London: Methuen, 1965).

Cao Guoqing 曹国庆, "Ming Qing shiqi Jiangxi de Huishang, 明请时期江西的徽商," Jiangxi shifan daxue xuebao (zhexue shehui kexue bao), 江西师范大学学报(哲学社会科学报) 1988.1, 22–27.

Cao Lin 曹琳, Mingdai shangren shangye jingying yanjiu 明代商人商业经营研究 (Beijing: Zhongguo shehui kexue, 2013).

John Chaffee, The Thorny Gates of Learning in Sung China (Cambridge: Cambridge University Press, 1985).

John Chaffee and Denis Twitchett, eds., The Cambridge History of China, v. 5, pt. 2, The Five Dynasties and Sung China, 960–1279 (Cambridge: Cambridge University Press, 2015).

Chan Hok-lam, "The Chien-wen, Yung-lo, Hung-hsi, and Hsüan-te Reigns, 1399–1435," 182–304, in Frederick W. Mote and Denis Twitchett, eds., The Cambridge History of China, v. 8, The Ming Dynasty, 1368–1644, pt. 2 (Cambridge: Cambridge University Press, 1998).

Chang Hsun and Benjamin Penny, eds., Religion in Taiwan and China: Locality and Transmission (Taipei: Institute of Ethnology, Academia Sinica, 2017).

Chang Jianhua 常建华. Mingdai zongzu yanjiu 明代宗族研究 (Shanghai: Renmin, 2005).

Michael G. Chang, A Court on Horseback: Imperial Touring and the Construction of Qing Rule, 1680–1785 (Cambridge, MA: Harvard University Asia Center, 2005).

Chen Baoliang 陈宝良, Piaoyao de chuantong: Mingdai chengshi shenghuo changjuan 飘摇的传统, 明代城市生活长卷 (Changsha: Hunan, 1998).

Boyi Chen, "Borders and Beyond: Contested Power and Discourse around Southeast Coastal China in the Sixteenth and Seventeenth Centuries," International Journal of Asian Studies 15.1 (Jan. 2018), 85–116.

Chen Chizhao 陈智超, ed., *Mingdai Huizhou Fangshi qinyou shouzha qibai tong kaoshi* 明代徽州方氏親友手札七百通考釋 (Hefei: Anhui daxue, 2001).

Chen Dakang 陈大康, *Mingdai shanggu yu shifeng* 明代商贾与世风 (Shanghai: Shanghai wenyi, 1996).

Chen Feng 陈锋, ed., *Ming Qing yilai Chang Jiang liuyu shehui fazhan shilun* 明清以来长江流域社会发展史论 (Wuchang: Wuhan daxue, 2006).

Fu-mei Chen and Ramon H. Myers, "Coping with Transaction Costs: The Case of Merchant Associations in the Ch'ing Period," 317–41, in *The Second Conference on Modern Chinese Economic History, v. 1* (Taipei: Institute of Economics, Academia Sinica, 1989).

Chen Keyun 陈柯云. "Ming Qing Huizhou de xiupu jianci huodong 明清徽州的修谱建祠活动," *Huizhou shehui kexue (zhexue shehui kexue ban)* 徽州社会科学(哲学社会科学版) 1993.4, 40–45.

"Ming Qing Huizhou diqu shanlin jingyingzhong de 'lifen' wenti 明清徽州地区山林经营中的'力分'问题," *Zhongguo shi yanjiu* 中国史研究 1987.1, 83–98.

"Ming Qing Huizhou zongzu dui xiangcun tongzhi de jiachiang 明清徽州宗族对乡村统治的加强," *Zhongguo shi yanjiu* 中国史研究 1995.3, 1,039–48.

"Ming Qing Huizhou zuchan de fazhan 明清徽州族产的发展," *Anhui daxue xuebao* 安徽大学学报 1996.2, 55–61.

"Ming Qing shanlin miaomu jingying chutan 明清山林苗木经营初探," *Pingjun xuekan* 平準學刊 4, shang (Beijing: Zhongguo shangye, 1989), 139–60.

Ch'en Kuo-tung Anthony, *The Insolvency of the Chinese Hong Merchants* (Nankang: Institute of Economics, Academia Sinica, 1990).

Chen Rui 陈瑞, "Ming Qing shiqi Huizhou zongzu neibu tiaoyue de kongzhi gongneng 明清时期徽州宗族内部条约的控制功能," *Huixue* 徽学 6 (2010), 152–76.

"Ming Qing shiqi Huizhou zongzu tang de kongzhi gongneng 明清时期徽州宗族堂的控制功能," *Zhongguo shehui jingji shi yanjiu* 中国社会经济史研究 2007.1, 54–63.

Chen Xuewen 陳學文, "Huishang yu Jiadingxian jingji di fazhan 徽商与嘉定县经济的发展," 149–55, in his *Zhongguo fengjian wanqi di shangpin jingji* 中國封建晚期的商品經濟 (Changsha: Hunan renmin, 1989).

Ming Qing shehui jingji shi yanjiu 明清社會經濟史研究 (Taipei: Daohe and Jingxiao daoxiang, 1991).

"Suzhou de shangye 苏州的商业," 156–74, in his *Zhongguo fengjian wanqi di shangpin jingji* 中國封建晚期的商品經濟 (Changsha: Hunan renmin, 1989).

Chen Zhiwu 陈志武, Peng Kaixiang 彭凯翔, and Yuan Weipeng 袁为鹏, "Qingchu zhi ershi shiji qianqi Zhongguo lishuai shi chutan – ji yu zhongguo lishuaishi shuzhuku (1660–2000) de kaocha, 清初至二十世纪前期中国利率史初探 – 基于中国利率史数据库 (1660–2000) 的考察," *Qingshi yanjiu* 清史研究 2016.4, 36–52.

Cheng Biding 程必定, Wang Jianshe 汪建设, et al., *Huizhou wuqian cun, Qimen juan* 徽州五千村, 祁门卷 (Hefei: Huangshan shushe, 2004).

Cheng Chenggui 程成贵, "Huizhou wenhua gucun – Liudu 徽州文化古村 – 六都" (Hefei: Anhui daxue, 2000, informal publication).

Cheng Yansheng 程演生, *Tianqi Huangshan dayu ji* 天啟黃山大獄記 (Taipei: Wenhai, 1971).

Cecilia Lee-fang Chien, *Salt and State: An Annotated Translation of the Songshi Salt Monopoly Treatise* (Ann Arbor: University of Michigan, Center for Chinese Studies, 2004).

Chow Kai-wing, *Publishing, Culture, and Power in Early Modern China* (Stanford: Stanford University Press, 2004).

The Rise of Confucian Ritualism in Late Imperial China: Ethics, Classics, and Lineage Discourse (Stanford: Stanford University Press, 1994).

Murat Çizakça, *A Comparative Evolution of Business Partnerships: The Islamic World and Europe, with Specific Reference to the Ottoman Archives* (Leiden: Brill, 1996).

Ronald H. Coase, *The Firm, the Market, and the Law* (Chicago: University of Chicago Press, 1988).

Sherman Cochran, Andrew C.K. Hsieh, and Janis Cochran, trans., ed., and introd., *One Day in China: May 21, 1936* (New Haven: Yale University Press, 1983).

Cooper, Thomas Thornville, *Travels of a Pioneer of Commerce in Pigtail and Petticoat: An Overland Journey from China towards India* (London: John Murray, 1871).

Oláh Csaba, "Brokers, Officials, and Foreign Trade in Ming China," 21–40, in Angela Schottenhammer, ed., *Tribute, Trade, and Smuggling* (Wiesbaden: Otto Harrassowitz, 2014).

John J. Dardess, *A Ming Society: T'ai-ho County, Kiangsi, Fourteenth to Seventeenth Centuries* (Berkeley: University of California Press, 1996).

Di Tunjian, Zhou Xiaoguang, and Bian Li, 翟屯建, 周晓光, 卞利, eds., *Huizhou wenhua shi* 徽州文化史(Hefei: Anhui renmin, 2015).

Ding Yi 丁易, *Mingdai tewu zhengzhi* 明代特務政治 (Beijing: Zhongwai, 1951).

Dohi Yoshikazu 土肥義和, "Tō Hoku Sō kan no 'sha' no soshiki keitai ni kansuru ichi kōsatsu, Tonkō no baai o chūshin ni 唐北宋間の'社'の組織形態に関する一考察、敦煌の場合を中心に," 691–703, in 'Chūgoku kodai no kokka to minshū' henshū iinkai '中国古代の国家と民衆'編集委員会, ed., *Chūgoku kodai no kokka to minshū: Hori Toshikazu sensei koki kinen* 中国古代の国家と民衆: 堀敏一先生古稀記念 (Tokyo: Kyūko shoin, 1995).

Dong Jian 董建, *Ziran yu yishu de lingguan huiying – Xi Xi'nan* 自然与艺术的灵光辉映 – 西溪南 (Hefei: hefei gongye daxue, 2005).

Edward Dreyer, "Military Origins of Ming rule," 58–106, in Frederick W. Mote and Denis Twitchett, eds., *The Cambridge History of China, v. 7, The Ming Dynasty, 1368–1644, pt. 1* (Cambridge: Cambridge University Press, 1988).

Du Yongtao, *The Order of Places: Translocal Practices of the Huizhou Merchants in Late Imperial China* (Leiden: Brill, 2015).

Patricia Buckley Ebrey, trans. and introd., *Chu Hsi's Family Rituals: A Twelfth-Century Chinese Manual for the Performance of Cappings, Weddings, Funerals, and Ancestral Rites* (Princeton: Princeton University Press, 1991).

Confucianism and Family Rituals in Imperial China: A Social History of Writing about Rites (Princeton: Princeton University Press, 1991).

"Conceptions of the Family in the Sung Dynasty," *Journal of Asian Studies* 43.2 (Feb. 1984), 219–45.

Family and Property in Sung China: Yüan Ts'ai's "Precepts for Social Life" (Princeton: Princeton University Press, 1985).

George Elisonas, "The Inseparable Trinity: Japan's Relations with China and Korea," 235–300, in John Whitney Hall, ed., *The Cambridge History of Japan, v. 4, Early Modern Japan* (Cambridge: Cambridge University Press, 2015).

Elizabeth Endicott-West, "Merchant Associations in Yuan China: The Ortogh," *Asia Major* 2.2 (1989), 127–54.

Fan Jinmin 范金民, "Cantian Dongting biandi Hui: Mingdai diyu shangban de xingqi 鑽天洞庭遍地徽: 明代地域商幫的興起," *Tōhō gakuhō* 東方学報 80 (March 2007), 83–131.

Fushui jia tianxia: Ming Qing Jiangnan shehui jingji tanxi 赋税甲天下: 明清江南社会经济探析 (Beijing: Shenghuo, dushu, xinzhi sanlian shudian, 2013).

Ming Qing Jiangnan shangye de fazhan 明清江南商业的发展 (Nanjing: Nanjing daxue, 1998).

Ming Qing shangshi jiufen yu shangye susong 明清商事纠纷与商业诉讼 (Nanjing: Nanjing daxue, 2007).

"Ming Qing shiqi huoji yu Suzhou de waidi shangren 明清时期活跃于苏州的外地商人," *Zhongguo shehui jingji shi yanjiu* 中国社会经济史研究 1989.4, 39–46.

"Mingdai Huishang randian de yige shilie 明代徽商染店的一个实列," *Anhui shixue* 安徽史学 2001.3, 2–4.6.
Fan Jinmin 范金民, and XiaWeizhong 夏维中, "Ming Qing Huizhou dianshang shulūe 明请徽州典商述略," *Huixue* 徽学 2 (2002), 129–38.
Fan Shuzhi 樊树志, Ming Qing de nupu yu nupuhua diannong 明清的奴仆与奴仆化佃农," *Xueshu yuekan* 学术月刊 1983.4, 68–73.
  Ming Qing Jiangnan shi zhen chuantong de bianqe 明清江南市镇传统的变革 (Shanghai: Fudan daxue, 2005).
Fang Lishan 方利山, *Huizhou zongzu citang diaocha yu yanjiu* 徽州宗族祠堂调查与研究 (Hefei: Anhui daxue, 2016).
Fang Weibao 方维保 and Wang Yingze 汪应泽, *Huizhou gu keshu* 徽州古刻书 (Shenyang: Liaoning renmin, 2004).
Fang Xing 方行, Jing Junxian 经君键, and Wei Jinyu 魏金玉, *Zhongguo jingji tongshi, Qing* 中国经济通史, 请 (Beijing: Zhongguo shehui kexue chubanshe, 2007).
David Faure, *China and Capitalism* (Hong Kong: Hong Kong University Press, 2005).
  "The Lineage as Business Company: Patronage versus Law in the Development of Chinese Business," 347–84, in *The Second Conference on Modern Chinese Economic History* (Taipei: The Institute of Economics, Academia Sinica, 1989).
David Faure, and Anthony Pang, "The Power and Limit of the Private Contract in Ming–Qing China and Today," 57–76, in Leo Douw and Peter Post, eds., *South China: State, Culture and Social Change during the 20th Century* (Amsterdam: Royal Netherlands of Arts and Sciences, 1996).
Si-yan Fei, *Negotiating Urban Space: Urbanization and Public Space in Nanjing* (Stanford: Stanford University Press, 2009).
Antonia Finnane, *Speaking of Yangzhou: A Chinese City, 1550–1850* (Cambridge, MA: Harvard University Asia Center, 2004).
Laurence Fontaine, *The Moral Economy: Poverty, Credit, and Trust in Early Modern Europe* (Cambridge: Cambridge University Press, 2014).
Maurice Freedman, *Chinese Lineage and Society* (London: Athlone Press, 1966).
  Lineage Organization in Southeastern China (London: Athlone Press, 1958).
  The Study of Chinese Society, comp. and introd. by G. William Skinner (Stanford: Stanford University Press, 1979).
Fu Chonglan 傅崇兰, *Zhongguo yunhe chengshi fazhan shi* 中国运河城市发展史 (Chengdu: Sichuang renmin and Sichuan sheng Xinhua shudian, 1985).

Fu Yiling 傅衣凌, *Ming Qing shidai shangren ji shangye ziben* 明清時代商人及商業資本 (Beijing: Renmin, 1956; 2nd ed., 1980).

Fujii Hiroshi 藤井宏, "Shin'an shōnin no kenkyū 新安商人の研究," *Tōyō gakuhō* 東洋学報 36.1 (June 1953), 1–44; 36.2 (Sept. 1953), 32–60; 36.3 (Dec. 1953), 65–118; and, 36.4 (March 1953), 115–45.

Fukuda Motoko 福田素子, "Chikurui shōsai-tan no denrai to henka – sono kingaku hyōgen o chūshin ni 畜類償債譚の伝来と変化 — その金額表現を中心に," *Tōhō gaku* 東方学 129 (Jan. 2015), 69–86.

Fuma Susumu 夫馬进, "Late Ming Urban Reform and the Popular Uprising in Hangzhou," in Linda Cooke Johnson, ed., *Cities of Jiangnan in Late Imperial China* (Albany: State University of New York Press, 1993).

"Shilun Mingmo Huizhoufu de sijuan fendan fenzheng 试论明末徽州府的丝绢分担纷争," 271–90, in Zhao Huafu 赵华富, ed., *'98 Guoji Huixue shu taolunhui lunwenji* '98国际徽学术讨论会论文集 (Hefei: Anhui daxue, 2000).

Furuta Kazuko 古田和子, "Kindai Chūgoku ni okeru shijō chitsujo to jōhō no hi-taishōsei: 19 seki matsu-20 seki shuto 近代中国における市場秩序と非対称性：19世紀末20世紀初頭," 135–64, in Furuta Kazuko, ed., *Chūgoku no shijō chitsujo: 17-seiki kara 20-seiki zenhan o chūshin ni* 中国の市場秩序：17世紀から20世紀前半を中心に (Tokyo: Keiō gijuku daigaku shuppankai, 2013).

Robert Gardella, "Contracting Business Partnerships in Late Qing and Republican China: Paradigms and Patterns," 326–47, in Madeleine Zelin, Jonathan K. Ocko, and Robert Gardella, eds., *Contract and Property in Early Modern China* (Stanford: Stanford University Press, 2004).

"Squaring Accounts: Commercial Bookkeeping Methods and Capitalist Rationalism in Late Qing and Republican China," *Journal of Asian Studies* 51.2 (May 1992), 317–39.

Hill Gates, *China's Motor: A Thousand Years of Petty Capitalism* (Ithaca: Cornell University Press, 1996).

Ge Qinghua 葛庆华, "Huizhou wenhui chutan 徽州文会初探," *Jiang Huai luntan* 江淮论坛, 1997.4, 78–84.

Clifford Geertz, *The Rotating Credit Association: A Middle Rung in Development* (Cambridge, MA: MIT Center for International Studies, 1956).

James Geiss, "The Reign of the Chia-ching Emperor, 1522–66," 440–510, in Frederick W. Mote and Denis Twitchett, eds., *The Cambridge History of China, v. 7, The Ming Dynasty, 1368–1644, pt. 1* (Cambridge: Cambridge University Press, 1988).

Jacques Gernet, "Introduction," i–xlv, in Stuart R. Schram, ed., *The Scope of State Power in China* (London and Hong Kong: School of Oriental and African Studies and the Chinese University Press, 1985).

François Gipouloux, "Partnerships and Capital Pooling in Late Imperial China," paper at the Eurasia Trajecto Gecem Conference, Empire, State and Law Across the Eurasian Continent, at Pablo de Olavide University, Seville, October 2018.

William N. Goetzmann and Elisabeth Köll, "The History of Corporate Ownership in China: State Patronage," 149–84, in Randall K. Morck, ed., *A History of Corporate Governance around the World: Family Business Groups to Professional Managers* (Chicago: The University of Chicago Press, 2005).

S.D. Goitein, *A Mediterranean Society: The Jewish Communities of the Arab World as Portrayed in the Documents of the Cairo Genizah, v. 1, Economic Foundations* (Berkeley: University of California Press, 1967).

Peter Golas, "Early Qing Guilds," 555–80, in G. William Skinner, ed., *The City in Late Imperial China* (Stanford: Stanford University Press, 1977).

"Mining," in Joseph Needham, *Science and Civilisation in China, v. 5, Chemistry and Chemical Technology*, pt. 13 (Cambridge: Cambridge University Press, 1999), 278–88.

Noël Golvers, *François de Rougemont, S.J., Missionary in Ch'ang-shu (Chiang-nan): A Study of the Account Book (1674–1676) and the Elogium* (Leuven: Ferdinand Verbiest Foundation and Leuven University Press, 1999).

Gong Shengsheng, "Lun 'HuGuang shu, tianxia zu' 论'湖广熟, 天下足'," *Nongye kaogu* 农业考古 1995.1, 130–40.

Bryna Goodman, *Native Place, City, and Nation: Regional Networks and Identities in Shanghai, 1853–1937* (Berkeley: University of California Press, 1995).

L. Carrington Goodrich and Chaoying Fang, eds., *Dictionary of Ming Biography, 1368–1644* (New York: Columbia University Press, 1976).

Vincent Goossaert and David A. Palmer, *The Religious Question in Modern China* (Chicago: The University of Chicago Press, 2011).

Frederick Delano Grant Jr., *The Chinese Cornerstone of Modern Banking: The Canton Guaranty System and the Origins of Bank Deposit Insurance 1780–1933* (Leiden: Brill Nijhoff, 2014).

Linda Grove and Christian Daniels, eds., *State and Society in China: Japanese Perspectives on Ming–Qing Social and Economic History* (Tokyo: University of Tokyo Press, 1984).

Gu Lu 顧祿, *Tongqiao yizhuo lu* 桐橋倚棹錄 (Shanghai: Guji, 1980).

Gu Yingtai 谷應泰, *Mingshi jishi benmo* 明史記事本末 (Beijing: Zhonghua, 1977).

Guo Qitao, *Exorcism and Money: The Symbolic World of the Five-Fury Spirits in Late Imperial China* (Berkeley: University of California, Berkeley, Institute of East Asian Studies, 2003).

Ritual Opera and Mercantile Lineage: The Confucian Transformation of Popular Culture in Late Imperial Huizhou (Stanford: Stanford University Press, 2005).

Hamashima Atsutoshi 浜島敦俊, "Min Shin jidai Chūgoku no chihō kangoku 明清時代中国の地方監獄," *Hōsei shi kenkyū* 法制史研究 33 (1983), 1–60.

Sōkan shinkō: kinsei Kōnan nōson shakai to minkan shinkō 総管信仰: 近世江南農村社会と民間信仰 (Tokyo: Kenbun, 2001).

Han Dacheng 韩大成, "Mingdai Huishang zai jiaotong yu Shangyeshi shang de zhongyao gongxian 明代徽商在交通与商业史上的重要贡献," *Shixue yuekan* 史学月刊 1988.4, 35–43.

Mingdai shehui jingji chutan 明代社会经济初探 (Beijing: Renmin, 1986).

Han Dacheng 韩大成, and Yang Qin 杨欣, *Wei Zhongxian zhuan* 魏忠贤传 (Beijing: Renmin, 1997).

Han Xiutao 韩秀桃, *Ming Qing Huizhou de minjian jiufen ji qi jiejue* 明清徽州的民间纠纷及其解决 (Hefei: Anhui daxue, 2004).

Ron Harris, "The Institutional Dynamics of Early Modern Eurasian Trade: The Commenda and the Corporation," *Journal of Economic Behavior and Organization* 71.3 (2009), 606–22.

Charles Hartman, "Sung Government and Politics," 19–138, in John W. Chaffee and Denis Twitchett, eds., *The Cambridge History of China, v. 5, pt. 2, The Five Dynasties and Sung China, 960–1279* (Cambridge: Cambridge University Press, 2015).

He Bingdi (aka Ho Ping-ti) 何炳棣, *Zhongguo huiguan shilun* 中國會館史論 (Taipei: Xuesheng, 1966).

Martin Heijdra, "The Socio-economic Development of Rural China during the Ming," 417–578, in Frederick W. Mote and Denis Twitchett, eds., *The Cambridge History of China, v. 8, The Ming Dynasty, 1368–1644, pt. 2* (Cambridge: Cambridge University Press, 1998).

Hino Kaisaburō 日野開三郎, "Kyakushō no torihiki shunari 客商の取引助成," 154–98, in his *Tōyō shigaku ronshū* 東洋史学論集, v. 17, *Tōdai teiten no kenkyū* 唐代邸店の研究 (Tokyo: San'ichi shobō, 1992).

"Sōdai chōseiko no hatten ni tsuite 宋代長生庫の発展について," 213–46, in his *Tōyō shigaku ronshū* 東洋史学論集, v. 6, *Sōdai no kahei to kin'yū (ge)* 宋代の貨幣と金融 (下) (Tokyo: San'ichi shobō, 1983).

Bibliography

Hino Kaisaburō 日野開三郎, and Kusano Yasushi 草野靖, "Tō Sō jidai no gōhon 唐宋時代の合本," 485–98, in his *Tōyō shigaku ronshū* 東洋史学論集, v. 5, *Tō Godai no kahei to kin'yū (ge)* 唐五代の貨幣と金融(下) (Tokyo: San'ichi shobō, 1982).

Ho Ping-ti (aka He Bingdi), *The Ladder of Success in Imperial China* (New York: Columbia University Press, 1965).

Hong Huanchun 洪煥椿, *Ming Qing shi oucun* 明清史偶存 (Nanjing: Nanjing daxue, 1992).

Horichi Akira 堀地明, *Min Shin shokuryō sōjō kenkyū* 明清食糧騷擾研究 (Tokyo: Kyūko Shoin, 2011).

Hoshi Ayao 星斌夫, *Dai unga, Chūgoku no sōun* 大運河, 中国の漕運 (Tokyo: Kondō shuppansha, 1971).

    Mindai sōun no kenkyū 明代漕運の研究 (Tokyo: Nihon gakujutsu shinkōkai, 1963).

    "Transportation in the Ming Dynasty," *Acta Asiatica* 38 (1980), 1–30.

Hu Tieqiu 胡铁球, "Ming Qing maoyi lingyu zhong de 'kedian,' 'xiejia,' 'yashang,' deng mingyi shitong kao 明请贸易领域中的 '客店,' '歇家,' '牙商' 等名异实同考," *Shehui kexue* 社会科学 2010.9, 144–53.

    Ming Qing xiejia yanjiu 明清歇家研究 (Shanghai: Guji, 2015).

Hu Zhongsheng 胡中生, "Cong 'Huizhou huishe zonglu' kan Qingdai Huizhou de jipin yu shiwu 从'徽州会社总录'看清代徽州的祭品与食物," *Huixue* 徽学 9 (2014), 48–65.

    "Jindai Huizhou qianhui de leixing yu tedian 近代徽州钱会的类型与特点," *Huixue* 徽学 4 (2006), 200–16.

Huang Jianhui 黄鉴晖, "Qingchu shangyong huipiao yu shangpin jingji de fazhan 请初商用会票与商品经济的发展," *Wenxian* 文献 1987.1, 3–16.

Huang Laisheng 黄来生 and Chen Liyun 陈丽云, "Shuma cun de chuantong jingji, zongzu, yu minjian fojiao xinyang 蜀马村的传统经济, 宗族与民间佛教信仰," *Huixue* 徽学 7 (2012), 158–81.

Ray Huang, *Taxation and Governmental Finance in Sixteenth-Century Ming China* (Cambridge: Cambridge University Press, 1974).

Huang Xingzeng 黄省曾, *Wufeng lu* 吳風錄 (Xuehai leibian ed.).

Huangshan shi zhengbian wenshi ziliao weiyuanhui 黄山市整编文史资料委员会, ed., *Huizhou daxing* 徽州大姓 (Hefei: Anhui daxue chubanshe, 2005).

Arthur W. Hummel, ed., *Eminent Chinese of the Ch'ing Period (1644–1912)* (Washington, DC: United States Government Printing Office, 1943).

Imabori Seiji 今堀誠二, *Chūgoku hōken shakai no kōsei* 中国封建社会の構成 (Tokyo: Keisō shobō, 1991).

Inoue Susumu 井上進, *Min Shin gakujutsu hensen shi, shuppan to dentō gakujutsu no rinkai ten* 明清学術変遷史, 出版と伝統学術の臨界点 (Tokyo: Heibonsha, 2011).

Inoue Tōru 井上徹, *Chūgoku no sōzoku to kokka no reisei: sōhōshugi no shiten kara no bunseki* 中国の宗族と国家の礼制: 宗法主義の視点からの分析 (Tokyo: Kenbun, 2000).

Peter Jackson, *The Mongols and the West, 1221–1410* (Harlow: Pearson Longman, 2005).

Jiang Hong 江洪, comp., *Suzhou cidian* 苏州词典 (Suzhou: Suzhou daxue, 1999).

Jiang Shounan 江授南, "Lanxi Huizhou de shanggui suyue 兰溪徽州的商规俗约," 926–29, in *Huixue* 徽学 4 (Tunxi: Anhui sheng Huizhou diqu huixue yanjiuhui, 1990).

Jiang Taixin 江太新, "Lun Qingdai Huizhou tudi maimai zhong zongfa guanxi de songchi 论清代徽州土地买卖中宗法关系的松弛," *Huizhou shehui kexue* 徽州社会科学 1995.1-2, 1,079-86.

Jiang Yonglin, introd. and trans., *The Great Ming Code/Da Ming lü* (Seattle: University of Washington Press, 2007).

Jing Jia (aka Kei Ka) 景嘉, *Chūgoku bujutsu shinpi tatsujin siuki Chō San den* 中国武術神秘達人酔鬼張三伝, trans. Koyama Kanji 小山寛二 (Tokyo: Shin jinbutsu ōraisha, 1973).

William C. Jones, trans., *The Great Qing Code* (Oxford: Clarendon Press, 1994).

Kang-I Sun-Chang, "Literature of the Early Ming to Mid Ming (1375–1572)," 25–90, in Kang-i Sun Chang and Stephen Owen, eds., *The Cambridge History of Chinese Literature, v. 2* (Cambridge: Cambridge University Press, 2010).

Katō Shigeshi 加藤繁, *Shinagaku zassō* 支那學雜草 (Tokyo: Seikatsusha, 1944).

Kawakatsu Mamoru 川勝守, *Min Shin Kōnan nōgyō keizaishi kenkyū* 明清江南農業経済史研究 (Tokyo: Tokyo daigaku shuppankai, 1992).

Min Shin Kōnan shichin shakaishi kenkyū, Kūkan to shakai keisei no rekishigaku 明清江南市鎮社会史研究: 空間と社会形成の歴史学 (Tokyo: Kyūko shoin, 1999).

Min Shin kōnōsei to kyodai toshi rensa: Chōkō to Dai unga 明清貢納制と巨大都市連鎖: 長江と大運河 (Tokyo: Kyūko shoin, 2009).

"Minmatsu Shinsho ni okeru dakkō to bōda 明末清初における打行と访打," *Shien* 史淵 119 (1982), 65–92.

William Kirby, "China Unincorporated: Company Law and Business Enterprise in Twentieth-Century China," *Journal of Asian Studies* 54.1 (Feb. 1995), 43–63.

Kishimoto Mio 岸本美緒, *Min Shin kōtai to Kōnan shakai: 17-seiki Chūgoku no chitsujo mondai* 明清交替と江南社会: 17世紀中国の秩序問題 (Tokyo: Tokyo daigaku shuppankai, 1999).

Shindai Chūgoku no bukka to keizai hendō 清代中国の物価と経済変動 (Tokyo: Kenbun, 1997).

Elisabeth Köll, *From Cotton Mill to Business Empire: The Emergence of Regional Enterprises in Modern China* (Cambridge, MA: Harvard University Press, 2002).

Kuroda Akinobu, "What Prices Can Tell Us about 16th–18th Century China," *Chūgoku shigaku* 中国史学 13 (December 2003), 101–17.

John Lagerwey, "Ethnographic Introduction," in Bu Yongjian 卜永坚 and Bi Xinding 毕新丁, eds., *Wuyuan de zongzu, jingji yu minsu* 婺源的宗族, 经济与民俗 (Shanghai: Fudan daxue, 2011).

"Village Religion in Huizhou: A Preliminary Assessment," *Minsu quyi* 民俗曲藝 174 (December 2011), 305–59.

Étienne de La Vaissière, *Sogdian Traders: A History* (Leiden: Brill, 2005).

Li Aixian 李爱贤, "Mingdai shangren zhuanji daliang chuxian zhi yinyuan chutan 明代商人传记大量出现之原因初探," *Xiangyang zhiye zhishu xueyuan xuebao* 襄阳职业技术学院学报 13.5 (Nov. 2014), 68–70.

Li Bozhong 李伯重, "Ming Qing shiqi Jiangnan diqu de mucai wenti 明清时期江南地区的木材问题," *Zhongguo shehui jingji shi yanjiu* 中国社会经济史研究 1986.1, 86–96.

Li Linqi 李琳琦 and Liang Renzhi 梁仁志, comp., *Huishang huiguan gongsuo zhengxinlu huibian* 徽商会馆公所征信录汇编 (Beijing, Renmin, 2016).

Li Tao 李涛, *Xu Zizhi tongjian changbian* 续资治通鉴长编 (Beijing: Zhonghua, 1979–95).

Li Yushuan 李玉栓, *Mingdai wenren jieshe kao* 明代文人结社考 (Beijing: Zhonghua, 2013).

Liang Fangzhong 梁方仲, comp., *Zhongguo lidai hukou, tiandi, tianfu tongji* 中国历代户口, 田地, 田赋统计 (Shanghai: Shanghai renmin, 1980).

Liang Mingwu 梁明武, Li Li 李莉, and Chen Jiancheng 陈建成, "Ming Qing Huishang mucai jingying zhong de ziben xingtai chutan 明请徽商木材经营中的资本形态初探," *Linye jingji* 林业经济 Nov. 2007, 63–67.

Liang Xiaomin 梁小民, *Zouma kan shangbang* 走马看商帮 (Shanghai: Shanghai shudian, 2011).

Lin Ji 林济, "Mingdai Huizhou zongzu jingying yu citang zhidu de xingcheng 明代徽州宗族精英与祠堂制度的形成," *Anhui shixue* 安徽史学 2012.6, 90–97.

Lin Meiling 林美玲, *WanMing Liaoxiang* 晚明辽饷 (Fuzhou: Fujian renmin, 2007).

Ling Mengchu, *Slapping the Table in Amazement*, trans. Shuhui Yang and Yunqin Yang (Seattle: University of Washington Press, 2018).

Liu Boshan 刘伯山, "Ming Qing Huizhou zongzu yu xiangcun shehui de wending 明请徽州宗族与乡村社会的稳定," *Huixue* 徽学 8 (2012), 179–202.

Liu Liying 刘丽英, "Ming Qing shiqi Yixian shangren yanjiu gaishu 明请时期黟县商人研究概述," *Heilong jiang shizhi* 黑龙江史志 336 (2014.23), 105–6.

Liu Miao 刘淼, "Chuantong nongcun shehui de zongzi fa yu citang jiji zhidu – jianlun Huizhou nongcun zongzu de zhenghe 传统农村社会的宗子法与祠堂祭祀制度 – 兼论徽州农村宗族的整合," *Zhongguo nongshi* 中国农史, 21.3 (2002), 81–88.

Cong Huizhou Ming Qing jianshe kan Huishang lijun de zhuanyi 从徽州明清建设看徽州商人利润的转移," *Jiang Huai luntan* 江淮论坛 1982.6, 21–29.

"Qingdai Huizhou cichan tudi guanxi – yi Huizhou Shexian Tangyue Baoshi, Tangmo Xushi wei zhongxin 清代徽州祠产土地关系 – 以徽州歙县棠樾鲍氏、唐模许氏为中心," *Zhongguo jingji shi yanjiu* 中国经济史研究 1991.9, 831–45.

"Qingdai Huizhou de 'hui' yu 'huiji': yi Qimen Shanhe li Chengshi wei zhongxin 清代徽州的 '会' 与 '会祭' 以祁门善和里程氏为中心," *Jiang Huai luntan* 江淮论坛 1995.4, 235–40.

"Qingdai Qimen Shanhe li Chengshi zongzu de 'hui' zhuzhi 清代祁门善和里程氏宗族的 '会' 组织," *Wenwu yanjiu* 文物研究, 8 (1993.10), 256–66, and 9 (1994.11), 268–74.

Liu Qiugen 刘秋根, "Mingdai gongshangye zhong hehuo zhi de leixing 明代工商业中合伙制的类型," *Zhongguo shehui jingji shi yanjiu* 中国社会经济史研究 2001.4, 58–64.

"Shidao shisi shiji de Zhongguo kehuo zhi 十到十四世纪的中国合伙制," *Lishi yanjiu* 历史研究 2002.6, 109–22.

comp., *Zhongguo diandang zhidu shi ziliaoji* 中国典当制度史资料集 (Baoding: Hebei daxue, 2016).

Zhongguo diandang zhidu shi 中国典当制度史 (Shanghai: Guji, 1995).

Liu Qiugen 刘秋根, *Zhongguo gudai hehuo zhi chutan* 中国古代合伙制初探 (Beijing: Renmin, 2007).

Liu Qiugen 刘秋根 and Xie Xiuli 谢秀丽, "Ming Qing Huishang shanggong ye pudian hehuozhi xingtai – san zhong Huishang zhangbu de biaomian fenxi 明清徽商商工业铺店合伙制形态 – 三种徽商帐簿的表面分析," *Zhongguo jingjishi yanjiu* 中国经济史研究 2005.3, 79–87.

Liu Shiji 刘石吉, *Ming Qing shidai Jiangnan shizhen yanjiu* 明清时代江南市镇研究 (Zhongguo shehui kexue: Xinhua shudian jingxiao, 1987).

Liu Xufeng 刘序枫, "Jindai Huanan chuantong shehui zhong 'gongsi' xingtai zaikau: yu Shanghai shang maoyi dao difang shehui 近代华南传统社会中'公司'形态再考: 由上海上贸易到地方社会," 227–67, in Lin Yuru 林玉茹, ed., Bijiao shiye xia de Taiwan shangye chuantong 比較視野下的臺灣商業傳統 (Taibei: Zhongyang yanjiu yuan Taiwan shi yanjiusuo, 2012).

Liu Yonghua, *Confucian Rituals and Chinese Villagers: Ritual Change and Social Transformation in a Southeastern Chinese Community, 1368–1949* (Leiden: Brill, 2013).

Lin Zhenhan 林振翰, *Yanzheng cidian* 鹽政辭典 (Zhengzhou: Zhongzhou guji, 1988; pref. 1926),

Liu Zhiwei 刘志伟, *Zai guojia yu shehui zhi jian: Ming Qing Guangdong diqu lijia fuyi zhidu yu xiangcun shehui* 在国家与社会之间: 明清广东地区里甲赋役制度与乡村社会 (2nd ed., Beijing: Zhongguo renmin daxue, 2010).

Long Denggao 龙登高, *Jiangnan shichang shi: shiyi zhi shijiu shiji de bianqian* 江南市場史: 十一至十九世紀的变迁 (Beijing: Qinghua daxue, 2003).

Robert S. Lopez, *The Commercial Revolution of the Middle Ages, 950–1350* (Cambridge: Cambridge University Press, 1976).

Lufrano, Richard John, *Honorable Merchants: Commerce and Self-Cultivation in Late Imperial China* (Honolulu: University of Hawai'i Press, 1997).

Luo Zhuandong 罗传栋, ed., *Chang Jiang hangyun shi* 长江航运史 (Beijing: Renmin jiaotong, 1991).

Laurence J. Ma, *Commercial Development and Urban Change in Sung China (960–1279)* (Ann Arbor: University of Michigan, Dept. of Geography, 1971).

Ma Yonghu 马勇虎, *Hexie youxu de xiangcun shequ: Chengkan* 和谐有序的乡村社区: 呈坎 (Hefei: Hefei gongye daxue, 2nd printing, 2007).

Joseph P. McDermott, "The Art of Making a Living in Sixteenth Century China," *Kaikodo Journal* (April 1997), 63–81.

  "Bondservants in the Tai-hu Basin in the Late Ming: A Case of Mistaken Identities," *Journal of Asian Studies* 40 (Nov. 1981), 675–702.

  "Emperor, Élites, and Commoners: The Community Pact Ritual of the Late Ming," 299–351, in Joseph P. McDermott, ed., *State and Court Ritual in China* (Cambridge: Cambridge University Press, 1999).

  "Family Financial Plans of the Southern Sung," *Asia Major*, 3rd ser., 4.2 (1991), 15–52.

  "For Students of Pre-modern Chinese Living Standards, a European Book to Read and Ponder, However Belatedly," *Chūgoku shigaku* 中国史学, 25 (Oct. 2015), 1–23.

"How to Succeed Commercially as a Huizhou Book Publisher, 1500–1644," 383–99, in Zhou Shengchun 周生春 and He Zhaohui 何朝晖, eds., *Yinshua yu shichang, Guoji huiyi lunwen ji* 印刷与市场, 国际会议论文集 (Hangzhou: Zhejiang daxue, 2012).

"The Making of a Chinese Mountain, Huangshan: Politics and Wealth in Chinese Art," *Ajia bunka kenkyū* アジア文化研究 *Asian Cultural Studies*, 17 (March 1989), 145–76.

The Making of a New Rural Order in South China, v. 1. Village, Land, and Lineage in Huizhou, 900–1600 (Cambridge: Cambridge University Press, 2013).

"Merchants and Markets in Late Imperial China," in Richard von Glahn and Ma Debin, eds., *Cambridge Economic History of China* (Cambridge: Cambridge University Press, forthcoming).

"Merchants in Late Imperial China: Obstacles and Solutions," in Francisco Bethencourt and Cátia Antunes, eds., *Early Modern Mercantile Culture* (Leiden: Brill, forthcoming).

"The Monastic Order and Monastic Landholdings,1000–1644: the Case of Fujian, Especially Fuzhou Prefecture" (paper presented at the Conference on Monastic Life in East Asia, held at Cambridge in July 2004).

"Private Non-commercial Publishing in Ming China and Its Private Uses," 201–25, in Michela Bussotti and Jean-Pierre Drège, eds., *Imprimer sans profit? Le livre non commercial dans la Chine impériale* (Paris: Droz, 2015).

A Social History of the Chinese Book (Hong Kong: Hong Kong University Press, 2006).

"The Urban Order of Suzhou, 1500–1650" (forthcoming).

Joseph P. McDermott, and Peter Burke, eds., *The Book Worlds of East Asia and Europe, 1450–1850* (Hong Kong: Hong Kong University Press, 2015).

Joseph P. McDermott and Shiba Yoshinobu, "Economic Change in China, 960–1279," 321–426, in John W. Chaffee and Denis Twitchett, eds., *The Cambridge History of China, v. 5, pt. 2, The Five Dynasties and Sung China, 960–1279* (Cambridge: Cambridge University Press, 2015).

Brian E. McKnight, *Law and Order in Sung China* (Cambridge: Cambridge University Press, 1995).

"Urban Crime and Urban Security in Sung China," *Chinese Culture*, 29 (December 1988), 23–66.

Susan Mann, *Local Merchants and the Chinese Bureaucracy, 1750–1950* (Stanford: Stanford University Press, 1987).

Mantetsu Shanhai jimusho chōsashitsu chōsabu 滿鐵上海事務所調查室調查部, ed., *Chūshi no minsengyō: Soshū minsen jittai chōsa hōkoku* 中支の民船業, 蘇州民船實態調查報告 (Tokyo: Hakubunkan, 1943).

Michael Marmé, *Suzhou: Where the Goods of All the Provinces Converge* (Stanford: Stanford University Press, 2004).
Masui Tsuneo 増井経夫, *Chūgoku no gin to shōnin* 中国の銀と商人 (Tokyo: Kenbun, 1986).
Mei Xinlin 梅新林 and Chen Guocan 陈国灿, eds., *Jiangnan nongcun chengshihua lishi yanjiu* 江南农村城市化历史研究 (Hangzhou: Zhejiang daxue, 2005).
Meilink-Roelofsz, M.A.P., *Asian Trade and European Influence in the Indonesian Archipelago between 1500 and about 1630* (The Hague: Martinus Nijhoff, 1962).
Steven R. Miles, *Upriver Journeys: Diaspora and Empire in Southern China, 1570–1850* (Cambridge, MA: Harvard University Asia Center, 2017).
Miyazaki Ichisada 宮崎市定, *Ajiashi kenkyū* アジア史研究, v. 3 (Kyoto: Tōyōshi kenkyūkai, 1975).
Mori Masao 森正夫, *Mindai Kōnan tochi seido no kenkyū* 明代江南土地制度の研究 (Kyoto: Dōhōsha, 1988).
Frederick W. Mote, "The Cheng-hua and Hung-chih reigns, 1465–1505," 373, in Mote and Twitchett, eds., *The Cambridge History of China, v. 7, The Ming Dynasty, 1368–1644, pt. 1* (Cambridge: Cambridge University Press, 1988).
Nakajima Gakushō 中島楽章, *Mindai gōson no funsō to chitsujo: Kishū monjo o shiryō to shite* 明代郷村の紛争と秩序: 徽州文書を資料として (Tokyo: Kyūko shoin, 2002).
Nakamura Jihei 中村治兵衛, *Chūgoku gyogyōshi no kenkyū* 中国漁業史の研究 (Tokyo: Tōsui shobō, 1995).
Negishi Tadashi 根岸佶, *Chūgoku no girudo* 中国のギルド (Tokyo: Nihon Hyōron shinsha, 1953).
H. Neville and H. Bell's Section, *Report of the Mission to China of the Blackburn Chamber of Commerce, 1896–7* (Blackburn: The North-East Lancashire Press Company, 1898).
Nie Zhuanyou 耿传友, "Wang Daokun 'Taihan ji' shangren zhuanji chutan 汪道昆 '太函集' 商人传记初探," *Guji yanjiu* 古籍研究 2001.3, 101–07.
Niida Noboru 仁井田陞, *Chūgoku hōseishi kenkyū, dorei nōdo hō· kazoku sonraku hō, v. 3* 中国法制史研究, 奴隷農奴法·家族村落法 (Tokyo: Tokyo daigaku shuppankai, 1962).
  Shina mibun hō shi 支那身分法史 (Tokyo: Tōhō bunka gakuin, 1942).
Thomas G. Nimick, *Local Administration in Ming China: The Changing Roles of Magistrates, Prefects, and Provincial Officials* (Minneapolis: Society for Ming Studies, 2008),
Nishijima Sadao, "The Formation of the Early Chinese Cotton Industry," 805–72, in Linda Grove and Christian Daniels, eds., *State and Society in*

China: Japanese Perspectives on Ming–Qing Social and Economic History (Tokyo: University of Tokyo Press, 1984).

Nishimura Gensho 西村元照, "Riu Roku Riu Chi no ran ni tsuite 刘六刘七の乱について," *Tōyōshi kenkyū* 東洋史研究, 32.4 (March 1974), 44–86.

Nishimura Kazuyo 西村かずよ, "Mingdai no doboku 明代の奴僕," *Tōyōshi kenkyū* 東洋史研究, 38.1 (June 1979), 24–50.

Niu Jianqiang 牛建强, "Mingdai Huizhou diqu zhi shehui bianqian 明代徽州地区之社会变迁," *Shixue yuekan* 史学月刊1995.4, 73–79.

Okano Shōko 岡野昌子, "Minmatsu Rinshin minhen kō 明末臨清民変考," 103–33, in Ono Kazuko 小野和子, ed., *Min Shin jidai no seiji to shakai* 明清時代の政治と社会 (Kyoto: Kyōtō daigaku Jinbun kagaku kenkyūjo, 1983).

Ōki Yasushi 大木康, *Min Shin bungaku no hitobito: shokugyō betsu bungakushi* 明清文学の人びと：職業別文学誌 (Tokyo: Sōbunsha, 2008).

Ono Kazuko, "Sansei shōnin to Zhang Juzheng 山西商人と張居正," *Tōhō gakuhō* 東方学報, 58.1 (March 1986), 555–92.

Ōta Izuru 太田出, *Chūgoku kinsei no tsumi to batu: hanzai, keisatsu, kangoku no shakaishi* 中国近世の罪と罰：犯罪・警察・監獄の社会史 (Nagoya: Nagoya daigaku shuppankai, 2015).

Oyama Masaaki 小山正明, "Min Shin jidai no kokōjin ritsu ni tsuite 明清時代の雇工人律につい て," 249–74, in Hoshi hakushi taikan kinen Chūgokushi ronshū iinkai 星博士退官記念中國史論集編集委員会, ed., *Hoshi hakushi taikan kinen Chūgokushi ronshū* 星博士退官記念中國史論集 (Yamagata: Hoshi Ayao sensei taikan kinen jigyōkai, 1978).

Pak Wŏn-ho 朴元熇, *Ming Qing Huizhou Fangshi zongzu de gean yanjiu* 明清徽州方氏宗族的个案研究 (Hefei: Huangshan shushe, 2013).

Geoffrey Parker, *Global Crisis: War, Climate and Catastrophe in the Seventeenth Century* (New Haven: Yale University Press, 2013).

Peng Chao 彭超, "Ming Qing shiqi Huizhou diqu de tudi jiage yu dizu 明清时期徽州地区的土地价格与地租," *Zhongguo shehui jingji shi yanjiu* 中国社会经济史研究 1988.2, 56–63.

  "Xiuning Chengshi zhichan bu pouxi 休宁'程氏置产簿'剖析," *Zhongguo shehui jingji shi yanjiu*, 7 (1983.4), 55–66.

Peng Xinwei 彭信威, *Zhongguo huobi shi* 中國貨幣史 (Shanghai: Renmin, 1988, 3rd pt. of 1958 ed.).

Peng Zeyi 彭泽益, ed., *Qingdai gongshang hangye beiwen jicui* 清代工商行业碑文集粹 (Zhengzhou: Zhongzhou guji, 1997).

  comp., *Zhongguo gongshang hanghui shiliao ji* 中国工商行会史料集 (Beijing: Zhonghua, 1995), 2 vols.

John H. Pryor, "The Origins of the Commenda Contract," *Speculum*, 52 (1977), 5–37.

Puk Wing-kin, *The Rise and Fall of a Public Debt Market in 16th-Century China: The Story of the Ming Salt Certificate* (Leiden: Brill, 2016).

Qi Yangkun 齐洋锟 and Chen Jun 陈君, "Ming Qing shiqi teshu de jinrong jigou 明清时期特殊的金融机构," *Chongqing keji xueyuan bao (shehui kexue ban)* 重庆科技学院报(社会科学版) 2012.8, 145–48.

Qiu Pengsheng 邱澎生, *Dang falü yu shang jingji: Ming Qing Zhongguo de shangye falü* 當法律遇上經濟: 明清中國的商業法律 (Taipei: Wunan tushu chuban gongsi, 2008).

"Ming Qing shidai Suzhou cheng gongshang ye zuzhi de biange 明清蘇州城工商業組織的變革," *Guoli daxue Taiwan daxue jianzhu yu chengxiang yanjiu* 国立大学台灣大學建筑与城乡研究, 5.1 (1990), 83–90.

"You shichan lüli yanbian kan Ming Qing zhengfu dui shichang de falü guifan 由市廛律例演變看明清政府對市場的法律規範," in *Shixue: chengtong yu bianqian xueshu yantaohui lunwen ji* 史學傳承與變遷學術研討會論文集, 5.1 (1990), 291–334.

"Yu Suzhou jingshang chongtu shijian kan Qingdai qianqi de guanshang guanxi 由蘇州經商衝突事件看清代前期的官商關係," *Wenshizhe xuebao* 文史哲學報, 43 (1995), 37–92.

Qu Yanbin 曲彦斌, *Zhongguo diandang xue* 中国典当学 (Shijiazhuang: Hebei renmin, 2002).

Quan Hansheng 全漢昇, "Zi Song zhi Ming zhengfu suiru zhong qianyin bili de biandong 自宋至明政府歲入中錢銀比例的變動," 355–67, in his *Zhongguo jingjishi luncong* 中國經濟史論叢, v. 1 (Hong Kong: Xianggang zhongwen daxue xinya shuyuan yanjiusuo, 1972).

Ren Fang 任放, "Ming Qing shizhen de fazhan zhuangguang ji qi pingjia zhipiao tixi 明清市镇的发展状光及其评价指标体系," 187–228, in Chen Feng 陈锋, ed., *Ming Qing yilai Chang Jiang liuyu shehui fazhan shilun* 明清以来长江流域社会发展史论 (Wuchang: Wuhan daxue, 2006).

David M. Robinson, *Bandits, Eunuchs, and the Son of Heaven: Rebellions and the Economy of Violence in Mid-Ming China* (Honolulu: University of Hawai'i Press, 2001).

Jean-Laurent Rosenthal and R. Bin Wong, *Before and beyond Divergence: The Politics of Economic Change in China and Europe* (Cambridge, MA: Harvard University Press, 2011).

William T. Rowe, "Approaches to Modern Chinese Social History," 236–96, in Olivier Zunz, ed., *Reliving the Past: the Worlds of Social History* (Chapel Hill: University of North Carolina Press, 1985).

Hankow: Commerce and Society in a Chinese City, 1796–1889 (Stanford: Stanford University Press, 1984).

Hankow: Conflict and Community in a Chinese City, 1796–1895 (Stanford: Stanford University Press, 1989).

David Tod Roy, trans., *The Plum in the Golden Vase, or Chin P'ing Mei* (Princeton: Princeton University Press, 2011), v.4.

Teemu Ruskola, "Conceptualizing Corporations and Kinship: Comparative Law and Development Theory in a Chinese Perspective," *Stanford Law Review* 52.6 (July 2000), 1599–1729.

Saeki Tomi 佐伯富, *Chūgoku ensei shi no kenkyū* 中国鹽政史の研究 (Kyoto: Hōritsu bunkasha, 1987).

Shindai ensei no kenkyū 清代鹽政の研究 (Kyoto: Tōyōshi kenkyūkai, 1956).

Paolo Santangelo, "Urban Society in Late Imperial Suzhou," 90–120, in Linda Cooke Johnson, ed., *Cities of Jiangnan in Late Imperial China* (Albany: State University of New York press, 1993).

Satoi Genshichirō 里井彦七郎, "Shindai kōgyō shihon ni tsuite 清代鉱業資本について," *Tōyōshi kenkyū* 東洋史研究, 11.1 (1950), 32–50.

Sawada Masahiro 澤田雅弘, "Bun Chōmei go ni okeru Gochū bungaku no henbō ni tsuite 文徴明後における呉中文学の変貌について," (*Daitō bunka daigaku sōritsu gojū-nen kinen*) *Chūgoku gaku ronshū* (大東文化大学創立五十周年記念)中国学論集 (Dec. 1984), 519–40.

Herbert Franz Schurmann, *Economic Structure of the Yüan Dynasty* (Cambridge, MA: Harvard University Press, 1956).

Shao Yiping 邵毅平, *Wenxue yu shangren, chuantong Zhongguo shangren de wenxue chengxian* 文学与商人, 传统中国商人的文学呈现 (Shanghai: Guji, 2010).

Shi Beisheng 施沛生, comp., *Zhongguo minshi xiguan daquan* 中国民事習慣大全 (Shanghai: Yishu zhu, 1924; reprt., Shanghai: Shanghai shudian, 2004).

Shi Tao 石涛 and Li Zhifang 李志芳, "Chanquan yu jili jizhi shi jiaoxia de Jin Shaan shangbang 产权与激励机制视角下的晋陕商帮," *Shanxi daxue xuebao (zhexue shehuike xuebao)* 山西大学学报 (哲学社会科学报), 30.6 (Nov. 2007), 124–27.

Shiba Yoshinobu 斯波義信, ed., *Chūgoku shakai keizai shi yōgo kai* 中国社会経済史用語解 (Tokyo: Tōyō Bunko, 2012).

Chūgoku toshi shi 中国都市史 (Tokyo: Tōkyō daigaku shuppankai, 2002).

"On the Emergence and Intensification of the Pattern Of Rural–Urban Continuum in Late Imperial Jiangnan Society," 149–207, in Billy K.L. So, ed., *The Economy of Lower Yangzi Delta in Late Imperial China:*

Connecting Money, Markets, and Institutions (London: Routledge, 2013).

"Shinkoku 'Kyakushō ichiran seimei Tenka suiriku rotei' ni tsuite 新刻 '客商一覽醒迷天下水陸路程' について," 903–18, in Mori Mikisaburō Hakushi shōju kinen jigyōkai 森三樹三郎博士頌寿記念事業会, ed., Tōyō gaku ronshū: Mori Mikisaburō Hakushi shōju kinen 東洋学論集: 森三樹三郎博士頌寿記念 (Kyoto: Hōyū shoten, 1979).

Sōdai Kōnan keizaishi no kenkyū 宋代江南経済史の研究 (Tokyo: Tokyo Daigaku Tōyō Bunka Kenkyūjo, 1988).

"Sōdai no toshika o kangaeru, 宋代の都市化を考える," Tōhōgaku 東方学 102 (Jan 2001), 1–19.

Sōdai shōgyōshi kenkyū 宋代商業史研究 (Tokyo: Kazama shobō, 1968).

Shibuya Yūko 渋谷裕子, "Min Shin jidai Kishū Kōnan nōson shakai ni okeru saiji soshiki ni tsuite 明清時代徽州江南農村社会における祭事組織について(1)," Shigaku 史学, 59.1 (1990), 103–34, and (2), in Shigaku 59.2–3 (1990), 93–129.

Shimizu Morimitsu 清水盛光, Chūgoku zokusan seido kō 中国族产制度考 (Tokyo: Iwanami shoten, 1949).

Tomoko Shiroyama, "Companies in Debt: Financial Arrangements in the Textile Industry in the Lower Yangzi Delta, 1895–1937," 298–326, in Madeleine Zelin, Jonathan K. Ocko, and Robert Gardella, eds., Contract and Property in Early Modern China (Stanford: Stanford University Press, 2004).

G. William Skinner, ed., The City in Late Imperial China (Stanford: Stanford University Press, 1977).

Joanna Handlin Smith, The Art of Doing Good (Berkeley: University of California Press, 2009).

Paul J. Smith, Taxing Heaven's Storehouse: Horses, Bureaucrats, and the Destruction of the Sichuan Tea Industry, 1074–1224 (Cambridge, MA: Harvard University, Council on East Asian Studies, 1991).

Paul J. Smith and Richard von Glahn, eds., The Song–Yuan–Ming Transition, 900–1500 (Cambridge, MA: Harvard University Asia Center, 2003).

Billy K.L. So, ed., The Economy of Lower Yangzi Delta in Late Imperial China (London: Routledge, 2013).

Sōda Hiroshi 相田洋, Hashi to ijin: kyōkai no Chūgoku chūsei shi 橋と異人: 境界の中国中世史 (Tokyo: Kenbun, 2009).

Song Lizhong 宋立中, Xianya yu fuhua: Ming Qing Jiangnan richang shenghuo yu xiaofei wenhua 闲雅与浮华: 明清江南日常生活与消费文化 (Beijing: Zhongguo shehui kexue chubanshe, 2010).

Suzuki Hiroyuki 鈴木博之, "Mindai Kishūfu no zokusan 明代徽州府の族産," *Tōyō gakuhō* 東洋学報, 71.1–2 (December 1989), 1–29.

Takamura Masahiko 高村雅彦, *Chūgoku no toshi kūkan o yomu* 中国の都市空間を読む (Tokyo: Yamakawa, 2000).

Tanaka Masatoshi, "Rural Handicraft in Jiangnan in the Sixteenth and Seventeenth Centuries," 79–100, in Linda Grove and Christian Daniels, eds., *State and Society in China: Japanese Perspectives on Ming-Qing Social and Economic History* (Tokyo: University of Tokyo Press, 1984).

Tang Lixing 唐力行, "Huishang zai Shanghai shizhen de qiantu yu dingju huodong 徽商在上海市镇的迁徒与定居活动," *Shilin* 史林 (Shanghai) 2002.1, 25–34.

Huizhou zongzu shehui 徽州宗族社会 (Hefei: Anhui renmin, 2004).

Shangren yu Zhongguo jinshi shehui 商人与中国近世社会 (Beijing: Commercial Press, 2017).

Suzhou yu Huizhou, 16–20 shiji liangdi hudong yu shehui bianqian de bijiao yanjiu 苏州与徽州：16–20世纪两地互动与社会变迁的比较研究 (Beijing: Shangwu, 2007).

"Zhongguo xiangcun jiwu shehui shenghuo de shitai 中国乡村急务社会生活的事态," *Zhongguo nongshi* 中国农史 21.4 (2002), 58–66.

Tang Lixing 唐力行, and Zhang Xiangfeng 张翔凤, "Guojia minzhong jian de Huizhou xiangshen yu jiwu shehui kongzhi 国家民众间的徽州乡绅与基屋社会控制," *Shanghai shifan daxue xuebao (zhexue shehui kexue ban)* 上海师范大学学报(哲学社会科学版), 31.6 (November 2002), 58–66.

Tang Wenji 唐文基, comp., *16–18 shiji Zhongguo shangye geming* 16–18世纪中国商业革命 (Beijing: Shehui kexue wenxian, 2008).

Tanii Toshihito 谷井俊仁, "Rotei sho no jidai 路程書の時代," 415–56, in Ono Kazuko 小野和子, ed., *Minmatsu Shinsho no shakai to bunka* 明清時代の社会と文化 (Kyoto: Kyōtō daigaku Jinbun kagaku kenkyūjo, 1996).

Tanii Yōko 谷井陽子, "Shindai chūki no Jūkei shōgyō kai to sono chosetsu 清代中期の重慶商業堺とその秩序," *Tōyōshi kenkyū* 東洋史研究, 74.3 (Dec. 2015), 133–65.

Tao Mingxuan 陶明选, "Zhang wang, Taizi ji xiangguan zhushen 张王、太子及相关诸神," *Huixue* 徽学, 5 (2008), 144–64.

Terada Takanobu 寺田隆信, "Guan yu Beijing Shexian huiguan 关于北京歙县会馆," *Zhongguo shehui jingji shi yanjiu* 中国社会经济史研究 1991.1, 28–38.

"Sansei Kōshū Kanshi no kasan bunkatsu monjo ni tsuite 山西绛州韓氏の家産分割文書について," *Bunka* 文化, 35.4 (Winter 1972), 127–40.

Sansei shōnin no kenkyū, Mindai ni okeru shōnin oyobi shōgyō shihon 山西商人の研究, 明代における商人および商業資本 (Kyoto: Dōhōsha, 1972).
François Théry, SJ, *Les sociétés de commerce en Chine* (Tientsin: Société française de libraire et d'édition, 1929).
Tonami Mamoru 礪波護, "Tō Sō jidai ni okeru Soshu 唐宋時代に於ける蘇州," 289–320, in Umehara Kaoru 梅原郁, ed., *Chūgoku kinsei no toshi to bunka* 中國近世の都市と文化 (Kyoto: Kyoto daigaku jimbun kagaku kenkyūjo, 1984).
Tong Guanzheng 童光政, *Mingdai minshi pandu yanjiu* 明代民事判读研究 (Guilin: Guangxi shifan daxue, 1999),
Conrad Totman, *Early Modern Japan* (Berkeley: University of California Press, 1993).
Denis C. Twitchett, "Merchant, Trade, and Government in Late T'ang," *Asia Major*, 14.1 (1968), 63–93.
"The T'ang Marketing System," *Asia Major*, n.s., 12.2 (1966), 202–48.
Abraham L. Udovitch, *Partnership and Profit in Early Medieval Islamic Trade* (Princeton: Princeton University Press, 1970).
Ueda Makoto 上田信. "Minmatsu Shinsho Kōnan no toshi no 'burai' o meguru shakai han de 明末清初江南の都市の'無頼'をめぐる社会判で," *Shigaku zasshi* 史学雑誌, 90 (Nov. 1981), 1–35.
"Ryūkako monogatari: Shindai Kōnan no ichi kōekiko ni ikita hitobito 清代江南の一公益子に生きた人々," *Chūgoku kindaishi kenkyū* 中国近代史研究 1988.9, 5–7.
Usui Sachiko 臼井佐智子, *Kishū shōnin no kenkyū* 徽州商人の研究 (Tokyo: Kyūko shoin, 2005).
Robert H. van Gulik, *Sexual Life and Practice in Ancient China: A Preliminary Survey of Chinese Sex and Society from ca. 1500 B.C. to 1644 A.D.* (Leiden: Brill, 1956).
Richard von Glahn, "Cycles of Silver in Chinese Monetary History," 17–71, in Billy K.L. So, ed., *The Economy of Lower Yangzi Delta in Late Imperial China* (London: Routledge, 2013).
The Economic History of China (Cambridge: Cambridge University Press, 2016).
"The Enchantment of Wealth: The God *Wutong* in the Social History of Jiangnan," *Harvard Journal of Asiatic Studies*, 51.2 (1991), 651–714.
Fountain of Fortune: Money and Monetary Policy in China, 1000–1700 (Berkeley: University of California Press, 1996).
The Sinister Way: The Divine and the Demonic in Chinese Religious Culture (Berkeley: University of California Press, 2004).
"Towns and Temples: Urban Growth and Decline in the Yangzi Delta, 1200–1500," 176–211, in Paul J. Smith and Richard von Glahn, eds.

The Song–Yuan–Ming Transition, 900–1500 (Cambridge, MA: Harvard University Asia Center, 2003).
Frederic Wakeman Jr., *The Great Enterprise: The Manchu Reconstruction of Imperial Order in Seventeenth-Century China* (Berkeley: University of California Press, 1985),
Wang Chongyuan 汪崇筼, "Bufen Huizhou Shexian yanshang guli ji jiazu 部分徽州歙县盐商故里及家族," *Sichuan ligong xueyuan xuebao (shehui kexueban)* 四川理工学院学报(社会科学版), 23.2 (April 2008), 11–17.
   "Huizhou diandang ziben de zengzhi, yi Cheng Xuyu jiazu wei lie 徽州典当资本的增值, 以程虚宇家族为列," *Zhongguo shehui jingji shi yanjiu* 中国社会经济史研究 2004.3, 41–47.
   Ming Qing Huishang jingying Huaiyan kaolüe 明清徽商经营淮盐考略 (Chengdu: Sichuan chuban jiduan Bashu shushe, 2008).
Wang Chunyu 王春瑜 and Du Wanyan 杜婉言, comp., *Mingdai huanguan yu jingji shiliao chutan* 明代宦官與经济史料初探 (Beijing: Zhongguo shehui kexue, 1986).
Wang Fangzhong 王方中, "Qingdai qianqi de yanfa, yanshang, yu yanchan shengchan 清代前期的盐法, 盐商, 与盐产生产," *Qingshi luncong* 清史论丛 1982.4, 1–48.
Wang Guoping 王国平 and Tang Lixing 唐力行, comp., *Ming Qing yilai Suzhou shehui shi beike ji* 明清以来苏州社会史碑刻集 (Suzhou: Suzhou daxue, 1998).
Wang Qingyuan 汪庆元, "Huishang huipiao zhidu kaolüe 徽商会票制度考略," *Wenxian* 文献 2000.1, 187–94.
Wang Rigen 王日根 and Cao Bin 曹斌, *Ming Qing hehaidao de shengcheng ji qi zhili yanjiu* 明请河海盗的生成及其治理研究 (Xiamen: Xiamen daxue, 2016).
Wang Shihua 王世华, "Ming Qing Huizhou dianshang de shengshuai 明清徽州典商的盛衰," *Qingshi yanjiu* 清史研究 1999.2, 62–70.
Wang Shiqing 汪世清, "Huizhou xue yanjiu de zhongda gongxian 徽州学研究的重大贡献," *Hefei xueyuan xuebao (shehui kexue ban)* 合肥学院学报(社会科学版), 21.1, 12–20.
Wang Shixin 汪士信, "Ming Qing shiqi shangye jingji fangshi de bianhua 明请時期商業經濟方式的變化," *Zhongguo jingji shi yanjiu* 中國經濟史研究 1988.2, 14–28.
Wang Tai Peng, *The Origins of Kongsi* (Selangur: Pelandunk Publications, 1994).
Wang Tingyuan 汪廷元, "Huishang congye renyuan de zuhe fangshi 徽商从业人员的组合方式," *Jiang Huai xuekan* 江淮学刊 2002.2, 119–125.
   "Huishang yu Shanghai 徽商与上海," *Anhui shixue* 安徽史学, 1993.1, 12–17.

"Lun Huizhou shangbang de xingcheng yu fazhan 论徽州商帮的形成与发展," *Zhongguo shi yanjiu* 中国史研究 1995.3, 39–46.

"Lun Ming Qing shiqi de Huizhou yashang 论明请时期的徽州牙商," *Zhongguo shehui jingji shi yanjiu* 中国社会经济史研究 1993.2, 54–60.

"Ming Qing Huishang yu Jiangnan mianzhi ye 明请徽商与江南棉织业," *Anhui shida xuebao* 安徽师大学报, 19.1 (1991), 61–69.

Wang Tingyuan 王廷元, and Wang Shihua 王世华, *Huishang* 徽商 (Hefei: Anhui renmin, 2005).

Wang Wenshu 王文书, *Songdai jiedai ye yanjiu* 宋代借贷业研究 (Baoding: Hebei daxue chubanshe, 2014).

Wang Xiaodong 王晓东, "Lun Huizhou wushu wenhua fazhan de yingxiang 论徽州武术文化发展的影响," *Shanghai tiyu xueyuan xuebao* 上海体育学院学报, 363 (May 2012), 27–31.

Wang Yajun 王亚军, *Ming Qing Huishang de susong yanjiu* 明请徽商的诉讼研究 (Beijing: Beijing shifan daxue chuban jiduan, 2013).

Wang Yuming 王裕明, "Ming Qing fenjia kuishu suojian Huizhou dianshang shulun 明清分家书所见徽州典商述论," *Anhui daxue xuebao (zhexue shehui kexue ban)* 安徽大学学报(哲学社会科学版) 2010.6, 94–102.

"'Renfeng ji' yu Ming zhongye Huizhou shehui '仁蜂集' 与明中叶徽州社会," *Anhui daxue xuebao (zhexue shehui kexue ban)* 安徽大学学报(哲学社会科学版), 29.5 (Sept. 2005), 106–11.

"Song Yuan shiqi de Huizhou shangren 宋元时期的徽州商人, *Anhui shixue* 安徽史学 2015.3, 123–28.

Wang Zhenzhong 王振忠, *Huizhou shehui wenhua shi tanwei: xin faxian de 16–20 shiji minjian dang'an wenshu yanjiu* 徽州社會文化史探微: 新发现的16–20世纪民间档案文书研究 (Shanghai: Shanghai shehui kexueyuan, 2002).

"Ming Qing Huainan yinye yu Yizhen minsu 明请淮南盐业与仪征民俗," *Yanye shi yanjiu* 盐业史研究 1994.4, 27–32, 64.

"Ming Qing yilai Hankou de Huishang yu Huizhou ren shequ 明清以来汉口的徽商与徽州人社区," 81–118, in Li Xiaodi 李孝悌, ed., *Zhongguo de chengshi shenghuo* 中国的城市生活 (Beijing: Beijing daxue, 2013).

Ming Qing yilai Huizhou cunluo shehui shi yanjiu 明清以来徽州村落社会史研究 (Shanghai: Renmin, 2011).

"Ming Qing yilai Huizhou de bao'an shanhui yu 'wuyu' zhuzhi 明清以来徽州的保安善会与 '五隅' 组织," *Minsu quyi* 民俗曲藝 (Taiwan), 174 (December 2011), 17–102.

Qianshan xiyang, Wang Zhenzhong lun Ming Qing shehui yu wenhua 千山夕阳, 王振忠论明清社会与文化 (Guilin: Guangxi shifan daxue, 2009).

Shehui lishi yu renwen dili 社会历史与人文地理 (Shanghai: Zhongxi shuzhu, 2017).

"Shexian Ming Qing Huizhou yanshang guli xunfang ji 歙县明清徽州盐商故里寻访记," *Yanye shi yanjiu* 盐业史研究 1994.2, 34–43.

"*Wang Zuofu tongnian aihuanlu* zhong de Huizhou dianshang shiyi 《汪作黼同年哀挽录》中的徽州典商事迹," *Huizhou shixue* 徽州史学, 2005.2, 115–17.

Wang Zongyi 汪宗义 and Liu Xuan 刘宣, "Qingchu jingshi shanghao huipiao 清初京师商号会票," *Wenxian* 文献 1985.2, 93–112.

Andrew Watson, trans., *Transport in Transition: The Evolution of Traditional Shipping in China* (Ann Arbor: University of Michigan, Center for Chinese Studies, 1972),

Ruby S. Watson, *Inequality among Brothers: Class and Kinship in South China* (Cambridge: Cambridge University Press, 1985).

Wei Jianlin 卫建林, *Mingdai huanguan zhengzhi* 明代宦官政治 (Taiyuan: Shanxi renmin, 1991).

Wei Tian'an 魏天安, *Songdai hanghui zhidu shi* 宋代行会制度史 (Beijing: Xinhua shudian jingxiao, 1997).

Whelan, T.S., *The Pawnshop in China* (Ann Arbor: University of Michigan, Center for Chinese Studies, 1979).

John E. Wills, "Relations with Maritime Europeans, 1514–1662," 333–75, in Frederick.W. Mote and Denis Twitchett, eds., *The Cambridge History of China, v. 8, The Ming Dynasty, 1368–1644, pt. 2* (Cambridge: Cambridge University Press, 1998).

Arthur P. Wolf and Chieh-shan Huang, *Marriage and Adoption in China, 1845–1945* (Stanford: Stanford University Press, 1980).

Sui-lun Wong, "The Chinese Family Firm: A Model," *Family Business Review*, 6.3 (Sept. 1993), 327–40.

W.W. Wood, *Sketches of China* (Philadelphia: Carey and Lea, 1830).

Wu Bingkun 吴秉坤, *Qing zhi Minguo Huizhou minjian jiedai lilü ziliao huibian ji yanjiu* 清至民国徽州民间借贷利率资料汇编及研究 (Shanghai: Shanghai jiaotong daxue, 2016).

Wu Fu 伍跌 and Yang Yanping 杨晏平, comp., "Beitu cang Xunzhi nianjian qiyue wenshu shiqi jian 北图藏顺治年间契约文书十七件," *Wenxian* 文献 1992.1, 197–209.

Wu Jingxian 吴景贤, "Ming Qing zhi ji Huizhou nubian kao 明清之际徽州奴变考," *Xuefeng yuekan* 学风月刊, 7.5 (June 1937), 6–20.

Wu Ren'an 吴仁安, *Ming Qing Jiangnan wangzu yu shehui jingji wenhua* 明清江南望族与社会经济文化 (Shanghai: Renmin, 2001).

Ming Qing shiqi Shanghai diqu de zhuxing wangzu 明清时期上海地区的著姓望族 (Shanghai: Shanghai renmin, 1997).

Wu Renshu 巫仁恕, *Pinwei shehua: wan Ming de xiaofei shehui yu shidafu* 品味奢华: 晚明的消费社会与士大夫 (Beijing: Zhonghua, 2008).

Wu Yulian, *Luxurious Networks: Salt Merchants, Status and Statecraft in Eighteenth-Century China* (Stanford: Stanford University Press, 2017).

Wu Zhaolong 吴兆龙, "Wang Daokun jiashi guan yanjiu 王道昆家史观研究," *Yichun xueyuan xuebao* 宜春学院学报, 33.11 (Nov. 2011), 70–73.

Wu Zhengfang 吴正芳, *Baiyang yuan, Huizhou chuantong cunluo shehui* 白杨源, 徽州传统村落社会 (Shanghai: Fudan daxue, 2011),

Xie Guozhen 谢国桢, *Mingdai shehui jingji shiliao xuanbian* 明代社会经济史料选编 (Fuzhou: Fujian renmin, 1981).

Xin Shufang 邢淑芳, "Gudai yunhe yu Linqing jingji 古代运河与临清经济," *Liaocheng shifan xueyuan xuebao (zhexue shehui ke xueban)* 聊城师范学院学报(哲学社会科学版), 1994.2, 68–75.

Xiong Yuanbao 熊遠報, *Shindai Kishū chiiki shakaishi kenkyū: kyōkai shūdan nettowāku to shakai chitsujo* 清代徽州地域社会史研究: 境界・集団・ネットワークと社会秩序 (Tokyo: Kyūko shoin, 2003).

"Sonraku shakai ni okeru 'senkai' – Shin Minkoku ki no Kishū chiiki o chūshin to shite 村落社会における'錢会'—清民国期の徽州地域を中心として," 395–418, in *Mindai shi kenkyūkai sōritsu sanjūgo nen kinen ronshū* 明代史研究会創立三十五年記念論集, v. 1 (Tokyo: Kyūko shoin, 2003).

"Sōzoku shihon no seiritsu to tenkai, Min Shin ki Kishū Kō shi Kōyūkai o chūshin to shite 宗族資本の成立と展開, 明清期徽州洪氏光裕会を中心として," 437–57, in Inoue Tōru 井上徹 and Endō Takatoshi 遠藤隆俊, eds., *Sō-Min sōzoku no kenkyū* 宋–明宗族の研究 (Tokyo: Kyūko shoin, 2005).

Xiu Xiaobo 修晓波, *Yuandai de semu shangren* 元代的色目商人 (Guangzhou: Guangdong renmin, 2013).

Xu Bin 徐斌, "Ming Qing Hebosuo chili ce yanjiu 明请河泊所赤历册研究," *Zhongguo nongshi* 中国农史 2011.2, 65–77.

Xu Dixin 许涤新 and Wu Chengming 吴承明, eds., *Zhongguo zibenzhuyi de fazhan shi, v. 1, Zhongguo zibenzhuyi yu guonei shichang de mengya* 中国资本主义发展史, v. 1, 中国资本主义与国内市场的盟芽 (Beijing: Renmin, 1985).

Xu Maoming 徐茂明, "Qingdai Hui Su liangdi de jiazu qiantu yu wenhua hudong – yi Suzhou Dafu Panshi wei li 清代徽苏两地的家族迁徒与文化互动 – 以苏州大阜潘氏为例," *Shilin* 史林 2004.2, 25–35.

Xu Tan 许檀, "Ming Qing shiqi de Linqing shangye 明请时期的临清商业," *Zhongguo jingji shi yanjiu* 中国经济史研究, 1986.2, 135–57.

Xu Xuelin 徐学林, *Huizhou keshu* 徽州刻书 (Hefei: Anhui renmin, 2005).

Yamane Yukio 山根幸夫, ed., Rinji Taiwan Kyūkan Chōsakai 臨時台湾旧慣調査会, comp., *Shindai keiyaku monjo, shokanbun ruishū: Keiji oyobi shokanbun ruishū* 清代契約文書・書簡文類集: 契字及書簡文類集 (Tokyo: Kyūko shoin, 1973).

Yan Guifu 严桂夫, *Huizhou lishi dang'an zongmu tiyao* 徽州历史档案总目提要 (Hefei: Huangshan shushe, 1996).

Yan Guifu 严桂夫, and Wang Guojian 王国键, *Huizhou wenshu dang'an* 徽州文书档案 (Hefei: Anhui renmin, 2006).

Yang Guozhen 杨国桢, *Ming Qing tudi qiyue wenshu yanjiu* 明清土地契约文书研究 (Beijing: Renmin, 1988).

 "Ming Qing yi lai 'heben' jingying de qiyue xingshi 明清以来'合本'经营的契约形式," *Zhongguo shehui jingji shi* 中国社会经济史, 3.1 (August 1987), 1–9.

Yang Lien-sheng, "Government Control of Merchants in Traditional China," 27–47, in his *Sinological Studies and Reviews* (Taipei: Shih-huo, 1982).

 Money and Credit in China: A Short History (Cambridge, MA: Harvard-Yenching Institute, 1952).

Yang Liwei 杨立威 et al., *Huizhou daxing* 徽州大姓 (Hefei: Anhui daxue, 2005).

Yao Pangzao 姚邦藻 and Mei Wen 梅文, "Huizhou gu citang tese chutan 徽州古祠堂特色初探," *Huangshan xueyuan xuebao* 黄山学院学报, 2.4 (Feb. 2001), 16–22.

Ye Xian'en 叶显恩, *Ming Qing Huizhou nongcun shehui yu dianpu zhi* 明清徽州农村社会与佃仆制 (Hefei: Anhui renmin, 1983).

Yin Lingling 尹玲玲, *Ming Qing Changjiang zhongxiayou yuye jingji yanjiu* 明清长江中下游渔业经济研究 (Ji'nan: Ji Lu shushe, 2004).

Yokoyama Suguru 横山英, "Shindai Kōseishō ni okeru ungyō no kikō 清代江西省における運業の機構," *Hiroshima daigaku bungakubu kiyō* 広島大学文学部紀要, 18 (1960.12), 49–89; part of this is included in his *Chūgoku kindaika no keizai kōzō* 中国近代化の経済構造 (Tokyo: Aki shobō, 1972).

Yu Yingshi 余英时, *Chinese History and Culture, v. 2, Seventeenth Century through Twentieth Century*, with the editorial assistance of Josephine Chiu-Duke and Michael S. Duke (New York: Columbia University Press, 2015).

 Shi yu Zhongguo wenhua 士与中国文化 (Shanghai: Xinhua shudian Shanghai faxing suojing xiao, 1987).

Yoneda Yūtarō 米田祐太郎, *Shina no shōnin seikatsu* 支那の商人生活 (Tokyo: Kyōsaisha, 1940).

Madeleine Zelin, "Chinese Business Practice in the Late Imperial Period," *Enterprise and Society*, 14.4 (Dec. 2013), 769–93.

"The Firm in Early Modern China," *Journal of Economc Behavior and Organization*, 71 (2009), 623–37.

The Magistrate's Tael: Rationalizing Fiscal Reform in Eighteenth-Century China (Berkeley: University of California Press, 1984).

The Merchants of Zigong: Industrial Entrepreneurship in Early Modern China (New York: Columbia University Press, 2005).

Madeleine Zelin, Jonathan K. Ocko, and Robert Gardella, eds., *Contract and Property in Early Modern China* (Stanford: Stanford University Press, 2004).

Zhang Changhong 张长虹, *Pinjian yu jingying, Mingmo Qingchu Huishang yishu canzhu yanjiu* 品鉴与经营, 明末清初徽商艺术赞助研究 (Beijing: Beijing daxue, 2010).

Zhang Haipeng 张海鹏, ed., *Huishang yanjiu* 徽商研究 (Hefei: Anhui renmin, 1995).

Zhang Haipeng 张海鹏, and Zhang Haiying 张海瀛, eds., *Zhongguo shida shangbang* 中国十大商帮 (Hefei: Huangshan shushe, 1993).

Zhang Shimin 张世敏, "Lun Ming zhongqi shangren zhuanji de fenlei yu fazhan mailuo 论明中期商人传记,的分类与发展脉络," *Xibu xuekan* 西部学刊 2014.12, 24–27.

Zhang Shouan 張壽安, *Yili dai li: Ling Tingkan yu Qing zhongye ruxue sixiang zhi zhuanbian* 以禮代理: 淩廷堪與清中葉儒學思想之轉變 (Shijia zhuang: Hebei jiaoyu, 2001).

Zhang Wei 张伟 and Tang Zi 汤怿, "Ming Qing haiwai maoyi zhong de hehuo zhi tanji 明请海外贸易中的合伙制探赜," *Zhongguo shehui jingji shi yanjiu* 中国社会经济史研究 2015.1, 35–41.

Zhang Xianqing 张显清, *Mingdai houqi shehui chuanxing yanjiu* 明代后期社会转型研究 (Beijing: Zhongguo shehui kexue, 2008).

Yan Song zhuan 严嵩传 (Hefei: Huangshan shushe, 1987).

Zhang Xiaoping 张小平, *Juzu er jubo sensen: Huizhou gu citang* 聚族而居柏森森: 徽州古祠堂 (Shenyang: Liaoning renmin, 2002).

Zhang Xu 张绪, "Shang xing er xia xiao: Qingdai zunlao yulao lizhi difang de shijian, yi Huizhou diqu wei li 上行而下效: 清代尊老优老礼制地方的实践, 以徽州地区为例," *Huixue* 徽学, 7 (2011), 198–208.

Zhang Youyi 章有义, *Ming Qing Huizhou tudi guanxi yanjiu* 明清徽州土地关系研究 (Beijing: Zhongguo shehui kexue, 1984).

Zhang Zhengming 张正明, *Chengxiong shangjie 500 nian Jinshang xingshuai shi* 称雄商界500年晋商兴衰史 (Taiyuan: Shanxi guji, 2001).

Ming Qing Jinshang ji minfeng 明请晋商及民风 (Beijing: Renmin, 2003).

Zhang Zhongmin 张忠民, *Jiannan de bianqian: jindai Zhongguo gongsi zhidu yanjiu* 艰难的变迁: 近代中国公司制度研究 (Shanghai: Shehui kexueyuan, 2002).

Zhao Chengzhong 赵承中, "Huangshan yuanan 黄山冤案," *Wenshi tiandi* 文史天地 2009.9, 30–33.

Zhao Huafu 赵华富, *Huizhou zongzu yanjiu* 徽州宗族研究 (Hefei: Anhui daxue, 2004).

—— "Lun Huizhou zongzu citang 论徽州宗族祠堂," *Anhui daxue xuebao* 1996.2, 48–54.

Jie Zhao, "Ties That Bind: The Craft of Political Networking in Late Ming China," *T'oung Pao*, 86 (2000), 136–64.

Zheng Limin 郑力民, "Huizhou shewu de zhu cemian, yi Shenan Xiaonühui tianye ge'an wei li 徽州社屋的诸侧面, 以歙南孝女会田野个案为例," *Jiang Huai luntan* 江淮论坛 1995.4, 67–75.

Zheng Xiaoruan 郑小娟, "Dui Mingdai Huizhou dianshang xingsheng de xin guancha 对明代徽州典商兴盛的新观察," *Fujian shangye gaodeng zhuanke xueyuan xuebao* 福建商业高等专科学院学报 2010.4, 6–10.

—— "'Xushui,' 'fanbu,' he xinxi zhongduan '蓄水,' '反哺,' 和信息终端," *Anhui daxue xuebao (zhexue shehui kexueban)* 安徽大学学报(哲学社会科学版), 33.1 (Jan. 2009), 109–12.

Zheng Xiaoruan 郑小娟, and Zhou Yu 周宇, *Shiwu-shiba shiji de Huizhou diandang shangren* 十五-十八世纪的徽州典当商人 (Tianjin: Tianjin guji, 2010).

Zheng Xiaowen 郑晓文, "Shilun Ming Qing yahang de shangye ziben 试论明请牙行的商业资本," *Kaifeng daxue xuebao* 开封大学学报, 19.1 (March 2005), 43–45.

Zheng Zhenman 郑振满, *Ming Qing Fujian jiazu zuzhi yu shehui bianqian* 明清福建家族组织与社会变迁 (Changsha: Hunan jiaoyu, 1992); trans. Michael Szonyi, *Family Lineage Organization and Social Change in Ming and Qing Fujian* (Honolulu: University of Hawai'i Press, 2001).

—— "Yangtian, mutian yu Huishang zongzu zuzhi, Shexi Xi'nan Wushi xianyang zhi 塋田, 墓田与徽商宗族组织, 歙西溪南吳氏先塋志," *Anhui shixue* 安徽史学 1988.1, 10–18.

Zhongguo guzhenyou bianjibu 中国古镇游编辑部, ed. (chief ed. Zhou Hong 周宏), *Guzhen yangxiangguan Huizhou* 古镇央像馆徽州 (Beijing: Shaanxi shifan daxue, 2003).

Zhongguo Renmin daxue Qingshi yanjiusuo 中国人民大学清史研究所 et al., comp., *Kang Yong Qian shiqi chengxiang renmin fankang touzheng ziliao* 康雍乾时期城乡人民反抗斗争资料 (Beijing: Zhonghua, 1979).

Zhou Shengchun 周生春 and Chen Qianqian 陈倩倩, "Jiazu shanghao zhuancheng yu zhili zhidu de yanbian 家族商号传承与治理制度的演变," *Zhejiang daxue xuebao (renwen shehui kexue ban)* 浙江大学学报(人文社会科学版), 44.3 (May 2014), 34–43.

Zhou Xiaoguang 周晓光, ed., *Huizhou wenhua shi, Ming Qing juan* 徽州文化史, 明清卷 (Hefei: Anhui renmin, 2015).

Zhu Changrong 朱昌荣, "Qingchu Cheng Zhu lixue 'fuxing' yuanyin chuyi 清初程朱理学 '复兴' 原因刍议," *Huixue* 徽学, 6 (2010), 152–76.

Zhu Xiaotian 朱小田, "Jindai Jiangnan miaohui jingji guankui 近代江南庙会经济管窥," *Zhongguo jingji shi yanjiu* 中国经济史研究 1997.2, 58–65.

Harriet T. Zurndorfer, *Change and Continuity in Chinese Local History: The Development of Hui-chou Prefecture 800–1800* (Leiden: E.J. Brill, 1989).

"Cotton Textile Production in Jiangnan during the Ming–Qing Era and the Matter of Market-Driven Growth," 72–98, in Billy K.L. So, ed., *The Economy of Lower Yangzi Delta in Late Imperial China: Connecting Money, Markets, and Institutions* (London: Routledge, 2013).

Index

ancestral hall, 60–124
  affiliated associations, 110
  assets, 122–23
  Buddhist temples, 410
  concentration, 62–64
  functions, 64–66
  legal restrictions, 69–77
  loans, 110–18, 120, 401
    interest rates, 123
  as master of bondservants, 391
  membership, 66–67
  membership issue, 60
  numbers, 60–124
  spirit tablets, 68, 80, 101–7
Anqing, 229
Antony, Robert, 131, 147

bankruptcy, 286–92
  legal history, 285
  liability, 289
  and reincarnation, 305
Bastid, Marianne, 33
Beijing, 196
bills of credit, 144
bondservant conditions, 401
bondservants
  conditions, 390
  rebellion, 390
Brokaw, Cynthia, 414, 417
brokerages
  division of labor, 174
  guild, 175
brokers, 170
  collusion, 176
  criticism of, 174–75
  excessive commitments, 174
  numbers
    Yangzhou, 172
  official and private, 172
  second jobs, 175
  Suzhou, 175, 185
  tasks and responsibilities, 171–72
Buddhist temples, 386
buiness staff
  salaries, 302

Carlettti, Francesco, 138
Changshu, 185, 230
Changshu county, 157, 179, 186–87, 196, 272
  pawnshops, 230
Changzhou
  trading, 26
Chaozhou prefecture, 40
Chen Guodong, 148
Chen Keyun, 66
Chen Kuo-tung, 148
Chen Zeng, 198
Cheng Lingxi, 405
Cheng Shizhong, 419
Cheng Shouxun, 198
Cheng Yi, 70–71, 76
Chengkan Luo, 92
Chens of De'an, 255
Chongqing, 185
Chow Kai-wing, 48, 414
climate problems, 388
Coase, Ronald, 281
commercial partnerships, 9, 238, 252–307, 397
  access to invested capital, 292
  "commenda," 247, 255–71
  dormant partners, 293
  joint-share, 175, 271–76
  lineage, 277–83
  personnel, 296
  practices, 304
commercial tax, late Ming, 14
  early Qing, 395
Congming, 272

Index

construction
  bargaining, 89–91
  dispute, 91–98
  fund raising, 83
construction costs, 77–82
Cortes, Adriano de las, SJ, 138
craft and trade associations, 150
credit associations, 83–84, 124, 273

Danyang county, 157
Daoist shrines, 386
debt
  law and custom, 288
Dizang, 419
Dongli Cheng
  "grassroots," 119–24
Dongting
  merchants, 40, 53, 269

eunuchs, 1, 49, 198–99, 222, 373, 377
Expansion Association, 107

Family Rituals, 76, 101, 407, 411
Fang Lishan, 61
Fang Yongbin, 118, 238
Faure, David, 214, 225, 281, 284
Fengjing town
  cotton industry, 24
Fishing Tax Offices, 133
flower drum songs, 3
frontier merchants, 213, 221, 223
Fu Yan, 138
Fuchi town, 340
Fujii Hiroshi, 258, 298, 308
Fuliang county, 392
Fuzhou, 230
Fuzhou prefecture, 53, 230, 232, 234

Gernet, Jacques, 195
Gipouloux, Francois, 270
Grand Canal, 7, 12–13, 15, 18, 20, 25, 27–28, 46, 129, 134, 148, 165, 202, 228, 230, 249–50, 357, 395
Gu Yanwu, 179, 298–99, 302–3, 369
Guan Zhidao, 35, 74
Guixi Xiang, 79, 89, 97, 104

Haiyan county, 118
Hangzhou, 185, 215, 282, 355
  brigands, 135, 141

crime, 158
emporium, 26
financial sector, 36
Huizhou merchants, 46, 51
merchant group, 40
porters, 170
salt merchants, 151
salt trade, 39
silk, 340
trading, 328–29
Hankou, 26
Hartman, Charles, 33
Heijdra, Martin, 23
hoarding, 222
Hong Yutu, 394
Hongren, 381
house firms, 9
Hu Song, 132, 137
Huang Jishui, 35
Huang, Ray, 207
Huang Xingceng, 34
Huangdun, 75
  dispute, 117, 416–18
Huangzhou, 26, 130–31, 133, 230, 247
Huizhou
  decline in wealth, 392, 395
  early Qing land-tenure change, 395
  elite surnames, 49
  grain shortage, 387
  military campaigns, 391
  pawnshops, 229
  popular cults, 405–6
  population, 8
  products, 44
  trading routes, 126
  wealth, 122–23
Huizhou lineages, 384
Huizhou merchants, 42, 57, 166, 283, 385, 393
  alliances, 41
  anticipated profit rates, 54
  biographies, 48
  commodities, 51
  common strategies, 225, 231
  criticism of, 179
  economic sectors, 50
  extralegal recourse to market abuses, 176
  frontier grain trade, 209
  house firms, 308–83

Huizhou merchants (cont.)
  insecurity, 129
  living standard, 55
  long-distance, 166
  major markets, 51
  native-place asociation
    Huizhou, 192
    Suzhou, 184–94
  niche within officialdom, 201
  origins, 47, 224
  pawnbrokers, 166
  pawnshops, 51
  pawnshops' practices, 232
  personnel management, 301
  pre-eminence, 48
  reasons for success, 53
  relations with government, 180, 191
  reputation, 55, 138
  salt monopoly
    interior merchants, 212
  salt trade elite, 213
  search for government niche, 200
  self-defense measures, 143
  Suzhou
    extralegal recourse to market abuses, 177
    legal recourse to market abuses, 178
  trading areas, 46
  trading goods, 44
  trading markets, 46
  trading routes, 127
  travel companions, 148
  wealth, 49, 54–57, 354
    location, 50
Huizhou pawnshops
  tax evasion, 167
Huizhou sources
  and Huizhou merchants, 56
Hunan, 272
Huzhou, 55, 134, 231, 240

Jiading county, 177
  cotton industry, 24
Ji'an county, 183, 191
Jiang Liangdong, 157
Jiang Village, 410
Jiangpu county, 244
Jiangxi and Huguang merchants
  salt monopoly
    river merchants, 212

Jiangxi merchants
  career patterns, 52–53
  markets and goods, 52–53
  origins, 52
  ties to Huizhou merchants, 52
Jiangyin, 239, 272
Jiangyin county, 131, 149, 231
Jin Sheng, 297, 393
Jin Yao, 76
Jingdezhen, 46–47, 55, 127, 232
Jiujiang, 15, 26, 129, 132–33, 230, 395

Kaifeng, 40, 46, 148, 185, 321, 336
Katō Shigeshi, 148
Kuang Zhong, 151

Lagerwey, John, 411
Lanxi, 261
legal handbook, 180
Li Jinde, 237
Li Mengyang, 213
Li Weizhen, 179
Li Yu, 240
lineage landholdings
  Qing, 400
lineages, 36–37, 277–307, 308–83, 396–401, 406–12
  military ties, 145
  ties with officialdom, 198
Linqing, 18, 46, 148, 185
  commercial taxes, 14
  Huizhou merchants, 46, 51, 197, 230–31, 355, 365, 372, 393
  native-place associations, 187
  pawnshops, 228, 246
Lishui, 234
Liu Shaoyi, 167
Liu Shiji, 13
Longfu Dai, 20
Longyu merchants, 53
Luo Dongshu, 92, 94
Luo Yinghe, 91
Luodian town, 177

Manchu invasion, 1, 384, 392
Mann, Susan, 172
market abuses
  legal recourse, 176
market nodes, 26
markets, 29

Index 465

Meilink-Roelofsz, M.A.P., 270
merchant guidebooks, 133, 138, 149
  warnings, 139
merchants
  career patterns, 44
  long-distance, 46
  outsiders, 166
    obstacles to trade, 168
  peddlers, 46
  regional groups, 40–42
    qualifications, 41
  relations with government, 197
    corruption, 201
  sojourning, 37, 181
Miaoshi zhi, 91
migration, 7, 92, 314, 337, 343, 394
  from Jiangxi, 52
military
  Yangzi presence, 133
Mingzhou Wu
  reform, 406–9
money exchange shops, 202
money shops, 50
Mt Huang disaster, 384

N.V. Bogoiavlenskii, 273
Nanchang, 47, 136
Nanjing, 2, 15, 18, 26, 44, 46–47,
    129–30, 133, 149, 177, 185,
    191, 196, 208, 228, 230, 234,
    244, 257, 328, 339, 341, 345,
    357, 363–64, 372, 389, 395,
    413, 436–37, 441
  military, 145
Nanxiang town, 177
native-place associations
  in Beijing, 182–83
  links with religious institutions, 191
  membership, 181
  Ming and Qing, 181–95
  in Suzhou, 182, 184, 187
  in Wuhu, 183
Ningbo, 23, 41, 134, 144, 298

Parker, Geoffrey, 388
pawnbrokerages, 50
pawnshops, 9, 116, 226–51
  antagonism to, 233
  early Qing number, 393
  interest rates, 234–42

  operations, 118–19, 232–34, 240–42
  tax, 227–29
  Xiuning, 50
  Yangzi Valley, 230
Pingwang, 135
Pinshi zhuan, 35
piracy, 1
  coastal, 131
  gang members, 130
  private arrangements, 147
  Spear Agencies, 148
  Suzhou, 160
  Yangzi, 128, 130, 132, 133, 136, 147
  Yangzi delta, 135, 165
  Yangzi river, 47
pirates, 1, 7, 128, 132, 148, 155
  Yangzi, 129
porters, 302
  Ningbo
    foreign trade, 173
public place
  in Changshu, Suzhou, 185–86
Puk Wing-kin, 214, 221, 225
purchase on credit, 144

Qi Biaojia, 158, 161
Qimen, 389
Qimen county, 389, 391–92
Qingjiang, 18, 21, 129
Qiu Jun, 34

Raozhou, 136
remittance notes, 144
river merchants, 212–13
Rosenthal, Jean-Paul, 237

salt
  trading, 44
salt administration
  malfunctioning, 207
salt certificates, 50, 216–26
  administrative problems, 223
  collusion, 143
  hoarding, 220, 223
  numbers, 206, 222
  reforms of 1617, 224
  sales in Lianghuai, 223
  wealth, 45
salt merchants, 385
  Hangzhou, 39

salt merchants (cont.)
　head merchant, 190
　post of Libationer, 356
　relation to government, 39
　reputation, 42
　role of Libationer, 187
　trading career, 39
　wealth, 38
　Yangzhou, 306
salt monopoly, 9, 33, 94
　boat protection, 149
　and credit associations, 118
　early Ming administrative
　　infrastructure, 207–9
　frontier merchants, 212
　level of capitalization, 225
　reforms of 1492, 43, 213–14
salt smuggling
　Yangzi, 129
salt taxes, 12, 167
salt trade, 46
salt trading, 34
　She and Xiuning traders, 50
Shandong, 272
Shangshan Wu, 37, 106, 115
Shanhe Chengs, 84, 386, 396–99
　decline, 397
　Doushan trust, 396
　migration, 397
Shanxi merchants, 42, 51, 54, 193, 268, 300
　markets and goods, 51
　salt monopoly, 51
　frontier merchants, 212
Shaxi Village, 410
She county, 388, 394
shed people, 395
Shen Qiqian, 36
Shiba Yoshinobu, 13, 23, 191, 261, 282
Shili county, 388–89
Shimen county, 241
Shuaidong Cheng, 145, 247, 274
Shuaikou Cheng, 105
Sichuan, 272
Single Whip tax, 10, 166
Skinner, G. William, 21–22, 25, 29, 437, 439, 451
Sōda Hiroshi, 148
Songjiang, 30, 55
　cotton, 226, 340

cotton industry, 24
pawnshops, 229, 347–48
trading, 328
Su Shi, 47
sumptuary, 140
sumptuary regulations, 31
Sun Long, 199
Suzhou, 13, 21, 27, 32, 34–36, 46, 55, 122, 130, 135–36, 141, 149–50, 152–57, 159, 163–66, 168, 171–73, 176–78, 185, 187, 191–94, 196–97, 199–200, 215, 227, 230, 232–34, 242, 269, 272, 276, 280, 298, 305, 329, 340–41, 351, 355, 362, 421, 428, 434, 436, 442, 446–47, 449–50, 452, 457
　ancestral hall, 185 n. 243
　　pawnshop, 122
　cotton, 24
　cotton weaving, 341
　crime, 135, 141, 156, 160, 165, 199
　　Ming changes in, 160
　　recourse to, 164
　emporium, 26, 126, 135, 151, 162, 229, 328–29
　guilds of beaters, 169
　Huizhou merchants, 51
　incidence of crime, 158
　literati, 40
　merchant culture, 34
　merchants, 38, 181
　military presence, 162
　pawnshops, 122, 229, 232, 341, 347–48
　policing, 161, 163
　popular cults, 414
　porters, 169
　regional character, 351
　shops, 243, 276
　silk, 226, 340
　taxes, 15, 28
　trade with Huizhou, 43
　wulai, 164
　yamen staff, 160

Taicang, 272
Taiping Army, 386
Taizhou, 272
Tang Shunzhi, 35

Index

Tangqi, 135
Tani Toshihito, 128
taxes
  on merchants, 196
Tianjin, 26, 357, 376, 379
Tibet, 191
timber trade
  in Song, Ming, and Qing, 50
Tongzhou, 272
travel
  bodyguards, 148
  risks, 134
Tunxi, 116, 402

Usui Sachiko, 298

village quartet, 8–9, 11, 59, 98, 386
village worship association, 386, 401
  Zhusheng, 401–3

Wan'an Wu, 82, 89, 91
Wang Daokun, 57, 146, 359
Wang Hua, 405
Wang (or Huang) Jianjie, 199
Wang Shiduo, 181
Wang Shixing, 52, 179, 268
Wang Shizhen, 40, 49
Wang Ti, 74, 76–77
Wang Yangming, 55
Wang Zhi, 147
Watson, James, 152
Watson, Rubie, 102
Wenchang, 419
Wong, R. Bin, 237
Wu Di, 412
Wu Shiqi, 49, 355
Wu Ziyu, 77
Wuchang, 129, 340, 343, 395, 434, 449
Wuhu, 20, 26, 42, 46, 127, 130, 132, 134, 151, 177–78, 183, 190, 230, 243–44, 246, 283, 340, 395
Wujiang, 233
  pawnshop loan rates, 234
Wujiang county, 13, 117
Wujin county, 130
Wuyuan county, 388

Xia Yan, 71, 74
Xin'an mingzu zhi, 36

Xi'nan Wus, 386
  rise and fall, 354–81
Xingguo
  regional character, 351
Xiong Yuanbao, 107
Xiuning, 388–89, 392
Xiuning county, 388, 392
Xiuning mingzu zhi, 37
Xu Jiuling, 131
Xu Pu, 211
Xu Sanxing, 174

Yan Song, 49, 195
Yangzhou, 39, 224, 282, 397
  emporium, 46
  Huizhou merchants, 48, 51, 354
  Huizhou migrants, 342, 350
  migrants, 212
  military, 145
  a node, 26
  pawnshops, 229
  population, 30
  salt, 222, 226, 347
  salt monopoly
    officials and merchants, 224
  salt production, 26, 51, 339
  salt trade, 130, 209, 343
  salt trading, 43
Yangzi
  pirates, 339
Yanyu gao, 153
Yanzhen, 118
Yaoan, 30
Ye Qi, 211
Yi county, 47, 388
Ying Jia, 153
Yizhen
  salt trade center, 245
Yoneda Yūtarō, 302
Yuan–Ming transition, 392
Yuezhou, 26
Yunnan, 272
Yushan county, 280

Zhang Han, 20–21, 46, 54
Zhang Shiche, 131, 137
Zhang Xun, 405, 412, 419
Zhao Huafu, 63
Zhao Jishi, 395
Zhen Jingfeng, 40

Zhenjiang, 26, 131
  pawnshops, 229
Zhou Hongmo, 71
Zhouzhuang, 233
Zhu Sheng, 151

Zhu Shirong, 242
Zhu Xi, 70, 73–75, 101, 413, 416
Zhujing town
  cotton industry, 24

Printed in the United States
By Bookmasters